On the Road around England and Wales

THOMAS COOK

On 5 July 1841 Thomas Cook, a 32-year-old printer from Market Harborough, in Leicestershire, England, led a party of some 500 temperance enthusiasts on a railway outing from Leicester to Loughborough which he had arranged down to the last detail. This proved to be the birth of the modern tourist industry. In the course of expanding his business, Thomas Cook and his son, John, invented many of the features of organised travel which we now take for granted. Over the next 150 years the name Thomas Cook became synonymous with world travel.

Today the Thomas Cook Group employs over 13,000 people across the globe and its Worldwide Network provides services to customers at more than 3000 locations in over 100 countries. Its activities include travel retailing, tour operating and financial services – Thomas Cook is a world leader in traveller's cheques and foreign money services.

Thomas Cook believed in the value of the printed word as an accompaniment to travel. His publication *The Excursionist* was the equivalent of both a holiday brochure and a travel magazine. Today Thomas Cook Publishing continues to issue one of the world's oldest travel books, the *Thomas Cook European Timetable,* which has been in existence since 1873. Updated every month, it remains the only definitive compendium of European railway schedules.

The *Thomas Cook Touring Handbook* series, to which this volume belongs, is a range of comprehensive guides for travellers touring regions of the world by train, car and ship. Other titles include:
Touring by train
On the Rails around France and Benelux (Published 1995)
On the Rails around the Alps (Published 1996)
On the Rails around Eastern Europe (Published 1996)
On the Rails around Europe (Third Edition Published 1998)
On the Rails around Britain and Ireland (Second Edition Published 1998)
Touring by car
On the Road around California (Second Edition Published 1996)
On the Road around Florida (Second Edition Published 1997)
On the Road around Normandy, Brittany and the Loire Valley (Published 1996)
On the Road around the Capital Region (Published 1997)
On the Road around the South of France (Published 1997)
On the Road around the Pacific Northwest (Published 1997)
Touring by car, train and bus
Touring Australia (Published 1997)
Touring Southern Africa (Published 1997)
Touring by ship
Greek Island Hopping (Published annually in February)
Cruising around Alaska (Published 1995)
Cruising around the Caribbean (Published 1996)

For more details of these and other Thomas Cook publications, write to Thomas Cook Publishing, at the address on the back of the title page.

ON THE ROAD AROUND

England and Wales

Driving holidays, short
breaks and day trips
by car

Eric and Ruth Bailey

A THOMAS COOK TOURING HANDBOOK

Published by Thomas Cook Publishing
The Thomas Cook Group Ltd
PO Box 227
Thorpe Wood
Peterborough PE3 6PU
United Kingdom

email: books@thomascook.com

Text:
© 1998 The Thomas Cook Group Ltd
Maps and diagrams:
© 1998 The Thomas Cook Group Ltd

ISBN 1 900341 10 7

Managing Editor: Stephen York
Project Editor: Deborah Parker
Map Editor: Bernard Horton
Route diagrams: Caroline Horton
Town maps drawn by ESR Cartography Ltd
Area and colour maps drawn by Lovell John
    Ltd
London Underground Map © London
    Regional Transport
Typesetting: Tina West

Cover illustration by Marianne Taylor
Picture research: Image Select International
Text design by Darwell Holland
Text typeset in Bembo and Gill Sans using
    QuarkXPress for Windows
Maps and diagrams created using Macromedia
    Freehand and GSP Designworks
Printed in Great Britain by Fisherprint Ltd,
    Peterborough

Written and researched by
Eric and Ruth Bailey

Additional research
Carol Sykes

Book Editor
Katy Carter

ABOUT THE AUTHORS

Eric and Ruth Bailey met as trainee journalists on a provincial English newspaper. They went their separate professional ways until their paths converged some years later, when they married and formed a freelance travel writing team, producing 15 books for five publishing companies and countless magazine and newspaper articles.

On the Road around England and Wales is their fourth in the 'On the Road...' series for Thomas Cook Publishing. They wrote *On the Road around the Capital Region* (1997), featuring Washington DC, Maryland, Virginia, Delaware and part of Pennsylvania. *On the Road around Florida* (1996) was written in association with the California-based travel-writing team, Fred Gebhart and Maxine Cass, and took them around northern Florida and southern Georgia. In 1996/97 they spent two months in South Africa, Lesotho, Swaziland and Botswana, contributing to *Touring Southern Africa* (1997). Other destinations the Baileys have written about include New England, Florida, Canada coast-to-coast, New York City and Ireland.

Eric and Ruth and their family are inland waterway enthusiasts. Their first book covered holiday boating in Britain, Ireland, France, Belgium and Holland. Among their other interests are rural life and dogs.

PHOTOGRAPHS

All the photographs in this book were supplied by Spectrum Picture Library with the exception of the following:
Back cover: CFCL/ISL

Between pp. 32 and 33
(i) Photographs of public houses reproduced courtesy of Greene King. Morris Dancers; S G York.
(iii) Needles: Image Select International.
(iv) Brighton Pavilion: Image Select International.
Between pp. 128 and 129
(i) Tarka Country: North Devon Marketing Bureau/Tom Teegan.
Between pp. 224 and 225
(i) London pagentry: CFCL/ISI.
(ii) Lakeland scenery: S G York.
(iii) Canterbury: Image Select International.
Between pp. 288 and 289
(ii) Beamish: B H Fox.
(iii) Salisbury: Image Select International.
(iv) York: Image Select International.

ACKNOWLEDGEMENTS

The authors and Thomas Cook Publishing would like to thank the many individuals and organisations who provided help during the production of this book. Among them are:

The English Tourist Board; Wales Tourist Board; regional tourist boards throughout England and Wales; Roy and Ros Anderson, Grantham; Jennifer Bennett, Hillcrest Hotel, Lincoln; Rob Bradley, City of Lincoln Tourism; Paddy and Jenny Broughton, Exeter; Rona Critchley, Greene King plc; Dora Goldberg, Image Select; Janet Reynolds, Devon Tourism; Geoff Saltmarsh, The Saltmarsh Partnership; Ian Weightman, Heart of England Tourism; and countless members of staff of Tourist Information Centres and attractions in the two countries.

5

CONTENTS

ROUTES AND CITIES – ENGLAND AND WALES

In alphabetical order. For indexing purposes, routes are listed in both directions – the reverse direction to which it appears in the book is shown in italics.

See also the Route Map, p. 8, for a diagrammatic presentation of all the routes in the book. To look up towns and other places not listed here, see the Index, p. 348–350.

6

7

REFERENCE SECTION

8

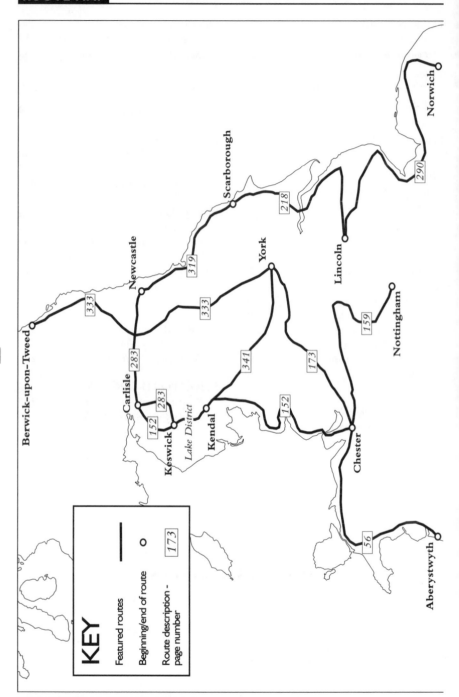

KEY

Featured routes

o Beginning/end of route

173 Route description - page number

Berwick-upon-Tweed

Newcastle

Scarborough

York

Lincoln

Nottingham

Carlisle

Keswick

Lake District

Kendal

Chester

Aberystwyth

Norwich

333

283

283

152

341

152

173

159

319

333

218

290

56

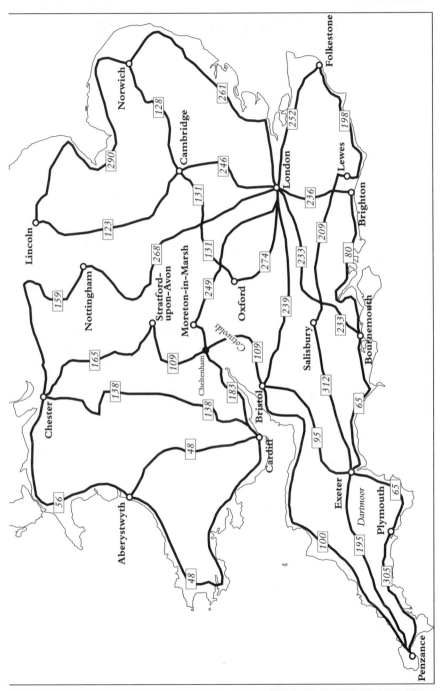

9

INTRODUCTION

Britons are now among the world's leading leisure travellers, but how many really know what lies just beyond their own doorstep? True, many families – all too many, you may think in a Bank Holiday traffic jam – take to the road for their annual trek to the South-West, the Lake District and major resorts in other parts of the country. But they tend to follow familiar routes, resulting in those awful jams and spoiling the holiday at both the beginning and the end.

This book attempts to introduce Britons, and visitors from elsewhere in the world, to the very best of England and Wales, while at the same time suggesting interesting alternatives to motorways and the more obvious routes. Some sections may prompt readers to devise their own day trips, either from home or a holiday base.

What surprises many visitors travelling England and Wales for the first time is the diversity of scenery and dialect, not only from one county to another but within a 30-mile stretch of countryside, too.

It is soon obvious, also, that you are never far from a building. England is a small country with 48 million people crammed into it. Wales is even smaller, with nearly three million people. Towns and villages are close together, particularly in the thickly populated southern half of England. Fortunately there are still great pastoral expanses, woodland, heath, moorland, downs and cornfields providing picturesque scenery in between.

One advantage of this is that you don't have to spend hours searching for a filling station or a place to eat. Nor is it difficult, outside the main tourist centres in high summer and holidays, to find somewhere to spend the night – though don't leave it too late in the day.

Budget accommodation is more readily available than ever before. The 'bed and break-fast' concept has developed considerably in recent years. It is no longer the sole domain of seaside landladies who expected guests to be out of the house by nine o'clock in the morning.

Host families today know they are an important part of the hospitality business. Regional tourist boards encourage them to provide information on local places of interest and how to reach them.

Hosts enjoy welcoming people into their comfortable homes – often country cottages, farmhouses or smart town properties. Guests from different countries can meet over breakfast and compare notes on what they have seen and done, and exchange recommendations.

Self-catering has also improved greatly. Thatched cottages are popular, and conversions have a special appeal – professionally converted barns, stables, chapels, or dairies, transformed into quaint, well-equipped holiday homes.

Between them England and Wales can provide a tremendous range of holiday pursuits. You can visit castles and historic stately homes, museums and art galleries with priceless collections. You can take a river trip or a steam train ride, tour historic ships, learn to hang-glide, go climbing, canoeing, horse-riding, cycling or hot-air ballooning. Sporting events and amusement parks by day, theatres and clubs by night – there are diversions and entertainments to suit all tastes.

England and Wales welcome you.

Eric and Ruth Bailey

HOW TO USE THIS BOOK

ROUTES AND CITIES

On the Road around England and Wales provides you with an expert selection of over 35 recommended routes between key cities and attractions of England and Wales, each designed to offer a practical and flexible framework for making the most of a touring holiday. Smaller cities, towns, attractions and points of interest along each route are described in the order in which you will encounter them. Additional chapters are devoted to key cities, towns or regions, which begin and end these routes. These chapters form the core of the book, from p.46 to p.340.

The routes have been to chosen to take in as many place of interest as possible. However, where applicable, an alternative route which is more direct is also provided at the beginning of each route chapter. This will enable you to drive more quickly between the places at the beginning and end of the route, if you do not intend to stop at any of the intermediate towns. To save space, each route is described in only one direction, but you can follow it in the reverse direction, too.

The arrangement of the text consists of a chapter describing a key destination followed by routes leading from that town or city to other major destinations, where applicable. For example, Bristol is covered in one chapter (pp.92–94), followed by routes from Bristol to Exeter (pp.95–99), Bristol to Penzance (pp.100–108) and Bristol to Stratford-upon-Avon (pp.109–117). The key towns and cities are arranged in alphabetical order, starting with Aberystwyth and continuing with Brighton, Bristol and Cambridge, and so on.

To find the page number of any route or city chapter quickly, use either the alphabetical list on the **Contents** pages, pp.6–7, or the master **Route Map** on pp.8–9. The routes are designed to be used as a kind of menu from which you can plan an itinerary, combining a number of routes which take you to the places you most want to visit.

WITHIN EACH ROUTE

Each route chapter begins with a short introduction to the route, followed by driving directions from the beginning of the route to the end, and a sketch map of the route and the places along it described in the chapter. This map, not to scale, intended to be used in conjunction with the driving direction, summarises the route; for a key to the symbols used, see p.13.

DIRECT ROUTE

This is the fastest, most direct and, sometimes, the least interesting drive, between the beginning and end of the route, usually along A roads or even motorways.

SCENIC ROUTE

This is the itinerary which takes in the most places of intrest, often using secondary and minor roads. Road directions are specific; always be prepared for detours due to road construction etc. The driving directions are followed by sub-sections describing the main attractions and places of interest along the way. You can stop at all of them and miss out those that do not appeal to you. Always ask at the local Tourist Information Office (TIC) for more information of accommodation, sights and places at which to eat.

 SIDE TRACK

This heading is occasionally used to indicate departures from the main route, or out-of-town trips from a city or town, which detour to worthwhile sights, described in full or highlighted in a paragraph or two.

CITY DESCRIPTIONS

Whether a place is given a half-page description within a route chapter or merits an entire chapter to itself, we have concentrated on practical details: local sources of tourist information; arriving in the city by car; getting around in town and city centres (public transport options are included for those who want a break from driving, or want to leave the car at their accommodation and let someone else tackle the local one-way system); accommodation and dining; communications; entertainment and shopping opportunities; events and sightseeing. The largest cities have all this detail; in smaller places some categories of information are less relevant and have been omitted or summarised.

Although we mention good independently owned lodgings in many places, we always also list the hotel chains which have a property in the area, indicated by code letters. Many travellers prefer to stick to one or two chains with which they are familiar and which give a consistent standard of accommodation. The codes are explained in **Hotel Codes** on p. 346, and central booking numbers for the chains are also given there.

MAPS

In addition to the sketch map which accompanies each route, we provide maps of major towns and cities (usually the central area). At the end of the book is a section of **colour road maps** covering the area described in this book, which is detailed enough to be used for trip planning.

THE REST OF THE BOOK

Arriving in England and Wales details arrival points for visitors travelling from abroad. **Travel Essentials** is an alphabetically arranged chapter of general advice for the tourist new to Britain and Ireland, covering a wide range subjects such as accommodation, opening hours and security. We have also included a glossary in this chapter (p.21), explaining unfamiliar British English words or phrases. **Driving in England and Wales** concentrates on advice for drivers on the law, rules of the road and so on. **Themed Itineraries** provides ideas and suggestions for putting together an itinerary of your own using the selection of routes in this book. At the back of the book, **Driving Distances** is a tabulation of distances between main towns and cities, to help in trip planning. The **Conversion Tables** decode British sizes and measures. Finally, the **Index** is the quick way to look up any place or general subject. And please help us by completing and returning the **Reader Survey** at the very end of the text; we are grateful for both your views on the book and new information from your travels in England and Wales.

KEY TO MAP SYMBOLS

Route diagrams

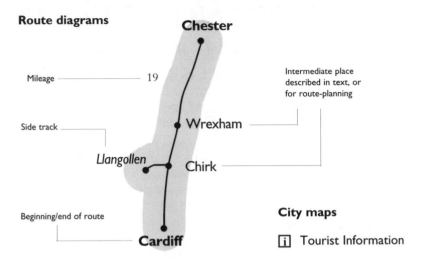

City maps

[i] Tourist Information

ABBREVIATIONS USED IN THE BOOK

(For hotel chains, see p. 346)

A	A Road, e.g. A1	hr(s)	hour(s)
AR	Advance reservations taken	Jan, Feb	January, February, etc.
Ave	Avenue (in addresses)	min(s)	minute(s)
B	B Road, e.g. B6318	M	Motorway, e.g. M25
BABA	Book a Bed Ahead scheme	Mon, Tues	Monday, Tuesday, etc.
BBG	Blue Badge Guides	NT	National Trust property
Bldg	Building	Pl.	Place (in addresses)
Blvd	Boulevard	Rd	Road (in addresses)
DP	Disabled persons (services)	SHS	Sympathetic Hearing Scheme
Dr.	Drive (in addresses)	St	Street (in addresses)
EH	English Heritage Property	TIC	Tourist Information Centre
GT	Guided tours booked	VC	Visitor Centre

13

KEY TO PRICE DESCRIPTIONS

It is impossible to keep up to date with specific tariffs for lodging and accommodation or restaurants. Instead we have rated establishments in broad price categories throughout the book, as follows:

Accommodation
(bed and breakfast, per person per night)

Budget	Under	£25
Moderate	Under	£50
Expensive	Under	£100

Meal
(for one person, excluding drinks or tip)

Cheap	Under	£7.50
Budget	Under	£12.50
Moderate	Under	£17.50
Pricey	£17.50 and above	

EXPLORING BRITAIN
by Rail and Air
with Thomas Cook Publishing

NEW RAIL MAP OF GREAT BRITAIN & IRELAND

This colour map covers the principal passenger railways of England, Scotland, Wales, Ireland and the Isle of Man, combining detailed rail information on local and high-speed rail routes with tourist guides to places of interest. Scenic rail routes are highlighted.

The new edition has been fully updated for 1998. **PRICE £5.95.**

EUROPEAN TIMETABLE

The Thomas Cook European Timetable is the most comprehensive schedule of pan-European rail services publicly available. Updated monthly, it is an essential tool for anyone planning independent rail travel around Europe. **PRICE: £8.40**

INTERNATIONAL AIR TRAVEL HANDBOOK

This handbook provides a directory of the world's major airports. It includes information on the main UK airports, with details of the airport facilities and transport connections. The 1998 edition has been enlarged, with over 40 more airports included and additional airport maps. **PRICE: £17.50**

THESE PUBLICATIONS ARE AVAILABLE FROM BOOKSHOPS AND THOMAS COOK UK RETAIL SHOPS, OR BY POST THOMAS COOK PUBLISHING, DEPT (OWN), PO BOX 227, THORPE WOOD, PETERBOROUGH, UK. PE3 6PU (EXTRA FOR POSTAGE AND PACKING.) TEL: 01733 503571/2.

AVAILABLE IN THE USA FROM FORSYTH TRAVEL LIBRARY INC, 226 WESTCHESTER AVENUE, WHITE PLAINS, NEW YORK 10604. TEL: 800 367 7984 OR 914 681 7250.

Thomas Cook

TRAVEL ESSENTIALS

The following is an alphabetical listing of helpful hints for overseas visitors planning a holiday around England and Wales.

ACCOMMODATION

Finding a Room

Tourist accommodation is plentiful in most places and you should be able to find something to suit your budget (remember that prices are often quoted per person, even for double rooms), from top-class hotels to simple bed-and-breakfast (b&b). Boards advertising the latter are to be seen everywhere. This very British institution consists of rooms offered by private individuals in their own homes. Though quality varies, it can be amazingly good value, particularly as you travel further away from London, and the welcome tends to be more personal than at hotels. Similar accommodation is offered in guest houses, farmhouses and inns – where evening meals may also be available.

If you haven't pre-booked, your best starting point on arrival at your destination will normally be the Tourist Information Centre (TIC), who almost always have free (or inexpensive) accommodation listings and (sometimes for a small fee) will make a booking for you. However, it is always a good idea to make advance bookings, if possible, especially if you are heading for major tourist destinations. In July–Aug there are usually long queues to book accommodation at TICs (particularly in London, Cambridge and Stratford) and, unless you arrive before 1400, you may be unable to find a bed. If you are travelling from outside the country, it's a good idea to book (at least for the first few nights) when you purchase your ticket. There are many published listings, including guides published by regional tourist boards – or you can obtain listings from relevant TICs in advance and book direct. Most TICs offer the invaluable 'book-a-bed-ahead' service (indicated in the text by BABA), whereby they will reserve a room at your next port of call (the booking fee can vary). This can take much of the anxiety out of late afternoon arrivals – and leave you more time to explore.

Hotel chains are well represented in Britain and, although they are not the cheapest option, do offer the security of consistent standards – as well as centralised reservations. The text uses initials to indicate which chains are represented in the main towns, e.g. *FP, MH* means that there are Forte Posthouse and Moat House properties (the initials are decoded in the *Hotel Chains* p.346). Precise details can be obtained from the chains' central reservations – or through a travel agent.

Hostelling International (HI)

For those on a tight budget, whatever their age, taking out membership of HI (the new name of the International Youth Hostel Federation) is recommended. In England and Wales the local version is YHA (Youth Hostel Association). Those who recall barrack-like dormitories endured on long-ago school trips need not quake: many hostels have been refurbished and, though still predominantly aimed at young, single travellers, HI imposes no age limit and caters for families. There are

15

some dormitories, but smaller rooms are also common. Some (usually the more remote) impose curfews and chores, but kitchen and laundry facilities can be excellent; some large hostels offer hot evening meals and, apart from camping, the accommodation is usually the cheapest available. There are 400 or so hostels in Britain and Ireland affiliated to HI and, where applicable, the accommodation sections of this book mention the nearest.

Individual UK membership (1998) is £10 (£5 for those under 18). There's also family membership: £19 covers both parents and all children under 18, while £9.50 covers one parent and all children under 18. On joining, you receive a copy of *The Guide*, which lists all hostels in England and Wales – with details of facilities, location, how to get there and opening times (so these details are not reproduced in this book).

Though hostels in small places tend to close in the daytime (minimum opening times for reception are 0800–1000 and 1700–2200), in cities they are often open 24 hours. Booking well in advance is sensible, and almost essential in summer. If you haven't pre-booked, check on arrival how long you can stay, as some impose a three-day limit at peak times. For information, to join, and to book accommodation before you start travelling: **Australia**, *tel: (02) 9261 1111;* **Canada**, *tel: (613) 237 7884;* **New Zealand**, *tel: (09) 379 4224;* **South Africa**, *tel: (21) 419 1853;* **USA**, *tel: (0202) 783 6161.*

Camping

If you are prepared to carry your own equipment, this is the cheapest option; campsites are plentiful and the local TICs supply details. Sites are often in caravan parks and tend to be some way out of town; details are given in the text. For more information about camping, contact the **Camping and Caravanning Club**, *Greenfields House, Westwood Way, Coventry CV4 8JH; tel: (01203) 694995,* open Mon–Fri 0845–1645. Membership (£26.50) entitles you to use over 4500 sites (you will receive a list detailing them). Non-members can have a free list of some 80 sites that are not restricted to members. **British Holiday & Home Parks Association**, *Chichester House, 6 Pullman Court, Great Western Rd, Glos GL1 3ND; tel: (01452) 526911,* produce an excellent annual guide, *Caravan & Chalet Parks Guide*, to over 1600 camping and caravan sites throughout Britain (no membership required). This is free, but stocks are limited.

Self-catering

There is a wide range of self-catering facilities, from luxurious to primitive, both in towns and in rural locations. Advance booking is the norm – and usually by the week, although shorter stays are sometimes possible. TICs have listings and there are many published guides.

BICYCLES

Cycling in the larger cities may be hair-raising (especially if you are not used to traffic driving on the left), but there are many quieter, rural areas where bicycles offer an excellent method of exploring. Books about bicycle touring are available and TICs usually have information about bike rental and routes. The **Cyclists' Touring Club**, *tel: (01483) 417217,* can provide information, including a list of rental firms.

BUSES

Buses offer a useful alternative if you are staying in a larger city or need a change from driving, but it should be noted that services in rural areas are often very poor. Services were deregulated in the 1980s and competition is resulting in constant changes to schedules and routes, so double-check any service that is important to your plans. Many towns and cities have a bewildering array of different companies, which may or may not operate from the same bus station – and not all display their destinations clearly. On most buses you pay the driver when you board (try to have plenty of change). On some, however, there's a conductor – sit down and wait for him/her to come to you. Press a bell button – once only (or pull the ceiling cord, if there is one) when you want the bus to halt at the next stop – necessary only if the next stop is a 'request'.

There is an efficient network of inter-city coaches, run in Britain mainly by **National Express**; *tel: (0990) 808080* (nationwide number).

CHILDREN

Many tourist destinations are now acknowledging the existence of young children, something at which the British are traditionally very bad, and providing children's menus, high chairs, and nappy-changing facilities. Children are not allowed in the bar area of pubs, though many pubs have separate restaurants, gardens and/or play areas. If hotels offer babysitting services, ask what that means – it may consist only of looking in occasionally. There are guidebooks that recommend attractions, restaurants and hotels where children are welcome – local newsagents sometimes have similar information. There are usually discounts (up to 50%) for children, and very young infants are often free, but be prepared for variations to the usual age definition: 5–15 years. Family rates are common – and usually good value if you have two or more children.

CLIMATE

The British climate is temperate and sustained periods of great heat/cold are unlikely, although brief spells of both cannot be ruled out in any season. Rain (or sleet/snow in winter) is probable, rather than possible, and the notoriously fickle weather can run through everything in one day – which at least has the advantage that if you awake to rain, there is a sporting chance of a fine afternoon! 'Rain before seven, fine by eleven' is a frequently expressed myth, especially in country districts.

Prevailing westerly winds bring noticeably more rain to the north and west than to the south and east. Generally, it gets hotter as you move south, with June–Sept being the warmest months. In Aug the average temperature in the south is 60–75°F (15–24°C). Whenever you are travelling, pack something warm, as well as rainproof footwear and clothing. Spring and autumn are probably the most rewarding seasons to travel, if you are not tied to school holidays.

CLOTHING

Travel as light as you can: however light your bag or suitcase may seem at home, it will seem infinitely heavier when you are lifting it in and out of the boot or lugging it to your accommodation. As well as a warm cover-up and rainproof outer wear, you may find yourself investing in the ubiquitous fold-up umbrella. Despite the generally mild climate, it is easy to get sunburnt in Britain; the unpredictability of the weather almost makes it more likely than if you are heading for the Mediterranean expecting sun, so the fair skinned and children should be especially careful to cover up and to use high-protection-factor sunscreen. Bring scarf, hat, gloves and plenty of layers in winter. There is no need for

17

formal clothes, even for evening wear, unless you are planning on upmarket dining or reserving the best seats at the Royal Opera House.

CURRENCY

The pound sterling (£) is divided into 100 pence (p). There are 1p, 2p, 5p, 10p, 20p, 50p and £1 coins (in an apparently confusing variety of sizes and weights but designed to help blind people), and £5, £10, £20 and £50 notes.

The usual rules for travellers apply: do not carry too much cash, take most of your money in traveller's cheques (preferably sterling) or Eurocheques, and use credit cards for large bills – the major cards are very widely accepted, though not by some small establishments (e.g. many b&bs). There are plenty of cash dispensers – outside banks, supermarkets and in other strategic positions. Commission rates tend to be high in exchange bureaux, particularly in London, so shop around. Banks in England and Wales open Mon–Fri 0930–1530 and usually Sat morning. **Thomas Cook** offices (listed throughout this book) cash any type of Eurocheque/traveller's cheque and replace Thomas Cook traveller's cheques if yours are lost/stolen; *tel: (0800) 622101.*

CUSTOMS

There are no limits on the amount of currency you may bring into the British Isles. Importing narcotics and offensive weapons is prohibited, so do not be tempted – and *never* carry anything for anyone else. If you need a prescribed drug on a regular basis, carry a prescription or doctor's letter to prove it's legitimate. Britain also prohibits the import of pornography, horror comics, fireworks, meat and poultry, plants, fruit and vegetables, as well as the obvious drugs, explosives, firearms and other weapons,

---

Thomas Cook Foreign Exchange

Thomas Cook operate over 600 foreign exchange bureaux around the UK, all offering a full foreign currency and traveller's cheque exchange service at competitive rates. Most bureaux offer other useful services for visitors to the UK, including *Moneygram*SM international money transfer, where money can be transferred to over 80 countries in as little as 10 mins, Worldwide Telephone cards and postage stamps.

There are over 40 bureaux in central London and 50 in major UK airports. All major tourist towns and cities, such as Edinburgh, Oxford, Bath and Stratford-upon-Avon, have Thomas Cook foreign exchange bureaux. Locations are mentioned within the appropriate chapters, but most Thomas Cook high street shops also have bureaux facilities.

---

while animals are subject to six months in quarantine. Similar rules apply when returning home: all countries have specified restrictions, so always check anything unusual with the relevant customs department.

Customs Allowances

The UK customs allowances for tobacco, alcohol and perfume are those set throughout the EU, and apply to anyone aged 17 or over. To all intents and purposes, there are no restrictions between EU countries for goods bought in ordinary shops but, if you have excessive amounts, you might be questioned as to whether everything is for your personal use.

Allowances are:

800 cigarettes, 200 cigars, 400 cigarillos and 1 kg tobacco.

+ 90 litres wine (max. 60 litres sparkling).

+ 10 litres alcohol over 22% volume (e.g. most spirits).
+ 20 litres alcohol under 22% volume (e.g. port and sherry).
+ 110 litres beer.

The allowances for goods bought outside the EU and/or in EU duty-free shops are: 200 cigarettes, 50 cigars, 100 cigarillos and 250 g tobacco.
+ 2 litres still table wine.
+ 1 litre spirits or 2 litres fortified/sparkling wine.
+ 50 g/60 ml perfume.
+ 0.5 l/250 ml toilet water.
+ other goods up to the value of £145.
For specific enquiries about UK customs, *tel: (0171) 202 4227.*

Allowances when Returning Home

Australia: goods to the value of A$400 (half for those under 18) plus 250 cigarettes or 250 g tobacco and 1 litre alcohol.
Canada: goods to the value of C$300, provided you have been away for over a week and have not already used up part of your allowance that year, plus 50 cigars plus 200 cigarettes and 1 kg tobacco (if over 16) and 40 oz/1 litre alcohol.
New Zealand: goods to the value of NZ$700. Anyone over 17 may also take 200 cigarettes or 250 g tobacco or 50 cigars or a combination of tobacco products not exceeding 250 g in all, plus 4.5 litres of beer or wine and 1.125 litres spirits.
South Africa: goods to the value of R.500 are duty free. A further R.10,000 is allowed on payment of 20%.
USA: goods to the value of US$400, as long as you have been out of the country for at least 48 hrs and only use your allowance once every 30 days. Anyone over 21 is also allowed 1 litre alcohol plus 100 (non-Cuban) cigars and 100 cigarettes.

DISABLED TRAVELLERS

England and Wales are increasingly well provided with facilities for disabled visitors, even though they sometimes fall short of what is advertised. Experienced travellers with disabilities will already know that planning is the key to ensure that you obtain suitable accommodation and travel with the minimum of hassle.

Travel

The Holiday Care Service, *2nd Floor, Imperial Buildings, Victoria Rd, Horley, Surrey, RH6 7PZ; tel: (01293) 774535,* and **RADAR** (the Royal Association for Disability and Rehabilitation), *12 City Forum, 250 City Rd, London EC1V 8AF; tel: (0171) 250 3222,* have got together to produce an annual guide, *Accessible Accommodation and Travel (£7).*

Accommodation

Help in finding accommodation is included in *Accessible Accommodation and Travel* (see above). The English Tourist Board grades all its approved accommodation, from hotels to self-catering, according to suitability, so TICs will be able to help on a local basis. Some hotel chains at the higher end of the market have bedrooms adapted for wheelchair users.

Visitor Attractions and Facilities

RADAR publishes a number of useful guides on access to visitor attractions. The National Trust and English Heritage also publish free booklets about access to their properties, including facilities for the visually and hearing impaired – these are available from all staffed sites. Again, TICs have information on access to local sites. A small number of sites offer the Sympathetic Hearing Scheme: SHS in the text indicates which TICs offer this service. TICs accessible to disabled persons are indicated in

19

the text by the initials DP. **Shopmobility** provide battery-powered scooters and wheelchairs in some towns: the phone number is given in the relevant *Getting Around* section.

Toilets for wheelchair users are increasingly being provided at museums and other tourist attractions, but they are by no means universal; a booklet, listing toilets (and a special key to them) is available from RADAR, but there is a charge for both (£5 book, £2.50 key).

DISCOUNTS

Prices change frequently and any you see printed (in this book and elsewhere) should be regarded as a guide, not gospel. In most instances, this book gives only the adult prices, but discounts for senior citizens, students, children and families are almost always available at tourist attractions and often on public transport and elsewhere. Students and senior citizens should carry proof of status; no student should be without the International Student Identity Card (ISIC), which allows many discounts as well as providing accident insurance – ask your local student travel office.

Membership of one of the national organisations which manage historic properties may be worthwhile if you are planning to visit several (see *Visiting Historic Places* box, p.24).

DRIVING

Driving in the British Isles is on the left. To hire a car you must be over 21/25 (according to agency) and have two years' driving experience. TICs can provide details of agencies – or you can book with the main companies in advance; some companies have offices at ports, airports and stations, or offer a delivery service. Non-EU nationals will need an International Driving Permit. US and Canadian licence holders can use their own for three months, but an international one may save hassle. A Green Card (International Insurance Certificate) is also required; car rental agencies will often include one in the package. Full information on road travel is given in *Driving in England and Wales* (see p.26).

ELECTRICITY

England and Wales use 230V (unlike the rest of Europe, which uses 220V) and plugs with three square pins, so bring an adapter.

FOOD AND DRINK

Usual eating hours are: breakfast 0730–0900, lunch 1200–1400, afternoon tea 1600–1700, dinner 1930–2130, but many eateries are open from very early to very late.

The stereotype of British food is of roast meat, heavy puddings, fish and chips – and afternoon tea featuring dainty cucumber sandwiches and cream cakes. All these are readily available, but not recommended on a daily basis if you value your cholesterol level. Most hotels and b&bs will offer you a full English breakfast: this is a wonderful institution, consisting of fried egg, bacon, sausage, tomato and fried bread (often also mushrooms, fried potatoes and/or baked beans), followed by toast and marmalade. If you can stomach this before 0900, you may decide to waive lunch.

Such is the ethnic mix in Britain that, particularly in bigger towns and cities, there is an enormous range of food available. At the budget end, most towns will have Chinese, Indian and Greek restaurants and/or takeaways, plus burger bars, pizza parlours and fish and chip takeaways, of varying quality. There are plenty of good sandwich bars/delis and it's never

20

British English

A few phrases which have different meanings in British and US English.

British	US
bank holiday	(public) holiday
bill	check
biscuit	cookie/cracker
car	automobile
car park	parking lot
carriage	railroad car
chemist	pharmacy/drugstore
coach	long-distance bus/railroad car
crisps	potato chips
first floor	second floor (and so on)
flat	apartment
fortnight	two weeks
gents	men's restroom
ground floor	first floor
ladies	women's restroom
lift	elevator
loo	restroom
nappy	diaper
note (bank)	bill
pavement	sidewalk
petrol	gasoline
phone box	telephone booth
platform	track
public holiday	holiday
pudding	dessert
quid	pound sterling
return ticket	round-trip ticket
single (ticket)	one-way ticket
subway	underground walkway
sweets	candy
timetable	schedule
traffic lights	stop light
Tube	London subway
Underground	subway

difficult to find ready-made sandwiches and other ready-to-eat snacks – often cheaper from supermarkets than small shops.

Pubs usually serve a good range, from the ubiquitous ploughman's lunch (bread, cheese and pickle) to three-course meals. They are your best bet if you are seeking traditional British fare at a reasonable price. Vegetarians are better provided for in Britain than in most of Europe. Most restaurants and even many pubs include vegetarian dishes on their menus. Contact the **Vegetarian Society**, *tel: (0161) 928 0793*, for a listing (£1).

Tea, usually served with milk, and coffee (specify black or white), are served everywhere, as is water – but specify tap (branch) water if you don't want to pay for the bottled variety. Spirits are expensive in Britain (due to heavy taxation), but naturally carbonated beer (heavier and more bitter than most European or American beer) is a speciality – be prepared for the fact that this is not served chilled. Lager is also ubiquitous. There are many different breweries and free houses (i.e. pubs not linked to any specific brewery) which serve a wide range for the connoisseur. Cider (fermented apple juice) is another English speciality, as is the rarer mead (based on honey) – try this if you get the chance. Wine bars serve better and cheaper wine than most pubs – and often have good food. Cocktail bars are also popular. Many drinking places have a happy hour (usually early evening), when drinks are served at half price. Pub hours are usually Mon–Sat 1100–2300 (though some close in the afternoon), Sun 1200–2230. Driving whilst drunk is illegal and socially unacceptable (see p.31 for more information).

GUIDED WALKS

An excellent way of getting your bearings in a new place is to take a guided walk. Accredited tour guides are known as Blue Badge Guides (BBG in the text), and details of the tours they offer can be

21

obtained from TICs. If you prefer your own company, ask the TIC to suggest a route: many have leaflets (usually free) showing themed trails.

HEALTH

You do not need any vaccinations before visiting the British Isles. If you are likely to have casual sex, take precautions against sexually transmitted diseases, including AIDS (condoms are widely available in pharmacies, pubs and supermarkets). It is safe to drink tap water, but wise to wash fresh food, especially if it's been on display. You are entitled to outpatient care at the Accident and Emergency department of public hospitals, but may have to pay if you need to be admitted (see *Insurance* below), unless your country has a reciprocal agreement. If you are from another EU country, obtain an E111 form. If you are on regular medication, carry a note of what you use.

HITCHHIKING

Hitchhiking on motorways (freeways) is illegal, but is allowed in motorway service areas and on ordinary roads. Most hitchhikers are perfectly normal people – usually students or young budget travellers – but it would be wise to exercise caution before deciding to give someone a lift. Theft and other offences have been committed by hitchhikers.

INSURANCE

If you are a visitor to Britain or Ireland, check that you have insurance to cover your health as well as your belongings (you might save unnecessary additional expense by checking whether your policies at home provide cover while travelling). Your insurance should also give cover in case of cancellation or the need for an emergency flight home.

OPENING HOURS

Virtually everything is closed (and there's no public transport) on Christmas Day, while very little functions on Boxing Day. Many places also close for at least one day (usually Good Friday) at Easter. Few close altogether on other public (bank) holidays, but some have shorter hours – normally as Sunday.

It is usual for attractions of all kinds to refuse entry 30–60 mins (some of the larger ones even longer) before closing time, so don't go late without checking.

Shops are typically open Mon–Sat 0900–1730; in smaller places they may close one midweek afternoon, while many areas and most supermarkets have at least one late-night opening (usually until 2000). Sunday opening is increasingly common in Britain, especially for supermarkets and small food shops (in cities these often stay open very late). **Museums** tend to open Mon–Sat 0900/1000 –1730/1800 and half-day Sun. **Parks and gardens** usually close at dusk in winter (1600 onwards). Many **tourist attractions** either close Mon except public holidays – or open Mon except public holidays! Some do not open in winter. All published times are subject to change (especially in the definition of seasons) and if you are intending to visit somewhere remote it's wise to check before you set out. **Stately homes** and similar places (e.g. National Trust properties) often have separate opening times and prices for different parts of the estate. This book often gives times only for the main house, but it is safe to assume that the gardens will be open on the same (and often extra) days for longer hours while the main grounds are usually open in daylight hours (and free) year-round. The price for the house almost invariably includes the estate's other attractions and that is the one quoted in this book, unless otherwise stated, but cheaper tickets are available for the gardens only – and other individual attractions. Most are out of town and close if there are special events, so check opening details before you set out.

PASSPORTS AND VISAS

All visitors to the United Kingdom must carry a valid passport, except nationals of other EU countries, Austria, Liechtenstein, Monaco and Switzerland – who can all use their national identity cards. Citizens of the EU (and most other West European) countries, Australia, Canada, Japan, New Zealand, South Africa and the USA do not need visas. Almost everyone else does.

POSTAGE

There is an excellent network of post offices and sub post offices (often located in local newsagents), opening hours are usually Mon–Fri 0900–1700, Sat 0900–1230. Smaller offices shut for lunch and Wed afternoon. Many shops and hotels sell stamps. Postboxes are usually bright red and easily found.

If you wish to receive mail, ask those writing to you to send their letters c/o the town's main post office, clearly marked 'poste restante'. Unclaimed mail is usually kept for a month. You will need some means of identification, such as a passport, to claim your mail.

SECURITY

England and Wales are reasonably safe places, and rural areas are generally less risky than conurbations, but theft is common and you should take sensible precautions wherever you are. Try not to become a target: keep valuables out of sight, carry travel documents and cash

inside a money-belt. Wear shoulder bags slung across your body; store your bag under the table in restaurants. Never leave large bags/suitcases unattended – not only to avoid theft, but because you might cause a security alert. If leaving your car, lock cases, bags and valuables in the boot.

Mugging is rare in rural areas and well-frequented areas of towns, but it's sensible to avoid deserted streets with poor lighting and women should dress in a way that does not attract undue attention. TICs can advise you about any areas that are best avoided by lone women.

Should you be unlucky, you must report any incident to the local police. Keep a note (separate from your valuables) of the numbers of your traveller's cheques, credit cards and insurance documents, together with a photocopy of the important page(s) of your passport, in case you are separated from the originals.

SMOKING

Smoking is banned in many public places in the UK, including most public transport, though it is usually allowed on the open top deck of tour buses/boats. Where allowed, it is usually in restricted areas. The same applies to many restaurants, shops and (indoor) shopping centres. The majority of drinking places, however, still allow unrestricted smoking.

TAXIS

There are taxi ranks at most stations and in town centres. Always tip (10–12% is normal) – unless you are dissatisfied with the driver. The box-like black cabs found in large towns and cities can be hailed in the street (they're available if the light at the front of the roof is on) and they are metered. If you are using a minicab service, make sure it is reputable and check the fare in advance.

23

Visiting Historic Places

For the avid stately home, castle and garden visitor, joining one of the national organisations responsible for running historic places can be a bargain, even if you are only on a short stay in Britain; once you join, you obtain free entry to all the other properties of that organisation. The best way to join is probably at one of the properties themselves, in which case the cost of your first visit will be deducted from the membership fee. Alternatively, you can join by post, or at many TICs. All the organisations offer various discounts: for joint membership, young people, senior citizens, families, etc.

Sightseeing sections of this book will tell you which organisations are responsible for particular properties: using the initials below. The **National Trust (NT)**, an independent charity, runs mainly historic houses (generally well furnished) and many gardens, as well as vast tracts of coast and countryside; most of its money goes on the land and buildings it protects. The adult annual subscription of £27 (family £51) gives free access to these and also to National Trust for Scotland (NTS) properties if you head north of the border(there is also a reverse arrangement). **English Heritage (EH)**, the government's official adviser on conservation matters and the main national body responsible for building conservation, manages many castles and abbeys, prehistoric and Roman remains. Often in ruins, their sites tend to be more peaceful and remote, although they include such prime attractions as Stonehenge and Dover Castle. Annual membership costs £23 (family £40). If you are concentrating on Wales, **Welsh Historic Monuments/Heritage in Wales (Cadw)** is the equivalents of English Heritage and have some superb properties; membership is £19, and there are reciprocal admission arrangements between both bodies.

Passes

The **Great British Heritage Pass** admits you free to nearly 600 historic properties all over Britain, some belonging to NT, EH, etc., others independent. The time (7 days £28, 15 days £39, 1 month £54) begins the first time you use the pass. You can buy it from many TICs, including Victoria (London), most international airports and ferry ports in England. **Cadw Explorer** passes give free access to all their properties for 3 or 7 days: get one at the first property you visit. In the Irish Republic, a **National Heritage Card** (£15) gives free admission to national parks and the historic properties and gardens run by the Office of Public Works.

TELEPHONES

In an emergency, freephone *999* or *112*, to call Police, Fire Brigade, Ambulance or Coastguard.

British telephone boxes were once bright red, but many are now far less conspicuous. They are usually located near shops, on street corners and at transport hubs. Some take only coins (minimum 10p), others only phonecards (available in various denominations from post offices, newsagents and Thomas Cook bureaux de change), but an increasing number accept both – and also ordinary credit cards. It makes sense to arm yourself with a card, to avoid the not uncommon predicament of finding that the only cash box is out of order. Except for emergencies/operator services, payment has to be inserted before you dial. With cash, try to use low-value coins – any that are unused are returned when you hang up.

Both the length of the call and the time of day affect the cost. There are two time bands: the cheapest is Mon–Fri 1800–0800 and all weekend; the more expensive is Mon–Fri 0800–1800. Numbers prefixed *0500/0800* are free, while those prefixed *0345/0645* are charged as local calls, irrespective of your location. Most other prefixes that do *not* begin *01* indicate premium rates, and an increasing number of information lines come into this category – many are recordings, so have plenty of change ready. Watch out, especially, for *0839/0891*, which are common and expensive.

To make an international call from the UK, dial *00* followed by the country code (*1* for USA, Canada and Caribbean, *62* for Australia, *64* for New Zealand, *27* for South Africa, *31* for the Netherlands, *33* for France, *43* for Germany, *32* for Belgium) and then the phone number, leaving out the initial *0* of the area code, if there is one.

To call a UK number from your own country, dial your country's international access code, followed by *44*, and then the number; remember to leave out the initial *0* of the area code. Area codes are always given in brackets in this book.

For UK domestic enquiries, *tel: 192*; for international enquiries, *tel: 153*.

TOILETS/WCs

Public facilities vary considerably in quality and ease of finding. Signposting varies: you may see signs for *Toilets, WCs, Ladies* and *Gentlemen*, or simply male and female figures (only a few are unisex). Be prepared, also, for such coy variations as *Adam and Eve* – often connected with the name of the establishment. If you can't find a public one, head for a large department store. Pub, restaurant and hotel facilities

are, of course, intended for customers. Most railway stations have toilets, but some make a small charge (20p is common).

USEFUL READING

There are so many guides to Britain that it would be invidious to single any out. Head for a bookshop and make your choice – but remember that a surprising amount of material is available free from TICs.

USEFUL ADDRESSES

British Tourist Authority (BTA), *Thames Tower, Black's Rd, London W6 9EL; tel: (0181) 846 9000; 551 Fifth Ave (Ste 701), New York, NY 10176-0799; tel: (212) 986 2266.* **English Heritage**, *23 Savile Row, London W1X 1AB; tel: (0171) 973 3000.* **National Trust**, *36 Queen Anne's Gate, London SW1H 9AS; tel: (0171) 222 9251.* **Welsh National Tourist Board**, *Brunel House, 2 Fitzalan Rd, Cardiff CF1 3NQ; tel: (01222) 499909.* **Cadw (Welsh Historic Monuments)**, *Welsh Office, Crown Building, Cathays Park, Cardiff; tel: (01222) 500200.*

VAT

Value added tax (sales tax) is automatically added to many goods and services in the UK, at a rate of 17.5%. On large purchases, you can reclaim VAT: ask the shop to fill in a tax refund form and get customs to certify it when you leave (within three months of purchase). To claim a refund, post this back to the shop.

WHAT TO TAKE

Few areas are so remote that you'll be unable to buy anything for which you discover a need, but it's sensible to get such things as a money-belt and electricity adapter (if needed) before you start travelling.

25

DRIVING IN ENGLAND AND WALES

This chapter provides hints and practical advice for those taking to the road in England and Wales and the focus is mainly on visitors from overseas who may be unfamiliar with various aspects of motoring in Britain.

ACCIDENTS AND BREAKDOWNS

If your car suffers a **breakdown**, move to the left-hand side of the road, if possible, stop and switch on hazard lights. On motorways (the British equivalent of freeways, autoroutes, autobahns, etc.) pull over to the hard shoulder. Free emergency telephones are placed at one mile intervals, with tenth-mile markers in between, so you should be able to work out which way to walk to the nearest telephone if you need help with a repair or a tow.

Roadside telephones are connected to the motorway police control centre and you will be asked where you are. An identifying number is written on the side of each telephone kiosk. You will also be asked if you would like the services of one of the major motoring organisations (AA, RAC, etc.). If, as occasionally happens, the telephones are out of order (this situation is usually indicated on roadside signs or overhead electronic boards) make sure your hazard lights are on, raise the car's bonnet and remain with the vehicle – a patrolling police car should be along shortly.

On other major roads limp, if you can, to a lay-by, where there may be a public telephone or an AA or RAC emergency

kiosk. Lay-bys are roadside parking bays holding anything from two or three to a number of cars and trucks, and are found at frequent intervals on trunk roads and even on some country lanes. Wherever you are when misfortune strikes, be prepared to pay a hefty charge if your vehicle has to be towed – unless you belong to a motoring organisation or one of its overseas affiliates, such as the American Automobile Association, or AA South Africa. AA (Automobile Association) or RAC (Royal Automobile Club) membership benefits are usually included in car hire agreements.

In the event of an **accident** involving another vehicle, property, people or animals (such as dogs, horses, sheep or pigs) you must stop. All persons involved should exchange names and addresses and drivers are required also to provide insurance details. If there has been personal injury or damage to property or animals, the accident must be reported to the police within 24 hours. Failure to stop or failure to report an accident are serious offences carrying heavy penalties.

Motorists in Britain do not need to carry their driving licences and insurance certificates at all times, but in the event of a reportable accident the police will require the documents to be produced within seven days, though drivers may produce them at a police station of their own choice. Again, failure to produce documents when required is an offence and could result in a large fine.

At the scene of an accident make

careful notes of the circumstances – the time, direction of travel of the vehicles involved, weather and road conditions, road widths, and the positions of road signs, traffic lights and witnesses – and if possible take photographs of the scene and damage. Make sure you note the names and addresses of any witnesses.

The least said at the scene, the better. Refrain from discussing the cause of the accident with anyone. Unwise words may result in an outbreak of road rage or prejudice a subsequent court case. Save any statements you may wish to make for your insurance company and, if necessary, the police.

Drivers from overseas – especially if they have travelled a long distance – are at their most vulnerable at the beginning and end of their holiday. After a long-haul flight it might be wiser to sleep off the effects of jetlag before picking up a hire car – possibly with an unfamiliar manual gear shift – and setting off on the left-hand side of the road. At the end of your trip allow plenty of time to get to the airport or ferry, remembering that such problems as traffic jams or punctures can occur at any time.

CAR HIRE

To make the most of a touring holiday in England and Wales, a car is undoubtedly the best option. You can set your own itinerary and change it at will, and although car rental and fuel costs in Britain are much higher than in some other parts of the world, especially North America, motoring is still the cheapest way to get from one place to another, especially for families.

You may get the best deal by reserving a car before you leave home, either through one of the major international rental agencies or through a tour operator's fly-drive package. If you turn up at a British airport without a pre-booked car it's worth checking at each of the rental desks to see who is offering the best rates. One or more of them may have special promotional deals on offer.

Major agencies operating in England and Wales include **Alamo**, *tel: (0990) 993000*; **Avis**, *tel: (0990) 900500*; **Budget**, *tel: (0800) 181181*; **Europcar** *tel: (0345) 222525*; **Hertz**, *tel: (0990) 996699*; **Holiday Autos**, *tel: (0990) 300453*.

To drive a car in England and Wales you will need a current driving licence issued in your own country, and this may need to be supplemented by an international driving permit, which can be obtained from national motoring organisations. If you arrive in your own car you must also have the vehicle's registration certificate or ownership document, and you must be insured – third party insurance is mandatory in Britain.

To rent a car you will need to be at least 21 years of age and not more than 65 or 70, depending on the hire company. You will be asked to show your driving licence and, if you do not pay by credit card, you will have to pay the rental charge in advance and leave a sizeable deposit. In addition to on-the-road breakdown coverage provided by either the AA or the RAC, the rental agreement will cover the mandatory third party insurance, but you are advised to take out a collision damage waiver (CDW) and personal injury insurance unless you are already covered by a policy issued in your own country – there can be a considerable saving if you are so covered.

Value Added Tax (VAT – see Travel Essentials) is imposed on car rentals, as on most goods and services, but is not refundable when you leave because the service is deemed to have been 'consumed' in Britain.

27

Most cars hired in England and Wales will be smaller than those found on North American roads, for instance, but standards of safety and comfort are high. Air-conditioning is a rare amenity but heaters are a universal fitting and will certainly be appreciated, sometimes even in the summer, in the mountain regions of Wales, the Peak District and the English Lakes.

British drivers seem to prefer hatch-backs to saloons (sedans), and convertibles are rare. Hatchbacks have the advantage that the back seats fold down to provide more luggage space, but this can raise a security problem if all your worldly possessions are exposed to public view when the car is parked. Unless you specify a preference for automatic transmission, the car you rent will almost certainly have a manual gear shift. You may have to pay a little more for an automatic, but it may be worth it if you are not used to DIY driving.

DIFFICULT DRIVING

You can be certain of one thing when driving in England and Wales: you won't be bored. British drivers are skilful, but can be impatient and aggressive. Unlike other Europeans, they do not make much use of the horn but they can be eloquent with flashing headlights and small but expressive hand gestures. Some of them treat most highways, especially motorways, as if they were circuits at Indianapolis or Daytona, regarding speed limits as a minimum rather than the maximum. The daunting habit of high-speed lane-switching enhances the feeling that you are not so much travelling as competing in a massive race.

It sometimes seems there are only two speeds on British roads: fast and stopped. **Traffic jams** into and out of many towns and cities are the norm at morning and evening rush hours, though 'rush' is hardly

the right word to use, and the back-up of cars, caravans and coaches brought to a standstill can be horrendous on popular holiday routes over summer weekends. It must be said, however, that many people seem to have a herd instinct when it comes to travelling by car, and you can often avoid the crowds by travelling on lesser roads, which more or less follow the course of popular major routes. This is the strategy we have encouraged in devising the alternative 'scenic' routes described in this book.

It won't be long – probably before you drive out of the airport or ferry terminus – before you encounter your first round-about (or traffic circle). **Roundabouts** are a peculiarly British system of traffic control, and it may be that there are more of them in the average English or Welsh town than in the whole of North America. The rule on approaching a roundabout is that you should give way to traffic from the right. On leaving a roundabout, check your rear-view mirror, ease over to the left and use your left-hand indicator to signal your intention to exit.

In some towns you may encounter a large roundabout surrounded by a number of smaller ones – rather like a frozen maelstrom. The 'yield to those on the right rule' still applies but many people, understandably, seem confused by the situation and the best advice is to stay cool, work out which way you want to go and don't move until there is a reasonable gap in the traffic. Remember, you can easily stall an unfamiliar car by moving off too quickly.

Motorways, you will be glad to know, do not have roundabouts.

The narrow, twisting country **lanes** that lead off major highways offer an opportunity to encounter the 'real' England and Wales, with sleepy villages, centuries-old churches and enchanting pubs. They can also present some unusual hazards – usually on a hairpin bend. Among these are hikers, cyclists, herds of cattle on their way to or from the milking sheds, tractors towing heavily laden trailers (often giving off a powerful agricultural odour), and horses ridden by over-confident little girls who maintain a haughty indifference to other road users. You won't encounter these perils on every bend in the road, of course, but bear them in mind, drive with care, and enjoy the scenery.

MAPS

Although there is a colour map section at the back of this book, you will need a more detailed road map to make the most of your travels. Good, inexpensive and up-to-date road maps and atlases are available everywhere. A popular choice is the *AA Road Atlas of Great Britain*. Most road atlases are dated so that you can check you have the latest edition, as the road network is constantly changing. For more detailed maps with a larger scale, Ordnance Survey do several series, available from larger bookshops.

PARKING

Street parking is allowed only on meters in most town centres, which are prowled by **traffic wardens**, men and women who wear navy blue uniforms and caps with a yellow band. Traffic wardens can issue fixed penalty notices for parking offences, for parking a car without lights, where required, and for failure to display an excise licence – the road fund tax disc usually located on the left side of the front windscreen.

Yellow lines painted on the edge of a street indicate on-street parking restrictions. A broken line means free parking is allowed for the period stated on a nearby sign, usually an hour or less. A single continuous line means parking is not allowed at certain times, usually Mon–Sat between 0830 and 1830 – again, the restriction will be posted on a nearby sign. A double yellow line indicates a total ban on parking.

Other places where parking is forbidden include the white zigzag lines indicating the approach to a pedestrian crossing, on a pedestrian crossing, within 32 ft of a junction and within 25 yds of a traffic light.

Fines for **parking offences** can be heavy and in some places – notably London and other large cities – illegally parked vehicles may be clamped or towed away. Unclamping or recovering your vehicle can be costly as well as time-consuming.

Off-street parking in open-air lots or more usually multi-storey car parks (parking garages) can be found in many places by following blue and white signs bearing the letter P. Most are 'pay and display' parks with machines where you buy an adhesive ticket to stick on the windscreen. In some cases you may obtain a ticket at the entry barrier and insert it into a machine and pay (on foot) for validation on exit. Some towns offer free parking and this will be indicated on the blue and white signs.

Some cities and popular holiday destinations operate 'Park and Ride' schemes, with car parks situated some distance from the town centre to which free transport is provided. There have been security problems in some of these car parks, so make sure your car is locked, with windows closed and nothing of value in sight.

PETROL

The first thing to point out is that fuel in Britain is expensive, with diesel and lead-free petrol the cheapest – though not by much – thanks to a lower rate of tax in the

29

interests of clean air. Fuel prices are at their highest at motorway service stations. You will find the best deals in suburban areas, especially at filling stations operated by supermarket chains (e.g. ASDA, Sainsbury and Tesco).

Motorway service stations and some town centre filling stations are open 24 hours a day, and those on major highways usually open from 0700 to around 2300. In rural areas, however, most petrol stations close in the evening and on Sun.

POLICE

It should not be difficult to recognise British police cars, which have become increasingly flamboyant in recent years. Motorway patrol cars and traffic police vehicles are generally painted white with a pattern of orange, red or blue stripes – sometimes all three. They have blue and white lights mounted on the roof, which flash when they mean business. The police sometimes use what they call 'unmarked' cars on highway patrol – vehicles indistinguishable from other cars. An officer in plain clothes should show his identity card as a matter of course if he stops you.

Police (and traffic wardens) can demand your name and address, and in the event of an accident or traffic offence a police officer can demand the name and address of the vehicle's owner, if he or she is not the driver. An officer can also demand to see your driving licence and insurance certificate, and if they are not available can order you to produce them at a police station of your choice within seven days.

ROAD SIGNS

There are four major types of signs used on British roads, mostly bearing conventional international symbols. **Information signs**, conveying information on such matters as parking zones, traffic priorities

and lane closures are always rectangular. **Warning signs**, indicating some danger or hazard ahead, are red-edged triangles surrounding a black pictogram denoting the kind of hazard. **Instructional signs** fall into two sub-categories. Signs on blue circular discs give positive indications – 'Turn Left', 'Keep Right' – while those on red discs with white borders or vice versa mostly indicate prohibitions – 'No Stopping', 'No Right Turn', and so forth. **Directional signs**, found just before and again at motorway exits and other road junctions, are large, clear and unmistakable. On motorways they are the size of advertising hoardings, with white lettering on a blue background. They indicate the distance to the next exit, the places it leads to and in the bottom left-hand corner the motorway junction number.

Motorways also have a system of electronic hazard warning lights, consisting of flashing lights, numbers and symbols to warn of things like accidents, fog or ice. Roadside electronic boards provide up-to-the-minute information on such matters as traffic congestion, highway work and junction closures.

There are two types of **pedestrian crossing** on British roads. 'Zebra' crossings have black and white stripes painted across the road and are indicated at night by spotlights and flashing amber beacons. 'Pelican' crossings are controlled by traffic lights and you must stop if the lights are red or flashing amber.

ROAD SYSTEM

British roads fall into four categories. **Motorways** are fast, multi-lane highways with limited access. They may not provide the shortest journey between two points but they should provide the quickest. They are indicated on blue and white road signs by the letter M followed by one or two numbers, e.g. M1, M63. Many of them cover great distances, but there are frequent service areas with cafeterias, shops, toilets, filling stations and sometimes a hotel.

The major non-motorway highways, **'A' roads** – the arterial roads that cross the country more or less north–south and east–west – are indicated by the letter A and a number. A road's importance diminishes as its number increases. Thus A2 is the major route south-east from London to Dover; A23 travels south from London to Brighton and A272 is a cross-country route from East Sussex to Hampshire.

'B' roads, shown by the letter B and three or four digits are minor roads, usually two lanes wide, connecting small villages and market towns.

The fourth category, known simply as **unclassified roads**, carry no letters or numbers. They meander across the countryside from hamlet to hamlet. In some parts of England and Wales they may be only one lane wide, with passing places at fairly frequent intervals.

RULES OF THE ROAD

The rules of driving in England and Wales are not much different from those in other parts of the world – except, of course, that traffic travels on the left. Even that is not unique. Many countries, from Australia to Zimbabwe (most of them, admittedly, part of the old British Empire), also drive on the left.

So the basic rule is – **keep left**, overtake on the right. Add to that ' Keep your head and think left all the time', and

perhaps switch your watch to the other wrist as a reminder, and you should be all right.

A useful publication for those unfamiliar with British roads is *The Highway Code*, obtainable from most newsagents and bookshops. It is a small, cheap publication, published by HM Stationery Office, the official government publishers, and is required reading for student drivers. But it contains everything you need to know about driving in Britain.

Speed limits are 70mph on motorways and dual carriageways (divided highways), 60mph on single carriageways and 30 or 40mph in towns and urban areas. The rule in urban areas is to drive at no more than 30mph on streets with lighting unless signs show a higher or lower limit.

You must stop at appropriate road signs or traffic lights; if required by a police officer in uniform or a traffic warden supervising traffic or pedestrians; for a pedestrian on a zebra or pelican crossing; for the warden of a school crossing (wearing a white topcoat and cap and carrying a round sign on a stick with the words 'Stop! Children Crossing' – the sign has caused female wardens to be known as 'lollipop ladies'); and for a workman controlling traffic at road works.

Britain has very strict laws on **drinking and driving**. At the time of writing, a drink-driving offence is established if a driver is found to have 35 or more milligrams of alcohol per 100 millilitres in breath, 80mg per 100ml in blood or 107mg per 100ml in urine. New legislation could reduce these limits.

31

BACKGROUND
ENGLAND AND WALES

England and Wales, which together form the bulk of the island of Great Britain, are linked geographically, historically and socially, yet there are cultural and topographical differences which create a kaleidoscope of experiences for anyone touring the two countries by car. This chapter is an introduction to some of the factors that contribute to the uniqueness of each and the unity of the two.

ENGLAND

GEOGRAPHY

32

With a population of more than 48 million (out of the United Kingdom total of 58 million) and an area covering just over 50,000 square miles, England is the largest of the three nations that make up Great Britain. It covers the southern and eastern parts of the island, bordering Scotland to the north and Wales to the west. In the south-east it is a mere 18 miles from France at the narrowest part of the English Channel; now, of course, England and France are linked by the Channel Tunnel, which emerges on the English side just outside the seaside resort of Folkestone.

England is divided into three major land regions: the Pennines, the south-west peninsula and the English lowlands.

The Pennines, often called the backbone of England, are a mountain range stretching south from the Scottish border for about 170 miles – more or less halfway down the length of the land. In the north-

west area of the Pennines is the Lake District, known for its scenic beauty. Scafell Pike, England's highest point at 3210 ft above sea level, is in the Lake District.

The south-west peninsula, a low plateau with granite highlands and a rugged coastline with frequent towering cliffs, encompasses the counties of Devon and Cornwall and parts of Somerset, and also contains England's westernmost point, Land's End, and the southernmost point in the British Isles, Lizard Point. The region's high rainfall and rich pastures are ideal for dairy farming and sheep are found in the high moorlands. The generally mild climate and the sheltered coves and sandy beaches along the coast make the peninsula a popular holiday area.

The English lowlands, containing much of England's farmlands, industry and most densely populated cities, cover the rest of the country. The north-western part of the lowlands form the rich plains of Lancashire, while those of Yorkshire are found in the north-east. The central lowlands – the Midlands – are a heavily

Colour section (i): Images of England: picturesque country pubs and welcoming town taverns; Morris Dancers.
(ii): Welsh scenes: the Pembroke Coastal Path (see p. 50) and Tenby (p. 51).
(iii): The Needles, on the Isle of Wight (p. 88); Portmeirion, North Wales (p. 58)
(iv): HMS Victory at Portsmouth (p. 86); Brighton Pavilion (p. 79)

populated area which has seen much industrial development since the end of the 18th century. The major city here – the UK's second largest after London – is Birmingham.

South of the Midlands, the hills and woodlands of the Thames Valley sweep gently towards London, and south of London are the chalk hills known as the Downs. The North Downs stretch through Surrey and Kent to Dover, where they end as the famous white cliffs. The South Downs run through Sussex and part of Hampshire.

The lowlands region to the north-east of London is low and flat and includes Lincolnshire and the counties of Cambridge, Essex, Norfolk and Suffolk, known collectively as East Anglia. The Fens, rich farmland bordering the Wash, is an area of land reclaimed by drainage during the 18th century.

CLIMATE

The English seem to be obsessed by their climate, and the weather looms large in their conversations. In truth, however, it isn't as bad as they often seem to think. Light winds blowing in off the surrounding seas and the warm waters of the Gulf Stream keep the climate mild, usually preventing temperatures from falling much below freezing point or rising to the swooning summer levels experienced in parts of mainland Europe. In London, the average summer temperatures are a high of 21°C and a low of 12°C.

In general (and it is difficult to be specific about British weather) the further north you go the colder it gets. The warmest regions are London, the south-east and the West Country; the wettest are the south-west peninsula, the Lake District and other areas west of the Pennines. The eastern side of England – from Northumbria down to Kent – is the driest part of the UK. That said, rain *can* fall anywhere at any time of the year and, unless you arrive during an unmistakable drought, it pays to be prepared by keeping a light raincoat handy at all times – or go native and buy an umbrella.

The thick 'pea soup' fogs every foreigner expects – thanks to the adventures of Sherlock Holmes and his ilk – are largely a thing of the past. They were caused in London and other large cities by smoke from factory chimneys and domestic coal fires. Anti-pollution legislation has put an end to smog. However, mild fogs do swirl around in some places from time to time – usually around international airports and on motorways!

HISTORY

England has always attracted immigrants. The country's first human inhabitants were small bands of hunters who were superseded around 4000 BC by farming peoples from Europe. Settled among the chalk hills around Salisbury Plain, these were the Stone Age people who built Stonehenge, the Avebury Ring and many other ceremonial circles found in the area.

The next wave of newcomers were the Celts, who began arriving from central Europe around 800 BC, bringing with them the skills of smelting bronze and iron. They also brought the Celtic language, which survives to this day as Gaelic in Ireland and Scotland and as the Brythonic dialect spoken in Wales and Cornwall.

Although Julius Caesar made exploratory incursions in 55 and 54 BC, it was AD 43 – nearly a century later – before the legions of Emperor Claudius swept across the English Channel in what has become known as the Roman invasion. Although they met considerable resistance

33

in the early years from the Welsh and tribes led by the warrior queen Boudicca, the Romans advanced steadily and by AD 80 controlled Wales and England to the far north. The Scots were a different matter – so troublesome and difficult to overcome, in fact, that in 122 the Emperor Hadrian ordered a wall to be built coast-to-coast across England's northern border to mark Rome's northern frontier.

England and Wales prospered under the Romans, who built paved roads linking London – their major port – with important regional centres, such as Canterbury, Chester, Lincoln and York. Many of the old Roman routes form the basis of major highways in use today. Trade flourished, there was economic and social stability and the living was good.

In 313, under Emperor Constantine, the Romans brought Christianity to their island colony. Then, as the Roman Empire went into decline, Britain began to feel the pinch: money became short, military garrisons were abandoned. From the early 5th century, when Roman power finally faded, suffered attacks from Germanic tribes of Jutes, Angles and Saxons who set up kingdoms and began pushing the Britons north and west. The Anglo-Saxons soon became the most powerful tribes in England, and by the 7th century the country had been divided by them into seven major kingdoms.

Viking raids on the Anglo-Saxon kingdoms began in the late 8th century, and in the following century the Vikings conquered them all, except Wessex, where King Alfred the Great defeated them in battle and sent them packing to the north-east.

The Norman Invasion
The next – and as it happened, the last – successful invasion of England came in

1066 when William Duke of Normandy earned himself the sobriquet 'the Conqueror' by defeating the English King Harold at the Battle of Hastings. Crowned king of England on the Christmas Day of that historic year, William set up a strong central government with Norman nobles in high positions. His reign saw the building of many cathedrals and castles – including the Tower of London – and in 1087, shortly before his death, he ordered a comprehensive survey of England. Known as the Domesday Book, it remains a treasure house of information about early medieval life.

William's death brought the beginning of a series of power struggles, civil wars, and wars with neighbouring Wales, Scotland and France that were to bedevil England over the next 470 years – almost five centuries that witnessed the murder in Canterbury Cathedral of Thomas à Becket, the Hundred Years War with France, the Black Death, the Wars of the Roses and the turbulent reign of Henry VIII, whose wives came and went, who had himself established as head of the church in England and who closed the monasteries.

On the positive side, those five centuries also saw the signing at Runnymede of Magna Carta, the establishment of the English system of common law, the beginnings of parliament, the founding of Oxford and Cambridge universities, and the birth of English as a language of great literature through the publication of such works as William Langland's *The Vision of Piers Plowman* and Geoffrey Chaucer's *The Canterbury Tales*.

The Golden Age
During the reign of Henry VIII's daughter, Elizabeth I 1558–1603, England became a major player in international

trade, with merchant adventurers sailing to ports around the world and exploring the islands of the Caribbean and the coasts of North and South America. English literature blossomed, nurtured by the pens of such writers as Francis Bacon, Christopher Marlowe, Edmund Spenser and, of course, the great bard William Shakespeare.

Elizabeth's successor, James I (James VI of Scotland) belonged to the House of Stuart, and his coming to the throne effectively sealed the union of England, Wales and Scotland, although the three countries continued to be ruled separately. During his reign English colonies were established at Jamestown and Plymouth in America.

Charles I, James's son, found himself in conflict with parliament over moves to limit the monarch's powers. The result was a civil war which broke out in 1642 and culminated in the beheading of Charles by the Parliamentarians in 1649. England became a republic under the dictatorship of Oliver Cromwell. The monarchy was restored, with Charles II on the throne, in 1660, two years after Cromwell's death.

The death of Charles II in 1685 brought his brother, James II, to the throne. James was a Roman Catholic and wanted to restore Catholicism and absolute monarchy, ambitions which were not shared by the majority of the people, who were looking forward to his death when his Protestant daughter Mary would inherit the throne. James then had a son, so to prevent the restoration of Catholicism, leading politicians invited Mary's husband, William of Orange, to take over the throne and restore English liberties. William landed in England in 1688 and James fled to France.

William and Mary became joint rulers of England after accepting the Bill of Rights, assuring basic civil rights to the people and banning the monarch from keeping a standing army, levying taxes or being a Roman Catholic.

Mary died before William and on his death, in 1702, Mary's sister Anne ascended to the throne, heralding another age of great literature and flourishing commerce. Parliament gained total control over the monarchy, and in 1707 the Act of Union legally completed the union of the Kingdom of England and Wales with the Kingdom of Scotland to form the Kingdom of Great Britain, forerunner of the United Kingdom of Great Britain and Northern Ireland.

WALES

GEOGRAPHY

Occupying a broad peninsula on the west coast of Great Britain, Wales covers an area of just over 8000 square miles. It is about 170 miles, with a maximum width north–south/east–west of about 100 miles, and is bounded by England to the east and the Bristol Channel to the south. The Irish Sea to the north and St George's Channel to the west separate Wales from Ireland.

Much of the country is mountainous with upland plateaux. It has two main mountain ranges – the Brecon Beacons and Black Mountains in the south and the more rugged Snowdonia in the north. At 3560 ft, Mt Snowdon is the highest peak in England and Wales. The ranges in central and southern Wales are flatter, forming large plateaux covered by forests, pastures, moors and bogs and cut by deep, narrow river valleys, and there are many waterfalls and small lakes.

About a third of the country is covered by coastal plains and river valleys. Its longest rivers are the Severn and the Wye, both rising near Aberystwyth and flowing

35

eastward into England to drain into the Bristol Channel. In the north the River Dee is part of the boundary with England, and the main rivers along the west coast are the Dyfi, Teifi and Tywi.

Wales has a little over 600 miles of coastline, much of stunningly beautiful, with many bays, beaches and natural harbours. In the north, however, some fine beach areas are blemished by long lines of mobile homes and beach cottages. Off the north-west coast, separated by the Menai Strait, lies the island of Anglesey.

The great concentration of population is in the south-east, between Swansea and Cardiff, and in the old coal-mining towns along the valleys that stretch north to the Brecon Beacons.

CLIMATE

The weather is as capricious in Wales as it is in England, but since it is in the wetter, western part of the island, there is probably an even stronger reason for keeping a raincoat in the back of the car. An umbrella, however, might not be such a wise accessory – strong winds sometimes blow in from the sea.

Inland, the mountainous terrain creates local mini-climates which can vary from valley to valley, and there can be sharp differences of temperature between day and night. Even in summer, it would be wise to take waterproof footwear and a warm top when out walking. When driving in the mountains, bear in mind that low cloud can cause a sudden and severe reduction of visibility.

HISTORY

People were living in caves in north-eastern Wales more than 200,000 years ago and stone burial chambers – *cromlechs* – built by Neolithic people can still be seen in parts of the country. The migration

from Europe around 6000 years ago brought farming and the use of stone and flint as tools and weapons. Bronze artefacts emerged with the next wave of immigrants, this time from central and western Europe, about 2000 BC. The Celts, ancestors of the present-day Welsh people, arrived during the mid 7th century BC, introducing iron-smelting and building hill forts.

Between AD 50 and 78 the region was occupied by the Romans, who controlled it for more than three centuries. Christianity was brought to Wales, probably by Irish missionaries, in the 5th century and absorbed into the old Celtic beliefs.

The Germanic invaders who gained control over much of England had little success in Wales. The Celts of Wales kept their independence for several hundred years by maintaining constant resistance against the Anglo-Saxons, although they were not politically united. One man emerged as a leader some time during this period and has remained as a figure of legend if not of history: the mysterious King Arthur.

In the late 8th century Offa, the king of Anglo-Saxon Mercia, built a dyke from the River Dee to the River Severn to keep Welsh raiders out of his kingdom. Offa's Dyke, a ditch and earthen wall, still exists and may be followed by walkers.

After the Norman invasion, William the Conqueror gave lands along the Welsh borders to Norman barons. Known as the Marcher Lords, the barons built castles and advanced into central and southern Wales, which they soon controlled. The country's heartland, however, remained unconquered and in the 12th century the Welsh regained much of their territory from the Normans.

During the 12th century Llywelyn the Great gained control of northern Wales and his grandson, Llywelyn II was acknowledged as Prince of Wales by England's Henry III in 1267. In return Llywelyn acknowledged Henry as his king. When Henry died in 1272 Llywelyn refused to accept Henry's son, Edward I, as king and fighting broke out. The Welsh prince was killed in 1282 during a battle with English troops.

Edward I placed Wales under English control, building a number of great castles, including those at Conwy, Caernarfon and Harlech, to maintain his authority. In 1301 he gave the title Prince of Wales to his eldest son, a tradition which has continued with the British monarchy to this day.

Dissatisfaction with the English grew and in 1400 Owen Glendower, a Welsh prince, headed a rebellion. Within four years he had driven the English out of much of Wales, but by 1410 they were back in control. Glendower died an outlaw in 1416, but his exploits made him a lasting hero of the Welsh people.

Union with England

When Henry Tudor, a Welsh nobleman, became King Henry VII of England in 1485, the notion of uniting with England began to appeal to the Welsh. The Acts of Union, passed in 1536 and 1543, during the reign of Henry Tudor's son, Henry VIII, brought English law, parliamentary representation and trade opportunities to Wales, but the Welsh language was not recognised officially.

The industrial revolution brought great changes to Wales. Copper, iron and slate began to be extracted in quantity and ironworks opened up in the Merthyr Tydfil and Monmouth areas of south Wales. Coal

mining began in the Rhondda valleys in the 1860s and by 1875 Wales led the world in the production of tin plate. Today, tourism is the country's major industry.

Small rural communities in south Wales grew into heavily populated industrial towns. Poor working conditions and industrial disputes led to the formation of trade unions and some people of Wales began to think again about their individuality.

Ever since the union with England, Wales has struggled to maintain its language and culture. Although the Welsh Bible was published in 1588 and the Society for the Promotion of Christian Knowledge, founded in 1699, helped in the publication of Welsh religious books, the language was not legally acceptable in the United Kingdom until 1942 – and then only after members of the Welsh Language Society had resorted to acts of civil disobedience.

The national eisteddfod, a celebration of Welsh literature, music and art, became the centrepiece of a campaign to preserve the Welsh language and culture after 1893 when the University of Wales was formed from the colleges of Aberystwyth, Bangor and Cardiff.

Step by step, Wales has won a more prominent role on the British political stage. In 1955 Cardiff became the country's official capital. 1964 saw the appointment of a minister of state for Wales with cabinet rank in the UK government, and two years later a member of Plaid Cymru, the Welsh Nationalist Party, was elected to parliament. A Welsh language television channel opened in 1982.

37

ARRIVING IN ENGLAND AND WALES

The following are brief details of the main gateways to England and Wales for visitors arriving from abroad.

Public transport from the air terminal or port to the nearest city centre is shown first. Frequency, where shown, applies between 0600 and 1800. Outside these hours, and on Sundays, frequency may be reduced. For more information about UK airports and their transport connections, consult Thomas Cook's *International Air Travel Handbook*. See p.14.

Brief details of taxi services to the nearest city then follow. After this information we give a brief description of the road system surrounding the airport or port, for visitors taking their rented car straight from the terminal.

BIRMINGHAM INTERNATIONAL AIRPORT

Up to seven trains an hour from the airport rail terminal to Birmingham New Street rail station (city centre). Journey time: 10–15 mins. Fare: £2.10. Long distance train services also operate to many parts of the country. Bus service 900 to St Martin's Circus, Queensway (close to New Street Station). Journey time: 30 mins. Frequency: 20 mins. Operator: West Midlands Travel; *tel: (0121) 200 2700.* Fare: £1.30 (£0.95 off-peak).

Taxi fare is £11, journey time 20 mins. Taxi ranks at exit from both terminals.

There is direct access to the motorway system surrounding Birmingham. Drive north from the airport to join M42 at Junction 7. Head south on the M42 for the M5 to South Wales and western England or for the M40 to Oxford and London. Head north for a few miles to join the M6. The M6 runs north-west to Chester, North Wales, Lancashire and the Lake District, and south-east to merge with the M1. The M1 takes you north to the Midlands and north-eastern England, or south to London.

CARDIFF AIRPORT

Trains run to Cardiff central rail station. Bus services direct from airport to city, frequency approximately hourly, fare £2.10 one way. Taxis available at international arrivals hall, fare £14.

From the airport drive east along the A4226, joining the A4050 road which runs east and north until it meets the main A4232 road. Head east on the A48 to Cardiff or north on the A4232 to Junction 33 of the M4. Eastbound the M4 runs to Bristol, from where the M5 runs north to the Midlands or south to south-western England; alternatively stay on the M4 eastwards to London. The M4 westbound from Junction 33 takes you to Swansea and southern Wales

DOVER

Dover is the principal port of entry for car ferries from France. Sailings include very frequent ship ferries, split between three operators – contact P&O, *tel: (0990)*

980980, Stena Line, *tel: (0990) 707070* and SeaFrance, *tel: (01304) 204204.* Crossing time 1¼–1½ hrs. There is also a hovercraft service, taking 35 mins, and a catamaran, 55 mins: for both contact Hoverspeed, *tel: (01304) 240241.*

Immediately outside the port area take the A2 road through Kent to Canterbury and, joining the M2, onto London. See Folkestone below for Dartford crossing.

FISHGUARD

This Welsh town is the port for ferries from Rosslare in Ireland. Ships take 3 hrs 30 mins, 2 sailings per day; the catamaran services travel 3–4 times daily and take 1 hr 40 mins. Stena Line, *tel. 0990 707070.*

Fishguard is on the south-west coast of Wales. The A40 road south connects with the A48 and then onto the M4 motorway to Cardiff, Bristol, western England and London. The A487 minor road north out of Fishguard travels the scenic west coast of Wales.

FOLKESTONE

Just outside the port of Folkestone, on the south coast, lies the the terminus for the *Le Shuttle* car-carrying trains which cross by the Channel Tunnel. From the terminal you can drive straight onto the M20 to parts of Kent and on to London. Connections to all other parts of England can be made by transferring onto the M25 motorway just before reaching the outer suburbs of London. See under Gatwick for notes on the M25. By heading east along the M25 from either the M20 or the M2 (see under Dover), you soon reach the Dartford crossing. This road tunnel and bridge complex allows you to cross the Thames estuary and enter Eastern England without driving through London.

Folkestone itself is the terminal for fast catamaran sailings from the French port of Boulogne. There are 5 crossings daily, taking 55 mins. Information from Hoverspeed, *tel: (01304) 240241.*

HOLYHEAD

This is a port on Anglesey, a large island off the north-west Welsh coast. Ferries from Dublin and Dun Laoghaire (pronounced Dunleary) dock here. Dublin to Holyhead takes 3 hrs 15 mins (2 per day): information from Irish Ferries, *tel: (01) 855 2222.* The crossing from Dun Laoghaire takes 1 hr 40 mins (4–5 daily): Stena Line, *tel: 0990 707070.*

Anglesey is connected to the mainland by bridges at Bangor. Take the main A5 road from Holyhead to Bangor. East of Bangor the road splits; the A5 leads into the English Midlands via Shrewsbury and Birmingham, the A55 heads north-east along the north coast of Wales to Chester and from there to north-west England via the M56 and M6 motorways.

LONDON GATWICK AIRPORT

Gatwick Express non-stop train service to London Victoria rail station (southern edge of central London) from the airport terminal. Journey time: 30 mins. Frequency: 15 mins. Fare: £9.50. Also, frequent Connex South Central trains to Victoria (journey time: 35 mins; fare: £7.50) and Thameslink (journey time 45–60 mins; fare £9.50). Taxis take 1 hr 30 mins–1 hr 50 mins to central London.

The airport is directly on the M23, a short motorway which leads north onto the M25 motorway, which circles London and feeds onto motorways and main roads to every part of the country as well as into central London. (The M25 sees very heavy traffic at all times, which crawls very slowly at peak hours; plan to join it after 1000 or before 1530.)

39

To reach Brighton and the south coast, head south down the M23 for a few miles and take the A23 continuation.

LONDON HEATHROW AIRPORT

Frequent Piccadilly Line underground (subway) trains from Heathrow direct to many stops in central London and suburban stations. There are two separate embarkation stations, for Terminals 1, 2 and 3 and for Terminal 4, respectively. Journey time: approx. 45 mins, depending on destination. Operator: London Underground Limited; *tel: (0171) 222 1234*. Fare: £3.30 single.

The new main-line rail service to Paddington station takes 30 mins. A shuttle bus connects the airport terminals to the airport station. Taxis are available from outside all terminals. The journey to central London takes about 1 hr, longer at peak periods, and the fare is £35.

You can drive straight from Heathrow onto the M4 motorway. The eastbound direction heads into central London; westbound the motorway travels to western England, Bristol and South Wales. A few miles west of Heathrow the M4 interchanges with the circular M25 motorway, which gives access to all other parts of England and Wales (see warning on M25 under Gatwick above).

LONDON STANSTED AIRPORT

Direct train service to London Liverpool Street rail station (in the City, on the eastern edge of central London) from the airport terminal building. Journey time: 30 mins. Frequency: half-hourly. Fare: £10.40.

Hire cars to central London can be booked at a desk in the international arrivals area, costing £60 for the 1½ hr

journey. Just outside Stansted Airport, the A120 road westbound connects almost immediately with the M11. Going north, this motorway leads quickly to Cambridge, the driving gateway to East Anglia. Southbound the M11 leads to the M25 (see above) and then into east London.

An easier but slower way to enter East Anglia, especially Colchester and the east coast, is to turn east along the A120 after leaving the airport.

LONDON WATERLOO INTERNATIONAL RAIL STATION

This is the British terminus for the high-speed Eurostar trains from Paris, Lille and Brussels. On the southern edge of central London, frequent London Underground (subway) trains and plentiful taxis connect it to all parts of the capital.

MANCHESTER AIRPORT

Frequent train service to Manchester Piccadilly rail station (central) direct from the airport terminal building. Journey time: 15–20 mins. Fare: £2.55. Also through services to many cities in north-west and north-east England.

Taxis to central Manchester from each terminal take 30 mins, fare £12–15.

The airport is on the A56 motorway. Head along it south-west to reach Chester and North Wales, or to reach the M6 and then south to the Midlands and western England.

Alternatively, turn north-east onto the M56 and proceed a few mles to the junction with the M63. Take the northbound direction along the M63 to reach M61/M62. here, the westbound direction leads to Lancashire and the Lake District; the eastbound lanes connect to roads into Yorkshire and the north-east of England.

THEMED ITINERARIES

This chapter consists of a series of ideas for planning your own itineraries, using key cities and recommended routes to take in sights found in those chapters which are connected with the theme of the itinerary.

These itineraries are intended both as guides for planning journeys, which you can follow or adapt to your tastes as you choose, and also as a source of ideas for developing your own themed itineraries along similar lines.

PLANNING AN ITINERARY

Themes can make a trip more fun but to make sure tours are practical, here are some tips:

1. Work out driving distances and times and allow plenty of time for your visit to the attraction or town.
2. Stay longer to look around or build time for a meal or coffee break into your stay.
3. Double-check the opening times of a museum or gallery which you definitely want to see so that you don't miss the whole point of your visit.
4. Pre-book accommodation if you plan to arrive fairly late in the evening or after the tourist office is closed.
5. If you are a real enthusiast about the theme you have chosen, an obscure place that is a real gem might be worth a long drive; otherwise it might be more interesting to fit in a couple of other more accessible locations.

6. Be flexible. If you discover that real gem, stay longer to explore it and discard something else planned for another day.
7. Allow plenty of time to get back to your departure point, whether it's an airport, station or ferry port.

ROUND ENGLAND AND WALES

The following itinerary links many of the recommended routes in this book, in whole or in part, to provide a round England and Wales super-route, enabling you to see as much of the country as possible in a series of journeys which make up one circular itinerary beginning and ending in London. Suggested day trips from London are added at the end. The time the itinerary will take depends entirely on how much sightseeing you plan to do between journeys.

The Route Map on pp.8–9 and the Driving Distances and Times chart on p.345, coupled with the recommended routes throughout this book, will reveal many ways of modifying this grand tour to take in the sights important to you.

London–Cambridge (pp.246–248).
Cambridge–Norwich (pp.128–130).
Norwich–Lincoln (pp.290–295).
Lincoln–Scarborough (pp.218–222).
Scarborough–Newcastle (pp.319–322).
Newcastle–Carlisle (p.283) – following first part Newcastle–Lake District route.
Carlisle–Chester (pp.152–158)
Chester–Cardiff (pp.138–146).
Cardiff–Cheltenham (p.183) – following part of the Cotswolds–Cardiff route;

41

this section of the route and the next can be shortened considerably by taking the Severn Crossing to Bristol.
Cheltenham–Bristol (pp.109–117) – taking part of the Stratford-upon-Avon–Bristol route.
Bristol–Penzance (pp 100–108).
Penzance–Exeter (pp.195–197).
Exeter–Salisbury (pp.312–316).
Salisbury–Lewes (pp.209–213).
Lewes–Folkestone (pp.198–202).
Folkestone–London (pp.252–260).
London (pp.223–232) and day trips to:
Bath (p.243).
Bournemouth (pp. 62–64).
Brighton (pp. 76–79).
The Cotswolds (pp. 180–182).
Oxford (pp. 298–302).
St Albans (p. 269).

ROYAL BRITAIN

The history of England and Wales is inextricably linked with the history of their kings and queens, and many of the most famous features of Britain's heritage have royal connections some legendary, some genuine, some firmly rooted in the past, others continuing to the present day. The following route and city chapters take in some of the most celebrated as well as some of the less well known.

1. **London** (pp.223–232)
    As the official home of the royal family and the seat of British government for centuries, London has a wide range of sights associated with the monarchy, including Buckingham Palace, Westminster Abbey, the Tower of London and the Banqueting House, Whitehall. Just out of town are Hampton Court and the Queen's House, Greenwich. The capital is also an excellent base from which to visit other places with royal connections.

2. **Lincoln** (pp.214–217).
    The Magna Carta.
3. **Brighton** (pp.76–79)
    George IV's Royal Pavilion.
4. **Brighton–Bournemouth** (pp.80–91)
    Henry VIII's flagship Mary Rose, Portsmouth; Osborne House and Charles I's one-time prison, Carisbrooke Castle, Isle of Wight; the New Forest.
5. **London–Oxford** (pp. 274–278)
    Windsor Castle.
6. **Cambridge** (pp. 118–122)
    Sandringham.

LITERARY TOUR OF BRITAIN

Britain has a particularly rich literary heritage, stretching from Geoffrey Chaucer, whose Canterbury pilgrims never reached their destination in the unfinished *Canterbury Tales*, through Shakespeare, who has a heritage industry all to himself, to the present day. The following itineraries take in a wide range of places associated with some of the world-famous figures of literary Britain.

1. **London** (pp.223–232)
    London has one of the greatest concentrations of literary attractions in the world, from the various houses lived in by Charles Dickens, for whom London was almost a symbol of human life, through the Bloomsbury of Virginia Woolf and her associates, to Dr Johnson's house in Gough Square and John Keats' in Hampstead. Karl Marx wrote *Das Kapital* in the British Museum Reading Room and is buried in Highgate Cemetery. Other literary figures to have made London their home include Oscar Wilde, Thomas

42

Carlyle, Robert Browning and Elizabeth Barrett Browning, George Eliot and Samuel Pepys. The city is also a good starting point for literary tours to the south and west and to the Midlands.

2. **Folkestone–Lewes** (pp. 198–202)
   Henry James's Lamb House in Rye; Vanessa Bell and Duncan Grant's Charleston Farmhouse, Lewes.

3. **London–Folkestone** (pp. 252–260)
   Charles Dickens Centre, Rochester.

4. **Bournemouth–Plymouth** (pp. 65–75).
   Gateway to Thomas Hardy's Wessex; Hardy's birthplace at Higher Bockhampton; Hardy's house, Max Gate, Dorchester.

5. **Stratford-upon-Avon** (pp. 323–327)
   The Shakespeare properties.

6. **Nottingham** (pp. 296–297)
   D. H. Lawrence Birthplace Museum, Eastwood; Lord Byron's home, Newstead Abbey.

7. **The Lake District** (pp. 203–208)
   One-time haunt of the Romantic Lake Poets, Wordsworth and Coleridge. The area also has associations with the perennially popular children's author, Beatrix Potter. Places described include: Windermere; Wordsworth's Dove Cottage, Grasmere; Rydal Mount, Ambleside; Beatrix Potter's Hill Top.

8. **Chester–York** (pp. 173–179)
   The Brontë Museum, Haworth.

HISTORIC HOUSES AND GARDENS

Britain boasts an enormous number of historic houses, ranging from palaces to relatively modest country seats, many of which are also famous for their gardens. This itinerary lists routes and cities close to a wide selection of some of the country's most celebrated houses and gardens. The

array of places worth visiting is so wide that we have included under the appropriate route or city some houses and gardens which you may want to visit even though they are not covered in our text; handbooks of organisations such as the National Trust and English Heritage will alert you to many architectural and horticultural gems which we had no space to describe.

1. **London** (pp. 223–232)
   The capital has more than its share of famous addresses and is also home to some of Britain's most renowned gardens. Historic houses include Buckingham Palace, Hampton Court, Kenwood House, Chiswick House and Osterley Park, while Polesden Lacy is a short journey south. Kew and Syon Park are among the jewels in Britain's horticultural crown; on the fringe of London.

2. **London–Brighton** (pp. 236–238)
   Hever Castle; Knole House; Chartwell; Ightham Mote; Emmetts Garden; Penshurst Place; Scotney Castle Garden; Sissinghurst Castle Garden; Royal Pavilion; Sheffield Park Garden; Leonardslee Gardens; Nymans; Wakehurst Place Garden.

3. **London–Folkestone** (pp. 252–260)
   Leeds Castle.

4. **Brighton–Bournemouth** (pp. 81–91)
   Goodwood House; Osborne House; Broadlands; Kingston Lacy.

5. **Lewes–Salisbury** (pp. 209–213)
   Petworth House; Uppark.

6. **Exeter** (pp. 187–189)
   Montacute House; Tintinhull House and Garden; Knightshayes Court; Castle Drogo.

7. **Plymouth–Penzance** (pp. 305–309)
   Lanhydrock; Trelissick Gardens; Trewithen House Garden; Glendurgan Garden.

8. **London–Norwich** (pp. 261–267)

43

Helmingham Hall Gardens; Felbrigg Hall; Blickling Hall; Somerleyton Hall.

9. **Cambridge–Norwich** (pp. 128–130)
Ickworth.
10. **London–Norwich** (pp. 261–267)
Melford Hall; Kerbrell Hall.
11. **Norwich–Lincoln** (pp. 290–295)
Holkham Hall; Oxburgh Hall; Sandringham House.
12. **London–Oxford** (pp. 274–278)
Cliveden; Hughenden Manor; West Wycombe Park; Windsor Castle; Savile Garden.
13. **Oxford** (pp. 298–302)
University Botanical Gardens; Blenheim Palace.
14. **London–Nottingham** (pp. 268–273)
Hatfield House; Luton Hoo; Knebworth House; Wrest Park House and Gardens; Woburn Abbey; Boughton House; Rockingham Castle; Deene Park; Althorp House; Charlecote Park.
15. **Nottingham** (pp. 296–297)
Belvoir Castle; the Dukeries (a collection of stately homes north of Nottingham in the Sherwood Forest area, including Clumber Park).
16. **Bristol** (pp. 92–94)
Sudeley Castle; Hidcote Manor Garden; Westonbirt Arboretum; Westbury Court Garden; Dyrham Park; Bowood House and Gardens; Lacock Abbey.
17. **Chester–Nottingham** (pp. 159–164)
Shugborough; Little Moreton Hall; Tatton Park; Chatsworth; Haddon Hall; Hardwick Hall; Lyme Park.
18. **Chester–York** (pp. 173–179)
Harewood House.
19. **York** (pp. 328–332)
Castle Howard.
20. **Newcastle** (pp. 279–282)
Bamburgh Castle.

SCENIC COUNTRYSIDE

For small countries, England and Wales boast a wide variety of countryside and natural features, from the green rolling hills so often thought of as the archetypal English landscape to the rugged grandeur of Snowdonia and the Brecon Beacons. The following routes give access to some of these natural wonders.

1. **Norwich** (pp. 286–289)
Norfolk Broads.
2. **Brighton–Bournemouth** (pp. 80–91)
The Needles; Alum Bay; the New Forest; Portland Bill.
3. **Bristol–Penzance** (pp. 100–108)
Quantock Hills; Blackdown Hills; Exmoor; St Michael's Mount.
4. **Salisbury–Exeter** (pp. 312–316)
Salisbury Plain.
5. **Exeter–Penzance** (pp. 195–197)
Dartmoor.
6. **Plymouth–Penzance** (pp. 305–309)
Lizard Point; Land's End; Cornwall Coastal Path.
7. **Cardiff–Chester** (pp. 138–146)
Malvern Hills; Brecon Beacons; Sugar Loaf Mountain; Symonds Yat.
8. **Chester–Stratford-upon-Avon** (pp. 160–166)
The Wrekin; Shropshire Hills.
9. **The Cotswolds** (pp. 180–182).
10. **Aberystwyth–Cardiff** (pp. 48–55)
Brecon Beacons; The Mumbles; Gower Peninsula; Elan Valley; Cenarth Falls; Pembrokeshire Coastal Path.
11. **Aberystwyth–Chester** (pp. 56–62)
Snowdonia National Park; Snowdon; Lake Bala.
12. **Chester–Carlisle** (pp. 152–158)
The Lake District, including Scafell Pike, Coniston Water, Windermere.
13. **Chester–Nottingham** (pp. 159–164)
Heights of Abraham; Peak District; Blue John Cavern and Mine; Pool's

44

Caves; Peak Cavern; Speedwell Cavern.
14. **Bristol–Exeter** (pp. 95–99)
Glastonbury Tor; Cheddar Gorge;
Wookey Hole Caves; Mendip Hills.
15. **York–Berwick-upon-Tweed**
(pp. 333–340)
North Yorkshire Moors Railway;
Swaledale; Kielder Water.
16. **York–Lake District** (pp. 341–344)
Yorkshire Dales, including Malham
Cove, Malham Tarn and Gordale Scar,
Wensleydale, the Buttertubs and
Aysgarth Falls.
17. **The Lake District** (pp. 203–208).

VINTAGE RAILWAYS

England and Wales have a wealth of small,
privately run railways, many operated by
enthusiastic volunteers to preserve some of
the romance of the steam age.
Aberystwyth–Chester (pp. 56–62)
Ffestiniog Railway; Snowdon Mountain
Railway; Talyllyn Railway.
Bournemouth–Plymouth (pp. 66–76)
Paignton and Dartmouth Steam Railway.
Brighton–Bournemouth (pp. 81–91)
Isle of Wight Steam Railway.
Bristol–Penzance (pp. 99–107)
West Somerset Railway.
Cardiff–Chester (pp. 135–142)
Severn Valley Railway.
Chester–York (pp. 167–174)
Keighley and Worth Valley Railway.
Folkestone–Lewes (pp. 193–197)
Bluebell Railway; Romney, Hythe and
Dymchurch Railway.
Lake District (pp. 198–204)
Ravenglass and Eskdale Railway.
Lincoln–Scarborough (pp. 214–218)
Legbourne Railway Museum; Cleethorpes
Coast Light Railway.

Scarborough–Newcastle (pp. 319–322)
North Yorkshire Moors Railway.
York–Lake District (pp. 341–344)
Settle–Carlisle Railway.

MARITIME HERITAGE

The sea has always played an important
role in the history of England and Wales.
Many places have maritime museums or
waterside trails.
Aberystwyth–Cardiff (pp. 48–55)
Fishguard; Swansea.
Bournemouth–Plymouth (pp. 65–75)
Weymouth.
Brighton–Bournemouth (pp. 80–91)
Portsmouth; Southampton.
Bristol (pp. 92–94)
SS Great Britain; Maritime Walk.
Cardiff (pp. 134–137)
Industrial Maritime Museum.
Chester–Carlisle (pp. 152–158)
Liverpool.
The Cotswolds–Cardiff (pp. 183–188)
Gloucester.
Lincoln–Scarborough (pp. 218–222)
Grimsby; Hull.
London (pp. 223–232)
HMS Belfast; St Katharine's Dock.
London–Folkestone (pp. 252–260)
Chatham; Dover.
London–Norwich (pp. 261–267)
Ipswich; Lowestoft; Great Yarmouth; The
Broads.
Newcastle (pp. 279–282)
Trinity Maritime Centre.
Norwich–Lincoln (pp. 290–295)
King's Lynn; Boston.
Plymouth (pp. 303–304)
Plymouth Hoe; Plymouth Dome.
Scarborough–Newcastle (pp. 319–322)
Whitby; Middlesbrough; Hartlepool.

45

ABERYSTWYTH

Located midway along the crescent curve of Cardigan Bay, and the largest coastal town in mid-Wales, Aberystwyth is a sedate, slightly old-fashioned resort which houses a university and the National Library of Wales. Its castle was built in the 13th century by Edward I.

TOURIST INFORMATION

TIC: *Terrace Road, Aberystwyth, Dyfed SY23 2AG; tel: (01970) 612125*, open daily 1000–1700 (July–Aug); Mon–Sat 1000–1700 (Sept–June). DP Services offered, local bed-booking and BABA (10% of first night taken as deposit). *Ceredigion West Wales* and an accommodation guide are available free.

ARRIVING AND DEPARTING

The resort is reached from the English Midlands by A44, with A487 providing access to North and South Wales.

GETTING AROUND

The attractions in town are all within walking distance of the centre. Free town maps and transport details are available from the TIC. The main bus operator is **Crosville Wales**, *tel: (01970) 617951.*

The main **taxi** rank is at the railway station in *Alexander Rd*. For details of registered taxi companies contact the TIC.

STAYING IN ABERYSTWYTH

There is a good range of accommodation available, particularly mid-range hotels and guesthouses. Cheaper accommodation is located mainly in outlying villages. It is generally easy to book on arrival, except

July–Aug (due to university graduation, the annual Ian Rush Soccer Tournament and school holidays). The only chain is *Mo.* **University** accommodation is available during the holidays; *tel: (01970) 622899.*

Conrah Country House Hotel, *Chancery, Rhydgaled, Aberystwyth SY23 4DF; tel: (01970) 617941; fax: (01970) 624546.* Set in 22 acres of quiet grounds, the hotel has 20 en suite rooms, an award-winning restaurant, elegant drawing and writing rooms, heated swimming pool and sauna; moderate.

Marine Hotel, *Marine Terrace, Aberystwyth SY23 2BX; tel: (01970) 612444; fax: (01970) 617435.* A family-run seafront hotel with 34 en suite rooms; budget–moderate.

Glyn-Garth Guest House, *South Road, Aberystwyth SY23 1JS; tel: (01970) 615050.* This family-run guesthouse is totally non-smoking and is near the harbour and castle. Six of its ten rooms have en suite facilities. Budget.

The Miners Arms, *Pontrhydgroes, Ystrad Meurig SY25 6DN; tel: (01974) 282238,* a 20 min drive east of Aberystwyth, lies in the heart of red kite country close to Cors Caron nature reserve, an area renowned for walking, bird-watching, horse-riding and fishing.

The Aberystwyth area has a wide range of self-catering accommodation and about half a dozen holiday parks, all with static caravans and most with pitches for touring caravans and tents. The nearest to town is **Aberystwyth Holiday Village,** *Penparcau Rd; tel: (01970) 624211,* only half a mile south of the centre.

Pwllclai Holiday Cottages, *Ardwyn, Capel Bangor, Aberystwyth SY23 3LL; tel: (01970) 880640*. Self-catering accommodation in four well-equipped cottages with panoramic views across the Vale of Rheidol, 4 miles east of the town.

HI: There are two YHA hostels within 10 miles of Aberystwyth. **Borth Hostel**, *Morlais, Borth, Ceredigion SY24 5JS; tel: (01970) 871498; fax: (01970) 871827*. **Ystumtuen Hostel**, *Glantuen, Ystumtuen, Ceredigion SY23 3AE; tel: (01970) 890693*.

Edward I's **Aberystwyth Castle** is freely accessible at all times, offering excellent views. At the other end of the promenade, the **Aberystwyth Electric Cliff Railway**; *tel: (01970) 617642*, operates daily every 10–15 mins 1000–1800 (Easter–Oct); £2 round-trip, running to the summit of Constitution Hill, from which there are views to Snowdonia. The **Great Aberystwyth Camera Obscura**, *tel: (01970) 617642*, open daily 1000– 1800; free, offers an unusual means of viewing the town.

North of town lies the **National Library of Wales**, *Penglais Hill; tel: (01970) 623816*, open Mon–Fri 0930– 1800, Sat 0930–1700; free. As well as books and manuscripts, this houses fine prints, watercolours and drawings relating to Wales.

Aberystwyth Arts Centre, *Penglais Hill; tel: (01970) 622887*, open Mon–Sat 1000–2000, Sun 1400–1700 (July–mid May); price varies according to event. Every conceivable aspect of the arts (performing and otherwise) can be found here at some time.

The **Ceredigion Museum**, *Terrace Rd; tel: (01970) 617911*, open Mon–Sat

1000–1700 (Sept–July); daily 1000–1700 (Aug); free. The emphasis of the permanent displays is on the three main occupations of the area: agriculture, lead-mining and seafaring, but they are by no means limited to these subjects and are supplemented by changing exhibitions from the museum's extensive collections.

If you have time for only one excursion, take the narrow-gauge **Vale of Rheidol Steam Railway**; *tel: (01970) 625819*. This runs from Aberystwyth to Devil's Bridge, departures twice daily (Apr–Oct); four times a day at peak times; £10 round-trip. The train climbs for 12 miles up the Rheidol valley, to the spectacular gorges and waterfalls spanned by three bridges at Devil's Bridge, one of Wales' most popular beauty spots. **Devil's Bridge Falls**, *Devil's Bridge; tel: (01970) 85233*, open all year (entry by coin-operated turnstiles), attendant on duty 1000–1700 (Easter–Sept); £2.20. 12 miles south-east.

47

Borth Animalarium, *Borth; tel: (01970) 871224*, open daily 1000–1800 (Easter–Sept); daily 1100–1630 (Oct); £2.75. 6 miles north. Committed to the captive breeding of endangered species, Borth lets you get close to some enchanting exotic creatures (such as lemurs and racoons), as well as more familiar species. There are also aviaries, as well as sections devoted to bats, reptiles and exotic insects.

Cilgerran Castle (Cadw), *Cilgerran; tel: (01239) 615007*, open daily 0930–1830 (late Mar–late Oct); Mon–Sat 0930–1600, Sun 1400–1600 (late Oct–late Mar); £1.70. 30 miles south-west. Thirteenth-century Cilgerran is a stirring sight, with its massive stone towers perched on a crag above the steep gorge of the River Teifi.

ABERYSTWYTH–CARDIFF

This trip offers three alternative routes. In addition to the direct route, one more or less follows the coast south along Cardigan Bay, then east along the Bristol Channel; the other heads inland from Aberystwyth through mountains and valleys before dropping southwards to the capital of Wales. Whichever route is chosen, the traveller is in for a treat. The first alternative to the direct route traverses the Ceredigion Heritage Coast and, in Pembrokeshire, Britain's only coastal National Park, both areas of spectacular seascapes. The second takes in the Brecon Beacons, another national park.

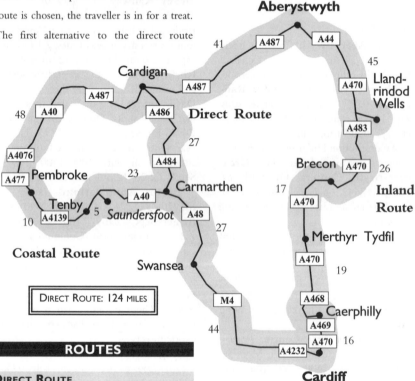

Aberystwyth

41 · A487 · A44

45

Cardigan

A487 · A487 · A470 · Lland-rindod Wells

48 · A40 · A486 · **Direct Route**

A483

27

A4076 · A484 · **Brecon** · A470 · 26

A477 · **Pembroke** · 23 · **Carmarthen** · 17 · **Inland Route**

A40 · A470

Tenby · 5 · *Saundersfoot* · A48 · A470

10 · A4139 · 27

Coastal Route · A470

Swansea · 19

DIRECT ROUTE: 124 MILES · M4 · A468

44 · A469 · **Caerphilly**

A470 · 16

A4232

Merthyr Tydfil

Cardiff

48

ROUTES

DIRECT ROUTE

Allow 2 hrs 45 mins to cover this 124-mile route. Head south on A487 for 24 miles, then turn inland on A486 for 14 miles to connect with A484 just south of the village of Pentre-cwrt. Follow this road south for a further 13 miles to A40, just east of **Carmarthen**, then head west, following signs to A48, which is reached in 2 miles. Follow this road south-east for 14 miles then join M4, which heads east to reach the outskirts of Cardiff after

52 miles. Junction 33 of the M4 connects with A4232 which reaches the city centre in about 5 miles.

COASTAL ROUTE

This is the longest route, covering just over 205 miles and taking around 5 hrs. From Aberystwyth follow A487, which hugs the coast for 16 miles south to Aberaeron, then turns a couple of miles inland to reach **Cardigan** after a further 25 miles and the ferry port of Fishguard in another 22 miles.

From Fishguard A40 heads due south for 15 miles towards Haverfordwest, skirting the town on A487 to connect with A4076, which should be followed for 4 miles. This leads to the A477 which heads for **Pembroke**, a further 7 miles away. From Pembroke A4139 reaches **Tenby** in 10 miles. Take B4316 to reach the pretty fishing harbour and yacht haven of Saundersfoot in less than 5 miles, then continue on B4316 to re-connect with A477 within another 3 miles.

Carmarthen is reached in a further 20 miles via A477 and A40. From Carmarthen A484 heads south, then east, and Swansea is reached in 27 miles. The M4 offers the best connection between Swansea and Cardiff – follow directions as in the direct route.

INLAND ROUTE

Heading inland, this route covers 123 miles and takes at least 3 hrs, taking into account the mountainous terrain.

From Aberystwyth head east on A44 for 25 miles and at Llangurig turn south on to A470, passing through Rhayader, and 15 miles from Llanturig turn east on to A4081. This reaches **Llandrindod Wells** within 5 miles. A483 heads south, reaching Builth Wells in 8 miles.

Follow A470 south to reach **Brecon** in

18 miles. You are now on the northern edge of the spectacular Brecon Beacons National Park. A470 continues south through the park, reaching **Merthyr Tydfil** in a further 17 miles. Continue south on A470 for 16 miles, then head east on A468 to reach **Caerphilly** in 3 miles. From Caerphilly A469 and A470 head south, reaching Cardiff in a further 16 miles.

CARDIGAN

TIC: *Theatr Mwldan, Bath House Rd, Cardigan SA43 1JY; tel: (01239) 613230; fax: (01239) 626566,* open Mon–Thur 1000–1700, Fri 1000–1630, Sat 1000–1700 (Oct–Apr); daily 1000–1800 (July–Sept).

ACCOMMODATION

Much of Cardigan's accommodation is in guesthouses and self-catering cottages in the outlying countryside.

Penbontbren Farm Hotel, *Glynmarthen SA44 6PE; tel: (01239) 810248; fax: (01239) 811129.* Two miles from Cardigan Bay, the hotel is in converted stone farm buildings with tasteful pine furnishings. It has ten en suite rooms, restaurant, bar, lounges, a farm museum and a nature trail. Moderate.

Garth Guest House, *Gwbert Road, Cardigan SA43 1AE; tel/fax: (01239) 613085.* Family and en suite rooms are available in this informally run guesthouse. Evening meals on request. Budget.

Brongwyn Mawr Farm, *Penparc, near Cardigan SA43 1SA; tel: (01239) 613644.* Pretty cottages with private patios and lovely gardens are set in unspoilt countryside 3 miles out of town. Static caravans and pitches for caravans and tents are also available.

SIGHTSEEING

Overlooking the estuary of the River Teifi, Cardigan stands in magnificent

49

walking country at the start of the **Pembrokeshire Coastal Path**, and there are splendid beaches in the area.

PEMBROKE

TIC: *Commons Rd, Pembroke, Pembrokeshire SA71 4EA; tel: (01646) 622388; fax: (01646) 621396,* open daily 1000–1730 (Easter–Oct); Tues, Thur, Sat 1000–1600 (Nov, Feb–Easter). DP services offered; local bed-booking (10% of first night refundable deposit) and BABA (booking fees: £1 for Wales, £5 for London and £3 for the rest of the UK, plus refundable deposit of 10% of first night). The *Pembrokeshire Guide* is free and includes an accommodation listing. **National Parks Information Centre**, *Westgate Hill; tel: (01646) 682148.*

GETTING AROUND

Most attractions are within walking distance of the centre, and free town and transport maps are available from the TIC.

The main local bus operators are **Silcox Motors**; *tel: (01646) 683143,* and **South Wales Transport**; *tel: (01792) 580580.*

Bus services are good to major towns, but less frequent to rural areas. There is no town **taxi** rank. For taxis contact **Castle Cars**, *tel: (01646) 622440*; or **Fred's Taxis**, *tel: (01646) 682226.*

ACCOMMODATION

There is a limited choice of hotel and b&b accommodation, including one hotel in the *BW* chain, and some farm accommodation in the outlying area. It is advisable to book in advance June–Sept.

High Noon Guest House, *Lower Lamphey Rd, Pembroke SA71 4AB; tel: (01646) 683736,* is close to Pembroke Castle, open year-round. Budget.

Poyerston Farm, *Cosheston, Pembroke; tel: (01646) 651347,* is a 200 year old farm-

house 2 miles east of town, open Apr–Oct. Two en suite rooms; budget.

HI: *Manorbier; tel: (01834) 871803.* The closest **campsite** is **Windmill Campsite**, *St Daniel's Hill; tel: (01646) 682392,* 1 mile south; no public transport.

SIGHTSEEING

Boat trips to **Skomer Island** are run by the **National Parks Authority**; *tel: (01646) 682148,* departing from Martin's Haven; £6 plus £6 landing fees.

Pembroke is within the stunningly unspoilt **Pembrokeshire Coast National Park** and is a good place from which to explore the coastal path.

This small town has one of the largest castles in south Wales. **Pembroke Castle**, *Main St; tel: (01646) 684585.* Open daily 0930–1800 (Apr–Sept); 1000–1700 (Mar, Oct; 1000–1600 (Nov–Feb); £2.95. Built by the Normans in the early 13th century, it has an 80 ft high circular keep and is surrounded by water on three sides.

OUT OF TOWN

Lamphey Bishops Palace (Cadw), *Lamphey; tel: (01646) 672224.* Accessible at all times; minimal charge (£1–£2) when manned – free in winter. 2 miles east. The ruined 13th-century palace was once a residence of the bishops of St David's.

Carew Castle, Cross and Mill, *Carew; tel: (01646) 651782,* open daily 1000–1700 (Easter–Oct); £2.50 (castle and mill), or £1.70 (either one). 4 miles north-east. The impressive Norman castle became an Elizabethan residence and has a restored tidal mill dating from 1558. There's a Celtic cross nearby.

On a moated site stands magnificent **Manorbier Castle**, *Manorbier; tel: (01834) 871394,* open daily 1030–1730 (Easter–Sept). 5 miles south-east.

TENBY

TIC: *The Croft, Tenby SA70 8AP; tel: (01834) 842404; fax: (01834) 845439,* open Mon–Sat 1000–1600 (Nov–Mar); daily 1000–1800 (Apr–mid July); 1000–2100 (mid July–end Aug); daily 1000–1730 (Sept–Oct).

ACCOMMODATION

Tenby and neighbouring Saundersfoot together offer a very wide choice of accommodation, with most hotels and guesthouses in the budget–moderate category, though standards are high.

The Imperial Hotel, *The Paragon, Tenby, Pembrokeshire SA70 7HR; tel: (01834) 843737; fax: (01834) 844342,* has a clifftop location 2 mins walk from the town centre. It has 44 en suite rooms. Moderate–expensive. **Rhodewood House Hotel**, *St Bride's Hill, Saundersfoot, Pembrokeshire SA69 9NU; tel: (01834) 812200,* has 44 well-equipped en suite rooms and a restaurant offering five-course evening meals. Budget–moderate.

The two resorts have some 30 caravan and holiday parks, many with self-catering cottages and tent and caravan pitches.

SIGHTSEEING

Tenby and Saundersfoot are attractive and popular seaside resorts, very busy in summer. A specific attraction is the **Tudor Merchant's House** (NT), *Quay Hill, Tenby; tel: (01834) 842279,* open Mon–Tues, Thur–Sat 1000–1700, Sun 1300–1700 (Easter–Sept); Mon–Tues, Thur–Fri 1000–1500, Sun 1200–1500 (Oct); £1.60. 10 miles east. This fine 15th-century town house is furnished in period style and recalls a period of maritime prosperity.

CARMARTHEN

TIC: *113 Lammas St, Carmarthen, Carmarthenshire SA31 3AQ; tel: (01267)* *231557/221901,* open daily 0930–1730 (Easter–Oct); Tues–Sat 1000–1630 (Nov–Easter). DP services offered; local bed-booking and BABA. Tickets for local events sold. *Coast and Countryside in Carmarthenshire,* including an accommodation listing, is available free.

GETTING AROUND

With the exception of Carmarthen Museum, the town's attractions are within easy walking distance of the centre. Free transport maps are available from the TIC.

The local bus service is reasonable within the town, but very infrequent to outlying areas. For **bus enquiries**, *tel: (01267) 231817.*

There is a **taxi** rank on Lammas St, or contact: **Carmarthen Taxi Company**; *tel: (01267) 237704,* or **Chris Cars**; *tel: (01267) 234438.*

ACCOMMODATION

There is a small range of hotel and b&b accommodation. It is generally possible to book on arrival, except during the Agricultural Show – one of the largest in Wales – in the second week of Aug.

Falcon Hotel, *Lammas St, Carmarthen; tel: (01267) 237152; fax: (01267) 2211277.* Private hotel with 15 en suite rooms and an à la carte restaurant which has earned an AA rosette. Moderate.

Boars Head Hotel, *Lammas St, Carmarthen SA31 3AE; tel: (01267) 222789; fax: (01267) 222289.* A 17th-century coaching inn in the centre of town, with 15 en suite bedrooms and a restaurant open daily, all day. Budget.

The closest **campsites** are **Pant Farm Caravan Park**, *Llangunnor; tel: (01267) 235665,* 2 miles east, and **Church House Farm**, *Llangain,* near *Llansteffan; tel: (01267) 283274,* 4 miles south.

51

SIGHTSEEING

For information about **guided walks**, starting from St Peter's Civic Hall; *tel: (01267) 232075.*

This ancient county town on the banks of the river Towy retains some steep and narrow streets. The remains of a 5000-seat **Roman Amphitheatre**, *Priory St,* are open at all times; free. The **Norman Castle**, open Mon–Fri 1000–1630; free, is also largely a ruin, but an impressive gatehouse survives.

Oriel Myrddin Art Gallery, *Church Lane; tel: (01267) 222775*, open Mon–Sat 1030–1645; free, contains changing displays of local arts and crafts.

For an insight into the history of the region, which is prime agricultural country, visit **Carmarthen Museum**, *Abergwili; tel: (01267) 231691*, open Mon–Sat 1000–1630; free. 1½ miles east.

OUT OF TOWN

On the coast, at the attractive town of **Laugharne**, is the boathouse where Dylan Thomas, Wales' most famous 20th-century poet, spent his last years. **The Boat House**, *Dylan's Walk, Laugharne; tel: (01994) 427420*, open 1000–1800 (Easter–Oct); reduced opening hours in winter, so check; £2.50. 13 miles south-west of Carmarthen.

Picturesque **Laugharne Castle**, *tel: (01994) 427906*, open 1000–1700 (May–Sept); £1.70, stands on a low ridge overlooking the wide Taf estuary; one of a string of fortresses that controlled the coast of south Wales.

Museum of the Welsh Woollen Industry, *Dre-fach Felindre, Llandysul; tel: (01559) 370929*, open Mon–Fri 1000–1700 (also Sat Easter–Sept); £2.50. 16 miles north; This is the place to see working historical exhibits and regular demonstrations of the various processes involved in converting wool into fabric.

LLANDRINDOD WELLS

TIC: *Old Town Hall, Memorial Gdns, Llandrindod Wells LD1 5DL; tel: (01597) 822600*, open Mon–Fri 0900–1800, Sat–Sun 0930–1730 (May–Sept); Mon–Fri 0900–1700 (Oct–Apr). DP services offered; local bed-booking and BABA (latest 30 mins before closing). Cadw membership and local theatre tickets sold. *Heart of Wales*, including accommodation listing, available free.

GETTING AROUND

Most of the attractions are out of town, and a free transport map and town map (10p) are available from the TIC. Local bus services are infrequent. The main bus companies are **Roy Browns**, *tel: (01982) 552597;* **Cross Gates**, *tel: (01597) 851207;* **Williams**, *tel: (01597) 824588;* and **Postbus**, *tel: (01597) 822925.* Most buses operate from *High St.* For **taxis**, contact: **Adeys**, *tel: (01597) 822118;* or **Grimwood**, *tel: (01597) 822864.*

ACCOMMODATION

Llandrindod Wells has a small selection of hotels and a good range of b&bs and guesthouses. It is usually possible to book on arrival, except during the Royal Welsh Agricultural Show – the biggest agricultural show in Wales (at Builth Wells in July) and the Victorian Festival (Aug).

The Metropole, *Temple St, Llandrindod Wells, Powys LD1 5DY; tel: (01597) 823700; fax: (01597) 824828.* A spacious, Victorian-style hotel, with 122 en suite rooms and a superb leisure complex. Moderate. **Holly Farm**, *Howey, Llandrindod Wells, Powys LD1 5PP; tel: (01597) 822402.* This charming old farmhouse, dating from Tudor times, has five ensuite rooms, lounge and restaurant, all set in beautiful countryside. Budget.

The nearest **campsites** are: **Disserth**

Farm Caravan Park, *Disserth, Howey; tel: (01597) 860277*, 2 miles south, and **Park Motel Caravan and Camping**, *Crossgates; tel: (01597) 851201*, 3 miles north.

SIGHTSEEING

Llandrindod Wells is surrounded by the wild and remote **Cambrian mountains** and was a popular inland spa in Victorian times. The town's heyday is celebrated during the **Victorian Festival** (Aug), when the streets come alive with street entertainers and horse-drawn vehicles.

Llandrindod Wells Museum, *Temple St; tel: (01597) 824513*, open Thur–Tues 1000–1230 and 1400–1630; £1.

BRECON

TIC: *Cattle Market Car Park, Brecon LD3 9DA; tel: (01874) 622485*, open daily 1000–1800 (Easter–Oct), daily 1000–1630 (Nov–Easter). DP services offered; local bed-booking and BABA. Tickets for local events sold.

ACCOMMODATION

Castle of Brecon Hotel, *Castle Sq. Brecon LD3 9DB; tel: (01874) 624611; fax: (01874) 623737*. This hotel, close to the town centre, with extensive views of the Brecon Beacons has 45 rooms and a restaurant. Moderate.

Brecon Beacons Holiday Cottages, *Talybont-on-Usk, Brecon LD3 7YS; tel: (01874) 676446; fax: (01874) 676416*, offers a wide selection of cottages, farmhouses and other properties – including a water mill, medieval tower, chapel and a castle – throughout the Brecon Beacons, Black Mountains and the Wye Valley.

SIGHTSEEING

Brecon stands at the confluence of the Usk and Honddu rivers on the edge of

he **Brecon Beacons National Park**, which covers 519 square miles of exhilarating landscapes. Activities in the area include rambling, horse-riding, mountain biking, caving, angling, gliding and canal and river boating.

Brecknock Museum, *Captain's Walk, Brecon, LD3 7DW; tel: (01874) 624121)*, open Mon–Fri 1000–1700 (year round), Sat 1000–1300, 1400–1700, to 1600 (Nov–Feb), Sun 1000–1300 (and 1400–1700 Apr–Sept); free.

Waterfolk Canal Centre, *Old Storehouse, Llanfrynach, Brecon LD3 7LJ; tel: (01874) 6655382*, open Sun–Thur and Sat 1000–1730; £1.50. Memorabilia focusing on the Monmouth and Brecon Canal is featured in the canal museum and craft shop. Horse-drawn boat trips (£3.25) available along the canal.

Welsh Distillers Visitor Centre, *No. 2 Parc Menter, Brecon LD3 1XX; tel: (01874) 610009*; £2, open Mon–Sat 0900–1700, Sun 1200–1700. The centre details the history of Welsh whisky, with sampling for adults.

MERTHYR TYDFIL

TIC: *14a Glebeland St; Merthyr Tydfil CD47 8AU; tel: (01685) 379884; fax: (01685) 350043*, open Mon–Sat 0930–1730. DP services offered; local bed-booking and BABA.

ACCOMMODATION

Merthyr Tydfil has a limited choice of accommodation, although options widen in the surrounding areas.

Tregenna Hotel, *Park Terrace, Merthyr Tydfil CF47 8RF; tel: (01685) 723627; fax: (01685) 721951*. Family-run hotel with 24 en suite rooms. Farmhouse accommodation and a self-catering three-bedroom cottage are also available in the Brecon Beacons National Park nearby. Moderate.

53

Brynawel Guest House, *Queens Road, Merthyr Tydfil CD47 0HD; tel: (01685) 722573*, offers b&b in a quiet location. Three en suite rooms. Budget.

Grawen Camping and Caravan Park, *Cwm Taf, Cefn Coed, Merthyr Tydfil CF48 2HS; tel: (01685) 723740*, has 20 caravan pitches in a forest and reservoir setting just north of the town.

SIGHTSEEING

Brecon Mountain Railway, *Pant Station, Dowlais, Merthyr Tydfil CF48 2UP; tel: (01685) 722988*; £5, open daily 1100–1700 (June–Aug), closed Mon, Fri and Sat (Oct) and Mon and Fri (April, May, Sept). A 7-mile round trip into the **Brecon Beacons** starts at the station 3 miles north of Merthyr Tydfil, off the A465 (signposted), where there is a collection of locomotives and rolling stock from around the world.

Cyfarthfa Castle Museum and Art Gallery, *Merthyr Tydfil CF47 8RE; tel: (01685) 723112*; £1, open daily 1000–1800 (Apr–Sept), Mon–Fri 1000–1530, Sat–Sun 1200–1530 (Oct–Mar). The museum, set in the cellars of this castellated Regency mansion, displays artefacts covering 3000 years of local history and has an impressive art collection.

Ynysfach Iron Heritage Centre, *Ynysfach Rd, Merthyr Tydfil CF48 1AG; tel: (01685) 721858*; £1.15, open Mon–Fri 1000–1700, Sat–Sun 1200–1700 (Easter–Sept), closed weekends (Oct–Easter). In the 18th and 19th centuries, Merthyr Tydfil was world famous for the production of iron and steel. The story is told in this converted beam engine house which houses exhibitions and life-size models.

CAERPHILLY

TIC: *The Twyn, Castle St, Caerphilly, Mid Glamorgan, CF83 1XX; tel: (01222)*

880011, open daily 1000–1800 (Easter–Sept); 1000–1700 (Oct–Dec); 1000–1600 (Jan–Easter). DP services offered; local bed-booking service (free) and BABA (latest 30 mins before closing; variable fee). *Rhymney Valley*, including an accommodation guide, is available free.

GETTING AROUND

A free town map is available from the TIC. **Caerphilly Castle**, the town's main attraction, is an easy walk from the centre.

Most bus services are operated from Station Terrace, by **Cardiff Bus**; *tel: (01222) 396521*, and **Caerphilly Bus**; *tel: (01222) 396521*.

There is a **taxi** rank at the station, or you can contact: **Brad Cars**, tel: (01222) 885000; **Castell Cars**, *tel: (01222) 869333*; **Civic**, *tel: (01222) 851011*; **Caerphilly Cars**, *tel: (01222) 868686;* or **BTM Taxis**, *tel: (01222) 885808.*

ACCOMMODATION

Accommodation is very limited: four hotels, a YMCA, several guesthouses and b&b establishments. It is usually possible to book on arrival, except during the peak holiday period.

The closest **campsite** is **Cwmcarn Forest Drive Campsite**, *Nant Carn Rd, Cwmcarn, Crosskeys; tel: (01495) 272001.* 8 miles north-east.

SIGHTSEEING

Caerphilly is a small town, famous for its castle and its crumbly cheese.

The massive 13th-century **Caerphilly Castle** (Cadw), *Castle St; tel: (01222) 883143*, open daily 0930–1830 (Apr–Oct); Mon–Sat 0930–1600, Sun 1100–1600 (Nov–Mar); £2.20. With its seemingly impregnable series of concentric stone and water defences, it is one of Western Europe's most powerful fortresses, while the tower outleans Pisa's.

54

SWANSEA

TIC: *Singleton St, Swansea SA1 3QG; tel: (01792) 468321,* open Mon–Sat 0930–1730. DP SHS services offered; local bed-booking and BABA (latest 1700), guided tours booked. *Swansea Bay, Mumbles, Gower* holiday guide is free and has an accommodation listing.

GETTING AROUND

Most attractions in the town are within walking distance of the centre. Free town and transport maps are available from the TIC.

Most local bus services are run by **SWT,** *tel: (01792) 580580,* from **Quadrant Bus Station,** *off Westway.* Coverage is good in the centre and to outlying areas, but there are no Sun services to the Gower Peninsula. The main **taxi** ranks are at St Mary's Church, Whitewalls and off King's Way.

ACCOMMODATION

There is a good choice of hotel and guest-house accommodation, in Swansea itself and in Mumbles and the Gower Peninsula. It is generally easy to book on arrival. Hotel chains in Swansea include *FP, Hn, Ja* and *Ma.*

HI: *Port Eynon, Gower; tel: (01792) 390706.* There are half a dozen **campsites** on the Gower Peninsula, details of which are included in the TIC's free holiday guide.

SIGHTSEEING

Swansea is a busy industrial port, where oil terminals have ensured continuing prosperity after the decline of coal. The docklands have been made into an attractive marina, while a statue in **Dylan Thomas Square** and eponymous theatre commemorate the poet, who was born here in 1914.

Swansea itself, together with the pretty village of **Mumbles** and the unspoilt **Gower Peninsula,** offers a wide variety of magnificent bays, beaches and cliffs. The area is sports-oriented and there are facilities for everything from paragliding to horse-riding, from fishing to go-karting.

Glynn Vivian Art Gallery, *Alexandra Rd; tel: (01792) 655006,* open Tues–Sun, public holidays 1000–1700; free. Permanent exhibits include a collection of the rare and richly-decorated Swansea pottery, fine and decorative art.

Swansea Museum, *Victoria Rd; tel: (01792) 653763,* open Tues–Sun, public holidays 1000–1700; free, covers archaeological, natural and local history, pottery and porcelain.

Maritime and Industrial Museum, *Museum Sq.; tel: (01792) 650351,* open Tues–Sun, public holidays 1000–1700; free. Complex includes a complete working woollen mill, floating exhibits and displays on Swansea's maritime history.

Plantasia, *Parc Tawe; tel: (01792) 474555,* open Tues–Sun, BH 1000–1700; £1.70. Here you can see over 5000 tropical plants, housed in an impressive glass pyramid with three climatic zones, as well as fish, reptiles, birds, butterflies and creepy-crawlies.

55

ABERYSTWYTH–CHESTER

There is something for everyone on this route: historic castles, the stunning scenery of Snowdonia National Park, charming coastal and country villages and the popular seaside resorts of north Wales.

DIRECT ROUTE: 89 MILES

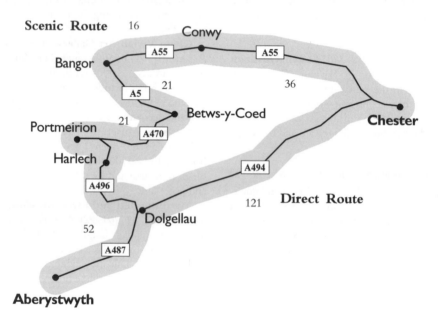

56

Scenic Route 16 Conwy

Bangor A55 A55

A5 21 36

Portmeirion 21 Betws-y-Coed Chester

A470

Harlech

A496 A494

121 Direct Route

Dolgellau

52

A487

Aberystwyth

ROUTES

DIRECT ROUTE

This 89-mile route takes about 2 hrs. From Aberystwyth head north-east on A487 for 32 miles to Dolgellau, then bear right on to A494 which passes through the towns of Ruthin and Mold to reach A55 after a total of 79 miles. Turn right on to A55 for 6 miles, then turn left on to A483 which reaches Chester in 4 miles.

SCENIC ROUTE

From Aberystwyth head north on A487 for 36 miles and at Llanelltyd turn left on to A496, reaching **Harlech** in a further 16 miles. Continue on A496, crossing the estuary at Penrhyndeudraeth and bearing left on to A487 to reach **Portmeirion**.

Return on A487, then bear left on A496 and join A470 at Blaenau Ffestiniog to reach **Betws-y-coed** 21 miles from Portmeirion.

Leave Betws-y-coed on A5 and continue west to reach **Bangor** in 21 miles. From Bangor, A55 heads east to **Conwy** (16 miles) where A546 continues to Llandudno. Return to A55 on A470 and head east to Colwyn Bay. At Abergele, 6 miles east of Colwyn Bay, follow A548 to Rhyl and Prestatyn.

From Prestatyn A548 follows the River Dee upstream to reach Chester after 30 miles.

HARLECH

TIC: *Gwyddfor House, High Street, Harlech, Gwynedd LL46 2YA; tel: (01766) 780658,* open daily 1000–1800 (Easter–Oct). Services offered: local bed-booking (latest booking 1750; *free*), BABA (latest booking 1730; *variable fee*). *Harlech and District* brochure is free and an accommodation list can be sent on request.

GETTING AROUND

The TIC has free town and transport maps. Harlech Castle, towering above the rail station, is the town's main attraction and is walkable from the town centre. For **general transport enquiries**, *tel: (01286) 679535.* Local bus services are limited and there are no evening or Sun services.

There are no **taxi** ranks. For taxis, contact **Morfa Garage**; *tel: (01766) 780288,* or **Parry's**; *tel: (01766) 780392.*

ACCOMMODATION

There is a small range of hotel, guesthouse and b&b accommodation, and it is generally easy to book on arrival, except during August.

St David's Hotel, *Harlech, Gwynedd*

LL46 2PT; tel: (01766) 780366; fax: (01766) 780820, has 60 en suite rooms and views across Cardigan Bay. Budget–moderate.

Croeso Cader Idris Farm Holidays, *Dolffanog Fach, Tywyn, Gwynedd LL36 9AJ; tel/fax: (01654)761235,* offer farmhouse bed and breakfast or self-catering in the Cader Idris area of Snowdonia National Park. Budget–moderate.

HI: The closest hostel is **Plas Newydd Youth Hostel**, *Llanbedr; tel: (01341) 23287.* The closest **campsite** is **Min Y Don**, *Beach Rd; tel: (01766) 780286,* 1 mile west.

EATING AND DRINKING

South of Harlech, the **Penhelig Arms**, *Aberdovey, Gwynedd LL35 0LT; tel: (01654) 767215; fax: (01654) 767690,* serves bar food and restaurant meals, and there's a sea-wall patio for outdoor eating. Budget–moderate.

The **Victoria Inn**, *Llanbedr, Gwynedd LL45 2LD; tel: (01341) 241213; fax: (01341) 241644,* serves bar meals. The three-crown inn has the Wales Tourist Board commendation. Budget.

SIGHTSEEING

The TIC has information on a variety of **walking tours** (with Snowdonia National Park Guides); from £1.50.

This little town of steep, narrow streets boasts probably the most famous of Edward I's 'iron ring' of castles, built to contain the Welsh in the 13th century. **Harlech Castle** (Cadw), *tel: (01766) 780552,* open daily 0930–1830 (Easter–Oct); Mon–Sat 0930–1600, Sun 1100–1600 (Nov–Easter); £3. Dominating the town, the castle dates from 1283–90 and is memorable, not only for its strength, but also for the panoramic views from its battlements of Snowdonia, the Lleyn Peninsula and the sea.

OUT OF TOWN

Llanfair Slate Caverns, *Llanfair; tel: (01766) 780247*, open daily 1000–1700 (Easter–mid Oct); £2.50. 1½ miles south. These tiny slate caverns are less crowded than their Snowdonian counterparts. They were created over a century ago and the slate was used for roofs all over Britain: much of it is still in place.

Maes Artro Museum, *Llanbedr; tel: (01341) 23467*, open daily 1000–1730 (May–Sept); £3. 3 miles south. This is a tourist attraction based in a genuine wartime RAF camp, which has been converted to house a variety of displays, including an original air-raid shelter.

PORTMEIRION

Tourist Information: *Hotel Portmeirion, Portmeirion, Gwynedd LL48 6ET; tel: (01766) 770228*, open at all reasonable hours.

ACCOMMODATION

Portmeirion Hotel, *Portmeirion, Gwynedd LL48 6ET; tel: (01766) 770228 fax: (01766) 771331.* The deluxe four-crown hotel with 37 ensuite rooms is set in subtropical woodland on its own private peninsula overlooking Cardigan Bay. There are also self-catering cottage suites. Moderate–expensive.

SIGHTSEEING

Portmeirion is open as an attraction daily 0930–1730; £3.50. There are various shops and a self-service restaurant – non-residents can also eat in the Hotel Portmeirion dining room. As there are many steps and steep slopes, the village is not suitable for wheelchairs.

This bizarre village – given popular fame by the cult TV series *The Prisoner* – is well worth a day's detour. It was the product of the imagination of Sir Clough Williams-Ellis, a Welsh architect who dreamed of creating a perfect village which would not mar the beauty of its natural setting. His fantastic creation, built 1925–72, has a distinctly Italianate flavour, with its colourful domes and towers, castle and lighthouse, cobbled squares and pastel-coloured villas, the plush hotel serving as a focus. The site, a rocky peninsula overlooking Cardigan Bay, has miles of paths through its deep, subtropical woodlands, leading to rocky coves and sandy beaches along the headland.

BETWS-Y-COED

TIC: *Snowdonia National Park Visitor Centre, Stablau'r Royal Oak, Betws-y-coed, Gwynedd LL24 0AH; tel: (01690) 710426,* open daily 1000–1800 (Apr–Oct); 0930–1630 (Nov–Mar). DP services offered; local bed-booking and BABA (latest 30 mins before closing). Guided tours booked. *Betws-y-coed Guide* costs 85p.

ACCOMMODATION

There are a few hotels in town and a good choice of guesthouses and b&bs. The TIC can provide accommodation listings. It is usually easy to book on arrival, except over Easter.

The three-crown **Swallow Falls Hotel**, *Betws-y-coed LL24 0DW; tel: (01690) 710796; fax: (01690) 710191,* stands opposite the falls just outside Betws-y-coed. Home-cooked food is served in its licensed tavern. Budget.

Princes Arms Hotel, *Trefriw, near Betws-y-coed LL27 0JP; tel: (01492) 640592, fax: (01492) 640559,* has 18 ensuite bedrooms, award-winning restaurant and log fires. Moderate.

Ferns Guest House, *Holyhead Rd, Betws-y-coed LL24 0AN; tel/fax: (01690) 710587,* is a Victorian home with nine ensuite rooms. Budget. Also from the

Victorian era is **Henlly's Hotel**, *Old Church Rd, Betws-y-coed LL24 0AL; tel/fax: (01690) 710534*, which has been converted from the former magistrates' court. Budget–moderate.

HI: Capel Curig (5 miles west), *Plas Curig; tel: (01690) 720225*; and **Lledr Youth Hostel** (4 miles south-west). There are two **campsites** in the town itself: at **Hendre Farm** (no telephone) and **Riverside**, *tel: (01690) 710310*.

EATING AND DRINKING

White Horse Inn, *Capel Garmon, Betws-y-coed, near Llanrwst LL26 0RW; tel: (01690) 710271*. A member of the Taste of Wales scheme which promotes the use of fresh local produce and good Welsh fare. Budget–moderate.

Meadowsweet Hotel and Restaurant, *Station Rd, Llanrwst LL26 0DS; tel/fax: (01492) 642111*, has a high reputation for its food. Budget–moderate.

SIGHTSEEING

Guided walks are available, starting from the TIC.

Lying at the meeting place of three valleys, Betws-y-coed makes a perfect – though busy – place from which to explore the **Snowdonia National Park**, with its dramatic mountains, lakes and forest trails. A popular walk is to the lovely **Swallow Falls**, open at all times; 40p (through turnstile). 2 miles west on A5.

Betws-y-coed Motor Museum; *tel: (01690) 710760*, open daily 1000–1800 (Easter–Oct); £1.30. The collection of vintage and classic vehicles includes some rare models.

Conwy Valley Railway Museum, *Station Rd; tel: (01690) 710568*, open daily 1000–1730 (Easter–Oct); Sat–Sun 1030–1630 (Nov–Easter); £1. Miniature (25% of full size) steam trains leave frequently

(from 1015) for a scenic journey (75p) and you can ride on a tramcar a third of full size (complete with buffet) from 0900 onwards (60p). Both stop running around 1700, but times vary.

OUT OF TOWN

Victorian mining conditions have been recreated at the multi-award-winning **Llechwedd Slate Caverns**, *Blaenau Ffestiniog; tel: (01766) 830306*, open daily 1000–1715 (Mar–Sept); 1000–1615 (Oct–Feb); £6.25 per ride; £9.50 for both. 13 miles south. **Miners' Tramway** follows the original route taken by the miners in 1846. The **Deep Mine** tram descends very steeply into the depths (the steepest passenger train in Britain), then there's a 25 min walk featuring ten *son et lumière* sequences.

Welsh Slate Museum, *Llanberis; tel: (01286) 870630*, open daily 0930–1730 (Easter–Sept); daily 1000–1600 (Mar, if Easter's late); £3. This contains most of the machinery and plant salvaged when Dinorwig quarry closed in 1969 and there are demonstrations of various skills.

Llanberis Lake Railway, *Llanberis; tel: (01286) 870549*, operates most days Easter–Oct; £3.90. 13 miles west. The 40-min return journey provides spectacular vistas of Snowdon and surrounding mountains.

The **Snowdon Mountain Railway** (13 miles west) and **Ffestiniog Railway** (13 miles south) also offer a good means of viewing the scenery.

BANGOR

TIC: *Town Hall, Deiniol Rd, Bangor, Gwynedd LL57 2RE; tel: (01248) 352786*, open daily 1000–1800. Services offered: local bed-booking and BABA (latest 1630). *Bangor Guide* is free, as is an accommodation list.

59

GETTING AROUND

With the exception of **Penrhyn Castle**, the town's attractions can be reached on foot from the centre. A free town map is available from the TIC. Bus services (reduced Sun and after 2000) are run by **Crosville**, *tel: (01248) 351879*. The main **taxi** rank is on *Ffordd Gwynedd*.

ACCOMMODATION

There is a small choice of hotels (*BW* is the only chain), and a larger range of b&bs and guesthouses. It is usually easy to book on arrival.

HI: *Tan-y-Bryn; tel: (01248) 353516*. The closest **campsite** is: **Treborth Hall**, *Treborth Hall Farm; tel: (01248) 364104*, 2 miles west.

SIGHTSEEING

A half-mile walk from *High St* takes you to the plateau at the top of **Bangor Mountain**. Bangor, lying between the mountains of Snowdonia and the island of Anglesey, has a small but charming **cathedral**, *High St; tel: (01248) 370693*, open daily 0645–1800; free. This was restored by Sir George Gilbert Scott in the 1870s. Beside the cathedral, the tranquil **Bible Garden**, open at all times; free, is planted with trees, shrubs and flowers referred to in the Bible.

Bangor Museum and Art Gallery, *Ffordd Gwynedd; tel: (01248) 353368*, open Tues–Fri 1230–1630, Sat 1030–1630; free, covers the history of north Wales.

The large island of **Anglesey**, across the Menai Strait and spanned by two great bridges built by Telford and Stephenson, has many good beaches.

Take a stroll along the 1500 ft Victorian **Bangor Pier**, *Garth Point; tel: (01248) 352421*, open 0830-2130 (Apr–Oct); 1000-1600 (Nov–Mar); 20p.

OUT OF TOWN

Bangor is a good base from which to explore some of Wales' finest castles. **Penrhyn Castle** (NT), *Llandegai; tel: (01248) 353084*, open Wed–Mon 1200–1700 (Easter–June, Sept–Oct); Wed–Mon 1100–1700 (July–Aug); £4.60. 1 mile east. Built 1820–45, the mock-Norman structure has a richly decorated Victorian interior, a countryside exhibition and lovely gardens with extensive collections of trees and shrubs.

Beaumaris Castle (Cadw), *Beaumaris, Anglesey; tel: (01248) 810361*, open daily 0930–1830 (Easter–Oct); Mon–Sat 0930–1600, Sun 1100–1600 (Nov–Easter); £2.20. 10 miles north. Located on Anglesey, moated Beaumaris is Britain's most perfect example of a concentrically planned castle.

Caernarfon Castle (Cadw), *Castle Ditch, Caernarfon; tel: (01286) 677617*. Open daily 0930–1830; £3.80. 9 miles south-west. Hugely impressive Caernarfon was the mightiest of the fortresses built by Edward I after his conquest of Wales.

Plas Newydd (NT), *Llanfairpwll, Anglesey; tel: (01248) 714795*, house open Sun–Fri 1200–1700 (Apr–Sept); Fri, Sun 1200–1700 (Oct); £4.20. 8 miles south-west. Overlooking the Menai Strait, Plas Newydd is an impressive 18th-century house in unspoilt surroundings, with lovely lawns and parkland.

CONWY

TIC: *Castle Buildings, Castle St, Conwy, Gwynedd LL32 8LD; tel: (01492) 592248*, open daily 0930–1830 (Apr–Oct); Mon–Sat 1000–1600, Sun 1100–1600 (Nov–Mar). DP services; local bed-booking (free) and BABA (latest 30 mins before closing; fee variable). Accommodation listing and leaflets on attractions are available free.

GETTING AROUND

Attractions are within walking distance of the centre. The TIC has free town maps and timetables. Most local bus services are operated by **Crosville Cymru**; *tel: (01492) 596969*. Services are good, but reduced after 1800 and winter Sun. **Elwyn's Taxis**; *tel: (01492) 592344*.

ACCOMMODATION AND FOOD

There is a small range of hotels and a reasonable choice of guesthouse and b&b accommodation. It is generally easy to book on arrival.

The Old Rectory, *Llansanffraid Glan Conwy, Conwy LL28 5LF; tel: (01492) 580611; fax: (01492) 584555,* is a deluxe hotel; its cuisine has received Egon Ronay's recommendation. Expensive.

HI: Conwy, *Larkhill, Sychnant Pass Rd; tel: (01492) 593571.* The nearest **campsite** is **Conwy Touring Park**, *Llanrwst Rd; tel: (01492) 592856*, 1½ miles south.

Castle Inn, *High St, Conwy, LL32 8DB; tel: (01492) 592324* dates from the early 16th century. Budget–moderate.

SIGHTSEEING

River trips are available; for details see notices on The Quay, or *tel: (01492) 592284.*

Ask the TIC about the *Conwy Town Trail*: a walk which takes in the major sights, including the **Stephenson rail bridge** (1848) and Telford's drawbridge-like **Conwy suspension bridge** (NT); *tel: (01492) 573282*, open daily 1000–1700 (July–Aug); Wed–Mon 1000–1700 (Easter–June, Sept–Oct); £1. Dating from 1826, this was one of the world's first suspension bridges and the toll house has been refurbished in style. On the harbourfront you can see what is reputedly **Britain's smallest house**.

Conwy's surviving medieval walls are possibly the most complete in Britain, but surprisingly few old buildings remain. The oldest is the carefully refurbished 14th-century **Aberconwy House** (NT), *Castle Street; tel: (01492) 592246*, open Wed–Mon 1100–1700; £2, or £2.50 to include the suspension bridge. Each room reflects a different period.

Conwy Castle and Town Walls (Cadw), *Castle St; tel: (01492) 592358,* open daily 0930–1830 (Easter–Oct); Mon–Sat 0930–1600, Sun 1100–1600 (Nov–Easter); £3. Edward I's castle dominates the town with its massive towers and barbicans, seemingly hewn from its narrow rocky promontory. From it you can walk around the town walls.

Teapot World, *Castle St; tel: (01492) 593429*, open Mon–Sat 1000–1730, Sun 1100–1730 (Easter–Oct); £1.50. If you thought teapots were just for making tea, this marvellous mixture of antiques and fun designs will make you think again.

Only a few hundred yards from the town centre are tropical butterflies, birds and plants to delight the senses, at **Conwy Butterfly Jungle**, *Bodlondeb Park; tel: (01492) 593149*, open daily 1000–1730 (Apr–Sept); 1000–1600 (Oct); £3.

Conwy RSPB (Royal Society for the Protection of Birds) Reserve, *Llandudno Junction tel: (01492) 584091*, open daily 1000–1700/dusk, £1, is a haven for waterfowl, with nature trails varying in length from half a mile to 2 miles.

OUT OF TOWN

Bodnant Garden (NT), *Tal-y-Cafn; tel: (01492) 650460*, open daily 1000–1700 (mid-Mar–Oct); £4.20. 7 miles south. Set in the lush Conwy Valley, Bodnant is an outstandingly lovely garden, with wonderful displays most of the year – and the bonus of views to Snowdonia.

61

BOURNEMOUTH

With seven miles of beaches set in a sheltered bay, Bournemouth is a dedicated seaside holiday resort which aims to cater for everybody's needs. There are dog-free and dog-friendly beaches; some beaches are strictly no-smoking zones and there are traffic-free promenades. A zoning system prevents clashes between the interests of water sports enthusiasts and bathers. Bournemouth's 2000 acres of parks and gardens are complemented by striking floral displays which decorate the town centre and its approaches.

TOURIST INFORMATION

TIC: *Westover Rd, Bournemouth, Dorset BH1 2BU; tel: (01202) 451700,* open Mon–Sat 0930–1730 (early Sept–mid May); Mon–Sat 0930–1730, Sun 1030–1700 (mid May–mid July); Mon–Sat 0930–1900, Sun 1030–1700 (mid July–early Sept). 24 hr information touchpad in TIC window. DP SHS services offered; local bed-booking (latest 10 mins before closing), BABA (latest 30 mins before closing). *Bournemouth Holiday Guide* (primarily an accommodation listing) is £1, but free by post.

ARRIVING AND DEPARTING

A complex of routes converges on Bournemouth, but the main access is provided by A338, which links with A31, which in turn connects to the north-east with M27 from Southampton and the South Coast and the M3 from London. From Ringwood A338 continues north to

Salisbury. A35 travels west to connect with A30, the major route to Devon and Cornwall.

Bournemouth has plenty of car parks in the town centre area.

GETTING AROUND

The majority of attractions are within walking distance of the centre. A free transport map is available from the TIC. **Yellow Buses**, *tel: (01202) 522661,* cover Bournemouth.

The main **taxi** rank is in the centre, just off the main square. Registered taxi companies include: **United Radio Cabs**, *tel: (01202) 556677;* **Mobile Radio Cars**; *tel: (01202) 522500,* and **Ariel Taxis**, *tel: (01202) 766707.*

STAYING IN BOURNEMOUTH

Accommodation

To book ahead, *tel: (01202) 451700* and state your requirements – you will be given a list of places that meet your criteria and you can book directly.

The choice of accommodation is excellent, ranging from five-star hotels to guesthouses; something for every budget. Hotel chains include *BW, Ct, DV, MH, Mo, ST* and *SW*.

A royal romance is recalled at the **Langtry Manor**, *26 Derby Rd, East Cliff, Bournemouth BH1 3QB; tel: (01202) 553887; fax: (01202) 290115.* The 25-room hotel was built in 1877 for the actress Lillie Langtry by the Prince of Wales, later Edward VII, and there is an abundance of Edwardian memorabilia. Expensive.

De Vere Royal Bath Hotel, *Bath Rd, Bournemouth BH1 2EW; tel: (01201) 555555; fax: (01202) 554158*, is the classic clifftop Victorian seaside resort hotel. It stands in 3 acres of grounds, and many of its 131 rooms overlook the sea. Expensive.

The Grove Hotel, *2 Grove Rd, East Cliff, Bournemouth BH1 3AU; tel: (01202) 552233; fax: (01202) 292233*, is an attractive country house style hotel a 5 min walk from beaches. Budget–moderate.

Ravenstone Hotel, *36 Burnaby Rd, Alum Chine, Bournemouth BH4 8JG; tel: (01202) 761047*. This small budget hotel is in a quiet road close to a beach.

The TIC has lists of **campsites**. The nearest are: **Mt Pleasant Touring Park**, *Matchams Lane, Christchurch; tel: (01202) 475474*; and **Port View Caravan and Camping Park**, *Matchams Lane, Christchurch; tel: (01202) 474214*. Both 5 miles north.

Eating and Drinking

There is a wide selection of eateries, including upmarket restaurants, trendy café-bars and traditional inns.

Money

There is a **Thomas Cook bureau de change** at *Midland Bank, 59 Old Christchurch Rd*.

ENTERTAINMENT AND EVENTS

For all **bookings**, *tel: (01202) 456456*. The **International Centre** and **Pavilion** attract big-name performers and West End productions. The **Bournemouth Symphony Orchestra** presents a series of summer concerts at the **Winter Gardens**. Live entertainment is part of the scene in pubs, clubs and hotel bars.

Major annual events include **Bournemouth Garden and Flower Show** (Apr–May), **Music Makers Festival** (June–July), **Carnival and Regatta** (July–Aug), and **Festival of Lights** (Aug).

SHOPPING

A traffic-free stroll from one end of town to the other takes you through ornate arcades, malls and the pedestrianised main square. All the main chain and department stores are well represented.

SIGHTSEEING

The TIC can book **BBG guided walks**, several **bus tours** (£3.70 half-day, £4.85 full-day) and **Waverley boat trips** from Bournemouth Pier (from £7 half–day).

Bournemouth has 2000 acres of parks and gardens and prides itself on high standards of cleanliness and safety, habitually winning awards for both. The 7 miles of sandy beaches, set in a sheltered bay, stretch from Hengistbury Head in the east to Alum Chine in the west and are interrupted only by two piers – at Boscombe and Bournemouth. For families, new Kidzones and radio-linked inspectors increase the natural safety of the beaches.

On Bournemouth's East Cliff is the **Russell-Cotes Art Gallery and Museum**, *Russell-Cotes Rd; tel: (01202) 451800*, open Tues–Sun 1000–1700; free, with extensive collections of Victorian and Edwardian paintings, furniture, decorative and modern art.

Shelley Rooms, *Boscombe Manor, Beechwood Ave, Boscombe; tel: (01202) 303571*, open Tues–Sun 1400–1700; free. This small museum cum library is devoted to Percy Bysshe Shelley and his artistic circle, while **St Peter's Church**, *Hinton Rd; tel: (01202) 290986*, open all day; free, is the last resting place of Shelley's heart – and Mary Shelley's rather more complete remains.

Three very different exhibitions: *Bournemouth Bears* (the teddy bear variety),

63

Mummies of the Pharaohs and *Dinosaur Safari* are contained in **Expo Centre**, *Old Christchurch Lane; tel: (01202) 293544,* open 0930–1730; £3.50 per exhibition.

OUT OF TOWN

Kingston Lacy House and Gardens (NT), *Wimborne Minster; tel: (01202) 883402,* house open Sat–Wed 1200–1730; £5.50 (house and garden). 10 miles northwest, Kingston Lacy is a fine example of a 17th-century mansion, in wooded parkland (with waymarked walks) and housing valuable art treasures, notably ancient Egyptian artefacts and an outstanding collection of paintings.

Corfe Castle (NT), *Wareham; tel: (01929) 481294,* open daily 1000–1630/ 1730 (Mar–Oct); daily 1100–1530 (Nov–Feb); £3.50. The impressive ruin is what's left of a Norman castle destroyed by Cromwell's Roundheads in 1646.

For a fun family day out, head for **Paultons Park**, *Ower, Romsey, nr Southampton; tel: (01703) 814455,* open 1000–variable closing times (mid Mar–Oct); £8 (all attractions). 30 miles northeast. There are over 40 (very varied) amusements, scattered through pleasant woodlands.

Beaulieu's veteran car exhibition charts a century's motoring achievement, with over 250 vehicles and displays. Other attractions at Beaulieu include the palace house and grounds, abbey ruins, a monorail and river cruises to the 18th-century village of **Buckler's Hard**, where ships for Nelson's fleet were built. **Beaulieu**, *tel: (01590) 612123,* open daily 1000– 1800; £8.50. 20 miles east.

Tank Museum, *Bovington, nr Wareham; tel: (01929) 405096,* open 1000–1700; £5. 25 miles west. The tanks in question are the fighting type and the museum covers every aspect of their construction and

Building Styles

Britain and Ireland have a legacy of historic buildings and monuments second to none. Here are some brief definitions of terms used in this book to describe periods and styles of building. A specialist guide will provide more detail.

Anglo-Saxon: dating from the period after the Roman occupation of Britain until the Norman Conquest (c. AD 650–1066).

Classical/baroque: style of the 17th and 18th centuries, characterised by formal symmetry and inspired by the architecture of ancient Greece and Rome.

Edwardian: early 20th-century period, recognisable by its revival of vernacular or countryside styles.

Georgian: a development of the Classical style, characterised by elegance and symmetry (1760–1840).

Gothic: architecture of the later Middle Ages, (c. 1180–1500), characterised by larger, higher and lighter buildings than the preceding Norman style – and by pointed arches. Loosely divided into three phases, successively more elaborate in character: Early English (1190–1300), Decorated (1280–1377), and Perpendicular (1370–1500).

Gothic Revival: style of the 19th-century.

Jacobean: used to describe buildings of the early 17th century.

Norman: (c. 1066–1190), characterised by solidity and round-headed arches.

Tudor: 1485–1600, typically using timber framing and/or elaborate brickwork, chimneys and decorative bay windows.

Victorian: late 19th-century period (c. 1840–1900), notable particularly for use of red brick and the revival of Gothic styles.

use, employing some interactive displays and with frequent action-filled special events.

BOURNEMOUTH–
PLYMOUTH

This route more or less follows the coast of southern England, passing through picturesque Dorset – with shades of Thomas Hardy and *The French Lieutenant's Woman* – and on into Devon. After skirting the estuary of the River Exe it enters the languid subtropical ambience of the English Riviera before heading west for historic Plymouth.

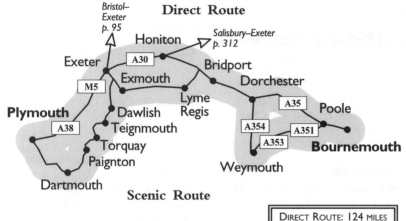

Bristol–
Exeter
p. 95

Direct Route

Honiton

Salisbury–Exeter
p. 312

Exeter

A30

Bridport

Exmouth

Dorchester

M5

Lyme
Regis

A35

Poole

Plymouth

Dawlish

A38

Teignmouth

A354

A351

Torquay

A353

Bournemouth

Paignton

Weymouth

Dartmouth

Scenic Route

65

DIRECT ROUTE: 124 MILES

ROUTES

DIRECT ROUTE

Allow 2 hrs 45 mins to cover this 124-mile route. Leave Bournemouth on A338 to **Poole**, then head west on A35. This passes through **Dorchester** and **Bridport** and reaches Honiton, Devon (see p. 316), after 66 miles, where A30 heads west towards Exeter (see p. 192). After another 12 miles, just outside Exeter, head south on M5, which connects with A38 in 5 miles. Skirting the southern edge of Dartmoor National Park (see p. 189), the route continues west to reach Plymouth in another 41 miles.

SCENIC ROUTE

This is a longer, more leisurely route, covering 180 miles and taking at least 5 hours.

Head for Poole, as above, then follow A35 west to the village of Lytchett Minster, 3 miles from Poole, take A351 to Wareham, then join A352 west for 11 miles to Warmwell, where a left turn on to A353 leads to **Weymouth**. From here A354 heads north to Dorchester, where you follow A35 west to Bridport.

Seven miles west of Bridport follow A3052 through **Lyme Regis** and Seaton to 3 miles west of Sidmouth where a right turn on to B3178 leads to Budleigh Salterton and **Exmouth**. From Exmouth head north on A376, joining A379 after 7½ miles and turning south on the opposite side of the Exe estuary. **Dawlish** marks the start of the English Riviera as the B3199 passes through **Teignmouth**, to the principal resort of **Torquay**. From Torquay follow the coast road, via **Paignton**, to Kingswear, where a car ferry crosses the River Dart to Dartmouth where A379 continues for 35 miles to Plymouth.

POOLE

TIC: *The Quay, Poole BH15 1HE; tel: (01202) 673322*, open Mon–Fri 0930–1730, Sat–Sun 1000–1700 (June, July, Sept); Mon–Fri 0900–1800, Sat–Sun 1000–1800 (Aug); Mon–Fri 0900–1700, Sat–Sun 1030–1630 (Apr–May); Mon–Fri 0900–1700, Sat–Sun 1030–1530 (Oct–Mar).

ACCOMMODATION

Salterns Hotel, *38 Salterns Way, Lilliput, Poole BH14 8JR; tel: (01202) 707321 fax: (01202) 707488*. The hotel stands by a 14-acre marine. It has a waterside patio and views across the harbour. Expensive.

Harmony Hotel, *19 St Peter's Rd, Parkstone, Poole BH14 1NZ; tel: (01202) 747510*. In a quiet residential area close to local amenities, the 11-room hotel can provide lunches and dinners. Most rooms are en suite. Budget–moderate.

Pear Tree Caravan Park, *Organford, Poole BH16 6LA; tel: (01202) 622434*. A quiet family country park with electric hook-ups, shop and modern toilet block. Budget.

EATING AND DRINKING

Corkers, *1 High St, The Quay, Poole BH15 1AB; tel: (01202) 681393, fax:*

(01202) 667393. Bistro and café-bar, restaurant specialising in seafood and four b&b rooms. B&b budget, restaurant moderate.

King's Head, *High St, Poole BH15 1BP; tel: (01202) 674919*. Just a stroll from the Quay, this popular inn dates from the 17th century. Extensive fish menu. Lunch 1200–1500, dinner 1900–2200. Moderate.

The Darby's Corner, *Waterloo Rd, Poole BH17 7LD; tel: (01202) 693700*. Vegetarian and vegan dishes are served as well as traditional meat choices. The Library is a room for non-smokers. Moderate.

SIGHTSEEING

Poole's Sandbanks Peninsula stretches from the cliffs of Bournemouth to the entrance to Poole Harbour. More than 3 miles of safe sandy beaches regularly receive the European Blue Flag award. Poole Harbour, one of Europe's largest natural harbours, is a popular sailing and windsurfing venue. Although it is a busy port, Poole, with its quaint Old Town streets, famous pottery and quayside, has much to offer the holidaymaker.

Aquarium Complex, *Poole Quay; tel: (01202) 686712*, open daily year-round, also evenings in summer. Admission charge. More than an aquarium, this all-weather attraction also has a serpentarium, insectarium, crocodile pool, model railway and a pirates and smugglers section.

Waterfront Museum, *4 High St, Poole; tel: (01202) 683138*, open daily Easter–Oct 1000–1700. Admission charge. Poole's seafaring history and associations with trade with Newfoundland are illustrated in fine displays, and there is a reconstructed Victorian street.

Brownsea Island (NT), *within Poole Harbour; tel: (01202) 707870*. £2.20, open Apr–Sept 1000–1800. Regular ferries from Poole Quay (£3.60 return) and from Sandbanks £2.20 return. The 500-acre site has interesting flora and fauna in natural surroundings. A 200-acre nature reserve is managed by Dorset Wildlife Trust. The castle on Brownsea Island was built by Henry VIII.

Compton Acres Gardens, *Canford Cliffs Rd, Poole; tel: (01202) 700778. £4.20, open Mar–Oct.* Nine distinctive gardens, including greatly admired Japanese, Italian, rock and water gardens.

Poole Pottery, *The Quay; tel: (01202) 666200. £2.50, open year-round.* The pottery is on the same site where it was established in the 1870s, and as well as watching craftspeople at work there is much visitor participation. A museum and shop selling 'seconds' can be visited.

DORCHESTER

TIC: *11 Antelope Walk, Dorchester DT1 1BE; tel: (01305) 267992,* open Mon–Sat 0900–1700, Sun 1000–1500 (May–Sept); Mon–Sat 0900–1700 (Apr, Oct); Mon–Sat 0900–1600 (Nov–Mar). DP SHS services offered; local bed-booking and BABA (latest 30 mins before closing). Tickets sold for local transport, theatres and events. *Dorchester Historical Guide and Town Trails* is 50p, but *West Dorset Where to Stay* and *West Dorset Exploring* are free.

GETTING ARROUND

Most of Dorchester's attractions are easily reached on foot. A town map and transport map are available free from the TIC. Local buses are operated by a number of different companies; for information, phone the TIC or **Dorset County Council**, *tel: (01305) 251000.* The main operator is **Southern National**, *tel: (01823) 272033.* Most buses stop on *Acland Rd.*

The main **taxi** rank is on *Trinity St.* Registered companies include: **Abcars**,

tel: (01305) 269696; **A-Line Taxis/ Dorchester Taxi Services**, *tel: (01305) 262888/264747/251666*; **Fast Cabs**, *tel: (01305) 251655*; **Pete's Cabs**, *tel: (01305) 251122*; **Bob's Cars**, *tel: (01305) 269500*; **Starline Taxis**, *tel: (01305) 263922*; and **Wessex Taxi Hire**, *tel: (01305) 251800.*

ACCOMMODATION

There are no large hotels and only a few small ones, but a good selection of b&bs, pubs and inns offer rooms throughout the town and outlying area. It is generally easy to book on arrival – except over public holidays and in school holidays. The only chain is PL.

Higher Waterston Farm Cottages, *Piddlehinton, Dorchester, Dorset; tel: (01305) 848208, fax: (01305) 848894.* Well-equipped cottages on a sheep farm, 8 miles from the sea. Tennis and games barn, open all year. Budget–expensive.

Casterbridge Hotel, *49 High East St, Dorchester, Dorset, DT1 1HU; tel: (01305) 264043; fax: (01305) 269884.* En suite rooms in Georgian town house. Moderate–expensive.

Accord Inn Hotel, *Fore St, Evershot, near Dorchester, Dorset DT2 0JW; tel: (01935) 83228.* Four-poster bedrooms, oak-beamed bars, log fires and candlelit restaurant (one non-smoking) in this pretty village. Moderate.

The Stables, *Hyde Crook, Frampton, Dorset DT2 9NW; tel: (01300) 320075.* Mainly equestrian 20-acre property 5 miles from Dorchester. Budget.

Clay Pigeon Caravan Park, *Warden Hill, Evershot, Dorchester, Dorset DT2 9PW; tel: (01935) 83492.* Modern facilities on site with shop for tents, touring caravans and motorhomes. Dogs welcome. Budget.

EATING AND DRINKING

The best roads for restaurants are *High*

67

West St and *High East St*: a list is available (free) from the TIC. Dorset Blue Vinney cheese, Dorchester chocolates and fudge and Moores Dorset biscuits are all local specialities.

The Mock Turtle, *34 High West St, Dorchester, DT1 1UP*. Pleasant surroundings with well-thought-out starters and main courses. Expensive.

Red Lion, *Winfrith, near Dorchester; tel: (01305) 852814*. A full range of pub meals in a place which welcomes families. On A352 Dorchester–Winborne road, has b&b accommodation and Caravan Club facilities. Budget–moderate.

SIGHTSEEING

A variety of **guided walks** (from £2.50) can be booked at the TIC, who also arrange individual guides for Dorchester and the surrounding area.

Remains of what was an important provincial centre are scattered around the town, including the vast amphitheatre which the Romans created out of **Maumbury Rings**, a Bronze Age circle (near Dorchester South railway station).

The county town of Dorset, Dorchester seems to have changed little since it featured so prominently as *Casterbridge* in the novels of Thomas Hardy (1840–1928), whose rather sombre statue broods at the end of *High West St*. Hardy was also an architect and designed his own last home, **Max Gate** (NT), *Alington Ave; tel: (01305) 262538*. Dining and drawing rooms open Sun–Mon, Wed 1400–1700 (Easter–Sept); £2.

A reconstruction of Hardy's study is in the **Dorset County Museum,** *High West St; tel: (01305) 262735*, open Mon–Sat 1000–1700 (all year), Sun 1000–1700 (July–Aug); £2.75. It also contains Hardy memorabilia, and is an excellent starting point for exploring Dorset's history, both

human and animal – from dinosaurs to butterflies.

Dorchester is also home to the **Dinosaur Museum**, *Icen Way; tel: (01305) 269880*, open daily 0930–1730 (Apr–Oct); 1000–1630 (Nov–Mar); £3.50. Britain's only museum devoted entirely to this subject comes complete with audio-visual and touch-screen displays.

The **Tutankhamun Exhibition**, *High West St; tel: (01305) 269571*, open daily 0930–1730; £3.50, presents a walk-through reconstruction of the tomb and facsimiles of its fabulous contents.

The site of the Assizes for four centuries is **Old Crown Court and Cells**, *Shire Hall, Stratton House, High West St; tel: (01305) 252241*. The recreated court is where, in 1834, the Tolpuddle Martyrs were sentenced to transportation (for demanding fair wages for agricultural workers) and they were held in the cells pending their departure. The court is open Mon–Fri 1000–1200 and 1400–1600; there are tours of the cells Tues–Fri at 1415 and 1615, Wed at 1015 and 1215 (late-July–early-Sept); court is free, but cells are 50p.

The Keep Military Museum, *The Keep, Bridport Rd; tel: (01305) 264066*, open Mon–Sat 0930–1700; £2. In a listed building, this contains an interesting mix of genuine military paraphernalia and interactive computer displays.

Teddy Bear House, *Antelope Walk; tel: (01305) 263200/269741*, open daily 0930–1730 (Easter–Oct); 1000–1630 (Nov–Easter); £2. Mr Edward Bear welcomes you to his home – to meet his human-size family at work and play.

OUT OF TOWN

Maiden Castle (EH), open at all reasonable times; free. 2 miles south-west. Arguably the finest Iron Age fort in Britain, the castle dates from the 1st century BC. The massive defensive earthwork powerfully evokes the presence of the pre-Roman British.

One of the finest 15th-century manor houses in England is the delightful **Athelhampton House**, *Athelhampton, Puddletown; tel: (01305) 848363.* House open Sun–Fri 1100–1700 (Easter–Oct); £4.50 (house and gardens). 6 miles east. The house contains magnificent rooms and is set in gardens that include topiary pyramids, several fountains and spectacular floral displays.

Kingston Maurward Park, *Stinsford; tel: (01305) 264738,* open daily 1000–1730 (Easter–Oct); £3. 1½ miles north-east. The 35 acres of exceptionally fine 18th-century style gardens and lawns, with a 5-acre lake, feature sweeping lawns and gloriously varied pockets of colour and scent. There are also a farm animal park and a mile-long nature trail.

Minterne Gardens, *Minterne Magna; tel: (01300) 341370,* open daily 1000–1900 (Apr–Oct); £3. 10 miles north. A fine collection of rare trees and shrubs is gathered in valley gardens, landscaped in the 18th century and enlivened by cascades and streams. En route from Dorchester, you pass the immodest **Cerne Giant**, the extraordinary Romano-British hill carving of a club-bearing man revealing his all to the village below.

Mill House Cider and Clock Museum, *Overmoigne; tel: (01305) 852220,* open daily 0900–1700; £1. 7 miles south-east. In this rather unusual museum, old cider-making equipment rubs shoulders with a selection of antique clocks.

Thomas Hardy's Cottage (NT), *Higher Bockhampton; tel: (01305) 262366,* open Sun–Thur, Good Fri 1100–1700/ dusk (Easter–Oct); £2.50. 3 miles north-

east. The small thatched cottage where Hardy was born (in 1840) was built by his great-grandfather and has changed very little.

New Barn Field Centre, *Bradford Peverell; tel: (01305) 267463,* open daily 1000–1700; £3.50. 3 miles north-west. This Iron Age homestead recreates life 2000 years ago, with a working pottery and exhibitions of tools and equipment.

Eldridge Pope & Co, *Weymouth Ave; tel: (01305) 251251,* offer group tours of their working real-ale brewery (samples included in the cost: £4).

WEYMOUTH

TIC: *The Kings Statue, The Esplanade, Weymouth DT4 8ED; tel: (01305) 785747,* open daily 0930–1830 (mid-June–mid July); 0930–1700 (Easter–mid-June, mid July–Nov); 1030–1500 (Dec–Easter). DP SHS services offered; local bed-booking and BABA (latest bookings 30 mins before closing). *Weymouth, Portland and South Dorset guide* is available for £1 and has accommodation listings. There is a free guide, *Royal Manor of Portland.*

GETTING AROUND

The town falls into two parts: mainland Weymouth and Portland 'Island' (actually linked to the mainland by a narrow strip of land). Buses between them (and other areas surrounding the centre) are frequent (less so after 1800) and transport maps are available from the TIC (25p). Weather permitting, the **White Motor Boats ferry**, *tel: (01305) 813246,* links Portland Castle with Brewer's Quay (Apr–Oct). There are **taxi** ranks on the Esplanade.

ACCOMMODATION

There is an excellent range of accommodation, from large independents to b&bs. **Accommodation hotline** (free-phone): *tel: (0800) 765223*. It is always a good idea to book in advance, essential for Carnival Week (mid Aug). Cheaper accommodation is mainly around the centre. The only chain is *Court*. Youth accommodation is provided at the **RSPB Lighthouse**, *Portland; tel: (01305) 820553*. The nearest **campsites** are **Waterside Holiday Park**, *Bowleaze Cove; tel: (01305) 833103*, 2 miles north; **East Fleet Farm**, *Chickerell; tel: (01305) 785768*, 2 miles west; and **Pebble Bank**, *90 Camp Road, Wyke Regis; tel: (01305) 774844*, between Weymouth and Portland.

SIGHTSEEING

A Dorset County Council book of **guided walks** is £1.60 from the TIC, who can also advise about **boat trips** and supply a list of **special events**.

Weymouth is an old harbour town, notable for its handsome late-Georgian buildings and beautiful bay. Two striking landmarks are the **Jubilee Clock** and the elaborately painted and gilded statue of **George III** on the Esplanade; the **Gloucester Hotel** was the king's summer home during his visits.

Dominating the old harbour is a 19th-century fort now housing a museum of coastal defence: **Nothe Fort**, *Barrack Rd; tel (01305) 787243*, open daily 1030–1730 (mid May–mid Sept); Sun, public holidays 1400–1600 (mid Sept–mid May); £2.50.

Deep Sea Adventure and Titanic Story, *9 Custom House Quay; tel: (01305) 76069* open daily 0930–1700 (winter); daily 0930–1800 (summer); £3, offers three floors of animated and interactive displays, including a *Titanic* exhibition.

Brewers Quay, *Hope Sq, Old Harbour; tel: (01305) 777622*, is a Victorian brewery that has been imaginatively redevel-oped in period style and is now a complex offering a variety of shops, eateries and craft workshops. It also houses: **The Timewalk**, open daily 0930–1730 (2130 in school holidays); 0930–1830 (Easter and public holidays weekends); £3.75, which takes you back through six centuries of Weymouth's history; and **Discovery** – a hands–on multimedia attraction with over 60 exhibits, open daily 1000–1730 (Mar–Dec); 0930–2100 (school holidays); Wed–Sun variable times (Jan–Feb); £3.30.

Sea Life Park, *tel: (01305) 788255*, open daily 1000–1700; £5.95 (all-day ticket). There are over 30 displays, scattered over 6 acres of land within the 350-acre **Lodmoor Country Park** (a little north of the centre), which makes for a very pleasant day out.

Portland Island is a limestone peninsula 4½ miles long and less than 2 miles wide, just south of Weymouth. At its southern tip is **Portland Bill**: a marvellous view rewarding anyone with the energy to climb to the top of the famous **Lighthouse** – open most days 1000–1700; £1.50, with a TIC in the bottom that's open Wed–Mon (mid July–Aug); sporadic days (Sept–mid July).

Portland Castle (EH), *Castletown; tel (01305) 820539*, open daily 1000–1800/dusk (Easter–Oct); £2.20. The castle, built of white Portland Stone, overlooks the harbour and is one of the best-preserved Tudor coastal forts.

The maritime nature of the area, with emphasis on shipwrecks and smuggling, is reflected in **Portland Museum and Shipwreck Exhibition**, *217 Wakeham; tel: (01305) 821804*, open Fri–Tues 1030–1300 and 1330–1700; £1.40.

Chesil Bank is a natural wonder extending westwards from the Isle of Portland almost as far as Bridport; some

18 miles. This vast bank of shingle, 40 ft high in places, is unique in Europe. The pebbles which make it up increase in size consistently from west to east. The sea deposits the pebbles, but experts disagree about where they all come from.

At **Bennetts Water Garden**, *Chickerell; tel: (01305) 785150,* open daily 1000–1700 (Apr–Oct), but check; £3.75, 2 miles north of the centre, the prime attraction is 6 acres of natural lakes, with over 100 varieties of water lilies.

BRIDPORT

TIC: *32 South St, Bridport DT6 3NQ; tel: (01308) 424901,* open Mon–Sat 0900–1700 (1 Apr or Easter–Oct); Mon–Fri 1000–1500, Sat 1000–1400 (Oct–Dec); Mon–Sat 1000–1400 (Jan–Mar or Easter Mon). A full range of services is offered.

ACCOMMODATION

The Greyhound Hotel, *East St, Bridport, Dorset DT6 3LF; tel: (01308) 422944.* The family-owned and run town centre hotel has 15 rooms, some with private bathrooms. It is a friendly, relaxed place with roomy bars where locals and visitors mix. Bar snacks and restaurant meals are available. Budget–moderate.

The Westpoint Tavern, *The Esplanade, Bridport DT6 4HG; tel: (01308) 423636,* faces the beach. All rooms are en suite and have sea views. Budget.

Durbyfield Guest House, *10 West Bay, Bridport DT6 4EL; tel: (01308) 423307.* On Dorset's Heritage Coastline, one minute from the beach and harbour, this Georgian home welcomes families.

Rudge Farm, *Chilcombe, Bridport, Dorset DT6 4NF; tel: (01308) 482630; fax: (01308) 482635.* Here you have the choice of a large en suite b&b room in a licensed farmhouse or self-catering in one of the converted barns and outbuildings

around a cobbled yard. The property is in beautiful countryside, 2 miles from the sea. Budget–moderate.

EATING AND DRINKING

George Hotel, *4 South St, Bridport DT6 3NQ; tel: (01308) 23187.* The public can call in for breakfast from 0830. Good choice of fish dishes and savoury snacks. Local beers are served. Cheap–budget.

Riverside Restaurant, *West Bay, Bridport DT6 4EZ; tel: (01308) 422011,* open daily lunch 1130–1430, dinner 1830–2100, closed for dinner Sun, phone as times may vary. Fish restaurant with a great reputation. There's a waterside patio for outdoor dining. Expensive–pricey.

SIGHTSEEING

A mixture of historic architectural styles sit happily together in Bridport – a medieval parish church, Tudor museum and Georgian town hall.

Bridport is a prime example of a town that grew up around its industry, and its layout reflects this. The industry was rope- and twine-making, and the cords were stretched between the buildings in the wide streets and straight alleys.

Bridport is still Britain's main source of twine. At one time rope from the town was shipped to many parts of the world from the harbour, a shipbuilding centre until 1879. The harbour, 1½ miles from the town centre, is now known as **West Bay**, where there are beaches. Beach fishing and fossil hunting are rewarding pastimes along the shore.

OUT OF TOWN

Parnham, *Beaminster; tel: (01308) 862204,* open April–Oct Sun, Wed and public holidays 1000–1700. £4. On the A3066 5 miles north of Bridport. Something different – a country house without antiques. It celebrates the living arts with interiors containing fine contemporary furniture, glass, textiles and ceramics. The house was restored by John and Jennie Makepeace. The workshop where John Makepeace produces his furniture is also open to visitors.

Mapperton Gardens, *Beaminster; tel: (01308) 862645*. Open daily Mar–Oct 1400–1800. £2.50. 5 miles from Bridport off the B3163. Italianate terraced gardens with topiary, fishponds, fountain court, orangery, croquet lawn, ornamental birds and views of Thomas Hardy country.

LYME REGIS

TIC: *Guildhall Cottage, Church St, Lyme Regis, Dorset DT7 3BS; tel: (01297) 442138*, open daily 1000–1700 (Apr, Oct); Mon–Fri 1000–1800, Sat–Sun 1000–1700 (May–Sept); Mon–Fri 1000–1600, Sat 1000–1400 (Nov–Mar). SHS services offered; local bed-booking and BABA. Tickets booked for excursions, theatres and local attractions. The useful guide to *Lyme Regis, The Pearl of Dorset* is 30p. Separate accommodation listings are free.

GETTING AROUND

Lyme Regis is very busy and crowded during peak holiday periods and parking is extremely difficult. A park and ride scheme operates from the western side of the town. The main bus operator is **Southern National**, *tel: (01305) 783645*. A good town shuttle service operates, with an hourly service to outlying areas: mostly 0600–2000. There are two useful passes: a daily **Explorer** (£4.50) and the weekly **Silver** (£14.25). The main **taxi** rank is at *The Square, Broad St*.

ACCOMMODATION

There is a good range of guesthouses and b&bs, with cheaper accommodation available in the centre. It is generally easy to book on arrival, except July–Aug.

Hotel Buena Vista, *Pound St, Lyme Regis, Dorset DT7 3HZ; tel: (01297) 442494*. Regency-style property with sea views, close to town and beach. Closed Dec and Jan. Moderate–expensive.

Coverdale Guest House, *Woodmead Rd, Lyme Regis, Dorset DT7 3AB; tel: (01297) 442882*. Views of sea or garden and countryside, open Feb–Nov. Budget.

Kersbrook Hotel and Restaurant, *Pound Rd, Lyme Regis, Dorset, DT7 3HX; tel: (01297) 442596*. Country house hotel by the sea. Moderate.

The TIC has details of **campsites**. The nearest are: **Hook Farm**, *Gore Lane, Uplyme; tel: (01297) 442801*, 1 mile west of the centre; **Wood Farm**, *Axminster Rd, Charmouth; tel: (01297) 560697*, 2 miles east; and **Newlands**, *Charmouth; tel: (01297) 560259*, 2 miles east.

SIGHTSEEING

The TIC books **bus tours** and **guided walks**. Lyme Regis was a fashionable seaside resort in the 18th and 19th centuries; a regular visitor was Jane Austen, who set part of *Persuasion* here. More recently, John Fowles set much of *The French Lieutenant's Woman* in the town. The harbour is sheltered by a stone breakwater known as **The Cobb**, site of the fascinating **Lyme Marine Aquarium**, *tel: (01297) 443678*, open daily 1000–dusk (Easter–Oct); £1.20.

The 'Jurassic Coast' is famous for fossils and two establishments devoted to the subject can arrange for you to join fossil searches: **Dinosaurland**, *Coombe St; tel: (01297) 443541*, open 1000–approx. 1700–1900 (according to demand); £3.20; and **Charmouth Heritage Coast Centre**, *Charmouth; tel: (01297) 560772*, open daily 1030–1700 (Easter, Whitsun–Sept); free, but donations welcomed. An excellent display of fossils can be seen at the **Lyme Regis Philpot Museum**, *Bridge St; tel: (01297) 443370,* open Mon–Sat 1000–1700, Sun 1000–1200 and 1430–1700; £1.

OUT OF TOWN

Pecorama, *Underleys, Beer, Seaton; tel: (01297) 21542,* open Mon–Fri 1000–1730, Sat 1000–1300 (Easter–May, Sept); Sun–Fri 1000–1730, Sat 1000–1300 (Oct–Easter); £3.20 covers the gardens, an exhibition and a train ride; small additional charges for some minor attractions. 8 miles west.

Seaton Electric Tramway, *Riverside Depot, Harbour Rd, Seaton; tel: (01297) 20375,* open daily 0840/0940–1720 (Easter–Oct); £4.20. 7 miles west.

LYME REGIS–TORQUAY

Although the route runs within a mile or so of the coast after leaving Lyme Regis, there are few glimpses of the sea unless you actually drive into the small and sleepy resorts of **Seaton**, **Sidmouth** and **Budleigh Salterton**. The River Exe estuary also disappears for much of the way between Exmouth and Dawlish.

EXMOUTH

The 2-mile stretch of sandy beach, with amusements for youngsters, make for a relaxed family holiday. The town's prosperity comes from its working docks as well as tourism.

Two miles north of Exmouth on A376 is **A La Ronde (NT)**, *tel: (01395) 265514.* Admission charge, open late April–Oct Sun–Thur. A curious-looking 16-sided house built in the late 18th century, with some unusual decorations.

Lord Nelson's mistress, Lady Emma

Hamilton, lived at **The Beacon**, Exmouth. Nelson's wife, Frances, is buried in neaby Littleham churchyard.

Imperial Hotel, *The Esplanade, Exmouth, Devon EX8 2SW; tel: (01395) 274761; fax: (01395) 265161.* Many of the 57 rooms have sea views. There is an outdoor swimming pool. Moderate.

Devoncourt Hotel, *Douglas Ave, Exmouth, Devon EX8 2EX; tel: (01395) 272277.* Set in 4 acres of subtropical gardens, the hotel overlooks the Torbay coastline. Generous low-season offers; high season prices moderate.

DAWLISH

Charles Dickens featured the town in *Nicholas Nickleby* and Jane Austen brought Dawlish and its long stretch of sand and shingle beach into *Sense and Sensibility*.

West Hatch Hotel, *34 West Cliff, Dawlish, Devon, EX7 9DN; tel: (01626) 864211,* has ten en suite bedrooms, some with four-posters. Budget–moderate.

TEIGNMOUTH

This family seaside resort (pronounced Tinmouth) has been popular since Victorian days. Visitors are taken back to Georgian times on Wednesdays in the peak holiday season, when a craft market takes place with costumed stallholders and evening entertainment.

A plaque on a house at *20 Northumberland Place* records that John Keats wrote his epic poem *Endymion* while living there.

Teignmouth's **Grand Pier**, *tel: (01626) 774367;* open daily 1000–2230, free admission to pier, offers a range of amusements.

TORQUAY

TIC: *Vaughan Pde, Torquay, Devon TQ2 5JG; tel: (01803) 297428,* open Mon–Sat 0900–1700 (Nov–Mar); Mon–Sat 0900–

73

1715 (Apr–May); Mon–Sat 0900–1800, Sun, public holidays 0900–1700 (June–Oct). DP SHS services offered; local bed-booking (latest 1700; variable fee), BABA (latest 1600; variable booking fee), tickets booked for theatre, bus and train. The *English Riviera Guide* (including accommodation list) is free.

GETTING AROUND

The majority of Torquay's attractions are within walking distance of the centre. Town maps (£1) are available from the TIC.

The main **bus** operator is **Stagecoach**, *tel: (01803) 613226*. Services are good in the centre and between towns up to 2300. The main **taxi** rank is opposite *Cary Pde*.

ACCOMMODATION

There is a good range of accommodation available, particularly mid-range hotels and guesthouses. Budget accommodation is located in the *Avenue Rd* area. It is usually easy to book on arrival, except July–Aug. Accommodation can be booked through the **Torquay Hotels and Catering Association**, *12 Walnut Rd; tel: (01803) 605808*. Chains represented are *BW, Ct* and *Mo*. The TIC has details of **campsites** in the area.

SIGHTSEEING

Wallace Arnold, *tel: (01803) 211729*, offer **bus tours**, while **boat trips** can be arranged by **Western Lady**, *tel: (01803) 852041*, from Princess Pier.

The palm-fringed town has elegant Victorian terraces, sandy beaches, well-kept gardens and a continental feel. It is associated with crime writer Agatha Christie, born here in 1890, so both **Torquay Museum**, *529 Babbacombe Rd; tel: (01803) 293975*, open Mon–Fri 1000–1645 (all year); Sat 1000–1645, Sun

1330–1645 (Easter–Oct); £2, and **Torre Abbey**, *The Kings Drive; tel: (01803) 293593*, abbey open daily 0930–1800 (Apr–Oct); £2.50, have special exhibitions on her life.

Allow at least an hour for **Kents Cavern**, *Ilsham Rd; tel: (01803) 215136*. Tours: Sun–Fri 0930–1730, Sat 0930–1700 (July–Aug); daily 1000–1700 (Apr–June, Sept); daily 1000–1600 (Oct–Mar); £3.75. The show caves date from 2,000,000 BC and there are evening 'ghost tours' (June–Sept).

Thousands of figures and hundreds of models, all on a scale of 1:12, with animation, sound effects and lovely gardens, make up the **Model Village**, **Babbacombe**: *Hampton Ave; tel: (01803) 315315*, open daily 0900–2200 (Easter–Sept); 0900–2100 (Oct); 0900–dusk (Nov–Easter); £3.80.

For a nostalgic look at life in Victorian times, visit **Bygones**, *Fore St; tel: (01803) 326108*, open Mon–Fri 1000–2200, Sat–Sun 1000–1800 (June–mid Sept); daily 1000–1500/1600 (Nov–Feb); daily 1000–1800 (Mar–May, mid Sept–Oct); £2.75.

PAIGNTON

The neighbouring resort is 3 miles south-west of Torquay and is worth a brief visit.

Paignton and Dartmouth Steam Railway, *Queens Park Station, Torbay Rd; tel: (01803) 555872*. Operates daily (June–Sept); less frequently (Mar–Oct); £6. Contact them directly for schedules.

Paignton Zoo, *Totnes Rd; tel: (01803) 557479*, open daily 1000–1800 (Apr–Sept); 1000–1700 (Oct–Mar); £7.60 (reduced to £5.95 Oct–Easter). This is one of the largest zoos in the country, with over 300 species. The new *Desert Habitat* is a hothouse full of appropriate flora and fauna.

Compton Castle (NT), *Marldon; tel: (01803) 872112,* open Mon, Wed–Thur 1000–1215 and 1400–1700 (Mar–Oct); £2.70. 4 miles west; This is a fortified manor house with curtain wall that was built between the 14th and 16th centuries.

DARTMOUTH

TIC: *Newcomen Engine House, Mayors Ave, Dartmouth, Devon TQ6 9YY; tel: (01803) 834224,* open Mon–Sat 1000–1600 (Oct–Easter); Mon–Sat 0930–1730, Sun 1000–1600 (Easter–Sept). DP services offered; local bed-booking and BABA (both 10% deposit of first night); some concessions to attractions sold. The annual guide, *Welcome to Dartmouth,* is available free and includes accommodation listings, ferry information and events.

In summer (June–Sept) the **Paignton and Dartmouth Steam Railway** runs between Paignton and Kingswear (see above).

GETTING AROUND

Most attractions are within walking distance of the centre. Bus services are good in the centre, patchy to outlying areas. Most services start from *South Embankment,* in the centre. The two main bus companies are **Western National**, *tel: (01752) 222666,* and **Stagecoach**, *tel: (01803) 613226.* A **taxi** rank is situated on *South Embankment.*

ACCOMMODATION

There are few hotels of any type in Dartmouth and only one chain: *FH.* Budget accommodation in guesthouses and b&bs is plentiful and can be found in the town centre. There are also several inns offering accommodation in the villages of Blackawton (5 miles west) and Dittisham (7 miles north). Though it is generally easy to find accommodation, it is advisable to book in advance during the Regatta (late Aug).

The TIC can provide **campsite** information. The two closest are: **Little Cotton Caravan Park**, *Little Cotton; tel: (01803) 832558,* 1 mile north, and **Leonards Cove Campsite**, *Stoke Fleming; tel: (01803) 770206,* 3 miles south.

SIGHTSEEING

Guided walking tours of the town are available (from £2) – contact **Peter King**, *tel: (01803) 832611.*

Boat trips from Dartmouth to Totnes (£6 round-trip) are offered by: **River Link**, *tel: (01803) 834488* or *(01803) 862735;* and **Red Cruisers**, *tel: (01803) 832109.* Both operate daily (Easter–Oct); infrequently (Nov–Easter). Contact them directly for schedules and details of other cruises. Departures are from North and South Embankments.

Dartmouth lies near the mouth of the River Dart, in an area of outstanding natural beauty – countryside and moorlands on one side, a scenic coastline on the other. On a piece of land jutting into the estuary is the 15th-century **Dartmouth Castle** (EH), *Castle Rd; tel: (01803) 833588,* open daily 1000–1800 (Easter–Oct); Wed–Sun 1000–1300 and 1400–1600 (Nov–Easter); £2.40. 1 mile south-east. The castle ferry usually runs over Easter, then weekends until Whit, then daily until Sept – but check.

Newcomen Engine House, *Mayors Ave; tel: (01803) 834224,* open Mon–Sat 0930–1730, Sun 1000–1600 (Apr–Sept), Mon–Sat 1000–1600 (Oct–Mar); 50p. The atmospheric steam engine was a milestone in the industrial revolution and this one (built late-18th-century) is a direct descendant of the 1712 original invention of Thomas Newcomen.

75

BRIGHTON

'London-by-the-Sea', Brighton began to develop as a seaside town after a local doctor had extolled the curative virtues of sea-bathing, introducing the taste for seaside holidays. It became hugely fashionable as a result of the patronage of the Prince Regent, later George IV: Georgian and Regency terraces sprang up everywhere after Brighton's royal admirer had built the exotic Royal Pavilion. Today, Brighton's combination of elegant buildings, exclusive shops and typical seaside amusements gives it a unique, raffish charm; it deserves at least a day's exploration.

TOURIST INFORMATION

TIC: *10 Bartholomew Sq., Brighton BN1 1JS; tel: (01273) 323755,* open Mon–Fri 0900–1700 (Sept–May); Sat 1000–1700, Sun 1000–1600 (Sept–mid July); Mon–Fri 0900–1800 (June–July); Sat 1000–1800, Sun 1000–1700 (mid July–Aug). DP SHS services offered; local bed-booking service (latest 1630 except Sun, fee £1.00 per person and 10% deposit of total stay), BABA (latest one hour before closing; fee £2.50 and 10% deposit of first night) – afternoons are busiest, especially during major conferences and public holidays. Guided tours booked. Tickets sold for National Express, local coach tours, Guide Friday and local events. *Brighton and Hove,* a booklet that includes accommodation listings, is free.

ARRIVING AND DEPARTING

Brighton's main artery is A23, stretching from London, 59 miles to the north. The main east-west link is A27, which by-passes the town some 5 miles to the north but has good links to the centre. A259 provides an east-west link, mainly along the coast, between Folkstone and Chichester.

GETTING AROUND

The majority of attractions are within walking distance of the centre, except for Preston Manor, Booth Natural History Museum and Brighton Marina. Free town and transport maps are available from the TIC. The transport map is also available from the local bus offices.

Buses

Two main bus companies operate in Brighton and Hove: **Brighton & Hove Bus & Coach Co.**, *Conway St, Hove, tel: (01273) 886200;* and **Brighton Blue Bus**, *Lewes Road, Brighton; tel: (01273) 674881.* Other services are provided as part of the county council's **Rider** network; *tel: (01273) 482123/478007.* Most buses pass through *Old Steine,* in the town centre.

Taxis

The chief **taxi** ranks are at *East St, Queens Sq., St Peters Place* and the railway station in *Queen's Rd.*

STAYING IN BRIGHTON

Accommodation

Thomas Cook has a hotel reservation desk on the main concourse of the railway station.

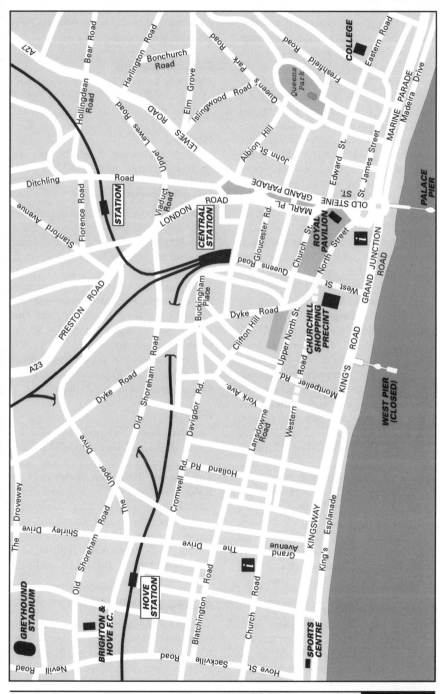

There is a good choice of accommodation in the town, affording a wide range of prices. Cheaper accommodation is mostly located near the seafront, in the town centre. There is no accommodation in pubs or inns in Brighton itself, but a wide choice is available in the outlying villages. It is generally easy to find accommodation on arrival, except during major conferences, public holidays and summer weekends: If you have made a reservation, it is advisable to arrive before 2000, because small hotels are reluctant to hold rooms any later. Hotel chains in Brighton include *BW, DV, Ja, Mo, ST* and *Th*. If you are staying for a week (or multiples), the **University** offers accommodation in self-contained flats during the summer holidays (July–Sept); *tel: (01273) 643667*.

HI: *Patcham Place, London Rd; tel: (01273) 556196*. **Brighton Backpackers** is an independent hostel at *75–76 Middle St; tel: (01723) 777717*, open daily from 1000.

There is one **campsite** in Brighton, but space for tents is limited and there's a maximum stay of two nights: **Sheepcote Valley Caravan Club Site**, *East Brighton Park; tel: (01273) 626546*. Outside town, the closest are: **Downsview Caravan Park**, *Bramlands Lane, Woodmancote, near Henfield; tel: (01273) 492801*; **New Barn Farm**, *New Barn Lane, Henfield; tel (01273) 494105*; **Farmhouse Campsite**, *Tottington Drive, Small Dole, Henfield; tel: (01273) 493157* (all 8 miles north-west); and **Hampden Vale Caravan Centre**, *South Heighton, Newhaven; tel (01273) 713530*, 8 miles east along the coast.

Eating and Drinking

There are over 400 eating places – more per head of population than anywhere else in the UK outside London. Many are excellent, so finding somewhere to suit

your taste and pocket is not difficult. Pubs are often good value.

Communications

The main **post office**, *Ship St*, is open Mon–Fri 0900–1730, Sat 0900–1230. It has poste restante facilities.

Money

There is a **Thomas Cook bureau de change** at *Midland Bank, 153 North St*.

ENTERTAINMENT

Details of current entertainment can be found in the TIC's publications *Brighton Scene* (25p), *What's On* (50p) and *Latest* (30p); all are available from newsagents as well as the TIC.

Brighton has two major entertainment venues: **Brighton Centre**, on the seafront, *Kings Rd; tel: (01273) 202881*; and **The Dome** concert hall, next to the Royal Pavilion, *Church St; tel (01273) 709709*. The town also offers some 35 pubs with live music (two withtheatres), six other theatres, three casinos and 25 discos.

EVENTS

The **Brighton Festival** (May) is an annual international arts festival that takes place at venues all over town. The **London to Brighton Veteran Car Rally** (first Sun Nov), a colourful event immortalised in the film *Genevieve*, monopolises the roads between the two places – the final stage is along the seafront.

The TIC's publications *Brighton Scene* and *Annual Diary of Events* (25p each) list all the events in town.

SHOPPING

The main department stores and high street shops are in *Churchill Sq.* and *Western Rd*. **The Lanes** form an area famous for antiques, gifts and high-class boutiques,

North Laine for arts and crafts and specialist shops. There is also the **Upper Gardner Street Market** (flea market) in the middle of the town centre, open Sat 0700–1300, and **Brighton Station Market** (general and car boot sale), Sun 0900–1400. Brighton rock (a peppermint stick with the town's name through the middle) is a traditional British seaside treat that can be purchased from all souvenir shops – and the TIC.

SIGHTSEEING

Various **sightseeing tours** provide an excellent introduction to Brighton; details from the TIC.

Fishing trips are available from Brighton Pier, organised by **Fred Cox**, tel: (0181) 647 8414.

BBG guided walks can be arranged at the TIC; £3. A stroll down Brighton's broad **Promenade**, which backs the pebbly beach, is a must, or you could take a ride on **Volk's Electric Railway**, 288 Madeira Drive; tel: (01273) 292718, which operates daily 1100–1700 (Easter–Sept); £1. This runs along the seafront: it was the first electric railway in Britain. No visitor to Brighton should miss the 100-year-old **Palace Pier**, Marine Parade, tel: (01273) 609361, open daily all year; free – alive with flashy amusements, as well as a museum of slot machines. The earlier **West Pier**, built in 1866, was a mere ruin, but is being restored and there are now tours; contact **West Pier Trust**, tel: (01273) 321499.

The **Sealife Centre**, Marine Parade; tel: (01273) 604234, open daily 1000–1800 (longer during summer); £4.95, specialises in British marine life and boasts the longest underwater tunnel display in Europe.

Brighton's famous **Lanes** are what survives of the old village before George IV and the fashionable hordes descended.

Only 3 ft wide in places, these 17th-century alleyways lie south of North St.

Behind the seafront, white stucco terraces abound, with **Kemp Town** just to the east, centred around Lewes Crescent, a fine example of early 19th-century planning. But the magnetic attraction is the **Royal Pavilion**, Old Steine; tel: (01273) 290900, open daily 1000–1700/1800; £4.10. George IV's bizarre confection of a seaside palace is a fitting monument to Regency high living. Its Indian-inspired onion domes and minarets were contributed by John Nash between 1815 and 1822, while the recently restored interior, famed for its elaborate chinoiserie and rich decor, is one of the most extraordinary in Europe. Particularly breathtaking is the opulent music room, but even the Great Kitchen has cast-iron palm trees.

Brighton Museum and Art Gallery, Church St; tel: (01273) 290900, open Mon–Tues, Thur–Sat 1000–1700, Sun 1400–1700; free. Built as the Prince Regent's stables and riding school, this has interesting collections of musical instruments, pottery, paintings and some excellent art nouveau and art deco furniture.

OUT OF TOWN

Booth Museum of Natural History, 194 Dyke Rd; tel: (01273) 290900, open Mon–Wed, Fri–Sat 1000–1700, Sun 1400–1700; free, 1½ miles north-west, boasts an original bird collection, as well as many other specimens, including a magnificent assortment of animal skeletons.

Preston Manor, Preston Drove; tel: (01273) 290900, open Tues–Sun and public holidays Mon 1000–1700, other Mon 1300–1700, Sun 1400–1700; £2.95. 2 miles north; a brilliantly presented Georgian manor house, allowing an insight into the 'upstairs and downstairs' lifestyles in a genteel Edwardian home.

BRIGHTON– BOURNEMOUTH

This largely coastal route covers the seaside resorts of West Sussex, historic Arundel and Chichester, the maritime centres of Portsmouth and Southampton – with a side track to the Isle of Wight – and the tranquil beauty of the New Forest.

DIRECT ROUTE: 94 MILES

ROUTES

DIRECT ROUTE

➡ Allow 1 hr 45 mins to cover this route. From the Palace Pier, Brighton, proceed west along A259 (the seafront road) for 11 miles to **Worthing**, then head north for 1 mile on A24 to connect with A27. Continue west on A27 for 34 miles, passing **Arundel**, **Chichester** and the outskirts of **Portsmouth** to join M27 at Cosham. From here, the motorway continues west for 27 miles, bypassing Southampton and connecting with A31 at Cadnam. Follow A31 for 12 miles west, then head south on A338 to reach Bournemouth in 9 miles.

SCENIC ROUTE

➡ Diverting from the main route to take in the coastal resorts of Sussex, plus Portsmouth, Southampton and the New Forest adds 25 miles and about 90 minutes to the journey.

Proceed to Worthing as above and continue on A259 to **Littlehampton**. Head north on A284, then west on A27 to Arundel. At Fontwell, 4 miles west of Arundel, turn south on A29 to **Bognor Regis**, where A259 bears north-west to Chichester. Then follow A27 west as in the direct route, following signs to Portsmouth and Southampton centres.

From Southampton follow A35 southwest across the **New Forest** to Lyndhurst, where A337 heads due south to Lymington, then turns west to reach Bournemouth in 17 miles.

WORTHING

TIC: *Chapel Rd, Worthing BN11 1HL; tel: (01903) 210022*, open all year May–Sept Mon–Fri 0930–1700, Oct–Apr 0945–1245, 1430–1615. Second office at *Marine Parade, Worthing BN11 3PX, same tel no*, open 1 May–30 Sept and four days over Easter. BABA and accommodation booking service for personal callers.

ACCOMMODATION

Holiday accommodation is mainly in hotels and guesthouses in the budget to moderate brackets. **Northbrook Farm Caravan Club Site**, *Titnore Way, Worthing BN12 6NY; tel: (01903) 502962*, open Apr–Oct, has 120 pitches.

SIGHTSEEING

Worthing is one of a string of resorts along the Sussex coast. It is less extrovert than Brighton. Its sea frontage, good shopping, entertainment scene and proximity to the countryside make it a popular place for retirement.

The **Lido**, *Marine Parade, Worthing; tel: (01903) 213486*, open daily 1000–1900 (early Mar–late Oct); free. Rides and games at indoor and outdoor entertainment complex, with fish restaurant, ice-cream parlour and gift shop.

Worthing Museum and Art Gallery, *Chapel Rd; tel: (01903) 204229*, open Mon–Sat 1000–1800, (Apr–Sept) Mon–Sat 1000–1700 (Oct–Mar); free. Anglo-Saxon jewellery and glass can be seen in the important archaeology collection. Two centuries of fashion are displayed, there are doll and toy collections

and English paintings, pottery, glass and other art works and a presentation of downland life. A shop and sculpture garden can be visited.

ARUNDEL

TIC: *61 High St, Arundel, West Sussex BN18 9AJ; tel: (01903) 882268*, open Mon–Fri 0900/0930–1730, Sat–Sun 1000–1730 (mid July–early Sept); Mon–Fri 0900/0930–1700, Sat–Sun 1000–1700 (Apr–mid July, early Sept–Oct); Sat–Tues 1000–1200 and 1300–1500, Wed–Fri 0930–1200 and 1300–1500 (Nov–Mar). Services offered: local bed-booking and BABA (latest bookings 30 mins before closing). A free *Sussex by the Sea* brochure, which includes accommodation listings, is available at the TIC.

GETTING AROUND

The town is small and walkable – a free map is available from the TIC. A free transport map can be obtained from **Public Transport Section**, *County Hall; tel: (01243) 777556*. The main local bus company is **Stagecoach**, *tel: (01903) 237661*.

ACCOMMODATION

Most accommodation is b&b and it's usually easy to find something on arrival, except during the Arundel Festival (late Aug). The only chain represented is *CI*.

HI: *Warningcamp, Arundel; tel: (01903) 882204*. There are several **campsites** within 5 miles. These include: **Maynards Caravan & Camping Park**, *Crossbush; tel: (01903) 882075*, ¾ mile east; **Ship and Anchor Marina**, *Station Rd, Ford; tel: (01243) 551262*, 2 miles south-west; train to Ford, then half a mile; and **White Rose Touring Park**, *Mill Lane, Wick, Littlehampton; tel: (01903) 716176*, 2½ miles south.

SIGHTSEEING

Skylark Cruises, *tel: (0378) 438166 (daytime)* or *(01903) 717337 (evenings)*, offer boat trips; £3–£5.

Arundel is a picturesque town on the banks of the River Arun. The town had a turbulent past, but now the fairytale **Arundel Castle**, *tel: (01903) 883136*, open Mon–Fri, Sun 1200–1600 (Apr–Oct); £5.50, offers turrets, a massive keep and stunning views of the countryside.

At the **Wildfowl and Wetlands Centre**, *Mill Rd; tel: (01903) 883355*, open daily 0930–1730 (Easter–Sept); 0930–1630 (Oct–Easter); £4.25, 60 acres of ponds, lakes and reed-beds attract many species of waterfowl. Some are tame enough to feed from your hand and hides let you observe the wild ones from reasonably close quarters.

West Sussex Brass Rubbing Centre, *61 High St; tel: (01903) 850154*, open Tues–Sun 1000–1700; centre free, but there are charges for brass rubbing.

The town's colourful past is depicted by wide-ranging exhibits in the **Arundel Museum and Heritage Centre**, *61 High St; tel: (01903) 882344*, open Mon–Sat 1030–1700, Sun 1400–1700 (Easter–Oct); £1.

A very extensive collection can be seen at the **Arundel Toy and Military Museum** *23 High St; tel: (01903) 507446*, usually open daily (June–Sept); £1.25, but ring for confirmation and times.

OUT OF TOWN

Amberley Museum, *Amberley; tel: (01798) 831370*, open Wed–Sun, public holidays 1000–1600/1700 (Mar–Nov); daily in school holidays; £5. 4 miles north. The museum was established to preserve the area's working heritage and you can watch a variety of craftspeople at work, using traditional tools and materials, and

ride a vintage bus or train around the extensive site.

CHICHESTER

TIC: *29A South St, Chichester, West Sussex PO19 1AH; tel: (01243) 775888*, open Mon–Sat 0915–1715 (all year); Sun 1000–1600 (Apr–Sept). Services offered: local bed-booking and BABA (latest 15 mins before closing), YHA/HI membership, tickets for concerts and coach excursions. Free *Chichester Visitors Guide* and accommodation listing.

GETTING AROUND

Unless you are attending the races, you should avoid Goodwood while they are on. Town and transport maps are available at the TIC. There are many local bus companies, but all enquiries are handled by **Traveline**; *tel: (0345) 959099*. There are daily and weekly **Explorer** tickets.

ACCOMMODATION

Chichester has quite a good choice of accommodation throughout the city and in outlying areas. There is a wide range of b&b establishments and cheaper hotels can be found on the edge of town and in the nearby countryside. Pre-booking is recommended during the Goodwood Festival of Speed (June), the Chichester Festivities (July) and Glorious Goodwood (July–Aug). Hotel chains include *Ja* and *Ma*. The closest **campsites** are: **Southern Leisure Lakeside Village**, *Vinnetrow Rd; tel: (01243) 787715* (families and couples only), 2 miles from the centre; and **Ellscott Nursery**, *Sidlesham Lane; Birdham; tel: (01243) 512003*, 4 miles from town. A full list is obtainable at the TIC.

ENTERTAINMENT AND EVENTS

Major events in Chichester include: the **Chichester Festival of Music, Dance** and Speech (mid Feb–mid Mar); the Chichester Festivities (first three weeks July), a flamboyant mix of exhibitions, theatre, music, poetry, dance and street entertainment, for details *tel: (01243) 785718*; the **British Open Polo Championships**, *Cowdray Park, Midhurst* (late June–mid July); and the premier horseracing meeting known as '**Glorious Goodwood**', *Goodwood racecourse; tel: (01243) 774107* (late July–early Aug). **Chichester Festival Theatre**, *Oaklands Pk; tel: (01243) 781312,* is one of the country's best theatres outside London and the summer (Apr–Oct) productions normally feature star actors

Chichester Harbour Water Tours, *tel: (01243) 786418* (talking timetable and answerphone), operate 90-min **boat trips** around the picturesque harbour, with its 48-mile shoreline (£4, no booking); departures from Itchenor. The pleasant 4-mile path along the canal to Chichester Harbour is rich in wildlife and makes an excellent walk.

Much of the encircling Roman wall remains, partly rebuilt in medieval times, and the **Wall Walk** is a good way of orienting oneself; the four main streets within it, meeting at the ornate 16th-century **Market Cross**, are also Roman in origin.
Chichester District Museum, *29 Little London; tel: (01243) 784683,* open Tues–Sat 1000–1730; free, provides a good introduction to the area's Roman and later history.

Chichester Cathedral, *West St; tel: (01243) 782595,* open daily 0730–1700/ 1900 (all year, except during services), with tours Mon–Sat at 1100 and 1415 (Easter–Oct); free, but £2 donation requested. There are many concerts

during the Chichester Festivities; no official charge, but a donation is expected. The 900-year-old cathedral, mainly Norman and Early English, has a graceful nave, some superb Norman sculpture and an unusual detached bell tower. It's an eye-catching sight, with its spire, visible for miles around, rising high above South Downs farmland. Close up it does not disappoint and the beautiful structure is enhanced by many art treasures, ranging from Romanesque stone carvings to 20th-century tapestries.

Both within the tranquil precinct and elsewhere there are some fine 18th-century houses, particularly in the area around **Pallant House**, *9 North Pallant; tel: (01243) 774557,* open Tues–Sat 1000–1715; £2.50. This is a Queen Anne town house, painstakingly restored and used as a small gallery, with good collections of porcelain and modern British art.

Fishbourne Roman Palace, *Salthill Rd, Fishbourne; tel: (01243) 785859,* open daily 1000–1800 (Aug); daily 1000–1700 (Mar–July, Sept–Oct); daily 1000–1600 (late Feb, Nov–mid Dec); Sun 1000–1600 (mid Dec–mid Feb); £3.80. 1½ miles west. Discovered in 1960 – excavations are still in progress – Fishbourne (*c.* AD 75) is the largest Roman residence ever unearthed in Britain: it boasts 20 remarkable mosaic floors and a reconstructed dining room. The museum traces the story of the site.

Mechanical Music and Doll Collection, *Church Rd, Portfield; tel: (01243) 785421/372646,* open Sun–Fri 1300– 1700 (Easter–Sept); Sun 1300–1700 (Oct–Nov, Jan–Easter); £2. 2 miles north-east. In the Victorian hall of music, you can listen to some of the collection of music-makers, such as street pianos, organs and music boxes. The doll collection features many that are Victorian or Edwardian.

Stansted Park, *Rowlands Castle, Hants; tel: (01705) 412265*, open Sun–Tues 1400–1730 (early July–late Sept); public holidays Sun–Mon 1400–1730 (late Sept–early July); £4. 8 miles north-west. An elegant stately home rebuilt Wren-style in 1900 (after a fire), with a series of period rooms – you can also see 'below stairs'. Set in glorious parkland, with a lovely old chapel, which inspired Keats, and Victorian walled gardens.

Tangmere Military Aviation Museum, *Tangmere; tel: (01243) 775223*, open daily 1000–1730 (Mar–Oct); daily 1000–1630 (Feb–Nov); £3. 3 miles east. Tangmere was one of the Battle of Britain airfields and its collection spans 70 years of military aviation.

Weald & Downland Open Air Museum, *Singleton; tel: (01243) 811348*, open daily 1030–1800 (Mar–Oct); Wed, Sat–Sun 1030–1600 (Nov–Feb); £4.90. 5 miles north. At the well-sited museum over 40 rescued rural buildings, including a 19th-century schoolhouse, medieval watermill and Tudor market hall, have been reconstructed. Nearby, in a peaceful downland setting, are the **West Dean Gardens**, *West Dean; tel: (01243) 811301*, open daily 1100–1700 (Mar–Oct); £3.50. They incorporate ornamental gardens, a walled kitchen garden, an arboretum, sunken gardens and a parkland walk, and are used for a selection of alfresco events in summer.

Goodwood House, *Goodwood; tel: (01243) 774107*, open Sun–Mon 1300–1700 (Easter–July and Sept), Sun–Thur 1300–1700 (Aug). Closed event days, £5.50. Set in glorious parkland, the house contains the superb Ducal Collection of paintings, including works by Canaletto and Stubbs, furniture, porcelain and tapestries.

PORTSMOUTH

TIC: *The Hard, Portsmouth PO1 3QJ; tel: (01705) 826722*, open daily 0930–1745 (Apr–end Oct); daily 0930–1715 (end Oct–Mar). DP SHS services offered; local bed-booking and BABA (latest bookings 30 mins before closing; 10% commission). Mayflower Theatre tickets sold. *Portsmouth – Flagship of Maritime England* is available free from the TIC and contains accommodation listings.

City Centre: *102 Commercial Rd, Portsmouth PO1 1EJ; tel: (01705) 838382*, open Mon–Sat 0930–1700 (all year); and *Clarence Esplanade, Southsea PO5 3ST; tel: (01705) 832464*, open 1000–1745 (Apr–Sept), both offer the full range of TIC services.

GETTING AROUND

Most attractions are within walking distance of the centre and the TIC provide free town and transport maps. The centre and surrounding towns are covered by frequent and reliable bus services, with reduced frequency 1800–2300 and on Sun. Route maps are also freely available from local bus operators. The **central bus depot**, *The Hard*, is the base for the main bus companies: **Provincial**, *tel: (01705) 650967*; **Stagecoach Coastline Buses**, *tel: (01705) 498894*; **Hampshire Buses**, *tel: (01962) 852352*; and **Southampton City Buses**, *tel: (01703) 553011*. **Provincial weekly tickets** (£7.50) can be used around the city.

ACCOMMODATION

Most accommodation is in the form of b&bs and guesthouses, but there are also many large independent hotels. It is generally easy to find accommodation on arrival, except during the annual VE Weekend (early May). Most of the cheaper establishments are in Southsea (the resort area just along the coast). National chains include BW, FP, Hn, Ib, Ma, MC and Mo. University accommodation is available in the holidays; tel (01705) 843178.

HI: Wymering Manor, Cosham, Portsmouth; tel: (01705) 375661. YMCA: Penny St; tel: (01705) 864341. The TIC provide information on campsites. The nearest is Southsea Caravan Park, Melville Rd, Southsea; tel: (01705) 735070, 1½ miles south-east.

SIGHTSEEING

Guide Friday operate bus tours around Portsmouth and Southsea, with various joining locations – the TIC have full details a couple of weeks before the season starts (May or June). Boat trips are operated by Butchers Blue Boats, tel: (01705) 822584, leaving daily from The Hard (Easter–Oct); £2.20 for a 45-min trip. Portsmouth Tourism Guiding Services offer guided walks, which can be booked at The Hard TIC. There are also free Guildhall guided tours, tel: (01705) 834092 (Civic Information desk), Mon, Wed, Fri at 1000 and 1130 (May–Sept).

The city of Portsmouth offers beaches, historic ships and maritime museums. Portsmouth's dockyard – the traditional home of the Royal Navy – is now a centre of maritime heritage, with the Royal Navy Museum and three historic ships: Henry VIII's Mary Rose (sunk in 1545 and raised from the seabed in 1982); Nelson's flagship HMS Victory, which fought at the Battle of Trafalgar in 1805; and Queen Victoria's HMS Warrior, 1860.

Portsmouth Historic Ships, HM Naval Base, The Hard; tel: (0839) 407080,

open daily 1000–1730 (Mar–Oct); 1000–1700 (Nov–Feb); entry to the dockyard itself is free, but it's £5.15 to board a single ship – or £10 to board all three.

Charles Dickens Birthplace Museum, 393 Old Commercial Rd, Portsmouth; tel: (01705) 827261, open daily 1000–1630 (Apr–Sept); £2. The small terraced house has been restored and furnished in Regency style.

Southsea, Portsmouth's seaside resort, is 2 miles south-east. Its D-Day Museum and Overlord Embroidery, Clarence Esplanade; tel: (01705) 827261, is open daily 1000–1730; £4.50. The magnificent Overlord Embroidery is part of the museum's depiction of the D-Day story, which also includes archive films, military displays and everyday scenes of life in Britain in 1944.

Sea Life, Clarence Esplanade; tel: (01705) 734461, open daily 1000–1800 (Oct–Easter); 1000–2100 (Easter–Sept); £4.75.

Southsea Castle, Clarence Esplanade; tel: (01705) 827261, open daily 1000–1730 (Apr–Oct); Sat–Sun 1000–1630 (Nov–Mar); £1.70. Built by Henry VIII in 1545 to protect the harbour, the castle now has audiovisual (and other) displays covering Tudor, Civil War and Victorian military life.

OUT OF TOWN

Portchester Castle (EH), Castle St, Portchester; tel: (01705) 378291, open daily 1000–1800/dusk (Easter–Oct); daily 1000–1600 (Nov–Easter); £2.50. 10 miles north-west. A royal palace and military rendezvous Portchester's history goes back 2000 years and some intact Roman walls can still be seen.

Staunton Country Park, Middle Park Way, Havant; tel: (01705) 453405, open daily 1000–1700 (Easter–Sept); 1000–

85

1600 (Oct–Easter); £3.30. 14 miles north-east. The 1000-acre park offers tropical glasshouses, Victorian gardens, woodland walks, lakes and a farm (you can feed the animals).

 ### SIDE TRACK FROM PORTSMOUTH

RYDE (ISLE OF WIGHT)

TIC: *81/83 Union St, Ryde PO33 2DY; tel: (01983) 562905*, open daily 0915–1745 (Easter–June, Sept); Fri–Sat 0915–2045, Sun–Thur 0915–1845 (July–Aug); Fri–Wed 1000–1600 (Oct–Easter). Services offered: local bed-booking and BABA (deposit 10% of first night for all bookings). Bookings made for the theatre and boat trips. *Isle of Wight Holiday Guide* available free of charge.

Ferries: There are regular sailings daily from Portsmouth Harbour to Ryde Pier Head, the journey taking about 20 mins. **Wight Link Ferries**; *tel: (0990) 827744*, and **Hovertravel**, *tel: (01983) 811000 (Ryde) or (01705) 8111000 (Southsea)*, will help with travel enquiries and arrangements.

GETTING AROUND

The majority of Ryde's attractions are within walking distance of the centre. The only remaining public train service links Ryde, Sandown and Shanklin. Free transport and town maps (summer only) are available from the TIC and *Things to See and Do* is obtainable from **Southern Vectis Bus Company**, *tel: (01703) 562264*. The majority of services in and around the town are operated by Southern Vectis, with buses serving the whole island, and the service is very good. All main routes operate until 2230 and the 'Night

Clubber' bus runs from 2300, visiting all the island's main towns.

The main **taxi** rank is located on The Esplanade, near the TIC.

ACCOMMODATION

Accommodation in Ryde and the surrounding area consists mainly of guesthouses and b&b establishments and it is usually easy to book on arrival, except during Aug Bank Holiday. There are no youth hostels

Two **campsites** are within 2 miles: **Beaper Farm**, *Sandown Rd; tel: (01983) 615210*, 1½ miles north-east, and **Pondwell Campsite**, *Seaview Rd; tel: (01983) 612330*, 2 miles east.

ENTERTAINMENT AND EVENTS

The premier event in the Isle of Wight calendar is **Cowes Week** (Aug), Britain's most important yachting regatta.

Entertainment facilities include **LA Bowling Alley**, *The Esplanade; tel: (01983) 617070*, and the **Ice Skating Rink**, *The Esplanade; tel: (01983) 615155*.

SIGHTSEEING

Southern Vectis coach tours starting from the bus station are bookable at the TIC. Bus 7 is an island explorer with commentary.

Wight Line Cruises; *tel: (01983) 564602*, operate a choice of **boat trips** from the end of the pier; £9.95–£10.50, bookings at the TIC.

Ryde offers all the pleasures of a traditional seaside town, having miles of sandy beaches with safe bathing, as well as attractive parks and gardens. The town owes much of its atmosphere to spectacular growth during Victorian times, when the half-mile long pier and many elegant houses were built. The main thoroughfare is *Union St*, sweeping down to the seafront and lined with cafés, gift shops, fashion boutiques and antique shops.

OUT OF TOWN

The island itself, 23 miles west–east and 13 miles north–south, is a popular holiday destination, offering pleasant scenery as well as the usual seaside attractions. There are plenty of safe, sandy beaches and many marked footpaths across the chalk downlands. **Shanklin Chine**, a picturesque cleft in the high chalk downs, is a popular walking spot.

It was Queen Victoria who made the island fashionable, by establishing a seaside retreat here. **Osborne House** (EH), *East Cowes; tel: (01983) 200022*, open daily 1000–1700 (Apr–Oct); £6 (house and grounds). 4 miles northeast. Overlooking the Solent, this elaborate Italianate villa, her favourite home, is richly decorated and gives a remarkably intimate glimpse of the family life of Victoria, Albert and their many children. In the extensive formal gardens is the charming Swiss Cottage, a chalet where the royal children learnt the arts of cookery and gardening.

Inland are the impressive ruins of **Carisbrooke Castle** (EH), *Newport; tel: (01983) 522107*, open daily 1000–1600 (Oct–Mar); 1000–1800 (Apr–Sept); £4. 7 miles west. Best known as Charles I's prison in 1648, immediately preceding his execution, the castle dates from Norman times and offers an imaginative range of things to do and see, including fine views from the ramparts and a 16th-century waterwheel that is still worked by donkeys.

The east coast of the island is the most developed. Heading south down the Ryde–Shanklin railway towards the great sweep of Sandown Bay is Brading, where a timber-framed house dating from *c.*1500 houses the worthwhile **Wax Works Brading**, *High St, Brading, Sandown; tel: (01983) 407286*, open daily 1000–2200 (May–Sept); 1000–1700 (Oct–Apr); £4.50. 2–3 miles south.

Waltzing Waters, *Old Leisure Centre, Brading Rd; tel: (01983) 811333*, open Mon–Fri, offers shows every hour on the hour until 1600, 6 miles south. The synchronisation of coloured lights, music and moving water is delightful.

For steam railway buffs there is a direct interchange with the Ryde–Shanklin line at Smallbrook Junction, for the **Isle of Wight Steam Railway**, *The Station, Haven Street; tel: (01983) 882204*. Phone for schedules. The steam railway runs 5 miles west to Wootton, using restored engines and rolling stock from the original service; £3.50 round trip, or £7.50 first class.

To the west of the island is the pretty port of **Yarmouth**, with its castle built by Henry VIII guarding the harbour. **Yarmouth Castle (EH)**, *Yarmouth; tel: (01983) 760678*, open daily 1000–1800 (Apr–Oct); £2. 15 miles west. The **Freshwater Peninsula** beyond tapers to the dramatic chalk pinnacles known as the **Needles**, with the inevitable pleasure park nearby. From here you can take a chairlift down to Alum Bay, famous for its multi-coloured sand.

Part of the peninsula is known as **Tennyson Down** – after the Victorian poet, who walked here daily from his home, Farringford (in Freshwater), now a hotel. ◢

87

SOUTHAMPTON

TIC: *9 Civic Centre Rd, Southampton, Hampshire SO14 7LP; tel: (01703) 221106*, open Mon–Wed, Fri–Sat 0900–1700, Thur 1000–1700. DP services offered; local bed-booking (latest booking 1645), BABA (latest booking 1600). Nuffield Theatre tickets sold. The *Southampton Visitors Guide* is free and includes accommodation listings.

GETTING AROUND

Most attractions are within walking distance of the centre. A town map, with local transport details, is to be found (inside the back cover) in the free *Visitors Guide*. Local bus services are excellent: very frequent in the centre and good to surrounding towns and villages. Most city services operate until 2200. There is no central bus station and most buses terminate around the city centre (*Pound Tree Rd, Castle Way, Bargate Rd, Vincents Walk*). **City Buses** *tel: (01703) 224854,* provide services mostly in the centre, while **Solent Blue Line**, *tel: (01703) 226235* cover a wider region.

There are **taxi** ranks opposite Marlands Shopping Centre (in *Above Bar*), in *Bedford Pl, Queensway, High St*, at transport terminals and opposite the Cenotaph (in *Above Bar*).

ACCOMMODATION

There are some large independent hotels and a wide range of other accommodation, particularly mid-range hotels and guesthouses. It is generally easy to find accommodation on arrival, except during the Southampton Boat Show (mid Sept). The majority of cheaper accommodation lies on the outskirts of the centre (*Hill Lane/Howard Rd*). **Town or Country**, *The Old Rectory, School Rd, Bursledon; tel: (01703) 405668,* is a self-catering agency

and does not charge a booking fee. Credit card bookings can be made with **The Leisure and Visitor Centre**; *tel: (01703) 221106*. Hotel chains include *DV, FP, Hn, Ib*, and *Nv*. **University** accommodation is available during the holidays; *tel: (01703) 593720*. The TIC can provide information on **campsites**, but there is also a **Forestry Commission** (New Forest), **camping enquiry line**; *tel: (0131) 314 6505*. The nearest campsite is a Forestry Commission site, *Lyndhurst Rd, Ashurst, nr Totton*, 6 miles west of Southampton. There is also **Riverside Park**, *Satchell Lane, Hamble; tel: (01703) 453220*, 6 miles east.

SIGHTSEEING

There are various sightseeing options which give an excellent introduction to Southampton. **Guide Friday** and others offer **bus tours** which can be booked at the TIC. A wide variety of **boat trips** is possible with **Solent Enterprise**; *tel: (01705) 524551*. Visitors can join a variety of **free guided walks** which start at *The Bargate*. Alternatively, guides can be hired from the **Southampton Tourist Guides Association**; *tel: (01703) 868401* (around £25 per guide; £30 for foreign-language guides), with a maximum of 30 people per group.

The **ferry**, *tel: (01703) 840722,* which operates frequently between Southampton and Hythe, is another good way to view the area.

Southampton is famous for its free **balloon festival**, which takes place annually (first weekend June).

The historic port of Southampton has a rich heritage and is the cultural centre for the region. Learn about the city's history and monuments by taking the **Walls Walk** – a path round the remains of the well-preserved medieval town walls.

Explore the lively waterfront at **Ocean Village** and **Town Quay**, with shops, entertainment and dozens of sailing boats. Southampton has several excellent museums. **Maritime Museum**, *The Wool House, Bugle St; tel: (01703) 635904*, open Tues–Sat 1000–1300 and 1400–1700, Sun 1400–1700; free, portrays the heyday of the port, when it was home to famous transatlantic liners such as the *Queen Mary* and *Queen Elizabeth*; it also features a *Titanic* exhibition. Housed in a beautiful timber-framed building is the **Tudor House Museum**, *Bugle St; tel: (01703) 635904*, open Tues–Fri 1000–1200 and 1300–1700, Sat 1000–1200 and 1300–1700, Sun 1400–1700; free. This displays the domestic and social life of Victorian and Edwardian England. The **Museum of Archaeology**, otherwise known as **God's House**, *Winkle St*, shares a phone and opening times with Tudor House; free.

Medieval Merchant's House (EH), *French St; tel: (01703) 221503*, open daily 1000–1800/dusk (Apr–Oct); £2. Originally a prosperous wine merchant's shop, the recreated premises are a vivid evocation of the 13th century.

OUT OF TOWN

A leisure park with gardens, lake, exotic birds and over 40 attractions, with rides for the whole family is **Paultons Park**, *Ower, nr Romsey; tel: (01703) 814455* (24 Hrs), open daily 1000–1800 (mid Mar–Oct); £8 (inc. rides). 6 miles north-west.

New Forest Nature Quest, *Longdown, Ashurst; tel: (01703) 292408*, open daily 1000–1700 (Mar–Oct), opening may be extended into winter months; £5.50. 5 miles west. Covering 25 acres of indoor and varied outdoor habitats, all types of British wildlife can be found here, while domestic creatures abound at the

nearby **Longdown Dairy Farm**, *Deerleap Lane, Longdown, Ashurst; tel: (01703) 293326*, open daily 1000–1700 (Apr–Oct); £3.80. 4 miles east. Visitors can touch and feed many of the often young animals, which include all of the common farm species.

Netley Abbey (EH), *1 Abbey Hill, Netley; tel: (01703) 378291*, open daily at any reasonable time; free. 4 miles east. The picturesque remains of the Cistercian abbey, founded in 1239 and later converted into a Tudor home, are reputed to be haunted.

LITTLEHAMPTON

TIC: *Windmill Complex, Coastguard Rd, Littlehampton BN17 5LH; tel: (01903) 713480*, open four days over Easter and weekends in May and Sept 1000–1700 (closed 1300–1400); daily 1000–1700 (June–Aug).

The main road here is built up virtually from Worthing, with attractive Rustington in between. The town has long been popular for its seaside scene. Much of the accommodation is in family-run hotels and guesthouses.

Harbour Park Ltd, *Seafront, Littlehampton; tel: (01903) 721200*, open late Mar–late Sept, times vary, phone for details. Free admission, charge for rides. Amusement arcades, roller coaster, dodgems and other rides. Also a museum and maritime artefacts. The complex has restaurant, cafe, gift shop and beach goods.

Windmill Theatre, *Windmill Entertainment Complex, The Green, Windmill Rd, Littlehampton; tel: (01903) 724929*. Variety shows, January pantomime and when no live performances are scheduled the theatre becomes a cinema.

The Body Shop Tour, *Watersmead, Littlehampton; tel: (01903) 844044*, open

Mon–Fri – book in advance; £3.95. The Body Shop thrives by selling environmentally friendly products. This is your chance to find out more about their operation.

BOGNOR REGIS

TIC: *Belmont St, Bognor Regis PO21 1BJ; tel: (01243) 823140.* BABA scheme operates, and helpful staff have a wide range of tourism information. The office covers Littlehampton TIC during its closed winter period.

Much of the Sussex coast is fringed with shingle, but Bognor has a sandy beach.

Butlin's Southcoast World, *Bognor Regis; tel: (01243) 822445*, open all year, daily summer hours and some off-peak weekends 1000–2300, varied hours and weekends only in part of winter, so phone for details. Visitors can enjoy the Water World's subtropical climate, funfair rides, indoor adventureland, games complex, boating lake, children's theatre and family shows, café, restaurant and continental food court.

The town has the usual choice of accommodation and there is a **Caravan Club Site**, *Rowan Way, Bognor Regis; tel: (01243) 828515.* The site, about a mile from the beach, is screened by trees.

THE NEW FOREST

TIC: *High St, Lyndhurst, Hampshire SO43 7NY; tel: (01703) 282269*, open daily 1000–1800 (Easter–Sept); 1000–1700 (Oct–Easter). DP services offered; local bed-booking and BABA. *Where to Stay Guide* is available free. Free town maps of Lyndhurst, the forest's 'capital', and details of transport around the New Forest are available.

GETTING AROUND

The main bus company is **Wiltshire and Dorset (W&D)**; *tel: (01590) 672382*, which operates from **Lymington Bus Station**, *High St, Lymington.* Most services run hourly or half-hourly. There's a **Day Explorer** ticket, valid on all their services in the area; £4.40.

ACCOMMODATION

A good range of accommodation is available, particularly b&bs. It is generally easy to book on arrival, except over public holiday weekends.

HI: **Burley**, *Cottismore House, Cott Lane, Burley, Ringwood; tel: (01425) 403233.* Forest Enterprise Holidays (part of the Forestry Commission); *tel: (0131) 314 6505*, runs ten campsites in the New Forest – contact them for details. The nearest to Lyndhurst is at Ashurst.

SIGHTSEEING

The area is most rewarding when you leave the beaten track, so non-walkers should ask the TIC about hiring bicycles or horses: many riding schools have facilities for both experienced riders and beginners. **The Forestry Commission**, *Queen's House, Lyndhurst, Hants SO43 7NH; tel: (01703) 283141*, arrange ranger-guided walks in the New Forest at Easter and throughout the summer (from £1); some are general and others have specific themes. Contact them for the programme and booking form.

English monarchs from William the Conqueror onwards have protected and enlarged this area, originally for the pleasures of hunting. Customs and institutions peculiar to the New Forest and dating from the Middle Ages survive to this day. 'Forest' originally did not imply continuous woodland and, in fact, the area contains woods linked by moorland and villages. It is well known for its unique woodland scenery, coastal views, ponies and wildlife. **Lymington** is the main town on the coast south of Lyndhurst.

Hurst Castle; *tel: (01590) 642322*, open daily 1000–1730 (Apr–June, Sept); 1000–1800 (July–Aug); 1000–1600 (Oct); £2. Built by Henry VIII and completed in 1544, the fortress was used for defensive purposes (on and off) right up to World War II, when it held gun batteries and searchlights. It stands at the end of a shingle spit extending almost to the Isle of Wight and provides splendid panoramas.

Hurst Castle Ferry, *19 Everton Rd, Hordle, Lymington; tel: (01425) 610784*, links Keyhaven and the castle. The ferry operates hourly during the day (Apr–Oct); £2.50 roundtrip. It also runs to **Yarmouth (Isle of Wight)** several times daily (Easter–Oct); £5.50 round trip. The same company operates **boat trips** in the area; from £4.

New Forest Museum and Visitor Centre, *Main Car Park, High St, Lyndhurst; tel: (01703) 283914*, open daily 1000–1800 (Apr–July, Sept); 1000–1900 (Aug); 1000–1700 (Oct–Mar); £2.50. The museum covers every aspect of the New Forest and has been designed to interest children as much as adults.**Nature Quest**, *Ashurst; tel: (01703) 292408*, open

daily 1000–1700 (Mar– Dec); £5.50. This is a revolutionary new wildlife attraction which enables you to observe the natural behaviour of such wild creatures as foxes, deer, minks and badgers as they go about their daily business, completely unaware of the human presence. Some (such as the badgers) are on camera, but most are just the other side of one-way glass. Sightings are not guaranteed, but – if you allow plenty of time and are prepared to be patient – you can usually see most of them: you can wander backwards and forwards at will and stay as long as you like.

For virtually guaranteed sightings (and a truly unforgettable experience), join the **New Forest Badger Watch**; at 2030 for approx. one hour every evening Mar– Oct. From constructed hides (with seats) you can watch (at close quarters) a family of wild badgers, above ground and/or in their sett, separated from them only by a sheet of one-way glass. Numbers are necessarily limited and early booking is essential (especially for weekends); *tel: (01425) 403412*, manned 0900–1000 (Feb–Oct). It is accessible from Lyndhurst and anyone booking will be given directions. Casual visitors are discouraged for the badgers' sake.

91

BRISTOL

The poet John Betjeman described Bristol as 'the most beautiful, interesting and distinguished city in England'. Beautiful parks and gardens lead on to interesting alleys, and dignified Georgian houses climb the hills, culminating in Brunel's masterpiece, the Clifton suspension bridge. Part of Bristol's appeal stems from its many historic maritime features.

TOURIST INFORMATION

TIC: *St Nicholas Church, St Nicholas St, Bristol BS1 1UE; tel: (0117) 926 0767,* open daily 0930–1730. DP services offered; local bed-booking (latest 30 mins before closing; 10% deposit of first night), BABA (latest 30 mins before closing; 10% of first night as deposit). The free *Essential Guide*, outlines just about everything; the *Official Visitors Guide* is £1.50.

ARRIVING AND DEPARTING

Two motorways converge on Bristol: M4 east from London, and west from Cardiff and Swansea; and M5 which links Birmingham and Exeter. Alternative east–west and north–south routes are provided by A4 and A38 respectively.

GETTING AROUND

Most of the town attractions can be reached on foot from the centre. Free town and transport maps from the TIC.

STAYING IN BRISTOL

Accommodation and Food

There is a good range of accommodation in Bristol, from large hotels to b&bs, but it's always advisable to book in advance. The TIC have a 24hr accommodation information line; *tel: (0117) 946 2211.* Most cheaper accommodation is located around the town centre. Hotels chains represented are: *BW, Ct, FP, Hn, Ja, MH, ST, SW* and *Th.* The University of Bristol offers self-catering flats in two locations during the holidays; *tel: (0117) 926 5698* and *923 8366.*

HI: Hayman House, *14 Narrow Quay; tel: (0117) 922 1659.* The TIC can provide information on **campsites**. The closest are: **Baltic Wharf Campsite**, *Cumberland Rd; tel: (0117) 926 8030* (stay limited to 21 days); and **Boars Head Campsite**, *Boars Head Public House, Main Rd; tel: (01454) 632278,* 7 miles north-west.

The TIC provides a list of local restaurants and there are some excellent ones, both in the centre and in outlying areas. Restaurants cluster around *Park St*, while *Whiteladies Rd* (Clifton) is packed full of trendy bars and restaurants. The **Galleries Shopping Centre**, *Broadmead,* offers a range of cheap and varied ethnic eateries, but at lunchtime only (it closes 1700).

Communications and Money

The main **post office**, *13 Castle Gallery,* is open Mon–Sat, 0900–1730. It has a poste restante facility. There are **Thomas Cook bureaux de change** at *Midland Bank, 49 Corn St* and *Bristol Airport.*

ENTERTAINMENT AND EVENTS

The events calendar is both full and varied (ranging from jazz to regattas), so it's

92

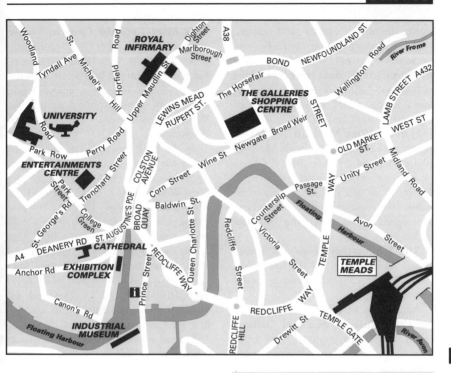

worth checking: a free annual brochure, *Events Guide*, is published every April and available from the TIC, who also provide a twice-monthly *Bristol Entertainments Bulletin*. **Colston Hall**, *Colston St; tel: (0117) 922 3686*, hosts many concerts; **Bristol Hippodrome**, *St Augustine's Parade; tel: (0117) 926 5524*, is a centre for those with a taste for the arts; and the prestigious **Bristol Old Vic**, *King St; tel: (0117) 949 3993*, is a 'must' for theatre-lovers.

Many major events are hosted by the **Ashton Court Estate**, *Long Ashton; tel: (0117) 963 9174*, 2½ miles south-west of town, including the International Balloon Fiesta, the world's second largest event of its kind, when around 150 hot-air balloons take to the air together (Aug); and the Bristol Community Festival, an enormous pop and folk music event (July).

SHOPPING

The TIC can provide a free shopping guide. The main shopping areas in the city are the **Galleries Shopping Centre**, **Broadmead** (100 retailers under one roof), *Park St, Queens St* and *Gloucester Rd*. **Clifton Village** (towards the bridge) is the place for antiques and jewellery. Bristol has a number of markets, including **St Nicholas**, *St Nicholas St* (Mon–Sat 0900–1700); and **Sun markets** (0900–1500) at *Bristol City Football Ground* and *Eastville Stadium*.

SIGHTSEEING

The Maritime Walk, along the south side of Bristol's historic harbour, takes in some of the city's most famous landmarks and ends with a return trip by harbour ferry. This is just one of a range of possible themed walks arranged by the TIC, most

94

lasting around 1½ hours and costing £2.50. It is possible to use the ferry (subject to season; tel: (0117) 927 3416) to visit specific attractions. Boat trips (around the harbour and further afield) and city bus tours in open-deck buses can also be arranged through the TIC.

Harveys Wine Museum 12 Denmark St; tel: (0117) 927 5036, open Mon–Sat 1000–1700; £4. Harveys Bristol Cream has been renowned for two centuries and the attractions of a visit range from refurbished 18th-century cellars and ancient wine vessels to a free glass of the Cream for adults.

The Exploratory Bristol Old Station, Temple Meads; tel 907 5000, open daily 1000–1700; £4.75. A fascinating hands-on science centre.

Among the art galleries and museums are: City Museum and Art Gallery, Queen's Rd, Clifton; tel: (0117) 922 3571, open daily 1000–1700; £2; and Bristol Industrial Museum, Princes Wharf, Wapping Rd; tel: (0117) 925 1470, open Tues–Sun, some public holidays 1000–1700; £1. Interesting buildings include: The Georgian House, 7 Great George St; tel: (0117) 921 1362, and The Red Lodge, Park Row; tel: (0117) 921 1360, both open Tues–Sat, some public holidays 1300–1700; £1 each. There are also several noteworthy religious buildings, including Bristol Cathedral, College Green; tel: (0117) 926 4879, open daily 0800–1800; free. Don't miss the Norman chapter house and Early English lady chapel.

John Wesley's Chapel, 36 The Horsefair; tel: (0117) 926 4740, open Mon–Sat 1000–1300 and 1400–1600 (Apr–Sept); Mon–Tues, Thur–Sat 1000–1300 and 1400–1600 (Oct–Mar); free. The world's oldest Methodist building, founded by Wesley himself, in 1739.

St Mary Redcliffe Church, Redcliffe Way; tel: (0117) 929 1487, open daily 0800–2000 (July–Aug); 0800–1700 (Sept–June); free. Admired by Queen Victoria, this is an unusually fine example of Gothic architecture – and the burial place of Sir William Penn, father of the 'founder' of Pennsylvania.

In the dock area you can just sit and watch the world go by, near to the spot from which John Cabot set sail for the New World in 1497, or stroll around the Maritime Heritage Centre, Wapping Wharf, Gas Ferry Road; tel: (0117) 926 0680, open daily 1000–1800; free. This covers the history of Bristol shipbuilding.

ss Great Britain, Gt Western Dock, Gas Ferry Rd; tel: (0117) 926 0680, open 1000–1630/1730; £3.70. Designed by Isambard Kingdom Brunel, she was the first of the great steamships (launched 1843) and is being restored in the dock where she was built.

OUT OF TOWN

Don't miss the Clifton suspension bridge, tel: (0117) 973 2122, open all year. Two miles north-west of the centre. The bridge itself is deservedly world famous and the views it provides of the Avon Gorge are breathtaking. While in the area, visit Bristol Zoo Gardens, Clifton; tel: (0117) 973 8951, open daily 0900–approx. 1700/1730; £6.50 (slightly reduced Oct–Easter). More than 300 species, many endangered, in attractive surroundings.

Clevedon Court (NT), Tickenham Rd, Clevedon; tel: (01275) 872257, open Wed–Thur, Sun, public holidays Mon, 1400–1700 (Easter–Sept); £3.60. 12 miles south-west. The 14th-century manor house incorporates a 12th-century tower and 13th-century hall and there's a lovely terraced garden.

BRISTOL–EXETER

Meandering across the neck of England's south-west peninsula, this route links two cities with a maritime heritage. It skirts the Mendip Hills and takes in two great spiritual centres – the cathedral city of Wells and mystic Glastonbury. From ancient Taunton the route leads to the country town of Tiverton and then follows the Exe Valley south to Exeter.

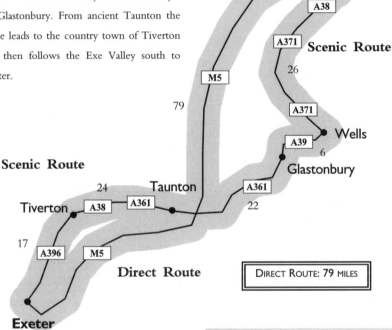

Direct Route

Bristol

A38

A371 **Scenic Route**

M5

79 A371

A39 Wells

Scenic Route 6

Glastonbury

26

24 Taunton A361

Tiverton A38 A361 22

17

A396 M5

Direct Route

DIRECT ROUTE: 79 MILES

Exeter

ROUTES

DIRECT ROUTE

Allow 1 hr 20 mins for the 79-mile trip. From central Bristol follow signs to M5, which can be joined 8 miles to the north at either Junction 18 or 19. Take M5 west for 68 miles, leave at Junction 29 and follow signs to Exeter city centre.

SCENIC ROUTE

From central Bristol follow signs to A38 and continue south for 14 miles, then turn left on to A371, passing through Cheddar to reach **Wells** after a further 12 miles. From Wells head south on A39, reaching **Glastonbury** in 6 miles, then follow A361 and the A38 for 22 miles to **Taunton**. Continue south-west on A38 and A361 for a further 24 miles to **Tiverton**, then follow A396 south for 17 miles to Exeter.

WELLS

TIC: *Town Hall, Market Pl., Wells, Somerset BA5 2RB; tel: (01749) 672552,* open daily 0930–1730 (Apr–Oct); 1000–1600 (Nov– Mar). DP services offered; local bed-booking service (bookings to closing time; 10% commission), BABA (bookings to closing time; 10% commission), guided tours booked. Discount tickets booked for local attractions. *Wells Information and Accommodation Pack* is 50p.

GETTING AROUND

Most attractions are within walking distance of the town centre. Town and transport maps are available from the TIC. **Badgerline** is the main operator for local buses, *tel: (01749) 673084.* Public transport is generally good to all areas of Wells, but infrequent at weekends and on public holidays. The main **taxi** rank is on *Saddler St, tel: (01749) 670200.*

ACCOMMODATION

There is seldom a problem finding accommodation on arrival, except during weekends July–Aug, when it is advisable to book in advance. There are a few hotels and guesthouses and a good selection of cheaper accommodation. The only hotel chain is *BW.***HI**: The Chalet, Ivythorn Hill, Street; tel: (01458) 42961, 1½ miles south of Glastonbury. The nearest **campsites** are: **Homestead Park**, *Wookey Hole; tel: (01749) 673022,* and **Ebborlands**, *Wookey Hole; tel: (01749) 672550,* both 1½ miles west of Wells.

SIGHTSEEING

Wells lies at the foot of the Mendip Hills and is perhaps best known for being the smallest city in England, while **Vicars' Close** is claimed to be Europe's most complete medieval street.

The 12th-century **Wells Cathedral**, *tel: (01749) 674483,* open 0700–dusk; £3, can be seen from a distance, its Early English Gothic architecture standing out against the surrounding countryside. Approaching through one of the medieval gateways, you are faced with the superb west front with 293 pieces of medieval sculpture extending across the whole façade – an array of figures unique in Europe.

Wells is also known for its annual **Literary Festival** (Oct–Nov); speakers from previous years have included novelists Joanna Trollope and Penelope Lively. This is staged in the **Bishop's Palace**, *The Henderson Rooms, The Palace; tel: (01749) 678691.* Away from the festival, the palace is open Tues–Fri, public holidays 1100–1800, Sun 1400–1800 (Easter–Oct); daily 1000–1800 (Aug); £3.

Wells Museum, *8 Cathedral Green; tel: (01749) 673477,* open daily 1000–1730 (Easter–June, Sept–Oct); daily 1000–2000 (July–Aug); Wed–Sun 1100–1600 (Nov–Easter); £2.

OUT OF TOWN

Wookey Hole Caves and Papermill *Wells; tel: (01749) 672243,* open daily 0930–1730 (Easter–Oct); 1030–1630 (Nov– Easter); £6.50 (reduction of £1.50 if you buy tickets in advance from the TIC). 1½ miles west. Cut through the limestone of the Mendip Hills by the River Axe, and lived in by man more than 2000 years ago, the caves are shrouded in legend. Tours of the underground complex combine fact and fantasy – your hostess in one cavern is a witch! At the mill you can try your hand at making paper and there are other attractions that make for an unusual day out.

Cheddar Gorge, one of the greatest natural fissures in the country, is noted for a series of caves with limestone rock formations and collections of prehistoric weapons. **Cheddar Showcaves**, *The Gorge, Cheddar; tel: (01934) 742343*, open daily 1000–1700 (Easter–Sept); 1030–1630 (Oct–Easter).

GLASTONBURY

TIC: *The Tribunal, 9 High Street, Glastonbury, Somerset BA6 9DP; tel: (01458) 832954/832949*, open Sun–Thur 1000–1700, Fri–Sat 1000–1730 (Apr–Sept); Sun–Thur 1000–1600, Fri–Sat 1000–1630 (Oct–Mar). Local bed-booking service (up to 30 mins before closing; refundable deposit of 10% of first night), BABA (up to 30 mins before closing; refundable deposit of 10% of first night). *Glastonbury and District Accommodation and Services Guide* is free, *Glastonbury Guide* costs £1.50.

GETTING AROUND

Attractions are all within walking distance of the town centre. Free town and transport maps are available from the TIC. The main bus operator is **Badgerline**, *tel: (01749) 673084*. Services are very patchy. The main **taxi** rank is outside the Town Hall. For details of registered taxi companies contact the TIC.

ACCOMMODATION

Most accommodation consists of b&bs and there are several guesthouses. It is generally easy to book on arrival, except during the Glastonbury Carnival (Nov), over Easter and in the summer holidays. The TIC has details of youth hostels and campsites in the area – the nearest **HI** is at Street (see Wells, above).

The nearest **campsites** are: **Ashwell Farmhouse**, *Ashwell Lane, Glastonbury; tel: (01458) 832313*; **Isle of Avalon Caravan & Camping Site**, *Godney Rd,*

Glastonbury; tel: (01458) 833618, and **The Old Oaks Touring Park**, *Wick Farm, Wick; tel: (01458) 831437*, 2 miles from the centre.

SIGHTSEEING

Bus tours are arranged by **Avalon Coaches**, *Northload St; tel: (01458) 832293*, and guides are available from **Gothic Image Bookshop**, *High St*, and **Robert Baulch**, *tel: (01458) 43164*.

Not to be missed are the **Miracle Plays**, performed in the abbey grounds (June–July). Among the young, the town is more famous for the **Pilton Pop Festival** – officially the **Glastonbury Festival of Performing Arts**, which takes place most years (last weekend June). The **Glastonbury Carnival** (second Sat Nov) is great fun, with around 100 illuminated floats.

Apart from being a shrine of religion, history and legend, Glastonbury is the ideal base from which to explore the many beauties of central Somerset. **Glastonbury Abbey**, *Magdalene St; tel: (01458) 832267*, open 0900–1800 (June–Sept); 0930–1630 (Oct–May); £2.50, was the first Christian sanctuary in the British Isles, so ancient that only legend can recall its origin. It is said to have been founded in the first century and to be the burial place of King Arthur.

Somerset Rural Life Museum, *Chilkwell St; tel: (01458) 831197*, open Tues–Fri 1000–1700, Sat–Sun 1400–1800 (Easter–Oct); Tues–Fri 1000–1700, Sat 1100–1600 (Nov–Easter); £1.80. A medieval barn and Victorian farmhouse display Somerset's history, including demonstrations of local crafts.

Glastonbury Lake Village Museum, *The Tribunal, 9 High St; tel: (01458) 832954*, open Sun–Thur 1000–1700, Fri–Sat 1000–1730 (Apr–Sept); Sun–Thur

97

1000–1600, Fri–Sat 1000–1630 (Oct–Mar); £1.50. Sharing a roof with the TIC, the museum presents displays of life in the Iron Age.

Chalice Well Gardens, *Chilkwell St; tel: (01458) 831154*, open daily 1000–1800 (Mar–Oct); 1300–1600 (Nov–Feb); £1. A constant provider of completely pure water, the well is steeped in history and legend. It was probably used in Neolithic times, almost certainly by the Druids and Joseph of Arimathea (hence the name), and is traditionally a sacred place maintained as a peaceful sanctuary.

OUT OF TOWN

The impressive **Glastonbury Tor**, *Wellhouse Lane* (always open; free), some 525 ft above sea level, rewards energetic climbers with panoramic views, while **St Michael's Tower** is a landmark for many miles around: it's what's left of a church on a tor of the same name and is freely accessible.

TAUNTON

TIC: *The Library, Paul St, Taunton, Somerset TA1 3PF; tel: (01823) 336344*, open Mon–Tues, Thur 0930–1730, Wed, Fri 0930–1900, Sat 0930–1600, public holidays Mon 1000–1600. DP SHS services offered; local bed-booking and BABA (latest 30 mins before closing). The *Welcome to Taunton Deane* brochure is free and includes accommodation.

Somerset Vistors Centre: *Sedgemoor Services, M5 Motorway (south), Axbridge, tel: (01934) 750833*, will provide general advice and information about the whole county.

GETTING AROUND

A free town map is available from the TIC. Most services within Taunton are operated by **Southern National**, *tel:*

(01823) 272033, from the **bus station**, *Tower St.* **Somerset County Council**, *tel: (01823) 358299*, issues timetables. Services are good in the centre, less frequent to country areas. A variety of passes is available.

The main **taxi** rank is on *Corporation St.*

ACCOMMODATION

There is a reasonable range of accommodation, including large and small hotels, but it's advisable to pre-book. The majority of guesthouse and b&b accommodation is on the edge of the centre and in outlying areas. A number of pubs and inns offer accommodation, mostly in the villages around Taunton. The only chain is *FP*.

The closest **campsites** are: **Holly Bush Farm**, *Culmhead; tel: (01823) 421515*, 5 miles south-east; **Ashe Farm Caravan and Camping Site**, *Thornfalcon; tel: (01823) 442567*, 4 miles south-east; **Gamlin's Farm**, *Greenham, Wellington; tel: (01823) 672596*, 8 miles south, and **Quantock Orchard Caravan Park**, *Crowcombe; tel: (01984) 618618*, 10 miles north-west.

SIGHTSEEING

This small county town has some fine old buildings, such as **Gray's Almshouses**, *East St*, dating from 1635. Part of the restored Norman **castle** houses the **Somerset County Museum**, *Taunton Castle, Castle Green; tel: (01823) 355504*, open Tues–Sat, public holidays Mon 1000–1700 (Easter–Oct); Tues–Sat 1000–1500 (Nov–Easter); £2. Another Taunton landmark is the sandstone tower of the 15th-century parish church of **St Mary's**, *Church Sq*.

The annual **Taunton Flower Show** (Aug) is held in **Vivary Park**. Horse-racing meetings are held (Sept–Apr) at

98

Taunton Racecourse, *Orchard Portman; tel: (01823) 337172.* The town is home to Somerset County Cricket Club, *The County Ground; tel: (01823) 272946,* which hosts matches Apr–Sept. Displays of Somerset CC memorabilia, housed in a renovated 16th-century priory barn, form the Somerset Cricket Museum, *7 Priory Ave; tel: (01823) 275893,* open Mon–Fri 1000–1600 (Easter–Oct); 60p. On first-class match days, access to the museum is available only if you have a ground ticket.

OUT OF TOWN

Hatch Court, *Hatch Beauchamp; tel: (01823) 480120,* house open Thur 1430–1730 (mid June–mid Sept); £3.50 (house and garden). 6 miles south-east. The 1750 Palladian mansion, of Bath stone, is beautifully maintained by the family. It contains good collections of paintings and furniture and is surrounded by a deer park and extensively restored gardens.

Hestercombe Gardens, *Hestercombe House, Cheddon Fitzpaine; tel: (01823) 413923,* open daily 1000–1700 (all year); £3. 2½ miles north. There are 50 acres of formal gardens and parklands, including a multi-terraced Edwardian garden – designed by Sir Edwin Lutyens and Gertrude Jekyll. Other features are lakes, temples and the county's highest waterfall.

The Vale of Taunton Deane is prime cider country and you can visit a traditional farm where the cider-making process is well explained with demonstrations and samples: Sheppy's Farmhouse Cider, *Three Bridges, Bradford-on-Tone; tel: (01823) 461233,* open Mon–Sat 0830–1800 (post Christmas–Easter); Mon–Sat 0830–1800 (Oct–Apr); Sun 1200–1400 (Easter–pre Christmas); £1.75 (entrance), £3.75 (guided tour). 3 miles south.

TIVERTON

TIC: *Phoenix Lane, Tiverton EX16 6LU; tel: (01884) 255827; fax: (01844) 257594,* open Mon–Sat 0915–1700 (Easter–end Oct), Mon–Fri 0915–1700, Sat 0915–1500 (Nov–Easter).

ACCOMMODATION

There are a few small hotels and b&bs in the area. Details from the TIC.

Bickleigh Cottage Country House Hotel, *Bickleigh Bridge, Tiverton EX16 8RJ; tel: (01884) 855230.* A converted 17th-century cottage, partly thatched, on the banks of the River Exe, the property has nine rooms, some non-smoking. Moderate.

Hartnoll Country House Hotel, *Bolham Rd, Bolham, Tiverton EX16 7RA; tel: (01884) 252777; fax: (01844) 259195.* A millstream runs through the grounds of this delightful Georgian hotel, which has 16 rooms, some non-smoking, some with four-poster beds. The restaurant serves English and continental dishes. Moderate.

SIGHTSEEING

Tiverton Museum, *St Andrew St, Tiverton; tel: (01884) 256295,* open Mon–Fri 1030–1630, Sat 1030–1300, 1400–1630; £1. The museum traces local history from Roman times and has galleries featuring agriculture and railways.

Knightshayes Court (NT), *Bolham; tel: (01884) 254665,* house open Fri–Wed 1100–1730; garden daily same times (Apr–Oct); £5.10. A fine collection of Old Masters and English furnishings from the 18th and 19th centuries are displayed in this National Trust property, a Gothic house built in the late 19th century. The gardens, among the first in Devon, have formal terraces and topiary depicting a fox and hounds.

99

BRISTOL–PENZANCE

Rarely more than a mile or so from the sea, this route traverses the length of the south-west peninsula, crossing the Somerset Levels and the very hilly moorlands of North Devon and Cornwall and taking in a number of classic English holiday resorts along the way. It's a switchback route – one moment at sea level, the next soaring along 400ft clifftops. It finishes at the end of the road – so far as southern England is concerned – Land's End, with only the Isles of Scilly and 2000miles of ocean between here and North America.

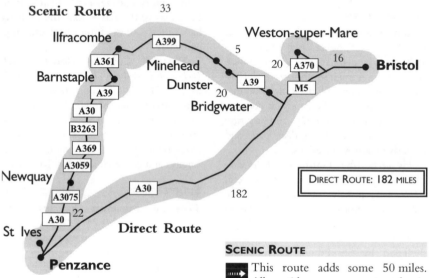

Scenic Route   33
Ilfracombe   A399
A361
Barnstaple   Minehead
A39   Dunster   A39
A30   Bridgwater   20
B3263
A369
A3059
Newquay
A3075   A30   182
22
A30
St Ives   Direct Route
Penzance

Weston-super-Mare
5
20   A370   16   Bristol
M5

DIRECT ROUTE: 182 MILES

ROUTES

DIRECT ROUTE

➡ The 182-mile route takes 3 hrs 30 mins. From central Bristol follow signs to M5 west (8 miles) and head for 72 miles, leaving at Junction 31 to join A30, which continues for 110 miles to Penzance.

SCENIC ROUTE

⇢ This route adds some 50 miles. Allow 6 hours – more to take in refreshment and sightseeing trips. There are plenty of places for overnight stops.

Leave central Bristol as above and travel west on M5 for 12 miles. Leave at Junction 21 and follow A370 east for 4½ miles into **Weston-super-Mare**. After visiting Weston return to M5 and continue south for 14 miles, leaving at Junction 23 to join A38 south, arriving at **Bridgwater** in 3 miles. Leave Bridgwater on A39 and continue for 25 miles to **Minehead** (via **Dunster**) and a further

25 miles to Blackmoor Gate, then bear right on to A399, which leads to Ilfracombe in 8 miles.

From **Ilfracombe** follow A361 to **Barnstaple**, then A39 west to **Bideford**. A39 continues south for 80 miles, passing Bude and joining A30 at Indian Queens. South of Bude, B3263 leads to Tintagel Head. Beyond Wadebridge A389 heads for Padstow, and **Newquay** is accessed via A3059. From Newquay leave on A3075 to join A30 at Blackwater. From here to **Penzance**, via **St Ives**, is 22 miles.

WESTON-SUPER-MARE

TIC: *Beach Lawns, Weston-super-Mare, Somerset BS23 1AT; tel: (01934) 888800/ 634512*, open Mon–Sat 0930–1700 (mid Oct–Mar); Mon–Sun 0930–1730 (Apr–mid Oct). DP SHS services offered; local bed-booking service and BABA (latest bookings 1 hr before closing; fee 10% of total stay). Theatre and attraction tickets sold. The *Weston-super-Mare Holiday Guide* is available free and includes accommodation listings.

GETTING AROUND

The majority of attractions are in the centre. A free transport map is available from the TIC or from **Badgerline**, *9–13 High St,* who operate most of the local services. These are good in the town centre and to major towns nearby. **Timetable hotline** *tel: (0117) 955 3231.* A **Day Rover** is £4.40 and **Rovercards** covering longer periods are available. **Taxi** ranks are located in *Alexander Parade.*

ACCOMMODATION

There is a reasonable range of hotels, guesthouses and b&bs, so it is generally easy to find accommodation on arrival, except over public holidays weekends.

The resort's leading hotel is the **Grand**

Atlantic, *Beach Rd, Weston-super-Mare BS23 1BA; tel: (01934) 626 543; fax: (01934) 415048.* A modernised Victorian establishment, with 76 bedrooms and commanding views across Weston Bay. Moderate–expensive.

The Commodore, *Beach Rd, Sand Bay, Kewstoke BS22 9UZ; tel: (01934) 415778; fax: (01934) 636483.* 1½ miles north-west of the town centre, the hotel developed from a group of 17th-century fishing cottages. The restaurant has an imaginative, good value menu. Moderate.

The majority of pub accommodation is located in the suburbs and neighbouring villages. There are a number of **campsites** within easy reach of town, of which the closest are: **Airport View**, *Moor Lane, Worle; tel: (01934) 622168,* 2 miles east; **Country View**, *Sand Bay; tel: (01934) 627595,* 3 miles north, and **West End Farm**, *Locking; tel: (01934) 822529,* 2 miles east.

SIGHTSEEING

Bakers Coaches; *tel: (01934) 415000,* offer a wide variety of **guided bus tours**; from around £4. **Waverley & Balmoral Pleasure Steamers**; *tel: (01446) 721221,* offer a variety of **boat trips** (from £7), which can be booked at the TIC.

Weston-super-Mare is a busy resort, with all the traditional features of a seaside town: piers, gardens and a wide sandy beach. Many of the town's attractions are situated on the 2 mile-long **Marine Parade**, including traditional offerings on the **Grand Pier**, *Marine Parade; tel: (01934) 620238,* open daily 1000–dusk (Easter–Oct); free. **Sea Life Centre**, *Marine Parade; tel: (01934) 613361,* open daily 1000–1800; £4.75, has a new section, Jurassic Seas, which explains how early life on earth developed.

A lively museum about local life that

101

includes finds from a nearby Iron Age camp is known as the **Time Machine**, *Burlington St; tel: (01934) 621028*, open daily 1000–1700 (Mar–Oct); 1000–1600 (Nov–Feb); £1.80.

International Helicopter Museum, *Locking Moor Rd; tel: (01934) 635227*, open daily 1000–1800 (Mar–Oct), 1000–1600 (Oct–Mar); £3. 2½miles east. The world's largest collection of helicopters is fascinating and there's a flight simulator if you don't fancy the real thing.

BRIDGWATER

TIC: *50 High St, Bridgwater TA6 3BL; tel: (01278) 427652*, open Mon–Fri 0900–1700. For a full range of information on attractions, events, special interests and accommodation throughout the county call at the **Somerset Visitor Centre**, *Sedgemoor Services, M5 motorway (south), Axbridge BS26 2UF; tel: (01934) 750833; fax: (01934) 750755*. The county also offers a *Welcome to Somerset* central booking service for all types of accommodation: *tel: (01934) 750834*.

ACCOMMODATION

Friarn Court Hotel, *37 St Mary St, Bridgwater TA6 3LX; tel: (01278) 452859; fax: (01278) 452988*. This family-run hotel in the town centre has 16 ensuite rooms. Budget–moderate.

Admiral's Rest Guesthouse, *5 Taunton Rd, Bridgwater TA6 3LW; tel/fax: (01278) 458580*. This elegant Victorian house close to the town centre has four luxurious en suite rooms and a private car park. Budget.

SIGHTSEEING

Admiral Blake Museum, *Blake St, Bridgwater; tel: (01278) 456127*, open Mon–Sat 1100–1700, Sun 1400–1700; free. The supposed birthplace of Oliver

Cromwell's admiral Robert Blake features the Battle of Sedgemoor, which was fought just outside the town in 1685.

OUT OF TOWN

Cannington College Heritage Gardens, *off A39; tel: (01278) 652226*, open daily 1400–1700 (Apr–Oct, 1–24 Dec); £2.25. 2 miles west. Established more than 75 years, the gardens contain extensive plant collections.

Coleridge Cottage, *35 Lime St, Nether Stowey; tel: (01278) 456127*, open Mon–Sat 1100–1700, Sun 1400–1700; £1.70, 6 miles west. The 'miserable cottage' (as his wife called it) in which Samuel Taylor Coleridge wrote *The Rime of the Ancient Mariner*.

DUNSTER

On the A396, 2 miles south of Minehead, Dunster is a small and picturesque market town, dominated by **Dunster Castle** (NT); *tel: (01643) 821314*, open Sat–Wed 1100–1600/1700; £5 (castle and grounds). In 1870 the ancestral home of the Luttrells was remodelled, but the fine 17th-century staircase and plaster ceilings were retained and there are still traces of the original 13th-century castle. The terraced woodland garden is home to some rare shrubs.

The town owed its past prosperity to the wool trade, an unusual relic of which is the octagonal 17th-century **Yarn Market** (EH), *Dunster High St*, open at any reasonable time; free. Built in 1609 and repaired in 1647, the building was used for the sale of locally woven cloth.

Nearby is the partially ruined but atmospheric **Cleeve Abbey** (EH), *Washford, Watchet; tel: (01984) 640377*, open daily 1000–1800/dusk (Easter–Oct); daily 1000–1300 and 1400–1600 (Nov–Easter); £2.40. 4 miles east, off A39. This is one of the rare places where you can see a reasonably complete set of 13th-century monastic cloister buildings – including a refectory with an outstanding timber roof.

MINEHEAD

TIC: *17 Friday St, Minehead TA24 5UB; tel: (01643) 702624,* open daily 0930–1700 (Apr–Sept); Mon–Fri 1000–1700, Sat 1000–1300 (Oct–Mar). Services offered: local bed-booking service, BABA.

ACCOMMODATION

A busy and popular seaside resort, Minehead has a good choice of small hotels and b&bs.

Beaconwood Hotel, *Church Rd, North Hill, Minehead TA24 5SB; tel: (01643) 702032.* Standing in terraced gardens overlooking Exmoor and the sea, the hotel has 16 rooms, some with balconies. Budget–moderate. **Benares Hotel**, *Northfield Rd, Minehead TA24 5PT; tel: (01643) 704911; fax: (01643) 706373.* Close to beaches and town centre, the Edwardian building has 19 ensuite rooms, some with views over the bay.

HI: *Alcombe Combe, Minehead TA24 6EW; tel: (01643) 702795.* **Minehead and Exmoor Caravan Park**, *Porlock Rd, Minehead TA24 8SN; tel: (01643) 703074,* is a mile west of the town and has 50 touring pitches – 30 with electrical hook-ups.

SIGHTSEEING

The railway age transformed Minehead from a major port into a Victorian holiday resort divided into two districts – Higher Town and Quay Town – connected by steep lanes of old houses.

Bossington Farm and Birds of Prey Centre, *Allerford, Minehead; tel: (01643) 862816,* open daily 1030–1630 (Mar–Oct); £3.50. Farm animals and rare breeds on show as well as birds of prey and owls. Flying displays staged daily.

West Somerset Railway, *Railway Station, Minehead; tel: (01643) 704996,* open daily (June–Sept); Tues–Thur and Sat–Sun (Oct and Apr–May); check for opening times on public holidays and other periods. Preserved steam trains operate on Britain's longest independent railway – 20 miles between Minehead and Bishops Lydeard, near Taunton.

West Somerset Rural Life Museum, *The Old School, Allerford, Minehead; tel: (01643) 862529,* open Mon–Fri 1030–1230, 1400–1630, Sat 1400–1630 (Apr–midOct); Sun 1400–1630 (midJuly–earlySept); £1. The museum is housed in an old school building and a smaller thatched schoolroom with a riverside garden.

ILFRACOMBE

TIC: *The Promenade, Ilfracombe, Devon EX34 9BX; tel: (01271) 863001; fax: (01271) 862586,* open Mon–Fri 1000–1700, Sat 1300–1700, Sun 1000–1400. Services offered: local accommodation reservations, BABA. Books, maps, souvenirs and leaflets covering Ilfracombe, Exmoor and North Devon; information and tickets for coach trips and cruises.

ACCOMMODATION

North Devon's major holiday resort, Ilfracombe has no shortage of accommodation, mainly in small hotels and guesthouses, but it would be wise to book ahead for a stay during July or August when the area's lovely coastline, with magnificent beaches and many undeveloped coves and inlets, attracts holidaymakers.

Among the most popular hotels is the **Ilfracombe Carlton**, *Runnacleave Rd, Ilfracombe EX34 8AR; tel: (01271) 862446; fax: (01271) 865379.* 48 well-equipped rooms and traditional cuisine. Budget–moderate.

103

Belvedere, *12 Broad Park Ave, Ilfracombe EX34 8DZ; tel: (01271) 862710,* is an elegant Victorian guesthouse. 'Real farmhouse' breakfast served and home-cooked dinner by arrangement. Budget.

HI: *Ashmour House, 1 Hillsborough Terrace, Ilfracombe EX34 9NR; tel: (01271) 865337; fax: (01271) 862652.*

SIGHTSEEING

Ilfracombe's magnificent harbour is a magnet for visitors, with its lively cafés, restaurants and maritime pubs. There are excellent walks along the coast, and trips to Lundy Island and neighbouring resorts may be taken aboard the paddle steamer *Waverley* or the MS *Oldenburg* (information and bookings at the TIC).

Watermouth Castle, *A399 3 miles east of Ilfracombe; tel: (01271) 867474,* is an amusement park, not a stately home, though it is centred on a 19th-century mansion, open Sun–Fri 1000/1100 (Easter, mid May–mid Sept); Sun–Thur 1300/1400 (Easter–mid May, mid Sept–Oct) – you should allow 3 hours and the last admission is 1600; £4.85 (covers all attractions except slot machines).

BARNSTAPLE

TIC: *36 Boutport St, Barnstaple, Devon EX31 1RX; tel: (01271) 75000,* open (public holidays excepted) Mon–Sat 0930–1700 (minimum – usually, but unofficially, closes much later in summer). DP services offered; local bed-booking (10% refundable deposit), BABA (10% refundable deposit), ferry tickets sold. The *Barnstaple Town Guide* costs 80p, but the *North Devon Guide, This Month in Devon* and accommodation listings are free.

ACCOMMODATION

It is always advisable to book accommodation in advance and essential in July–Aug.

There are few hotels in Barnstaple. Cheaper b&b accommodation can be found on the edge of town and in the suburbs of Newport (1½ miles east) and Sticklepath (1 mile south-west).

HI: *Worlington House, New Rd, Instow; tel: (01271) 860394.* The nearest **campsite** is **Brightlycott Farm**, *on the A39 (towards Lynton),* 2 miles north.

SIGHTSEEING

Guided walks of historic Barnstaple are organised by Tom Evans – ask for him at the TIC. **Coach tours** are available daily with **Loverings Coaches**, *tel: (01271) 863673,* which start from the bus station and cost approx. £4–£8. The 21 mile **Tarka Cycle Trail** takes in the surrounding countryside; featured in Henry Williamson's novel, *Tarka the Otter.* The TIC can provide information and make bookings for boat trips to Lundy.

North Devon Museum, *The Square; tel: (01271) 346747,* open Tues–Sat 1000–1630; £1 – but free Sat 1000–1200. As well as displays about the natural and human history of the region, this incorporates the **Royal Devon Yeomanry Museum**.

For a garden centre with a difference, visit **Jungleland**, *St John's Lane; tel: (01271) 43884,* open Mon–Sat 0900–1730, Sun 1030–1600; free. The worlds of desert and jungle meet here, under cover, beside a large pool and waterfall. Added colour is provided by chipmunks, terrapins, birds and fish.

Sanders Sheepskin Works and Tannery, *Pilton Causeway; tel: (01271) 42335,* open Mon–Fri 0900–1700, Sat 0915–1200; free entry and free optional tours at 1100 and 1400. You can purchase natural and dyed sheepskin products and hand-thrown pottery in the shop.

Brannams Pottery, *Roundswell; tel: (01271) 343035,* open Mon–Fri 0915–

1615; £3.50 including tour. 1½ miles south-west.

OUT OF TOWN

Those interested in exquisite hand-made glassware, should not miss **Dartington Crystal**, *Great Torrington; tel: (01805) 626266.* Visitor Centre open daily 1000–1600; £2.75. 12 miles south.

BIDEFORD-PADSTOW

This section of the route covers the stunningly beautiful north coasts of Devon and Cornwall, with sweeping sea views and wild countryside dotted with the relics of old industry.

TICs: *Victoria Park, The Quay, Bideford, Devon EX39 2QQ; tel: (01237) 477676; fax: (01237) 421853; The Crescent, Bude, Cornwall EX23 8LE; tel: (01288) 354240; fax: (01288) 353111; Red Brick Building, North Quay, Padstow, Cornwall PL28 8AF; tel: (01841) 533449; fax: (01841) 532356.* Each offers local accommodation reservations and BABA.

Britain's largest port in the 16th century, **Bideford** today is an estuary town of narrow streets leading to a bustling tree-lined quay where you can take a boat to Lundy Island. The town has an impressive 16th-century 24-arch bridge across the River Torridge and a thriving centre with shops, markets, pubs and cafés. A statue of the author Charles Kingsley on the quayside commemorates the fact that part of *Westward Ho!* was written in the town.

Riverside Hotel, *Limes Lane, Bideford EX39 2RG; tel: (01237) 474239; fax: (01237) 421661,* is set in 3 acres of garden and has 16 rooms, some with four-poster beds. Fresh seafood is a feature of the à la carte menu. Moderate.

Three miles north-west of Bideford, **Westward Ho!** (complete with exclamation mark) owes its existence to Charles

Kingsley's swashbuckling novel of the same name. An undeveloped area of land overlooking stretches of sand and mud was soon covered with Victorian villas as speculators acted swiftly following the book's publication in 1855. Today, Westward Ho! is a popular family resort.

Clovelly, 8 miles west of Bideford, is the village that launched a thousand chocolate box tops. The picturesque streets of this archetypal picture-postcard place (try taking a photograph with no one in it) descend steeply to a tiny harbour and a stony beach.

A dozen miles south of Clovelly lies **Bude**, Cornwall. Once a busy port, the town today is a prime resort with fine sandy beaches, rock pools and a tidal swimming pool. It is a major centre for surfing. **Widemouth Bay**, just south of the town, has some of the cleanest water on the north Cornwall coast. There is a good selection of hotel and b&b accommodation, but advance booking is advisable for July–Aug.

A diversion on to B3263, 8 miles south of Bude, leads to rugged **Tintagel Head** with the ruined castle which legend says was the birthplace of **King Arthur**.

Padstow, near the mouth of the Camel river, has been Cornwall's ecclesiastical capital and a major fishing port. Its busy and colourful harbour is fringed by many medieval buildings. There are good bathing and surfing beaches in the area. Padstow has recently become something of a gourmet centre, thanks to TV chef Rick Stein, proprietor of **The Seafood Restaurant**, *Riverside; tel: (01841) 532485,* expensive.

NEWQUAY

TIC: *Municipal Buildings, Marcus Hill, Newquay TR7 1BD; tel: (01637) 871345,* open Mon–Fri 0900–1700, Sat 1000–1230

105

(Nov–end May); Mon–Sat 0900–1800, Sun 1000–1700 (end May–Sept). SHS services offered; local bed-booking and BABA (latest 1 hr before closing). Bureau de change. *Newquay Guide* and *Discover Cornwall* guides are free and include accommodation listings.

GETTING AROUND

Most attractions are within walking distance of the centre. A free town map is available from the TIC. Most bus services are operated by **Western National**; *tel: (01208) 79898*. Services are good in the centre and reasonable to nearby towns, but very poor to the north coast area.

The main **taxi** rank is on *Trebarwith Crescent*; or contact: **123 Taxis**; tel: *(01637) 851234;* **A1 Taxis**; *tel: (01637) 872325,* or **Ace Taxis**; *tel: (01637) 852121.*

ACCOMMODATION

There is a good range of accommodation, with over 130 hotels and 100 guesthouses and b&bs. Most of the cheaper accommodation is central. It is generally easy to find accommodation on arrival, except July–Aug. Hotel chains are *BW* and *Ct*. **Hostel** accommodation is available at **Backpackers**, *69–73 Tower Rd; tel: (01637) 879366*; **Fistral Backpackers**, *Headland Rd; tel: (01637) 873146*; **Matt's Surf Lodge**, *110 Mount Wise; tel: (01637) 874651*; **Rick's Hostel**, *8 Springfield Rd; tel: (01637) 851143*; and **Towan Backpackers**, *Beachfield Ave; tel: (01637) 874668*. The closest **campsites** are: **Trenance Chalet and Caravan Park**, *Edgcumbe Ave; tel: (01637) 873447,* ½ mile east of the centre; **Porth Beach Tourist Park**, *Alexandra Rd, Porth; tel: (01637) 876531,* 1½ miles north-west; **Trencreek Farm Holiday Park**, *Trencreek; tel (01637) 874210,* 1½ miles east; **Hendra Holiday Park**, *Lane; tel: (01637) 875778,*

2 miles east; and **Trevelgue Holiday Park**, *Trevelgue Rd; tel: (01637) 851851,* 2 miles north.

SIGHTSEEING

Grand Tour of Newquay, *tel: (01726) 860345,* is a town bus tour (£2). **Bus tours** of a wider area are operated by **Western National** and **R&M Coaches** – book at the TIC.

Boat trips (from short pleasure jaunts to full-day shark/conger fishing) are available from **Newquay Shooting & Fishing Centre**, *tel: (01637) 874139,* and **Dolphin**, *tel: (01637) 878696* (or *877048* evenings).

Trenance Leisure Park and Gardens, *off Edgcumbe Ave,* open daily dawn–dusk; free. Covering 26 acres of parkland and gardens, Trenance offers a variety of alfresco activities. It is also home to several of the town's attractions. **Newquay Zoo**, *Trenance Gardens; tel: (01637) 873342,* open daily 0930–1800 (Easter–Oct); 1000–1700 (Nov–Easter); £4.50. Close encounters with some of the creatures are encouraged and there are staggered feeding times. **Art & Craft Exhibition**, *Trenance Cottages,* open daily 1000–1730 (Apr–Sept); free.

Tunnels Through Time, *St Michaels Rd; tel: (01637) 873379,* open Sun–Fri 1000–1700, also some Sat (Apr–Oct); £3.30. The tableaux present a well-balanced mix of fact and fantasy to bring Cornwall's past to life.

Children under 12 can let off steam at **Fun Factory**, *St Georges Rd; tel: (01637) 877555,* open daily 1000–2100 (mid July–Aug); Wed–Sun 1000–1800 (Sept–mid July); adults free, children £3.50; and **Tumbletown**, *Gover Lane; tel: (01637) 875610,* open daily 0900–2200 (June–Sept); 0900–1730 (Oct–May); adults free, children £2.50.

OUT OF TOWN

Lappa Valley Railway, *Newlyn East; tel: (01872) 510317.* Operates daily 1030/1100–1600/1700 (Easter–Oct); £5.25 round trip; 6 miles south-east. This is not just for miniature railway buffs: the journey is through glorious countryside and you can alight at East Wheal Rose to enjoy a variety of (mostly free) alfresco pursuits – before boarding any return train.

Trerice Manor (NT), *Newlyn East; tel: (01637) 875404,* open Wed–Mon 1100–1730 (Apr–Sept); 1100–1700 (Oct); £3.80; 3 miles south-east. This is a small Elizabethan manor (1571) with fine fireplaces and ceilings, as well as oak and walnut furniture and some interesting clocks. The barn houses a small museum devoted to lawn mowers.

ST IVES

TIC: *The Guildhall, Street-an-Pol, St Ives, Cornwall TR26 2DS; tel: (01736) 796297,* open Mon–Sat 0930–1730/1800, Sun 1000–1300 (mid May–mid Sept); Mon–Fri 0930–1700/1730 (mid Sept–mid May); also Sat 1000–1300 (Apr–mid May). SHS services offered; local bed-booking and BABA (latest 1hr before closing) – for accommodation bookings, be prepared to queue 1200–1700. *West Cornwall Guide* (including an accommodation list) is free. *What's On* keeps abreast of events in the area.

GETTING AROUND

The main bus operator is **Western National**, *tel: (01209) 719988.* Services are good within the town, but reduced services run after 1000 and on Sunday.

Registered **taxi** companies are: **Goodways**; *tel: (01736) 794437;* **Nicholls**; *tel: (01736) 796361;* **Ayr Taxi**, *tel: (01736) 796144;* **D.J.'s Cars**; *tel: (01736) 798103;* and **Wheelchair Friendly**; *tel: (01736)*

793344, which has facilities for disabled travellers.

ACCOMMODATION

A good range of accommodation is available, particularly guesthouses and b&bs. It is usually easy to book on arrival, except July–Sept. The only chain represented is *BW*. The nearest **campsites** are: **Ayr Holiday Site**, *Higher Ayr; tel: (01736) 795855,* in town; and **Hellesveor Farm Caravan & Camping Site**, *Hellesveor Farm; tel: (01736) 795738,* 1mile out.

SIGHTSEEING

The TIC can supply a walking route round the historic town. **Bus tours** are operated by: **Oates Travel**, *tel: (01736) 795343;* **Western National**, *tel: (01736) 797577;* and **Harry Safari**, *tel: (01736) 711427;* while short **boat trips** (around the bay and to **Seal Island**) are offered by **Mr Stevens**, *tel: (01736) 797328,* and **Mr Laity**, *tel: (01736) 796080.*

Turner, Whistler and Sickert started the trend for artists to converge on St Ives and many works by them and later artists are now displayed in the **St Ives Tate Gallery**, *Porthmeor Beach; tel: (01736) 796226,* open Mon–Sat 1100–1900, Sun, public holidays 1100–1700 (Apr–Sept); Tues–Sun 1100–1700 (Oct–Mar); £3.50 – or £5.50 to include the **Barbara Hepworth Museum and Sculpture Garden**, *Barnoon Hill; tel: (01736) 796226,* opening times as for the Tate, but closes at dusk; £3.50. Run by the Tate since 1980, the sculptures are in positions chosen by Hepworth, whose will decreed the studios and garden should be open to the public.

St Ives Museum, *Wheal Dream; tel: (01736) 796005,* open daily 1000–1700 (Easter, mid-May–Sept); £1. Art, photography, model ships, fishing, mines,

107

railways and many other topics are covered in this museum of the area.

OUT OF TOWN

A deserted Romano-Cornish village site, with eight easily identifiable houses, is **Chysauster Ancient Village** (EH), *New Mill; tel: (0831) 757934*, open daily 1000–1800/dusk (Easter–Oct); £1.50. 8 miles south-west.

Don't miss the **Wayside Folk Museum**, *Old Mill House, Zennor; tel: (01736) 796945*, open daily 1000–1800 (mid Apr–Sept); daily 1100–1700 (mid Mar–mid Apr); Sun–Fri 1100–1700 (Oct); £2. 4 miles west. Before modern roads were built, Zennor was very inaccessible and had to be virtually self-sufficient. The collection in this, Cornwall's oldest private museum, is drawn from the immediate area and gives a real taste of traditional Cornish life.

108

PENZANCE

TIC: *Station Rd, Penzance, Cornwall TR18 2NF; tel: (01736) 362207*, open Mon–Fri 0900–1700, Sat 1000–1300 (Oct–May); Mon–Sat 0900–1700 (June–Sept). DP SHS services offered; local bed-booking and BABA (latest 1 hr before closing), but no booking services Sat Oct–May. The *West Cornwall Guide* is free and includes accommodation listings.

GETTING AROUND

A free town map is available from the TIC and free transport maps are available from bus and train stations. The main bus operator is **Western National**, *tel: (01209) 719988*. For details of **taxi** companies contact the TIC.

ACCOMMODATION

There is a good range of accommodation, particularly mid-range hotels and guest-

houses. It is generally easy to book on arrival. The only chain represented is *Mo*.

HI: Castle Horneck, *Alverton; tel: (01736) 62666*. The TIC has details of **campsites** in the area.

SIGHTSEEING

Only 10 miles from Land's End, the town is as much a busy market and fishing centre as a seaside resort. *Chapel St*, running from market to harbour, has some remarkable Georgian houses, most notably the exotic **Egyptian House** (*c.*1835).

You can operate some of the exhibits at **Trinity House National Lighthouse Museum**, *Wharf Rd; tel: (01736) 360077*, open daily 1100–1700 (Mar–Oct.); £2.50. With one of the world's finest collections of related artefacts, the museum gives a dramatic insight into the history of lighthouses over the past two centuries – before automation began to take over.

OUT OF TOWN

Don't miss the fairytale **St Michael's Mount** (NT), *Marazion; tel: (01736) 710507*, open Mon–Fri 1030–1730 (Apr–Oct); as tide and weather permits (Nov–Mar); £3.80. 3 miles east. The great rock, an island at high tide, is capped by a spectacular castle dating from the 14th century, which contains a maze of narrow passageways. Access is by ferry – or on foot across the cobbled causeway at low tide.

Inevitably, **Land's End** has a themed visitor attraction of the same name: **Land's End**, *Sennen; tel: (01736) 871220*, open daily 1000–dusk. 10 miles south-west. It's £2 to park – how much you spend after that depends on which of the attractions interest you. However, a short walk south along the cliffs allows you to savour, in relative peace, some of England's most dramatic coastal scenery.

BRISTOL–
STRATFORD-UPON-AVON

This route traverses part of the region known as the Heart of England. The area offers the contrasts of elegant Georgian architecture and picturesque half-timbered buildings; and of the sweeping heights of the Malvern Hills and the gentle meanderings of the Avon and Severn rivers.

DIRECT ROUTE: 77 MILES

26

Worcester · A422 · A46 · A422

Scenic Route

7

A449

Great Malvern

Stratford-upon-Avon

8

A46

A449

Tewkesbury

Ledbury · A438

Direct Route

14

A46

M5

A438

10

A4019 · Cheltenham

A46 · Cotswolds–Cardiff p.183

Direct Route

18 · Scenic Route

A417

M5

Cirencester

M4

A429

35

M4 · London–Bristol p.239

Bristol

109

ROUTE

ROUTES

DIRECT ROUTE

➡️ This 77-mile route takes 1hr 30mins. From central Bristol follow signs to M4 (about 5miles) and head west on the motorway for 4 miles. Join M5 and continue north for 37miles, leaving at Junction9 to join A46 for 3 miles east. Head north on A46, skirting Evesham and continuing for 18miles to the outskirts of Alcester, then head east on A46, which reaches Shottery in 6miles. From here A422 takes the final 4miles to reach Stratford-upon-Avon.

SCENIC ROUTE

➡️ Allow 3 hours for this route, which covers 123 miles. From central Bristol follow the signs as above to M4, then head east for 18miles, leaving the motorway at Junction 17 to travel north on A419 for 17miles to **Cirencester**. Leave Cirencester on A417 north for 13miles, then turn right on to A46 which reaches **Cheltenham** in 5miles.

From Cheltenham head north-west on A4019 to intersect with A38 in 6 miles. A38 leads north to reach **Tewkesbury** in 4 miles. A438 travels west for 14miles to **Ledbury**, where we turn north again on A449 to reach **Great Malvern** in 8miles and **Worcester** in a further 7miles. From Worcester A422 leads to Stratford-upon-Avon, 26miles to the east.

CIRENCESTER

TIC: *Corn Hall, Market Pl., Cirencester, Glos GL7 2NW; tel: (01285) 654180/ 655526*, open Mon 0945–1700, Tues–Sat 0930–1700 (Nov–Mar); Mon 0945–1700/ 1730, Tues–Sat 0930–1700/1730 (Apr–Oct). Services: local bed-booking (latest 15 mins before closing), BABA (latest 30 mins before closing). NT membership and tickets for local events sold. *Cirencester Official Town Guide (£1), Cirencester Mini Guide* (25p) and *Accommodation in the Cotswolds* (50p).

GETTING AROUND

Most attractions are near the centre and can be reached on foot. A free transport map is available from the TIC. Bus coverage is reasonable in town, but patchy to outlying areas, with no local services after 1845 nor on Sun. For **general transport enquiries**, *tel: (01452) 425543*. Most local bus services are operated from *Market Place* by a number of companies.

The main **taxi** rank is on *Market Place*.

STAYING IN CIRENCESTER

There is a small number of hotels, including one chain, *Ja,* and a range of guesthouses, b&bs and pubs. It is generally easy to book on arrival, except during the International Air Tattoo (July, at nearby Fairford).

King's Head Hotel, *Market Pl, Cirencester GL7 2NR; tel: (01285) 653322; fax: (01285) 655103.* This archetypal market town inn, with panelled walls, paintings and lots of atmosphere, has been in business since the 17th century. Moderate–expensive.

HI: *Duntisbourne Abbots; tel: (01285) 821682.* The closest **campsites** are: **Mayfield Touring Park,** *Cheltenham Rd, Perrotts Brook; tel: (01285) 831301,* 2miles north, and **Cotswold and Coburne,** *Broadway Lane, South Cerney; tel: (01285) 860216,* 3miles south.

SIGHTSEEING

Guided town walks are available May–Sept; £1.

Cirencester, now a typical Cotswold town, was once an important Roman settlement and has impressive Roman artefacts in the **Corinium Museum**, *Park St; tel: (01285) 655611,* open Mon–Sat 1000–1700 (Apr–Oct); Tues–Sat 1000–1700 (Nov–Mar); Sun 1400–1700 (all year); £1.75. The grassed-over remains of **Cirencester Amphitheatre**, *off Cotswold Ave,* are open at all times; free.

The finest building in this attractive town is **St John Baptist Parish Church**, *Market Pl.; tel: (01285) 653142,* open daily Mon–Sat 0930–1700, Sun 1415–1730; free. This 15th-century church has a magnificent interior and tower. Note the 12th-century Norman arch in the grounds behind the church.

The 40 ft yew hedge in front of **Cirencester Park**'s Mansion House is reputed to be the highest in Europe.

Brewery Arts, *Brewery Court; tel: (01285) 657181,* is a craft centre where resident craftspeople with various skills have their studios and sell the results of their labours.

OUT OF TOWN

For tours of the area, the TIC operates **Cotswold Scenic Bus Tours**; £7.50. Cirencester makes an ideal base for exploring the Cotswolds – see pp. 180–182.

Barnsley House Garden, *Barnsley; tel: (01285) 740281,* open Mon, Wed–Thur, Sat 1000–1800; £2. 3 miles north. A highlight is the splendid *potager ornée* (decorative vegetable garden).

Chedworth Roman Villa (NT), *Yanworth; tel: (01242) 890256,* open Tues–Sun, public holidays 1000–1730 (Mar–Oct); Wed–Sun 1100–1600 (Nov); £2.60. 10 miles north. Built for a wealthy landowner, there are remains of two bath houses and some fine mosaics.

Cotswold Water Park, *Keynes Country Park, Shornecote; tel: (01285) 861459,* covers 30 square miles of countryside to the south of Cirencester. It encompasses over 100 man-made lakes, with many water- and land-based activities.

CHELTENHAM

TIC: *77 Promenade, Cheltenham, Glos GL50 1PP; tel: (01242) 522878/264136,* open Mon–Fri 0930–1800, Sat 0930–1715, Sun 0930–1330 (July–Aug); Mon–Sat 0930–1715 (Oct–June); public holidays 0930–1330. Services offered: local bed-booking and BABA (10% refundable deposit taken for both – or £2.50 for BABA), guided tours booked. Tickets sold for theatre, events and coach tours; membership sold for YHA/HI. *Cheltenham Spa, Centre for the Cotswolds* (50p) includes an accommodation listing. Out of hours, there's a touch-screen information system in the window of Waterstone's – opposite the TIC.

GETTING AROUND

Most attractions are within walking distance of the centre. The TIC has free town and transport maps.

Cheltenham and Gloucester local buses operate from **Royal Well Bus Station**, *off Royal Well Rd; tel: (01242) 511655.* The service is good in the town centre and to some villages, but reduced after 1800. **Shopmobility**; *tel: (01242) 255333.* There are **taxi** ranks on *High St, Royal Well Rd* and *The Promenade* – or *tel: (01242) 580580/242777.*

STAYING IN CHELTENHAM

Accommodation and Food

Accommodation is plentiful, with a particularly wide choice of smaller hotels, guesthouses and b&bs. It is generally easy to book on arrival, except during the Cheltenham Gold Cup (Mar). Hotel chains include *BW, FH* and *Th.*

Cotswold Grange Hotel, *Pittville*

111

Circus Rd, Cheltenham GL52 2QH; tel: (01242) 515119; fax: (01242) 241537. Near the town centre, the hotel has 25 air-conditioned rooms. Budget–moderate.

YMCA, *Victoria Walk; tel: (01242) 524024*, in the town centre. Nearest campsites are: **Cheltenham Caravan Clubsite**, *Cheltenham Racecourse, Prestbury Park; tel: (01241) 523102*, 1 mile north, and **Beggars Roost Caravan and Camping Park**, *Bamfurlong Lane, Staverton; tel: (01452) 712705*, 1½ miles north.

There is a very good range of eateries, including several gourmet restaurants. Many of the upmarket places are located in the Montpellier area.

Communications

The main **post office**, *High St*, is open Mon–Fri 0900–1700, Sat 0900–1300.

ENTERTAINMENT AND EVENTS

The TIC can provide free events listings, including the *Cheltenham and Gloucester Bulletin*. The main theatre is **Everyman Theatre**, *Regent St; tel: (01242) 572573*. For concerts and other entertainment, the main venue is the **Town Hall and Pittville Pump Room**, *Imperial Sq.; tel: (01242) 227979*. Some restaurants regularly have live music.

For spectator sports, there is horse-racing at **Cheltenham Racecourse**, *Prestbury; tel: (01242) 513014*. 1 mile north. Every March it hosts one of England's most prestigious race meetings, the **Cheltenham Gold Cup** (National Hunt Festival). The **Festival of Music** (July) and the **Festival of Literature** (Oct) are other major annual events, both staged at various venues in the centre.

SHOPPING

Cheltenham has a few very good shopping areas: *The Promenade, Regent Arcade* (with

its interesting Fishing Wish Clock), *Regent St, High St, Beechwood Place* and, particularly, the areas of Montpellier and Suffolk, where there are many antiques shops.

SIGHTSEEING

For **guided walks**, contact the TIC, which also has details of **bus excursions** around the **Cotswolds.**

Cheltenham developed as a fashionable spa in the 18th century and is exceptionally elegant, with many fine Regency buildings laid out in spacious crescents, squares and terraces, all built of attractive golden Cotswold stone. For such a well-preserved place, it is surprisingly free of tourist trappings. If time is short, head for the *Promenade* and *Montpellier Walk*.

The renowned spa waters may be sampled at the town hall or at the **Pittville Pump Room Museum**, *Pittville Park; tel: (01242) 523852*, open Wed–Mon 1000–1420, Sun, public holidays 1100–1420 (June–Sept); £1. 1½ miles north. This is perhaps Cheltenham's finest building, with its Greek revival colonnade and dome. It now houses a museum of costume and jewellery, with fashions ranging from Regency to art nouveau.

Cheltenham Art Gallery and Museum, *Clarence St; tel: (01242) 237431*, open Mon–Sat 1000–1720; closed public holidays; free, has a good arts and crafts collection, as well as displays covering Cheltenham's history.

Holst Birthplace Museum, *4 Clarence Rd; tel: (01242) 524846*, open Tues–Sat 1000–1620; closed public holidays; free. Located in the Regency house where the composer of *The Planets* was born in 1874, the museum explores his life and music. It has been well restored to reveal the workings of domestic life from Regency to Edwardian times.

At Cheltenham's prestigious racecourse,

the **Hall of Fame**, *tel: (01242) 513014*, is open Mon–Fri 0900–1700 (all year); free except on race days. It recounts the history of steeplechasing.

OUT OF TOWN

Sudeley Castle and Gardens, *Winchcombe; tel: (01242) 604357*, open daily 1100–1700 (Apr–Oct); £5.50. 8 miles north-east. Chief among local attractions is this charming inspiration for P. G. Wodehouse's fictional castle Blandings, in real life the home of Queen Katherine Parr, after the death of Henry VIII.

Hailes Abbey (EH), *Hailes, near Winchcombe; tel: (01242) 602398*, open daily 1000–1800/dusk (Apr–Oct); Sat–Sun 1000–1300 and 1400–dusk (Nov–Mar); £2.40. 10 miles north-east. The graceful ruin is situated in a peaceful woodland setting and there are some fine medieval sculptures in its museum.

TEWKESBURY

TIC: *The Museum, 64 Barton St, Tewkesbury, Glos GL20 5PX; tel: (01684) 295027/272277*, open Mon–Sat 0900–1700 (all year); Sun, public holidays 1000–1600 (Easter–Sept). SHS services offered; local bed-booking and BABA. *Visitor Guide to Tewkesbury and Winchcombe* is free and includes an accommodation listing.

GETTING AROUND

Most of Tewkesbury's attractions are within walking distance of the centre. A street map (90p) and a free bus route map are available from the TIC. There are various companies operating local services, including: **Swanbrook Coaches**, *tel: (01242) 574444*; **Cheltenham and District**, *tel: (01242) 522021*; **Midland Red West**, *tel: (01905) 763888*; and **Boomerang Bus Company**, *tel: (01684) 292108*. **Tewkesbury Town**

Taxis, *tel: (01684) 294122*, operate from High St. Other taxi companies include: **Abbey Taxis**, *tel: (01684) 292028*; and **Avonside Taxis**, *tel: (01684) 293916*.

ACCOMMODATION

There is a choice of hotels and b&bs in the town as well as a range of guesthouse and b&b establishments in the surrounding villages. It is generally easy to book on arrival, except during the Cheltenham Gold Cup (Mar). The only chain is *Mo.*

Royal Hop Pole Hotel, *Church St, Tewkesbury GL20 5RT; tel: (01684) 293236; fax: (01684) 296680*. Mentioned in Charles Dickens' *Pickwick Papers*, the 29-room hotel has a charming riverside garden. Moderate.

Bell Hotel, *52 Church St, Tewkesbury GL20 5SA; tel: (01684) 293293; fax: (01684) 295937*. Standing opposite Tewkesbury Abbey, the timber-fronted building dates from 1696 and has 25 rooms. Moderate.

There are a number of **campsites** around Tewkesbury; ask for details at the TIC. The closest is in the town itself: **Abbey Caravan Club Site**, *Gander Lane; tel: (01684) 294035*.

SIGHTSEEING

Guided town walks in the summer are run by **Cotswold and Gloucestershire Tourist Guides**, *tel: (01242) 226554*; £1.50. The TIC has *Tewkesbury's Alleyways* and the *Battle Trail Walk* leaflets (20p), for themed walks around the town. For **boat trips** on the Severn and Avon (£3.50, from Tolsey Quay), contact **The Pride of Avon**, *tel: (01684) 275906*. The TIC has **bus tours** of the surrounding area, including the **Cotswolds** and the **Forest of Dean**; £7.50.

This attractive town lies at the confluence of the rivers Severn and Avon, on the

113

very edge of the Cotswolds. The main attraction is **Tewkesbury Abbey**, *Church St; tel: (01684) 850959,* open Mon–Sat 0730–1700/1730, Sun 0730–1800; donations. As one of the largest abbey churches to survive Henry VIII's Dissolution, it is one of the country's finest examples of Romanesque architecture.

Tewkesbury was the site of an important battle during the Wars of the Roses: **Tewkesbury Town Museum**, *64 Barton St; tel: (01684) 295027,* open daily 1000–1300 and 1400–1630 (Easter–Oct); 50p, has models of both town and battle.

John Moore Museum, *Church St; tel: (01684) 297174,* open Tues–Sat, some Sun, public holidays 1000–1300 and 1400–1700 (Apr–Oct); £1. Housed in a 15th-century timber-framed building, this natural history collection is aimed at children.

LEDBURY

TIC: *3 The Homend, Ledbury, Herefordshire HR8 1BN; tel: (01531) 636147,* open daily 1000–1700 (Apr–Oct); Mon–Sat 1000–1700 (Nov–Mar). DP SHS services offered; local bed-booking (latest booking 1645) and BABA (latest booking 1630). *Ledbury Town Guide* costs £1; an accommodation listing is free.

GETTING AROUND

The TIC can provide free town and transport maps. Most buses run from the Market House or The Memorial (*High St*). Daytime services are good within Ledbury and to many nearby towns, but stop at 2000 and there are no Sun services. For **bus enquiries**, *tel: (0345) 125436.* For **taxis**, ring: **Ledbury Taxis**, *tel: (01531) 633596*; **M. Powell**, *tel: (01531) 635249*; **Merediths**, *tel: (01531) 632852*; **R. Wadley**, *tel: (01531) 635574*; or **Venture**, *tel: (01531) 633822.*

ACCOMMODATION

There is a small range of hotels, and a wider choice of guesthouses and b&bs. A few pubs in the centre let out rooms. It is advisable to book ahead at weekends and holiday times. The closest **campsites** are **Keepers Cottage**, *Falcon Lane; tel: (01531) 670269,* 1½ miles south-west, and **Eastnor Deer Park**, *Eastnor; tel: (01531) 632302,* 2½ miles east.

SIGHTSEEING

Guided walks start from the timbered **Market House** (1650), *High St; tel: (01531) 634229*; £2.50.

A small market town of great charm, Ledbury has many well-preserved timbered houses. Cobbled Church Lane, often used as a film set, is particularly picturesque; it leads to the large Norman and Perpendicular **Church of St Michael and All Angels**, open 1000–1800 (May–Sept); free. In winter, ask the TIC. This has an unusual detached tower. **The Painted Room**, *Council Offices, Church Lane,* is so named after a series of 16th-century frescos and can be visited (free) when staff are there: Mon–Fri 1100–1400. If you want a guide, an appointment is necessary.

OUT OF TOWN

National Birds of Prey Centre, *nr Newent; tel: (01531) 820286,* open daily 1030–1730 (Feb–Nov); £4.50. 10 miles south. More than 200 birds of about 80 species live at the centre – and many breed, so there are often fledglings to admire. Eagles, owls, vultures, hawks, buzzards and falcons are among the species flying free at daily demonstrations.

Eastnor Castle, *Eastnor; tel: (01531) 633160,* open Sun–Fri 1100–1630 (July–Aug); Sun, public holidays 1100–1630 (Easter–June, Sept); £4 (castle and grounds). 2½ miles east (on M438). The splendid Georgian castle has richly decorated interiors and contains tapestries, fine arts, armour and furniture. The surrounding grounds encompass a deer park, arboretum and lake.

GREAT MALVERN

TIC: *21 Church St, Malvern, Worcs WR14 2AA; tel: (01684) 892289*, open daily 1000–1700. DP SHS Services offered: local bed-booking and BABA. *The Malverns*, including an accommodation listing, is free.

GETTING AROUND

Town and transport maps are available free from the TIC. Buses are frequent within the town and every 2 hours to outlying areas – until 1800 (later to Worcester). The main **taxi** rank is outside the **post office**, *Abbey Rd.* Details of registered taxi companies are available from the TIC.

ACCOMMODATION

There are a fair number of hotels, b&bs and guesthouses. Hotel chains include *BW* and *DV*.

Sidney House, *40 Worcester Rd, Great Malvern WR14 4AA; tel: (01684) 574994.* Delightful Georgian guesthouse with spectacular views across the Severn Valley. Budget–moderate.

Mount Pleasant Hotel, *Belle Vue Terrace, Great Malvern WR14 4PZ; tel: (01684) 561837; fax: (01684) 569968.* Set in 60 acres of terraced gardens, the Georgian building has an orangery and 14 rooms with all facilities. Moderate.

HI: Hatherley, *18 Peachfield Rd, Malvern Wells; tel: (01684) 569131.* The nearest **campsites** are 5–6 miles away.

SIGHTSEEING

The TIC has details of local **bus tours** and **guided walks**.

Great Malvern is the largest of the five towns known as the Malverns, which lie beneath the 9 mile range of the **Malvern Hills**; the hills and countryside around the towns are very popular with walkers. The Malverns developed in the 18th century, after the beneficial effects of the local spring waters were discovered: sample them at **St Ann's Well**. This is a Victorian café open daily 1000–1800 (Easter–Sept); Sat–Sun 1000–1800 (Oct–Easter). It is perched on the side of a 1395 ft hill known as the **Worcestershire Beacon**: reaching it involves a climb of 95 steps from Rose Bank Gardens, *Belle Vue Terrace*, but the views are great.

Great Malvern has many connections with **Sir Edward Elgar**; ask the TIC for a copy of the *Elgar Route* leaflet.

Great Malvern Priory, *Church St; tel: (01684) 561020*, open 0900–1800; free, is a beautiful Norman building with superb 15th-century stained glass. The **Malvern Museum**, *Abbey Rd; tel: (01684) 567811*, open 1030–1700; 80p, traces the town's history.

OUT OF TOWN

There are lovely gardens at **Little Malvern Court**, *Little Malvern; tel: (016984) 892988*, open daily 1415–1630 (mid Apr–mid July); £4 (house and garden). 4 miles south, on A449. Almost adjoining the courthouse (open at the same times; free) is **Little Malvern Priory**, which retains its tower and east end, where some 15th-century stained glass depicts Edward IV and his family.

WORCESTER

TIC: *The Guildhall, High St, Worcester WR1 2EY; tel: (01905) 726311*, open Mon–Sat 1030–1730 (mid Mar–Oct); Mon–Sat 1030–1600 (Nov–mid Mar). DP services offered; local bed-booking and

115

BABA (latest 30 mins before closing). Guided tours booked, YHA/HI membership sold. Tickets sold for day trips, events and entertainment. *The Worcester Visitor*, including an accommodation listing, costs 75p (free by post).

DIAL Worcester: *54 Friary Walk, Crowngate Centre; tel: (01905) 27790,* open Tues–Wed, Fri 0900–1500, Mon, Thur 0900–1300. Disablement Information Advice Line available. *Mini Com: (01905) 22191.*

GETTING AROUND

Most attractions are within walking distance of the centre. A free map is available from the TIC. For **general transport enquiries**, *tel: (0345) 125436.* Most services are operated by **Midland Red West**, *tel: (01905) 763888,* from the **bus station**: *Crowngate, Angel Place.* Services are excellent in town, running until 2330, but less frequent to rural areas. The main **taxi** rank is at The Cross. For details of registered taxi companies, contact the TIC.

STAYING IN WORCESTER

Accommodation

There are a reasonable number of hotels and a good choice of b&bs and guesthouses, with cheaper accommodation mainly outside town. It is generally easy to book on arrival, except during the Three Choirs Festival (Aug 1999). The TIC has details of **campsites**. The closest are: **Ketch Caravan Park**, *Bath Rd, Worcester; tel: (01905) 820430,* 2 miles; **Millhouse**, *Hawford; tel: (01905) 451283,* 3 miles north; and **Lenchford Meadow Park**, *Shrawley; tel: (01905) 620246,* 7 miles north-west.

Eating and Drinking

There is a fair range of eateries, both in the centre and on the outskirts, with a small choice of gourmet restaurants. **King Charles II Restaurant**, *King Charles House, 29 New St*, is situated in a beautiful listed building – the house from which King Charles II escaped his enemies after the Battle of Worcester in 1651.

Communications

The main **post office**, *Foregate St*, opens Mon–Fri 0900–1730, Sat 0900–1230. It has poste restante facilities.

ENTERTAINMENT AND EVENTS

Where and When (a poster displayed around town) is a guide to what is currently on. *Worcester Evening News* (25p) also has entertainment listings.

There are the **Swan Theatre**, *The Moors; tel: (01905) 27322* (for drama), and **Huntingdon Hall**, *Deansway; tel: (01905) 611427* (for live music), as well as five nightclubs, and many pubs and wine bars. **Worcester Races**, *The Racecourse, Pitchcroft; tel: (01905) 25364,* are held throughout the year; the TIC has a fixture list. The **Three Choirs Festival**, *Worcester Cathedral*, takes place every third year in Aug – next time is 1999.

SHOPPING

Worcester is well endowed with pretty, pedestrianised shopping areas, such as *Worcester High St, Crowngate, Crown Passage, Reindeer Court, Friar St* and *The Hopmarket*. The **Royal Worcester Porcelain Factory**, *Severn St*, has bestware and factory-seconds shops.

SIGHTSEEING

Guided walks are run by **Faithful City Guides**, *tel: (01905) 451894,* bookable from the TIC, where they start (£2). Worcester has many connections with the composer **Sir Edward Elgar**; ask for the

Elgar Route leaflet. In summer there are 45 min **river trips** on the Severn, operated by **Bickerline**, *South Quay; tel: (01531) 67067, 1100– 1700 (Mar–Nov); £3.*

The town is dominated by the outline of the graceful **Worcester Cathedral**, *College Green; tel: (01905) 28854,* open 0800–1800; donation. The 14th-century tower is not the only attraction; notable inside are the beautiful 11th-century crypt and a number of fine monuments including King John's tomb, with its Purbeck marble effigy.

Worcester's old buildings can easily be seen on foot: they include **Greyfriars** (NT), *Friar St; tel: (01905) 23571,* open Wed–Thur, public holidays 1400–1730 (Apr–Oct); £2.20, a well-restored, half-timbered Franciscan friary of 1480, with a peaceful garden; the 14th-century **Edgar Tower**, *College Precinct*; **King Charles House** (1577), *New St* (it now houses a restaurant); and the ornate **Guildhall** (1722), *High St; tel: (01905) 723471,* open Mon–Sat 0900–1700; free.

Worcester was strongly Royalist during the 17th-century civil wars; the story of that conflict, focusing on Charles' defeat at Worcester in 1651, is traced at **The Commandery, Civil War Centre**, *Sidbury; tel: (01905) 355071,* open Mon–Sat (1000–1700), Sun 1330–1730; £3.40. This is housed in a building that was the Royalist headquarters and is now the setting for frequent events, including garden parties and ghost tours.

The town is famous for its distinctive, brilliantly coloured porcelain. Learn all about this and watch some of the production at the **Royal Worcester Porcelain Factory**, *Severn St; tel: (01905) 23221;* tours Mon–Fri from 1025 (except public holidays and factory holidays); £4.95. Then see the world's best collection in the adjacent **Museum of Worcester Porcelain**, open Mon–Fri 0930–1700, Sat 1000–1700; £1.75 (but covered by the factory tour ticket).

The **Museum of Local Life**, *Tudor House, Friar St; tel: (01905) 722349,* open Mon–Wed, Fri–Sat 1030–1700; £1.50, explores Worcester's social history over the past 200 years. **City Museum and Art Gallery**, *Foregate St; tel: (01905) 25371,* open Mon–Wed, Fri 0930–1800, Sat 0930–1700; free. A continuous programme of art exhibitions, a gallery about the River Severn and a 19th-century chemist's shop are among the attractions.

OUT OF TOWN

Elgar's Birthplace Museum, *Crown East Lane, Lower Broadheath; tel: (01905) 333224,* open Thur–Tues 1030–1800 (May–Sept); 1330–1630 (Oct–mid Jan, mid Feb–Apr); £3. 3 miles west. The museum houses a collection of musical scores, photos and memorabilia, in the cottage where this quintessentially English composer was born in 1857.

Spetchley Park Gardens, *Spetchley Park; tel: (01905) 345224/345213,* open Tues–Fri, public holidays 1100–1700, Sun 1400–1700 (Apr–Sept); £2.70. 3 miles east. Thirty acres of gardens, with rare trees, shrubs and plants, incorporate a park with red and fallow deer.

Witley Court (EH), *Great Witley; tel: (01299) 896636,* open daily 1000–1800/dusk (Easter–Oct); Wed–Sun 1000– 1600 (Nov–Easter); £2.75. 10 miles north-west of town. The shell of the vast Victorian Italianate mansion, with John Adam interiors, is redolent with the atmosphere of high-society house parties and noted for its Poseidon and Flora fountains; the equally lavish **parish church** nearby was Witley Court's private chapel and has a remarkable 18th-century baroque interior.

117

CAMBRIDGE

Settlers have been attracted to this fenland site since prehistoric times, but Cambridge's fame rests with its university, reputedly founded in 1209 by a handful of rebel scholars from Oxford. The colleges, many of which back on to the River Cam, are the town's chief architectural glory. Together with many other fine buildings, they are best explored at a leisurely pace to savour the atmosphere of a town which has nurtured countless great scientists, philosophers and poets.

TOURIST INFORMATION

TIC: *Wheeler St, Cambridge CB2 3QB; tel: (01223) 322640*, open Mon–Fri 0900–1800/1900, Sat 0900–1700, Sun, public holidays 1030–1730 (Easter–Aug); Mon–Fri 0900–1730/1800, Sat 0900–1700 (Sept–Easter). DP SHS services offered; local bed-booking (latest 30 mins before closing; fee £3 plus 10% of first night), BABA (latest 1 hr before closing; fee £3 plus 10% of first night): be prepared to queue for accommodation, especially on summer afternoons. Guided tours booked, Heritage passes sold. *Cambridge Official Guide* (including accommodation list) is £3.95, *Where to Stay In and Around Cambridge* is 50p.

Guide Friday, *Station Forecourt; tel: (01223) 362444*, offer an accommodation-finding service (commission charged) 0930–1700.

ARRIVING AND DEPARTING

M11 forms the major route from London to Cambridge, with A10 as an alternative.

A45 provides links to the east and west, and the city is encircled by a ring road which gives good access to and from the centre. Parking becomes sparser as you approach the centre.

GETTING AROUND

Most attractions are within a walkable area. Town and transport maps are available at a small charge from the TIC.

Public transport information, *tel: (01223) 317740*. There's a free city centre shuttle (Mon–Sat, except public holidays) and transport is generally quite good in the centre, but very patchy to outlying areas. The main **taxi** rank is on *St Andrew's St*, by St Andrew's Church.

STAYING IN CAMBRIDGE

Accommodation and Food

There is a small range of hotels and a larger choice of guesthouses and b&bs, with cheaper places 2–3 miles from the centre. It is always advisable to book in advance, fairly essential June–Sept. Availability is affected by the Cambridge Folk Festival (July), races at Newmarket (throughout the summer) and Mildenhall Air Show (May). Hotel chains in Cambridge include *BW, DV, FP, Hd* and *MH*. Accommodation is not available in the university.

HI: *97 Tenison Rd; tel: (01223) 354601*. **YMCA**: *Gonville Pl.; tel: (01223) 356998*. The nearest **campsite** is **Highfield Farm Camping Park**, *Highfield Farm, Long Rd, Comberton; tel: (01223) 262308*, 4 miles west.

There is a good selection of restaurants

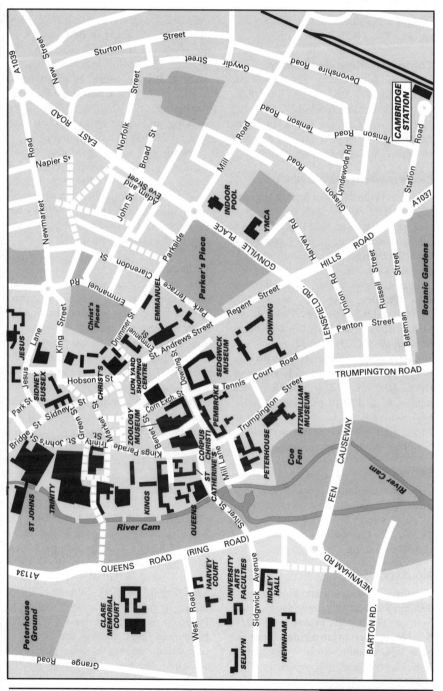

of many nationalities, to suit all tastes and pockets. The TIC has a list for 50p.

Communications and Money

The main **post office**, *St Andrew's St*, opens Mon–Fri 0900–1730, Sat 0900–1900. Poste restante facilities.

There are **Thomas Cook bureaux de change** at *Midland Bank, 32 Market Hill* and *138 Shaftesbury Avenue*.

Events and entertainment lists are available from the TIC. *Summer in the City* covers in some detail what's on July–Sept. The main entertainment venue is the **Cambridge Corn Exchange**, *Wheeler St; tel: (01223) 357851*, a combined concert hall, theatre, cinema and pop venue. Other theatres: **Arts Theatre**, *Peas Hill; tel: (01223) 352000*; **ADC Theatre**, *Park St; tel: (01223) 504444*; and **Mumford Theatre**, *East Rd; tel: (01223) 352932*.

Events of special note are: **Cambridge Folk Festival** (last weekend July), *Cherry Hinton Hall; tel: (01223) 463346*, 3 miles south-east, and **Bumps Races** (June–July); on the River Cam: rowing races in which each boat has to bump those in front to improve its league position.

The main areas for shopping are *Lion Yard* and *Grafton* centres, *Rose Crescent, Trinity St, King's Parade, St John's St* and *Green St*. There is also **Cambridge market**, *Market Hill*, Mon–Sat, for general goods.

Various sightseeing tours provide an excellent introduction to Cambridge – details from the TIC. **Guide Friday**, *tel: (01223) 362444*, operate a **Cambridge Tour** on open-topped double-decker buses, starting from Cambridge station. A ticket (£7) is

valid all day, and you can get on/off at any of the stops. A variety of **BBG walks**, of the town and colleges, is offered by the TIC; £5.75 – book at least half an hour in advance. **Private tours** can be arranged, *tel: (01223) 457574*. **Cambridge Punting Company**, *tel: (01223) 327280*, offer **walking and punting tours**: 2 hrs, half walking and half chauffeur-punting.

Punting is a very good way to see Cambridge. Punts, rowing boats and canoes can be hired (Easter–early Oct): from *Mill Lane* (for the Backs or upriver to Grantchester); or from *Quayside* (only for the Backs). Details of chauffeur-punt companies are available from the TIC.

Colleges

The university is made up of about 30 colleges, scattered around the town. Visitors are usually welcome to wander freely (but quietly!) through the courts, to visit the chapels and, in some cases, halls and libraries. Most colleges open roughly 0930–1630 and in some cases an admission fee is charged, but there's no extra charge for attractions within the college. Access is generally restricted during examination time (mid Apr–late June).

A good place to start is along the **Backs**, the area between *Queens Rd* and the west bank of the River Cam, where there are classic views of some of the most beautiful colleges. Unmissable is **King's College** (£2.50), founded by Henry VI. Royal patronage is reflected in the splendour of **King's College Chapel**, open Mon–Sat 0930–1630, Sun 1000–1700 (out of term); Mon 0930–1630, Tues–Sat 0930–1515/1530, Sun 1315–1415 (during term). This is arguably the finest Perpendicular (15th-century Gothic) building in England and its fan vaulting is magnificent. Among its other glories are Rubens' *Adoration of the Magi* (1639), hanging behind the altar, and the brilliantly coloured 16th-century narrative stained-glass windows.

Picturesque **Queens' College** (£1), founded by not one queen but two, is unusual for its half-timbered 16th-century **President's Lodge** and the **Mathematical Bridge** over the Cam. This wooden bridge was built in 1749, on mathematical principles – without the aid of a single nail; curious Victorians who dismantled it had to resort to bolts to hold it together again. Beautifully proportioned **Clare College** (£1.50) has notable gardens across its elegant bridge, the oldest surviving in the city.

Trinity College (£1.50) boasts a 2-acre **Great Court**, claimed to be the largest university court in the world; apparently this is where Sir Isaac Newton first measured the speed of sound. Trinity's magnificent **Library**, designed by Christopher Wren, is open to the public.

Beyond Trinity lies **St John's** (£1.50), which has a beautiful Tudor gatehouse. Its enclosed river bridge is known as the **Bridge of Sighs**, modelled on the famous Venetian bridge. Within St John's garden and across the river lies the 12th-century **School of Pythagoras**, the oldest house in Cambridge.

Further north, and around the river bend, is **Jesus College** (free), which has many medieval buildings and spacious, secluded grounds.

Away from the river, highlights among the other (free) colleges include **Corpus Christi**, which has the best surviving early medieval court; the chapel at **Pembroke**, which was Wren's first building; **Emmanuel chapel**, also by Wren, which contains a plaque to former student John Harvard who, after sailing on the *Mayflower*, founded another great university; and **Pepys' Library** at **Magdalene**, where

the diarist's collection, as well as his shorthand manuscripts, is displayed.

Other Attractions

The **Round Church**, *Round Church St*; free, is one of only four circular churches surviving in England. Built in 1130, it was based on the shape of the Holy Sepulchre in Jerusalem. Tiny **St Bene't**, *Bene't St*, is one of Britain's earliest surviving Saxon churches and the oldest church in the county; free. There are panoramic views from **Great St Mary's Church**, *King's Parade*; *tel: (01223) 350914*, open Mon–Sat 1000–1700, Sun 1300–1700; £1.50 for the tower, otherwise free.

The **Fitzwilliam Museum**, *Trumpington St*; *tel: (01223) 332900*, open Tues–Sat 1000–1700, Sun, public holidays 1415–1700; free. Housed in a grandiose 19th-century edifice, its outstanding collections include Canaletto, Rembrandt, Turner, Titian and French Impressionists; Egyptian, Greek and Roman antiquities; and medieval illuminated manuscripts, ivories, miniatures, carvings and armour.

Scott Polar Research Institute, *Lensfield Rd; tel: (01223) 336540/337733*, open Mon–Sat 1430–1600; free. Museum of polar life and exploration, including Eskimo and Lapp arts. Reopens mid 1998.

Other Museums and Galleries

Folk Museum, *Castle St; tel: (01223) 355159*, open Mon–Sat 1030–1700, Sun 1400–1700 (Apr–Sept); closed Mon (Oct–Mar); £1. An eclectic array of Cambridgeshire artefacts. **Museum of Zoology**, *Free School Lane; tel: (01223) 336650*, open Mon–Fri 1415–1645; free. Zoological specimens, encompassing sea creatures, insects and mammals. **Sedgwick Museum**, *Downing St; tel: (01223) 333456*, open Mon–Fri 0900– 1300 and 1400–1700, Sat 1000–1300; free. Extensive geological

121

specimens. **University Museum of Archaeology and Anthropology**, *Downing St; tel: (01223) 333516*, open Mon–Fri 1400–1600, Sat 1000–1230; free. Worldwide prehistoric and modern cultures.

OUT OF TOWN

Anglesey Abbey and Garden (NT), *Lode; tel: (01223) 811200*, house open Wed–Sun, public holidays 1300–1700 (end Mar–mid Oct). Gardens open on the same days 1100–1730, also Mon–Tues (July–Aug); £5.60 (house and gardens), £3.30 (gardens only). On Sun and public holidays, tickets for the house are timed – and you may not get in at all on public holidays. 6 miles north-east. The house, built *c.*1600, has beautiful Georgian-style gardens including an arboretum, statues and a watermill.

Duxford Airfield and Imperial War Museum, *Duxford; tel: (01223) 835000*, open daily 1000–1800 (Easter–Oct); 1000–1600 (Nov–Easter); £6.40. 8 miles south. Home to most of the Imperial War Museum's collection of historic military aircraft and vehicles. Civil aircraft include the prototype Concorde 01.

Nearer at hand, you can walk (or punt) 2 miles along the River Granta from *Silver St* to the little village of **Grantchester**, immortalised in Rupert Brooke's poem, *The Old Vicarage, Grantchester*.

SIDE TRACK FROM CAMBRIDGE

Ely is on A10, 16 miles north-east of Cambridge

ELY

TIC: *Oliver Cromwell's House, 29 St Mary's St, Ely CB7 4HF; tel: (01353) 662062/663653*, open daily 1000–1800 (Apr–Sept); Mon–Sat 1000–1715 (Oct–Mar). DP services; local bed-booking (latest 30 mins before closing),

BABA (latest 1½ hrs before closing). *Discovering East Cambridgeshire, Places to Eat, Visitors' Guide* and an accommodation guide are all free.

ACCOMMODATION

There are few hotels, but many b&b establishments in Ely and the surrounding area, plus a few pubs with rooms. It is usually easy to book on arrival, except during the Mildenhall Air Show (May). Hotel chains include *Ct*. The nearest **campsite** is **Two Acres Caravan and Camp Site**, *Ely Rd, Little Thetford; tel: (01353) 648870*, 2 miles south.

SIGHTSEEING

Surrounded by flat East Anglian landscape, Ely was effectively an island until the fens were drained in the 17th and 18th centuries. There are many attractive buildings and the small town is dominated by its wonderful cathedral. The octagonal 14th-century lantern tower is a miracle of medieval engineering, while the Lady Chapel (1321) is breathtakingly beautiful. **Ely Cathedral**; *tel: (01353) 667735*, open daily 0700–1900 (summer: i.e. BST); Mon–Sat 0730–1830, Sun 0730–1700 (winter: GMT); subject to services; £3 (including guided tour). The adjacent **Stained Glass Museum**; *tel: (01353) 667735*, open Mon–Fri 1030–1630, Sat 1030–1730, Sun 1200–1800; £2.50, gives an insight into how stained-glass windows are designed and made.

Oliver Cromwell's House (address and hours as the TIC); £2.30, dates from the 13th century.

The history of the Isle of Ely, from the Ice Age to World War II, is covered by the **Ely Museum**, *Market St; tel: (01353) 666655*, open Tues–Sun, public holidays 1030–1600; £1.80. ▣

122

CAMBRIDGE–LINCOLN

From scholarly Cambridge to ecclesiastical Lincoln, this route links towns and villages which have witnessed the ebb and flow of English history for centuries. This is Big Sky country, with the wide acres of Cambridgeshire giving way to broad-leafed woodland, grandly rolling vistas and some surprisingly steep hills – to dispel the widely held British belief that the whole of Lincolnshire is as flat as a pancake.

Lincoln

A15

A607

Grantham   30

A1

20

Stamford   123

10

A1

Peterborough

DIRECT ROUTE: 100 MILES

A1   20

A1   **Huntingdon**

20

A14

M11

Cambridge

ROUTE

This 100-mile journey takes 2hrs 30mins. From central Cambridge follow A1303 west for 2miles, joining M11 north at Junction13. After a further 2miles follow A14 north for 17miles to **Huntingdon**. Leave Huntingdon on A14, joining A1 north in 5miles. A further 12miles turn right on to A1139 and follow the signs to **Peterborough** city centre. From Peterborough, follow A47 west for 7miles back to A1 and travel north to reach **Stamford** via A43 after a further 7 miles. **Grantham**, 20 miles to the north of Stamford, is accessed via A52.

Leave Grantham on A52 north and turn right on to A607 which continues north through villages and countryside reminiscent of The Cotswolds to join A15 at Bracebridge Heath after 11 miles. From here Lincoln is reached in just over 3 miles.

HUNTINGDON

TIC: *The Library, Princes St, Huntingdon PE18 6PH; tel: (01480) 425831*, open Mon–Fri 0930–1730, Sat 0900–1630 year round except public holidays. Usual services, including BABA.

ACCOMMODATION

Old Bridge Hotel, *1 High St, Huntingdon PE18 6TQ; tel: (01480) 452681; fax: (01480) 411017*. The Terrace, where guests can eat informally in the riverside hotel, has a mural occupying all its walls. There is also a non-smoking restaurant. There are nearly 30 well-equipped rooms of varying sizes in the 18th-century creeper-clad property. Moderate–expensive.

The George, *George St, Huntingdon PE18 6AB; tel: (01480) 432444; fax: (01480) 453130*. Approached from the ring road – the property faces the pedestrianised *High St* – the George has some non-smoking bedrooms. Moderate.

Park Lane Caravan Park, *Park Lane, Godmanchester PE18 8AF; tel/fax: (01480) 453740*, open mid Mar–Oct. The park has 50 touring pitches with electrical hook-ups. Amenities include hot showers, laundry and play area.

SIGHTSEEING

Before the re-shuffle of county boundaries in 1974, Huntingdon was the county town of the former small rural county of Huntingdonshire. Now it is in Cambridgeshire and has grown, but retains its character and many of its fine old buildings.

Still a busy market town – markets are held on Wed and Sat – Huntingdon originated around a crossing on the River Great Ouse. Its importance and prosperity increased in the 18th century when roads improved and it became a staging post for coaches travelling along the Great North Road. The George (see 'Accommodation' above), a former coaching inn, is still a popular local rendezvous.

Huntingdon's most famous son was Oliver Cromwell, whose family home was **Hinchingbrooke House**, now a school but open to the public on summer Sunday afternoons. Another local political figure served as Prime Minister in the 1990s, Huntingdon being John Major's parliamentary constituency.

The town's great asset is the river, crossed by a 14th-century stone bridge which separates Huntingdon from Godmanchester. Day boats may be hired from the **Bridge Boatyard** (Huntingdon Marine Leisure Ltd); *tel: (01480) 413517*.

Cromwell Museum, *Grammar School Walk, Huntingdon; tel: (01480) 425830*. The former schoolroom where Cromwell, Lord Protector and effective ruler of England 1653–58 (and, later, diarist Samuel Pepys) were educated, claims the most comprehensive collection of Cromwell documents and personal items in the country. Admission charge, opening times vary widely throughout the year, closed Mon. Phone for details.

PETERBOROUGH

TIC: *45 Bridge St, Peterborough PE1 1HA; (01733) 452336*, open Mon–Fri 0900–1700; public holidays, Sat 1000–1600.

Services offered: local bed-booking and BABA, tours booked. *Where to Stay in Peterborough* and *Greater Peterborough Visitors Guide* are free.

ACCOMMODATION

Bull Hotel, *Westgate, Peterborough PE1 1RB; tel: (01733) 561364; fax: (01733) 557304.* A busy 18th-century city centre establishment with comfortable en suite rooms. Moderate.

Orton Hall Hotel, *Orton Longueville, Peterborough PE2 7DN; tel: (01733) 391111; fax: (01733) 557304.* Set in 20 acres of parkland 2½ miles from the city centre, the 17th-century manor has spacious guestrooms, some of which are for non-smokers. Moderate.

Swallow Hotel, *Peterborough Business Park, Lynchwood, Alwalton PE2 6GB; tel: (01733) 371111; fax: (01733) 236725.* The modern four-star hotel opposite the East of England Showground has 163 rooms, more than half of which are non-smoking. The hotel is 3½ miles from Peterborough city centre. Moderate–expensive.

SIGHTSEEING

The magnificent **Peterborough Cathedral**, *Minster Precincts; tel: (01733) 343342* is well worth a visit, open Mon–Sat 0830–1715/1745, Sun 1200–1715/1745; free, but £2 donation requested. Begun in 1118, the church was given the status of cathedral by Henry VIII in 1541. Katherine of Aragon, Henry's first queen, is buried here and it was the original burial place of Mary, Queen of Scots. Among the cathedral's architectural features are the splendid west front, with its three huge arches, the eastern building (1496–1508), offering exquisite fan vaulting, and the painted nave ceiling (*c.* 1220), unique in England. A visitor centre explains the building's history.

Outside the city centre is an ongoing archaeological excavation, with a recreation of a Bronze Age farm (*c.* 1000 BC). **Flag Fen Excavations**, *Fengate; tel: (01733) 313414*, open daily 1100–1700; £3.50. 2 miles east.

STAMFORD

TIC: *Stamford Arts Centre, 37 St Mary's St, Stamford, Lincolnshire PE9 2DL; tel: (01780) 755611*, open Mon–Sat 0930–1700; public holidays, Sun 1000–1600 (Apr–Sept). DP Services offered: local bed-booking and BABA (latest 15 mins before closing), tours booked. An accommodation list is available free.

GETTING AROUND

Apart from Burghley House, the town's attractions are within easy walking distance of the centre. Free town and transport maps are available from the TIC. **General transport enquiries**, *tel: (01522) 553135.* Most services operate from *Sheepmarket*.

Taxis often wait on *Red Lion Sq.*, or you can contact: **Direct Line**, *tel: (01780) 481481*; **Merritt**, *tel: (01781) 766155*, or **Star Taxis**, *tel: (01780) 762345.*

ACCOMMODATION

There is a very small range of hotels, but a good number of guesthouses, pubs with rooms and b&bs. Cheaper accommodation can be found in both the centre and the suburbs. It is generally easy to book on arrival, except during the Burghley Horse Trials (late Aug–mid Sept) and public holidays weekends. The only chain represented is *BW*.

Garden House Hotel, *St Martin's, Stamford, PE9 2LP; tel: (01780) 763359; fax: (01780) 763339.* The family-run 18th-century town house hotel has 20 prettily presented en suite rooms. Good

125

dining with fresh produce is offered. Moderate.

The George Hotel, *71 St Martin's, Stamford PE9 2LB; tel: (01780) 555171; fax: (01780) 557070.* This 400 year old former coaching inn has a warren of rooms, with much oak panelling, the Garden Lounge for breakfast and casual dining and a more formal restaurant where the jacket and tie dress code applies. There are nearly 50 ensuite guestrooms. Expensive.

Birch House, *4 Lonsdale Rd, Stamford PE9 2RW; tel: (01780) 754876.* Non-smoking b&b in comfortable home 10 mins walk from the town centre. Budget.

HI: *16 High St, Thurlby, Bourne; tel: (01778) 425588.* The closest **campsite** is **Road End Farm**, *Great Casterton; tel: (01780) 763417,* 1 mile north.

SIGHTSEEING

BBG walks of the town start from the TIC Sat–Sun (May–Sept); approx. £2.50. Stamford is generally regarded as the finest stone-built town in England, its wealth of medieval and Georgian buildings forming an extraordinarily unspoilt whole. In 1967 it was declared a conservation area and there are delights around every corner. Highlights include five medieval churches, including the Perpendicular **St Martin's**, *High St; tel: (01780) 751233;* free, but not always open, so ring to check. The church dates from 1430 and contains the tombs of the Cecil family.

Browne's Hospital, *Broad St; tel: (01780) 751226,* open Sat–Sun 1100–1600 (May–Sept); £1.50, is one of the finest surviving medieval almshouses in England, founded in 1483 and still in use. The hospital contains medieval stained glass (in the chapel and audit room) and also a museum about almshouse life.

Stamford Steam Brewery Museum,

All Saints St; tel: (01780) 752186, open Wed–Fri 1000–1600, Sat, Sun 1000–1800 (Apr–mid-Oct); £1.20. The brewery was established in 1825 and remained in business until 1974. It now displays the 19th-century equipment.

Stamford Museum, *Broad St; tel: (01780) 766317,* open Mon–Sat 1000–1700 (all year); Sun 1400–1700 (May–Sept); free. Unusual exhibits in this museum, which interprets the town's history, are life-size models of General Tom Thumb and England's largest man.

You do not have to leave Stamford to visit the magnificent **Burghley House and Park**; *tel: (01780) 752451,* house open daily 1100–1700 (Easter–Sept); £5.60. 1 mile south-east of the centre. Burghley is the vast palace built by Elizabeth I's chief minister, William Cecil, Lord Burghley. The 18 state rooms are crammed with porcelain, paintings and tapestries collected over the centuries. The park was landscaped by Capability Brown and is open all year; free.

The **Burghley Horse Trials**, a major event in the equestrian calendar, are held here every Sept.

OUT OF TOWN

Rutland Water, *Information Centre: Sykes Lane, Empingham, Oakham LE15 8PX; tel: (01572) 653026/027,* open daily Easter–end Sept, variable opening or may be closed winter. Rutland Water open all year. **Cycle Hire Centre**, *tel: (01780) 720888* and **Nature Reserve**, *tel: (01572) 770651,* open all year. **Butterfly Aquatic Centre**, open Easter–end Oct. For opening hours of **water sports**, *tel: (01780) 460464.* Admission charge for car parking £1 weekdays, £2 weekends and public holidays.

Rutland Water, 5 miles from Stamford, covers 3100 acres and was the largest man-made lake in Western Europe when it opened more than 20 years ago. A major recreational area, Rutland Water has 25 miles of cycle tracks, a sailing club and facilities for visitors to launch and sail their own dinghies and rowing boats, trout fishing, birdwatching, botanic and other nature study pursuits, including guided rambles.

GRANTHAM

TIC: *The Guildhall Centre, St Peter's Hill, Grantham, Lincs NG31 6PZ; tel: (01476) 566444,* open Mon–Sat 0930–1700, Sun and public holidays 1000–1500 year-round. BABA and usual services, including accommodation reservations.

ACCOMMODATION

The **Angel & Royal Hotel**, *High St; tel: (01476) 565816; fax: (01476) 567149,* is one of England's finest medieval inns where past guests have included King John, Richard III, Charles I and Edward VIII. It has 30 rooms, some non-smoking. Moderate.

The area also has the **Blue Cow Inn**, *High St, South Witham, Grantham NG33 5QB; tel: (01572) 768432,* an old village stone pub (budget), several other hotels and inns and some warmly welcoming budget-priced b&bs and guesthouses, like the 17th-century **Archway House**, *Swinegate, Grantham NG31 6RJ; tel: (01476) 561807.*

SIGHTSEEING

The pleasant redbrick town, bordered by the River Witham and surrounded by old stone villages is the birthplace (in 1925) of Britain's first woman prime minister, Margaret Thatcher, later Baroness Thatcher. Sir Isaac Newton, the scientist, was born a few miles away at Woolsthorpe in 1642. Both are featured in Grantham

Museum. A monument to Newton, cast in bronze, stands outside the **Guildhall**. The **Guildhall Arts Centre** is a venue for the performing arts. Thursday and Saturday markets are held in the town.

Belton House (NT), *Grantham; tel: (01476) 566116,* open Wed–Sun and public holidays except Good Fri 1100–1730, house open 1300 (Apr–end Oct). Admission charge. Stone mansion with international art treasures. The 1000-acre grounds include landscaped gardens, woodland deer park and children's adventure parkland.

Harlaxton Manor Gardens, *Grantham; tel: (01476) 592131;* open Tues–Sun and public holidays 1100–1700 Apr–Oct. £2.50. Classical European garden styles on seven levels. Woodland nature trail, picnic area and tea room.

Grantham Museum, *St Peter's Hill; tel: (01476) 568783,* open Mon–Sat 1000–1700 year round; admission charge. Grantham was a Royal Manor when the Domesday Book was compiled. The museum's displays reflect the town's long history, with special sections on Sir Isaac Newton and Lady Thatcher, whose family had a grocery shop in the town. The building is still there but in different use.

St Wulfram's Church, dating from the late 13th century, has a 282 ft spire, said to be the sixth highest in England.

OUT OF TOWN

Belvoir Castle, *tel: (01470) 870443,* open Tues–Thur and Sat 1100–1700, Sun and public holidays 1100–1800 Apr–end Sept, also Sun in Oct 1100–1700. £4.50. 7 miles south-west. Priceless paintings and antique furniture, tapestries and porcelain in the splendid castle which has been home to the Dukes of Rutland since the reign of Henry VIII.

CAMBRIDGE-NORWICH

Two of England's finest cities are connected on this route, which provides an opportunity to take in the world-famous horse racing town of Newmarket and ancient Bury St Edmunds, named after a Saxon king. Almost entirely rural, the route also skirts the southern edge of Thetford Forest Park.

Norwich

A11

34

Thetford

DIRECT ROUTE: 65 MILES

A134 13

A11

Direct Route

Scenic Route

A14

A1304

Bury St Edmunds

128

13

A1304 **Newmarket**

A14

Cambridge

A1303 12

A1304 for a further 2 miles to arrive at **Newmarket** just over 12 miles from Cambridge. Continue east on A1304 for 3 miles, then turn right on to A14 which reaches **Bury St Edmunds** in a further 10 miles. From Bury A134 leads to the outskirts of Thetford after 13 miles. From here A11 reaches Norwich after another 34 miles.

ROUTES

DIRECT ROUTE

This 65-mile trip takes 1 hr 20 mins. From Cambridge follow A1303 east for 3½ miles, continue east on A14 for a further 12 miles, then A11 for 48 miles and follow signs to the city centre.

SCENIC ROUTE

Follow the route from Cambridge to the A14, as above, and after 4½ miles follow A1303 east for 2.2 miles, then

Colour section (i): 'Tarka Country', North Devon (p. 104); inset, Cardiff Castle (p. 137). (ii): A view from the Malvern Hills (p. 115) to Hereford; punting by King's College, Cambridge (p. 120). (iii): Albert Dock in Liverpool (p. 155); Blackpool's Promenade (p. 156). (iv): Chatsworth House (p. 164).

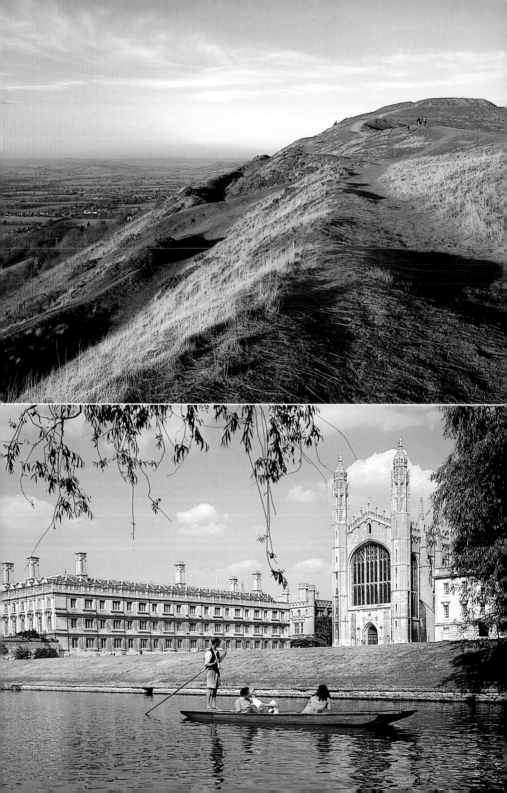

NEWMARKET

TIC: *63 The Rookery, Newmarket, Suffolk CB8 8HT; tel: (01638) 667200,* open Mon–Fri 0900–1700, Sat 1000–1300. DP services offered; local bed-booking and BABA, guided tours booked. Town guide and accommodation listing are free.

GETTING AROUND

With the exception of the National Stud, racecourses and some trainers' yards, attractions are accessible on foot from the centre. Town maps are free from the TIC. **Cambus** is the main operator for local buses, which operate from the **bus station**, *The Rookery*. The main **taxi** rank is on *High St*.

ACCOMMODATION

There is a small range of accommodation, roughly half hotels, half guesthouses/b&bs. It is generally possible to book on arrival, except over spring public holidays, during the Mildenhall Air Show (May) and during race meetings. The only chain is *BW*.

HI: Brandon, *Bury Rd, Brandon; tel: (01842) 812075* – or **Cambridge**. The nearest **campsite** is at **Rowley Mile Racecourse**, *tel: (01638) 663235,* 2 miles south-west of town; no public transport.

SIGHTSEEING

Buildings worth noting in the centre are the **Rutland Arms Hotel**, *Palace St,* and, further along the street, **Nell Gwynne's House**, home of the colourful mistress of Charles II.

Newmarket is world famous for its **horse racing**, and this dominates the attractions of the town, race meetings are at irregular intervals (mid Apr–mid Aug and Oct). Many attractions can be visited only by prior appointment, so it's easiest to take a **guided tour**. One Newmarket guide service, **Hoofbeats**, *66 Old Station*

Rd; tel: (01638) 668455, offers a 'menu', comprising the various attractions and race meetings; prices begin at £10.

Don't miss the **National Horseracing Museum**, *99 High St; tel: (01638) 667333,* open Tues–Sat, public holidays 1000–1700, Sun 1200–1600 (Mar–Oct); also Mon (July–Aug); £3.30. This tells the story of the development of horseracing. The museum also offers **Newmarket Equine Tours**, Mon–Sat 0920 sharp (Mar–Oct); £20 – numbers are limited, so book.

The **National Stud**, *Newmarket; tel: (01638) 666789,* tours (by appointment only) start Mon–Fri 1115 and 1430, Sat 1115, Sun 1430 (Mar–Aug and autumn race days); £3.80. 2 miles south-west of town. This is the home of horse-breeding and visitors are able to meet stallions, mares – and foals, if the timing's right.

For enquiries about horseracing at the **Rowley Mile** and **July racecourses**, contact the TIC – or the Clerk of the Course, *tel: (01638) 663482.*

You can see horses training daily (0600–1230) on **Newmarket Heath**, west of town. Parking off *Moulton Rd*.

OUT OF TOWN

Mildenhall, 10 miles north-east, is a pleasant market town with an ancient church and interesting museum. It becomes a hive of activity every May, when it hosts NATO's largest **Air Show**: call the 24-hr newsline; *tel: (01638) 543341.*

BURY ST EDMUNDS

TIC: *6 Angel Hill, Bury St Edmunds, Suffolk IP33 1UZ; tel: (01284) 764667/ 757083,* open Mon–Sat 0930–1730, Sun 1000–1500, public holidays 1000–1600 (Easter–Oct); Mon–Fri 1000–1600, Sat 1000–1300 (Nov–Easter). Services offered: local bed-booking and BABA (latest

129

30 mins before closing). Membership sold for YHA/HI, NT, Great British Heritage passes, concert tickets, local travel information and bookings. A visitors' information pack is free.

GETTING AROUND

Many of Bury's attractions are in the centre. The TIC can provide free town and transport maps. For local transport enquiries, call **Travel Line**; *tel: (0645) 583358*. Many local bus services terminate at the **bus station**, *St Andrew's St; tel: (01284) 702020*. The main **taxi** rank is on *Cornhill*.

ACCOMMODATION

Bury has a handful of good hotels and a reasonable number of b&b establishments, but it's advisable to pre-book. The TIC has listings for accommodation of all kinds, including campsites. The only chain represented is *BW*.

The nearest **campsites** are **The Dell Touring Park**, *Beyton Rd, Thurston; tel: (01359) 270121*, 3 miles east; **Snuff Box Farm**, *Bradfield Combust; tel: (01284) 828164*, 5 miles south; and **Metcalfe Arms Meadow**, *Lawshall Rd, Hawstead; tel: (01284) 386321*, 5 miles south.

SIGHTSEEING

The cathedral town retains its 12th-century grid street plan, so it's easy to explore on foot. The TIC organises an interesting variety of **guided town walks** – and a Walkman tour of the abbey ruins.

There are some attractive streets and many splendid Georgian buildings, including the **Athenaeum**, *Angel Hill*, where Charles Dickens gave public readings, and the **Theatre Royal** (NT), *Westgate St; tel: (01284) 769505*, open Mon–Fri 1000–2000, Sat 1200–2000 (except during rehearsals/performances); free.

A wonderfully eccentric collection within a rare Norman house is offered by **Moyse's Hall Museum**, *Cornhill; tel: (01284) 757488*, open Mon–Sat 1000–1700, Sun 1400–1700; £1.25.

The town's name comes from a 9th-century martyred Saxon king. On the strength of his shrine, the medieval **Abbey** (EH) became one of the most powerful in England. Its fragmentary but graceful ruins form the centrepiece of the award-winning floral **Abbey Gardens**, open 0900–dusk all year; free. **Abbey Visitor Centre**, *Samson's Tower, West Front; tel: (01284) 763110*, open daily 1000–1700 (Easter–Oct); free. Winter opening is limited, so check. Bizarrely, later houses have been built into the church's west front. Two fine gatehouses remain: the magnificent 14th-century **Abbeygate** and the **Norman Tower** – which forms the belfry of the adjacent 16th-century **St Edmundsbury Cathedral**, *Angel Hill; tel: (01284) 754933*, open daily 0830–2000 (June–Aug); daily 0830–1800 (Sept–May); free.

OUT OF TOWN

West Stow Country Park, *Icklingham Rd, West Stow; tel: (01284) 728718*, open 0800–dusk (all year); free. 6 miles west of Bury. The 125-acre park is rich in wildlife, especially birds (there are two hides). Within the park is a remarkable reconstruction of an **Anglo-Saxon village**, open daily 1000–1700; £3.20. This was built on the excavated site of an actual Anglo-Saxon settlement.

Ickworth House (NT), *Horringer; tel: (01284) 735270*. House open Tues–Wed, Fri–Sun, public holidays 1300–1700 (Easter–Oct); £4.75. 3 miles south-west of Bury. The extraordinary house, with its 100 ft high oval rotunda, boasts a fine art collection, including works by Titian, Gainsborough and Velasquez.

CAMBRIDGE–OXFORD

England's greatest centres of scholarship are linked on this route, which takes in the riverside town of Bedford – where such unlikely bedfellows of fame as John Bunyan and Glenn Miller are commemorated – Woburn Abbey, seat of the Dukes of Bedford, and the historic county town of Buckingham.

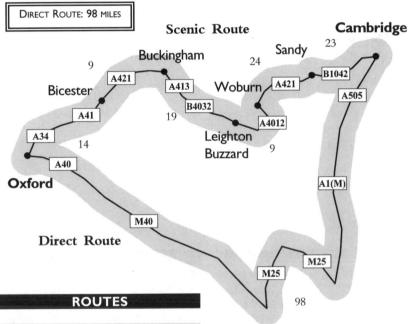

DIRECT ROUTE: 98 MILES

Scenic Route

Cambridge

Buckingham — Sandy — Woburn — Leighton Buzzard — Bicester — A421 — A413 — A4032 — A421 — B1042 — A505 — A4012 — A41 — A34 — A40 — Oxford — A1(M) — M40 — Direct Route — M25 — M25

9 24 23 19 14 9 98

131

ROUTES

DIRECT ROUTE

This 98-mile journey takes 1 hr 50 mins. From central Cambridge follow signs for about 4 miles to A10 and continue west for 9 miles, then follow A505 for 11 miles to Baldock, picking up A1(M) at Junction 9. Continue south on A1(M) for 23 miles then head west on M25 for 15 miles, leaving at Junction 16 to follow M40 west for 30 miles. Leave M40 at Junction 8 and follow A40 for 4 miles and A420 for 2 miles to reach Oxford.

SCENIC ROUTE

About the same distance, but allow an hour extra for the journey. From central Cambridge take A603 south-west for 12 miles, then follow B1042 for a further 11 miles to **Sandy**. Continue on A603 west for 9 miles to **Bedford**. Leave Bedford on A6 north for 2½ miles, then head west on A421 for 9 miles, A507 for 1 mile and A4012 which reaches **Woburn** in a further 2 miles.

A4012 continues south to reach **Leighton Buzzard** in 9 miles. From Leighton Buzzard take B4032 for 11 miles north-west to Winslow, then A413 for 6 miles north and A421 for 2 miles west to **Buckingham**. A421 continues south-west to reach **Bicester** in 9 miles. Follow A41 south-west for 2 miles, then A34 for 12 miles to reach the Oxford ring roadsystem; you can 'Park 'n' Ride' or follow signs for about 2 miles to the city centre.

SANDY

The small town of Sandy, Bedfordshire, is home to the headquarters of the Royal Society for the Protection of Birds. The neighbouring 160-acre nature reserve is open to the public and the reserve has heath, lake and woodland habitats that attract many bird species, including rare ones. There are many trails. Guided nature walks take place on Sun afternoons.

RSPB Nature Reserve, *Sandy, Beds; tel: (01767) 680551*, open daily year round, except Christmas Day and New Year's Day; £2 (RSPB members free).

BEDFORD

TIC: *10 St Paul's Sq., Bedford MK40 1SL; tel: (01234) 215226*, open Mon–Sat 0930–1700, Sun 1100–1500. BABA, local accommodation bookings and usual services.

ACCOMMODATION

County Hotel, *2 St Mary's St, Bedford MK42 0AR; tel: (01234) 799955; fax: (01234) 340447.* A town centre riverside hotel. Moderate.

Embankment Hotel, *Bedford MK40 3PD; tel: (01234) 261332; fax: (01234) 325085*, has a riverside garden. Moderate.

SIGHTSEEING

Bedford is a business and administrative

centre. It is set on the River Great Ouse, beside which are public gardens, and many visitors crossing the river bridge notice the waterside **Swan** pub and stop there for an enjoyable meal.

Bedford's trump card is the **Cecil Higgins Art Gallery and Museum**, *Castle Close; tel: (01234) 211222*, open Tues–Sat and Sun afternoon and public holiday Mondays; free. This large Victorian house contains the works of some of the world's greatest painters.

Another celebrity in Bedford is **Glenn Miller**, the American big band leader who helped keep spirits high in the UK during World War II. His bust in bronze can be seen at the *Corn Exchange, St Paul's Sq.*, from which many of the band's performances were broadcast.

John Bunyan arrived in Bedford in the mid-1660s in his late twenties and became a popular preacher. **John Bunyan Museum**, *Castle St; tel: (01234) 358870*, open Tues–Sat 1400–1600 (Apr–Oct), also mornings July–Aug; admission charge, relates aspects of Bunyan's life.

WOBURN

Woburn Abbey, *tel: (01525) 290666*, open Sat–Sun 1100–1600 (Dec–Easter); Mon–Sat 1100–1600, Sun, public holidays 1100–1700 (Easter–Nov); £7, was remodelled in the 18th century. It contains a magnificent collection of paintings, including works by Velasquez, Rembrandt, Reynolds and a superb sequence of Canalettos – and of 18th-century furniture. One area within the grounds (about a mile from the house) forms Woburn's **Safari Park**; *tel: (01525) 290407*, open Sat–Sun 1100–1500 (Jan–Feb, subject to weather); daily 1000–1700 (Mar–Oct); £9 (including free entry to deer park and reduced entry to abbey). Nine species of deer roam freely within the 3000-acre

Deer Park, open Sat–Sun 1030–1545 (Dec–Easter); daily 1000–1630/1645 (Easter–Nov); £5 per car, 50p per pedestrian/cyclist. There is also a 51-shop **Antiques Centre** at the abbey; tel: (01525) 290350, open daily 1000–1730 (May–Sept), 1100–1630 (Oct–Apr); 20p.

LEIGHTON BUZZARD

The Swan, High St, Leighton Buzzard; tel: (01525) 372148; fax: (01525) 370444, Georgian former coaching inn in the town centre. Moderate.

This small Bedfordshire town on the Grand Union Canal provides a good stopping place for boat crews to replenish supplies. It was once an important railway town.

Leighton Buzzard Railway, Billington Rd (off A4146); tel: (01525) 373888, open Sun and public holidays only (Easter– Sept), also Wed, Thur, Sat in Aug, Wed in June and July and weekends in Dec; admission charge. About 50 locomotives from different parts of the world are displayed. Steam-hauled trains take passengers 5½ miles into the countryside from Page's Park station. Industrial heritage displays at the Stonehenge Works terminus.

BUCKINGHAM

TIC: Old Gaol Museum, Market Hill, Buckingham MK18 1EW; tel: (01280) 823020, open Mon–Sat 1000–1600; to 1700 and Sun 1400–1700 (July–Aug). Services offered: BABA, National Express and some theatre bookings.

ACCOMMODATION

Buckingham Lodge, Ring Rd South, Buckingham MK18 1RY; tel: (01280) 822622; fax: (01280) 823074. Seventy ensuite rooms and indoor pool. Moderate.

SIGHTSEEING

Buckingham is less important than it once was, now lying in the shadow of Milton Keynes, but it retains a wealth of Georgian buildings.

Stowe Landscape Gardens (NT), 3 miles north-west of Buckingham; tel: (01280) 822850, opening times of house and gardens are different and vary greatly – telephone for details; gardens £4.20, house £2. Capability Brown, Vanbrugh, Kent and Gibbs all had a hand in the extravagant and spectacular 18th-century landscaping of Stowe. Lakes, statues, temples, monuments and wonderful views. The house is not a National Trust property.

Old Gaol Museum, Market Hill; tel: (01280) 823020, open Mon–Sat 1000–1600 (Apr–late Dec); to 1700 and Sun 1400–1700 (July–Aug). Local hisotry is outlined in the museum.There is an audiovisual presentation in one of the gaol's original cells.

133

BICESTER

TIC: Unit 6A, Bicester Retail Village, Pingle Drive, Bicester OX6 7WD; tel: (01869) 369055, open daily 1000–1800.

Founded as a frontier fort on the border between Mercia and Wessex, Bicester has a wealth of 16th- and 17th-century buildings, and some which are much older. **St Edburg's Church**, founded as a Saxon Minster, was rebuilt and extended between the 11th and 14th centuries. The Causeway is a narrow medieval street. An **Historic Town Trail** has been devised, along which a dozen or more historic buildings can be seen. Now the town is drawing in many visitors to **Bicester Village**, an American-style direct-sell retail park where designer fashions and other goods can be bought at discounted prices. The village is open daily 1000–1600.

CARDIFF

The Welsh capital, Cardiff, is a city whose relatively recent growth owes much to the influence of the Earls of Bute in the 19th century. It was their interest in the iron and coal industries which transformed the town into the greatest coal port in the world during the heyday of the South Wales coalfield. Although the Welsh coal industry has now shrunk beyond recognition – the Rhondda Heritage Park providing a glimpse into the ways of life formerly associated with it – Cardiff itself retains a cosmopolitan air, with good cultural and shopping facilities. Its public spaces and buildings, many of which date from around the turn of the century, have a well-cared-for look, and it is worth allowing a day or two to explore.

134

TOURIST INFORMATION

TIC: *Cardiff Central Station, Central Square, Cardiff, South Glamorgan CF1 1QY; tel: (01222) 227281*, open Mon, Wed–Sat 0900–1830, Tues 1000–1830, Sun 1000–1600, public holidays 1000–1700 (Apr–Sept); Mon, Wed–Sat 0900–1730, Tues 1000–1730, Sun 1000–1600 (Oct–Mar). DP services offered; local bed-booking service (free), BABA (latest 30 mins before closing, £1 fee taken for Wales, £5 for London, £3 for rest of UK), bureau de change. British Heritage Pass and Cadw 7 day Explorer Pass sold. *Where to stay in Cardiff* is available free, as is an A4 leaflet, *Cardiff and Glamorgan Heritage Coast.*

ARRIVING AND DEPARTING

Cardiff has good connections with other parts of Wales, the English Midlands and, thanks to M4 and the River Severn Crossings, the West of England. M4 is the key to most routes into and out of the city, which can be accessed from the motorway via junctions 29, 32 and 33.

More than a dozen car parks are dotted around the city centre.

GETTING AROUND

Town and transport maps are available from the TIC – get the *pocket Cardiff map* (20p). Most of the attractions in town are within walking distance or an easy bus journey from the city centre. The rapidly growing **Cardiff Bay** development area is about a mile south of the centre.

Most **bus** services operate from **Central Bus Station**, *Central Square*. The main local operator is **Cardiff Bus**, *tel: (01222) 396521*. Services are good in the city centre and to the suburbs, running until 2300 on the most popular routes, with reduced services on Sun. Cardiff Bus have a **Capital Day-Out** ticket for £3 a day, covering all their services. The main **taxi** ranks can be found at Central Station, *The Hayes, Park Place* and *St Mary St*.

STAYING IN CARDIFF

Accommodation

There is a good range of accommodation in all categories, with cheaper establishments located on the edge of the city, in the suburbs of Whitchurch and Heath – and in Llandaff, 2.4 miles north. Most b&bs are located along *Cathedral Rd*

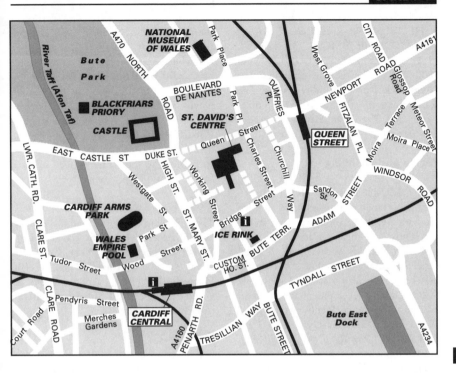

(10 mins from the centre) and *Newport Rd* (15 mins from the centre). It is generally possible to book on arrival, except during Rugby International weekends (late Jan–early Mar). Hotel chains in Cardiff include *Cp, FP, Ja, Ju, Ma, MH, QI* and *Th.* For advance accommodation bookings you can contact **Cardiff Marketing Ltd**, *PO Box 48, Cardiff CF1 1XQ; tel: (01222) 395173*, manned Mon–Fri 0900–1730 (10% deposit taken).

Within 5 minutes of the city centre is **Churchill's Hotel**, *Cardiff Rd, Llandaff, Cardiff CF5 2AD; tel: (01222) 462372; fax: (01222) 568347.* A town house with 22 en suite rooms, each one different, and 13 mews cottages suitable for families. Budget–moderate.

In the shadow of Cardiff Castle is **Austins**, *11 Coldstream Terrace, Cardiff CF1 8LJ; tel: (01222) 377148*, a small fam-ily-run hotel overlooking the River Taff. Three of its 11 rooms are en suite. Budget.

The de luxe four-star five-crown **Park Thistle Hotel** in the city centre, *Park Place, Cardiff, CF1 3UD; tel: (01222) 383471; fax: (01222) 399309*, is adjacent to the pedestrianised shopping precinct. Expensive.

Jury's Cardiff Hotel, *Mary Ann St, Cardiff CF1 2EQ; tel: (01222) 341441; fax: (01222) 223742*, is handy for the main shopping and entertainment areas. Moderate.

In a lakeside setting, the 135-room **Copthorne Hotel**, *Copthorne Way, Culverhouse Cross, Cardiff CF5 6XJ; tel: (01222) 599100; fax: (01222) 599080*, has the Wales Tourist Board's de luxe five-crown rating; nevertheless its room rates fit easily into the moderate category. Moderate.

HI: *2 Wedal Rd, Roath Park; tel: (01222) 462303*. **Cardiff YMCA**, *The Walk; tel: (01222) 497044*, open 0900–1300 and 1800–2200. The closest campsites are: **Lavernock Point Holiday Estate**, *Fort Rd, Penarth; tel: (01222) 707310*, 5 miles south; and **Tredegar House**, *Newport; tel: (01633) 815880*, 10 miles east.

Eating and Drinking

It's worth investing £1 in *Where to eat in Cardiff*, available from the TIC. There is a very good range of restaurants in all price categories, with the most expensive in the city centre, and cheaper places in the areas of Roath, Cathays and Canton. A good variety of eateries can be found in Cardiff's new restaurant quarter at *Mill Lane*, while the Cardiff Bay development area offers an ever-growing choice. Renowned for good Welsh food is **Blas-Ar-Gymru** (A Taste of Wales), *48 Crwys Rd, Cathays; tel: (01222) 382132* (booking recommended). Try some **Brains** beer, the distinctive local brew.

Communications

The main **post office**, *24 Hill St, The Hayes; tel: (01222) 227305*, is open Mon–Fri 0900–1730, Sat 0900–1630, and has poste restante facilities.

Money

There is a **Thomas Cook bureau de change** at *Midland Bank, 56 Queen St*.

ENTERTAINMENT

Various entertainments listings, including *Buzz*, are available free from the TIC. There is a wide variety of clubs and pubs, catering for all tastes.

The main concert halls are **St David's Hall**, *The Hayes; tel: (01222) 371236*, and **Cardiff International Arena**, *Bute Terrace; tel: (01222) 224488*. For theatre, there is **New Theatre**, *Park Pl.; tel: (01222) 394844*

(home of Welsh National Opera), and the **Sherman Theatre**, *Senghennydd Rd; tel: (01222) 230451*.

Cardiff Ice Rink, *Hayes Bridge Rd; tel: (01222) 383451*, is home to the Cardiff Devils ice hockey team. The famous Welsh home of international rugby, **Cardiff Arms Park**, *Westgate St*, is being demolished and will be replaced by a new stadium – this should be finished in time for the World Cup in Sept 1999.

EVENTS

The following are popular annual events: **Welsh Proms** (July – St David's Hall), **Welsh Singer of the Year Competition** (June – St David's Hall), **Welsh Harp Festival** (June, every two years – St David's Hall), **Cardiff Summer Festival** (Aug – various venues).

SHOPPING

For shopaholics, the TIC can provide *Where to shop in Cardiff* (50p). The town has many Edwardian arcades, department stores, malls, indoor and outdoor markets. The main shopping centres are **St David's Centre**, **Capitol Centre**, **Queen's West**, **St David's Market** and **Central Market**. **Cardiff Market**, *St Mary's St*, is a daily indoor market; **Splott Market**, *East Tyndall St, Splott*, takes place Sun; and **Jacob's Antique Market**, *West Canal Wharf*, is best visited Thur and Sat, 0900–1730.

SIGHTSEEING

Bus tours of the city are operated by **Leisurelink**, in association with **Guide Friday**; *tel: (01222) 522202*, starting from central station; £6. **Boat trips** round the Bristol Channel area are run by **Waverley Excursions**; *tel: (01446) 720656*. They start from Penarth Pier and can be booked at the TIC; from £7.95. For details of

guided walks, contact **Cardiff Official Guides**; *tel: (01222) 811970.*

Cardiff Castle, *Castle St; tel: (01222) 878100,* open daily 0930–1800 (Apr–Sept); 0930–1630 (Nov–Feb); 0930–1700 (Mar, Oct); £4.80 (tour), £2.40 (grounds only). The castle has Roman stonework in its outer walls and an 11th-century keep, but its character is overwhelmingly Victorian, thanks to the 3rd Marquess of Bute, who transformed it in the mid 19th century in the most lavish of styles; the result is an opulent, mock-medieval interior.

The **National Museum and Gallery**, *Civic Centre, Cathays Park; tel: (01222) 397951,* open Tues–Sun, public holidays 1000–1700; £3.25, has excellent collections, including particularly fine French Impressionist paintings and an Evolution of Wales exhibition.

St John's Church, *Church St, The Hayes; tel: (01222) 395231,* open Sun–Thur 0800–1800, Fri–Sat 0800–1630; free, but donations welcomed.

From the city centre, you can take a lovely riverside walk to **Llandaff Cathedral**, *The Green, Llandaff; tel: (01222) 564554,* open daily 0700–1900; free, but donations welcomed. Two miles north-west. Originally Norman, the cathedral was reconstructed after it was heavily bombed in 1941 and it has a striking Epstein sculpture, *Christ in Majesty.*

Techniquest, *Stuart St, Cardiff Bay; tel: (01222) 475475,* open Mon–Fri 0930–1630, Sat–Sun, public holidays 1030–1700; £4.50, is one of the largest hands-on science centres in the UK, ideal for children.

Welsh Industrial and Maritime Museum, *Bute St, Cardiff Bay; tel: (01222) 481919,* open Tues–Sun, public holidays 1000–1700; £2. This is a hands-on museum depicting the history of Welsh industry and shipping.

Norwegian Church, *Harbour Dr., Cardiff Bay; tel: (01222) 454899,* open daily 1000–1600; free. The attractive deconsecrated church is now an arts centre, offering a wide variety of events and entertainments.

Cardiff Bay Visitor Centre, *tel: (01222) 463833,* open Mon–Fri 0930–1930, Sat–Sun, public holidays 1030–1930 (May–Sept); Mon–Fri 0930–1630, Sat–Sun 1030–1700 (Oct–Apr); free. The award-winning 'Tube' presents futuristic displays about the development.

OUT OF TOWN

Highly recommended is the **Museum of Welsh Life**, *St Fagans; tel: (01222) 569441,* open daily 1000–1800 (July–Sept); daily 1000–1700 (Oct–June); £5.25 (Easter–Oct); £4.25 (Nov–Easter). 6 miles west of town. Buildings ranging from a toll gate to a chapel have been assembled from all over Wales in the 100-acre St Fagans Park, to give an insight into Wales' rural past.

Castell Coch (Cadw), *Tongwynlais; tel: (01222) 810101,* open Mon–Sat 0930–1830 (Apr–Oct); Mon–Sat 0930–1600 (Nov–Mar); Sun 1100–1600 (all year); £2.20. 4 miles north-west. Like Cardiff Castle, it was extensively altered by the 3rd Marquess of Bute and his architect William Burges: the result is a fairy-tale castle, its conical sandstone towers rising romantically from the Welsh hillside.

The **Rhondda Heritage Park**, *Lewis Merthyr, Coed Cae Rd, Trehafod, Rhondda; tel: (01443) 682036,* open daily 1000–1800 (Easter–Sept); Tues–Sun 1000–1800 (Oct–Easter); £4.95. 17 miles north-west. This is one of many ex-collieries in south Wales where tourism has taken over from heavy industry. The original colliery buildings have been converted to provide a record of a coal-mining community and the tour guides are ex-miners.

137

CARDIFF–CHESTER

This attractive route leads from mountainous south Wales into countryside that epitomises rural England – a landscape dotted with churches, castles, black-and-white timbered buildings, small villages and ancient market towns.

Chester

A483   19

Wrexham

Llangollen

A483

A5

Chirk

A5

Oswestry   24

16   A483   A5

A458   **Shrewsbury**

Welshpool   19   A49   **Direct Route**

Scenic Route   A4117   A456   **Kidderminster**

Ludlow   A49

Leominster

Scenic Route   A49   **Direct Route**

Hereford

Abergavenny   A49

17   A4137   60

A40   **Monmouth**

A4042   A40

A449

34   41

M4

Cardiff

DIRECT ROUTE: 149 MILES

138

ROUTES

DIRECT ROUTE

This route of 149 miles takes 3 hrs 15 mins. From central Cardiff follow signs to M4 (8 miles) and follow the motorway east for 9 miles. At Junction 24 turn north on to A449 and after 13 miles bear right on to A40, continue for 11 miles then head north again on A4137, which joins A49 in 5 miles. A49 heads north for 60 miles to **Hereford**, **Leominster**, **Ludlow** and **Shrewsbury**, where the route continues north on A5 for 24 miles to Chirk. From Chirk A483 leads past **Wrexham** to reach Chester in 19 miles.

SCENIC ROUTE

▶ This adds about 46 miles to the trip – allow another hour. Leave central Cardiff as above and head east on M4, leaving at Junction 26 to head north on A4042, which reaches Abergavenny after 17 miles.

From **Abergavenny** head east on A40 to reach Monmouth in another 17 miles. Continue on A40 from Monmouth to join A4137 after 6 miles. From here continue to A49 as on the direct route and follow it to Shrewsbury.

Leave Shrewsbury on A458 west to reach **Welshpool** in 19 miles. From Welshpool follow A483 north for 16 miles to the outskirts of **Oswestry**, where it links up with A5, which continues to Chester as in the direct route.

MONMOUTH

TIC, *Shire Hall, Agincourt Sq., Monmouth NP5 3DY; tel: (01600) 713899*, open daily 1000–1730 (Apr–Oct). BABA and local accommodation reservations.

ACCOMMODATION AND FOOD

Riverside Hotel, *Cinderhill St, Monmouth NP5 3EY; tel: (01600) 715577*. 18th-century inn. Moderate.

Steeples, *7 Church St, Monmouth NP5 3BX; tel: (01600) 712600; fax: (01600) 772832*. Town centre b&b. Budget.

Steppes Farm Cottages, *Rockfield, Monmouth NP5 5EW; tel: (01600) 716273*. Self-catering in stone, oak-beamed cottages for two to six people. Moderate–expensive according to season.

Punch House, *Agincourt Sq., Monmouth; tel: (01600) 713855*. Flower bedecked inn with good bar menu. Budget–moderate.

The Trekkers, *The North, nr Trellech, Monmouth; tel: (01600) 830367* offering a good selection of freshly cooked food, including vegetarian choices. Moderate.

SIGHTSEEING

With its medieval heritage and its associations with Admiral Lord Nelson, King Henry V and Charles Stuart Rolls (of Rolls-Royce fame), Monmouth is a distinctive and interesting place to visit. At its heart is *Agincourt Square*, with old coaching inns and the Georgian **Shire Hall**, which has an arcaded market floor.

The 13th-century gatehouse on the **Monnow Bridge** is the only complete example in Britain. The town grew up around two rivers – the Monnow and the Wye.

The Nelson Museum, *Priory St, Monmouth; tel: (01600) 713519*, open Mon–Sat 1000–1300, 1400–1700, Sun 1400–1700; admission charge. The museum has an amazing collection of items connected with the life of the Norfolk-born admiral – weapons, pictures, model ships, silver and glass, as well as displays depicting Monmouth's history and the exploits of Rolls-Royce co-founder Stuart Rolls.

Monmouth Castle, where Henry V was born in 1387, is a ruin, but herbs and plants typical of his time grow in the King's Garden at **Great Castle House**. **The Castle and Regimental Museum**, *The Castle, Monmouth; tel: (01600) 772175*, open daily 1400–1700 (summer), Sat–Sun 1400–1600 (winter). This displays Monmouth's military history from the establishment of the Roman Blestium, to modern times.

139

HEREFORD

TIC: *1 King St, Hereford HR4 9BW; tel: (01432) 268430*, open daily 0900–1700 (May–Sept); Mon–Sat 0900–1700 (Oct–Apr). DP services; local bed-booking (latest booking 1630; fee £1.50 or 10% refundable deposit), BABA (latest booking 1630; fee £2.50 or 10% refundable deposit). Guided tours booked, YHA/HI membership sold. *Places to eat/stay/visit* and the annual *Hereford What's On Guide* are available free.

GETTING AROUND

Free town and transport maps are available from the TIC. Local bus services, run by **Midland Red**, *tel: (01905) 763888*, operate from **Hopper Bus Station**. The main **taxi** rank is on *Widemarsh St*.

ACCOMMODATION

It is generally easy to find accommodation on arrival, except over summer public holidays and during the Three Choirs Festival (Aug 2000). There is a reasonable range of places to stay, with rather more choice of b&bs and guesthouses than large hotels, and a few inns with rooms outside the town. The only hotel chain is *FH*.

In the summer holidays, rooms are available at the **Royal National College for the Blind**; *tel: (01432) 265725*. The closest **campsite** is: **Hereford Racecourse Campsite**, *Roman Rd; tel: (01432) 272364*, 2 miles north.

SIGHTSEEING

This ancient county town has some pleasant streets through which to roam and the TIC has information on **guided walks** and **bus tours** of the area. Walks, conducted by **Hereford Guild of Guides**, leave the TIC Mon–Sat at 1030, Sun at 1430 (mid May–mid Sept); £1. They last 60–90 mins.

The much altered 12th-century cathedral has two great treasures: the *Mappa Mundi*, a world map drawn in 1289, and the medieval Chained Library, where nearly 1500 rare books are chained to the bookcases. **Hereford Cathedral**; *tel: (01432) 359880*. Cathedral open Mon–Sat 0930–1600, Sun 1230–1530; free. *Mappa Mundi* and Chained Library open Mon–Sat 1000–1615, Sun 1000–1515 (Easter–Sept); Mon–Sat 1030–1515 (Oct–Easter); £4.

Hereford is renowned for cider: **Bulmers** have been making it for over 100 years, and there are 2-hr group tours of the **Cider Mills**, *Plough Lane*; £2.95. Booking necessary; *tel: (01432) 352000*. To learn about cider-making through the ages, visit the **Cider Museum and King Offa Distillery**, *21 Ryelands St; tel: (01432) 354207*, open daily 1000–1730 (Apr–Oct); Mon–Sat 1300–1700 (Nov–Mar); £2.

OUT OF TOWN

Hereford is surrounded by lush countryside and it's a pretty trip to **Dinmore Manor and Gardens**, *tel: (01432) 830322*, open daily 0930–1730; £2.50. 6 miles north. The climb to the manor, once a monastery, is well worth while, for a happy mix of real and mock medieval.

LEOMINSTER

TIC: *1 Corn Sq., Leominster HR6 8LR; tel: (01568) 616460*, open Mon–Sat 0930–1730 (Apr–Oct); Mon–Sat 1000–1600 (Nov–Mar). Services offered: accommodation reservations.

ACCOMMODATION AND FOOD

The town serves an agricultural community and accommodation is available on farms and at b&bs in the surrounding villages.

One of the main places to stay in town is the **Royal Oak Hotel**, *South Street, Leominster HR6 8JA; tel: (01568) 612610*, dating from the early 1700s. Moderate.

The Talbot Hotel, *West St; tel: (01568) 616347*, has a restaurant and coffee lounge open for lunch and dinner. Moderate.

SIGHTSEEING

The medieval streets of black-and-white timbered buildings with overhanging gables in the centre of this busy country town lure visitors with their cameras, but it is wise to take photographs very early on a summer morning before the crowds of shoppers get there. The town's name is pronounced 'Lemster'.

Priory Church, at the heart of the town, retains a number of its original Norman features within its reddish walls.

OUT OF TOWN

Croft Castle (NT), *Yarpole; tel: (01568) 780246*, open Wed–Sat 1400–1800 (May–Sept); Sat–Sun 1400–1700 (Apr and Oct); £3.20. Off A4110 5 miles northwest. The sturdy walls have stood since the 14th and 15th centuries, though the interior dates from the 18th century. The castle stands in 1000 acres of parkland with important avenues of silver birch trees and centuries-old chestnuts.

LUDLOW

TIC: *Castle St, Ludlow, Shropshire SY8 1AS; tel: (01584) 875053*, open Mon–Fri 1000–1700, Sat 1000–1600 (Nov–Mar); Mon–Sat 1000–1700, Sun 1030–1700 (Apr–Oct). DP services offered; local bed-booking (extremely busy public holidays Sat) and BABA (latest 30 mins before closing). Tickets booked for local coach day trips. *South Shropshire Guide*, including accommodation listing, is free.

GETTING AROUND

The attractions in Ludlow are all within walking distance of the town centre. For **general transport enquiries**, *tel: (0345) 056785*. To book **taxis**: **Annette's Taxis**, *tel: (01584) 878787*; **Ludlow Travel**, *tel: (01584) 876000*.

ACCOMMODATION

There is a moderate choice of accommodation in the town, with a few hotels, b&bs, guesthouses and pubs offering rooms. There is more on offer in the surrounding area. It is generally easy to book on arrival, except during public holiday weekends and the Ludlow Festival (last week June–first week July). Hotel chains include *BW* and *Rg*.

HI: **Ludlow**, *Ludford Bridge; tel: (01584) 872472*. There is a **campsite** at **North Farm**, *Whitcliffe; tel: (01584) 872026*, 1 mile west of town.

SIGHTSEEING

Guided walking tours are led by members of **Ludlow Historical Research Group**, *tel: (01584) 873197*; £1. Tours start at 1430 by the cannon at the castle entrance and run Sat–Sun (Easter–Sept); daily during the **Ludlow Festival** (last week June–first week July).

The loveliest border town on the English side of the Marches, Ludlow exudes serenity and charm. The market town boasts nearly 500 listed buildings and preserves its Norman street pattern almost intact. *Broad St* is particularly impressive, with its many timber-framed Tudor and elegant 17th–19th-century brick buildings.

Only the impressive 11th-century castle is a reminder of more turbulent times. **Ludlow Castle**; *tel: (01584) 873355*, open daily 1030–1600 (Feb–Apr, Oct–Dec); 1030–1700 (May–Sept); closed

Jan; £2.50 (castle); extra £1.50 for Holo-deck. The long history of the castle, with its massive red sandstone keep, little round Norman chapel, medieval and Tudor additions, provides a startling contrast to the foretaste of the 21st century provided by hologram displays on **The Holodeck** (the castle's latest attraction).

The ashes of Shropshire's poet A.E. Housman (1859–1936) are buried in the churchyard of the fine, late medieval **St Laurence's Church**; *tel: (01584) 872073*, open all year, stewards on duty 1000–1700 (Easter–Oct); free, but donations welcome. **Ludlow Museum**, *Castle St; tel: (01584) 873857*, open Mon–Sat 1030–1300 and 1400–1700 (Apr–Sept); Sun 1030–1700 (July–Aug); £1.

SIDE TRACK
FROM LUDLOW

KIDDERMINSTER

TIC: *Station Approach, Comberton Hill, Kidderminster, Worcestershire DY10 1QX; tel: (01562) 829400*, open daily 1100–1630 (May–Sept). At other times, contact **Bewdley TIC**, *Load St, Bewdley, Worcs DY12 2AE; tel: (01299) 404740*. DP SHS services offered; local bed-booking and BABA (latest booking 1600; 10% of first night taken as deposit for all bookings). The free guide *Discover Worcestershire's Wyre Forest* includes accommodation.

ACCOMMODATION

There are few places to stay, so it is advisable to book in advance when there are gala weekends at the Severn Valley Railway (see below). Accommodation information from the TIC. There are two **campsites** quite close: **Wolverley Camping and Caravan Park**, *Brown Westhead Park, Wolverley;*

tel: (01562) 850909, 2 miles north-east, and **Shorthill Caravan, Camping and Leisure Park**, *Worcester Rd South, Crossway Green, Hartlebury; tel: (01299) 250571*, 5 miles south.

SIGHTSEEING

Kidderminster, 18 miles east of Ludlow, was once the centre of carpet manufacture and a variety of mills and chimneys remain along the canal as a monument to its industrial heritage. But the real reason for stopping off is for a 16-mile wallow in nostalgia on the **Severn Valley Railway**, which runs from the old station alongside. One of Britain's finest steam railways, this takes you on a picturesque riverside trip via pretty Georgian **Bewdley** to cliffside **Bridgnorth**, whose two halves are linked by funicular railway.

Hereford and Worcester County Museum, *Hartlebury Castle, Hartlebury; tel: (01299) 250416*, open Mon–Thur 1000–1700, Fri, Sun 1400–1700; £1.90. 4 miles south. **West Midland Safari and Leisure Park**, *Spring Grove, Bewdley; tel: (01299) 404604*, open daily 1000–1700 (Apr–Oct); £4.50. 2 miles west.

SHREWSBURY

TIC: *The Music Hall, The Square, Shrewsbury, Shropshire SY1 1LH; tel: (01743) 350761*, open Mon–Sat 0930–1715 (Oct–Apr); Mon–Sat 0930–1800 (May–Sept); Sun 1000–1600 (June–Sept); 1000–1600 (Easter, late May public holidays). DP SHS services offered; local bed-booking and BABA (latest 30 mins before closing), guided tours booked. YHA/HI membership, coach and events tickets sold. *Shrewsbury (annual) brochure* includes an accommodation list and is available free of charge.

GETTING AROUND

Most attractions are within easy walking distance of the centre. Free town and transport maps are available from the TIC. There are several local bus companies, operating mainly from the **bus station**, *Raven Meadows; tel: (0345) 056785.*

ACCOMMODATION

There is a good range of hotels, pubs, b&b and guesthouse accommodation, with cheaper establishments located on the edge of the town centre. It is generally easy to book on arrival, except during the West Midlands Agriculture Show (May), and the Shrewsbury Flower Show (Aug). Hotel chains in Shrewsbury include *Ct.*

HI: **Shrewsbury**, *The Woodlands, Abbey Foregate; tel: (01743) 360179.* The nearest **campsite** is **Severn House**, *Monford Bridge; tel: (01743) 850229;* 4 miles north-west.

SIGHTSEEING

Guided walks of the town leave the TIC daily at 1430, and also at 1100 Sun (May–Sept); £2.

Shrewsbury has a long history and occupies a lovely setting on a loop of the River Severn. A plethora of well-cared-for half-timbered buildings, especially in the lanes around the *High St,* includes **Abbot's House** (1450), *Butcher Row,* and **Ireland's Mansion** (1575), *High St.*

The 16th-century **Rowley's House**, *Barker St; tel: (01743) 361196;* open Tues–Sat 1000–1700, Sun 1000–1600; £2, displays finds excavated from the nearby Roman city of Wroxeter.

Clive House Museum, *College Hill; tel: (01743) 354811,* open Tues–Sat 1000–1700, Sun 1100–1600; £1, was once the home of Clive of India, Shrewsbury's MP in the 1760s.

The much altered **Shrewsbury**

Castle; *tel: (01743) 358516,* open 1000–1630; £2, dates from Norman times and contains a refurbished regimental museum.

Across English Bridge is the restored church of **Shrewsbury Abbey**, *Abbey Foregate; tel: (01743) 232723,* open 0930–1730 (Easter–Oct); 1030–1500 (Nov–Easter); free. Founded in 1083 as a Benedictine abbey, this was the home of Ellis Peters' fictional medieval monk-sleuth, Brother Cadfael. The monastery was dissolved in 1540 and is now simply a parish church, but fragments of a medieval shrine to St Winefride survive.

A striking sunken flower garden is the centrepiece of Shrewsbury's riverside park: **Quarry Park and The Dingle** (Percy Thrower Gardens), *The Quarry; tel: (01743) 231456,* open 0800–dusk; free, except for the Aug Flower Show.

For an unusual themed attraction, visit **Shrewsbury Quest**, *Abbey Foregate; tel: (01743) 366355,* open daily 1000–1700 (Apr–Oct); 1000–1600 (Nov–Mar); £3.95. This is a recreation of 12th-century monastic Shrewsbury, in which you can create an illuminated manuscript, solve a mystery and relax in a medieval herb garden.

OUT OF TOWN

Attingham Park (NT), *Atcham, nr Shrewsbury; tel: (01743) 709203,* house open Sat–Wed 1330–1700 (Apr–Sept); £3.80. 4 miles south-east. Has an impressive picture collection and a landscaped deer park.

Wroxeter Roman City (EH), *Wroxeter; tel: (01743) 761330,* open daily 1000–1800/dusk (Easter–Oct); Wed–Sun 1000–1400/1600 (Nov–Mar); £2.75 (including audio tour). 5 miles east. These are the fascinating remains of one of Rome's largest British settlements.

CHIRK

Chirk is famous for Thomas Telford's sensational 1000ft **Pontcysyllte Aqueduct,** which carries the beautiful Llangollen Canal 126ft above the River Dee. Beside it is an even longer and higher viaduct. The aqueduct can be crossed by self-drive day boat hired at Trevar or Chirk. A **restaurant boat** takes passengers over the aqueduct from Chirk Marina, near Wrexham; *tel: (01961) 773384.*

SIDE TRACK FROM CHIRK

LLANGOLLEN

TIC: *North Wales Borderlands Centre, Town Hall, Llangollen; tel: (01978) 860828,* open daily year round.

ACCOMMODATION AND FOOD

There is a wide choice of good quality accommodation around Llangollen, most of it surprisingly inexpensive.

The Royal Hotel, *Bridge St, Llangollen LL20 8PG; tel: (01978) 860202; fax: (01978) 861824.* Standing beside the River Dee, this hotel has 33 en suite rooms. Moderate.

Ty Cerrig Guesthouse, *Bryneglwys, Corwen LL21 9NN; tel: (01490) 450307.* An emphasis on Welsh dishes using local produce. Budget.

Plas Offa Farm, *Whitehurst, nr Llangollen LL14 5AN; tel: (01691) 773760.* 17th-century farmhouse alongside Offa's Dyke. Budget.

SIGHTSEEING

Llangollen is 5 miles east of the A5 a few miles south of Wrexham. Set on the banks of the River Dee, the town is a pleasant tourism centre which bursts into life when its famous **International**

Musical Eisteddfod takes place in July.

Plas Newydd, *Hill St; tel: (01978) 861314,* open daily 1000–1700 (Apr–Oct); £2. This was the stately home where the 'Ladies of Llangollen' lived for nearly 50 years from 1780.

Llangollen Railway, *Abbey Rd; tel: (01978) 860951.* Site open daily 0900–1930 (May–late Oct); weekends throughout the year and some other dates e.g. Christmas period. Steam train trips through the Dee Valley with a dinner dance on board on Saturdays. Admission charge.

Lower Dee Exhibition Centre, *Mill St; tel: (01978) 860584,* open daily 1000–1700; admission charge. Dr Who memorabilia with sound and light effects. Also Model Railway World, Hornby Dublo collection and a Museum of Inland Waterways.

WREXHAM

TIC: *Lambpit St, Wrexham LL11 1WN; tel: (01978) 292015,* open daily 1000–1730. BABA, local accommodation reservations; bookings taken from guided tours, theatre seats and events.

ACCOMMODATION

Abbotsfield Priory Hotel, *29 Rhosddu Rd, Wrexham LL11 2LP; tel: (01978) 161211; fax: (01978) 291413.* Family-run hotel with 14 en suite rooms. Budget.

Aldersey Guest House, *25 Hightown Rd, Wrexham LL13 8EB; tel: (01978) 365687.* Near the town centre. Budget.

SIGHTSEEING

The large and busy market town of Wrexham dates from Saxon times. It has three permanent indoor markes open daily, except Sun and an outdoor market on Mon.

Minera Lead Mines and Country Park, *Wern Rd, Minera, Wrexham; tel: (01978) 753400,* open Tues–Sun 1000–1700 (Easter–end Sept; also Mon in Aug and Bank Holidays); £1. Lead mining history here goes back to medieval times.

County Borough Museum, *County Bldgs, Regent St, Wrexham; tel: (01978) 358916,* open Mon–Fri 1030–1700, Sat 1030–1500; free. Displays reflect local social and industrial history.

Bersham Ironworks and Heritage Centre, *Bersham, nr Wrexham; tel: (01978) 261529,* open year round (Heritage Centre); Apr–Sept (Ironworks); £1. Cannon for the American War of Independence and cylinders for James Watt's steam engine were made in the furnaces and foundries here.

ABERGAVENNY

TIC and Brecon Beacons National Park Information Centre, *Swan Meadow, Monmouth Rd, Abergavenny, Gwent NP7 5HH; tel: (01873) 857588,* open daily 1000–1800. DP services offered; local bed-booking and BABA (latest 1730). *Browsing Around Abergavenny* and a comprehensive guide to accommodation and activities are free of charge.

GETTING AROUND

The town's area of interest is small and walkable – a free town map and transport timetables are available from the TIC. Most local bus services are operated from **Swan Meadow**, *Monmouth Rd,* by **Red and White**, *tel: (01633) 266336;* and **Phil Anslow**, *tel: (01495) 792323.* For **taxis**, contact: **Lewis's**, *tel: (01873) 854140;* **Park Taxis**, *tel: (0800) 654321;* or **Carlton Taxis**, *tel: (01873) 850716.*

ACCOMMODATION

There is a small number of hotels, includ-

ing the *MC* chain, and a good choice of guesthouses and b&bs. Cheaper places can be found within the town and in farmhouses in the surrounding area. It is generally easy to book on arrival. The closest **campsites** are **Pyscodlyn Farm**, *Llanwenarth Citra; tel: (01873) 853271,* 2 miles north-west, and **Clydach Gorge**, *tel: (01633) 838838,* 4 miles south-west.

SIGHTSEEING

A busy market town on the River Usk, Abergavenny regards itself as the gateway to Wales. Lying on the fringe of the 500 square miles of the **Brecon Beacons National Park**, it makes a superb base for walking the hills which rise all around. An extinct volcano, **Sugar Loaf Mountain** (1950 ft), lies 2½ miles north.

Abergavenny Castle and Museum, *Castle St; tel: (01873) 854282,* open Mon–Sat 1100–1300 and 1400–1700, Sun 1400–1700 (Mar–Oct); Mon–Sat 1100–1300 and 1400–1600 (Nov–Feb); £1. You can see remains of the original castle's walls, towers and gateway, while the museum recreates old rooms and displays traditional furnishings and crafts.

St Mary's Priory Church, *Monk St; tel: (01873) 853168,* open daily 1000–1400 (closes Wed–Fri 1200–1400), Sun visits must be between services; free. This contains one of the largest collections of medieval art in the UK.

OUT OF TOWN

The imposing, moated, 11th-century **White Castle** (Cadw), *Llantilio Crossenny; tel: (01600) 780380,* is accessible at all times; around £1 when manned, otherwise free. 5½ miles east. This is one of the highlights of the 18-mile *Three Castles Walk* – the other two are Skenfrith and Grosmont. Details from the TIC, or *tel: (01222) 465511.*

145

The once-thriving south Wales coalfield is immortalised at the excellent **Big Pit Mining Museum**, *Blaenafon; tel: (01495) 790311*, open daily 0930–1700 (Mar–Oct); underground tours 1000–1530; telephone for winter opening; £4.50. 8 miles south-west. Ex-miners guide visitors down the 300ft shaft of a colliery that closed in 1980.

Raglan Castle (Cadw), *Raglan; tel: (01291) 690228*, open daily 0930–1830 (Easter–Oct); Mon–Sat 0930–1600, Sun 1100–1600 (Nov–Easter); £2.20. 10 miles south-east. This elegant, 15th-century castle, with its hexagonal towers, is the most complete of the local fortresses. According to local legend, an underground passage links the castle with the **Beaufort Arms**, in the High Street. Moderate.

WELSHPOOL

TIC: *The Vicarage Gdns, Church St, Welshpool, Powys SY21 7DD; tel: (01938) 552043/553215*, open daily 0900–1730. DP services offered; local bed-booking and BABA. NT membership and local theatre and events tickets sold. *Montgomeryshire Guide*, with accommodation list, is free of charge.

GETTING AROUND

Welshpool's attractions are within walking distance of the centre, and free town and transport maps are available from the TIC. The main bus company is **Crosville**, *tel: (01691) 652402.* .

ACCOMMODATION

There are two hotels, one in the *Ct* chain, and a reasonable range of guesthouse and b&b accommodation. It is usually easy to book on arrival. The closest **campsites** are: **Severn**, *Cilcewydd, Forden; tel: (01938) 580238*, 1½ miles south; **Maes yr Afon**, *Berriew; tel: (01686) 640587*, 4 miles west; and **Derwen Mill**, *Guilsfield; tel: (01938) 554365*, 3miles from Welshpool.

SIGHTSEEING

The Georgian architecture and pleasant walks along the attractive canal make this small market town worth lingering over.

Welshpool and Llanfair Light Railway, *The Station, Llanfair Caereinion; tel: (01938) 810441*, open on specific days (most days mid June–Aug), call for schedules; £7.30. This offers an 8-mile trip through some delightful countryside.

Montgomery Canal Cruises, *Severn St Wharf; tel: (01938) 553271*, run daily at 1300 and 1500 (Easter–Oct); also at 1100 (July–Aug, public holidays); £2.75, and the trip lasts 1 hr 30 mins.

Powysland Museum and Montgomery Canal Centre, *Canal Wharf; tel: (01938) 554656*, open Mon–Tues, Thur–Fri 1100–1300 and 1400–1700, Sat–Sun 1000–1300 and 1400–1700 (May–Sept); Sat 1400–1700 (Oct–Apr); free.

OUT OF TOWN

Powis Castle and Garden (NT), *nr Welshpool; tel: (01938) 554336*. Castle and museum open Wed–Sun, public holidays 1200–1600 (May, Sept–Oct); Tues–Sun 1200–1630 (June–Aug); £6 (covers castle, museum and garden). 1 mile south; footpath from town. Dominating the town, this medieval stronghold has one of the finest country house collections in Wales.

CARLISLE

Guarding the western end of England's border with Scotland, Carlisle is well worth a day's stopover to appreciate its castle, museum and cathedral; it also has some excellent shops.

TOURIST INFORMATION

TIC: *Old Town Hall, Carlisle, Cumbria CA3 8JH; tel: (01228) 512444*, open Mon–Sat 0930–1700 (Mar–May, Sept–Oct); Mon–Sat 0930–1730 (June); Mon–Sat 0930–1800/1830 (July–Aug); Mon–Sat 1000–1600 (Nov–Feb); Sun 1030–1600 (Easter, May–Oct). DP SHS services offered; local bed-booking service and BABA (latest 30 mins before closing; free), guided walks and tours booked. *Carlisle Holidays and Short Breaks Guide* is free.

There is a **Thomas Cook bureau de change** at *Midland Bank, 29 English St*.

ARRIVING AND DEPARTING

Carlisle is intersected by A6 from the south and A7 from the north, with links to Newcastle and the west coast provided respectively by A69 and A595. M6, which terminates 4 miles north of Carlisle, skirts the town 2 miles to the east.

GETTING AROUND

The town's attractions are within easy walking distance of the centre, and a free town map is available from the TIC. Most local bus services operate from the **bus station**, *Lonsdale St*.

STAYING IN CARLISLE

There is a good range of hotel, guest-house and b&b accommodation, including hotels in the *BW, FP, MC* and *SW*

chains. It is generally easy to book on arrival, but best to book in advance July–Aug. Accommodation is available (Aug–Sept only) at the **Cumbria College of Art and Design**, *tel: (01228) 599058*.

HI: **Etterby House**, *Etterby; tel: (01228) 23934*. The nearest **campsite** is **Orton Grange**, *Wigton Rd; tel: (01228) 710252*, 4 miles south-west.

SIGHTSEEING

Carlisle's turbulent history as a border town is told at the excellent **Tullie House Museum and Art Gallery**, *Castle St; tel: (01228) 34781*, open Mon–Sat 1000–1700, Sun 1200–1700; £3.50. Across the street lies the imposing 11th-century castle, with its long history of warfare – don't miss the graffiti (supposedly carved by prisoners). **Carlisle Castle** (EH); *tel: (01228) 591922*, open daily 0930–1800/dusk (Easter–Oct), 1000–1600 (Nov–Easter); £2.70. There are some interesting streets and alleys around the red sandstone **Carlisle Cathedral**, *Castle St; tel: (01228) 48151*, open Mon–Sat 0730–1815, Sun 0730– 1700; donation requested. This features a curiously truncated Norman nave and a striking 19th-century ceiling.

OUT OF TOWN

Explore the western end of **Hadrian's Wall** – including **Birdoswald Roman Fort** (EH), *Gilsland, Brampton; tel: (01697) 747602*, open daily 1000–1730 (Easter–Oct); £1.95. 18 miles east.

Lanercost Priory (EH), *Lanercost; tel: (01697) 73030*, open daily 1000–1800 (Easter–Oct); £1.20. 12 miles east. Ruined priory buildings and roofed nave.

147

CHESTER

Lying just outside the Welsh border, Chester was originally a Roman stronghold, and a flourishing medieval port before the tidal estuary of the Dee silted up (from the 15th century). This legacy has left the best-preserved city wall in England and an exceptional architectural heritage within it, which Chester has an enviable record for preserving.

TOURIST INFORMATION

TIC: *Town Hall, Northgate St, Chester, Cheshire CH1 2HJ; tel: (01244) 317962,* open Mon–Sat 0900–1645/1700 (Nov–Apr); Mon–Sat 0900–1930 (May–Oct); Sun 1000–1600 (all year). DP services offered; local bed-booking service and BABA (latest 30 mins before closing; 10% refundable deposit taken). Bookings made for guided walks, bus tours and National Express/Eurolines; tickets sold for theatre and events. Free *Chester Visitor Guide* includes accommodation listing. Accommodation bookings busiest in afternoons.

TIC: *Chester* **Visitor Centre**, *Vicar's Lane; tel: (01244) 351609,* open 0900–1900 (Nov–Mar); 0900–2100 (Apr–Oct). DP services offered; local bed-booking service and BABA (latest 1700 winter, 1900 summer). Other bookings as for the main TIC.

TIC: *Chester Railway Station, Station Rd; tel: (01244) 322220.* DP services offered; local bed-booking service, BABA, guided tours booked.

ARRIVING AND DEPARTING

Chester is surrounded by a mesh of major routes, giving good access into North Wales, the North-West and the English Midlands. M56, 5 miles north of the city, provides a fast link with Manchester, and M53, 2 miles west, heads north to Birkenhead and Wallasey, where the Mersey Tunnel provides access to Liverpool.

GETTING AROUND

Free town maps are available from the TICs. Local and regional bus transport is regular and frequent, but evening and Sun services to outlying areas are limited. Most bus services operate from the **Bus Exchange Point**, *Princess St.* For **enquiries** *tel: (01244) 602666.* The main **taxi** rank is at the Bus Exchange Point.

STAYING IN CHESTER

Accommodation and Food

Chester and the surrounding area can provide an extremely wide choice of accommodation in all categories, particularly b&b. It is usually easy to book on arrival, except during the Chester Races (held on specific dates May–Sept; check with TIC).

Hotel chains in Chester include *BW, FH, FP, Ja* and *MH* – also *Hd* at Ellesmere Port. The majority of cheaper rooms can be found in the suburbs of Hoole and Hough Green (1½ miles from the centre: respectively east and west). For self-catering accommodation, contact **Chester Holiday Homes**, *PO Box 799, Chester CH1 3GB; tel: (01270) 610633.*

HI: *Hough Green House, 40 Hough Green; tel: (01244) 680056.*

The nearest **campsites: Thornleigh**

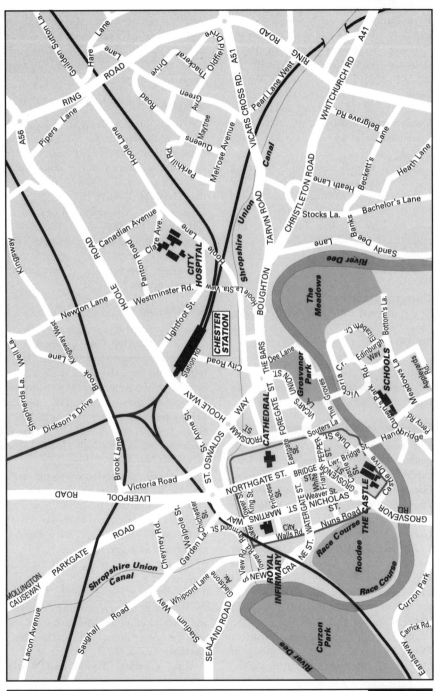

149

Park Farm, *Ferry Lane, Sealand Rd; tel: (01244) 371718* (1½ miles west); Chester Southerly Caravan Park, *Balderton Lane, Marlston-cum-Lache; tel: (01244) 270791* (3 miles south); Birchbank Farm, *Stamford Lane, Christleton; tel: (01244) 335233* (3 miles east); and Fairoaks Caravan and Camp Park, *Rake Lane, Little Stanney; tel: (0151) 355 1600* (3 miles north).

Chester is well endowed with eating places, from gourmet to takeaway. The main areas for restaurants are around *Eastgate St, Watergate St, Lower Bridge St* and *Northgate St*. The TIC has a free restaurant guide. Cheshire cheese (in red, white and blue) and fresh Dee salmon are local specialities.

Communications

The main post office, *St John St*, is open Mon–Fri 0900–1730 (Wed from 0930), Sat 0900–1230. Poste restante facilities.

Money

There is a Thomas Cook bureau de change at *Midland Bank, 47 Eastgate St.*

The TIC has a free monthly *What's On* guide, and there are listings in the local papers. The main arts venue is Chester Gateway Theatre, *The Forum, Hamilton Place; tel: (01244) 340392*, and the main spectator sports venue is Chester Racecourse, *The Roodee; tel: (01244) 323170.*

Among Chester's more important annual events are Chester Races, *The Racecourse, The Roodee* (specific dates May–Sept); Chester Regatta (oldest in the world), on the River Dee (June); River Carnival and Raft Race, on the River Dee (July); Chester Summer Music Festival, various locations in town (July); Literature Festival, various

locations (Oct); Lord Mayor's Show and Festival of Transport, City Centre and *The Roodee* (May). Every five years (next in 2002) The Chester Mystery Plays are performed.

The main shopping areas are *Foregate St, Watergate St, Eastgate St, Northgate St* and *Grosvenor Precinct* (a covered mall). Chester has a large number of antique shops, many of which are on *Watergate St*. Don't miss the Cheshire Candle Shop, *Bridge St Row*, or the Cheshire Workshops, *Burwardsley, Tattenhall; tel: (01829) 70401*, open daily 1000–1700 (8 miles east) – the largest hand-carved candle manufacturer in Europe. The Forum, *off Northgate St*, houses a market Mon–Sat.

Guided town walks and ghost trails are offered by Chester City Council (£3). Among the many tours available, boat trips on the attractive river and canal are particularly recommended. Most tours can be booked through the TIC: Guide Friday bus tours (£6); trips on Bithell's Boats, *tel: (01244) 325394* (£3); canal trips and cruises from Mill Hotel, *Milton St; tel: (01244) 350035* (from £1).

An excellent introduction to the city's history is provided at the Chester Heritage Centre, *Bridge St Row; tel: (01244) 317948*, open Mon–Sat 1100–1700, Sun 1200–1700; £1. It has displays, models and video presentations.

Chester is fairly compact and the ideal way to get your bearings is to walk the 2 mile circuit of the city walls. Much of the Roman wall survives, with two towers and gates added in the Middle Ages. Look out for the elaborate, if anachronistic, Eastgate Clock (1897), *Eastgate St.*

King Charles' Tower and Water

Tower, *City Walls; tel: (01244) 402008,* open daily 1100–1600 (mid June–mid Sept); 40p for King Charles' Tower; 90p for Water Tower. The exhibition is concerned with the long siege of Chester during the Civil War.

Historic buildings abound, but don't miss the famous **Rows** – two tiered galleries of walkways and shops, built in medieval and Tudor times in elaborate half-timbered style. The principal Rows are *Eastgate, Northgate, Watergate* and *Bridge St*, and they now form a thriving shopping area. A life-size recreation of the Rows in Victorian times can be seen at the **Chester Visitor Centre**, *Vicar's Lane; tel: (01244) 351609,* open daily 0900–1800; free.

Chester Castle dates from Norman times, but what remains is principally 19th-century restoration: the castle now houses the **Cheshire Military Museum**, *tel: (01244) 327617,* open daily 1000–1700; 50p, which contains memorabilia of the Cheshire Regiment.

Chester Cathedral, *St Werburgh St; tel: (01244) 324756,* open daily 0700–1830; free. The squat, sandstone structure is mainly 14th-century, though it was well restored in the 1870s; it has some fine medieval woodcarving.

The three bridges spanning the Dee – the **Old Dee Bridge**, *Lower Bridge St,* the elegant **Suspension Bridge**, *The Groves,* and **Grosvenor Bridge**, *Grosvenor St* – are also worth a look.

Roman finds are well displayed at the **Grosvenor Museum**, *27 Grosvenor St; tel: (01244) 402008,* open Mon–Sat 1030–1700, Sun 1400–1700; free. Chester's history is covered from the time when dinosaurs left footprints to today's countryside.

You can see part of the largest Roman **amphitheatre** in Britain outside Newgate on *Vicar's Lane* while at **Deva Roman**

Experience, *Pierpoint Lane, off Bridge St; tel: (01244) 343407,* open daily 0900–1700; £3.80, a Roman galley transports visitors to a recreation of Roman Chester, complete with smells.

Chester Toy & Doll Museum, *13A Lower Bridge St; tel: (01244) 346297,* open daily 1100–1700; £1.50, boasts a vast collection of Dinky cars, an original Punch and Judy, a large model of the Coronation Coach and an operational jukebox.

On the Air, Broadcasting Museum & Vintage Sound Shop, *42 Bridge St Row; tel: (01244) 348468,* open daily 1000–1700; £1.95. The history of broadcasting is related by exhibits ranging from *Germany Calling* (in an air-raid shelter) to a television studio – and everything in between.

OUT OF TOWN

Beeston Castle (EH), *Beeston,* open daily 1000–1800 (Apr–Oct); daily 1000–1600 (Nov–Mar); £2. 6 miles east. The ruined 13th-century castle has unusual crusader-like defences and stupendous, panoramic views. On the next hill lies **Peckforton Castle**, *Peckforton near Tarporley; tel: (01829) 260930,* open daily 1000–1800 (Easter–mid Sept); £2.50, a fine 19th-century mock-medieval fortress. Both castles are landmarks visible from miles around, rising above the Cheshire Plain.

One of the best zoos in Britain, with its animals in semi-natural enclosures, is **Chester Zoo**, *Upton-by-Chester; tel: (01244) 380280,* open daily 1000–1900; £6.50. 2 miles north-east.

Further north is the **Boat Museum**, *Ellesmere Port; tel: (0151) 355 5017,* open daily 1000–1700 (Oct–Apr); Sat–Wed 1000–1600 (Nov–Mar); £4.50. Occupying a historic canal dock, this has the world's largest floating collection of canal craft, large and small.

CHESTER–CARLISLE

This route covers much of north-west England, starting just north of the border with Wales and finishing just south of the border with Scotland, and – if you choose not to travel directly – following the varied coastlines of Merseyside, Lancashire and Cumbria for almost the whole length of the journey and traversing the Lake District for the last 70 miles.

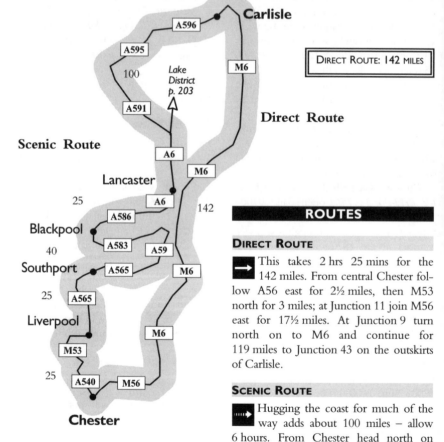

DIRECT ROUTE: 142 MILES

ROUTES

DIRECT ROUTE

This takes 2 hrs 25 mins for the 142 miles. From central Chester follow A56 east for 2½ miles, then M53 north for 3 miles; at Junction 11 join M56 east for 17½ miles. At Junction 9 turn north on to M6 and continue for 119 miles to Junction 43 on the outskirts of Carlisle.

SCENIC ROUTE

Hugging the coast for much of the way adds about 100 miles – allow 6 hours. From Chester head north on A540 for 6 miles, then follow A550 north-east for 3 miles and join M53. After 7 miles leave the motorway at Junction 3, following A552 to the Mersey Tunnels (toll) from which you emerge on the **Liverpool** side of the river.

From Liverpool follow A59 towards M57, then head west on A5207 for miles to join A565 north, which leads to **Southport** in 13 miles. At Southport continue east on A565 for 9½ miles, joining A59 for 8 miles to the outskirts of Preston; then follow A583 and signs for **Blackpool** 14 miles away. **Lancaster**, 20 miles north of Blackpool, is reached by way of A586 and A6. Continue north on A6 for 22 miles to Levens, then bear right on to A591. This leads through the heart of the Lake District (see p. 203) for 52 miles to Bothel, where A595 heads north-east for the last 18 miles to Carlisle.

LIVERPOOL

TIC: *Merseyside Welcome Centre, Clayton Sq., Liverpool, Merseyside L1 1QR; tel: 709 3631,* open Mon–Sat 0930–1730, public holidays 1000–1700. Services offered: local bed-booking and BABA; bureau de change; tickets booked for tours, theatre, local events; YHA/HI membership sold. The excellent *Pocket Guide* is £1, but an accommodation listing is free.

TIC: *Atlantic Pavilion, Albert Dock; tel: 708 8854,* open 1000–1730. DP SHS services offered; local bed-booking and BABA; tours and tickets for theatre and local events booked.

GETTING AROUND

Most attractions are within walking distance of the centre. There is good train and bus coverage of the city and surrounding area, with reduced frequency in the evenings and on Sun. **Merseytravel**, *tel: 236 7676,* handle all local transport enquiries, including ferries. **Shopmobility**, *Clayton Sq.; tel: 708 9993.*
The **central bus station**, *Paradise St,* is

the terminal for local buses; services are run by many different companies.

Regular **ferries** cross the Mersey, from Liverpool Pier Head to the Wirral Peninsula.

There are several **taxi** ranks in the centre. Look out for the special Tourist Taxis (which display a badge).

STAYING IN LIVERPOOL

Accommodation

There is a reasonable selection of hotel accommodation in and around the city, but not much in the way of guesthouses and b&bs. It is generally easy to find accommodation on arrival, except during the Grand National meeting (Apr). Hotel chains include *Ca, MH* and *Th.* University accommodation is available in summer, at **North Western Hall**; *tel: 707 8452,* and **Cathedral Park**; *tel: 709 3197.*

There is one private hostel: **Embassie Youth Hostel**, *1 Faulkner Sq.; tel: 707 1089,* and a **YMCA**, *56 Mt Pleasant; tel: 709 9516.* The nearest **campsite** is **Wirral Country Park**, *Station Rd, Thurstaston, Wirral; tel: 648 4371/3884,* adjacent to the Visitor Centre.

Eating and Drinking

Liverpool has the oldest **Chinatown** in Europe, just outside the city centre, as well as restaurants of many nationalities – and to suit all pockets. *Lark Lane* is a lively area (likened to New York's Greenwich Village), with a good choice of eating places, as is the **Cavern Quarter**.

Communications

The main **post office**, *2333 Whitechapel,* opens Mon–Fri 0900–1730, Sat 0900–1230. Poste restante facilities are available. Liverpool's **telephone area code** is *0151.*

153

ENTERTAINMENT AND EVENTS

There's an enormous choice of evening entertainment: get the TIC's free entertainment list, *In Touch*. Local newspapers also carry listings. Some major venues are: **Music: Bluecoat Arts Centre**, *School Lane; tel: 708 9050*; **The Cavern Club**, *Mathew St; tel: 236 9091* (where the Beatles first played); **Royal Liverpool Philharmonic Orchestra**, *Hope St; tel: 709 3789*.

Theatres: Liverpool Empire, *Lime St; tel: 709 1555* (the city's main theatre) **Liverpool Playhouse/Studio**, *Williamson Sq.; tel: 709 8363* (Britain's oldest continuing repertory theatre); **Flora Pavilion**, *Promenade, New Brighton, The Wirral; tel: 639 4360*.

Nightclubs: The Grafton, *West Derby Rd; tel: 263 2303*.

Sports: Aintree Racecourse, *Ormskirk Rd; tel: 5232600*; **Everton Football Club**, *Goodison Park; tel: 330 2200*; **Liverpool Football Club**, *Anfield Rd; tel: 263 2361*.

The most important annual events are: **The Grand National**, *Aintree Racecourse* (Apr); **Liverpool Festival of Comedy**, various venues (June); the **Mersey River Festival**, *River Mersey* and *Albert Dock* (June) – Britain's largest water-based festival; the **Beatles Convention**, *Adelphi Hotel* (Aug); and the **Mathew Street Festival** (Aug).

SHOPPING

There are three modern precincts: *Clayton Square*, *St John's Centre* and *Cavern Walks*, as well as the shopping areas of *Bold St*, *Church St* and *Lord St*. The beautifully restored Albert Dock is also popular. A number of excellent **markets** include: **Quiggins Centre**, *School Lane*, Mon–Sat; **St John's Market**, *Eliot St*, Mon–Sat; and **Stanley Dock Sunday Market**.

SIGHTSEEING

The 1 hr **City Sightseeing Tour** is a good introduction to the city and, for Beatles fans, there is a 2 hr **Magical History Tour**. Both are by bus; details from the TIC. For a cruise on the Mersey (daily, year round), contact **Mersey Ferries**, *tel: 630 1030*.

In the 18th century, Liverpool developed from a humble fishing town into Europe's most important Atlantic seaport. The enormous **Royal Liver Building** (1911) still dominates the Mersey waterfront; it is easily identified by the liver birds perched on the top. Other fine municipal buildings can be seen around *William Brown St*, such as **St George's Hall**, which dates from 1854 and is one of the finest neoclassical buildings in the country.

Walker Art Gallery, *William Brown St; tel: 478 4199*, open Mon–Sat 1000–1700, Sun 1200–1700; free, houses an internationally renowned collection of European art from 1300 onwards – don't miss the award-winning sculpture gallery. Britain's largest Anglican cathedral is the Victorian Gothic **Liverpool Cathedral**, *St James Rd; tel: 709 6271*, open daily 0800–1800; free, but donations welcomed. It is superbly well-proportioned and the triforium gallery contains a unique collection of Victorian and Edwardian embroidery. Climb the tower for great views (access 1100–1700; £2).

A striking example of modern ecclesiastical architecture is provided by the city's other cathedral, the Roman Catholic **Metropolitan Cathedral of Christ the King**, *Mount Pleasant; tel: 709 9222*, open daily 0800–1700/1800; free, but donations welcomed.

Albert Dock, once bustling with shipping, now teems with visitors to the complex of museums, exhibitions and shops.

Outstanding are the **Merseyside Maritime Museum, Anything to Declare?** (try your hand at catching smugglers), and **Museum of Liverpool Life**, all under the same roof: *Albert Dock; tel: 478 4499,* open daily 1000–1700; £3 (joint ticket).

At **The Beatles Story**, *Britannia Vaults, Albert Dock; tel: 709 1963;* open daily 1000–1800; £5.45, you can relive the Fab Four's progress, from gigs at the Cavern to modern legend.

The **Tate Gallery**, *The Colonnades, Albert Dock; tel: 709 0507,* is the national collection's northern wing and contains superb examples of modern painting and sculpture. A grand re-opening (after redevelopment) is scheduled for summer 1998. Probable opening times Tues–Sun, public holidays 1000–1800; free.

A rare chance to see what goes on behind the scenes at a museum is provided by the **Conservation Centre**, *Whitechapel; tel: 478 4499,* open Mon–Sat 1000–1700, Sun 1200–1700; £1.50.

Liverpool Museum and Planetarium, *William Brown St; tel: 478 4399.* Museum open Mon–Sat 1000–1700, Sun 1200–1700; free. Call for Planetarium performance details. The collections cover everything from outer space to the Amazonian rain forests.

Western Approaches, *1 Rumford St; tel: 227 2008,* open Mon–Thur, Sat 1030–1630; £4.75. This was the secret wartime headquarters for the Battle of the Atlantic.

OUT OF TOWN

Across the Mersey, on the Wirral peninsula, is Port Sunlight – the original garden village, which was built by William Hesketh Lever in 1888 for his soap factory workers. The story of the community is told at the **Port Sunlight Heritage Centre**, *95 Greendale Rd, Port Sunlight,* *Wirral; tel: 644 6466,* open daily 1000–1600 (Apr–Oct); 1200–1600 (Nov–Mar); 40p. 5 miles west.

An outstanding collection of 18th-century furniture, porcelain, tapestries, embroidery, sculptures and paintings can be seen at the **Lady Lever Art Gallery**, *Port Sunlight; tel: 478 4136,* open Mon–Sat 1000–1700, Sun 1200–1700; free.

SOUTHPORT

TIC: *112 Lord St, Southport, Merseyside PR8 1NY; tel: (01704) 533333,* open Mon–Fri 0900–1730, Sat–Sun, public holidays 1000–1600. Services offered: local bed-booking and BABA (latest booking for both 30 mins before closing; fee 10% of first night). Tickets sold for attractions and transport. Two *Southport* guides (one general, the other with accommodation) are 50p (for both), but free by post.

GETTING AROUND

Most attractions are within walking distance of the centre. The TIC has town maps (35p) and free timetables. Local **bus** services are run mainly by **Mersey Travel**; *tel: (0151) 236 7676.*

For **taxis**, call: **Yellow Tops**, *tel: (01704) 531000*; **All White**, *tel: (01704) 537777*; **Central Cabs**, *tel: (01704) 544414*; **Kwik Cars**, *tel: (01704) 547000.*

ACCOMMODATION

There is a wide choice of accommodation, particularly small hotels, b&bs and guesthouses, with budget places in the centre. It is usually easy to book on arrival, except during the annual Southport Flower Show (Aug).

Hotel chains include *BW* and *Mn*. The closest **campsite** is **Brooklyn Country Club**, *Gravel Lane, Banks; tel: (01704) 28534,* 3 miles north.

155

SIGHTSEEING

Beach Aviation, *tel: (01704) 547811*, offer pleasure flights from Southport Sands (from £9.50).

This gracious Victorian resort has extensive beaches and dunes, well-laid-out parks and the second longest pier in Britain. *Lord St*, a conservation area, is a fine thoroughfare with canopied shops.

Southport Zoo, *Prince's Park; tel: (01704) 538102*, open daily 1000– variable, according to season; £3. Over 800 animals live and breed in family groups and all revenue goes towards their welfare in this family-run zoo.

Pleasureland Amusement Park, *Southport Sands; tel: (01704) 532717*, open daily 1100–2000 (June–early Sept); Sat– Sun (mid Feb–early Nov); free. There are over 100 attractions. You can pay individually for rides (£1 is the norm) or get wristbands covering them all.

BLACKPOOL

TIC: *1 Clifton St, Blackpool, Lancashire FY1 1LY; tel: (01253) 21623*, open Mon– Thur, Sat 0900–1700, Fri 0930–1700, Sun 1000–1545 (late May–early Nov); Mon– Thur 0845–1645, Fri 0930–1615, Sat 0900–1645 (early Nov–late May). Services offered: free local bed-finding – no bookings made. *The Blackpool Festival* brochure (including accommodation listings) is free.

GETTING AROUND

General transport enquiries, *tel: (01253) 23931*. Many attractions are within easy walking distance of the centre and the town is well served by public transport: a free transport map is available from the TIC. Blackpool has had **trams** since 1885. The network stretches along the seafront for 12 miles. Most local services are operated by **Blackpool Transport**, *tel: (01253) 23931*. The main

taxi rank is on *Talbot Sq.* and the TIC has details of registered taxi companies.

ACCOMMODATION

There are nearly 3000 hotels and guest-houses in the town, so there is seldom a problem in finding somewhere to stay on arrival. However, it is advisable to pre-book during the Blackpool Illuminations (Sept–Oct), especially at weekends. Accommodation can be booked through the **Blackpool Hotel and Guest House Association**, *87a Coronation St; tel: (01253) 21891* (commission charged). Hotel chains include *Ct, DV, FP, Gr, Mo, ST* and *TI*.

There are various **campsites** within easy reach of town; the following are all approx. 3–4 miles inland: **Gillett Farm**, *Peel Rd, Peel; tel: (01253) 761676*; **Mariclough–Hampsfield**, *Preston New Rd; tel: (01253) 761034*; **Pipers Height**, *Peel Rd, Peel; tel: (01253) 763767*; and **Underhill Farm**, *Preston New Rd; tel: (01253) 763107*.

SIGHTSEEING

The **tram** is a pleasant way to travel the 7-mile promenade and view the **Illuminations** (usually Fri following Aug Bank Holiday–end Oct/early Nov). **Seagull coaches** operate tours of the area; book at the TIC.

Blackpool, *the* major seaside resort in north-west England, developed in the mid 18th century, catering for huge numbers of workers from industrial Lancashire. Millions still arrive during the summer season, in search of traditional seaside fun. Along the famous **Golden Mile** of beach, with its three piers (north pier is open all year), are any number of amusements, all dominated by the 518 ft **Blackpool Tower**, *Promenade; tel: (01253) 22242*, open daily 1000–late (Easter–early Nov);

from £5. This smaller copy of the Eiffel Tower boasts an indoor theme park and has a renowned ballroom at its foot. **The Magic of Coronation St**, *Sandcastle Bldg, South Promenade; tel: (01253) 299555*, open daily 1000–2200 (during the illuminations); daily 1000–1800 (the rest of the year); £5.99. Wander down a replica of British television's most famous street and experience the characters' lives in nine separate film shows. Or go to **Chromokey** to have yourself photographed and superimposed on genuine footage, so that you appear as a character (£7.99). The **Rovers Return** is a genuine pub, replicating the fictional one (but with extra space) and you can visit it (1100–2300) without going into the Street or Chromokey.

If state-of-the-art stomach-churning rides are your passion, don't miss **Blackpool Pleasure Beach**, *South Promenade; tel: (01253) 341033*, open 1100–late (Easter–Nov); free, but charges for rides. The latest attraction is the UK's first Space Shot: riders are thrown up 210 ft, then free-fall at 80 mph!

Blackpool Zoo Park, *East Park Drive; tel: (01253) 725610*, open daily 1000–dusk; £5.50. 2 miles east; is a modern zoo, with over 400 animals.

As a contrast to the relentless fun, try the **Grundy Art Gallery**, *Queen St; tel: (01253) 751701*, open Mon–Sat 1000–1700; free, which has a good 19th- and 20th-century British collection.

LANCASTER

TIC: *29 Castle Hill, Lancaster, Lancashire LA1 1YN; tel: (01524) 32878*, open Mon–Sat 1000–1700, Sun (public holidays weekends only) 1000–1600 (Apr–June, mid–late Sept); Mon–Sat 1000–1800, Sun 1200–1600 (July–early Sept); Mon–Sat 1000–1600 (Oct–Mar). DP SHS services

offered; local bed-booking and BABA (latest 30 mins before closing); bureau de change; bookings for tours, hire cars and local events; YHA/HI membership sold. Accommodation and eating guides are free.

GETTING AROUND

Most of the attractions are within easy walking distance of the centre, and free town and transport maps are available from the TIC. **General transport enquiries**, *tel: (01524) 841656*.

Most local buses are operated by **Ribble**, *tel: (01524) 424555*, from the **bus station**, *Damside St*. Services are good in the centre, to Morecambe and to some outlying villages.

The main **taxi** rank is by the bus station, or contact: **Lancaster Radio Taxis**, *tel: (01524) 844844*; **City Cabs**, *tel: (01524) 35666*; **John's Taxis**, *tel: (01524) 845210*; **Beatstream**, *tel: (01524) 32090*; or **Tiger Taxis**, *tel: (01524) 844122*.

ACCOMMODATION

There are a few hotels, as well as a small range of b&b, guesthouse and pub accommodation, with cheaper places located on the edge of town. It is generally easy to book on arrival. Accommodation is available at **Lancaster University** during the holidays, *tel: (01524) 65201*.

HI: *Oakfields Lodge, Redhills Rd, Arnside, Carnforth; tel: (01524) 761781*. One of the nearest **campsites** is **Detrongate Farm**, *Bolton-le-Sands, Carnforth; tel: (01524) 732842*, 3 miles north.

SIGHTSEEING

The TIC can provide information on **bus tours**, **guided walks** (including walks across the vast – and treacherous – sands of **Morecambe Bay**), **canal cruises** and **boat trips**.

A city with a historic heart, Lancaster is dominated by its massive castle: the keep dates from *c.*1170 and the Shire Hall contains a fine heraldic display. **Lancaster Castle**, *Shire Hall, Castle Hill; tel: (01524) 64998*, open Sat–Sun 1030–last tour 1600 (Easter–Oct). Also open for tours on weekdays when crown courts are not in operation; £3 (full tour), £2 (short tour if court is sitting), £1.50 external tour. Also on the hill is **Lancaster Priory/St Mary's Church**; *tel: (01524) 65338*, open daily 0930–1700 (Easter–Oct); free, but donations requested. The structure is mainly 14th–15th century – don't miss the magnificent carved choir stalls.

Housed in the fine 18th-century Customs House on the quay, a reminder that this was once a great port, is the **Lancaster Maritime Museum**, *St George's Quay; tel: (01524) 64637*, open daily 1100–1700 (Easter–Oct); 1400–1700 (Nov–Easter); £2.

The **Cottage Museum**, *15 Castle Hill; tel: (01524) 64637*, open daily 1400–1700 (Easter–Sept); 75p, is furnished as an artisan's house of *c.*1820, while the **Judges' Lodgings**, *Church St; tel: (01524) 32808*, open Mon–Sat, public holidays Sun 1400–1700 (Easter–June, Oct); Mon–Fri 1000–1300 and 1400–1700, Sat–Sun 1400–1700 (July–Aug); £2, contain a collection of furniture by Gillow, the famous Lancaster cabinet-maker, and a museum of childhood.

Another place to get a feel for history is the **City Museum and King's Own Regimental Museum**, *Market Sq.; tel: (01524) 64637*, open Mon–Sat 1000–1700; free. This is a fine Georgian house, with exhibits showing local life since Neolithic times, as well as the regimental artefacts.

The domed **Ashton Memorial** (1906); 50p, stands in a fine landscaped city park of 38 acres (free), which is also home to other attractions, including the **Butterfly House**, *Williamson Park; tel: (01524) 33318*, open daily 1000–1700 (Easter–Oct); Mon–Fri 1100–1600, Sat–Sun 1000–1600 (Nov–Easter); £2.75 (covers butterfly house, foreign bird enclosure and 'mini-beast' house, i.e. insects, reptiles, etc.).

Dating from 1859, but in medieval style and recently renovated, is the Catholic **St Peter's Cathedral**, *St Peter's Rd; tel: (01524) 61860*, open daily 0800–1900; free.

OUT OF TOWN

Of particular appeal to Wild West fans is **Frontierland Western Theme Park**, *Morecambe; tel: (01524) 410024*, opening times vary enormously, so check locally (mid March–Oct); £8–£10 (seasonal) for a day's unlimited rides. 4 miles north-west. There are over 40 rides and other attractions, including the 160 ft Bay Polo Tower. Also live shows in summer.

Leighton Moss Wildlife Park, *Myers Farm, Silverdale, Carnforth; tel: (01524) 701601*. Vistor Centre open daily 1000–1700; Park open 0900–2100/dusk; £3.50 – plus £2 for special events (arranged throughout the year). 8 miles north. Owned by the Royal Society for the Protection of Birds, this is primarily a reed-marsh, with nature trails and bird-watching hides.

Leighton Hall, *Carnforth; tel: (01524) 734474*, open Tues–Fri, Sun 1400–1700 (May–July, Sept); 1100–1700 (Aug); £3.40. 8 miles north. Gillow furniture is among the treasures at this neo-Gothic mansion set in fine parkland.

CHESTER–NOTTINGHAM

This route ranges over the lush landscapes of Cheshire, into the stunning moorlands of the Pennines and the Peak District National Park. It brushes with South Yorkshire at the steel city of Sheffield, then heads back into Derbyshire before descending towards Nottingham.

ROUTE: 127 MILES

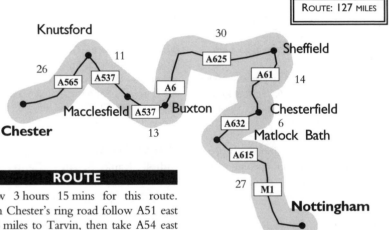

159

ROUTE

Allow 3 hours 15 mins for this route. From Chester's ring road follow A51 east for 6 miles to Tarvin, then take A54 east for 2 miles, picking up A556 east for 18 miles to **Knutsford**. A537 then heads east to reach **Macclesfield** in 11 miles and continues to **Buxton** in a further 13 miles. Follow A6 north for 6 miles to Chapel-en-le-Frith, where A625 heads east to reach **Sheffield** in 24 miles. From Sheffield follow signs to A61 south to reach **Chesterfield** in 14 miles. A632 then heads west and reaches Matlock after 6 miles. Leave **Matlock** on A615 east and after 9 miles join A38 east for 3½ miles, joining M1 south at Junction 28. Leave M1 after 9 miles at Junction 26 and follow local signs to reach Nottingham city centre after a final 5½ miles.

KNUTSFORD

TIC: *Council Offices, Toft Rd, Knutsford, Cheshire WA16 6TA; tel: (01565) 632611,* open Mon–Thur 0845–1700, Fri 0845–1630. Services offered: BABA and local accommodation reservations; information on sites associated with Mrs Elizabeth Gaskell's novel *Cranford,* for which Knutsford was the model.

ACCOMMODATION AND FOOD

The town's finest hotel is **Cottons**, *Manchester Rd, Knutsford WA16 0SU; tel: (01565) 650333; fax: (01565) 755351.* Amenities include indoor pool, gym, sauna, tennis and squash. Expensive.

Longview Hotel and Restaurant, *55 Manchester Rd, Knutsford WA16 0LX; tel: (01565) 632119; fax: (01565) 652402.* The hotel has 23 en suite rooms. Moderate.

La Belle Époque Brasserie, *60 King St, Knutsford WA16 6DT; tel: (01565) 6330600; fax: (01565) 634150.* This well-known restaurant has a distinctly Parisian ambience and seven b&b rooms. Accommodation moderate; restaurant pricey.

SIGHTSEEING

Cranford aficionados will be happy trying to identify buildings mentioned in the book. Mrs Gaskell is buried in the Unitarian churchyard, *Toft Rd.* The town, has a wealth of 18th-century houses along its winding streets.

Tatton Park, *Knutsford (signposted from M6, Junction 19, and M56, Junction 7); tel: (01565) 750250,* open daily (Easter–Sept), Sat–Sun (Oct). The 1000-acre park includes **Tatton Hall**, a huge Regency edifice, and magnificent formal gardens. Each section has different opening times and admission charges.

OUT OF TOWN

Salt Museum, *162 London Rd, Northwich; tel: (01606) 41331,* open Tues–Fri 1000–1700, Sat–Sun 1400–1700; £1.75. 6 miles west. Britain's only museum dedicated to this taken-for-granted substance.

MACCLESFIELD

TIC: *Town Hall, Market Pl., Macclesfield SK10 1DX; tel: (01625) 504114; fax: (01625) 504203,* open Mon–Thur 0845–1700, Fri 0845–1630. Services offered: BABA, local accommodation reservations and usual services.

ACCOMMODATION

Sutton Hall, *Bullocks Lane, Sutton, Macclesfield SK11 0HE; tel: (01625) 253211; fax: (01625) 252538.* Usefully combined as a pub, restaurant and hotel. Accommodation: moderate; food: budget–pricey.

Moorhayes House Hotel, *27 Manchester Rd, Tytherington, Macclesfield SK10 2JJ; tel: (01625) 433228.* Half a mile from the town centre. Budget–moderate.

SIGHTSEEING

Until the advent of man-made fibres soon after World War II, Macclesfield was a leading silk-spinning and weaving town. The industry's tale is told in the **Macclesfield Silk Museum**, *The Heritage Centre, Roe St; tel: (01625) 613210,* open Mon–Sat 1100–1700, Sun 1300–1700; £2.40. Demonstrations of silk production are given at **Paradise Mill** in nearby *Park Lane; tel: (01625) 618228,* open Tues–Sun 1300–1700; £2.40. A joint ticket gives access to both places.

OUT OF TOWN

Jodrell Bank Science Centre and Arboretum, *nr Holmes Chapel, tel: (01477) 571339,* open daily 1030–1730 (late Mar–Oct), Sat–Sun and school winter holidays 1100–1630 (Nov–late Mar); £3.80. On A535, 8 miles west. The world-famous Lovell radio telescope dominates the countryside. There are hands-on science exhibits, a Planetarium and grounds with trails and an arboretum.

BUXTON

TIC: *The Crescent, Buxton, Derbyshire SK17 6BQ; tel: (01298) 25106,* open daily 0930–1700 (Mar–Oct); 1000–1600 (Nov–Feb). DP services; local bed-booking (latest 15 mins before closing), BABA (latest 30 mins before closing). Membership sold for YHA/HI. *Buxton Town Guide*: 85p. *High Peak Where to Stay*: 20p. TIC has details of wheelchairs for free use.

GETTING AROUND

The majority of attractions are within walking distance of the centre. The TIC

160

can provide travel information and has maps for sale. Information on local bus services from **Busline**, *tel: (01298) 23098*. **Taxi** ranks are at *Grove Parade* and *Market Pl.*

ACCOMMODATION

There is seldom a problem in finding accommodation on arrival, except during the Opera Festival and Gilbert and Sullivan Festival (July–Aug). There is a good selection of hotels, guesthouses and b & bs, with cheaper accommodation about 10 mins' walk from the centre. Hotel chains include *BW* and *Ct.*

HI: *Sherbrook Lodge, Harpur Hill; tel: (01298) 22287.* A list of hostels in the Peak District area is available from the TIC. There are four **campsites**: **Cold Springs Farm**, *tel: (01298) 22762*; **Grin Low Caravan Club Site**, *tel: (01298) 77735*; **Lime Tree Park**, *tel: (01298) 22988*; and **Staden Grange**, *tel: (01298) 24985.*

SIGHTSEEING

High Peak BBG offer a programme of **guided walks**, starting from the TICs in Buxton and Castleton; *tel: (01433) 621824.* The annual leaflet *Places to Visit* (40p from the TIC) details all the possibilities in the area.

Buxton owes its mellow grandeur to its development as a fashionable Georgian spa town. Its many beautiful 18th- and 19th-century buildings are centred on the lovely hillside **Pavilion Gardens**, crowned by the magnificent iron and glass **Pavilion** (1871) and the Edwardian **Opera House**, setting for Buxton's annual festival (July–Aug); *tel: (01298) 72190.*

The town is surrounded by the **Peak District National Park**, which offers over 1600 miles of public footpaths and 80 square miles of open-access country. **Buxton Country Park**, on the edge of

town, has good views of some typical High Peak scenery. **Poole's Cavern**, *Green Lane; tel: (01298) 26978*; open daily 1000–1700 (Mar–Oct); £3.80 is one of many limestone cave complexes in the region.

OUT OF TOWN

Castleton, 8 miles north-east, is the heart of High Peak walking and caving country. Nearby **Peak Cavern**, *tel: (01433) 620285*, open daily 1000–1700 (Easter–Oct); £3, is perhaps the most spectacular of the caves. Access to **Speedwell Cavern**, *tel: (01433) 621888*, open daily 0930–1630/1730; £5, is by boat. Other complexes are: **Blue John Cavern and Blue John Mine**, *tel: (01433) 620638/ 620642*, open daily 0930–1730/dusk (all year, but Jan–Feb only if weather permits); £4.50; **Treak Cliff Cavern**, *tel: (01433) 620571*, open daily 0930–1730 (Mar–Oct); 1000–1600 (Nov–Feb); £4.50.

Peveril Castle (EH), *Castleton; tel: (01433) 620613*, open daily 1000–1800 (Apr–Oct); 1000–1600 (Nov–Mar); £1.60. The climb up to this Norman castle is rewarded by a panoramic view over surrounding hills and moors.

Chestnut Centre Conservation Park, *Castleton Rd, Chapel-en-le-Frith; tel: (01298) 814099*, open daily 1030–1730 (Mar–Dec); Sat–Sun 1030–1730 (Jan–Feb); £4.50. 7 miles north. Europe's largest collections of multi-specied otters and owls, in near natural surroundings.

SHEFFIELD

TIC: *Peace Gardens, Sheffield, South Yorkshire S1 2HH; tel: (0114) 273 4671/4672*, open Mon–Fri 0930–1715, Sat 0930–1615. DP SHS services offered; local bed-booking service (10% of first night refundable deposit) and BABA (latest one hour before closing; fee £2 for

161

London – otherwise 10% of first night deposit). YHA/HI membership arranged; tickets sold for National Express and local theatres and events. *In and Around Sheffield Guide* and accommodation lists are free.

GETTING AROUND

Most attractions are either in the city centre or on the outskirts of the city and accessible by bus from the centre. Free city and transport maps are available from the TIC. A good bus service runs throughout the city, operated by **Mainline** from the **Transport Interchange**, *Pond St; tel: (01709) 515151.*

The main **taxi** rank is on *Barkers Pool*. Among the registered taxi companies are: **Abbey Taxis**, *tel: (0114) 275 1111*; and **Mercury**, *tel: (0114) 267 0707.*

ACCOMMODATION

There is a good range of accommodation in the town and the outlying area. **TIC accommodation hotline**, *tel: (0114) 273 4673.* Most budget accommodation is in Millhouses (3 miles south-west), Broomhill (1½ miles west), Ecclesall (1 mile south-west) and Grenoside (4 miles north). Accommodation can be difficult to find if a major event is being held in the city. Hotel chains include *FP, Hd, MH, Nv, ST* and *SW*. During the holidays, accommodation is available at both Sheffield's **universities** – ask the TIC.

HI: Hathersage, *Hathersage, Derbyshire; tel: (01433) 650493.* The nearest **campsite** is **Fox Hagg Farm**, *Lodge Lane; tel: (0114) 230 5589*, 4 miles west.

ENTERTAINMENT

Sheffield is home to a number of international sports and entertainment venues, including **Sheffield Arena**, *Broughton Lane*, which often hosts indoor pop concerts; **Don Valley Stadium**, for international athletics and outdoor pop concerts; **Ponds Forge International Sports Centre**; and the **Crucible Theatre**, where the televised **Embassy World Snooker Championship** is held (every Apr).

SHOPPING

Meadowhall Shopping Centre is one of the largest indoor shopping centres in Europe. **Fargate** and **The Moor** are also major shopping areas.

SIGHTSEEING

Since Victorian times Sheffield has been renowned for steel, cutlery, engineering and tool-making. Diversification has changed the emphasis and Sheffield is now a major leisure centre, as Britain's first official 'National City of Sport'. The TIC has details of walks and registered guides.

The story of Sheffield's industrial development is well told at the lively **Kelham Island Industrial Museum**, *Alma St; tel: (0114) 272 2106*, open Mon–Thur 1000–1600, Sun 1100–1645; £2.50.

The attractively landscaped **Weston Park** is 1 mile west of the city centre and is the setting for two of Sheffield's attractions: the **City Museum**, *tel: (0114) 276 8588*, open Wed–Sat 1000–1700, Sun, public holidays 1100–1700; free, which has a good display of Sheffield plate and cutlery; and the **Mappin Art Gallery**, *tel: (0114) 272 6281*, open Wed–Sat 1000–1700, Sun, public holidays 1100–1700; free. This is renowned for its Victorian paintings.

One of the city's few surviving pre-Victorian buildings, a 16th-century house, is home to the museum of Sheffield life in Tudor and Stuart times: **Bishop's House Museum**, *Meersbrook Park; tel: (0114) 255 7701*, open Wed–Sat 1000–1630, Sun

1100–1630; £1. 3 miles south of the centre. Other galleries include: **Graves Art Gallery,** *Surrey St; tel: (0114) 273 5158,* open Tues–Sat 1000–1700; free, which includes a diverse collection of British art and Chinese ivories; and **Ruskin Art and Craft Gallery,** *Norfolk St; tel: (0114) 273 5299,* open Tues–Sat 1000–1700; free, which is the Sheffield collection of John Ruskin's works.

When there are no services you can look round **Sheffield Cathedral,** *Church St; tel: (0114) 275 3434,* open daily; free. A major new attraction, due to open in late 1998, is the **National Centre for Popular Music;** *tel: (0114) 279 8941.* 5 mins' walk from the rail and bus stations; proposed price £5.75.

CHESTERFIELD

TIC: *The Peacock Centre, Low Pavement, Chesterfield, Derbyshire S40 1PB; tel: (01246) 345777; fax: (01246) 345770,* open Mon–Sat 0900–1730 (Easter–end June); 0900–1800 (July–Aug); 0900–1730 (Sept–Oct); 0900–1700 (Nov–Easter). Services offered: BABA, local accommodation bookings and all services; official tourist guides available.

ACCOMMODATION

Chesterfield Hotel, *Malkin St, Chesterfield S41 7UA; tel: (01246) 271141; fax: (01246) 220719.* 73 en suite rooms, and a modern leisure centre. Moderate. **Abbeydale Hotel,** *Cross St, Chesterfield S40 4TD; tel: (01246) 277849.* Comfortable hotel near *Market Sq.* Moderate. **Abigail's Guesthouse,** *62 Brockwell Lane, Chesterfield S40 4EE; tel: (01246) 279391,* has seven rooms. Budget.

SIGHTSEEING

Chesterfield's famous landmark is the **Crooked Spire,** *Church of St Mary and All Saints, St Mary's Gate; tel: (01246) 206506,* open Mon–Sat 0900–1700; church free, tower visit £2.50. The 'corkscrew' spire is 228ft high and leans 9ft 5ins from its true centre.

Chesterfield Market, *Market Sq.,* trades Mon, Fri, Sat, when more than 250 stalls pack the town centre. The story of the market's development and the background to the building of the parish church are told in **Chesterfield Museum and Art Gallery,** *St Mary's Gate; tel: (01246) 345727,* open Mon, Tues, Thur–Sat 1000–1600; free.

OUT OF TOWN

Revolution House, *High St, Old Whittington; tel: (01246) 453554,* open daily 1000–1600 (Easter–end Oct); free. 3 miles north. This 17th-century thatched cottage was where three noblemen met to plot their part in the Revolution of 1688. **Hardwick Hall** (NT), *tel: (01246) 850430,* open Wed–Thur, Sat–Sun, public holidays 1230–dusk (Apr–Oct); £5.80, 7 miles south-east, is an exceptionally well-preserved Elizabethan mansion.

MATLOCK BATH

TIC: *The Pavilion, Matlock Bath, Derbyshire DE4 3NR; tel: (01629) 55082,* open daily 0930–1715 (Mar–Oct); Wed–Mon 1000–1600 (Nov–Feb). DP SHS services offered; local bed-booking service and BABA (latest 1 hr before closing), guided tours booked. *Illustrated Guide to Matlock Bath* is 40p. Free accommodation guide.

GETTING AROUND

Matlock Bath (the area of interest to tourists) is about 1 mile south of residential Matlock. Town maps and transport maps are available from the TIC. Most attractions are within walking distance of

163

Matlock Bath centre. For **bus information**, *tel: (01298) 23098*. **Matlock Taxis**, *tel: (01629) 584195*, operate the taxi service at the station.

ACCOMMODATION

There is a reasonable range of b&b and guesthouse accommodation, but few hotels – the only chain is *FH*. Advance booking is always desirable and essential for public holidays and peak periods.

HI: *40 Bank Rd, Matlock; tel: (01629) 582983*. The closest **campsite** is **Wayside Farm**, *Matlock Moor; tel: (01629) 582967*. 2 miles north-east.

SIGHTSEEING

Matlock Bath's **spa water** is renowned – there is a pump for sampling at the TIC. **Well-dressing** is an ancient art seldom seen outside Derbyshire; the TIC have a leaflet detailing dates and venues.

Matlock Bath is a good base for exploring the beautiful dales of the southern Peak District: **Derbyshire Tourist Guides**, *tel: (01629) 534284*, operate a full programme of local town and village **guided walks** – book at the TIC.

The town lies in a dramatic gorge on the edge of the **Peak District National Park**. The **Heights of Abraham Country Park and Caverns**, *Matlock Bath; tel: (01629) 582365*, open daily 1000–1700 (Easter–Oct); call for winter opening hours; £5.95. Towering over the town, the summit can be reached by cable car. There are two sets of caverns.

The **Whistletop Countryside Centre**, *Old Railway Station; tel: (01629) 580958*, open daily 1000–1700 (Apr–Oct); Sat–Sun 1200–1600 (Nov–Mar); free. This offers a good introduction to Derbyshire flora and fauna, while the excellent **Peak District Mining Museum**, *South Parade; tel: (01629)*

583834, open daily 1100– 1600; £3 (joint ticket) or £2 each museum/mine, tells the story of lead mining from Roman times.

Children will enjoy **Gulliver's Kingdom**, *Matlock Bath; tel: (01629) 57100*, open daily 1030–1700 (Easter holidays, late May–early Sept); Sat–Sun (Easter–early May, late Sept–Oct); £5.25.

Riber Castle Wildlife Park, *Matlock; tel: (01629) 582073*, open daily 1000–1700 (1500 Oct–Mar); £4. Includes the world's most comprehensive collection of lynx.

OUT OF TOWN

The grandest and most famous of several historic houses in the area is **Chatsworth**, *nr Bakewell; tel: (01246) 582204*, open daily 1100–1630 (Easter–Oct); £5.90. 10 miles north. Nearby is the atmospheric medieval **Haddon Hall**, *Bakewell; tel: (01629) 812855*, open daily 1100–1700 (Apr–July, Sept); Mon–Sat 1100–1700 (Aug); £4.75. 6½ miles north-west.

Arkwright's Cromford Mill, *Cromford; tel: (01629) 824297*, open daily 0900–1700; free. Tours 1000–1600; £2. 1 mile south. The world's first water-powered cotton mill.

Middleton Top Engine House, *Wirksworth; tel: (01629) 823204*, open (static) Sun 1030–1700; 35p, open (working) first Sat of month 1030–1700 (Easter–Oct); 60p. 4 miles south. Middleton boasts a steam engine of 1829 which, until 1963, hauled wagons up the steep Middleton incline on the Cromford and High Peak Railway.

National Tramway Museum, *Crich; tel: (01773) 852565*, open Mon–Fri 1000–1730; Sat–Sun, public holidays 1000–1830 (Apr–Oct), but variable: call for details; £4.50. 6 miles south-east. This marvellous tram museum has many working examples.

CHESTER– STRATFORD-UPON-AVON

Black-and-white timbered buildings abound on this route, which curves south-east from the walled city of Chester on the banks of the River Dee, through the Potteries of Arnold Bennett's Five Towns – there are, in fact, six – and the county town of Stafford to the great city of Birmingham, then on to the riverside birthplace of the Bard.

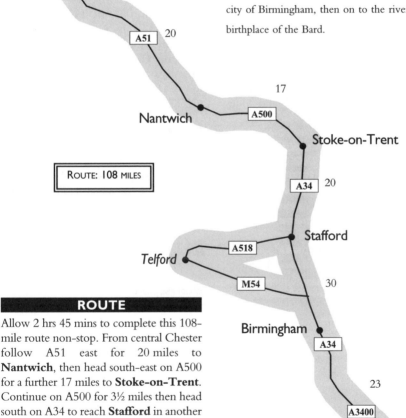

ROUTE: 108 MILES

165

ROUTE

Allow 2 hrs 45 mins to complete this 108-mile route non-stop. From central Chester follow A51 east for 20 miles to **Nantwich**, then head south-east on A500 for a further 17 miles to **Stoke-on-Trent**. Continue on A500 for 3½ miles then head south on A34 to reach **Stafford** in another 17 miles. Follow A34 south for 10½ miles to just south of Cannock, then take A460 south-west for 1½ miles, joining M6 at Junction 11. After driving south on M6 for 10 miles, leave at Junction 7 and follow

A34 for 5½ miles into central **Birmingham**. Leave Birmingham on A34 south. After 8 miles this joins A3400 (at M42 intersection), which continues south to reach Stratford-upon-Avon after 14 miles.

NANTWICH

TIC: *Church House, Church Walk, Nantwich, Cheshire CW5 5RG; tel: (01270) 610983/610880,* open Mon–Fri 0845–1715; Sat 0845–1300 (July–Aug). Services offered: BABA, local accommodation reservations and official tour guides.

ACCOMMODATION

Crown Hotel, *High St, Nantwich CW5 5AS; tel: (01270) 625283; fax: (01270) 628047*. Atmospheric black-and-white timbered hotel. Moderate.

Rookery Hall, *Worleston, nr Nantwich CW5 6DQ; tel: (01270) 610016; fax: (01270) 626027*. 45 luxuriously decorated rooms (expensive–pricey) and a noted dining room (pricey).

Stoke Grange Farm, *Chester Rd, Nantwich CW5 6BT; tel: (01270) 625525*. A b&b with three rooms. Budget.

Churche's Mansion, *Hospital St, Nantwich; tel: (01270) 74256*. Exquisite food in Elizabethan surroundings. Pricey.

SIGHTSEEING

Nantwich has been an important salt-producing centre for centuries and the threat to the industry posed by the 16th-century fire in the town was so great that Queen Elizabeth I herself donated £1000 and launched a national restoration fund for the town. Today, Nantwich has one of the country's finest sets of Elizabethan timber-framed buildings. The 14th-century **Church of St Mary**, a survivor of the great fire, contains ribbed vaulting with bosses depicting the life of the Virgin.

STOKE-ON-TRENT

TIC: *Quadrant Rd, Hanley, Stoke-on-Trent, Staffs ST1 1RZ; tel: (01782) 284600,* open Mon–Sat 0915–1715. DP services offered; local bed-booking and BABA (latest 1630). Tickets booked for factory tours, some events and theatres. *The China Experience* and an accommodation listing are free.

GETTING AROUND

Stoke-on-Trent comprises six separate towns, known as the **Potteries**. From north to south these are **Tunstall**, **Burslem**, **Hanley**, **Stoke**, **Fenton** and **Longton**. Hanley is the centre. The city's attractions are spread throughout its six towns. **General transport enquiries**, *tel: (01782) 747000*.

ACCOMMODATION

There is a good choice of accommodation in and around Stoke-on-Trent including hotels, b&bs, guesthouses and farmhouses; reservations recommended. **TIC hotline**, *tel: (01782) 284222*. Hotel chains include FP, Gr, Ja, MH, Pn and ST.

The nearest **campsite** is **Trentham Gardens**, *Stone Rd, Trentham; tel: (01782) 657341*, 3 miles south.

SIGHTSEEING

The Stoke area has been the centre of pottery-making in Britain since before the Romans came. Its many pottery factories, shops and museums are scattered throughout the six towns: the TIC's *China Experience* leaflet has full details.

A good place to start is the **City Museum and Art Gallery**, *Bethesda St, Hanley; tel: (01782) 232323*, open Mon–Sat 1000–1700, Sun 1400–1700; free, which displays a huge collection of ceramics, especially Staffordshire pottery.

You can tour the factories of many of

the world-famous names, but it's essential to pre-book your tour by telephone. **Royal Doulton: Visitor Centre**, *Nile St, Burslem; tel: (01782) 292434*, open Mon–Sat 0930–1700, Sun 1000–1600. 90-min factory tours Mon–Fri from 1030; £2.50, or £5 including tour. The world's largest public collection of Royal Doulton can be seen in the **Minton Museum**. This is due to reopen some time in 1998, so ask at the TIC.

The oldest pottery in England still on its original site is **Spode: Visitor Centre and Museum**, *Church St, Stoke-on-Trent; tel: (01782) 744011*, open Mon–Sat 0900–1700, Sun 1000–1600; £2, or £3.50 including tour.

Traditional skills are demonstrated at the **Gladstone Pottery Museum**, *Uttoxeter Rd, Longton; tel: (01782) 319232*, open daily 1000–1700; £3.75. This has been preserved as a working Victorian pottery, retaining its giant bottle kiln.

Etruria Industrial Museum, *Lower Bedford St, Etruria (west of Hanley); tel: (01782) 287557*, open Wed–Sun 1000–1600; £2. The 19th-century Etruscan Bone and Flint Mill, which ground materials for the potteries, is being restored as working condition as a museum.

OUT OF TOWN

You can see potters and decorators at work at the **Wedgwood Visitor Centre**, *Barlaston; tel: (01782) 204218*, open Mon–Fri 0900–1700, Sat 1000–1700, Sun 1000–1600; £3.25. 6 miles south.

When pottery threatens to overwhelm you, one of the biggest visitor attractions in the country awaits – a blend of stomach-churning rides and fantasy experiences. **Alton Towers**, *Alton; tel: (01538) 204060*, open daily 0900–1700/1900 (Easter–Oct); rides begin 1000; £18.50. 16 miles east.

For a more restful experience, you can visit a fascinating survival of an unusual Victorian garden, divided into smaller plots which comprise a miniature 'world tour' of gardening, including such diverse features as a Chinese pagoda and pinetum. **Biddulph Grange Garden** (NT), *Biddulph; tel: (01782) 517999*, open Wed–Fri 1200–1800, Sat–Sun and public holidays 1100–1800 (Easter–Oct); Sat–Sun 1200–1600/dusk (Nov–mid Dec); £4 (reduced to £2 Nov–Dec). 7 miles north.

Arnold Bennett's 'Bursley', in his Five Town novels, was based on **Burslem** and the TIC has a *Bursley Trail* leaflet, outlining a walking route that takes in many of the places featured.

STAFFORD

TIC: *Ancient High House, Greengate St, Stafford ST16 2HS; tel/fax: (01785) 240204*, open Mon–Fri 0900–1700, Sat 1000–1600 (Apr–Oct), 1000–1500 (Nov–Mar). BABA, local accommodation reservations and usual services.

ACCOMMODATION

There is a reasonably good selection of hotels, guesthouses and b&bs close to the town centre. The free booklet *Things to Do and Places to Stay*, available at the TIC, contains details of hotels and guesthouses in Stafford and the surrounding areas. It also has a short list of restaurants and pubs.

De Vere Tillington Hall, *Eccleshall Rd, Stafford ST16 1JJ; tel: (01785) 253351; fax: (01785) 259223*. A spacious and comfortable hotel. Moderate.

Abbey Hotel, *65/69 Lichfield Rd, Stafford ST17 4LW; tel: (01785) 258531; fax: (01785) 246875*. Family-run hotel. Moderate.

Vine Hotel, *Salter St, Stafford ST16 2JU; tel: (01785) 244112; fax: (01785)*

167

246612. Handy for the main shopping area, the Vine dates in part from the 13th century. Moderate.

SIGHTSEEING

A busy but attractive county town, Stafford has excellent shops, relaxing parks and a mixture of architectural, cultural and historic attractions. Picturesque *Church Lane* has a number of timbered buildings and *Mill St* is the setting for lively restaurants and pubs.

Ancient High House, *Greengate St; tel: (01785) 240204,* open Mon–Fri 0900–1700, Sat 1000–1600 (Apr–Oct), 1000–1500 (Nov–Mar); £1.60. Dating from 1595 and a refuge for CharlesI during the English Civil War, this timber-framed town house houses an extensive collection of period furniture and the regimental museum of the Staffordshire Yeomanry.

Shire Hall Gallery, *Market Sq.; tel: (01785) 278345,* open Mon–Sat 1000–1700; free. One of Staffordshire's most attractive historic buildings, the gallery retains original panelled courtrooms and is an attractive venue for exhibitions of art, craft and photography.

Stafford Castle and Visitor Centre, *Newport Rd; tel: (01785) 257698,* open Tues–Sun 1000–1700 (Apr–Oct), 1000–1600 (Nov–Mar); £1.60. Norman castle in grounds which encompass an historic trail, medieval herb garden and picnic area.

OUT OF TOWN

Izaak Walton's Cottage, *Worston Lane, Shallowford, nr Great Bridgeford; tel: (01785) 760278,* open Tues–Sun, public holidays 1100–1630 (Apr–Oct); admission charge. 4 miles north. The charming thatched cottage in which the author of *The Compleat Angler* lived is now dedicated to the history of fishing and literature.

Museum of Cannock Chase, *Valley Heritage Centre, Valley Rd, Hednesford; tel: (01543) 877666,* open daily 1100–1700 (Easter–Sept), Mon–Fri 1100–1600 (Oct–Easter); free. 12 miles south. The history of Cannock Chase from medieval hunting forest to 19th-century coalfield.

Shugborough Estate (NT), *Milford; tel: (01889) 881388,* open daily 1100–1700 (Easter–Sept); Sun 1100–1700 (Oct); £8 (house, museum and farm). 6 miles east. Magnificent building containing some outstanding collections. The surrounding grounds are being restored as a 19th-century working estate.

↩ SIDE TRACK
FROM STAFFORD

Telford is 20 miles west of Stafford, taking A518.

TIC: *The Telford Centre, Management Suite, Telford, Shropshire TF3 4BX; tel: (01952) 291370,* open Mon–Thur, Sat 0900–1800, Fri 0900–2000. DP services offered; local bed-booking (latest 30 mins before closing; free). The brochure *Telford and Ironbridge Gorge & The Wrekin Visitor Guide,* including an accommodation listing, is available free.

TIC: *The Wharfage, Ironbridge; tel: (01952) 432166,* open Mon–Fri 0900–1700, Sat–Sun 1000–1700 (usually closes earlier in winter). Offers the same services as the main TIC.

ACCOMMODATION

There is a good selection of hotels, guesthouses and b&bs in Telford and Ironbridge, so it is usually not difficult to book on arrival.

Hotel chains include *BW, Ct, Hd, MH* and *PL.*

HI: **Ironbridge**, *Paradise, Coalbrookdale, nr Ironbridge; tel: (01952) 433281.* The nearest **campsite** is the **Severn Gorge Caravan Park**, *Bridgnorth Rd, Tweedale; tel: (01952) 684789*; 2 miles south.

OUT OF TOWN

This new town, a burgeoning business centre, is the jumping-off point for Britain's best industrial heritage museum. The nearby River Severn gorge witnessed a key event in the industrial revolution: Abraham Darby discovered how to mass produce iron. He built the world's first **Iron Bridge** in 1779 and this is the focal point of the seven sites that spread over 6 square miles and make up the **Ironbridge Gorge Museum**, *Ironbridge; tel: (01952) 433522 (432166 at weekends).* All open daily 1000– 1700 (Easter–Oct); some (including Blists Hill) remain open year round; £8.95 (passport ticket covering all seven). 5 miles south-west.

One of the largest aviation-related collections in the UK is located at the **Aerospace Museum**, *Cosford, Shifnal; tel: (01902) 374872,* open daily 1000– 1700 (all year); £4.50. 8 miles east. 80- plus aircraft on show ranging from World War II fighters to modern pas- senger airliners.

Weston Park, *Weston-under-Lizard, nr Shifnal; tel: (01952) 850207.* House open 1300–1700 (Easter–Sept); £5 (house, park and gardens). Often closed for 'routine' visits; check before going. 5–6 miles east. This is a 17th-century mansion with contents that include Aubusson and Gobelin tapestries, paint- ings by such masters as Van Dyck, Gainsborough, Holbein and Stubbs and superb antique furniture. ◾

BIRMINGHAM

TIC: *2 City Arcade, Birmingham, West Midlands B2 5TX; tel: 643 2514 or 605 7000,* open Mon–Sat 0930–1730, closed public holidays. DP SHS services offered; local bed-booking (fee £2 or 10% of first night) and BABA (latest 1700; 10% of first night or variable fee). Busy for accom- modation bookings during major events at the **National Exhibition Centre (NEC)**. The *Pocket Guide to Birmingham* is free and includes an accommodation list.

TIC: *Exhibition Centre, Birmingham; tel: 780 4321,* open Mon–Thur 0845–1700, Fri 0845–1645, open weekends during major exhibitions. DP services offered; local bed-booking, BABA.

TIC: *130 Colmore Row, Birmingham, B3 3AP; tel: 693 6300,* open Mon–Sat 0930–1800, Sun 1000–1600. Usual infor- mation services plus half-price theatre ticket booking service.

Information Desk, *Birmingham Airport; tel: 767 5511,* open 24 hours. DP Accommodation lists available, with courtesy telephones for bookings.

ARRIVING AND DEPARTING

Airport: **Birmingham International Airport**, 9 miles east of centre; *tel: 767 5511.* See p.38 for transport details from the airport.

A taxi into the centre costs about £11. **Station**: The main rail stations are **Birmingham International**, at the air- port (see above), and **Birmingham New St**, *New St,* in the city centre, where a taxi rank and car hire service are available.

GETTING AROUND

Although Birmingham and its satellite towns stretch for miles in all directions, most attractions are within walking dis- tance of the centre. Town and transport maps are available free from the TICs. For

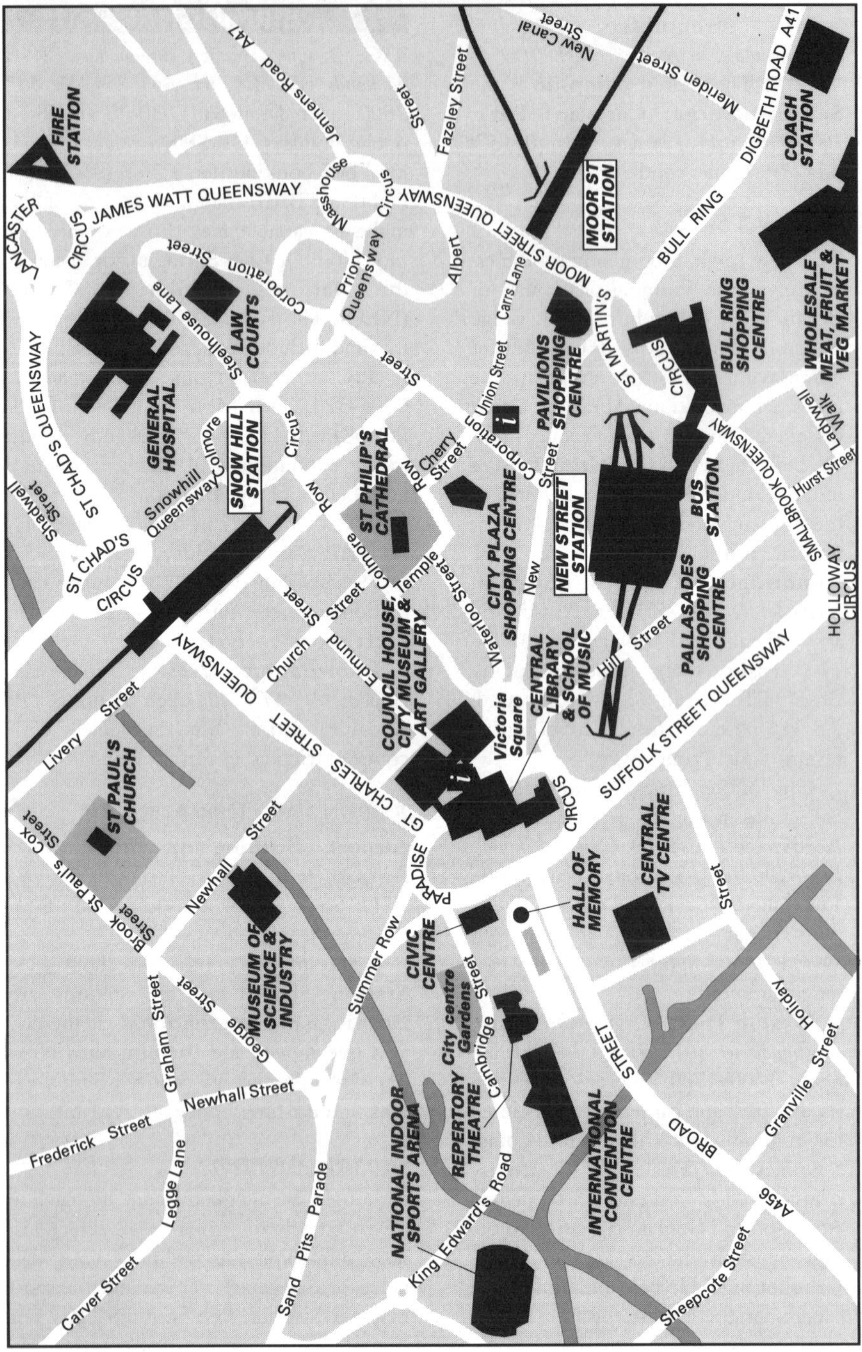
FIRE STATION
LANCASTER CIRCUS
JAMES WATT QUEENSWAY
A47
Jennens Road
Masshouse Circus
Fazeley Street
New Canal Street
Meriden Street
MOOR ST STATION
MOOR STREET QUEENSWAY
BULL RING
DIGBETH ROAD A41
COACH STATION
WHOLESALE MEAT, FRUIT & VEG MARKET
BULL RING SHOPPING CENTRE
ST MARTIN'S CIRCUS
PAVILIONS SHOPPING CENTRE
Carrs Lane
Albert Street
Priory Queensway
Corporation Street
Steelhouse Lane
LAW COURTS
GENERAL HOSPITAL
ST CHAD'S QUEENSWAY
Shadwell Street
Snowhill Queensway
Colmore Circus
SNOW HILL STATION
ST CHAD'S CIRCUS
ST PHILIP'S CATHEDRAL
Cherry Street
Colmore Row
Temple Row
Union Street
CITY PLAZA SHOPPING CENTRE
New Street
NEW STREET STATION
BUS STATION
Ladywell Walk
Hurst Street
SMALLBROOK QUEENSWAY
PALLASADES SHOPPING CENTRE
HOLLOWAY CIRCUS
Hill Street
SUFFOLK STREET QUEENSWAY
CENTRAL LIBRARY & SCHOOL OF MUSIC
Victoria Square
Waterloo Street
COUNCIL HOUSE, CITY MUSEUM & ART GALLERY
Edmund Street
Church Street
GT CHARLES STREET QUEENSWAY
Livery Street
ST PAUL'S CHURCH
Cox Street
St Paul's Street
Brook Street
Newhall Street
MUSEUM OF SCIENCE & INDUSTRY
PARADISE CIRCUS
CIVIC CENTRE
HALL OF MEMORY
CENTRAL TV CENTRE
Summer Row
City centre Gardens
Cambridge Street
REPERTORY THEATRE
BROAD STREET
Holliday Street
Granville Street
A456
INTERNATIONAL CONVENTION CENTRE
NATIONAL INDOOR SPORTS ARENA
King Edward's Road
Sheepcote Street
Sand Pits Parade
George Street
Graham Street
Frederick Street
Legge Lane
Carver Street

general transport information call the **Centro Hotline**; *tel: 200 2700*. The majority of local **bus** services are operated from the **Midland Red Bus Station**, behind Birmingham New St. Services are frequent, both within the city and to the suburbs, and an hourly night service operates on main routes.

Main **taxi** ranks can be found on *New St, Corporation St* and *Colmore Row*. For a black cab, *tel: 427 8888*.

STAYING IN BIRMINGHAM

Accommodation and Food

It is usually easy to book on arrival, except during major events at the **NEC**, when it is advisable to book in advance. There is a good range of hotel, guesthouse and b&b accommodation, with cheaper establishments located just outside the centre. Hotel chains in Birmingham include *BW, Ca, CI, Cp, FP, Hd, Ib, MC, MH, Nv, QI, ST, SW* and *Th*. During the holidays, **university** accommodation is available; *tel: 359 8489*. For **campsite** information contact the TICs for a list. None of the sites is within easy reach of the centre.

A free list of restaurants is available from the TICs. There is a large choice of international cuisine in all price ranges. Birmingham is well known for its many Balti restaurants (Kashmiri cooking) to the south of the city – in Sparkbrook, Bamsall Heath and Moseley – and its lively Chinatown around *Hurst St*.

Communications

The main **post office**, *Victoria Sq.*, is open Mon–Fri 0910–1710, Sat 0900–1200, and has poste restante facilities.

Birmingham's **tel. area code** is *0121*.

Money

Thomas Cook has **bureaux de change**

in the centre: *99 New St* and *50 Corporation St*, and at Midland Bank, *130 New St*.

ENTERTAINMENT

Free events listings and *What's On* magazine are available from the TICs. Birmingham has plenty of entertainment to offer, a sample of which is listed below.

Theatre, Opera and Ballet: **Alexandra Theatre**, *Suffolk St, Queensway; tel: 643 1231* (home to the D'Oyly Carte Opera Company). **Birmingham Hippodrome**, *Hurst St; tel: 622 7486* (home to the Birmingham Royal Ballet). **Birmingham Repertory Theatre**, *Broad St; tel: 236 4555*.

Music: **National Indoor Arena**, *King Edward's Rd; tel: 200 2000*. **NEC Arena Birmingham**, *National Exhibition Centre; tel: 780 4133*. **Symphony Hall**, *Broad St; tel: 212 3333* (home of the City of Birmingham Symphony Orchestra).

Sport: **National Indoor Arena**, *King Edward's Rd; tel: 200 2000* (home to the television Gladiators). **Warwickshire County Cricket Club**, *County Ground, Edgbaston; tel: 446 4422*.

SHOPPING

There are various shopping centres to explore, including the **Arcadian Centre**, *Hurst St*; **Bull Ring Shopping Centre**, *Bull Ring*; **City Plaza**, *Cannon St*; **Pallasades Shopping Centre**, *The Pallasades*; and **The Pavilions**, *High St*. Pay a visit to the **Jewellery Quarter** in Hockley, which has been the centre of the British jewellery industry for almost 200 years.

There are also markets for bargain hunters: **Bull Ring Centre Market Hall**, *Bull Ring*, open Mon–Sat; **Rag Market**, *Edgbaston St*, open Tues, Fri and Sat, with an antiques market on Mon;

171

Row and Flea Markets, *adjacent to Rag Market*, open Tues, Fri and Sat.

SIGHTSEEING

Britain's second city (after London) cannot claim to be the most attractive of conurbations – it has been extensively rebuilt since World War II and is renowned more as a business and conference centre than a tourist venue. Despite this, it has a thriving cultural life, has built up a number of excellent visitor attractions and makes a good accommodation base for sightseeing in the Midlands.

For a trip around Birmingham's extensive old waterways network – which gives a whole new perspective on the city's many flyovers – contact **Brummagem Boats**, *Sherborne Street Wharf; tel: 455 6163*, departing at 1130, 1400 and 1600 (Easter–Oct). **Guide Friday**, *tel: 6432514*, offer sightseeing **bus tours** starting from *Waterloo St*; from £6.

The city offers a number of good art collections and museums. Notable for fine and decorative art is the **Birmingham Museum and Art Gallery**, *Chamberlain Sq.; tel: 235 2834*, open Mon–Sat 1000–1700, Sun 1230–1700; free. This is home to the world's finest Pre-Raphaelite collection.

Birmingham's important contribution to technology is celebrated at the **Museum of Science and Industry**, *Newhall St; tel: 235 1661*, open Mon–Sat 1000–1700, Sun 1230–1700; free.

For a glimpse of working life in another of the traditional local industries, try the **Jewellery Quarter Discovery Centre**, *77–79 Vyse Street, Hockley; tel: (0121) 554 3598*, open Mon–Fri 1000–1600, Sat 1100–1700; £2.

Among the other museums and galleries in town are: **Birmingham Shakespeare Memorial Room**,

Chamberlain Sq.; tel: 235 3382, open Mon–Sat 0900–1700 (by prior arrangement); free. **The Ikon Gallery**, *58–72 John Bright St; tel: 643 0708*, open Tues–Sat 1100–1800 (Thur–2000); free. **Railway Museum**, *670 Warwick Rd, Tyseley; tel: 707 4696*, open daily 1000–1700 (dusk in winter); free.

The city's latest major attraction is the **Sea-Life Centre**, *The Water's Edge, Brindleyplace; tel: 633 4700*, open daily 1000–1700; £6.50.

The city has several churches worthy of note. **St Chad's Cathedral**, *St Chad's Queensway; tel: 236 2251*, open daily 0910–1830; free. **St Martin's in the Bull Ring**, *Bull Ring; tel: 643 5428*, open Mon–Sat 1000–1600; free. **St Paul's Church**, *St Paul's Sq.; tel: 236 7858*, open Mon, Wed, Fri 1200–1430, Sun for services; free. **St Philip's Cathedral**, *Colmore Row; tel: 236 6323/4333*, open Mon–Sat 0800–1730, Sun 1300–1545; free. Among the historic buildings is 18th-century **Soho House**, *Soho Ave, Handsworth; tel: 554 9122*, open Tues–Sat 1000–1700, Sun 1200–1700; £2.

OUT OF TOWN

Cadbury World, *Lineen Rd, Bournville; tel: 451 4180* for opening times. It is advisable to book tickets in advance, *tel: 451 4159*; £6. 5 miles south. This is devoted to the development of one of Birmingham's industries: chocolate – with free samples to aid the understanding!

To see a fine Jacobean house, with 27 period rooms, visit **Aston Hall**, *Trinity Rd, Aston; tel: 327 0062*, open daily 1400–1700 (Easter–Oct); free. 3 miles north.

Another historic building is **Perrott's Folly**, *Waterworks Rd*, open Sun, public holidays 1400–1700 (Easter–Sept); £1.50. 2 miles west.

CHESTER-YORK

This route links two of England's ancient cities and provides an opportunity to visit some of the country's great commercial centres spawned by the Industrial Revolution. Manchester, Bradford and Leeds may have been hell-holes at times in the past, but today they are vibrant, go-ahead places with lively multi-ethnic communities and plenty to see and do.

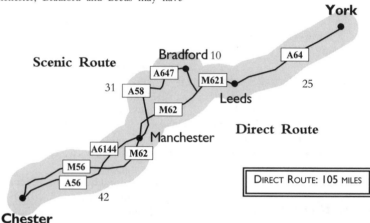

Scenic Route — Bradford 10 · A647 · A58 · 31 · M62 · Manchester · A6144 · M62 · M56 · A56 · 42 — **Chester**

York · A64 · M621 · Leeds · 25 · **Direct Route**

DIRECT ROUTE: 105 MILES

173

ROUTES

DIRECT ROUTE

The 105 miles can be covered in 2 hrs. From central Chester take A56 east for 2 miles, turn left on M23 north and continue for a further 3 miles to join M56 east at Junction 15. Follow this motorway for 17 miles to Junction 9, then join M6 north and after 6 miles, at Junction 21a, follow M62 east for 48 miles to Junction 27, just east of Bradford. Continue on M621 for 5 miles to the outskirts of Leeds, following signs to A64, which continues east for 20 miles to become part of the York ring road system. Follow signs for 4 miles into city centre.

SCENIC ROUTE

Adding some 27 miles and another hour to the journey, this route provides a chance to see something of the north Cheshire countryside and smaller towns, and the grandeur of the moors between **Manchester** and **Bradford**.

From central Chester take A56 north-east for 27 miles to Lymm, then continue on A6144 to Stretford and follow signs to Manchester city centre, reached after a total of 42 miles. Leave Manchester on A664 north to reach Rochdale after 11 miles. Head east on A58, which reaches Halifax after 15 miles, then follow A647 for 8 miles north-east to Bradford. M62 and M621 form the best route between Bradford and **Leeds**. Continue to York as in the direct route.

MANCHESTER

TIC: *Manchester Visitor Centre, Town Hall Extension, Lloyd St, Manchester M60 2LA; tel: (0161) 234 3157/8,* open Mon–Sat 1000–1730, Sun, public holidays 1100–1600. DP services offered; local bed-booking (latest 30 mins before closing) and BABA (latest bookings 1 hr before closing) – all accommodation bookings are subject to a (variable) fee. Tickets sold for city walking tours. *Manchester City Guide for Visitors* is £1, but *Where to Stay* is free. Out of hours 24-hr touch-screen outside the TIC – or *tel: (0891) 715533* (premium rate).

TIC: *International Arrival Hall, Terminal 1, Manchester Airport; tel: (0161) 436 3344,* open daily 0800–2100. DP services offered; local bed-booking and BABA. TIC: *International Arrival Hall, Terminal 2, Manchester Airport; tel: (0161) 489 6412,* open daily 0930–1230. DP services as Terminal 1.

ARRIVING AND DEPARTING

Airport: Manchester Airport, 10 miles south of the centre; *tel: (0161) 489 3000,* or – premium rate and you need the flight number – *(0839) 888747* (international flights), *(0839) 888757* (domestic flights). There are bureaux de change (including **Thomas Cook**) in both terminals and a courtesy bus between the terminals. **Rail connections** into **Piccadilly Station.** **GM Buses** 44/105/107 provide regular links with Piccadilly Bus Station; £1.80–£2 one-way. **Airtax,** *tel: (0161) 499 9000,* are black cabs based at the airport; about £12 to the centre. See p. 40 for road connections from the airport.

Stations: The two main rail stations are linked to each other (and the TIC) by Metrolink. The central **Piccadilly Station,** *off London Rd,* is the more important and a boarding point for Eurostar

trains. It has both a taxi rank and a **Hertz** car hire office; *tel: (0161) 236 2747.* **Victoria Station,** *off Corporation St,* is for suburban trains.

GETTING AROUND

Local **bus and rail enquiries,** *tel: (0161) 228 7811.* The city centre and surrounding suburbs are well served by Metrolink, and there are reasonable bus and train services, both within the city and to outlying towns. The TICs can provide free town and transport maps. Most in-town attractions are within walking distance of the centre. **Shopmobility,** *tel: (0161) 839 4060.*

Metrolink, *205 2000,* is an excellent **tram** system, running every 6–15 mins between the southern suburb of Altrincham and Bury (9 miles north), with eight stations in the city centre. Tickets from machines at stations.

The main local **bus** depot is **Piccadilly Bus Station,** *Piccadilly; tel: (0161) 228 7811.* There are many different bus companies in Manchester and a wide range of special tickets. Both the TIC and the Travel Centre in the bus station can give full information.

Main **taxi** ranks are at the airport, rail stations, *Albert Sq., Piccadilly Gdns* and *Whitworth St West.*

STAYING IN MANCHESTER

Accommodation and Food

The Manchester district has over 18,000 beds, across all accommodation categories, so it's usually easy to find somewhere to stay on arrival. There is a good choice of larger hotels in the centre and cheaper b&b, guesthouse, pub and self-catering accommodation in the suburbs, particularly to the south (Chorlton, Didsbury and Fallowfield). Hotel chains include *CI, Cp, Ct, FP, Hd, Ja, MH, Nv, Rm* and *Th.* **University** accommodation is available in the holidays at Woolton Hall (3 miles from the centre); *tel: (0161)224 7244.*

HI: *Potato Wharf, Castlefield; tel: (0161)839 9960.* The closest **campsites** are: **Gelder Wood Country Park**, *Ashworth Rd, Heywood, Rochdale; tel: (01706) 364858,* 9 miles north; **Burrs Country Park Campsite**, *Burrs, Woodhill Rd, Bury; tel: (0161)764 9649,* 10 miles north.

The TIC has a free *Food and Drink Guide.* The choice is overwhelming, with the cuisine of over 20 nationalities available and cheap eateries all over town. Manchester has the largest Chinese population in Britain, so **Chinatown** offers an exceptionally wide choice; **Rusholme** is the Indian area, the best range of eating places being in *Wilmslow Rd.*

Communications and Money

The main **post office**, *26 Spring Gardens,* opens Mon–Fri 0830–1800, Sat 0830–1900. Poste restante facilities.

There are **Thomas Cook bureaux de change** at *100 King St.* and *22 Cross St.*

The main entertainment magazine is the fortnightly *City Life* (£1.40 from newsagents and TICs). The city offers an enormous choice.

Theatre, Opera and Ballet

Dancehouse Theatre, *Oxford Rd; tel: (0161)237 9753* (theatre). **Green Room**, *Whitworth St West; tel: (0161)950 5900* (fringe theatre, cabaret). **Palace Theatre**, *Oxford Rd; tel: (0161)242 2503* (theatre, ballet, opera). **Royal Exchange Theatre**, *Upper Campfield Market; tel: 833*

9833 (theatre). **Royal Northern College of Music**, *Oxford Rd; tel: 273 4504* (opera, ballet, jazz). **Opera House**, *Quay St; tel: 242 2509* (theatre, musicals, opera, dance).

Music

Apollo Theatre, *Ardwick Green; tel: 242 2503* (concerts). **BBC Philharmonic**, *New Broadcasting House, Oxford Rd; tel: 244 4001* (classical). **GMEX**, *Windmill St, Mosley St; tel: 832 9000* (international exhibitions, events, pop concerts). **Bridgewater Hall**, *Lower Mosley St; tel: 907 9000* (international concert hall, home of the **Hallé Orchestra**).

Sport

Manchester City Football Club, *Maine Rd; tel: 224 5000.* **Manchester United Football Club**, *Old Trafford; tel: 872 1661.* **Lancashire County Cricket Club**, *Old Trafford, Talbot Rd; tel: 282 4040.* **Nynex Arena**, *behind Victoria Station; tel: (0161) 950 5000,* is home to Manchester's ice hockey and basketball teams, but also hosts diverse entertainments for large audiences.

The TIC produce an events calendar. Major annual events include the **Lord Mayor's Parade**, *City Centre* (mid June); and **Manchester Festival**, various venues (Sept–Oct), a live arts and television event.

Arndale Centre, *Market St,* has over 150 outlets. The pedestrianised area of *St Ann's Sq/King St* is the place for designer labels, while the **Northern Quarter** is best for speciality shopping. As well as **Arndale Market**, *Arndale Centre,* and **Castlefield Street Market**, *Castlefield,* there are weekly **flea markets** at Gorton,

175

Harpurhey, Longsight, Moss Side, Wythenshawe and Beswick.

SIGHTSEEING

Manchester is a new city by British standards, having developed as one of the centres of the industrial revolution. Much spruced up in recent years to counteract its once dour image, it boasts first-class museums and lively nightlife; while superb countryside, historic houses and parks are within easy reach. It is a convenient base for touring the north-west.

A variety of **BBG guided walks** is available, from £2.50, but pre-booking is advisable: contact the TIC for details. The TIC can also provide full information about 1-hr guided **minibus tours** of Manchester, which leave from the **Central Library**, *Peter St;* Mon–Fri at 1000, 1100, 1200, 1400 and 1500 (May–Sept); £9.50. Alternatively, **boat trips** on the canal system provide a good insight into how Manchester's wealth was created: contact **Bridgewater Packet-boat Service**, *tel: (0161) 748 2680*; **Egerton Narrow Boats**, *tel: (0161) 833 9878*; or **Irwell and Mersey Packet-boat Company**, *tel: (0161) 736 2108.*

If you want to see behind the scenes at a major television and film studio, don't miss the **Granada Studios Tour**, *Water St, Castlefield; tel: 832 4999* (24-hr information), open daily all year, but Granada is a working studio and times vary, so telephone for details; £12.99.

Just around the corner is the excellent **Museum of Science and Industry**, *Liverpool Rd; tel: 832 1830* (24-hr information), open daily 1000–1700; £5. There are 15 galleries, offering everything from intergalactic inventions to old steam engines, with a hands-on Visitor Centre and changing exhibitions.

The Pump House: People's

History Museum, *Left Bank, Bridge St; tel: 839 6061*, open Tues–Sun, public holidays 1100–1630; £1. This covers the lives of ordinary people, from Victorian cotton workers to contemporary footballers.

As well as excellent collections of ceramics, sculptures and decorative arts, there is a celebrated exhibition of Pre-Raphaelite paintings at the **City Art Galleries**, *Mosley St; tel: 236 5244*, open Mon 1100–1730, Tues–Sat 1000–1730, Sun 1400–1730; free.

Museum of Transport, *Boyle St, Cheetham; tel: (0161) 205 2122*, open Wed, Sat–Sun, public holidays 1000–1700; £2.50; 1 mile north. Dedicated to Greater Manchester's public transport systems, from horse-drawn carriages to the Metrolink.

Manchester Museum, *University of Manchester, Oxford Rd; tel: 275 2634*, open Mon–Sat 1000–1700; free. 1 mile south; buses 40–49. Wide-ranging displays take you from dinosaur prints to live reptiles. **Whitworth Art Gallery**, *University of Manchester, Oxford Rd; tel: (0161) 275 7450*, open Mon–Sat 1000–1700; Sun 1400–1700; free. There are collections of textiles, wallpapers, sculptures and all types of pictures. **Gallery of English Costume**, *Platt Hall, Rusholme; tel: (0161) 224 5217*, open Tues–Sat 1000–1730 (Mar–Oct); Tues–Sat 1000–1600 (Nov–Feb); free. 1 mile south of the centre. One of the country's finest collections of costumes from the 17th century onwards is contained in an elegant Georgian house.

Manchester United Museum and Tour Centre, *Sir Matt Busby Way, Old Trafford; tel: (0161) 877 4002*, open Tues–Sun, most public holidays 0930–1600 (on match days closes 30 mins before kick-off); £2.95 (museum), £5.50 (with tour). 3 miles south-west. For soccer enthusiasts, the 'backstage' tour is a must.

BRADFORD

TIC: *Central Library, Bradford; tel: (01274) 753678;* (there is a possibility of the TIC moving, but the telephone number should remain the same, so ring to check), open Mon–Fri 0900–1730, Sat 0900–1700. DP services offered; local bed-booking and BABA; *Haworth and Ilkley* guides and an accommodation listing are free.

GETTING AROUND

Most attractions are walkable from the centre. Town and transport maps are free from the TIC and the station. The main bus operator is **Yorkshire Rider** and services are quite good within the town. For bus and train information throughout west Yorkshire, contact **Metro**, *tel: (0113) 245 7676.*

ACCOMMODATION AND FOOD

There is a good range of accommodation, particularly guesthouses and b&bs. Cheaper accommodation is located mainly in outlying villages. It is generally easy to book on arrival. Hotel chains represented are *Ja, Ma, Nv* and *ST*. There is accommodation at the **university** during the holidays: *tel: (01274) 384889.* **HI**: **Haworth**, *Longlands Hall, Longlands Drive, Lees Lane, Haworth; tel: (01535) 642234.* The TIC has details of **campsites** in the area, including **Dobrudden Caravan Park**, *Baildon Moor, Baildon; tel: (01274) 581016,* 7½ miles north of the centre.

Bradford is noted for the enormous number of places offering food from the Indian sub-continent.

SIGHTSEEING

Wool and Bradford are almost synonymous, such was its importance in the 19th century after the industrial revolution brought steam power to the wool trade. Like many small market towns that

exploded into industrial cities almost overnight, Bradford's architecture is a mixture of grand civic buildings and factories.

You can step into the world of colour at the award-winning **Colour Museum**, *Providence St; tel: (01274) 390955,* open Tues–Fri 1400–1700, Sat 1000–1600; £1.50. The fascinating **National Museum of Photography, Film and Television**, *Pictureville,* is closed for major refurbishment, but due to re-open late 1998/early 1999, so ask at the TIC. In the meantime, some of its collection can be seen at *Treadwell's Art Mill, Upper Parkgate.*

For a different kind of experience, visit Bradford's Gothic Victorian **Undercliffe Cemetery**, *Undercliffe Lane; tel: (01274) 642276,* open daily 0900–dusk; free. Here you will find ornate tombstones, with weeping angels, marble obelisks and even an Egyptian tomb with sphinxes.

Set on a rise, its detailed carvings catching the eye, particularly the 20 angels supporting the nave roof, is **Bradford Cathedral**, *Church Bank; tel: (01274) 777720,* open daily 0830–1730; free.

OUT OF TOWN

Wool baron Henry Butterfield made Cliffe Castle his home and part of the building is still furnished and decorated in the lavish style of the 1880s. The museum specialises in natural history, geology and local history. **Cliffe Castle Museum**, *Spring Gardens Lane, Keighley; tel: (01535) 618230,* open Tues–Sat, public holidays 1000–1700, Sun 1200–1700; free. 10 miles north.

Once the home of the remarkable Brontë family, the small Georgian parsonage in Haworth is now an intimate museum. This is where the writers of *Jane Eyre* (Charlotte), *Wuthering Heights* (Emily) and *The Tenant of Wildfell Hall* (Anne), lived. **Brontë Parsonage Museum**,

177

Church St, Haworth; tel: (01535) 642323, open daily 1000–1700 (Apr–Sept); daily 1100–1630 (Oct–mid Jan, mid Feb–Mar); £3.80. 8 miles west.

A brick-roofed former spinning room in a Victorian woollen mill has been transformed into the **1853 Gallery**, *Salts Mill, Victoria Rd, Saltaire, Shipley; tel: (01274) 531163*, open daily 1000–1800; free. 4 miles north. This houses Europe's largest collection of the works of Bradford-born artist **David Hockney**.

Bolling Hall, *Bowling Hall Rd; tel: (01274) 723057*, open Wed–Fri, public holidays 1100–1600, Sat 1000–1700, Sun 1200–1700; free. 1 mile south. Bolling has a domestic atmosphere uncommon in stately homes.

Bradford Industrial and Horses at Work Museum, *Moorside Mills, Moorside Rd; tel: (01274) 631756*, open Tues–Sat, public holidays 1000–1700, Sun 1200–1700; £2. 3½ miles north-east. Bradford's heritage is reflected in this museum, which covers wool mills, steam engines and live shire horses.

East Riddlesden Hall (NT), *Bradford Rd, Keighley; tel: (01535) 607075*, open Sat 1300–1700, Sun 1100–1700, Mon–Wed 1200–1700 (Easter–Oct); also Thur 1200–1700 (July–Aug); £3. 8 miles north. The attractive 17th-century manor has panelled rooms, fine plasterwork and mullioned windows.

LEEDS

TIC, Gateway Yorkshire: *City Station, Leeds, West Yorkshire LS1 1PL; tel: (0113) 242 5242*, open Mon–Sat 0930–1800, Sun 1000–1600. Services offered: local bedbooking and BABA – one day ahead only. Guided walks booked. There are free accommodation and events listings, as well as sightseeing literature. A town map is 10p.

GETTING AROUND

The majority of the city's attractions are within walking distance of the centre. Free transport maps are available from the TIC. For bus and train information throughout west Yorkshire, contact **Metro**; *tel: (0113) 245 7676*.

A good bus service runs throughout the region, mostly from the **central bus depot**, *Duke St*. A reduced service operates after 2000 and Sun, but there are night buses in and around the city on Fri and Sat.

The main **taxi** rank is at Leeds railway station and there are others in the centre.

ACCOMMODATION

Accommodation of all types is available. The cheaper properties are in the suburbs, Headingley, Roundhay and Moortown, 2–4 miles north of the centre. It is generally easy to find accommodation on arrival, except July–Aug. **Accommodation hotline** freephone: *tel: (0800) 808050*. Hotel chains in Leeds include *Hd, Hn, Ma, MC, Mo* and *Th*.

Campsites include: **Roundhay Park**, *Princes Ave; tel: (0113) 2266 1850*, 4 miles north-east; and **Moor Lodge Caravan Park**, *Blackmore Lane, Bardsey; tel: (01937) 572 424*, 5 miles north-east.

SIGHTSEEING

Boat trips are operated by **Yorkshire Hire Cruises**, *tel: (0113) 2456195*, from Leeds Waterfront; £1.50. **Guided walks** of the city are organised by Leeds County Council every Wed and Sun (Easter–mid Sept); £2.50.

The city centre has some impressive Victorian buildings, including the **Corn Exchange**, which now houses speciality shops and exhibitions, and the magnificent **Town Hall**.

Paintings, sculptures and one of the best

20th-century collections in the country can be seen at **Leeds City Art Gallery**, *The Headrow; tel: (0113) 247 8248,* open Mon–Fri 1000–1700; Wed 1000–2000; Sat 1300–1700; free, while **Leeds City Museum**, *The Headrow; tel: (0113) 247 8275,* open Tues–Sat 1000–1700; free, offers an excellent natural history gallery and displays of Roman artefacts. **Henry Moore Sculpture Gallery**, *The Headrow; tel: (0113) 234 3158,* open daily 1000–1730 (2100 Wed); free, is dedicated to sculpture of all periods.

Royal Armouries Museum, *Armouries Drive; tel: (0990) 106666,* open daily 1000–1800 (Apr–Oct); 1000–1700 (Nov–Mar); (2200 first Thur each month); £6.95. This is a unique new development, with exciting live demonstrations, films and interactive displays that bring the history of arms and armour up to date.

Tetley's Brewery Wharf, *The Waterfront; tel: (0113) 242 0666,* open Tues–Sun, public holidays 1030–1730; £4.95. Tetley's are one of the country's leading brewers and beer is taken seriously. If you are over 14 you can tour the actual brewery (£2), but the rest of the complex is strictly for fun.

OUT OF TOWN

To see how medicine has changed over the last century and a half, visit the hands-on **Thackray Medical Museum**, *Beckett St, Burmantofts; tel: (0113) 244 4343,* open Tues–Sun 1000–1700; £3.95. 2 miles north-east.

Roundhay Park, *Prince's Ave,* a large, natural park 3 miles north of the centre. Opposite Roundhay are the formal **Canal Gardens**, home to **Tropical World**, *Prince's Ave; tel: (0113) 266 1850,* open daily 1000–dusk; free. Here you will find indoor tropical forests, tumbling waterfalls and clear pools, butterflies, fish, exotic birds and mammals.

On a river island site is 19th-century Thwaite Mill, a preserved water-powered grinding mill, complete with waterwheels. **Thwaite Mills Industrial Museum**, *Thwaite Gate, Stourton; tel: (0113) 249 6453,* open Tues–Sun 1300–1700 (Apr–Oct); £2. 2 miles south.

Kirkstall Abbey, *Kirkstall Rd; tel: (0113) 2275 5821,* open daily dawn–dusk; free. 3 miles west (A65). The ruins retain many impressive features: a transept, cloisters and chapter house. A colourful record of Victorian street life, including a toy gallery and reconstructed street, is presented by the nearby **Abbey House Museum**, *Kirkstall Rd; tel: (0113) 275 5821,* open Tues–Sat 1000–1700, Sun 1300–1700; £2.

Temple Newsam House, *off Selby Rd; tel: (0113) 2264 7321,* open Tues–Sun 1300–1700 (Apr–Oct); Sat–Sun 1300–1700 (Nov–Mar); £2; 4 miles east. This is a Tudor–Jacobean mansion with Chippendale furniture and an extensive collection of decorative arts, set in 1200 acres of parkland, encompassing a farm with some rare breeds.

Harewood House, *Harrogate Rd, Harewood; tel: (0113) 288 6331.* House open daily 1100–last entry 1630; £6.50. 7 miles north-east. The magnificent historic house has an excellent art gallery, a bird garden and beautifully landscaped grounds – courtesy of Capability Brown.

Edwardian Lotherton is also a treasure trove of decorative arts and costumes and has an exceptionally fine bird garden, with over 200 species. **Lotherton Hall**, *Aberford; tel: (0113) 281 3259,* open Tues–Sun 1300–1700 (Apr–Oct); Sat–Sun 1300–1700 (Nov–Mar); £2. 13 miles north-east.

179

THE COTSWOLDS

This mainly rural region, ideal for touring by car and bicycle, and for walking, covers about 800 square miles in Gloucestershire and Oxfordshire and small parts of Warwickshire and Worcestershire.

Lovely landscapes, cottages and substantial buildings of warm Cotswold stone, country pubs, many with home-cooked food, and market towns with small specialist shops make the region popular with visitors all year round, and parking often requires much patience.

Market towns and villages of the Cotswolds include Bourton-on-the-Water, Burford, Charlbury, Chipping Campden, Chipping Norton, Cirencester (see p.110), Fairford, Lechlade, Moreton-in-Marsh, Northleach, Stow-on-the-Wold and Tetbury.

TOURIST INFORMATION

TICs are at **The Brewery**, *Sheep St, Burford; tel: (01993) 823558* (seasonal opening); **Corn Hall**, *Market Place, Cirencester; tel: (01285) 654180* **Woodstaplers Hall Museum**, *High St, Chipping Camden; tel: (01386) 840101* **Cotswold Countryside Collection**, *Northleach; tel: (01451) 860715* (seasonal opening); **Hollis House**, *The Square, Stow-on-the-Wold; tel: (01451) 831082;* and *63 Long St, Tetbury; tel: (01666) 503552* (seasonal opening).

All offer BABA, local accommodation reservations and usual information services.

ACCOMMODATION AND FOOD

Much of the accommodation in the Cotswolds is in guesthouses and b&bs, working farms and village inns, offering tasteful rooms and warm hospitality. Some are non-smoking establishments. There is also a good choice of self-catering cottages. In good walking country, a number of them are dog-friendly. Larger hotels with 20 or 30 rooms are mainly in the bigger towns. Most accommodation is in the budget–moderate category. TICs sell the *Cotswold Accommodation Guide* at 50p.

HI: there is a YHA hostel in a former 19th-century glove factory at **Charlbury**; *tel: (01608) 810202;* and another in a 16th-century building at **Stow-on-the-Wold** town centre; *tel: (01451) 830497.*

There is no shortage of pubs for good lunches and evening meals and bar food. On sunny days it may be wiser to avoid the main towns and villages in the lunchtime peak and go to one of the hostelries on the road between popular centres.

SIGHTSEEING

Bourton-on-the-Water
Bourton–on–the–Water is one of the most popular Cotswold villages. The River Windrush flows alongside the road, crossed by a series of bridges.

Miniature World, *tel: (01451) 810121,* open 1000–1730 (mid Apr–mid Oct); £1.75. This collection shows exquisitely hand-crafted scenes and models, all in fine detail.

Model Village, *tel: (01451) 820467,* open year round; £1.50. This shows

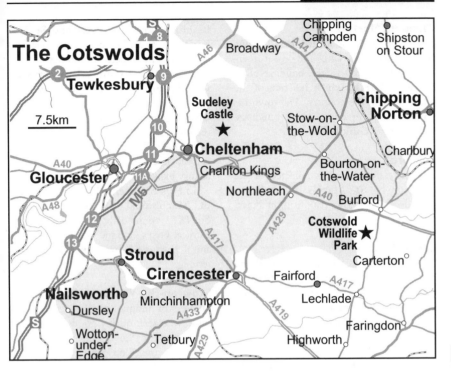

The Cotswolds

Tewkesbury

Broadway

Chipping Campden

Shipston on Stour

7.5km

Sudeley Castle ★

Stow-on-the-Wold

Chipping Norton

Cheltenham

Charlbury

A40

Gloucester

Charlton Kings

Bourton-on-the-Water

A48

Northleach

Burford

Stroud

Cotswold Wildlife Park ★

Cirencester

Fairford

Carterton

Nailsworth

Minchinhampton

Lechlade

Dursley

Wotton-under-Edge

Tetbury

Highworth

Faringdon

181

Bourton as it was in 1937, with its Cotswold stone houses, its gardens and trees at one-ninth of actual size.

Bourton Model Railway, *tel: (01451) 820686*, open daily April–Sept, weekends only Oct–Mar except Jan, when there is limited opening; £1.50. About 400 ft of scenic railway layout and working trains.

Cotswold Motor Museum and Toy Collection, *The Old Mill; tel: (01451) 821255*, open daily Feb–Nov; £1.40. Vintage advertisement signs and 1920s caravans, as well as cars and toys in an 18th-century watermill.

Bourton's newest attraction is the **Dragonfly Maze**, *Rissington Rd; tel: (01451) 822251*, open year round, 1000–dusk, admission charge. Reach the maze centre to discover the secret of the Golden Dragonfly.

Burford

Burford, in Oxfordshire, regarded as the gateway to the Cotswolds, dates from medieval times. The steep main street has Tudor and Georgian buildings. There are walks by the River Windrush.

Cotswold Wildlife Park, *Burford; tel: (01993) 823006*, open all year (narrow-gauge railway April–Oct); £5.10. There are lions and other creatures, an adventure playground and a children's farmyard area.

Charlbury

In the Wychwood Forest area, Charlbury was once a centre of the Quaker movement and the glove-making industry, has an annual street fair in September.

Chipping Campden

The **Market Hall** was built in 1627. Several shops offer local arts and crafts.

Chipping Norton

The wool trade flourished in Chipping Norton centuries ago, and wool merchants contributed to the building of **St Mary's Church**, which has one of the finest naves in the country. The town has some well-preserved medieval buildings, including the **Guildhall**.

Fairford

Prosperity from wool is reflected in the grandeur of **St Mary's Church**. Its stained-glass windows date from medieval times.

Lechlade

This is where the navigable part of the Thames begins. **Halfpenny Bridge**, which crosses the river to the town centre, has a built-in tollhouse.

Between Lechlade and Burford is the **Cotswold Woollen Weavers**, *tel: (01367) 860491*, where fleece is transformed into wool in an 18th-century mill. Woollen goods are sold in the mill shop.

Moreton-in-Marsh

The Tuesday street market in is the largest in the Cotswolds. Some 200 stalls are set up in *High St*, which is lined with 17th and 18th-century buildings.

The local skill of basket-making is commemorated at the **Inn on the Marsh** in *Stow Rd*. Dozens of baskets hang from the ceiling of the restaurant and photographs show local scenes depicting the old craft.

Cotswold Falconry Centre, *Batsford Park, Moreton-in-Marsh; tel: (01386) 701043*, open Mar–Nov; £3. Flying eagles, owls, falcons and other hawks.

Northleach

Few towns are richer in traditional Cotswold architecture than Northleach.

Its great church of **St Peter and St Paul** is in the Cotswold Perpendicular style, and there are some superb almshouses.

The Cotswold Countryside Collection, *Northleach; tel: (01451) 860715*, open late May–early Nov; £1.60. This museum in the former house of correction records many aspects of rural life, including a 'below stairs' presentation, a cell block and courtroom and agricultural history exhibits.

In *High St* is **Keith Harding's World of Mechanical Music**; *tel: (01451) 860181*, open daily 1000–1800; £5. Musical boxes, antique clocks and mechanical instruments are played in a period setting.

Stow-on-the-Wold

Hunters of antiques and collectibles, and those who seek quality goods in specialist shops flock to Stow, one of the busiest towns in the Cotswolds. The original stocks stand on the green, and there's a wide choice of pubs and teashops.

Cotswold Farm Park, *Guiting Power; tel: (01451) 850307*, open Apr–Sept; £3.50. Off B4068, 5 miles west. More than 50 breeding flocks and herds of the rarest breeds of British farm livestock can be seen rearing their young, including Gloucester Old Spot pigs and shire horses.

Tetbury

Tetbury's pillared **Market House**, dating from the 1650s, is just one of the much-photographed places in this pretty town.

Chavenage House, tel: (01666) 502329, open Sun–Thur 1400–1700; £3. 2 miles north-west. This Elizabethan house, with an interesting history and a blood-curdling legend, may seem familiar – it has featured in a number of TV programmes, including some Agatha Christie whodunnits.

COTSWOLDS–CARDIFF

Starting at the heart of the Cotswolds (see p. 180) – an area many people regard as the epitome of the English countryside – this picturesque route takes us to elegant Cheltenham (see p. 111) and the busy port and cathedral city of Gloucester, then on through one of Britain's oldest forests before following the western shore of the River Severn to the capital of Wales.

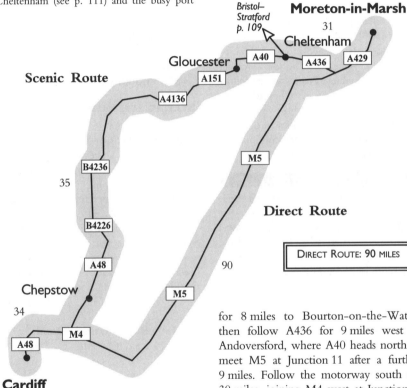

ROUTES

DIRECT ROUTE

➡ This 90-mile journey takes 1 hr 45 mins. From the Cotswold town of Moreton-in-Marsh head south on A429 for 8 miles to Bourton-on-the-Water, then follow A436 for 9 miles west to Andoversford, where A40 heads north to meet M5 at Junction 11 after a further 9 miles. Follow the motorway south for 30 miles, joining M4 west at Junction 20 to cross the River Severn. After 27 miles, leave M4 at Junction 29, joining A48, and follow local signs to reach the centre of Cardiff in 7 miles.

SCENIC ROUTE

⟶ Staying off motorways until the last 30 miles or so, this route adds about

10 miles and 45 minutes – without allowing for stops – to the direct route.

From Moreton-in-Marsh continue to Andoversford as in the direct route, then follow A40 north for 5½ miles into Cheltenham, then on for another 8 miles to Gloucester. Three miles beyond Gloucester, follow A48 south-west for 8 miles, then A4151 north to reach Cinderford in 4 miles. To see the best of the Forest of Dean, take B4226 west for 6 miles to Coleford, then head south on B4228 for 3½ miles – perhaps taking time to explore the network of unclassified forest roads – and B4234 for a further 3½ miles to Lydney. From Lydney follow A48 west for 9 miles to Chepstow. Just west of Chepstow join M48 west, which links with M4 after 6½ miles. From here the remainder of the route continues to Cardiff as in the direct route.

GLOUCESTER

TIC: *28 Southgate St, Gloucester GL1 2PD; tel: (01452) 421188*, open Mon–Sat 1000–1700. DP SHS services offered; local bed-booking (1630 latest; 10% refundable deposit), BABA (1630 latest; fee £2.50 or 10% refundable deposit). Guided tours (in summer), theatre and coach tickets booked. YHA/HI membership sold. The *Gloucester Travel Guide*, including information on where to stay, is available free of charge.

Tourist Information Point, *National Waterways Museum, The Docks*, open (to personal callers only) daily 1000–1800 (summer); 1000–1700 (winter). DP, SHS. No accommodation booking service available.

GETTING AROUND

The majority of attractions in Gloucester are within walking distance of the centre; free town and transport maps are available from the TIC. The public transport coverage is good in the centre and on popular routes, but rather patchy on some rural routes. Evening services are more limited and on Sun there are few services beyond the city centre.

A number of companies run local services from the **bus station**, *Market Parade*. The main operators are **Stagecoach Gloucester Citybus**, *tel: (01452) 527516*, who offer a range of bus passes.

The main **taxi** ranks are at the rail and bus stations. There are around eight registered taxi companies; telephone numbers available from the TIC.

Shopmobility, *tel: (01452) 396898*.

STAYING IN GLOUCESTER

Accommodation

There is a wide range of accommodation available, which is generally easy to book on arrival, except during events: Cheltenham Gold Cup (Mar), Three Choirs Festival (Aug 1998 and 2001) and Fairford International Air Tattoo (July). In addition to the many hotels, there is a good range of cheaper guesthouse and b&b accommodation – and also farmhouse accommodation within a few miles of the city. Hotel chains include *FP, HG, Ja, PL, RH* and *TI*.

Hatherley Manor Hotel, *Down Hatherley Lane, Gloucester, GL2 9QA; tel: (01452) 730217, fax: (01452) 731032*. The 56-room 17th-century hotel, five miles outside Gloucester, is set in 37 acres of parkland. Moderate.

Jarvis Bowden Hall Hotel and Country Club, *Upton St Leonards GL4 8ED; tel: (01452) 614121 fax: (01452) 611885*. Health facilities include a small gym. Expensive.

Denmark Hotel, *36 Denmark Rd, Gloucester GL1 3JQ; tel: (01452) 303808*.

Small family hotel. Moderate (some budget rooms).

Firview Guesthouse, *27–29 Heathville Rd, Gloucester GL1 3DS; tel: (01452) 521881.* Central property. Budget. **Springfield Farm**, *Witcombe, Gloucester GL3 4TU; tel: (01452) 863532.* Budget.

Witcombe Park Holiday Cottages, *Great Witcombe, Gloucester GL3 4TR; tel: (01452) 863591.* Five self-catering units for two people. Budget–moderate.

Briarfields, *Gloucester Rd, Cheltenham GL51 0SK; tel: (01242) 235324* (1 mile from Junction 11, M5). Five-acre caravan and camping site with 72 pitches with hook-ups and nearby water supply, open year-round. Budget. An 18-room motel is on site.

HI: Slimbridge, *Shepherd's Patch, Slimbridge; tel: (01453) 890275.* The closest **campsites** are: **Red Lion Camping and Caravan Site**, *Wainlode Hill, Norton; tel: (01452) 730251,* 4 miles north; **Gables Farm Camping and Caravan Site**, *Moreton Valence; tel: (01452) 720331,* 7½ miles south.

Eating and Drinking

Gloucester has a number of historic inns that offer a pleasant atmosphere, real ales and, in many instances, very good food. Outside the city there are various up-market restaurants offering excellent cuisine, such as **Kingshead House**, *Birdlip; tel: (01452) 862299,* 8 miles from Gloucester, and **Greenway Hotel**, *Shurdington Road; tel: (01242) 862352,* 9 miles from Gloucester.

Don't forget to try two of the famous local products: Double Gloucester cheese and Gloucester sausage.

Communications

The main **post office**, *King's Sq.*, is open Mon–Fri 0900–1730, Sat 0900–1230. Poste restante facilities are available.

ENTERTAINMENT AND EVENTS

Free entertainment listings, *Events in Gloucester* and the *Cheltenham and Gloucester Bulletin*, are available from the TIC; another listing is the *Gloucester Citizen* (30p from newsagents). The **Guildhall Arts Centre**, *Eastgate St; tel: (01452) 505089*, functions as the main theatre, cinema and music venue. Others are: **New Olympus Theatre**, *Barton St; tel: (01452) 505089* (box office in the Arts Centre); and **Kings Theatre**, *Kingsbarton St* (tickets available at the TIC). Gloucester has a good variety of lively nightclubs: try **Wild Wallies**, *Bruton Way*, **King of Clubs**, *Quay St* and **The Avenue**, *The Leisure Centre, Bruton Way*.

Gloucester has one of the largest dry-ski complexes in the south-west: **Gloucester Ski Centre**, *Robinswood Hill; tel: (01452) 414300*, open Mon–Fri 1000–2000, Sat–Sun 1000–1800 (Sept–July).

Gloucester, Hereford and Worcester take it in turns to host the annual **Three Choirs Festival** (Aug), of choral and sacred music, presented in the Cathedral. Gloucester's next turn is 1998, and the city will be crowded. The **Gloucester Festival** is an annual event (last week July–first week Aug), which includes many sporting and cultural activities at a variety of locations around the city. Nearby Fairford hosts a major aviation display, the **International Air Tattoo** (July).

Britain is noted for some eccentric events that have continued through the centuries. One of the better known is **Cooper's Hill Cheese Roll** (late May Bank Holiday), in which local athletes compete in chasing cheeses down *Cooper's Hill* (3 miles south-west).

SHOPPING

You can get a free shopping guide from the TIC. *North, South, East and Westgate Streets* are (or will be by end 1999) pedestrianised shopping areas, with branches of most chain stores. **Eastgate Market** contains 43 traders. Gloucester Docks also has an interesting shopping centre, including the **Gloucester Antiques Centre**, a converted warehouse with 67 antique shops.

SIGHTSEEING

Gloucester Civic Trust, *tel: (01452) 301903*, offers a programme of **walking tours**, including excellent city walks starting from *The Cross* – daily at 1430 (Aug); Sun, Wed (June–July, Sept). No charge is made, but donations are welcomed. Also tours of the docks every Sun at 1430 (Aug), starting from the information point at the Waterways Museum. The TIC can provide a walking trail that takes in some of the city's interesting churches.

Gloucester Cathedral, *Westgate St; tel: (01452) 528095*, open 0800–1700 (1800 May–Sept); closed during some events; free, but donations welcomed. The magnificent Norman cathedral would, on its own, make the town worth a visit. Its amazing riches include a vast east window with 14th-century stained glass; arguably the finest medieval cloisters in the country – featuring exquisite fan vaulting; and the painted tombs of Edward II and Robert, Duke of Normandy.

Gloucester has a small historic heart, centred on the cathedral precinct and the **Gloucester Folk Museum**, *99/103 Westgate St; tel: (01452) 526467*, open Mon–Sat 1000–1700 (all year); Sun 1000–1600 (July–Sept); free. Housed in a group of Tudor and Jacobean half-timbered houses, the museum offers hands-on displays, special exhibitions and

events, as well as a fascinating range of material covering every aspect of life in and around the city for over 500 years.

The House of the Tailor of Gloucester/Beatrix Potter Gift Shop, *9 College Court; tel: (01452) 422586*, open Mon–Sat 0930–1730; free, was the inspiration for Beatrix Potter's famous story and is now a unique gift shop that incorporates a display about her life and work.

Prison Museum *Barrack Sq.; tel: (01452) 529551, open* Mon–Sat 1000–1600 (Easter Tues–Sept); £1. The first prison museum to be part of a fully operational working prison (in the old Gate Lodge), it depicts the history of Gloucester Castle as a prison since 1792.

City Museum and Art Gallery, *Brunswick Rd; tel: (01452) 524131*, open Mon–Sat 1000–1700 (Oct–June); Mon–Sat 1000–1700, Sun 1000–1600 (July–Sept); free. Built with the Roman city wall as one of the (visible) foundations, with such intriguing exhibits as a Norman backgammon set and an Iron Age mirror.

As well as being a cathedral city, Gloucester was once a flourishing inland port, linked by canal to the River Severn. The **Docks** have been revitalised, and the 19th-century warehouses now contain some unusual museums. **National Waterways Museum**, *Llanthony Warehouse, The Docks; tel: (01452) 318054*, open daily 1000–1800 (1700 Oct–Apr); £4.50. This follows the development of Britain's inland waterways over the last two centuries: you can learn how families lived on barges, for instance, and drive a barge through a lock. They also organise 45-min **boat trips** at 1200, 1330, 1430 and 1530 (Easter–Oct); £2.50, on *Queen Boadicea II*, one of Dunkirk's 'little ships'.

Robert Opie Collection: Museum of Advertising and Packaging, *Albert*

Warehouse, The Docks; tel: (01452) 302309, open daily 1000–1700 (Mar–Oct); Tues–Sun 1000–1700 (Nov–Feb); £2.95. Follow the progress of some familiar brand names through a nostalgic look at changing fashions in advertising and packaging.

Soldiers of Gloucestershire Museum, *Custom House, The Docks; tel: (01452) 522682*, open public holidays, Tues–Sun 1000–1700 (July–Sept); £3.50. This follows the fortunes, in peace and war, of two regiments – the men and their families. You can lead a patrol through No Man's Land.

Blackfriars Priory (EH), *Southgate St*, is Britain's best example of a Dominican priory, but restoration is ongoing and access is restricted. For information, *tel: (0117) 975 0700*. Similarly, **Llanthony Priory**, with its distinctive medieval buildings, is being further restored and will be a living history centre. Already it has a nature reserve. To arrange a visit, *tel: (01452) 396620*.

OUT OF TOWN

There are scenic guided **bus tours** of the **Cotswolds** and the **Forest of Dean** (June–Sept). These are popular, so book (through the TIC) to avoid disappointment.

Nature in Art, *Wallsworth Hall, Twigworth; tel: (01452) 731422, open Tues–Sun, public holidays 1000–1700*; £2.95. 2½ miles north. The world's first museum devoted entirely to art inspired by nature – in any medium, from any period and from any country, so the exhibits are extraordinarily varied.

Prinknash Abbey Pottery, *Prinknash Abbey, Cranham; tel: (01452) 812239*, which is a working pottery (tours £1), in the grounds of the old abbey, an acknowledged beauty spot that provides

breathtaking views over the Vale of Gloucester. Entry to the grounds is free and the pottery shop is open daily 0900–1730; 4 miles east.

Berkeley Castle, *Berkeley; tel: (01453) 810332*, open Tues–Sun 1400–1700, public holidays 1100–1700 (Easter–May); Tues–Sat 1100–1700, Sun 1400–1700 (June, Sept); Mon–Sat 1100–1700, Sun 1400–1700 (July–Aug); Sun 1400–1630 (Oct); public holidays 1100–1700; £4.80. 16 miles south. The scene of Edward II's brutal murder, Berkeley is England's oldest inhabited castle. Since 1153, successive generations have gradually transformed it from a Norman fortress into a stately home, crammed with treasures and surrounded by sweeping lawns and Elizabethan terraced gardens. An added attraction is a butterfly farm, where hundreds of the beautiful creatures fly free, open same hours; £1.75.

Six miles north of Berkeley is the **Wildfowl and Wetlands Centre**, *Slimbridge; tel: (01453) 890065*, open daily 0930–1700 (May–Sept); 0930–1600 (Oct–Apr); £5. 12½ miles south. Sir Peter Scott's world-renowned collection of water birds can be viewed in 800 acres of varied wetland habitat. There are also indoor exhibits, a tropical house and heated observatory. This is an excellent place to find out about conservation in action.

CHEPSTOW

TIC: *Castle Car Park, Bridge St, Chepstow, Gwent NP6 5EY; tel: (01291) 623772*, open daily 1000–1800 (Easter–Oct). DP services offered; local bed-booking service and BABA (latest 1730). *Wye Valley and Vale of Usk* is available free and includes accommodation. There is also a *Chepstow Town Guide* which is produced annually (free, but supplies are limited).

GETTING AROUND

The TIC has free town maps and time-tables. Most local buses use the **bus station**, *Thomas St*, and are operated by **Red and White**, *tel: (01633) 266336* or **Badgerline**, *tel: (0117) 955 3231*. Services are reasonable Mon–Sat, infrequent after 2000, Sun and public holidays. For **taxis**, call: **AB**, *tel: (01291) 625696*; **MR Cabs**, *tel: (01291) 624482*; or **Bridge Cabs**, *tel: (01291) 623737*.

ACCOMMODATION

There is a small choice of hotels and a reasonable range of guesthouses, b&bs and farmhouses, usually easy to book on arrival.

George Hotel, *Moor St, Chepstow, Monmouthshire, NP6 5DB; tel: (01291) 625363*. Situated by the medieval town gate, the George has 14 en suite bedrooms. Real ales are served in the bar. Moderate.

Castle View Hotel, *16 Bridge St, Chepstow, NP6 5EZ; tel: (01291) 620349; fax: (01291) 627397*. Family-run hotel, 300 years old, with family rooms and commended cuisine in its restaurant. Moderate. **Beaufort Hotel**, *Beaufort Sq., Chepstow NP6 5EP; tel (01291) 622497*. The hotel dates from the 16th century. All guestrooms have bathrooms ensuite. The restaurant offers à la carte and table d'hôte menus and bar meals are served at lunchtimes and evenings. Moderate.

Upper Dedbury House, *Sedbury Lane, Sedbury, Chepstow NP6 7HN; tel: (01291) 627173*. Richly beamed country guesthouse allowing pets by arrangement. One mile from Chepstow. Budget.

The closest **campsite** is **St Pierre Caravan Park**, *Portskewett; tel: (01291) 425114*, 3 miles south-west.

SIGHTSEEING

Walking routes are suggested in the annual *Chepstow Town Guide* (free). A town of narrow, steep streets, Chepstow stands on cliffs at the southern entrance to the Wye Valley. Guarding this strategic position from a dramatic cliff above the Wye is **Chepstow Castle** (Cadw); *tel: (01291) 624065*, open daily 0930–1830 (Easter–Oct); Mon–Sat 0930–1600, Sun 1100–1600 (Nov–Easter); £3. Probably the earliest stone castle in the country, it was strengthened over the centuries and is remarkably intact. The **town walls**, 7 ft thick in places, were designed as an extension to this stronghold.

Chepstow Museum, *Gwy House, Bridge St; tel: (01291) 625981*, open Mon–Sat 1030/1100–1300 and 1400–1700/1730, Sun 1400–1700/1730; £1, covers the history of Chepstow and the lower Wye Valley area.

OUT OF TOWN

The TIC has details of two **long-distance walking paths**: along **Offa's Dyke** and the **Wye Valley**.

Caldicot Castle, *Caldicot; tel: (01291) 420241*, open Mon–Sat 1030–1700, Sun 1330–1700 (Mar–Oct); £1.50. 5 miles south-west. The restored Norman border castle is surrounded by peaceful gardens and a country park.

Tintern Abbey (Cadw), *Tintern; tel: (01291) 689251*, open daily 0930–1830 (Easter–Oct); Mon–Sat 0930–1600, Sun 1100–1600 (Nov–Easter); £2.20. 6 miles north. Founded in 1131 and set in a meadow by the Wye, the unmissable subject of one of Wordsworth's most famous poems is possibly the most complete of ruined British monasteries.

188

DARTMOOR NATIONAL PARK

Dartmoor's unique landscape, the highest in southern England, was formed by deep and violent subterranean eruptions more than 350 million years ago. Granite rocks have weathered over eons to curious shapes. Such places as Haytor Rocks and Vixen Tor illustrate this, forming dramatic landmarks. The highest tors, Yes Tor and High Wilhays, near Okehampton, are 2000 ft above sea level.

More than a dozen rivers rise in Dartmoor. Wooded valleys, miles of open moorland dotted with rounded rocks and a rich inheritance of prehistoric monuments – standing stones, hill forts and burial sites – make for varied scenery.

TOURIST INFORMATION

Dartmoor National Park Authority: **High Moorland Visitor Centre**, *Old Duchy Hotel, Princetown; tel: (01822) 890414*, open all year except Christmas Day, Boxing Day and a week in March.

The authority has information centres with car park and toilets at: *Postbridge, on B3312; tel: (01822) 880272, Newbridge (riverside); tel: (01364) 631303, Haytor, at lower car park on main road; tel: (01364) 661520.* These centres are open Easter–last weekend Oct.

Community Information Point, *The Square, Moretonhampstead; tel: (01647) 440043*, open all year, limited hours in winter.

Leaflets and maps are also available at a network of post offices and stores around Dartmoor.

TICs: *Museum Courtyard, 3 West St, Okehampton; tel: (01837) 53020*, open Easter–Oct, closed Sun except in peak season.

Lower free car park, Bovey Tracey (next to Riverside Mill, Devon Guild of Craftsmen centre); tel: (01626) 832047.

Town Hall Building, Bedford Sq., Tavistock; tel: (01822) 612938.

Leonard's Bridge, Ivybridge; tel: (01752) 897035.

Dartmoor National Park Authority issues a free newspaper, *Dartmoor Visitor* invaluable for anyone planning a Dartmoor holiday. It is crammed with information and also has a good map. To receive a copy, send a large stamped addressed envelope or International Reply Coupon to the High Moorland Visitor Centre at Princetown.

GETTING AROUND

Dartmoor covers about 365 square miles. About 40 per cent of the National Park is owned by the Duchy of Cornwall. The National Trust owns and manages more than 5500 acres of Dartmoor.

Among the more important towns and villages encompassed by or at the edge of Dartmoor are Okehampton (see p.195), Lydford, Tavistock, Yelverton, Ivybridge, Princetown, Buckfastleigh, Widecombe, Haytor, Bovey Tracey, Moretonhampstead, Postbridge, Whiddon Down and Chagford. Each is worth a visit.

189

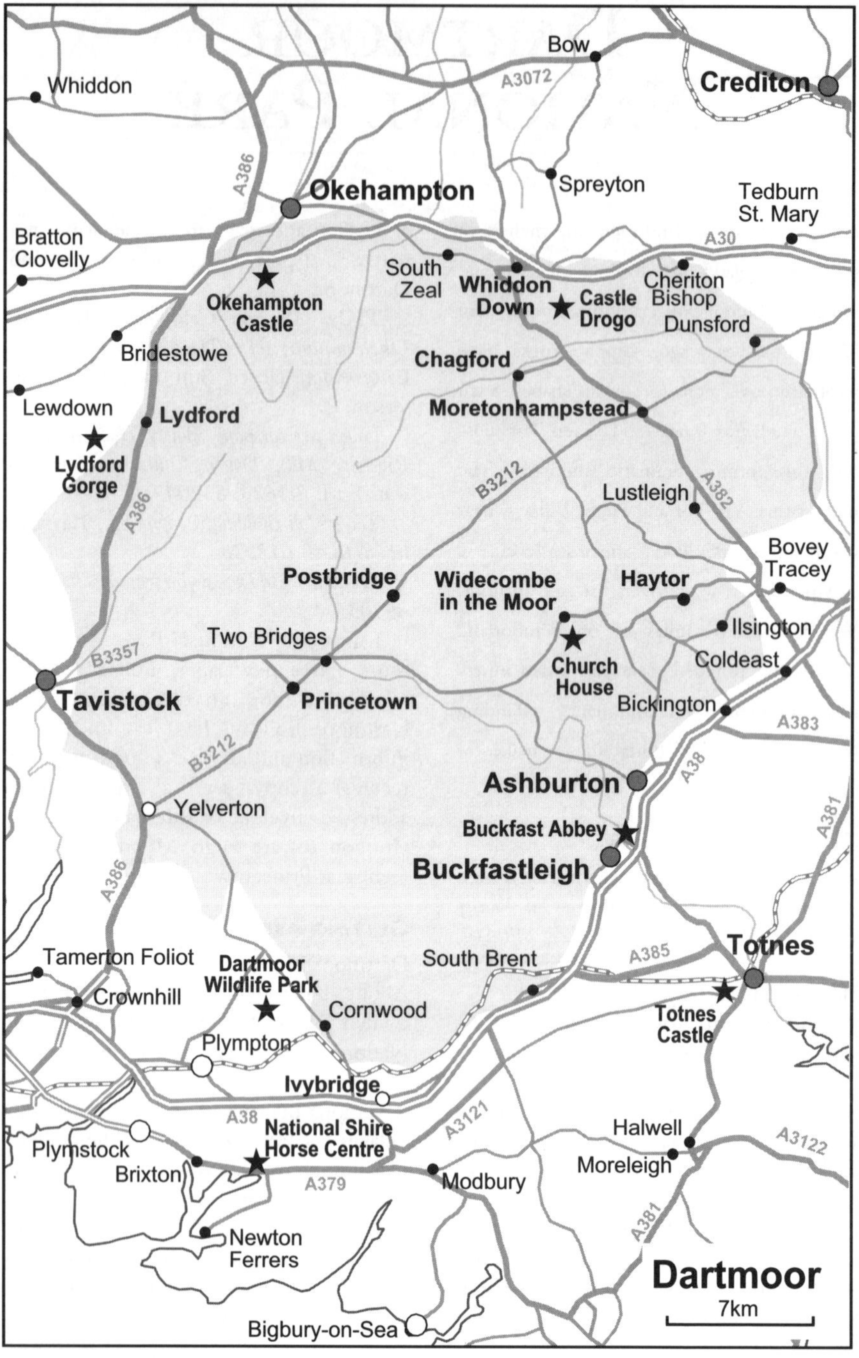
Bow
A3072
Crediton
Whiddon
A386
Okehampton
Spreyton
Tedburn
St. Mary
Bratton
Clovelly
A30
South
Zeal
Whiddon
Down
Cheriton
Bishop
Okehampton
Castle
Castle
Drogo
Dunsford
Bridestowe
Chagford
Lewdown
Lydford
Moretonhampstead
Lydford
Gorge
B3212
Lustleigh
A382
A386
Bovey
Tracey
Postbridge
Widecombe
in the Moor
Haytor
Ilsington
Two Bridges
B3357
Church
House
Coldeast
Tavistock
Princetown
Bickington
A383
B3212
Ashburton
A38
Yelverton
Buckfast Abbey
A381
A386
Buckfastleigh
Totnes
Tamerton Foliot
Dartmoor
Wildlife Park
South Brent
A385
Crownhill
Cornwood
Totnes
Castle
Plympton
Ivybridge
A38
National Shire
Horse Centre
A3121
Halwell
A3122
Plymstock
Moreleigh
Brixton
A379
Modbury
A381
Newton
Ferrers
Dartmoor
7km
Bigbury-on-Sea

Most of the lanes are narrow, twisty and steep. Sheep and wild ponies wander at will. Rain or mist can quickly reduce visibility and a speed limit of 40 mph is imposed. The best ways to explore Dartmoor's wild areas are on foot or horseback. A detailed map is essential, or there are experienced guides available to accompany walkers. For motorists and cyclists there are dozens of attractions and places of interest.

ACCOMMODATION AND FOOD

Small hotels are mainly in the moderate or expensive category. Guesthouses, farms, b&bs and inns tend to be budget price. Self-catering accommodation rates usually vary with the seasons. One of the largest agencies for self-catering cottages in Devon and Cornwall is **Helpful Holidays**, based on Dartmoor at *Chagford; tel: (01647) 433593; fax: (01647) 433694.*

Campers and caravanners are well catered for in campgrounds, holiday parks and farms. At Postbridge, where a primitive 13th-century **clapper bridge** is a famous landmark, is a **camping barn**; *tel: (01822) 880222.*

There are pubs and other good food outlets in every other town and village. Devon cream teas refresh thousands of visitors a year in picturesque villages of thatched cottages.

SIGHTSEEING

Barometer World and Museum, *Quicksilver Barn, Merton, Okehampton; tel: (01805) 603443.* Museum open Feb–Dec, Mon–Sat 1000–1600. Admission charge. Showroom open all year, Mon–Sat 0800–1700. Free. The fascinating 300 year old craft of making mercury barometers continues here. Hundreds of antique and new barometers are exhibited.

Buckfast Abbey, *Buckfastleigh; tel:*
(01364) 642519. Abbey open daily 0530–1900, visitor facilities open summer 0900–1730, winter 1000–1600; free. A thousand years of history are revealed at the abbey, home of the Benedictine monks. The abbey has a physic garden and shops selling books and monastic produce from all over Europe.

Canonteign Falls, *near Chudleigh; tel: (01647) 252434,* open daily 1000–1730, last admission 1630 (early Mar–mid Nov); Sun (winter); admission charge. Lakes and waterfalls including England's highest (220 ft).

Castle Drogo (NT), *Drewsteignton; tel: (01647) 433306,* open daily 1100–1730, gardens from 1030 (April–Oct); admission charge. This castle of granite and oak, presents the upstairs and downstairs aspects of early 20th-century life.

Dartmoor Earth Mysteries Centre, *Princetown Stores, Tavistock Rd, Princetown; tel: (01822) 890204,* open daily except Christmas Day; free. Megaliths, mining the moors and stone circles that can predict eclipses of the sun and moon provide a different slant on life.

Lydford Gorge, *The Stables, Lydford; tel: (01822) 820441,* open daily 1000–1730 (April–Oct); admission charge. A National Trust riverside walk along a woodland gorge with views of the 90 ft White Lady waterfall, Devil's Cauldron and a series of whirlpools.

Miniature Pony Centre, *2 miles west of Moretonhampstead; tel: (01647) 432400,* open 1030–1630 (Mar–Nov); admission charge. Hands-on experience of ponies, donkeys, goats and other creatures.

Yelverton Paperweight Centre, *Leg o' Mutton, Yelverton; tel: (01822) 854250,* open Mon–Sat 1000–1700 (two weeks before Easter–end Oct); Wed afternoon and Sat (winter). Hundreds of antique and modern glass paperweights.

191

EXETER

Exeter is an ancient city and, although its centre was heavily bombed during World War II and has been largely rebuilt, it still has its many old buildings, including Roman walls, the unscathed cathedral and some elegant Georgian terraces.

TOURIST INFORMATION

TIC: *Civic Centre, Paris St, Exeter, Devon EX1 1RP; tel: (01392) 265700; fax: (01392) 265260,* open Mon–Fri 0900–1700, Sat 0900–1300 and 1400–1700. DP services offered; local bed-booking service and BABA (latest 30 mins before closing; fee is 10% of first night). YHA/HI membership, tickets for National Express and day trips from local coach operators sold. *Exeter Visitor Guide,* available free, includes an accommodation listing.

ARRIVING AND DEPARTING

Exeter stands at the intersection of a number of important routes. A396 approaches from North Devon, crossing Exmoor National Park. A38 is the major route from Plymouth. M5 is the main route from Bristol and the Midlands. A30 connects with south-east England and Cornwall.

GETTING AROUND

The majority of attractions are within walking distance. A free town map and transport map are available from the TIC and local transport providers. Most bus services within Exeter and to surrounding area are on minibuses which are run by **Stagecoach**, *tel: (01392) 427711,* from the **central bus station**, *Paris St.*

The main **taxi** rank is located outside **Debenhams**, *Sidewell St.*

STAYING IN EXETER

Accommodation and Food

There is a good range of accommodation of all types in Exeter, and most guesthouses and b&b establishments are located in the city centre. Accommodation is generally easy to find except during mid July, due to the Exeter Festival and university graduation. Hotel chains in Exeter include *BW, Mn* and *Th.*

Exeter's oldest hotel – indeed the oldest in England – is the **Royal Clarence**, *Cathedral Yard, Exeter EX1 1HB; tel: (01392) 319995; fax: (01392) 439423.* It has 62 rooms and overlooks the magnificent cathedral. Moderate.

The largest hotel is the **Rougemont Thistle**, *Queen St, Exeter EX4 3SP; tel: (01392) 254982; fax: (01392) 420928.* It is a grand Victorian structure with opulent public areas. Moderate.

University accommodation is available during the holidays; *tel: (01392) 263509.* **HI**: *47 Countess Wear Rd; tel (01392) 873329.* The closest **campsites** accessible by public transport are: **Castle Brake Holiday Park**, *Woodbury; tel: (01395) 232431,* 8 miles south-east; and **Kennford International Caravan Park**, *Exeter; tel: (01392) 833046,* 4 miles south.

Exeter has a good choice of gourmet and cheap restaurants, inns and wine bars, mostly located in the city centre.

The timbered, low-ceilinged **Ship Inn**, *Martin's Lane,* is said to have been Francis Drake's favourite pub.

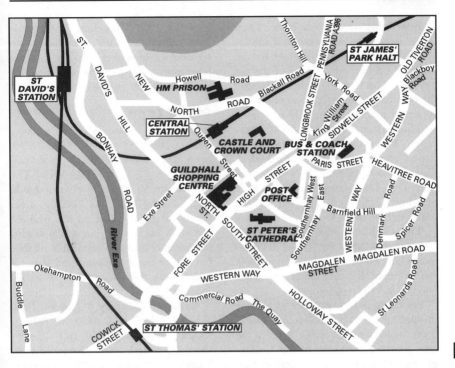

Maryam's, *28 South Street; (01923) 496776,* is an Italian restaurant handy for the cathedral and the Quay, open daily 1200–1400, 1800–2215. Budget–moderate.

Communications

The main **post office**, *Bedford St,* opens Mon–Fri 0900–1730, Sat 0900–1300. It has a poste restante facility.

Money

There is a **Thomas Cook bureau de change** at *Midland Bank, 38 High St.*

ENTERTAINMENT AND EVENTS

Entertainment and events listings can be found in *What's On* and *Exeter Events,* both available free from the TIC.

The **Northcott Theatre**, *Stoker Rd; tel: (01392) 493493/211080,* is a professional theatre which presents a wide range of plays, musicals, films and concerts, with regular visits from touring companies.

Two of the main annual events are the **Devon County Show** (mid May) – at Westpoint, 5 miles east, and the **Exeter Festival** (early July) – various venues.

SIGHTSEEING

Free **guided walks** are operated by **Exeter City Council's Guided Tours** service; *tel: (01392) 265212.* The main meeting point is the Royal Clarence Hotel. A leaflet is available from the TIC.

A variety of **bus tours** (May–Sept) may be booked at the TIC and all-day **coach excursions** around the surrounding area are run by **Dartline**, *tel: (01392) 444343;* **Hookways Greenslade**, *tel: (01392) 469210;* and **Turners Tours**, *tel: (01769) 580242.*

Boat trips depart from Exeter Quay (May–Sept) – pay as you board; £2.50.

Cathedral Close is a quiet haven, bounded on one side by part of the old city wall. This inspiring cathedral escaped the German bombing: it is one of the best preserved in England and Devon's finest building. Hunt out the 60 ft tall, 14th-century Bishop's Throne and the exotically carved choir stalls. **Exeter Cathedral**, *Cathedral Close; tel: (01392) 214219*, open daily 0715–1700 (except during services); free, but £2 donation suggested. Guided tours available (May–Oct).

The Guildhall, *High St; tel: (01392) 277888*, open Mon–Fri 1000–1700 (subject to civic functions); free. Built in 1330, this is reputedly the oldest municipal building in Britain still in use.

For the unusual experience of walking through medieval, subterranean water ducts, which supplied spring water to the city, take a guided tour of the **Underground Passages**, entrance *Roman Gate Passage* (next to Boots in the *High St*); *tel: (01392) 265887*, open Mon–Sat 1000–1700 (July–Sept and school holidays); Tues–Fri 1400–1700, Sat 1000–1700 (rest of year); £2.50 (Sept–June); £3.50 (July–Aug). The 13th-century passages are very narrow – unsuitable for anyone prone to claustrophobia.

St Nicholas Priory, *The Mint, off Fore St; tel: (01392) 265858*. Limited opening times, so telephone in advance; £1. Originally the guest wing of an 11th-century Benedictine priory, the building later became an Elizabethan merchant's home – but the Norman crypt, kitchen and main hall have survived.

Quay House Interpretive Centre, *46 The Quay; tel: (01392) 265213*, open daily 1000–1700 (Easter–Oct); free.

Royal Albert Memorial Museum, *Queen St; tel: (01392) 265858*, open Mon–Sat 1000–1700; free. The permanent collections cover everything from archaeology to zoology and the museum hosts many visiting exhibitions (for which there are variable charges).

OUT OF TOWN

Becky Falls Estate, *Manaton, nr Bovey Tracey, Dartmoor; tel: (01647) 221259*, open daily 1000–1800/dusk (mid Mar–mid Nov); £2.75. 15 miles west. The estate covers 50 acres of lovely woodlands, with walking trails, so opening times depend to some extent on the weather: Dartmoor can be tricky, especially in winter. Summer times are reasonably reliable, but ring to check mid Nov–mid Mar – at which time the entrance fee is usually reduced.

Crealy Country, *Crealy Park, Sidmouth Rd, Clyst St Mary; tel: (01395) 233211*, open daily 1000–1800 (Easter–Oct); 1030–dusk (Nov–Easter); £4.50. 5 miles south-east. Family entertainment park.

Killerton House and Gardens (NT), *Broadclyst; tel: (01392) 881345*. House open Wed–Mon 1100–1730 (Easter–Oct); £4.80 (inclusive). 7 miles north-east. The 18th-century house contains an outstanding collection of costumes from the 18th century to the present. It stands in an extensive estate, with beautiful gardens and woodland walking trails.

Powderham Castle, *Kenton; tel: (01626) 890243*, open Sun–Fri 1000–1730 (Easter–Oct); £4.95. 8 miles south. The ancestral home of the Earls of Devon dates from around 1390, but was greatly altered in the 18th and 19th centuries. There are lavishly furnished rooms and lovely grounds with views over the ancient deer park to the Exe estuary – don't miss the walled garden, nor the Secret Garden, opened in 1997.

EXETER–PENZANCE

The wild moorlands of Devon and Cornwall form the main feature of this route, and although there is a paucity of sizeable communities for much of the way there are some historic towns and attractive villages to be seen and stunning landscapes to be admired.

Direct Route

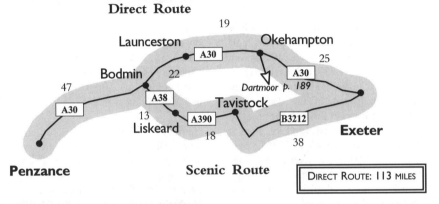

Launceston 19 Okehampton 25

Bodmin 22 A30

A38 Dartmoor p. 189

A30 Tavistock

13 A390 B3212

Liskeard 18 Exeter

38

Penzance Scenic Route

DIRECT ROUTE: 113 MILES

195

ROUTES

DIRECT ROUTE

Journey time for the 113-mile trip is 2 hrs 20 mins. From central Exeter follow signs to A30, which is our route all the way to Penzance, and head west to reach **Okehampton** in 25 miles. Continue for a further 19 miles to **Launceston** and for another 22 miles to **Bodmin**. From Bodmin A30 reaches Penzance in 47 miles.

SCENIC ROUTE

Heading across Dartmoor (see p. 185), this route adds about 12 miles and half an hour to the trip, though moorland mists may slow your progress. Follow B3212 out of Exeter (accessed by South Bridge over the River Exe) and continue for 17 miles to Moretonhampstead and a further 12 miles to Princetown, then head west on B3357 to reach Tavistock in 9 miles. A390 continues west to Liskeard, 18 miles away, then A38 carries on for 13 miles to Bodmin, where A30 continues to Penzance as above.

OKEHAMPTON

TIC: *3 West St, Okehampton, Devon; tel: (01837) 53020*, open Mon–Sat 1000–1700 (Apr–Oct), also Sun in peak season. BABA, local accommodation reservations. **Okehampton Information, Okehampton and District Chamber of Trade**, has a 24-hr phone line; *tel: (01837) 55565*.

ACCOMMODATION

Heathfield House, *Klondyke Rd, Okehampton; tel/fax: (01837) 54211*. Well situated hospitable home, open Feb–Nov. Budget–moderate.

Higher Cadham Farm, *Jacobstowe,*

Okehampton; tel: (01837) 851647; fax: (01837) 851410. Farm b&b with a family atmosphere. Budget–moderate.

Camping Barn, *Sticklepath Halt, near Okehampton.* This is one of seven on Dartmoor, for small groups, families and individuals. For information call booking office; *tel: (01271) 24420.* Budget.

SIGHTSEEING

Set in Dartmoor's northern foothills, North of Okehampton are the two highest peaks in the region, High Willhays and Yes Tor, both over 2000 ft. It has two rivers, the East Okement and West Okement. The southern part of the Tarka Trail pedestrian path goes through the area.

Museum of Dartmoor Life, *West St, Okehampton; tel: (01837) 52295,* open Mon–Sat 1000–1700 (April–Oct), also Sun (June–Sept); admission charge. Award-winning displays, interactive exhibits, working waterwheel.

Okehampton Castle (EH), *1 mile south-west of town centre; tel: (01837) 52844,* open daily 1000–1800 (late Mar–Oct); £2.20. Once the largest castle in Devon, the romantic ruins are situated on the fringe of Dartmoor and offer superb views, a woodland trail and a riverside picnic area.

OUT OF TOWN

Finch Foundry (NT), *Sticklepath; tel: (01837) 840046,* open Wed–Mon 1100–1730 (late Mar–end Oct); £2.50. 4 miles east. The 19th-century water-powered forge produced agricultural hand tools.

LAUNCESTON

TIC: *Market House Arcade, Market St, Launceston, Cornwall; tel: (01566) 772321,* open all year Mon–Fri 0845–1700, also Sat 0845–1700 (Apr–Oct). BABA, local bed reservations.

SIGHTSEEING

Launceston Steam Railway, *St Thomas Rd, Launceston; tel: (01566) 775665,* open daily (Easter–Oct); admission charge. Phone for timetable. Trips through the River Keney valley in carriages hauled by former Welsh slate quarry engines.

BODMIN

TIC: *Shire House, Mount Folly, Bodmin, Cornwall PL31 2DQ; tel: (01208) 76616,* open Mon–Sat 1000–1700 (mid May–mid Sept); Mon–Fri 1000–1300 (mid Sept–mid May). DP services offered; local bed-booking and BABA. *Bodmin Town and Moors Guide* is free.

GETTING AROUND

The majority of attractions are within walking distance of the centre. The main **bus** operator is **Western National**; *tel: (01208) 79898.* **Taxi** companies include: **Bodmin Taxis**, *tel: (01208) 73000* and **Parnells**, *tel: (01208) 72880.*

ACCOMMODATION

There's a wide choice of accommodation, both in town and in surrounding areas: hotels, guesthouses, b&b in farms and self-catering.

The TIC has details of **campsites** – the nearest is **Old Callywith Rd**, *Bodmin; tel: (01208) 73834,* 1 mile north, on the edge of Bodmin Moor.

SIGHTSEEING

Historically the county town of Cornwall, this small market town lies midway between the county's north and south coasts.

The steam **Bodmin and Wenford Railway**, *tel: (01208) 73666,* operates daily (May–Sept); sporadically (Oct–Apr); £7 Day Rover.

Bodmin's military past is reflected in

the **Duke of Cornwall Light Infantry Museum**, *Castle Canyke Rd; tel: (01208) 72810,* open Mon–Fri 1000–1700; £1.25. A different aspect of history is illustrated at **Bodmin Jail**, *Berrycombe Rd; tel: (01208) 76292* open Mon–Fri 1000–1800, Sat 1100–1600 (Apr–Oct); Mon–Sat 1100–1600 (Nov–Mar); £3.

OUT OF TOWN

Lanhydrock House and Gardens (NT), *Bodmin; tel: (01208) 74084.* House open Tues–Sun, public holidays 1100–1730 (Easter–Sept); Tues–Sun 1100–1700 (Oct); £6 (house and garden). 2½ miles south-east. The 17th-century house retains some elements of its origins. The gardens, formal and shrub, are of interest year-round.

Pencarrow House, *Washaway; tel: (01208) 841369.* House open Sun–Thur, public holidays 1100–1700 (June–mid Sept); 1330–1700 (Easter–May, mid Sept–mid Oct); £4 (house and garden). 4 miles north. Georgian house in 50 acres of formal gardens and woodland.

TAVISTOCK

TIC: *Town Hall, Bedford Sq., Tavistock; tel: (01822) 612938,* open Mon–Sat 1000–1700 (April–Oct), also Sun in peak season. BABA, local accommodation reservations.

ACCOMMODATION

The Bedford, *Plymouth Rd, Tavistock, PL19 8BB; tel: (01822) 613221; fax: (01822) 618034.* Castellated stone building near *Bedford Sq.* Moderate.

Moorland Hall, *Brentor Rd, Mary Tavy, near Tavistock; tel: (01822) 810466.* Small and welcoming Victorian hotel in spacious grounds. Moderate.

Harford Bridge Holiday Park, *Peter Yavy, near Tavistock PL19 9LS; tel: (01822) 810349; fax: (01622) 810028.* 120 pitches

priced from £2 to £8 a night. Showers, shop and leisure facilities on site.

SIGHTSEEING

In the mid 19th century, Tavistock, on the River Tavy, flourished as a result of the discovery of copper deposits, and the town's Victorian architecture reflects this prosperous period.

Almost every day is market day in Tavistock. The **Pannier Market**, *tel: (01822) 611003* is open Tues–Sat all year, specialising in different goods according to the day of the week.

Morwellham Quay, Morwellham and Tamar Valley Trust, *near Tavistock, PL19 8JL; tel: (01822) 832766,* open daily except Christmas 1000–1730 (earlier closing in winter when mine and grounds only are open); admission charge. Last admission 2 hours before closing. Visitors can take a unique train trip a mile into old copper mine workings, try on 1860s fashions, and ride in a wagonette drawn by shire horses. The ancient inland port became the greatest copper port in Queen Victoria's empire. The award-winning visitor centre presents a wide choice of activities. There is a separate admission charge for the **Tamar Valley Wildlife Reserve**, where visitors can use bird hides and follow trails among rare habitats in a 250-acre park.

LISKEARD

The small Cornish town near the green and wooded southern reaches of Bodmin Moor is a convenient base for walking, fishing, golf and other outdoor pursuits as well as motor touring.

Well House, *St Keyne, Liskeard PL14 4RN; tel: (01579) 342001; fax: (01579) 343891.* Small 100 year old hotel with croquet lawn, tennis court and swimming pool. Expensive.

197

FOLKESTONE–LEWES

This route follows the coast of the English Channel eastwards across mysterious Romney Marsh and into the lovely area where the lush pastures and forests of the Sussex Weald meet the steep and chalky slopes of the South Downs. It crosses landscapes which have inspired painters and poets and witnessed every conflict from the Roman and Norman invasions to the Battle of Britain.

Lewes
8
A26
Newhaven
A259
13
A259
Eastbourne
53
Hastings
A259
37
A259
Rye
24
A259
Folkestone

ROUTE: **74** MILES

198

ROUTE

This route of 74 miles takes 2 hrs. From Folkestone A259 west is the highway to follow for much of the route. It reaches **Rye** after 24 miles, **Hastings** after 37 and **Eastbourne** after 5 miles. From Eastbourne continue west on A259 for a further 13 miles and at Newhaven head north on A26. After 5 miles follow A27 west for 3 miles to Lewes.

RYE

TIC: *Heritage Centre, Strand Quay, Rye, East Sussex TN31 7AY; tel: (01797) 226696,* open daily 0900–1730 (mid Mar–Oct); Mon–Fri 1000–1300, Sat–Sun 1000–1600 (Nov–Dec); Mon–Fri 1000–1500, Sat–Sun 1000–1600 (Jan–mid Mar). DP SHS services offered; local bed-booking (latest 15 mins before closing), BABA (latest 30 mins before closing). Hoverspeed and White Rock Theatre,

Hastings, can be booked. *Rye Colour Guide* (including accommodation listing) is £1.50, *Rye 1066* town guide and *Simply Rye* are available free.

ACCOMMODATION

There is a good range of accommodation, including a number of mid-range hotels and pubs in the centre. Cheaper accommodation can be found on the edge of town. It is usually easy to book on arrival, except for Sat, public holidays and Aug. Hotel chains in Rye include *FH*. There is one **campsite**: **Rolvendene Farm**, *Love Lane; tel: (01797) 222311*; half a mile north-west. The TIC are able to supply details of other campsites.

SIGHTSEEING

Jane Fraser Hay, *tel: (01424) 882343,* offers **guided walks** of the town (£3), starting from the Heritage Centre. The TIC can supply an **audio tour**; £2.

Rye now lies 2 miles inland, but was once a coastal town, rife with smugglers. Narrow, cobbled lanes, such as *Watchbell St*, are lined with interesting old houses. **The Mermaid Inn**, *Mermaid St:* dating from 1420, is one of England's oldest pubs, with a history of smuggling and, of course, reputed to be haunted.

Find out more at the **Rye Town Model Sound and Light Show**, *Heritage Centre, Strand Quay; tel: (01797) 226696,* opening hours as TIC; £2. There are shows every half-hour, in which the history of Rye is dramatically brought to life. Events in the town include the **Rye Festival** (Sept) and **Medieval Festival** (Aug).

Rye Castle and Rye Museum, *Gungarden; tel: (01797) 226728,* open Sat–Sun 1100–1600 (Nov–Mar); daily 1030–1730 (Apr–Oct); £1.50.

A one-time home of novelist Henry James is **Lamb House** (NT), *West St, tel: (01892) 890651,* open Wed, Sat 1400–1800 (Apr–Oct); £2.20.

OUT OF TOWN

The **Romney, Hythe and Dymchurch Railway**, *tel: (01797) 362353,* is a popular miniature railway whose steam trains are replicas of full-size locomotives. Catch it at New Romney; 12 miles east. The railway runs daily (Apr–Sept); Sat–Sun (Mar, Oct) – check directly for schedules. There are six stations; £8.34 lets you ride all day and also covers the **Toy and Model Museum**, *New Romney station.*

HASTINGS

TIC: *4 Robertson Terrace, Hastings TN34 1JE; tel: (01424) 781111,* open Mon–Fri 0930–1700, Sat 1000–1700 (May); Mon–

Sat 0930–1700 (Oct–Easter); Mon–Fri 0930–1700, Sat 1000–1700 (Sept); daily 0930–1800 (July–Aug); Mon–Fri 0930–1700, Sat 1000–1730 (June). DP SHS services offered; local bed-booking (latest 15 mins before closing), BABA (latest 15 mins before closing). *Hastings Holiday Guide* (including accommodation list) is 50p (free by post). *1066 Country Discover Hastings* brochure (with accommodation list) is free. Le Shuttle, ferries, coach tours and theatre tickets booked.

Fishmarket TIC: *The Stade, Old Town, Hastings TN34 1E2; tel: (01424) 781111,* open Sat–Sun 1100–1600 (Nov, Feb); Sun 1100–1600 (Dec–Jan); Fri–Sun 1000–1700 (Mar–Apr, Oct); Tues–Sun 0930–1700 (May–June, Sept); Sun–Fri 0930–1800, Sat 0930–1900 (July–Aug).

GETTING AROUND

Free town and transport maps are available from the TIC. Local public transport is quite good in the centre, but very patchy in outer areas. **Bus enquiries**, *tel: (01424) 433711.* The main local operator is **Stagecoach South Coast Buses**. The main **taxi** rank is at *Havelock Rd.*

ACCOMMODATION

There is a good range of accommodation, particularly guesthouses and b&bs. Cheaper accommodation is located mainly in the centre. It is generally easy to book on arrival, but essential to book ahead for July–Aug and advisable during the annual Morris Dance Festival (May) and half-marathon (Mar). The only hotel chain is *BW*.

HI: Hastings, *Guestling Hall, Rye Rd, Guestling; tel: (01424) 812373.* The TIC has details of **campsites**. The nearest are: **Shearbarn Holiday Park**, *Barley Ln; tel: (01424) 423583,* approx. 2 miles north-east; and **Stalkhurst Camping and**

Caravanning Site, *Ivyhouse Lane; tel: (01424) 439015*, 2½ miles north.

SIGHTSEEING

Guide Friday operate open-top double-decker **bus tours** and the TIC has details of a variety of other tours.

The attractive seaside town of Hastings is an ideal base for exploring the Sussex coast and countryside. The Old Town nestles between two hills (which can be climbed by **cliff railways**), and has picturesque old houses and narrow, winding streets.

Hastings Castle: The 1066 Story, *West Hill; tel: (01424) 781112,* open daily 1000/1030–1700/1730; £2.80, uses sound and light in a 20min show that brings to life the events of the most famous date in British history.

The Hastings Embroidery, *Town Hall, Queens Rd; tel: (01424) 781113,* open Mon–Fri 1130–1500 (Oct–Apr); Mon–Fri 1000–1630 (May–Sept); £1.50. Executed by the Royal School of Needlework, the embroidery depicts events from the Battle of Hastings to modern times.

An attraction with a difference is the **Flower Makers Museum**, *Shirley Leaf and Petal Company, 58a High St, Old Town; tel: (01424) 427793,* open Mon–Fri 0930–1630, Sat 1100–1700; £1. You can usually see some work in progress.

Fishermen's Museum, *Rock-a-Nore Rd, Old Town; tel: (01424) 461446,* open daily approx. 1100–1700, but this varies (usually longer in summer, shorter in winter); free. **Shipwreck Heritage Centre**, *Rock-a-Nore Rd, Old Town; tel (01424) 437452,* open 1030–1700 (Apr–Oct); £1.95. Exhibition of underwater treasures from local shipwrecks over three millennia and audiovisual presentation.

Deep under *West Hill* is a labyrinth of tunnels arranged to enable visitors to relive the excitement of the old smuggling days: **Smugglers Adventure**, **St Clements Caves**, *West Hill; tel: (01424) 422964,* open daily 1000–1730 (Easter–Sept); 1100–1630 (Oct–Easter); £4.20.

OUT OF TOWN

The **Battle of Hastings** actually took place at Battle, where you can visit the site and the ruins of the abbey that William built on the site in thanksgiving for his victory. **Battle Abbey** (EH), *tel: (01424) 773792,* open daily 1000–1800 (Easter–Oct); 1000–1600 (Nov–Easter); £3.50. 6 miles north-west.

Pevensey Castle (EH), *Pevensey; tel: (01323) 762604,* open daily 1000–1800 (Easter–Oct); Wed–Sun 1000–1600 (Nov–Easter); £2. 12 miles west. The ruins of a medieval castle are enclosed within walls of Roman origin.

EASTBOURNE

TIC: *Cornfield Rd, Eastbourne BN21 4QL; tel: (01323) 411400,* open Mon–Sat 0900–1800, Sun 1000–1300 (May–Oct); Mon–Sat 0900–1700 (Nov–Apr). Services offered: local bed-booking and BABA (fee £2.50). Bus tours booked.

GETTING AROUND

The majority of attractions are within walking distance of the town centre. Free town and transport maps are available from the TIC. Bus services are operated by **Eastbourne Bus Company** and **South Coast Buses**. For **general enquiries**, *tel: (01323) 416416.* The main **taxi** ranks are at the rail station and *Bolton Rd*.

ACCOMMODATION

Eastbourne has a good range of accommodation, with a choice of cheaper establishments. It is advisable to book in advance during the Ladies Tennis Tour-

nament (June). Hotel chains include: *BW, Ct, DV, Hn, Mo, Pn* and *QI.*
HI: *East Dean Rd; tel: (01323) 721081.* The TIC can supply a list of **campsites**.

ENTERTAINMENT AND EVENTS

Eastbourne is a major entertainment centre, with an impressive choice of venues. Major annual events include **Eastbourne International Folk Festival** (early May), various venues; **Airborne RAF Show** (mid-Aug), various venues; and **1812 Firework Nights** (July–Sept), *Redoubt Fortress*. Get the full list from the TIC.

SIGHTSEEING

Eastbourne is an unspoilt seaside town of charm and elegance and an ideal touring base. Local bus 3 runs to the cliffs of **Beachy Head.**

Children enter the world of Long John Silver at the award-winning adventure theme park, **Treasure Island**, *Royal Pde; tel: (01323) 411077,* open daily 1000–1800 (Easter–Sept); £2 child; £1.20 adult.

Circling around Southbourne Lake, with its swans, ducks, geese and wild flowers, is **Eastbourne Miniature Steam Railway Fun Park**, *Lottbridge Drove; tel: (01323) 520229,* open daily 1000–1700 (Easter–Sept); Sat–Sun 1000–1700 (Oct); free, but £1.50 per train ride, £1 nature trail. A good place for children to let off steam.

Redoubt Fortress, *Royal Pde; tel: (01323) 410300,* open 1000–1730 (Easter–Nov); £1.85, is a circular fortress, built in 1810 to guard against Napoleonic invasion. It now houses three important military exhibitions.

RNLI Lifeboat Museum, *King Edward's Pde; tel: (01323) 730717,* open daily 1000–1600/1700 (Easter–Dec); free, but the RNLI relies entirely on donations to keep voluntary services going. The

museum features life-saving vessels from the early days of the fishing industry to high-tech modern boats.

Museum of Shops, *20 Cornfield Terrace; tel: (01323) 737143,* open 1000–1700; £2.50. This displays over 50,000 items in authentic settings.

Butterfly Centre, *Royal Parade; tel: (01323) 645522,* open daily 1000–1700 (Mar–Oct); £3.50. Wander through indoor tropical gardens, filled with hundreds of live butterflies.

LEWES

TIC: *187 High St, Lewes, East Sussex BN7 2DE; tel: (01273) 483448.*Open Mon–Fri 0900–1700, Sat 1000–1700, Sun 1100–1500 (Apr–Sept); Mon–Fri 0900–1300, 1400–1700 (Oct–Mar). BABA, local accommodation reservations.

GETTING AROUND

Lewes is a compact town, though its Saxon origins mean that no matter where you head you will almost certainly be going either up or down – and some of its side streets are especially steep.

ACCOMMODATION

The town and surrounding area has a reasonable selection of small hotels, guesthouses and b&bs. Accommodation maybe difficult to find during the Glyndebourne Festival (mid May–late Aug).

White Hart Hotel, *High St, Lewes BN7 1XE; tel: (01273) 476694; fax: (01273) 476695.* Historic coaching inn with a carvery. Moderate–expensive.

Shelleys Hotel, *High St, Lewes BN7 1XS; tel: (01273) 472361; fax: (01273) 483152.* 16th-century manor house in an acre of garden. Moderate–pricey.

Ousedale House, *Offham, Lewes BN7 3QF; tel: (01273) 478680; fax: (01273) 486510.* A mile from the town centre.

Hampers available for Glyndebourne and other picnics. Budget–moderate.

Ranscombe House, *Ranscombe Lane, Glynde, Lewes BN8 6AA; tel: (01273) 858538.* Set in a walled garden, handy for Glyndebourne. Budget.

HI: *Frog Firle, Alfriston; tel: (01323) 870423; fax: (01323) 870615.*

EATING AND DRINKING

Lewes is a town of many pubs, most of which serve meals and bar snacks, and there are a number of restaurants, cafés and tea shops.

Dorset Arms, *22 Malling St; tel: (01273) 477110.* Cheerful log fires are a feature of this 17th century inn, which serves real ales from Harvey & Son, who have been brewing in Lewes since 1790.

Pelham Arms, *St Anne's Hill, High St; tel: (01273) 475149.* This centrally located pub has a renowned restaurant.

La Cucina, *13 Station Rd; tel: (01273) 476707.* A popular Italian restaurant. Lunch served Thur–Sat 1200–1400; dinner Mon–Sat 1800–2230. Moderate.

EVENTS

Founded by John Christie in 1934, **Glyndebourne Festival Opera**, *Glyndebourne, Lewes BN8 5UU; tel: (01273) 812321; fax: (01273) 812783,* is the area's most famous event. International-class opera is presented (mid May–late Aug) in a new concert hall in a superb downland setting. Picnics on the lawn remain a tradition.

Lewes Bonfire Night (5 Nov) is a spectacular carnival. The event commemorates the Lewes Martyrs – 17 Protestants burned at the stake in 1556 – rather than the Gunpowder Plot of 1605.

SIGHTSEEING

Lewes has a history stretching back to

Saxon times and has had its share of violence over the centuries. Thomas Paine, author of *The Rights of Man*, lived and plotted in Lewes during his service as an excise officer.

Lewes Castle, *High St; tel: (01273) 486290,* open Mon–Sat 1000–1730; £3.25 (£4.25 combined ticket with Anne of Cleves House). The shell of the castle's Norman keep provides some spectacular views over the surrounding Downs. The adjoining **Museum of Sussex Archaeology** traces the impact of successive invasions in the region and houses a large collection of Romano-British, Saxon and medieval antiquities.

Anne of Cleves House, *52 Southover High St, Lewes; tel: (01273) 474610,* open Mon–Sat 1000–1730, Sun 1200–1730 (late Mar–early Nov), Tues, Thur, Sat 1000–1730 (Jan–late Mar and early Nov–Dec); £2 (£4.25 combined ticket with Lewes Castle). The house was the divorce settlement of Henry VIII to his fourth wife. It contains a folk museum.

Lewes Priory, *Priory St,* open daily dawn–dusk; free. The ruins of the great Cluniac priory, dating from 1077 and destroyed on the orders of Henry VIII.

OUT OF TOWN

Monks House, *Rodmell,* open Wed and Sat 1400–1700; £2.20. 4 miles south. The home of novelist Virginia Woolf and her husband Leonard from 1919 to 1969.

Firle Place, *Firle; tel: (01273) 858335,* open Wed, Thur, Sun and public holidays 1400–1700 (Apr–Sept); £4. Off A27 5 miles south-east. The house has important collections of English and European Old Masters, French and English furniture and porcelain, and documents relating to the Gage family, the occupants of Firle for 500 years, and their involvement in the American War of Independence.

THE LAKE DISTRICT

Some of England's most spectacular scenery and its highest mountains make the 700 square miles of the Lake District a greatly desirable holiday spot. Walking, climbing, sailing and fishing are popular activities, gentle pursuits like taking a lake cruise, visiting museums, gardens and beauty spots.

A literary vacation could take in places associated with William Wordsworth and his sister Dorothy, Beatrix Potter, Arthur Ransome, Samuel Taylor Coleridge, Robert Southey, Thomas de Quincey and John Ruskin.

With so much accessible natural beauty and so many people wanting to explore it, it is becoming increasingly difficult to safeguard the landscape for future generations. The region suffers the ravages of a surfeit of humanity and cars. To restrict damage by vehicles it is suggested that visitors go to some parts by coach, minibus, steam train, steamer or launch to enjoy the scenic delights. Details of tour options are available from Lake District TICs.

KENDAL

TIC: *Town Hall, Highgate, Kendal, Cumbria LA9 4DL; tel: (01539) 725758,* open Mon–Sat 0900–1700 (all year); Sun 1000–1600 (Easter–Oct). DP services offered; local bed-booking and BABA (latest 30 mins before closing). Tours booked, coach tickets sold. *Kendal Mini Guide* costs 45p, *Where to Stay in South Lakeland* costs £1.

GETTING AROUND

Most of Kendal's attractions are within easy walking distance of the centre. Free town and transport maps are available from the TIC. Local **bus** services are good within the town and on the main route through the Lake District, but patchy to outlying areas and poor on Sun. Most local buses are operated by **Stagecoach Cumberland**, *tel: (01946) 63222.*

The main **taxi** rank is on *Market Place,* or contact: **AA Taxis**, *tel: (01539) 740205;* **Ace Taxis**, *tel: (01539) 733430;* **Airport Taxis**, *tel: (01539) 724658;* **Blue Star Taxis**, *tel: (01539) 723670;* or **Castle Taxis**, *tel: (01539) 726233.*

ACCOMMODATION

There are only a few hotels in Kendal, but a good choice of b&b, guesthouse and pub accommodation, with cheaper establishments located in the centre. It is generally possible to book on arrival, except over public holiday, in high summer and at Christmas/New Year, when the area is extremely busy.

HI: *118 Highgate; tel: (01539) 724066.* The closest **campsites** are: **Millcrest**, *Skelsmergh, Shap Rd; tel: (01539) 741363,* 1½ miles north; and **Ashes Lane Caravan and Camping Park**, *Staveley; tel: (01539) 821119,* 3 miles north

SHOPPING

The bargain hunter cannot afford to miss **K Village**, Kendal's factory shopping outlet, with reductions on famous brands. These include Clarks Shoes, Laura Ashley, Denby Ware and Dartington Crystal. It is reached from the M6 (Junction 36).

203

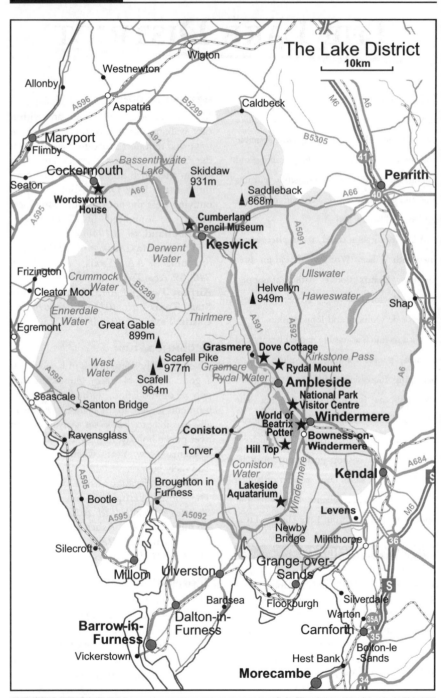

The Lake District

10km

Wigton
Westnewton
Allonby
A596
Aspatria
Caldbeck
B5299
M6
A6
B5305
41
Maryport
Flimby
Bassenthwaite Lake
Skiddaw 931m
Saddleback 868m
Penrith
Cockermouth
Seaton
A66
A66
40
Wordsworth House
A595
Cumberland Pencil Museum
A5091
Keswick
Derwent Water
Frizington
Crummock Water
Cleator Moor
B5289
Helvellyn 949m
Ullswater
Haweswater
Shap
Ennerdale Water
Egremont
Great Gable 899m
Thirlmere
A591
A592
Wast Water
Scafell Pike 977m
Scafell 964m
Grasmere
Rydal Water
Grasmere
Dove Cottage
Kirkstone Pass
Rydal Mount
Ambleside
A595
A6
Seascale
Santon Bridge
National Park Visitor Centre
Ravensglass
Coniston
World of Beatrix Potter
Windermere
Bowness-on-Windermere
Torver
Hill Top
A684
Coniston Water
Broughton in Furness
Lakeside Aquatarium
Kendal
A595
Bootle
A595
A5092
Levens
Windermere
M6
S
Newby Bridge
Milnthorpe
36
Silecroft
Grange-over-Sands
Millom
Ulverston
Bardsea
Flookburgh
Silverdale
Warton
35A
Barrow-in-Furness
Dalton-in-Furness
Carnforth
35
Vickerstown
Hest Bank
Bolton-le-Sands
34
Morecambe

SIGHTSEEING

There are pleasant strolls along the River Kent and many good fell walks within an easy radius – enquire at the TIC. Well-known for its major products – mint cake and shoes – Kendal lies just south of the **Lake District National Park** and is a good base from which to visit the rolling fells of the southern lakes. Numerous **bus tours** are bookable at the TIC.

Quieter than some other Lakeland towns, Kendal has some fine 17th- and 18th-century buildings and some excellent museums for rainy days: at **Abbot Hall**, the **Art Gallery** includes paintings by Turner, Romney and Ruskin, while the **Museum of Lakeland Life and Industry** captures the area's working and social life. **Art Gallery and Museum**, *Kirkland; tel: (01539) 722464*, open daily 1030–1700 (Apr–Oct); 1030–1600 (mid Feb–Mar, Nov–mid Dec); £2.50 each.

Kendal Museum of Natural History and Archaeology, *Station Rd; tel: (01539) 721374*, opening times as Abbot Hall; £2.50, includes one area devoted to Alfred Wainwright, famed for his Lakeland guidebooks.

Quakerism began in this area and 15 countries have contributed tapestries celebrating the movement to the collection at the **Quaker Tapestry**, *New Rd; tel: (01539) 722975*, open Mon–Sat 1000–1700 (Easter–Oct); £2.50.

Kendal Parish Church, *Kirkland; tel: (01539) 721248*, open daily 1030–1630 (Apr–Oct); free. Reduced opening Nov–Mar, so ring to check. The 13th-century church has an interesting multi-arched interior and brass rubbing is possible.

A wide variety of reptiles is on display at **Kendal Reptiles**, *117 Sticklandgate; tel: (01539) 721240*, open Mon–Sat 1000–1700, Sun 1030–1630 (Easter–Oct); £2.50.

OUT OF TOWN

Levens Hall and Topiary Garden, *Levens; tel: (015395) 60321*, open Sun–Thur 1100–1700 (Apr–Sept); steam collection 1400–1700; £4.80. 5 miles south. An Elizabethan hall and a famous topiary garden, where the trees were first shaped in 1694.

A 60ft high 14th-century tower and a limestone rock garden are two of the more unusual features at **Sizergh Castle** (NT), *Sizergh; tel: (015395) 60070*, open Sun–Thur 1330–1730 (Apr–Oct); £3.30. 3 miles south.

Lakeland Wildlife Oasis, *Hale, Milnthorpe; tel: (015395) 63027*, open daily 1000–dusk; £2.85. 4 miles south. This is a conservation-minded mixture of zoo and museum.

WINDERMERE

TIC: *Victoria St, Windermere, Cumbria LA23 1AD; tel: (01539) 446499*, open daily 0900–1800 (Easter–Oct); 0900–1700 (Nov–Easter). DP services offered; local bed-booking and BABA (latest 15 mins before closing), bureau de change. *Windermere and Bowness Mini Guide* costs 75p, *Where to Stay in South Lakeland* £1.

Lake District National Park Office, *Glebe Rd, Bowness-on-Windermere; tel (01539) 442895*, open 0930–1730 (Easter–Oct); Sat–Sun 1000–1600 (Nov–Dec).

GETTING AROUND

Most attractions are within an area of just over a mile across. Free transport maps are available from the TIC, who will provide photocopies (10p) of town maps. Local bus services are good within the town and on the main route through the Lake District, but patchy to outlying areas, and poor on Sun. Most local buses are operated by **Stagecoach Cumberland**, *tel: (01946) 63222*.

The main **taxi** rank is outside the station, or contact: **Coopers Cabs**, *tel: (01539) 445282*; **Cumbria Taxis**, *tel: (01539) 445246*; or **Lakes Taxis**, *tel: (01539) 446777*.

ACCOMMODATION

There is a good choice of accommodation and it is generally possible to book on arrival, except over public holiday weekends and in high summer. Hotel chains include *BW, FH* and *MC*.

Applegarth Hotel, *College Rd, Windermere, LA23 1BU; tel: (015394) 43206; fax: (015394) 46636*. Some family rooms. Budget–moderate.

Lakeside Hotel, *Newby Bridge, Windermere LA12 8AT; tel: (015395) 31207; fax: (015395) 31699*. On the shore of Lake Windermere. Expensive

The Linthwaite House Hotel, *Windermere LA23 3JA; tel: (015394) 88600; fax: (015394) 88601*. De luxe hotel in 14 acres of gardens overlooking Lake Windermere. Expensive.

Holly Park House, *1 Park Rd, Windermere LA23 2AW; tel: (015394) 42107*. Victorian guesthouse close to centre. Budget.

Quality self-catering cottages and apartments around the central and southern lakes are available through the well-established holiday home agency. **Lakelovers**, *The Toffee Loft, Ash St, Bowness-on-Windermere, Cumbria LA23 3RA; tel: (015394) 88855; fax: (015394) 88857*.

HI: *High Cross, Bridge Lane, Troutbeck; tel: (01539) 443543*. The nearest **campsite** is **Limefitt Park**, *Patterdale Rd, Troutbeck; tel: (01539) 432300*, 2½ miles north. **Park Cliffe Caravan and Camping Estate**, *Birks Rd, Windermere LA23 1PA; tel: (015394) 32300*. Family-run park with mountain views. Tent pitches.

EATING AND DRINKING

Roger's Restaurant, *4 High St, Windermere; tel: (015394) 44954*. Includes good English fare. Moderate–expensive.

Gilpin Lodge, *Crook Rd, near Windermere; tel: (015394) 88818*. Award-winning restaurant in country house hotel.

The Porthole, *3 Ash St, Bowness; tel: (015394) 45510*, provides Italian, English, French and vegetarian cuisine. Moderate.

Holbeck Ghyll, *Holbeck Lane, Windermere; tel: (015394) 34743*. Fresh local produce, imaginative dishes and a varied wine list make this a popular special occasion place. Expensive.

SIGHTSEEING

Numerous **bus tours, guided walks** and **boat trips** can be booked at the TIC.

On the eastern side of **Lake Windermere**, Britain's largest lake, Windermere town's Victorian villas and hotels bear witness to its established appeal. There are many viewpoints within walking distance, including **Orrest Head** – reached via the path beside the Windermere Hotel. A 1½-mile walk (or bus) will take you down to **Bowness**, the tourist trap on the lake shore; but even commercialisation cannot spoil the character of this vast expanse of water, with its wooded islands and shores.

The **Lakeside and Haverthwaite Railway**, *tel: (01539) 531594*, is a scenic 3½-mile privately owned steam railway. Take it from Haverthwaite to Lakeside, where a new attraction is the **Lakeside Aquatarium;** *tel: (01539) 530153*. This presents a unique series of naturally themed displays revealing the amazing variety of aquatic life found locally, both in the water and around it. A dramatic underwater walkway reveals Windermere's depths.

In Bowness itself, delightful 3D

tableaux are used to bring children's stories to life at the **World of Beatrix Potter**, *Rayrigg Rd, Bowness; tel: (01539) 488444,* open daily 1000–1830 (Easter–Sept); 1000–1600 (Oct–Easter); £2.95.

Windermere Steamboat Museum, *Rayrigg Rd; tel: (01539) 445565,* open daily 1000–1700 (Easter–Oct); £2.80. This combines displays of historic (but mostly functional) steam-, motor- and sail-boats, with steam-boat trips on the lake during summer – weather permitting.

OUT OF TOWN

There are countless excellent walking areas within easy reach. The best introduction to the district is provided by **Brockhole National Park Visitor Centre**, *Windermere; tel: (01539) 446601,* open daily 1000–1700 (Easter–Oct); free. 3 miles north-west.

Devotees of the Lakes' romantic poet, William Wordsworth, can visit **Dove Cottage and Wordsworth Museum**, *Grasmere; tel: (01539) 435544,* open daily 0930–1730 (closed early Jan–early Feb). 8 miles north-west. It was here that he wrote much of his best-known poetry. The poignant evidence of poverty displayed in this early home (including walls papered with newspapers of the day) contrasts with the grander **Rydal Mount**, *nr Ambleside; tel: (01539) 433002,* open daily 0930–1700 (Mar–Oct); 1000–1600 (Nov–Feb); £2; 7 miles north-west. Wordsworth spent his last years here.

To see the cottage where Beatrix Potter wrote many of the Peter Rabbit stories, take a ferry (from *Ferry Nab Rd*) to the quiet western shore, within reach of **Hill Top** (NT), *Near Sawrey, Ambleside; tel: (01539) 36269,* open Sat–Wed 1100–1700 (Apr–Oct); £3.30. 4 miles south-west. The cottage is tiny, so avoid peak periods.

AMBLESIDE

TIC: *The Old Courthouse, Church St; tel: (015394) 32582,* open daily 0900–1700 (Easter–Oct), Fri, Sat 0900–1700 (Nov–Easter). BABA and local bed bookings.

ACCOMMODATION AND FOOD

There are a couple of dozen hotels in and around Ambleside and a strong back-up of b&bs, guesthouses and farmhouse accommodation. A free guide to owner-managed properties is issued by **Cumbria and Lakeland Self Caterers' Association**; *tel: (0345) 585199,* for the association's vacancy advisory service.

Brantfell, *Rothay Rd, Ambleside LA22 0EE; tel: (015394) 32239.* Well situated for fell walks. Budget.

Kirkstone Foot Hotel, *Kirkstone Pass Rd, Ambleside LA22 9EH; tel/fax: (015394) 32232.* Noted for its traditional cuisine. Moderate.

Waterhead Hotel, *Ambleside LA22 0DB; tel: (015394) 32566; fax: (015394) 31255.* On Lake Windermere's shore. Moderate–expensive.

Windlehurst, *Millans Park, Ambleside LA22 9AG; tel: (015394) 34570.* Overlooking fields and fell. Budget.

The Grove Farm, *Stockghyll Lane, Ambleside LA22 9LG; tel: (915394) 33074; fax: (015394) 31881.* Three modern caravans sleeping two to six, open Mar–Oct; Budget–Moderate.

Ambles Bistro, *Lake Rd; tel: (015394) 33970.* Moderate.

Wateredge Hotel, *Waterhead Bay; tel: (015394) 32332.* Six-course meals with home-made truffles accompanying the coffee. Expensive.

SIGHTSEEING

At the northern tip of **Lake Windermere**, Ambleside provides a useful base for exploring the southern lakes

207

region. **Bowness-on-Windermere,
Grasmere, Coniston, Ullswater, Rydal
Water**, the **Kirkstone Pass** and other
National Park locations are close by.

**Windermere Submarine Informa-
tion Centre**, *Watered Pier, Ambleside; tel:
(015394) 33990.* Phone for times and
prices. Reservations essential. The deep
diving submarine dives through many
fathoms of Lake Windermere's water to
explore 'inner space' and little-known
parts of the earth's surface. Fish life,
including Arctic char, and unusual fauna
may be observed and tales are told of
wrecked boats and sunken aircraft.

KESWICK

TIC: *Moot Hall, Market Sq., Keswick
CA12 4JR; tel: (017687) 72645,* open
daily 0930–1900 (July, Aug), 0930–1730
(Apr–June and Sept, Oct). BABA, local
accommodation bookings and tour guide
services.

National Park Information Centre,
31 Lake Rd, Keswick; tel: (017687) 72803,
open daily 0930–1730 (Apr–Oct) 1000–
1600 (Nov–Mar).

ACCOMMODATION

At the heart of the northern Lakes area,
Keswick is a busy town with plenty of
accommodation, mostly in the form of
b&bs, guesthouses and small hotels. Even
so, at peak times, including winter and
spring bank holidays, it is wise to book
ahead.

Allerdale House, *1 Eskin St, Keswick
CA12 4DH; tel: (017687) 73891.* Handy
for town, theatre and lake. Budget.

**Applethwaite Country House
Hotel**, *Applethwaite, Underskiddaw, Keswick
CA12 4PL; tel: (017687) 72413; fax:
(017687) 75706.* Croquet lawn, bowling
green and putting course. Moderate.

Castle Inn Hotel, *Bassenthwaite, nr*

*Keswick CA12 4RG; tel: (017687) 76401;
fax: (017687) 76604.* Nearly 50 well-
equipped rooms and a leisure club.
Expensive.

Beckstones Farm, *Thornthwaite,
Keswick CA12 5SQ; tel: (017687) 78510.*
Converted Georgian farmhouse. Budget.

Dale Head Hall Lakeside Hotel,
*Lake Thirlmere, Keswick CA12 4TN; tel:
(0800) 454166; fax: (017687) 71070.*
16th-century manor. Moderate.

Scotgate Holiday Park, *Braithwaite,
Keswick CA12 5TF; tel: (017687) 78343.*
Caravans, motor caravan and tent pitches.
Budget.

SIGHTSEEING

Keswick, near **Derwent Water**, is rich in
enticing shops selling climbing and
hiking boots, tents, backpacks, fleeces and
wet weather gear. To the south is
Borrowdale, in the shadow of **Scafell**,
England's highest peak.

Cars of the Stars Motor Museum,
Standish St, Keswick; tel: (017687) 73757.
A display of vehicles made famous in films
and on TV – the James Bond collection,
Batmobile and many more, open mid
Feb–New Year; admission charge.

Cumberland Pencil Museum,
*Southey Works, Keswick; tel: (017687)
73626,* open daily 0930–1600; admission
charge. Fascinating story of pencil production from the discovery of graphite
onwards.

Keswick Museum and Art Gallery,
*Fitz Park, Station Rd, Keswick; tel:
(017687) 73263,* open Sun–Fri 1000–
1200, 1300–1600 (Easter–Oct); admission
charge. This traditional-style, purpose-
built Victorian museum depicts local history from Roman times and displays a
model of the Lake District made in 1834.
Library material from Walpole, Southey
and Wordsworth is exhibited.

LEWES–SALISBURY

This very attractive route traverses some of the best countryside in the south of England. It follows the South Downs westwards, passing through some quaint villages, historic towns and ancient Winchester with its glorious cathedral.

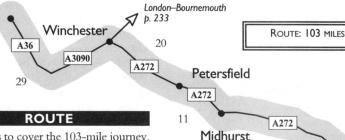

ROUTE: 103 MILES

ROUTE

Allow 3 hrs to cover the 103-mile journey. From Lewes head north on A275 and after 9 miles, at Chailey Common, turn left on A272, the road we follow for the next 70 miles to Winchester. It takes us through the West Sussex towns of **Haywards Heath**, **Billingshurst**, **Petworth** and **Midhurst** and through **Petersfield**, Hampshire. From **Winchester** head south-west on A3090 (A31) for 10 miles to Romsey, then follow A27 west for 8 miles, where it intersects with A36, which travels north-west to reach Salisbury in 6 miles.

LEWES–MIDHURST

TICs: *Market Sq., Petworth GU28 0AF; tel: (01798) 343523; North St, Midhurst GU29 9DW; tel: (01730) 817322*. Both centres offer information on local attractions and events and can assist with accommodation reservations.

ACCOMMODATION

Hotels, guesthouses, farmhouses, inns, b&bs and self-catering establishments are listed in *South East Accommodation Guide* and *The Beautiful South*, available (free) at TICs in the regions covered by the South East Tourist Board and the Southern Tourist Board.

The Anchorhold, *35 Paddock Hall Rd, Haywards Heath, West Sussex RH16 1HN; tel: (01444) 425468.* B&b in a peaceful cottage with large garden. Budget. **Hilton Park Hotel**, *Cuckfield, Haywards Heath RH18 5EG; tel: (01444) 545555; fax: (01444) 457222.* Country house hotel with magnificent views of the South Downs. It has 15 en suite rooms. Expensive.

Newstead Hall Hotel, *Adversane, Billingshurst, West Sussex RH14 9JH; tel: (01403) 783196; fax: (01403) 784228.* Tudor-style country house. Moderate.

The Angel Hotel, *North St, Midhurst,*

209

West Sussex GU29 9DN; tel: (01730) 812421; fax: (01730) 815928. The restored 16th-century coaching inn is said to have been given its name by a group of Pilgrim Fathers resting there while travelling to Southampton to board a ship for America. Expensive.

Spread Eagle Hotel, *South St, Midhurst GU29 9NH; tel: (01730) 816911; fax: (01730) 815668.* Coaching inn dating from 1430. Expensive–pricey.

Swan Inn, *Red Lion St, Market Sq., Midhurst GU29 9BP; tel: (01730) 812853.* 15th-century inn located in the centre of the old market square. Budget.

EATING AND DRINKING

Selsey Arms, *Coolham, A272 3 miles east of Billingshurst; tel: (01403) 741537.* Cosy and welcoming, the inn has a restaurant and serves food at the bar. B&b available in two ensuite rooms. Budget.

Six Bells, *76 High St, Billingshurst; tel: (01403) 782124.* Charming 15th-century pub. Real ales and bar food.

The Limeburners, *Newbridge, Billingshurst (signposted off A272 1 mile west of the village); tel: (01403) 782311.* An archetypal country pub, with an attractive garden, beamed ceiling and open fire. Discreet camping ground at the rear.

SIGHTSEEING

Borde Hill Gardens, *Balcombe Rd, Haywards Heath; tel: (01444) 4500326,* open daily 1000–1800; £2.50. An award-winning collection of azaleas, rhododendrons, magnolias and camellias and many champion trees.

The **Coolham Airfield D-Day Memorial**, *Selsey Arms, Coolham, A272 3 miles east of Billingshurst; tel: (01403) 741537,* commemorates the multi-national airmen who served and perished at Coolham Advanced Landing Ground

Airfield during Operation Overlord in June 1944.

Parham House and Gardens, *Parham Park, Pulborough (6 miles south of Billingshurst); tel: (01903) 744888,* open Wed, Thur, Sun and public holidays; house 1400–1800; gardens 1300–1800 (Apr–Oct); £4.50. Surrounded by a deer park at the foot of the South Downs, the Elizabethan house has a collection of Elizabethan and Stuart portraits, furniture, china, needlework, oriental carpets and tapestries. The gardens include a brick-and-turf maze.

Pulborough Brooks Nature Reserve, *Wiggonholt, Pulborough; tel: (01798) 875851,* open daily; nature reserve 0900–2100 (sunset if earlier); visitor centre 1000–1700; nature reserve £3; visitor centre free. This extensive nature reserve, managed by the Royal Society for the Protection of Birds, has nature trails, scenic views and viewing hides.

Petworth Cottage Museum, *346 High St, Petworth; tel: (01798) 342100,* open Tues–Thur, Sat–Sun, public holidays 1400–1630 (early Mar–Oct); £3. A 17th-century estate worker's cottage and garden, restored as they might have been in 1910.

Petworth House and Park; *tel: (01798) 342207,* open Mon–Wed, Sat–Sun 1300–1730; (end Mar–Oct); £4.50. The late 17th-century palace is set in an extensive deer park designed by Capability Brown and painted by Turner, whose paintings feature in the collection which also includes works by Van Dyck, Gainsborough and Reynolds. The house also contains fine collections of furniture and sculpture.

PETERSFIELD

TIC: *County Library, 27 The Square, Petersfield GU32 3HH; tel: (01730) 268829,* open Mon–Fri 1000–1700, Sat 1000–1600 (May–Sept); Mon–Wed and Fri 1000–1700, Sat 1000–1300 (Oct–Apr). Services offered: BABA, local accommodation bookings, sightseeing information.

ACCOMMODATION

Langrish House, *Langrish, Petersfield, Hampshire GU32 1RN; tel: (01730) 266941; fax: (01730) 260543.* 3 miles west of Petersfield, the hotel was originally a 16th-century farmhouse. Moderate.

Heath Farmhouse, *Sussex Rd, Petersfield GU31 4HU; tel: (01730) 264709.* Attractive Georgian house on B2146. Budget.

SIGHTSEEING

The Bear Museum, *35 Dragon St; tel: (01730) 265108*, open Tues–Sat 1000–1700; free. Britain's first museum dedicated to teddy bears.

Physic Garden, *rear of 16 High St*, open daily; free. A small walled garden laid out in the style of the 17th century.

OUT OF TOWN

Queen Elizabeth Country Park; *tel: (01705) 595040*, open daily 1000–1730 (Easter–Oct); Sat–Sun 1000–1730 or dusk (Nov–Mar); free. 4 miles south, on A3. Said to be one of the finest in England, the park is located on Butser Hill and covers more than 500 acres.

Butser Ancient Farm, *tel: (01705) 598838*, open daily 1000–1700 (Mar–Nov); admission charge. Signposted off A3, 5 miles north. Rare breeds can be seen at this restoration of a Celtic farm of 2000 years ago.

Uppark (NT), *South Harting; tel: (01730) 825317*, open Sun–Thur; exhibition, gardens, shop and restaurant 1130–1730; house 1300–1700; £5. 4 miles south off B2146. Completely restored after

a major fire in 1989, the paintings, textiles, furniture and ceramics which were fortunately saved from the blaze are again on show in this exquisite late 19th-century house.

WINCHESTER

TIC: *The Guildhall, The Broadway, Winchester SO23 9LJ; tel: (01962) 840500/ 848180*, open Mon–Sat 1000–1700 (Oct–May); Mon–Sat 1000–1800, Sun 1100–1400 (June–Sept). DP SHS services offered; local bed-booking (latest 30 mins before closing) and BABA (latest 1 hr before closing) – queue at designated booking desk, which can be busy in late afternoon. *Winchester Visitor's Guide* (includes accommodation) is £1. A large range of other guides is on sale.

GETTING AROUND

The majority of attractions in town are within walking distance of the centre. Town maps are free from the TIC. Public transport is good in the centre at all times and to outlying areas Mon–Sat (running to 2300), but Sun services are limited. **Stagecoach (Hampshire Bus)** is the main operator, *tel: (01256) 464501*; most services starting from the **bus station**, *The Broadway*. Some services display the **County Bus** sign. **Shopmobility**, *tel: (01962) 842626*. There are **taxi** ranks at the railway station, *Broadway* and *Silver Hill*. **Taxi** firms include: **Wessex Cars**, *tel: (01962) 877749*; and **Wintax**, *tel: (01962) 866208*.

ACCOMMODATION AND FOOD

It is advisable to pre-book accommodation, especially if you are arriving late. There is a range of high–medium priced hotels in the city and cheaper accommodation is mostly found a little way from the centre. Hotel chains include *BW* and *MH*.

211

HI: *City Mill, Water Lane; tel: (01962) 853723.* There are a number of **camp-sites** in the area and the TIC has a free list available. The closest is **Morn Hill Caravan Club Site**, *Morn Hill, tel: (01962) 869877,* 3 miles east; most pitches are for caravans, not for tents.

There is a good selection of restaurants of all nationalities, listed in the *Winchester Visitor's Guide*. Most eating places can be found in the *Jewry St, City Rd* and *High St* areas. The **Richoux Restaurant**, *God Begot House, 101 High St; tel: (01962) 841790,* is in a 14th-century building and has a good patisserie.

COMMUNICATIONS

The main **post office**, *Middle Brook St,* opens Mon–Fri 0900–1730, Sat 0900–1900. Poste restante facilities.

ENTERTAINMENT AND EVENTS

A quarterly list of events, *What's on in Winchester,* is free from the TIC. **Theatre Royal**, *Jewry St; tel: (01962) 843434,* is a major entertainment venue. It is due to reopen after refurbishment in late 1998.

The **Winchester Folk Festival** is staged every Apr at The Guildhall, *The Broadway.*

SHOPPING

The main areas for shopping are *High St* and the Brooks Centre. There is a **general market**, *Middle Brook St,* every Wed–Sat. **Kingswalk Antiques Market**, *Kingswalk; tel (01962) 862277,* takes place Mon–Sat from 0900.

SIGHTSEEING

The *Winchester Visitor's Guide* illustrates a suggested city walk that takes in the main sights and the TIC can supply several leaflets for other **self-guided walks**. **Guided walking tours** of the city start

from outside the TIC daily 1030 and 1430 (May–Sept); Mon–Sat 1430 (Apr, Oct); Sat–Sun 1100 (Nov–Mar); £2. They last around 90 mins; *tel: (01962) 840500* for information. Other types of **guided tours** can also be booked at the TIC.

Winchester was London's predecessor as capital of England and many early English kings are buried in **Winchester Cathedral**, *5 The Close; tel: (01962) 853137,* open daily 0715–1830; free, but £2.50 donation suggested. The present structure, started in 1079, contains many ancient treasures and is thought to be the second-longest medieval building in the world. Nearby are the ruins of the old palace of the bishops of Winchester: **Wolvesey Castle** (EH), *College St; tel: (01962) 854766,* open daily 1000–1800 (Apr–Sept); daily 1000–1800/dusk (Oct); £2.

The city is also famous for one of the oldest public schools in Britain, founded in 1382: **Winchester College**, *College St; tel: (01962) 868778.* To see round you must join an official tour (no booking required) – they leave daily at 1100, 1400 and 1515 (Apr–Sept); £2.50.

What is reputed to be the legendary **Round Table** of King Arthur is displayed in the surviving part of the 13th-century castle, the **Great Hall**, *off High St; tel: (01962) 846476,* open daily 1000–1700 (Apr–Oct); 1000–1600 (Nov–Mar); free. Times subject to variation.

Winchester has five magnificent military museums, four of which are at the Peninsula Barracks. **Royal Hussars Museum**, *Peninsula Barracks, Romsey Rd; tel: (01962) 828541,* open Tues–Fri 1000–1600, Sat–Sun, public holidays 1200–1600; free. **Gurkha Museum**, *Peninsula Barracks, Romsey Rd; tel: (01962) 828536,* open Tues–Sat, public holidays 1000–1700; £1.50. Museums covering the **Light Infantry** and the **Royal Green Jackets** are also housed in the barracks.

Royal Hampshire Regiment Museum, *Southgate St; tel: (01962) 863658*, open Mon–Fri 1000–1230 and 1400–1600, Sat–Sun, public holidays 1200–1600 (Apr–Oct); free.

Winchester Gallery, *Park Ave; tel: (01962) 852500*, open (only when there are exhibitions) Tues–Fri 1000–1630; free.

Intech (Interactive Technology Exhibition), *Hampshire Technology Centre, Romsey Rd; tel: (01962) 863791*, open daily 1000–1600; free. Designed to be educational and stimulating for children.

Westgate Museum, *High St; tel: (01962) 848269/869864*, open Mon–Fri 1000–1700 (Apr–Sept); Tues–Fri 1000–1700 (Feb–Mar, Oct); Sat 1000–1300 and 1400–1700, Sun 1400–1700 (Feb–Oct); 30p. This is a fortified medieval gateway which became a debtors' prison in the 17th century.

A small museum devoted to the history and archaeology of Winchester is the **City Museum**, *The Square; tel: (01962) 863064/868269*, open Mon–Fri 1000–1700 (Apr–Sept); Tues–Fri 1000–1700 (Oct–Mar); Sat 1000–1300 and 1400–1700, Sun 1400–1700 (all year); free.

Hospital of St Cross, *St Cross Rd; tel: (01962) 851375*, open daily 0930–1700 (Apr–Oct); 1030–1530 (Nov–Mar); £2. Founded in 1132, this is the oldest charitable institution in England.

City Mill (NT), *Bridge St; tel: (01962) 870057*, open Sat–Sun 1100–1645 (Mar); Wed–Sun, public holidays 1100–1645 (Apr–Oct); £1. The mill was rebuilt in 1744, using 15th-century materials.

OUT OF TOWN

Romsey Abbey, *Romsey; tel: (01794) 513125*, open daily 0830–1830; free, but £1 donation requested. 10 miles south-

west there are guided tours Thur at 1500 (May–Sept); £1.50. Saxon sculptures can be found in the (mainly) 12th-century abbey, which is the last resting place of Earl Mountbatten of Burma.

Most of **Mottisfont** village is encompassed by an estate of which the centrepiece is a 12th-century Augustinian priory, which features a room decorated by Rex Whistler. The prime attraction is the national collection of old-fashioned roses. The scent from these is best in the evening so, during the season (late May–June, but check), the gardens stay open until 2030. **Mottisfont Abbey and Gardens** (NT), *Mottisfont, nr Romsey; tel: (01794) 340757*. House open Sat–Wed 1300–1700; £4–£5 in the rose season. 10 miles southwest.

Jane Austen's House, *Chawton, nr Alton; tel: (01420) 83262*, open Sat–Sun 1100–1630 (Jan–Feb); daily 1100–1630 (Mar–Dec); £2. 15 miles east. The 17th-century structure, which has a large collection of memorabilia, is where Jane Austen spent her last eight years (1809–1817) – when she wrote most of her novels. She died in Winchester (in a house that can still be seen in *College St*) and is buried in the cathedral.

Sir Harold Hillier Gardens and Arboretum, *Jermyns Lane, Ampfield, nr Romsey; tel: (01794) 368787*, open daily 1030–1800 (Apr–Oct); 1030–1700/dusk (Nov–Mar); £4 (Apr–Oct), £3 (Nov–Mar). 7 miles south-west. The 166 acres of gardens are delightful in every season, with a superb selection of trees and shrubs.

Marwell Zoological Park, *Marwell, Colden Common; tel: (01962) 777406*, open daily 1000–1800 (1630 in winter); £7.50. 6 miles south-east. A large zoo with around 1000 animals, set in over 100 acres of parkland, Marwell specialises in the breeding of endangered species.

213

LINCOLN

Many people who have the impression that Lincolnshire is flat, perhaps because of its air force bases and fens, discover the truth when they drive through the rolling Wolds to Lincoln. Few English cities have such precipitous ascents (and descents) as this lovely historic place with its cathedral castle and range of attractions. One of the thoroughfares is aptly named Steep Hill.

TOURIST INFORMATION

TIC: *9 Castle Hill, Lincoln LN1 3AA; tel: (01522) 529828/564506*, open Mon–Thur 0900–1730, Fri 0900–1700, Sat–Sun, public holidays 1000–1700. Services offered: local bed-booking (latest 15 mins before closing), BABA (latest 30 mins before closing). Guided tours booked and tickets sold for local events. There is free literature covering accommodation and places to visit, as well as an official guide that costs £1.99.

ARRIVING AND DEPARTING

Out on a limb from England's major road routes, Lincoln is 14 miles north-east of Newark, and is accessed from A1 by A46. A quieter, more picturesque route to the city is provided by A15 from Peterborough to the south and Scunthorpe to the north.

GETTING AROUND

Lincoln's attractions are within walking distance of the town centre, and free town and transport maps are available from the TIC.

214

General transport enquiries, *tel: (01522) 553134;* **bus and train times**, *tel: (01522) 553135.* The main operator of services is **Lincoln City Transport/Lincolnshire Roadcar**, *tel: (01522) 532424.*

The only **taxi** rank is outside the railway station, *St Mary's St*, but a couple of the taxi companies have offices in *High St*.

STAYING IN LINCOLN

Accommodation

There is a good selection of hotels, b&bs and guesthouses. Cheaper places can be found in the centre, in the South Park area (1 mile south) and in the suburb of North Hykeham (3 miles south). It is usually easy to book on arrival, but pre-booking is essential during the Lincolnshire Show (June), Lincoln Christmas Market (mid Dec) and summer public holidays. Hotel chains include *CM, FH* and *FP*.

Castle Hotel, *Westgate, Lincoln LN1 3AS; tel: (01522) 538801, fax: (01522) 575457,* 19th-century property with views of the castle and cathedral. Expensive.

Hillcrest Hotel, *15 Lindum Terrace, Lincoln LN2 5RT; tel/fax: (01522) 510182.* A former Victorian rectory, the hotel is a 5 min walk from the cathedral. Moderate-expensive.

White Hart Hotel, *Bailgate, Lincoln LN1 3AR; tel: (01522) 526222.* The 14th-century commended hotel has single, twin, double and family rooms and suites. Breakfast not included. Pricey.

The Reindeer, *8 High St, Lincoln; tel: (01522) 520024.* A traditional English pub. Budget.

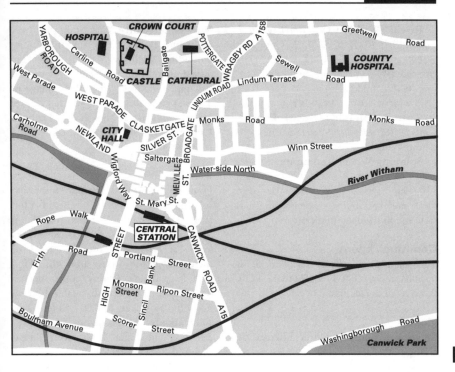

Tower Hotel, *38 Westgate, Lincoln, LN1 3BD; tel: (01522) 529999, fax: (01522) 560596.* Purpose-built in 1990. Moderate–expensive.

The Wren Guest House, *22 St Catherine's, Lincoln; tel: (01522) 537949.* Small and friendly. Budget.

The Headmaster's House, *4 Christ's Hospital Terrace, Lincoln LN2 1LY; tel: (01522) 569080, fax: (01522) 534622.* Self-contained non-smoking apartment in a lovely Georgian house, one minute from the cathedral. B & b or self-catering. Moderate.

HI: *77 South Park; tel: (01522) 522076.* **YMCA**, *St Rumbold St; tel: (01522) 511811.* The closest **campsites** are: **Hartsholme Country Park**, *Skellingthorpe Rd; tel: (01522) 686264,* 3½ miles south-west; **Shortferry Caravan Park**, *Ferry Rd, Fiskerton; tel: (01526) 398021,* 7 miles

east; and **Hazelwood Caravan Site**, *Moor Lane, Thorpe on the Hill; tel: (01522) 688245,* 5 miles south-west.

Eating and Drinking

Lincoln has a wonderful variety of places to eat – pubs serving full meals or bar snacks, wine bars, olde worlde restaurants, fish and chip shops, Indian, Chinese and Italian restaurants and American-style diners. *Steep Hill* has a cluster of good places to eat. The TIC can provide a free list of restaurants. Local specialities are Lincolnshire sausage, stuffed chine (ham stuffed with parsley), plum bread and haslet.

Brown's Pie Shop, *33 Steep Hill, tel: (01522) 527330,* sells home-made British food cooked on the premises. Budget.

Bistro 7, *7 Gordon Rd, off Bailgate, Lincoln; tel: (01522) 575777,* includes a vegetarian menu. Budget.

Royal William IV, *Brayford Pool, Lincoln; tel: (01522) 528159,* Good bar snacks and quick, efficient service. The riverside tables outside are popular in summer. Cheap-budget.

A wide selection of cask ales is available at **Tom Cobleigh's Nosey Parker**, *Crusader Rd, Lincoln; tel: (01522) 524401.* Cheap–budget.

Spinning Wheel Restaurant, *39 Steep Hill, Lincoln; tel: (01522) 522463,* open 1100–late, serves light snacks or main meals and has an extensive evening à la carte menu. Budget–moderate.

Communications

The main **post office**, *Guildhall St,* is open Mon–Fri 0900–1730, Sat 0900–1230. Poste restante facilities.

Money

There is a **Thomas Cook bureau de change** at *Midland Bank, 221 High St.*

ENTERTAINMENT AND EVENTS

The local papers carry listings. For drama, there is the **Theatre Royal**, *Clasketgate; tel: (01522) 525555.* For concerts (and the Midsummer Music Festival) there is **The Lawn**, *Union Rd; tel: (01522) 560306;* and **Lincoln Cathedral**, *tel: (01522) 544544.* Some pubs have live music and there is one night-club; **Ritzy 1 & 2**, *Silver St.*

A free events list is available from the TIC. The **Lincolnshire Show**, *Lincolnshire Showground,* takes place (third week June), the **Lincoln Christmas Market** (mid Dec) is held in the *Uphill* area: this is a major event with hundreds of decorated stalls manned by people in Victorian costume. The **Lincoln Mystery Plays** are staged in the cathedral (July–Aug).

SHOPPING

The main shopping areas are the **Waterside Centre**, *High St,* in the lower city; and **Bailgate**, in the upper city around the Cathedral – this is particularly aimed at tourists. *Steep Hill,* which joins the upper and lower areas, has a range of antiques and collectors' shops, craft centres and second-hand bookshops. **Lincoln Central Market**, *Sincil St,* takes place Mon–Sat 0800–1600.

SIGHTSEEING

Hour-long **guided walks** leave from outside the TIC daily at 1100 and 1400 (Easter, May public holidays, July–Aug); Sat–Sun (Sept–Oct); £2. **Ghost walks** leave Sat 1700 (all year); £3. Details of these and other tours from the TIC, including: **Guide Friday** double-decker open-top **bus tours** that offer hop-on hop-off day tickets; £4.50 (Easter–Oct); and **Cathedral City Cruises**, *tel: (01522) 546853* who offer **boat tours** from Brayford Pool (Easter–Sept); from £3.50.

Lincoln was developed by the Romans as *Lindum Colonia,* to command the meeting of their military roads, Ermine St and Fosse Way, and it later became the centre of the largest and wealthiest bishopric in England. There are substantial remains of the **Roman settlement** – they arrived in AD 48 and by the end of the century Lincoln was one of Europe's finest cities. The TIC can supply *Roman Trail* brochures.

The focal point of Lincoln is still **Lincoln Cathedral**, *Minster Yard; tel: (01522) 544544,* open Mon–Sat 0715–2000, Sun 0715–1800 (May–Aug); Mon–Sat 0715–1800, Sun 0715–1700 (Sept–Apr); but always subject to services; free, but suggested donation £2.50. Its triple towers stand out for miles around. One of the finest Gothic buildings in Europe, it lives up to all expectations, from the carved angels on the breathtaking west front to the elaborate decoration of the **Angel Choir** – look for the carving of the **Lincoln Imp** amongst the angels. The cathedral crowns the old city, which is tightly packed on the end of a high plateau above the River Witham; its steep cobbled streets deserve a day's exploration. Below the cathedral lie the ruins of the medieval **Bishop's Old Palace** (EH), *Minster Yard; tel: (01522) 527468,* open daily 1000–1800 (Easter–Sept); £1. Around *Minster Yard* are attractive medieval and Georgian houses.

Across from the west façade of the cathedral, beyond *Exchequergate*, is the much-restored **Lincoln Castle**, *Castle Hill; tel: (01522) 511068,* open Mon–Sat 0930–1730, Sun 1100–1730; 1100–1600 (Oct–Easter); £2. Two contrasting attractions are that the original Magna Carta is housed here and that there are marvellous views from the observatory tower.

Head down *Steep Hill* to see (exterior only) **Jews' Court**, *2–3 Steep Hill*; among the best surviving examples of 12th-century domestic architecture, a reminder of the thriving Jewish community prior to anti-Semitic expulsions in the 13th century.

Below the hill the city is unremarkable, but there are some good museums, notably the region's largest and most popular museum of social history, which includes frequent demonstrations of past skills: **Museum of Lincolnshire Life**, *Burton Rd; tel: (01522) 528448,* open Mon–Sat 1000–1730; Sun 1000–1730 (May–Sept); Sat 1000–1730, Sun 1400–1730 (Oct–Apr); £1.20.

The Lawn, *Union Rd; tel: (01522) 560306,* offers free admission to all the facilities (though not to concerts, shows, etc.). A former hospital in acres of lovely grounds, it has been turned into a visitor and conference centre, open Mon–Fri 0900–1700, Sat–Sun 1000–1700. The range of attractions includes **Sir Joseph**

Banks Conservatory (a 5000ft² tropical glasshouse), an **aquarium**, a hands-on **archaeological museum**, a small **RAF museum**, and a variety of shops, eateries and entertainment venues.

Ellis Mill, *Mill Rd,* open Sat–Sun 1400–1800 (May–Sept); Sun 1400–dusk (Oct–Apr); 70p, is the sole survivor (and still working) of a whole line of mills.

Incredibly Fantastic Old Toy Show, *26 Westgate; tel: (01522) 520534,* open Tues–Sat 1100–1700, Sun, public holidays 1200–1600 (Easter–Sept); Sat (and Tues–Fri in school holidays) 1100–1700, Sun 1200–1600 (Oct–Christmas); £1.90. Toys of every description can be found here – and not all are behind glass.

The city's superb collection of civic insignia can be seen in the **Guildhall**, *High St; tel: (01522) 564507,* open first Sat each month and assorted other days, tours: 1030 and 1330 – and by appointment; free. The neighbouring 15th-century **Stonebow** arch is on the site of the Roman and medieval southern gateways.

The major Lincolnshire venue for fine and decorative arts, is the **Usher Art Gallery**, *Lindum Rd; tel: (01522) 527980,* open Mon–Sat 1000–1700, Sun 1430–1700; £1.

OUT OF TOWN

Together, **Hartsholme Country Park** and **Swanholme Lakes**, *Skellingthorpe Rd*, 3½ miles south-west, form a large area of open space for alfresco activities.

The many country houses in the surrounding area testify to its agricultural wealth. These include **Doddington Hall**, *Doddington; tel: (01522) 694308.* House open Sun, Wed, public holidays 1400–1800 (May–Sept); £3.80. 4 miles south-west. The hall is a mellow Elizabethan manor house, with lovely walled rose gardens and Georgian interiors.

LINCOLN–SCARBOROUGH

This route gives an overview of eastern England's countryside and coast. It takes in The Wolds of Lincolnshire and the River Humber estuary, with the once great fishing port of Grimsby and Cleethorpes, its neighbouring resort, before crossing the river on the impressive Humber Bridge (toll) to Hull and on into North Yorkshire, where it meets the North Sea at Bridlington and follows the coast to Scarborough.

DIRECT ROUTE: **89** MILES

218

Scarborough

A165 9

Filey

A165 8

Bridlington

18

A165

Beverley

A164 8

Hull

Direct Route A15

M180 25

A180

Grimsby

Cleethorpes

A15

A16 16 **Scenic Route**

A158 A157

Louth

Lincoln 26

ROUTES

DIRECT ROUTE

Alow 2 hrs for this 89-miles journey. Leave Lincoln on A15 north for 23½ miles then head east on M180, leaving at Junction 5 after 7 miles. Rejoin A15 north and continue for 10 miles to join A164 just after the Humber Bridge crossing. After a further 9½ miles, near Beverley, head east on A1035 for 5½ miles then join A165 which reaches Scarborough in 33½ miles.

SCENIC ROUTE

Taking in the Lincolnshire Wolds and the Humber estuary adds around

39 miles and 1 hour 20 minutes. Leave Lincoln on A158 east for 12 miles and at Wragby head north-east to reach **Louth** in 14 miles. Follow A16 north for 11 miles and at Waltham turn right on to A1098 to reach **Cleethorpes** in 4 miles. Continue to **Grimsby**, then follow A180 north-west for 15 miles, heading north on A15, crossing the Humber Bridge and after 10 miles following the signs to central **Hull**. Leave Hull on B1231 and drive west for a mile to join A164 north, which reaches **Beverley** in 8 miles. From Beverley continue to **Bridlington**, **Filey** and Scarborough, as in the direct route.

LOUTH

TIC: *New Market Hall, off Cornmarket, Louth, Lincolnshire LN11 9NS; tel: (01507) 609289*, open Mon–Sat 0900–1700. Services offered: local accommodation reservations; BABA. Information on local attractions and antiques sources.

ACCOMMODATION

For a small market town with a population of just over 14,000, Louth has a good selection of accommodation, including hotels, inns, guesthouses and self-catering establishments.

Brackenborough Arms Hotel, *Cordeaux Corner, Louth LN11 0SZ; tel: (01507) 609169; fax: (01507) 609413.* On A16, 1½ miles north. Moderate.

Beaumont Hotel, *Victoria Rd, Louth LN11 0BX; tel: (01507) 605005; fax: (01507) 607758.* Moderate.

King's Head, *10 Mercer Row, Louth LN11 9JQ; tel: (01507) 602965.* Former coaching inn in town centre. Budget.

Masons Arms, *Cornmarket, Louth LN11 9PY; tel: (01507) 609525.* Refurbished 18th-century posting inn. Budget.

HI: *Woody's Top, Ruckland, nr Louth LN11 8RQ; tel: (01507) 533323.*

SIGHTSEEING

Known as the 'capital' of the Wolds, Louth is a compact town of red brick and pantile buildings, with many Georgian houses and a busy market that trades Wed, Fri, Sat. The 295 ft spire of **St James's Church** is a landmark for miles around.

Louth Museum, *4 Broadbank; tel: (01507) 601211*, open Wed 1000–1600; Fri–Sat 1400–1600; 50p. Includes Louth carpets and examples of local printing.

OUT OF TOWN

Legbourne Railway Museum, *The Old Station, Legbourne; tel: (01507) 603116*, open Tues–Sun and public holidays 1030–1700 (Easter–Sept); admission charge. 4 miles south-east on A157. Some 2000 railway relics at Britain's oldest preserved Great Northern Railway station.

CLEETHORPES/GRIMSBY

TICs: *42–43 Alexandra Rd, Cleethorpes, Humberside DN35 8LE; tel: (01472) 323111; fax: (01472) 323112*, open Mon–Thur 0930–1715, Fri 0930–1645, Sat–Sun 1000–1600.

National Fishing Heritage Centre, *Alexandra Dock, Grimsby, Humberside DN31 1UF; tel: (01472) 323222; fax: (01472) 323223*, open Mon–Thur 0930–1330, 1430–1715; Fri 0930–1330, 1430–1645; Sat–Sun 1000–1230, 1300–1600. In addition to BABA and local accommodation reservations, both centres provide information on local and national attractions and sell tickets for the Humber Bridge and local events.

ACCOMMODATION

Between them, Grimsby and Cleethorpes – running one into the other, they are virtually one place – offer a reasonable selection of accommodation. Grimsby has the better choice of larger hotels, while

219

Cleethorpes has a wide range of smaller establishments. Hotel chains in Grimsby include *FE*, *FP*.

Fleece Inn, *Lock Rd, North Cotes, Grimsby DN36 5UP; tel: (01472) 388233.* On A1031, 4 miles south of Cleethorpes. Traditional country inn. Budget.

Holmhirst Hotel *3 Alexandra Rd, Cleethorpes DN35 8LQ; tel: (01472) 692656.* Overlooks the sea. Budget.

Millfields, *53 Bargate, Great Grimsby DN34 5AD; tel: (01472) 356068; fax: (01472) 250286.* Offers a range of leisure facilities. Moderate.

The nearest campground is **Greenfields Camping Park**, *Providence Cottage, Barrow-upon-Humber DN19 7EE; tel: (01469) 530760.* 14 miles north-west off A1077.

SIGHTSEEING

Cleethorpes and Grimsby owe their development from small, unimportant communities to the arrival of the railway in the mid 19th century. Watched over by the Anglo-Saxon tower of Holy Trinity church, the ancient village of Clee grew dramatically into a popular seaside resort, thanks to its gently shelving sandy beaches. Grimsby shot into prominence as a fishing port when the railway enabled vast quantities of fish to be transported quickly throughout Britain. One of the fish docks which once covered 60 acres has now become a yacht marina.

Cleethorpes Coast Light Railway *Lakeside Station, Kings Rd, Cleethorpes; tel: (01472) 604657.* A nostalgic steam train trip with panoramic views of the Humber estuary, Good Friday–Sept; £1.35.

Discovery Centre *The Lakeside, Kings Rd, Cleethorpes; tel: (01472) 323232,* open daily 1000–1700; £1.70. Visitors can examine the ecology of the Humber estuary through hands-on exhibits.

Jungle World – The Mini-beast Zoo, *Lakeside, Kings Rd, Cleethorpes; tel: (01472) 602118,* open daily 1000–1700 (Apr–Oct), Sat–Sun 1000–1530 (Nov–Mar). An indoor rainforest houses birds and butterflies.

National Fishing Heritage Centre, *Alexandra Dock, Grimsby; tel: (01472) 344868,* open daily 1000–1800; £4.50. This prize-winning attraction vividly recreates the life of Grimsby's fishing community in the 1950s, when the town was the world's leading fishing port.

HULL

TIC: *1 Paragon St, Hull HU1 3NA; tel: (01482) 223559,* open Mon 1000–1800, Tues–Sat 0930–1800, Sun 1300–1700. DP Services: local bed-booking and BABA (latest 30 mins before closing). Membership sold for YHA/HI. *Hull Visitor Guide* (with accommodation listing) is free.

GETTING AROUND

The majority of attractions are within walking distance of the centre. Free town maps are available from the TIC. The two main bus operators are **Stagecoach (Hull)**, *tel: (01482) 222222,* and **East Yorkshire Motor Services**, *tel: (01482) 327146,* both based at the **main bus depot**, *Ferensway.* The main **taxi** rank is located at Paragon Station.

ACCOMMODATION

There is a wide range of accommodation in the centre, with cheaper places located mainly in the suburbs 2 miles north-west. It is generally easy to book on arrival, except during the first and last weeks in July (university graduation ceremonies). Hotel chains include *FP* and *TI*.

University self-catering accommodation is available in the holidays; *tel: (01482) 346351.* Nearest **campsites**:

Lakeminster Park, *Hull Rd, Beverley*; *tel: (01482) 882655*, 7 miles north; **Entick House**, *Ings Lane, Dunswell*; *tel: (01482) 807393*, 5 miles north, and **Burton Constable Caravan and Camping Park**, *Old Lodge, Sproatley*; *tel: (01482) 562508*, 7 miles north.

SIGHTSEEING

Guided walks of the area, incorporating the surrounding countryside, are organised by **Paul Schofield**, *tel: (01482) 878535*, and **Keith Daddy**, *tel: (01482) 781427*; £2. They start from the TIC at 1400 Mon, Wed, Fri, Sat (Apr–Oct).

Hull (Kingston-upon-Hull) is a blend of new attractions, such as the **Humber Bridge** and **Hull Marina**, and older ones, such as the **Old Town**, where Hull began about 800 years ago. Here, historic architecture, quiet narrow lanes, old pubs, colourful barges at anchor, preserved warehouses, formal gardens and wide views of the impressive Humber waterway provide many hours of interest.

Holy Trinity Church, *Market Pl.*; *tel: (01482) 324835*, open Tues–Fri 1000–1600, Sat 0930–1200 (all year); Mon 1400–1600, Wed 1200–1600 (Easter–Christmas); Thur 1200–1600 (Easter–Sept); free. Founded in 1285, this is England's largest parish church.

Hull has seven major **museums**; *tel: (01482) 613902*, open Mon–Sat 1000–1700, Sun 1330–1630; £1 each. **Town Docks (Maritime) Museum**, *Queen Victoria Sq.*, covers Hull's maritime heritage over seven centuries. At the **Streetlife (Transport) Museum**, *High St*, exhibits cover every conceivable type of transport, from penny-farthing bicycles to the *Arctic Corsair*, a large freezer-trawler from the 1960s. **Wilberforce House**, *High St,* was the birthplace of the 18th-century reformer and houses unique collections connected with his anti-slavery campaign. **Ferens Art Gallery**, *Queen Victoria Sq.*, offers an extensive collection of paintings, old and new. **Old Grammar School**, *Market Pl.*, is devoted to the story of the people of Hull.

Hull and East Riding Museum, *High St*, is the archaeological museum, with notable Roman, Saxon, Viking and Celtic exhibits, such as excellent Roman mosaic floors and the **Hasholme Carr Boat**: the largest prehistoric cop boat ever found, made from one giant tree. You can board the 1927 **Spurn Lightship**, *The Marina*, and see how it used to function (closed Nov–Mar).

BEVERLEY

TIC: *Beverley Guildhall, Register Sq., Beverley, North Humberside HU17 9AU*; *tel: (01482) 867430*, open Mon–Fri 0930–1730, Sat 1000–1700 (all year); Sun 1000–1400 (Easter–Sept). DP services offered; local bed-booking (latest 30 mins before closing), BABA (latest booking 1700 Mon–Fri, 1500 Sat). Ticketing agency for local events/performances. Beverley tourist brochure available free of charge, as well as an accommodation list.

GETTING AROUND

Most attractions are within a walkable area from the centre. Town and transport maps are available from the TIC. Buses are operated by **East Yorkshire Bus Company**, *tel: (01482) 327146*.

ACCOMMODATION

There is a good range of accommodation and the TIC has details of rooms within a 50 mile radius of Beverley. It is generally easy to find accommodation on arrival, except during the Beverley Music Festival (May) and the Folk Festival (June).

HI: **Beverley Friary**, *Friars Lane*; *tel:*

221

(01482) 881751. The TIC has details of **campsites** in the area – the nearest are: **Lake Minster Park**, *Bleach House Farm, Hull Rd; tel: (01482) 882655,* 1 mile south; and **Waudby's Caravan Site**, *Brough Rd, South Cave, Brough; tel: (01430) 422523,* 12 miles south-west.

SIGHTSEEING

Beverley is a tranquil and historic market town whose landmark, **Beverley Minster**, *tel: (01482) 868540,* open Mon–Sat 0900–2000 (1600 Oct–Easter), Sun 1430–1700; free, but donation invited, is a fine example of Gothic architecture.

Also of interest is **St Mary's Church**, *North Bar Within*, open daily 1000–1600; free. A now-famous carving here is reputed to have inspired the White Rabbit in Lewis Carroll's *Alice in Wonderland*.

BRIDLINGTON

222

TIC: *25 Prince St, Bridlington YO15 2NP; tel: (01262) 673474; fax: (01262 401797,* open Mon–Sat 0930–1730, Sun 0930–1700 (closed Sun Oct–Easter). BABA; local bed-booking.

ACCOMMODATION

Bridlington has a good selection of private, family hotels, guesthouses and self-catering establishments.

Expanse Hotel, *North Marine Drive, Bridlington YO15 2LS; tel: (01262) 675347; fax: (01262) 604928.* Moderate.

Glen Alan Hotel, *21 Flamborough Rd, Bridlington YO15 2HU; tel: (01262) 674650.* Family-run licensed hotel, in a pleasant residential area, with nine ensuite rooms. Home-cooked meals available. Budget.

The nearest campground is **Thornwick Bay Holiday Centre**, *Flamborough, Bridlington, East Yorkshire YO15 1AU; tel: (01262) 850369; fax: (01262) 851550.*

SIGHTSEEING

A traditional seaside resort, once more fashionable than it is today, Bridlington has the usual holiday attractions with the bonus of marvellous beaches.

Sewerby Hall, *Sewerby, Bridlington; tel: (01262) 673769.* Hall open daily 1000–1800 (Easter–late Oct); Sat–Tues 1100–1600 (late Oct–mid Jan, Mar–Easter); £2.60. Built 1714–20 and added to over the centuries, Sewerby has many period rooms and doubles as the **Museum of East Yorkshire**, with fine permanent displays and changing exhibitions. The beautiful and varied gardens enclose a small children's zoo.

FILEY

TIC: *John St, Filey YO14 9DW; tel: (01723) 513962,* open daily 1000–1730 (May–Sept), Sat–Sun 1000–1630 (Oct–Apr). Services offered: local accommodation reservations; BABA. When closed, information is available at Scarborough TIC (see p. 317).

Seafield Hotel, *9–11 Rutland St, Filey YO14 9JA; tel: (01723) 512715.* Close to town centre and beach. Budget.

Orchard Farm Holiday Village, *Hunmanby, Filey YO14 0PU; tel/fax: (01723) 891582.* Within walking distance of sandy beaches, the village has eight self-catering cottages, 90 caravan and tent pitches and has excellent facilities.

SIGHTSEEING

Serving as an inshore fishing station as well as a holiday resort, Filey is a quiet retreat from sophisticated Scarborough, seven miles to the north.

Filey Museum, *8–10 Queen St*, open Sun–Fri 1000–1200, 1400–1700, Sat 1400–1700 (late May–mid Sept); admission charge. Housed in the town's oldest domestic building, dating from 1696.

LONDON

London is indisputably one of the world's great cities. Renowned for pageantry, and with history oozing from her ancient stones, she has nevertheless kept pace with the changing times, and modern attractions compete with more traditional activities. If you feel the need for a bit of peace, you will never be far from one of the great parks or leafy squares.

However, London is certainly not a city to explore by car. The roads are congested, and parking is difficult to find and expensive. If you plan to do more than just pass through, it is better to use public transport. As this book focuses on exploring by car, we have kept the information in this chapter to a minimum.

TOURIST INFORMATION

The **British Travel Centre (BTC)**, *12 Lower Regent Street, London SW1* (tube: *Piccadilly Circus*), open Mon–Fri 0900–1830, Sat–Sun 1000–1600 (Sat extended June–Sept). Services offered: local b&b and BABA (£5 booking fee, plus redeemable deposit of first night); booking service for guided tours and theatres; transport passes; and comprehensive multi-lingual information. Last bookings 30 mins before closing.

TICs which offer the same services include: **Victoria Station**, *main concourse*; open daily 0800–1900 (Apr–Oct); Mon–Sat 0800–1800, Sun 0900–1600 (Nov–Mar). This is London's official tourist centre and always busy, so expect to queue – possibly for a long time. **Liverpool**

Street Station, *street level*; open Mon–Fri 0800–1800, Sat–Sun 0845–1730. **Waterloo International Station**, *arrivals hall*, open daily 0830–2100. **Selfridges**, *Oxford St, W1* (tube: *Bond St/Marble Arch*); open store hours.

London Tourist Board (LTB), *26 Grosvenor Gdns, SW1* (tube: *Victoria*); *tel: 730 3450*, open Mon–Fri 0900–1730.

ARRIVING AND DEPARTING

Airports

Heathrow Airport is 15 miles west of central London and has four terminals. There are TICs in *Terminal 3 (arrivals concourse)* and *Terminals 1/2/3 (tube station concourse)*, open daily 0830–1800. Services offered: as for BTC (see above).

Gatwick Airport is 27 miles south of central London. For flight enquiries: *tel: (01293) 535353*. **Stansted Airport** is 37 miles north-east of central London. For enquiries: *tel: (01279) 662379*.

For details of transport links from these airports to central London, see p. 40.

Trains and Buses

The **enquiry number** for trains is centralised; *tel: (0345) 484950*. London has 16 mainline rail stations, all linked to tube stations – usually of the same name (sometimes with separate entrances).

Victoria Coach Station, *Buckingham Palace Rd, SW1; tel: (0990) 808080*, is the main London terminal for long-distance coaches. Tickets for **National Express**, which covers most of England and Wales, can be bought at the coach station daily 0600–2400.

223

GETTING AROUND

The *A–Z Map of London* (available for £2.25 from most newsagents) covers the central area on a scale of 6 ins to the mile. It has a street index, highlights places of interest and also has maps showing West End cinemas and theatres.

Free bus and tube maps and other information about **London Transport (LT)**, including fares and a wide range of passes are available in most tube stations. If you want other information, try the main LT office at **St James's Park** tube station (ground level); *tel: 222 1234* (24 hours).

Taxis: London's famous 'black cabs' (which may not be black, but the shape is distinctive) are metered and drivers have to pass a rigorous test on their knowledge of London. Licensed minicabs (ordinary cars) must be booked by telephone – avoid the pirates touting for business on the street and at mainline stations.

224

A **cruise on the river** is a wonderful way to see London. Buy tickets at the pier. A widely available free leaflet, *Discover the Thames*, outlines the possibilities. For more information, contact **Thames Passenger Services Federation**, *tel: 345 5122*.

STAYING IN LONDON

Accommodation

London's accommodation ranges from world-renowned institutions as the Ritz and Savoy to youth hostels. All the major international hotel chains are represented and there are many small establishments.

LTB, *tel: 824 8844*, accepts telephone bookings for over 500 hotels and guesthouses within a 20 mile radius of central London: payment by MasterCard and Visa only. The major TICs book all types of accommodation throughout Britain. For telephone bookings through BTC, call **Expotel Reservations**, *tel: 930 0572*.

Thomas Cook have hotel booking desks at Gatwick Airport and at Charing Cross, St Pancras, King's Cross, Victoria and Paddington rail stations.

The nearest **campsites** are some way out of town. **Tent City**, *Old Oak Common Lane, Acton, W3* (tube: *East Acton); tel: (0181) 743 5708*, is easily the cheapest option (£6 per person per night), open June–Sept.

Eating and Drinking

London offers eating places of every conceivable type, from traditional British to those of countries you probably couldn't pinpoint on a map. The cost is equally varied. In the West End, **Soho** and **Covent Garden** offer a good choice of restaurants. Soho is also the centre of London's **Chinatown**.

There are **pubs** on almost every street and many do good value food.

Communications

Post offices usually open Mon–Fri 0900–1730, Sat 0900–1230, although some small branches close for lunch.

The post office near *Trafalgar Square (24/28 William IV St, WC2 4DL; tel: 930 9580)* is open Mon–Sat 0800/0830–2000/2100. It has a poste restante facility.

Telephone codes

Unless some other code is shown, all the telephone numbers in this chapter have the code *0171* and it is unnecessary to dial

Colour section (i): Tintern Abbey (p. 188); pagentry in London.
(ii): The Lake District (pp. 203–208): Lakeland scenery; Bowness on Lake Windermere.
(iii): Canterbury Cathedral (p. 257).
(iv): Bath (pp. 242–245): the Abbey towers over the Roman Baths.

UNDERGROUND

Travel Information 0171-222-1234
Travelcheck 0171-222-1200

225

Interchange stations

○ Interchange stations
⇄ Connections with British Rail
Connections with British Rail within walking distance
✈ Airport interchange
✶ Closed Saturdays and Sundays
✦ Closed Sundays
✶✶ Closed Saturdays and Sundays
◇ Mornington Crescent closed for rebuilding
† For opening times see poster journey planners
Certain stations are closed during public holidays

Key to Lines

Bakerloo
Central
Circle
District
East London
Hammersmith & City
Jubilee
Metropolitan
Northern
Piccadilly
Victoria
Waterloo & City †
Docklands Light Railway †
British Rail

© Copyright London Regional Transport

Registered User 98/E/890

Diary 2K 4.96

226

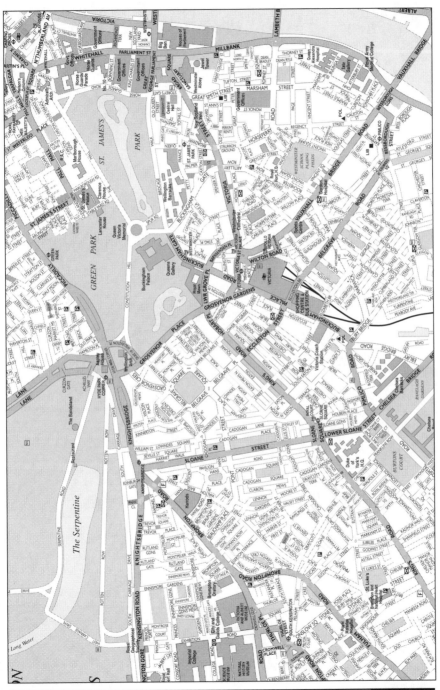

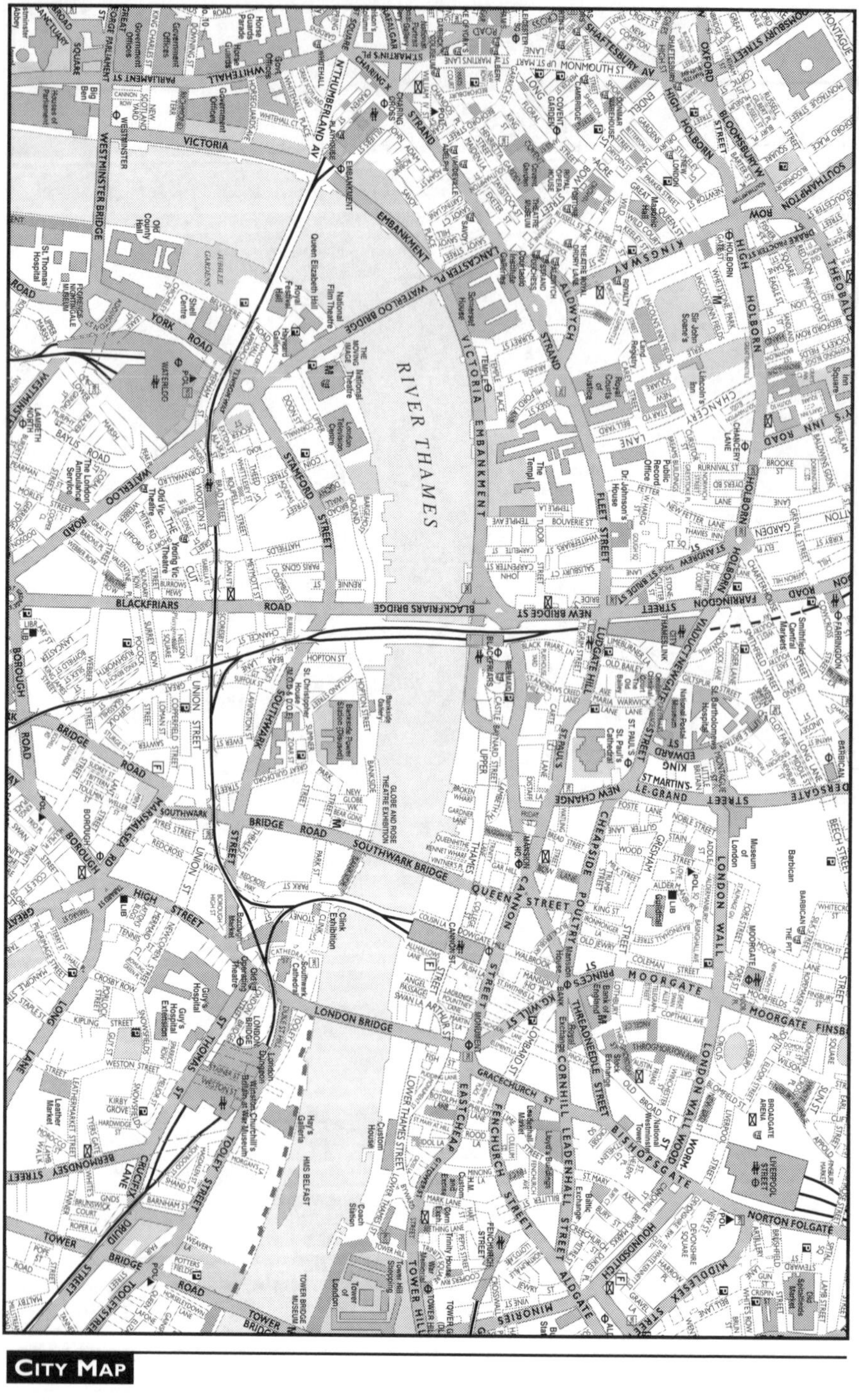
RIVER THAMES
VICTORIA EMBANKMENT
WATERLOO BRIDGE
BLACKFRIARS BRIDGE
SOUTHWARK BRIDGE
LONDON BRIDGE
WESTMINSTER BRIDGE
STRAND
ALDWYCH
KINGSWAY
HIGH HOLBORN
FLEET STREET
LUDGATE HILL
CHEAPSIDE
QUEEN VICTORIA STREET
CANNON STREET
MOORGATE
LONDON WALL
BISHOPSGATE
FENCHURCH STREET
LEADENHALL STREET
EASTCHEAP
TOWER HILL
TOOLEY STREET
BOROUGH HIGH STREET
BLACKFRIARS ROAD
STAMFORD STREET
SOUTHWARK STREET
YORK ROAD
WATERLOO ROAD
St. Paul's Cathedral
Museum of London
Barbican
Guy's Hospital
Tower of London
HMS BELFAST
Royal Festival Hall
Old County Hall
Royal Courts of Justice
Covent Garden

this if you are within the *0171* area – which covers central London. Surrounding areas have the code *0181*.

Money

There are banks and bureaux de change on virtually every main street. **Thomas Cook bureaux de change** can be found in every area of London and at all the airports. Locations include: *16 King St, Covent Garden; 1 Marble Arch; 92 Kensington High St; 79 Piccadilly; 152 Portobello Rd; 133 Regent St; 1 Woburn Pl., Russell Sq.; Kings Cross rail station;* and *Victoria rail station.*

ENTERTAINMENT

Countless special exhibitions and events, from royal pageantry to sporting contests, are staged throughout the year. The most comprehensive entertainments listings are the weekly magazines *Time Out* (£1.70) and *What's On in London* (£1.20), available from newsagents.

The *Evening Standard* (out around lunchtime Mon–Sat; 30p) has good theatre and cinema listings every day and on Thur a comprehensive supplement (*Hot Tickets*) details every type of activity.

SHOPPING

Oxford Street (tube: *Marble Arch/Bond St/Oxford Circus*) includes such department stores as Selfridges, Dickens and Jones and John Lewis. **Regent Street** (tube: *Oxford Circus/ Piccadilly Circus*) is noted for high-quality British clothing shops. For exclusive designer clothes, jewellery, antiques, art galleries, the auction house Sotheby's and upmarket window shopping, try **Bond Street** (tube: *Bond St*). **Brompton Road** (tube: *Knightsbridge*) is famous for Harrods and Harvey Nichols, which specialise in upmarket fashion.

SIGHTSEEING

Most attractions open daily, but a few do not (Monday is a common closing day for museums, Sunday for churches). **Entry is usually refused 30–60 mins before closing time.** *London Guide* and *Holiday London* (available from TICs) are reasonably comprehensive free booklets and include many places for which this book has no space, e.g. museums covering everything from tea and coffee to Sherlock Holmes.

The **London White Card** (£15 for 3 days, £20 for a week), gives free entry to over a dozen museums. Buy it from any of the participants.

Fleets of mainly open-topped **tour buses** offer an excellent introduction to London. The three major operators are: **Big Bus**, *tel: (0181) 944 7810*, who always have *live* English-only commentaries; **London Pride**, *tel: (01708) 631122*, and **Original London Sightseeing**, *tel: (0181) 877 1722*

Several companies offer themed **walking tours** (£4 is normal), usually starting from tube stations and at a leisurely pace. Some of the companies are: **Stepping Out**, *tel: (0181) 881 2933*; **Original London Walks**, *tel: 624 3978*; and **Dickens's London**, *tel: 624 3978* or *(0181) 980 5565*.

Westminster and the West End

Pigeon-filled **Trafalgar Square** is dominated by **Nelson's Column**, guarded by Landseer's great bronze lions. On the east side is the 18th-century **St Martin-in-the-Fields**.

National Gallery, *Trafalgar Square, WC2* (tube: *Charing Cross); tel: 839 3321*, open Mon–Sat 1000–1800 (some Wed –2000), Sun 1200–1800; free. One of the world's greatest galleries. Just around the corner, thousands of faces from British history stare down from the walls of the **National Portrait Gallery**, *St Martin's Place, WC2; tel: 306 0055,* open Mon–Sat 1000–1800, Sun 1200–1800; free.

Whitehall links Trafalgar Square to Westminster, passing the **Horse Guards**: mounted sentries of the Household Cavalry in full regalia – the guard changes Mon–Sat 1100, Sun 1000, and goes off duty 1600. The entrance to Downing Street (the London home of the Prime Minister) is protected by forbidding gates.

Dominated by **Big Ben**'s clock tower are the **Houses of Parliament**, *Parliament Square, SW1* (tube: *Westminster*); *tel: 219 3000.* When Parliament is in session (usually mid Oct–July, with breaks around Christmas and Easter), you can watch democracy in action from the Strangers' Gallery of the House of Commons – your best chance of getting in quickly is to go Mon–Thur at around 1700. The House of Lords is easier to get into.

Westminster Abbey opens daily 0800–1800; 0800–1945 (Wed); after 1800 is the only time flashlight/tripod photography is allowed). Visitors are admitted (free) to nave and cloister between services (*tel: 222 5152* for details of services). The choir, transepts and royal chapels can be visited Mon–Sat (£4). Bookings for comprehensive tours (£7) can be made in advance (advisable in mid-summer); *tel: 222 7110.*

Heading west brings you to **Buckingham Palace**, *SW1* (tube: *Victoria/St James's Park*); *tel: 839 1377.* The **Changing of the Guard** takes place in the forecourt at 1130, daily in summer, on alternate days in winter. **State Rooms** are open to the public daily 0930–1730 (Aug–Sept); £9 (numbers are limited, so purchase tickets in advance). The **Queen's Gallery**, open daily 0930–1630 has changing displays drawn from the royal collection.

Tate Gallery, *Millbank, SW1* (tube: *Pimlico*); *tel: 887 8008,* open Mon–Sat 1000–1750, Sun 1400–1750; free. Britain's greatest collection of indigenous and modern paintings and sculptures.

Bloomsbury and Covent Garden

The **British Museum**, *Great Russell St, WC1* (tube: *Russell Sq./Holborn/Tottenham Court Rd*); *tel: 580 1788,* open Mon–Sat 1000–1700, Sun 1430–1800; free, is indisputably one of the world's great museums.

To the south is **Covent Garden** (tube: *Covent Garden*), with a wide variety of attractions, including the **London Transport Museum**, *Covent Garden Piazza, WC2; tel: 836 8557,* open daily 1000/1100–1800; £4.50.

Regent's Park

Regent's Park itself (tube: *Baker St/Camden Town*) is one of London's pleasantest open spaces. Within it is **London Zoo** (tube: *Camden Town*); *tel: 722 3333,* open daily 1000–1730 (Mar–Sept); 1000–1600 (Oct–Feb); £7.80.

At the park's south-west corner is the ever-popular **Madame Tussaud's**, *Marylebone Rd, NW1* (tube: *Baker St); tel: 935 6861,* open daily 0900/1000–1730; £8.95. Shows at the adjacent **Planetarium** (same entrance; *tel: 486 1121)* last 30 mins and begin every 40 mins Mon–Fri 1220–1700, Sat–Sun and school holidays 1020–1700; £5.65. Both attractions £11.20.

Kensington and Chelsea

In **Kensington** (*SW7;* tube: *South Kensington*), three of the world's greatest museums are clustered together – all free Mon–Fri after 1630; Sat–Sun, public holidays after 1700: The **V&A (Victoria and Albert Museum)**, *Cromwell Rd; tel: 938 8500,* open Tues–Sun 1000–1750, Mon 1200–1750; £5; the **Natural History**

Museum, *tel: 938 9123*, open daily 1000/
1100–1750; £6 and the **Science Museum**,
Exhibition Rd; tel: 938 8000, open daily
1000–1800; £5.95.

Exhibition Rd leads north, past the
ornate circular **Royal Albert Hall**, to the
Albert Memorial in **Kensington
Gardens**, home to **Kensington Palace**
(tube: *High St Kensington/Queensway*); *tel:
937 9561*; open daily 1000–1800 (May–
Sept); £6, and **Hyde Park**.

The City of London
The medieval city was almost totally
destroyed by the Great Fire in 1666, an
event recalled by **The Monument**,
Monument St, EC3 (tube: *Monument*); *tel:
626 2717*, open Mon–Fri 0900–1740,
Sat–Sun 1400–1740 (Apr–Sept); Mon–Sat
0900–1540 (Oct–Mar); £1. When the
City was rebuilt, Sir Christopher Wren
designed 51 new churches: his masterpiece, completed in 1710, was **St Paul's
Cathedral**, *Ludgate Hill, EC4* (tube: *St
Paul's*); *tel: 236 4128*. Cathedral open
Mon–Sat 0830–1600; galleries 1000–
1615; Sun for worship only; £3.50, or £6
to include the galleries.

Tower of London, *Tower Hill, EC3*
(tube: *Tower Hill*; DLR; riverboat); *tel:
709 0765*, open daily 0900/1000–
1700/1800; £8.30. The enormous complex evokes the bloody past at every turn.
The dazzling **Crown Jewels** can be
examined at close quarters and Beefeaters
provide excellent free tours. The adjacent
Tower Bridge, *tel: 378 1928*, open
0930/1000–1800/1830; £5.50, is another
unmistakable landmark. To see it open,
tel: 378 7700 for times.

South of the Thames
Moored opposite the Tower, **HMS
Belfast**, *Morgan's Lane, Tooley St, SE1*
(tube: *London Bridge*); *tel: 407 6434*, open

daily 1000–1800; £4.40, is a World War II
cruiser, with seven decks equipped as they
were when she went to war, some 'crew'
and suitable soundtracks.

In gloomy vaults nearby is the **London
Dungeon**, *28/34 Tooley St, SE1* (tube:
London Bridge); *tel: 403 0606*, open daily
1000–1730/1830; £8.50.

The South Bank Centre (tube:
Embankment or *Waterloo* is an outstanding
arts complex. Its entertainment venues
include the **Royal National Theatre**, *tel:
928 2252;* the **National Film Theatre
(NFT)**, *tel: 928 3232;* the **Royal Festival
Hall** and **Queen Elizabeth Hall** and
Purcell Room, *tel: 960 4242;* the
**Museum of the Moving Image
(MOMI)**, *tel: 401 2636*, open daily
1000–1800; £5.95, includes high-tech
displays and hands-on exhibits.

A 10min walk alongside the Thames
is the **London Aquarium**, *County Hall,
Westminster Bridge Rd, SE1* (tube: *Waterloo*
or *Westminster*); *tel: 967 8000;* open daily
0930–1930 (June–Aug); daily 1000–1800
(Sept–May); £6.50.

Further south is the impressive
Imperial War Museum, *Lambeth Road,
SE1* (tube: *Lambeth North*; bus C10); *tel:
416 5000*, open daily 1000–1800; £4.50
(free after 1630).

Greenwich
Heading downriver, Greenwich is home
to the **National Maritime Museum**,
which has an interactive gallery; the fascinating **Old Royal Observatory**, and
the beautifully-refurbished **Queen's
House**. All three are open daily 1000–
1700 and covered by a single ticket;
£5.50; *tel: (0181) 858 4422*. At the waterfront, str the surprisingly small round-the-
world yacht **Gipsy Moth IV** and board
the historic tea clipper **Cutty Sark**; open
Mon–Sat 1000–1700/1800; £3.20.

231

LONDON–BOURNEMOUTH

This route travels from central London to the south coast, taking in a little of suburban Surrey before crossing into the more rural countryside of Hampshire and traversing the historic New Forest. The alternative scenic route follows the valley of the lovely River Test south from Andover to Romsey (see Lewes–Salisbury, p. 213) before entering the New Forest.

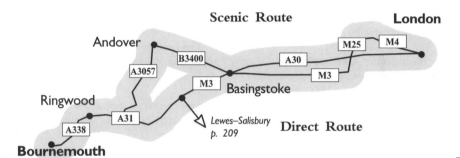

Scenic Route

London

Andover

M25 M4

B3400

A30

A3057

M3

M3

Ringwood

Basingstoke

A31

Lewes–Salisbury
p. 209

Direct Route

A338

Bournemouth

233

| DIRECT ROUTE: 107 MILES |

ROUTES

DIRECT ROUTE

➡ This journey of 107 miles will take around 2 hrs. From central London (Hyde Park Corner) head west on A4 (Brompton Rd) for 8 miles, then follow M4 north-west for 10 miles, M25 south for 7 miles and M3 for 51 miles. At Junction 14 of the M3 follow M27 west for 10 miles (Junction 1) then follow A31 west for 12 miles to Ringwood and A338 south for 9 miles to Bournemouth.

SCENIC ROUTE

➡ This adds about 2 miles and an hour's travelling time to the direct route. From central London follow the directions as above but leave M3 at Junction 3 and at Bagshot head west on A30, passing through Hartley Wintney and Hook to reach Basingstoke in 20 miles. From Basingstoke follow B3400 through Overton and Whitchurch, reaching Andover after 17 miles. Next, head south on A3057 for a further 17 miles and from Romsey continue west on A31 and complete the journey as from Junction 1 of M27 on the direct route.

BASINGSTOKE

TIC: *Willis Museum, Old Town Hall, Market Place, Basingstoke RG21 1QD; tel:*

(01256) 817618, open year round. Services offered: BABA; official tourist guide service can be booked. *Hampshire Borders Tourist Office, address as above; tel: (01256) 811660.*

ACCOMMODATION

Forte Travelodge, Stag and Hounds, *Winchester Rd, Basingstoke RG22 6HN; tel: (01256) 843566.* Modern en suite accommodation. Rooms are all one price and can sleep three adults and a child. Fill the room and the price is in the very modest budget category. No restaurant, but there's a 'Harvester' pub nearby.

Basingstoke Country Hotel, *Scures Hill, Nately Scures, Hook, Hants RG21 7QR; tel: (01256) 764161; fax: (01256) 768341.* Converted from a private residence, the low-level 100-room hotel is set in nearly 5 acres. There's a beautician in the five-crown, highly commended hotel, and leisure amenities include indoor pool, gymnasium, sunbeds, sauna and steam room. The Winchester Restaurant has won AA and RAC awards. Expensive.

Hilton National, *Old Common Rd, Black Dam, Basingstoke RG21 3PR; tel: (01256) 460460; fax: (01256) 840441.* Stylish luxury hotel in its own grounds, with 141 en suite rooms, gymnasium, sauna and indoor pool. Executive and family rooms, some non-smoking. Moderate–expensive.

Cherry Lodge, *Reading Rd, Hook, near Basingstoke RG27 9DB; tel/fax: (01256) 762532.* Country guesthouse, home cooking. Good rural walks. Budget.

ENTERTAINMENT

The Anvil, *Churchill Way; tel: (01250) 819797,* is an up-to-the-minute town centre conference and entertainment centre with music, dance and comedy performances, opened in 1994, it has been acclaimed as one of the finest concert halls in the south of England.

The **Haymarket Theatre,** *Wote St; tel: (01256) 323073,* in the old town area of cobbled streets, stages plays by noted writers with well-known casts.

SIGHTSEEING

Anyone who thinks of Basingstoke as a small town which has developed purely as a major business and shopping centre may be surprised to find a number of leisure facilities and places worth visiting in and around the borough.

The **Leisure Park** provides a venue for ice skating, swimming, bowling and bingo. A 10-screen cinema and a restaurant are on site.

Among literary figures associated with the area are Jane Austen, who was born at Chawton in 1775 and Richard Adams, who put Watership Down on the map with his book of that name. The **Wayfarers' Walk** in the Hampshire Borders goes over Watership Down.

At **Willis Museum** (*same address as TIC*) centuries of local history presented with displays and exhibits.

Whitchurch Silk Mill, *28 Winchester St, Whitchurch, Hants RG28 7AL; tel: (01256) 893882,* open Tues–Sun, 1030–1700 (year round); admission charge. Fine silk fabrics for theatrical costumes and period interiors are woven on antique machinery at this water mill, south west of Basingstoke. The site has riverside gardens, a shop and tearooms.

The Vyne (NT), *Sherborne St John, Basingstoke RG24 9HL; tel: (01256) 881337,* open weekends in March (grounds only), house Sat, Sun and Tues–Thur 1330–1730 (April–Oct), grounds same days as house 1230–1730 (April–Oct); admission charge. Also open Bank Holiday Mondays but closed on the Tuesday following.

Phone to check Bank Holiday times. The early 16th-century house was extensively altered in the mid 17th century, when the earliest classical portico to a country house was added. The Vyne has a tearoom and shop, the latter opens for Christmas shopping; *tel: (01256) 880039* for opening times.

OUT OF TOWN

About 7 miles east of Basingstoke is **Odiham**, a pleasant country town with Georgian facades. About 1 mile beyond it is **Galleon Marine**, *tel: (01256) 703691*, on the scenic **Basingstoke Canal**, where small boats can be hired.

ANDOVER

TIC: *Town Mill House, Bridge St, Andover SP10 1BL; tel: (01264) 324320*, open all year. Services offered: local accommodation reservations, BABA.

ACCOMMODATION

White Hart Hotel, *Bridge St, Andover, SP10 1BH; tel: (01264) 352266; fax: (01264) 325767*. Centrally located former coaching inn, well modernised with nearly 30 guestrooms. Cricket pictures and memorabilia decorate one of the bars. Moderate.

Amberley Hotel, *70 Weyhill Rd, Andover, SP10 3NP; tel: (01264) 352224; fax: (01264) 392555*. About a mile from the town centre, the hotel has 17 rooms, nine of which are en suite. Budget–moderate.

SIGHTSEEING

The busy little town is set in pretty countryside through which the renowned game-fishing waters of the River Test flow. The town has a modern indoor shopping centre. Villages in the vicinity have a wealth of thatched cottages.

Museum of the Iron Age, *Church Close, Andover; tel: (01264) 366283*, open Tues–Sat 1000–1700 (all year). Admission charge, free parking. A sensitive interpretation of the nearby **Danebury Hill Fort**. Exhibitions trace aspects of life in the pre-Roman Iron Age, with reconstructions and models alongside material and artefacts found during excavations. The entrance is guarded by a life-size replica of an Iron Age warrior.

Finkley Down Farm Park, *1½ miles north of A303, 2 miles east of Andover; tel: (01264) 352195*. Admission charge, open 1000–1800 (mid Mar–early Nov). Last admission 1700. Close encounters with goats, rabbits, horses and various farm animals which can be seen being fed and groomed. Also at the farm are gypsy caravans, a Barn of Bygones, picnic area and the Rooster's Rest tearoom.

RINGWOOD

This is one of the popular villages on the outskirts of the New Forest, in good walking and touring country.

St Leonards Hotel, *Ringwood Rd, St Leonards, Hants BH24 2NP; tel: (01425) 471220; fax: (01425) 480274*. The hotel, in attractive grounds and convenient for the New Forest, has 34 rooms, all with en suite facilities. Moderate. Special terms for two-night breaks including a Saturday (terms vary according to season).

Karelia Holidays, *The Studio, Ashley, Ringwood BH24 2EE; tel: (01425) 478920, fax: (01425) 480479*. Five self-catering Finnish-style log houses in a natural setting, backing on to Ringwood Forest. Amenities include sauna, plunge pool and games room. The log houses sleep two to 10 people. The property is ideal for children and pets. Christmas breaks available.

235

LONDON–BRIGHTON

The seaside resort of Brighton is a popular destination for day tripper from London, especially on weekends in the summer, when the direct route usually attracts a lot of traffic.

It's a good idea for those with the time to choose a weekday for the journey. The two routes described below follow more or less parallel courses, never more than 10 miles apart, but each quite different in character. The direct route incorporates 16 miles of motorway and a similar distance of excellent dual carriageway. It crosses some attractive countryside, but beyond south London's urban sprawl avoids towns and villages. The scenic route also involves dreary suburban traffic for the first 15 miles, but is soon among attractive places. Both routes provide superb views of the South Downs.

London

Scenic Route

A243

A23

43

A24

M23

236

Crawley **Direct Route**

A264

Horsham

A24

54

| DIRECT ROUTE: 54 MILES |

A272

A23

24

A281

ROUTES

DIRECT ROUTE

➡️ The 54 miles will take 1hr 30 mins. From Hyde Park Corner take A302 (Grosvenor Place) south, following signs to A23 and from Victoria continuing south on A202 to cross Vauxhall Bridge and pick up A23 after a total of 3 miles. Continue south on A23 for 15 miles, passing through Brixton, Streatham and the outskirts of Croydon to reach the M23, which passes the exits for Gatwick Airport (after 9 miles) and **Crawley** (11 miles) before losing its motorway status

Brighton

to become the A23 again at Pease Pottage (16 miles, service area). Continue south for a further 20 miles to Brighton.

SCENIC ROUTE

▐▶ From Hyde Park Corner proceed west along A4 (Knightsbridge and Brompton Rd) for 3 miles, then bear left on A308 and continue for 4 miles and turn on to A3 south. After a further 8 miles head south on A243 for 5 miles to Leatherhead then follow A24 south for 22 miles to **Horsham** and 16 miles to Poynings, from where A23 continues south to reach Brighton in 8 miles.

CRAWLEY

Information: *Town Hall, The Boulevard, Crawley, West Sussex RH10 1UZ; tel: (01293) 528744*, open Mon–Fri 0900–1700.

ACCOMMODATION

Thanks to Gatwick, there is no shortage of accommodation in the Crawley area. Hotel chains include: *Cp, Ev, FP, Hd, Hn, Md, MH, PL, Rm, Th, Tl.*

Stanhill Court Hotel, *Stanhill, Charlwood, Surrey RH6 0EP; tel: (01293) 862166; fax: (01293) 862773*. This four-crown Victorian country house is set in woodland close to Gatwick. Expensive. **Hunters Restaurant and Guesthouse**, *190 Three Bridges Rd, Crawley RH10 1LN; tel: (01293) 612190*. Seven bedrooms in a guesthouse used to international visitors. Lunch and evening meals available. Budget–moderate. **The Manor House**, *Bonnetts Lane, Ifield, Crawley RH11 0NY; tel: (01293) 512298*. Family-run b&b with six rooms. Courtesy transport to Gatwick, 5 mins away.

SIGHTSEEING

An ancient village that became a new town in the 1950s – traces of the old village are to be found in *High St* – Crawley today is best-known as a shopping centre. **County Mall** in the town centre is one of the largest indoor shopping centres in the region.

Gatwick Zoo, *Russ Hill, Charlwood; tel: (01293) 862312*, open daily 1030–1800 (Mar–Oct), daily 1030–dusk (Jan–Feb and Nov–Dec); £4. Monkeys, wallabies, otters and meerkats run free or in large enclosures, and there are free-flying butterflies in a tropical house. The bird collection includes flamingos, macaws, ducks and penguins.

Skyview Gatwick, *South Terminal, Gatwick Airport (tel: (01293) 502244*, open daily 0700–1900; £4.50. Simulated action rides, a multimedia cinema showing a day in the airport's life, a tour of an historic airliner, a view of aircraft activity from the spectators' gallery and a tour of the Internet. Spectator's gallery only, £1.50.

HORSHAM

TIC: *9 The Causeway, Horsham, West Sussex RH12 1HE; tel: (01403) 211661*, open Mon–Sat 1000–1700. Located in an attractive half-timbered Tudor building, which also houses the town's museum, the centre offers information on attractions throughout the region and operates BABA and local accommodation reservations.

A comprehensive list of hotels, guest-houses and b&bs is available at the TIC. The nearest campsite is **Raylands Caravan Park**, *Jackrells Lane, Southwater RH13 7HA; tel: (01403) 730218; fax: (01403) 732828*. 4 miles south, open May–Oct, the park has 80 touring pitches (60 with electricity).

Horsham's major town centre hotel is picturesque **Ye Olde King's Head**, *Carfax, Horsham RH12 1EG; tel: (01403) 253126; fax: (01403) 242291*. Built in 1401, the quaint old coaching inn has a minstrels' gallery, oak panelling and

Landscape

Where should you head for to see the kind of scenery that appeals to you? Despite its density of population, Britain has an extraordinary variety of countryside, from the domestic to the wild. Some of the best of English and Welsh scenery is to be found in the **National Parks**: for mountain scenery, the highest peaks are to be found in spectacular **Snowdonia**; the **Lake District** offers a magical combination of lakes, mountains and woodland; while the **Peak District**, and the less visited **Brecon Beacons**, are also dramatically beautiful. In many areas of the north and west, it seems unimaginable that such remoteness can exist on the same island as south-eastern England. In southern England: **Dartmoor** offers the largest expanse of open country; the **Cotswolds** and Dorset more domesticated, hilly landscapes, in which buildings seem in perfect harmony with their surroundings. Britain's irregular shape and diverse geology have resulted in an amazingly varied **coastline**: Dover's white cliffs are a symbol of this island nation but, for dramatic coastal scenery, the Cornish, Pembrokeshire, north Norfolk and Northumberland coasts are incomparable.

beams, as well as 42 rooms, restaurant and bar. Moderate–expensive. **Clarence Guest House**, *1 Clarence Rd, Horsham RH13 5JS; tel: (01403) 250826.* Family-run, with six rooms; 10 mins from town. Budget–moderate. **Quintrell House**, *13 Warnham Rd, Horsham RH12 1QS; tel: (01403) 260929.* Non-smoking b&b near town centre with 2 en suite rooms. Budget. **George Hotel**, *High St, Henfield, West Sussex BN5 9DB; tel: (01273) 492296.* 14th-century coaching inn on A281, 9 miles south, with 5 rooms. Home-cooked food available. Budget.

SIGHTSEEING

The birthplace of Percy Bysshe Shelley – a controversial fountain in the town centre commemorates the poet – Horsham is an attractive old market town whose character has been retained by sensible development. The town is built around the *Carfax*, a large square with a variety of architectural styles. *The Causeway*, running behind the old town hall, is a lovely street of mainly Tudor houses.

Horsham Museum, *9 The Causeway; tel: (01403) 254959,* open Mon–Sat 1000–1700; free. A treasure house of artefacts and documents – and a collection of historic bicycles. Frequently changing exhibitions.

OUT OF TOWN

Leonardslee Gardens, *Lower Beeding; tel: (01403) 891212,* open daily 1000–1800 (Apr and June–Oct), daily 0900–2000 (May); £4.50. On A281, 5 miles south. Set among seven lakes in a 240-acre valley, the gardens are noted for their spectacular displays of rhododendrons and azaleas in May, but there are things to enjoy in summer and autumn, too, including a wild flower walk, rock garden, bonsai exhibition, alpine house, and a display of Victorian cars.

Nymans Garden (NT), *Handcross; tel: (01444) 400321,* open Wed–Sun and public holidays 1100–1800 or sunset if earlier; £4.50. *On B2110, signposted off A23, miles south of Pease Pottage.* The partly walled garden has an outstanding collection of rare trees, shrubs and plants. There are woodland walks and a wild garden.

LONDON-BRISTOL

This route crosses the wide expanses of England's south country, an area of mellow towns, hidden villages and ancient stone circles, and visits Swindon – which earned fame as a railway centre – and Bath, founded by the Romans and now Britain's best-preserved Georgian city, justifiably a magnet for tourists from all over the world.

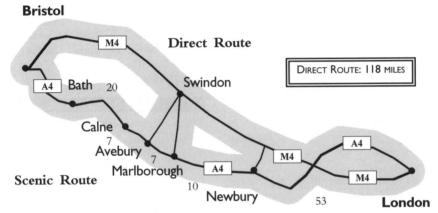

Bristol

M4 · **Direct Route**

DIRECT ROUTE: 118 MILES

A4 · **Bath** 20 · **Swindon**

Calne 7

Avebury 7 · A4 · M4 · A4

Scenic Route · **Marlborough** 10 · M4

Newbury 53 · **London**

239

ROUTES

DIRECT ROUTE

→ Allow 2hrs for this 118-mile map. From central London (Hyde Park Corner) follow A4 west for 8miles and join M4 at Chiswick. Continue on M4 for 104 miles to Junction 19 and follow M32 (Bristol Parkway) west for 6miles to the city centre.

SCENIC ROUTE

▰▶ From Hyde Park Corner you could follow A4 all the way to Bristol – indeed that is the route followed for most of this journey, which is about 26 miles longer than the direct route (allow 3½hours driving time). However, A4 is · not the most interesting road in its early stages and it would be better to proceed to M4 as above and follow the motorway for 49 miles to Junction 13, where A34 leads west to **Newbury** in 4 miles.

Leave Newbury on A4 and continue to **Marlborough**, 19 miles to the west. From Marlborough take A346 north and follow signs to **Swindon**, 12 miles away.

Head south from Swindon on A4361 for a further 12 miles to **Avebury**, where A4 again leads west, linking **Calne**, **Chippenham** and **Bath** to reach Bristol after 40 miles.

NEWBURY

TIC: *The Wharf, Newbury RG14 5AS; tel:* *(01635) 30267,* open all year. Services offered: Local bed-booking, BABA.

ACCOMMODATION

Foley Lodge Hotel, *Stockcross, Newbury RG20 8JU; tel: (01635) 528770, fax: (01635) 528398*. The former Victorian hunting lodge has 4 acres of landscaped gardens. Expensive; weekend leisure breaks moderate.

Millwaters Hotel, *London Rd, Newbury RG14 2BY; tel: (01635) 528838; fax: (01635) 523406*. The waterside Georgian manor house hotel has 30 rooms. Moderate. **Regency Park Hotel**, *Bowling Green Rd, Thatcham (just north-west of Newbury), RG13 3RP; tel: (01635) 871555; fax: (01635) 871571*. A 7-min drive from Junction 13 of M4, the hotel has 50 luxury rooms. Expensive.

SIGHTSEEING

Newbury has some lovely old buildings in the *High St* and some one-of-a-kind speciality shops.

St Nicholas Church, dating from the early 16th century, is especially noted for its pulpit. **The Kennet and Avon Canal**, re-opened in the early 1990s, runs through the town, and many people are attracted to the area by **Newbury Racecourse**.

Kennet Horse Boat Company, *32 West Mills, Newbury RG14 5HU; tel: (01635) 44154*, open mid April–end Sept. Traditional painted narrow boats converted to carry passengers, using peaceful 'green' horsepower instead of engines, just as they did 200 years ago when the Kennet and Avon was first built. Phone for time and duration of public trips and details of private group charters.

Newbury District Museum, *The Wharf; tel: (01635) 30511*. Free, open Mon–Sat 1000–1700 (Apr–Sept), Sun and public holidays 1300–1700, Mon–Sat 1000–1600 (Oct–Mar) closed Sun and public holidays in winter. (Closed Wed all

year except in school holidays.) Civil War battles in the area are one of the themes detailed. Displays include as local archaeology and history, costumes and crafts. The museum is housed in a 17th-century cloth hall and 18th-century granary.

Highclere Castle, *Highclere Park; tel: (01635) 253210. £5.50*, open Tues–Sun 1100–1700 (early May–late Sept). Last admission 1600. Magnificent early Victorian castle in landscaped parkland. As well as priceless Old Masters and 18th-century portraits, there is a display of antiquities collected by the fifth Earl of Caernarvon, famous for his later discovery of the tomb of Tutankhamun.

MARLBOROUGH

TIC: *Car Park, George Lane, Marlborough, SN8 1EE; tel: (01672) 513989*, open Mon–Sat 1000–1700, Sun 1030–1630 (April–Oct), Mon–Sat 1030–1630, Sun 1200–1500 (Nov–Mar). Services offered: tourist guide service (phone ahead for details and booking), local accommodation reservations and BABA.

Ivy House, *High St, Marlborough SN8 1HJ; tel: (01672) 515333; fax: (01672) 515338*. Privately owned Grade II listed Georgian house. Moderate. **The Old Vicarage**, *Burbage, Marlborough SN8 4AG; tel: (01672) 810495; fax: (01672) 810663*. Country guesthouse in 2 acres of gardens. Moderate.

Marlborough's broad *High St* and attractive buildings give the town an unstressed, open feel. It is a pleasant place for browsing in and it has good country walks near its boundaries. It is an ideal base for visitors wanting to spend time around Salisbury Plain and Stonehenge.

Barbury Castle Country Park, *Marlborough Downs*. Always accessible; free. Barbury is an Iron Age hill fort with spectacular views.

SWINDON

TIC: *37 Regent St, Swindon SN1 1JL; tel: (01793) 530328,* open Mon–Sat 0930–1730. DP Services offered: local bed-booking and BABA. The excellent *Swindon Visitors' Guide* is available free – this includes street (and other) maps and accommodation listings.

The attractions in town are within walking distance of the centre. The main **taxi** ranks are at the rail and bus stations.

ACCOMMODATION

There is a good range of accommodation, from top-class hotels to b&bs. Cheaper accommodation can be found around the centre and at the bus and rail stations. Advance booking is recommended at all times, and is essential for the International Air Tattoo (last weekend July). Hotel chains include: *DV, FP, Hn, Ib, Ma* and *MC*. The TIC has details of **campsites**.

SIGHTSEEING

Swindon is where the West Country meets the Cotswolds and it's a lively modern town surrounded by some of England's finest countryside. For 150 years it was one of the world's great railway towns, a heritage celebrated at two complementary museums dedicated to the era of steam: the **Great Western Railway Museum** and **Railway Village Museum**, both *Faringdon Rd; tel: (01793) 466555,* open Mon–Sat 1000–1700, Sun 1400–1700; £2.30 (covers both). GWR is dominated by five locomotives and contains all sorts of rail memorabilia, while the village recreates a Victorian rail worker's home.

Collections on archaeology, geology, nature and social history are in the **Swindon Museum**, *Bath Rd, Old Town; tel: (01793) 466556,* open Mon–Sat 1000–1700, Sun 1400–1700; free. The adjoining **Art Gallery** opens the same hours (free):

it contains a significant collection of British 20th-century art.

OUT OF TOWN

Among the attractions within reach of Swindon are the famous **White Horses** cut into the chalk hillsides. The nearest is the *Hackpen Horse,* 5 miles south. Others are at Marlborough, Alton Barnes, Cherhill, Westbury and Pewsey.

Lydiard Park, *Hook St, off Whitehill Way; tel: (01793) 770401,* house open Mon–Sat 1000–1300 and 1400–1700, Sun 1400–1700 (Mar–Oct); Mon–Sat 1000–1400 (Nov–Feb); 75p. 3 miles west. The restored Georgian house features a 17th-century painted window, fine furnishings and ornate plasterwork. Also in the 260-acre park is a small church that is worth seeing – get the key at the house.

AVEBURY

TIC: Information and leaflets on Avebury available at Marlborough TIC (see above).

Avebury Ring, *tel: (01672) 539250.* Freely accessible. The Avebury Ring is the largest and one of the most important megalithic monuments in Europe. Part of Avebury village is within an ancient stone circle, larger than that at Stonehenge although the stones themselves are not as big. An avenue of stones is also on the site of nearly 30 acres. The National Trust administrates the property and **Alexander Keiller Museum**; *tel: (01672) 539250.* £1.50, open daily 1000–1800 or dusk, whichever is earlier (Apr–Oct), daily 1000–1600 (early Nov–late Mar).

Avebury Manor and Garden; *tel: (01672) 539250.* £3.50 house and garden, £2 garden only, garden open daily except Mon and Thur, also Bank Holiday Mondays 1100–1730 (late Mar–early Nov), house open 1400–1730 Tues, Wed, Sun and Bank Holiday Mondays (late Mar–early Nov). Last admission 1700 or dusk if earlier. The house dates from the early 16th century, with Queen Anne alterations. The garden has medieval walls, ancient box and topiary.

CALNE

Bowood House, *Calne, Wilts; tel: (01249) 812102. £4.70, open Apr–Oct.* Woodland grounds and Capability Brown parkland and gardens in which a variety of features, including cascades, temples and fountains are encountered. There's an adventure playground and walks among rhododendrons of many colours can be enjoyed in May and June. The house has art treasures and antiques.

CHIPPENHAM

TIC: *The Neeld Hall, High St, Chippenham SN15 3ER; tel: (01249) 657733.* Local accommodation reservations, BABA.

ACCOMMODATION

Stanton Manor, *Stanton St Quintin, Chippenham, SN14 6DQ; tel: (01666) 837552; fax: (01666) 837022.* The small hotel 4miles north of Chippenham has a croquet lawn. Moderate–expensive.

White Hart Inn, *Ford, Wilts SN14 8RP; tel: (01249) 782213; fax: (01249) 783075.* Oak beams, inglenook fireplace, cosy bars and popular à la carte restaurant. Moderate.

SIGHTSEEING

Dyrham Park (NT), *Dyrham, nr Chippenham; tel: (0891) 335215 (premium-rate recording),* house open Fri–Tues 1200–1730/dusk (Easter–Oct); £5.20. Built 1691–1710, the rooms have changed so little that they correspond almost exactly with the then-housekeeper's inventory. The ancient park is home to fallow deer.

Sheldon Manor, *nr Chippenham; tel:*

(01249) 653120. £3.25, open 1230–1800 (garden), 1400–1800 (house) Sun, Thur and Bank Holiday Mondays (Apr–Oct). Wiltshire's oldest inhabited manor house. Panelled rooms and collections of porcelain and glass. Beautiful gardens with old-fashioned roses, terraces and water features. Home-made lunches and cream teas served in the barn.

Lacock Abbey, Fox Talbot Museum and Village, *Lacock, near Chippenham; tel: (01249) 730227 (abbey), (01249) 730459 (museum). £5.20,* open: abbey daily except Tues 1300–1730 (late Mar–early Nov); museum, cloisters and grounds daily 1100–1730 (late May–early Nov). Museum also open (£2 admission) weekends only 1100–1600 (Nov–Feb). Founded in 1232, the Abbey was converted to a country house around 1540. Medieval cloisters, sacristy, chapter house and monastic rooms are mainly intact. The garden is a delight. The museum depicts the work of William Fox Talbot (1800–1877), inventor of the photographic negative.

BATH

TIC: *Abbey Chambers, Abbey Church Yard, Bath BA1 1LY; tel: (01225) 477101,* open Mon–Sat 0930–1900, Sun 1000–1800 (early June–late Sept); Mon–Sat 0930–1700, Sun 1000–1600 (late Sept–early June). DP services offered; local bed-booking (up to closing time; £2.50 fee and 10% refundable deposit of first night, BABA (latest 1630; £2.50 fee and 10% refundable deposit) – be prepared to queue for accommodation bookings in summer. Great British Heritage Pass sold (for overseas visitors only) and tickets for bus tours.

The main **post office**, *New Bond St,* opens Mon–Sat 0900–1730. Poste restante facilities are available. **Thomas Cook bureaux de change** at *Midland Bank 45 Milsom St* and *41 Southgate*

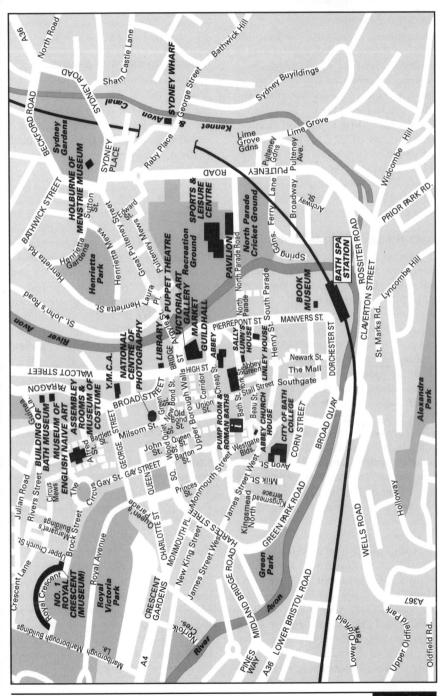

243

GETTING AROUND

Most attractions are within walking distance of the centre and a town map is available (25p) from the TIC. Minibuses covering the centre are very good, but are less frequent to outlying areas of the town. The main local bus operator is **Badgerline**, based at the **bus station**, *Manvers St; tel: (01225) 464446*, operating a frequent service within the city limits. There are **taxi** ranks at the rail station, *Orange Grove*, *Milsom St* and *New Orchard St*. The TIC can provide details of registered taxi companies.

ACCOMMODATION AND FOOD

It is always advisable to book in advance, particularly for Easter, summer, Christmas and public holidays weekends. During the Bath International Festival (May–June), accommodation must be booked well in advance. There is a wide range of hotels and guesthouses in the city, although the smaller ones are usually on the outskirts, a short bus ride from the centre. Hotel chains include: BW, FH, Hn, MC and ST.

HI: *Bathwick Hill; tel (01225) 465674*. There is also a **YMCA**, *Broad Street Place; tel: (01225) 460471*. A list of **campsites** is available free from the TIC. The nearest are: **Newbridge Caravan Park**, *Brassmill Lane; tel: (01225) 428778*, only half a mile west of the centre (on the main A4); and **Newton Mill Touring Centre**, *Newton St Loe; tel: (01225) 333909*, 3 miles west.

There is a good selection of restaurants and pubs, offering food of all nationalities. The TIC has a list of restaurants. **Sally Lunn's Refreshment House and Museum**, *4 North Parade Passage; tel: (01225) 461634*, is the oldest house in Bath, *c.*1482. Excavations in the Cellar Museum show remains of Roman, Saxon and medieval buildings. In 1680 Sally Lunn worked in this building, creating the

legendary Sally Lunn Bun. Other local delicacies are Bath Olivers and Bath Buns.

ENTERTAINMENT AND EVENTS

Entertainment listings are included in *This Month in Bath*, a useful booklet available free from the TIC, and the *Bath Chronicle* has a list of events and venues. The main annual event is the **Bath International Festival** (May–June) at various venues, a celebration of music and the arts.

SHOPPING

The main shopping areas are *Milsom St*, *Stall St* and *Union St*, for major stores and small boutiques and shops. *Northumberland Place* and *The Corridor* are pedestrianised, with small shops, while *Barlett St* and *Walcot St* specialise in antiques. Bath is noted for antiques and there are regular **antiques fairs**, as well as the **Antique Market**, *Guinea Lane*, Wed 0630–1430; and the **Paragon Antiques Market**, *3 Bladud Buildings, Paragon*, Wed 0630–1530.

SIGHTSEEING

Various sightseeing tours cover all aspects of Bath. An excellent introduction is a guided **bus tour** on an open-top double-decker; two companies offer tickets that enable you to hop on and off all day. If you stay on board, the (red bus) **City Tour**, *tel: (01225) 424157*, lasts about 45 mins (£5). The (green bus) **Badgerline/ Guide Friday**, *tel: (01225) 464446/ 444102*, lasts about an hour (£6.50). Get both leaflets before deciding.

A free 2 hr **walking tour** of central Bath includes the main points of historical and architectural interest – daily at 1030, Mon–Fri at 1400, Sun at 1430 (all year) and some summer evenings at 1900. The walk starts by the 'Free Walking Tours Here' notice in the Abbey Churchyard. For further information, *tel: (01225)*

477000. There are also **Ghost Walks of Bath**, from the Garrick's Head (next door to the Theatre Royal) at 2000 Mon–Fri (May–Oct); Fri only (Nov–Apr); £3.

Canal and river trips are available during the day (from £3). Punts and skiffs can be hired; details from the TIC.

Bath is the best-preserved Georgian city in Britain and has some superb architectural features, such as the shop-lined **Pulteney Bridge** (designed by Robert Adam in 1771), which spans the River Avon and has shops on both sides. If you are interested in seeing how the place developed, visit the **Building of Bath Museum**, *The Countess of Huntingdon's Chapel, the Vineyards, Paragon; tel: (01225) 333895*, open Tues–Sun, public holidays 1030–1700 (mid Feb–Nov); £3.

The picturesque streets around the centre are a hive of activity, with a variety of lively street entertainers. To the north of the city are many interesting streets, such as **The Circus** and the graceful **Royal Crescent**.

A restored and furnished Georgian residence is **No1 Royal Crescent**, *tel: (01225) 428126*, open Tues–Sun, public holidays, Bath Festival Mon 1030–1700 (mid Feb–Oct); Tues– Sun 1030–1600 (Nov–mid Feb); £3.50.

Bath is named for its Roman baths, a complex of ancient pools and saunas that are some of the best-preserved Roman remains anywhere in England. The baths were built around a natural hot spring (46.58°C). The adjoining 18th-century Pump Room has a hot spa-water pump and visitors can still taste the waters. **Roman Baths Museum and Pump Room**, *Abbey Churchyard; tel: (01225) 477785*, open daily 0900–1800 (Apr–Sept); also daily 2000–2200 (Aug); Mon–Sat 0930–1700, Sun 1030–1700 (Oct–Mar); £6, or £8 to include the

Museum of Costume, *Bennett St; tel: (01225) 477789*, open Mon–Sat 1000–1700; £3.60. Situated in the 18th-century **Assembly Rooms**, this fascinating museum shows the development of British fashion over the last 400 years.

Overlooking the Roman baths is **Bath Abbey**, which dates from the late 15th century, but has undergone many restorations, open (subject to services) daily 0900–1800 (Easter–Oct); daily 0900–1600 (Nov–Easter); free, but £1.50 donation requested. Situated in the south side of the abbey, under *Kingston Pavements*, are the **Bath Abbey Heritage Vaults**, *tel: (01225) 422462*, open Mon–Sat 1000–1600; £2. Carefully restored 18th-century cellars provide a setting for artefacts from the abbey's past.

OUT OF TOWN

Bath makes an ideal touring base, being surrounded by pleasant countryside dotted with attractions. **Iford Manor Gardens**, *Westwood, nr Bradford-on-Avon; tel: (01225) 863146*, open Sun 1400–1700 (Apr, Oct); Tues–Thur, Sat–Sun 1400–1700 (May–Sept); £2.20. 6miles south-east; train to Bradford-on-Avon, then 2 miles' walk south. The riverside Tudor House, with its 18th-century façade, belonged to a landscape artist and is surrounded by an Italianate terrace garden.

Longleat, *Warminster; tel: (01985) 844400*, house open daily 1000–1800 (Easter–Oct); 1000–1600 (Nov–Easter); Safari park open 1000–1730/dusk (Easter–Oct); £12 (all attractions), £4.80 (house only). Longleat, home of the Marquess of Bath, is a magnificent Elizabethan house (completed 1580) which contains Tintoretto paintings, Flemish tapestries, Titian-school ceilings and other priceless *objets d'art*. The renowned safari park is home to many rare and endangered species.

245

LONDON–CAMBRIDGE

Three counties are included on this relatively short route: Hertfordshire, Essex and Cambridge. It provides an opportunity to visit the supposed burial place of King Harold, who died at the Battle of Hastings, a medieval priory, the birthplace of Cecil Rhodes and a palatial house once owned by King Charles II.

246

Cambridge

16

A1301

Saffron Walden

B1383

12

Bishop's Stortford

A120

26

Scenic Route

Ware

M11

Waltham Cross **Waltham Abbey**

57

25 A10

Direct Route

DIRECT ROUTE: 57 MILES

London

ROUTES

DIRECT ROUTE

➡ This route of 57 miles takes 1 hr 15 min. From the City of London follow the signs for A11 east (follow Leadenhall St and Aldgate High St to Whitechapel). After 8 miles join A12 and follow signs to M11, reached in 2½ miles,

and continue on the motorway for 43 miles, leaving at Junction 11. Take A1309 east for 2½ miles, then follow A603 and signs for a mile to Cambridge city centre.

SCENIC ROUTE

Allow 2 hours driving time for this route which totals 69 miles. From Ludgate Circus proceed south along New

Bridge St and turn left into Queen Victoria St. Continue into Threadneedle St and bear left into Bishopsgate. You are now on A10, which reaches **Waltham Cross** after a total of 15 miles. Continue on A10 for a further 10 miles to Ware and 6 miles north of **Ware** turn right onto A120 to reach Bishop's Stortford in a further 10 miles. From **Bishop's Stortford** follow B1383 north for 12 miles to **Saffron Walden**. Leave Saffron Walden on B184 and after 6 miles continue north on A1301, which reaches Cambridge after a further 10 miles.

WALTHAM ABBEY

TIC: *54 Sun St, Waltham Abbey, Essex EN9 1EJ; tel: (01992) 652295*, open all year. Services offered: local accommodation reservations; BABA.

ACCOMMODATION

Swallow Hotel, *Old Shoe Lane, Waltham Abbey; EN9 3LX; tel: (01992) 717170, fax: (01992) 711841*. Modern low-level red brick hotel close to Junction 26 of the M25. Moderate.

SIGHTSEEING

Some attractive old buildings have been retained in the heart of Waltham Abbey. The town is conveniently close to **Epping Forest**. **Epping Forest District Museum**, *39–41 Sun St, Waltham Abbey; tel: (01992) 716882*, open Fri–Tues afternoons; free. A brightly-presented social history of the area with one of the galleries highlighting Victorian life.

Waltham Abbey Church, *Highbridge St; tel: (01992) 767897*, open variable hours, mainly daily 1000–1800 (summer) and 1000–1600 (winter), closed Wed 1000–1100 and Sun 1000–1200. King Harold is said to have been brought to the town after his defeat at the Battle of Hastings. His tomb supposedly rests at the abbey church, which has a fine Norman nave.

Hayes Hill Farm, *Stubbing Hall Lane, Crooked Mile, Waltham Abbey; tel: (01992) 89278*, open Mon–Fri 1000–1630, Sat, Sun and public holidays 1000–1800 all year; admission charge. Traditional farm-yard on working dairy and arable farm. Afternoon milking can be watched.

WARE

Once an important stopping place on the old North Road, Ware has retained much of its medieval aspect, with some attractive buildings in the *High St*. The town's maltings also contributed to its prosperity. Some of the houses by the River Lea have restored gazebos at the water's edge.

Hanbury Manor, *Ware, Herts, SG12 0SD; tel: (01920) 487722; fax: (01920) 487692*. For recreation there is a golf course designed by Jack Nicklaus. Pricey.

Ware Moat House, *Baldock St, Ware SG12 9DR; tel: (01920) 465011; fax: (01920) 468016*. Centrally situated in the town. Moderate.

BISHOP'S STORTFORD

TIC: *The Old Monastery, Windhill, Bishop's Stortford, Herts; tel: (01279) 655831*, open Mon 0900–1630, Tues–Thur 0900–1700, Fri 0900–1645, Sat 0900–1300. BABA, local accommodation booking.

ACCOMMODATION

Down Hall Country House, *Hatfield Heath, nr Bishop's Stortford; tel: (01279) 731441; fax: (01279) 730416*. Italianate Victorian property in 100 acres of grounds has a range of leisure activities. Expensive.

SIGHTSEEING

Bishop's Stortford, by the River Stort, was destined to thrive, lying on the Roman road between St Albans and Colchester, and in medieval times earning prominence as a staging post on the coaching route between London and Cambridge. Thur and Sat are market days. The **Bishop's Stortford Mural**, 28 ft long, outlines local history from the Ice Age to the 1990s.

Rhodes Memorial Museum and Commonwealth Centre, *Nettleswell House, South Rd, Bishop's Stortford; tel: (01279) 651746*, open Tues–Sat 1000–1600 all year; £1. Photographs, documents and memorabilia depict the life of Cecil John Rhodes, founder of Rhodesia (now Zimbabwe) in the pair of Victorian villas where he grew up.

Castle Mound, *The Castle, Bishop's Stortford; tel: (01279) 655261*. The mound, the remains of a castle built by William the Conqueror, provides a haven close to the town centre. You may need to borrow the key to the gate from the TIC.

SAFFRON WALDEN

TIC: *Market Place, Market St, Saffron Walden, Essex CB10 1HR; tel: (01799) 510444*. Services offered: town trail leaflets available; official tour guide can be booked; BABA.

ACCOMMODATION

Saffron Hotel, *High St, Saffron Walden CB10 1AY; tel: (01799) 522676; fax: (01799) 513979*. Seventeen rooms in 16th-century listed building. Moderate.

HI: *1 Myddylton Place, Saffron Walden, CB10 1BB; tel: (01799) 523117; fax: (01799) 520840*.

SIGHTSEEING

The saffron crocus from which the town takes its name blooms outside the local museum in autumn. This is a charming town of narrow alleyways, and centuries-old timber-framed houses with decorated plasterwork. Tues and Sat are market days – signs of the medieval market rows can still be seen. The parish church is said to be the largest in Essex.

Bridge End Gardens, *Bridge End, Saffron Walden; tel: (01799) 510445*, open daily dawn–dusk all year; free. This 3.5-acre site has some fine trees, a Victorian garden with roses and period ornaments and a Dutch garden. A hedge maze can be visited by appointment – call at the TIC.

Saffron Walden Museum, *Museum St, Saffron Walden; tel: (01799) 510313*. Open Mon–Sat 1000–1700, Sun and public holidays 1430–1700 (Mar–Oct), Mon–Sat 1000–1600, Sun 1400–1600 (Nov–Feb); £1. In the grounds are the ruins of the Norman castle. The museum, known for its ethnographic department, also has decorative arts, an Ancient Egyptian feature, natural history collections, geology displays and the Great Hall gallery of archaeology and early history. Many local Saxon finds are exhibited.

Fry Public Art Gallery, *Bridge End Gardens, Castle St, Saffron Walden; tel: (01799) 513779*, open Sat, Sun and public holidays 1445–1700 (Apr–late Oct). Artists of north-west Essex who have made a significant contribution to British art are represented here.

Audley End House and Park (EH), *Saffron Walden; tel: (01799) 522399*, open Wed–Sun, public holidays 1100–1800 (Easter–Sept), Wed–Sun 1000–1500 (Oct); £5.50. 1 mile west. The palatial house, dating from 1603, was built by the Earl of Suffolk and later owned by King Charles II. It has many fine interiors, including some by Robert Adam, and a magnificent Jacobean great hall. It is set in Capability Brown parkland.

LONDON–COTSWOLDS

This unashamedly meandering route is designed to enable visitors to experience the contrasting landscapes which are to be discovered in the space of a leisurely day out. It takes in the lush wooded slopes of the Chilterns and the open vistas of north Oxfordshire before entering the mellowness of the Cotswolds.

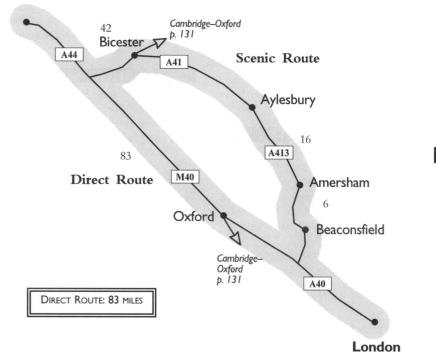

Moreton-in-Marsh

42   Bicester

A44   A41

Cambridge–Oxford
p. 131

Scenic Route

Aylesbury

16

83   A413

Direct Route   M40   Amersham

6

Oxford   Beaconsfield

Cambridge–
Oxford
p. 131

A40

DIRECT ROUTE: 83 MILES

London

249

Cambridge–Oxford p. 131

ROUTES

DIRECT ROUTE

➡ This 83-mile route takes 1 hr 45 mins. From Hyde Park Corner follow Park Lane north to Marble Arch and bear left into Bayswater Rd (A40 west). Continue on A40 for 18 miles, joining M40 at Junction 1. Leave the motorway after 31 miles at Junction 8 and continue towards Oxford on A40. After a little over 8 miles join A44 north to reach

Moreton-in-Marsh (See p.182) in a further 25 miles.

SCENIC ROUTE

▐▐▐▶ This journey is about 10 miles longer than the direct route – allow an extra half hour driving time. Proceed from central London as above, but leave the motorway after only 6 miles at Junction 2 and follow signs to **Beaconsfield**.

Depart Beaconsfield on A355 north to reach **Amersham** in 6 miles, then follow A413 north-west for 16 miles to **Aylesbury**. Leave Aylesbury on A41 west, arriving at Bicester after 17 miles. From Bicester follow B4030 west, connecting with A44 after 14 miles, just south of Chipping Norton. From here A44 reaches Moreton- in-Marsh in 11 miles.

BEACONSFIELD

250

Bellhouse, *Oxford Rd, Beaconsfield HP9 2XE; tel: (01753) 887211; fax: (01753) 888231.* Forty of the 136 rooms in the De Vere hotel are designated non-smoking. The Bellhouse has a leisure centre and a choice of bars and restaurants. Moderate–expensive.

White Hart, *Aylesbury End, Beaconsfield HP9 1LW; tel: (01494) 671211.* 16th-century inn with most rooms in modern annexe. The Toby Restaurant serves until 2200. Moderate.

Chequers Inn Hotel and Restaurant, *Kiln Lane, Wooburn Common, nr Beaconsfield HP10 0JQ; tel: (01628) 529575 fax: (01628) 850124.* Seventeen guestrooms in beamed village inn. Moderate.

Highclere Farm, *New Barn Lane, Seer Green, Beaconsfield HP9 2QZ; tel: (01494) 875665; fax: (01494) 875238.* Commended accommodation on a working farm in quiet countryside, yet only 20 miles from London. Moderate.

SIGHTSEEING

Bekonscot Model Village, *Warwick Rd, Beaconsfield HP9 2PL; tel: (01494) 672919*, open daily 1000–1700 (mid Feb–early Nov); £3.20. Actually there are six enchanting villages on the 1.5-acre site, dating from the 1930s, with a castle, churches, shops, houses, landscaped gardens, railway stations and a splendid model railway, all in miniature. Since 1978 the attraction has been run by the Church Army, who donate surplus profits to charity – well over £1 million so far. Facilities include a miniature tramway, children's playground, picnic areas, refreshment kiosk and souvenir shop.

AMERSHAM

TIC: *Tesco's Car Park, London Rd, Amersham, HP7 0AH; tel: (01494) 729492*, open Tues–Sun 1030–1630 (Apr–Sept). BABA and usual services.

The Crown, *High St, Amersham HP7 0DH; tel: (01494) 721541 fax: (01494) 431283.* This Forte Heritage hotel with a Georgian façade has original Elizabethan interior features. Its guestrooms are attractively decorated. Moderate.

Amersham Museum, *49 High St, Amersham; tel: (01494) 725754*, open Sat, Sun and Bank Holiday Mon 1430–1630 (Easter–end Oct), also Wed in Aug. The local history museum is in a small 15th-century half-timbered house with a herb garden.

The Climb, *Bensheim Way, Amersham; tel: (01494) 722202*, open daily; £3.85 per session, juniors £1.50. This is the Chiltern Indoor Climbing Centre, the new sports concept, with a wall nearly 36ft high, with overhangs, and a smaller wall for learners. Qualified instructors.

AYLESBURY

TIC: *8 Bourbon St, Aylesbury HP20 2RR;*

tel: (01296) 330559, open Mon–Sat 1000–1630. BABA and usual services.

ACCOMMODATION

Holiday Inn Garden Court, *Buckingham Rd, Watermead, Aylesbury, HP19 3FY; tel: (01296) 398839; fax: (01296) 394108.* Forty well-proportioned rooms, half non-smoking. Good weekend deals. Budget–moderate.

Hartwell House, *Oxford Rd, nr Aylesbury HP17 8NL; tel: (01296) 747444; fax: (01296) 747450.* The last word in comfort and luxury at this 40-room country house set in 90 acres of gardens and parkland with cherished architectural features from the 17th and 18th centuries. Indoor swimming pool, gym, spa bath, steam room, sauna, solarium, beauty and hair salon, and in the grounds croquet, tennis and fishing. Expensive.

Forte Posthouse, *Aston Clinton Rd, Aylesbury HP22 5AA; tel: (01296) 393388; fax: (01296) 392211.* Modern courtyard-style hotel with good standard of comfort. Three miles from town centre. Moderate.

Charterhouse, *103 London Rd, Aston Clinton, nr Aylesbury HP22 5LD; tel: (01296) 631313; fax: (01296) 631616.* B&b on A41 between Aylesbury and Tring. The listed, commended house has views over the Chiltern Hills. Budget.

SIGHTSEEING

Many of Aylesbury's visitors arrive by boat, cruising the Aylesbury arm of the **Grand Union Canal**. The lively town with its 90-unit Friars Square shopping centre, all under cover, has three markets a week, on Wed, Fri and Sat.

Buckinghamshire County Museum,
Church St, Aylesbury; tel: (01296) 331441, open Tues–Sun 1000–1600, public holidays 1400–1700, closed Christmas and Easter; museum free, Dahl Gallery £1.75. Visitors are advised to phone ahead to confirm opening hours as priority is given to school groups and admission may be limited at weekends and half-terms. Housed in restored buildings dating from the 15th century, a range of galleries display contemporary and traditional arts and crafts from the region. The new **Roald Dahl Gallery** is a child's delight with a giant peach which children can inside and a range of exciting features and inventions. Exhibitions are often held, and there are gardens and a gift shop.

Chiltern Brewery, *Nash Lee Rd (B4009), Terrick, Aylesbury; tel: (01296) 612983,* shop open Mon–Sat 0900–1700, conducted tours at noon on most Sats; prior confirmation advised. This is claimed to be Buckinghamshire's oldest working traditional brewery. Its **Breweriana Museum** was introduced in 1994.

Bucks Goat Centre, *Stoke Mandeville, nr Aylesbury; tel: (01296) 612983,* open daily except Mon all year; admission charge. All breeds of British goat are here, with other animals. Weekend donkey rides in summer. Goat products on sale.

Waddesdon Manor, *Waddesdon, nr Aylesbury; tel: (01296) 651211,* open (grounds) Wed–Sun and public holidays 1000–1700 (Mar–Dec) (house) Thur–Sun and public holidays 1100–1600 (Apr–Nov), also Wed in July and Aug; £9 house and grounds, £3 grounds only. The house, built in the French Renaissance style between 1874 and 1889, contains Baron Ferdinand Rothschild's collection of 18th-century art treasures.

251

LONDON–FOLKESTONE

Following in the footsteps of Geoffrey Chaucer's pilgrims – in part at least – this route heads east from London along a road constructed originally by the Romans. Neither the Romans nor the pilgrims would recognise much of the route today, of course, although the downlands along which parts of the Pilgrims' Way may still be followed would still be familiar to them. From historic Canterbury, the route continues south-east to Dover, always a port and fortress, then turns west to finish at Folkestone, the resort and cross-Channel ferry port, now famous as the English end of the Channel Tunnel.

London

29

A2

Rochester
Chatham   **Scenic Route**

A20

A2

Canterbury

M20

Sandwich

6

A2

A258

Direct Route

70

16

Deal

Walmer   2

A258

6

DIRECT ROUTE: 70 MILES

4

Dover

A20

St Margaret's Bay

9

Folkestone

ROUTES

DIRECT ROUTE

This 70-mile journey takes 1 hr 25 mins. From the City of London follow signs south to A2. These will take you across Blackfriars Bridge and along the New Kent Road (A201) to meet the A2 (here, the Old Kent Road) after 2 miles. Continue for 3 miles to Deptford, then head south for 12 miles on A20. Join M20 at Swanley and continue south-east to reach Folkestone in 53 miles.

HISTORIC ROUTE

The direct route is almost entirely motorway and, paradoxically, may be slow due to congestion caused by heavy goods vehicles and holiday traffic travelling to the Channel Tunnel terminus. The old route, following the Roman road yet still taking in a portion of motorway, is worth consideration. It adds about 27 miles and 40-mins' travelling time.

From the City of London (Ludgate Circus) follow signs to A13 east (East India Dock Road) and after 5 miles, at Poplar, bear right on to A102, go through the Blackwall Tunnel and after 3 miles join A2 south to reach Rochester in 21 miles. From Rochester or Chatham you may continue to Canterbury by following M2 to Boughton Street or by staying on A2 through Gillingham, Sittingbourne and Faversham. From Canterbury A2 continues south-east to reach Dover in 16 miles. From Dover follow A20 west for 9 miles to Folkestone.

ROCHESTER AND CHATHAM

TIC: *95 High St, Rochester, Kent ME1 1LX; tel: (01634) 843666*, open daily 1000–1700, Sun 1030–1700. Services offered: local bed-booking and BABA (latest bookings 1630; 10% deposit of first night for all bookings). The excellent *It's More, It's Rochester* guide and an accommodation guide are free.

GETTING AROUND

The attractions in Chatham and Rochester, except the Historic Dockyard, are within walking distance of either town (they are only half a mile apart). The whole area becomes very congested during the summer festivals. A free town and transport map is available from Rochester TIC. **Bus enquiries**; *tel: (0800) 696996*.

ACCOMMODATION

There is a variety of accommodation in the area, including several large independent hotels, but the maximum choice lies in guesthouses and b&b establishments. It is usually easy to find accommodation on arrival, except during festivals: notably Sweeps Festival (May), Dickens Festival (early June), Medway Arts Festival (late July), and Norman Rochester Festival (Aug). Chains represented are *BW* and *FP*.

HI: **Capstone Farm**, *37 Capstone Rd, Gillingham; tel: (01634) 400788*. Rochester TIC will provide information on **campsites**. The nearest is **Woolman's Wood Campsite**, *Rochester Rd, Bridgewood; tel: (01634) 867685*, 3 miles south.

SIGHTSEEING

The **City of Rochester Society**, *tel: (01634) 721886 (evenings)*, operate **guided walks** Wed, Sat–Sun, public holidays (Good Fri–Sept); free. They last 1½ hours, leaving the Dickens Centre at 1415. **Rochester Tours**, *tel: (01634) 405228*, operate **guided bus tours** (Apr–Oct) and also a shuttle bus linking the area's attractions. The TIC has information about various **boat trips** (from around £5).

The city of Rochester sits on the banks

253

of the River Medway, dominated by **Rochester Castle** (EH), *The Keep, Castle Hill; tel: (01634) 402276,* open daily 1000–1600 (Oct–Mar); 1000–1800 (Apr–Sept); £2.70. This has one of the finest Norman keeps in the country, while the cathedral, founded in 604, is the second oldest in England. **Rochester Cathedral**, *The Precinct, Rochester; tel: (01634) 843366,* open daily (subject to services) 0730–1700/1800; £2 donation suggested.

Rochester features in several of the novels of Charles Dickens, who spent many years in the area, and the Elizabethan **Eastgate House** brings to life the characters and scenes he created. **Charles Dickens Centre**, *High St, Rochester; tel: (01634) 844176,* open daily 1000–1730; £3. For a taste of shopping over the last century, visit the **Draper's Museum of Bygones**, *4 High St, Rochester; tel: (01634) 830647,* open daily 1000–1700; £2.25.

Historic Dockyard, *Chatham; tel: (01634) 812551,* open daily 1000–1700 (Easter–Oct); Wed, Sat–Sun 1000–1600 (Nov, Feb–Easter); £5.60. 3 miles north-east of Rochester. Once an important naval base, this is the most complete Georgian dockyard in the world – and now a working museum where ropes and flags are still being made.

OUT OF TOWN

Leeds Castle, *nr Maidstone; tel: (01622) 765400,* castle open 1100–1800 (Mar–Oct); 1015–1500 (Nov–Feb); £8.50 (castle and park). 14 miles south-east. The fairytale castle sits on two small islands in a lake surrounded by magnificent parklands. Its origins are way back in the 9th century – it was Henry VIII who turned it from a fortress into a royal palace.

Stoneacre (NT), *Otham, Maidstone; tel: (01622) 862871,* open Wed, Sat 1400–

1800 (Apr–Oct); £2.20. 12 miles south-east. A half-timbered, mainly 15th-century house, surrounded by a newly restored cottage garden.

TIC: *Canterbury* **Visitor Centre**, *34 St Margaret's St, Canterbury, Kent CT1 2TG; tel: (01227) 766567,* open Mon–Sat 0930–1730, Sun 1000–1500 (Easter–Oct); Mon–Sat 0930–1700 (Nov–Easter). SHS services offered; local bed-booking service (£2 fee and 10% refundable deposit of total stay) and BABA (latest 30 mins before closing; £4 fee and 10% deposit), bureau de change. Tickets booked for local events, festivals and major concerts. *Canterbury Accommodation Guide* is available free from the TIC.

TIC: *Longport Coach Park, Lower Chantry Lane,* open daily 0930–1700 (mid Mar–mid Oct). Services offered: local bed-booking service (latest 30 mins before closing); bureau de change.

GETTING AROUND

Most of Canterbury's attractions are within walking distance of the centre. Free town and transport maps are available from the TIC. Most **bus** services are operated by **Stagecoach East Kent**, *tel: (01227) 766151,* from the **Central Bus Station**, *St George's Lane*. Services are good to most areas of the city and in the surrounding area, but reduced Sun.

The main **taxi** rank is on St George's Lane companies include: **Andycabs Taxis**, *tel: (01227) 876111*; **Laser Cars**, *tel: (01227) 464422*; and **Blean Taxis**, *tel: (01227) 471553.*

STAYING IN CANTERBURY

Accommodation and Food

There is a reasonable range of hotels on

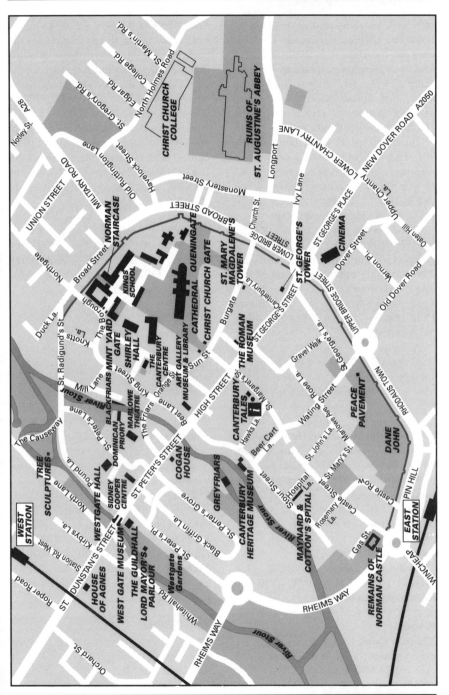

offer in Canterbury and over 80 guest-house and b&b establishments. The majority of the cheaper accommodation is located on the edge of the centre. It is generally easy to find accommodation on arrival, but advance bookings are recommended during university graduation (July) and Cricket Week (Aug).

Hotel chains in Canterbury include *FH*. There are only three pubs and inns offering accommodation near the city, one of which is in the centre. The other two are located in Chilham (7 miles southwest) and Boughton (7 miles west).

HI: **Ellerslie**, *54 New Dover Rd; tel: (01227) 462911*. The TIC has details of **campsites**. The nearest campsites are: **The Camping and Caravanning Club Site**, *Bekesbourne Lane; tel: (01227) 463216*, 1½ miles east; and **The Royal Oak**, *Broad Oak; tel (01227) 710448*, 3 miles north.

A list of local restaurants is available from the TIC. There is a good range of cheaper eating places in Canterbury and most major ethnic specialities are catered for.

There are two gourmet restaurants in the city: **Sully's**, *County Hotel, High St; tel: (01227) 766266*, and **Tuo e Mio**, *16 The Borough; tel: (01227) 761471*; and only one specialising in vegetarian food: **Fungus Mungus**, *34 St Peter's St; tel: (01227) 781922*. St Peters St is a particularly good area for restaurants.

Communications

The main **post office**, *28 High St*, opens Mon–Fri 0900–1730, Sat 0900–1230, and has a poste restante facility.

Money

Thomas Cook bureaux de change are to be found at *9 High St, Kingsmead, Coach Park* and *14 Mercery Lane*.

Entertainment listings can be found in the publication *What, Where, When*, available free and widely distributed throughout the city. The main theatre, **The Marlowe**, is located at *The Friars; tel: (01227) 787787*, in the city centre.

An events listing is available free from the TIC and covers both major and more unusual events taking place around the city, including the twice-yearly **Chaucer Festival**, *22 St Peters St*, in the city centre (Apr and during the summer).

Another major event is the **Canterbury Festival** (2 weeks in Oct), with over 200 events. For a full programme, contact the **Canterbury Festival Office**, *Christchurch Gate, The Precincts; tel: (01227) 452853*.

Long Market, High St, St Peters St, St George's St and *The Marlowe Arcade* are all good for gifts, clothes and accessories, while antique shops and a further selection of gift ideas can be found on *Palace St* and at *Burgate*. There's a **market** at *St George's St* (it spreads into adjacent streets) every Wed 0900–1700/earlier.

English wines can be sampled and the 'vine trail' walked at **Ash Coombe Vineyard**, *Coombe Lane, Ash; tel: (01304) 813396*, open Thur–Sat 1100–1700, Sun 1200–1600 (Apr–Oct); **Staple Vineyards**, *Church Farm, Staple; tel: (01304) 812571*, open Mon–Sat 1000–1700, Sun 1200–1600 (Easter–Christmas); and **St Nicholas Vineyard**, *Ash; tel: (01304) 812670*, open Sat–Sun 1000–1800 (all year); Mon–Fri 1000–1800 (Apr–Dec).

Three major events have shaped Canterbury's character: the arrival of St Augustine from Rome in 597, to begin the conversion of the English peoples; the brutal despatch of Thomas à Becket, in 1170, and German bombing in 1942. Despite the latter, much of the medieval streetscape of the small city survives, clustered around the cathedral to which Chaucer's pilgrims, among others, journeyed in the Middle Ages.

Guided walks of the town from the **Canterbury Guild of Guides**, *tel: (01227) 459779*, can be booked at the TIC. Joining location is the **Canterbury Visitor Centre**, from where departures are daily at 1400 (Easter–Nov); daily at 1100 (June–Sept); Fri at 2000 (July–Aug). **Ghost Tours** are also available – from the Canterbury Tales (see below).

If you prefer to walk alone, head first for **Canterbury Cathedral**, *The Precincts; tel: (01227) 762862*, open Mon–Sat 0845–1900 (Easter–Sept); 0845–1700 (Oct–Easter); Sun 1230–1430 and 1630–1730 (all year); £2.50. Occasionally the cathedral is closed to visitors at short notice, so check opening times prior to visit. The magnificent cathedral dates from Norman times: highlights include the amazingly beautiful 12th- and 13th-century stained glass; the largest Norman crypt in the country; the central tower ('Bell Harry'), and the tomb of the Black Prince. You can also see the site of the shrine of St Thomas à Becket in Trinity Chapel; an altar in the north transept marks the spot where he was martyred by Henry II's over-zealous knights.

The city itself is compact, lying mostly within the bounds of the city wall, which was built in the 13th and 14th centuries on Roman foundations.

Long stretches of wall survive, but only one gate, the **West Gate**, survived World War II bombing. This now contains an interesting arms museum: **West Gate Museum**, *St Peters St; tel: (01227)*

452747, open Mon–Sat 1100–1230 and 1330–1530; 80p.

The city's Roman history is explained at the **Roman Museum**, *Butchery Lane; tel: (01227) 785575*, open Mon–Sat 1000–1700 (all year); Sun 1330–1700 (June–Oct); £1.90. There is Saxon work, as well as the remains of a later Norman church, in the ruins of **St Augustine's Abbey**, (EH), *Longport; tel: (01227) 767345*, open daily 1000–1800/dusk (Easter–Oct); Tues–Sun 1000–1600 (Nov–Mar); £2. Further up *Longport* is **St Martin's Church**, parts of which date back to the 6th century and said to be the oldest parish church in England.

There are some fine medieval buildings along the River Stour, including some of the 'hospitals' built to accommodate pilgrims.

The lovely **Poor Priests' Hospital** houses the excellent **Canterbury Heritage Museum**, *Stour St; tel: (01227) 452747*, open Mon–Sat 1030–1700 (all year); Sun 1330–1700 (June–Oct); £1.90. Many of the city's treasures are displayed here, while the nearby 13th century **Greyfriars**, the first English friary built by the followers of St Francis (1267), is a charming building spanning the river.

Chaucer's 14th-century masterpiece, *The Canterbury Tales*, in which a group of ill-assorted pilgrims tell each other often bawdy stories en route from Southwark to Canterbury is, of course, not forgotten here. Allow an hour for **The Canterbury Tales**, *St Margaret's St; tel: (01227) 454888*, open daily 0900/0930–1730/1800 (Mar–Oct); 0930/1000–1630/1730 (Nov–Feb); £4.75.

Also worth a visit is the **Royal Museum, Art Gallery and Buffs Regimental Museum**, *18 High St; tel: (01227) 452747*, open Mon–Sat 1000–1700; free.

257

DOVER

TIC: *Townwall St, Dover, Kent CT16 1JR;* tel: (01304) 205108, open daily 0900–1800. DP SHS services offered; local bed-booking service and BABA (booking fee £5 or 10% of first night). Tickets sold for all cross-channel journeys, National Express, Euroline and theatres. YHA/HI membership sold. *White Cliffs Country Guide* is free and has accommodation listings.

ARRIVING AND DEPARTING

Ferries and Hovercraft: ferries to Calais are operated by **P&O European Ferries**, *tel: (0990) 980980,* **Stena**, *tel: (0990) 707070,* and **Seafrance**, *tel: (0990) 711711,* from the Eastern Docks in Dover; ferries operate at least hourly throughout the year. Buses run every 45 mins between the station and the Eastern Docks terminal 0545–0115 and are timed to coincide with ferry arrivals. Ferry tickets can be purchased at the terminal or at the TIC. Two **Thomas Cook bureaux de change** can be found at the *Eastern Docks.* **Hoverspeed**, *tel: (01304) 865000,* operate hovercraft and SeaCat services from the Hoverport on the Western Docks (For further details of Arriving in England, see p.40).

GETTING AROUND

Most of Dover's attractions are within walking distance of the town centre. Pick up free town and transport maps from the TIC. **Public transport helpline**, *tel: (0345) 696996.* Most **bus** services are operated by **Stagecoach East Kent**, *tel: (01227) 472082,* from the central bus depot on *Pencester Rd.*

For local **taxis** contact **A2B**, *tel: (01304) 225588;* **Central Cars**, *tel: (01304) 240441;* **Dover Taxis**, *tel: (01304) 201915;* **Invicta**, *tel: (01304)*

240604; **New Street Cars**, *tel: (01304) 242526;* or **Star Taxis**, *tel: (01304) 242526.*

STAYING IN DOVER

Accommodation and Food

There is not a wide choice of hotels, but there is a good range of guesthouse and b&b establishments, mostly located in the town centre. The only inn with accommodation is at *St Margaret's-at-Cliffe,* 4 miles east. It is generally easy to find accommodation on arrival, except July–Aug. Hotel chains in Dover include *BW, FP* and *TI.*

HI: *306 London Rd; tel: (01304) 201314.* **YMCA**: *4 Leyburne Rd; tel: (01304) 206138,* open from 1700. The closest **campsites** are: **Hawthorne Farm**, *Martin Mill; tel: (01304) 852658,* 3 miles north-east, and **St Margaret's Country Club**, *Reach Rd, St Margaret's-at-Cliffe; tel: (01304) 853262,* 3 miles east.

There is a good choice of cheapish eating establishments in Dover, mostly located in the town centre.

Communications

The main **post office**, *Pencester Rd,* is open Mon–Sat 0830–1730. A poste restante facility is available.

ENTERTAINMENTS

Entertainment listings can be found in the TIC's events list and in the two local newspapers *Dover Express* (40p) and *East Kent Mercury* (30p), which are available at local newsagents. An events listing is available free from the TIC.

SIGHTSEEING

Free **guided walks** from **White Cliffs Countryside Project**, *tel: (01304) 241806,* start at various locations around the town and can be booked at the TIC. The TIC can also supply leaflets showing suggested walking routes.

Dover Castle (EH), Castle Hill; tel: (01304) 201628 or 211067, open daily 1000–1800 (Apr–Sept); 1000–1600 (Oct–Mar); £6. Dover Castle is one of the most impressive medieval fortresses in Western Europe and you can spend hours exploring the vast castle (there's a land train to take you between the points of interest). Children love the Live and Let's Spy interactive room, while adults are fascinated by the labyrinth of Top Secret Wartime Tunnels, a secret operations HQ during World War II.

The best view of the fabled **White Cliffs** is from a boat, but a walk up the East Cliff footpath above Eastern Docks will bring you to the parkland of **Langdon Cliffs and South Foreland Lighthouse** (NT), Upper Rd; tel: (01304) 202756. Lighthouse open Sat–Sun, public holidays 1400–1730 (Apr–Oct); £1. Cliffs accessible all year; free.

Back in town, experience an exciting, multimedia show which tells the story of Britain through the eyes of Dover: **The White Cliffs Experience**, Market Sq.; tel: (01304) 214566, open daily 1000–1800 (Apr–Oct); 1000–1700 (Nov–Mar); £4 for one 'journey' of 1½ hrs (Roman Encounters or World War II – Our Finest Hour), or £5.50 for both (allow 2½ hrs) – tickets also cover Dover Museum.

The exceptionally well-preserved **Roman Painted House**, New St; tel: (01304) 203279, open Tues–Sun 1000–1700 (Apr–Sept); £2, is the genuine article, with wonderful frescos and a touch-table of archaeological finds.

Dover Museum, Market Sq.; tel: (01304) 201066, open daily 1000–1730/1800; £1.60 (or included in the White Cliffs Experience). This is the largest and newest museum in the district, with a range of objects reflecting the history of Dover. **Old Town Gaol**, Dover Town Hall, Biggin St; tel: (01304) 242766, open Wed–Sat 1000–1630 (Nov–Apr); Tues–Sat 1000–1630 (May–Oct); Sun 1400–1630 (all year); £3.40. This is a fully restored Victorian prison.

⤵ SIDE TRACKS
FROM DOVER

Deal and Walmer Castles are both forts built by Henry VIII in the 1530s: whereas Deal preserves its martial character, Walmer has the gentler atmosphere of a stately home, with attractive formal gardens.

Walmer Castle and Gardens (EH), Kingsdown Rd, Walmer; tel: (01304) 364288, open daily 1000–1800 (Apr–Oct); Wed–Sun 1000–1600 (Nov–Dec, Mar); £4. 6 miles northeast on the A258. **Deal Castle** (EH), The Stand, Deal; tel: (01304) 372762, open daily 1000–1800 (Apr–Oct); Wed–Sun 1000–1600 (Nov–Mar); £2.80. 7 miles north-east. Also at Deal are the **Maritime and Local History Museum**, St George's Rd; tel: (01304) 372679 (Deal TIC); open daily 1400–1700 (June–Sept); £1; **The Salter Collection**, 18 Gladstone Rd; tel: (01304) 361471; open Mon–Fri 1200–1700 (July–Aug); £1.50; and the **Time Ball Tower**, Seafront; tel: (01304) 201200, open Tues–Sun 1000–1700 (July–Aug); £1.20.

Further along the coast is the Cinque Port of **Sandwich**. Attractions include the **Precinct Toy Collection**, 38 Harnet St, Sandwich; tel: (01304) 621114, open Mon–Sat 1030–1630, Sun 1400–1630 (Easter–Sept); Sat–Sun 1400–1600 (Oct–mid Dec); £1. 10 miles north-east. Also at Sandwich

259

are the remains of the Roman **Richborough Castle** (EH), *Richborough Rd; tel: (01304) 612013,* open daily 1000–1800 (Apr–Oct); £2. ⛺

FOLKESTONE

TIC: *Harbour St, Folkestone, Kent CT20 1QN; tel: (01303) 258594; fax: (01303) 259754,* open daily 0900–1730; daily 0800–1815 (July–Aug). Right by the harbourside, the centre offers a full range of services, including local bed bookings and BABA.

ACCOMMODATION

There is no shortage of accommodation in this Channel ferry port-cum-holiday resort, with a good range of hotels, guesthouses, self-catering cottages and flats and b&bs.

The town's best known hotel, in a clifftop setting, is the Regency-style **Clifton Hotel**, *The Leas, Clifton Gardens, CT20 2FB; tel/fax: (01303) 851231.* Expensive.

Hotel Burstin, *The Harbour, CT20 1TX; tel: (01303) 257455; fax: (01303) 256786.* Said to be Britain's largest entertainment hotel. Moderate.

Langhorne Garden Hotel, *10-12 Langhorne Gardens, CT20 2EA; tel: (01303) 257233; fax: (01303) 242760.* Town centre hotel. Budget–moderate.

Shakespeare Hotel, *Shakespeare Terrace, The Leas, CT20 2DX; tel: (01303) 221075; fax: (01303) 221076.* Cosy hotel with sea views. Budget.

The nearest campsites are **Folkestone Camping and Caravanning Club Site**, *The Warren, Folkestone CT19 6PT; tel: (01303) 255093;* 1½ miles from town centre; **Little Satmar Holiday Park**, *Wine House Lane, Capel-le-Ferne, Folketone; tel: (01303) 251188,* 2 miles east; and **Varne Ridge Caravan Park**, *145 Old*

Dover Rd, Capel-le-Ferne, Folkestone; tel: (01303) 251765, 2 miles east.

SIGHTSEEING

A popular resort from the 19th century, Folkestone remains a place for bracing walks along clifftops or on a beach. There are the usual seaside amusements.

Folkestone Museum and Art Gallery, *2 Grace Hill; tel: (01303) 850123,* open Mon–Sat 093–1700; free. Displays of local, natural and social history and archaeology include a Saxon skeleton, and there are sections on World Wars I and II.

OUT OF TOWN

Butterfly Centre, *on A260, Swingfield; tel: (01303) 844244,* open daily 1000–1700 (Apr–early Oct); £2. 4 miles north. Butterflies from all over the world fly free in landscaped tropical gardens with a wide range of tropical plants. Garden centre, plant area and shop.

Kent Battle of Britain Museum, *Hawkinge Airfield, nr Folkestone; tel: (01303) 893140,* open daily 1000–1700 (Easter–Sept); daily 1100–1600 (Oct); £3. Off A260, 2 miles north of Folkestone.

Lympne Castle, *Lympne, B2067; tel: (01303) 267571,* open Mon–Thur 1030–1730 (late May–mid Sept); £2. 11 miles south-west. Built in 1360, the castle has a great hall flanked by Norman and medieval towers. Dolls, toys, reproduction medieval brasses and models of English cathedrals are displayed. Souvenirs, gardens and a picnic site.

Port Lympne Wild Animal Park, *Lympne; tel: (01303) 264647,* open daily 1000–1700 (last admission) (May–Sept), 1000–1530 (Oct–Apr); £6.99 (safari trailer £2). 11 miles south-west. The 300-acre park encompasses spacious paddocks containing herds of rare horses, deer, antelope, rhino, elephant, gorillas and other species.

LONDON-NORWICH

Almost entirely coastal, this scenic route takes in the counties of Essex, Suffolk and Norfolk and three popular seaside resorts, as well as the historic towns of Colchester – Britain's oldest – and Ipswich. It provides opportunities to visit scenes immortalised by the painter John Constable and Aldeburgh, a shrine for international music-lovers. Finally, it threads through the Norfolk Broads, that strange region of reed-fringed waterways, a popular destination for boating holidays and now a national park.

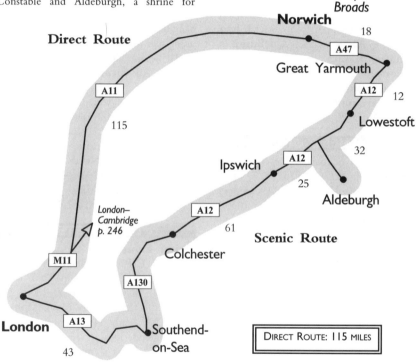

Direct Route

Norwich

Norfolk Broads

18

A47

Great Yarmouth

A11

A12 12

115

Lowestoft

32

261

Ipswich A12

25

Aldeburgh

London–Cambridge p. 246

A12

61 **Scenic Route**

M11

Colchester

A130

London A13

Southend-on-Sea

43

DIRECT ROUTE: 115 MILES

ROUTES

DIRECT ROUTE

Allow 2 hrs 15 mins for this 115-mile route. From the City of London follow the signs for A11 east (follow Leadenhall St and Aldgate High St to Whitechapel). After 8 miles join A12 and follow signs to M11, reached in 2½ miles, and continue on the motorway for 36 miles to Junction 9; head north-east on A11 for 63 miles, then follow signs for 5½ miles to central Norwich.

SCENIC ROUTE

▪➡ The mileage on this route is increased by about 77 miles – allow 4½ hours travelling time. From the City of London proceed as above to A11 east and within half a mile join A13, to arrive in **Southend-on-Sea** after 43 miles. Leave Southend on A127 and after 8 miles head north on A130 to join A12 on the outskirts of Chelmsford. A12 continues north-east to **Colchester** and **Ipswich** and beyond. 18 miles from Ipswich bear right on to A1094 to reach **Aldeburgh** in 6½ miles. Return to A12 to reach **Lowestoft** 32 miles from Aldeburgh. Continue north on A12 for 12 miles to **Great Yarmouth**, then follow A47 west to reach Norwich in 18 miles.

SOUTHEND-ON-SEA

TIC: *19 High St, Southend-on-Sea, Essex SS1 1JE; tel: (01702) 215118/9*, open Mon–Sat 0930–1700. DP SHS services offered; local bed-booking (latest 1630), BABA (latest 1600). *Southend-on-Sea and accommodation guide* are free.

GETTING AROUND

The majority of attractions are an easy walk from the centre. Free town and transport maps are available from the TIC. Most services operate from the **bus station**, *York Rd; tel: (01702) 434444*. The main **taxi** rank is on *London Rd*.

ACCOMMODATION

It is advisable to pre-book for weekends – especially the second May Bank Holiday (Southend Airshow). There is a fair range of hotels and guesthouses, with cheaper establishments on the edge of town and along the seafront. The nearest **campsite**

is **Eastbeach Caravan and Camping Site**, *East Beach, Shoeburyness; tel: (01702) 292466*, 4 miles east.

SIGHTSEEING

The TIC has information on **bus tours** and **boat trips**.

Royal Terrace preserves a glimpse of the town's faded Regency elegance, but Southend is primarily a popular seaside resort and the attractions are family oriented. **Southend Pier**, *Southend Seafront; tel: (01702) 215622*, open Mon–Fri 0800–2100, Sat–Sun 0800–2200 (May–Sept); daily 0815–1600 (Oct–Apr); £1.85 (including pier train).

All the fun of the fair is offered at **Peter Pan's Adventure Island**, *Western Esplanade; tel: (01702) 468023*, open daily 1100–2200 (May–Sept); Sat–Sun and school holidays 1100–1800 (Oct–Apr); £9 unlimited rides – or 50p per ride.

Children's favourite characters are recreated at **Never Never Land**, *Western Esplanade; tel: (01702) 460618*, open Sat–Sun 1100–2200 (Easter–Nov); daily during school holidays; £1.80.

COLCHESTER

Visitor Information Centre (VIC): *1 Queen St, Colchester, Essex CO1 2PG; tel: (01206) 282920*, open Mon–Tues, Thur–Sat 0930–1800, Wed 1000–1800, Sun 1000–1700 (Easter–early Nov); Mon–Sat 1000–1700 (early Nov–Easter). DP services offered; local bed-booking service and BABA (latest 30 mins before closing). YHA/HI membership sold. *Treat Yourself to Colchester*, the mini guide, *Where to Stay*, *Where to Eat* and *Time Out* (a monthly entertainment guide) are all free.

GETTING AROUND

With the exception of Colchester Zoo, the town's attractions are within walking distance of the centre. Town and transport maps are available free from the VIC. The main local bus operator is **Eastern National**, *tel: (01206) 571451.* **Shopmobility**, *tel: (01206) 369099.* The main **taxi** ranks are at the bus station and on High St (outside the Red Lion), or *tel: (01206) 766767.*

ACCOMMODATION

There are over a dozen hotels and masses of b&b establishments, so it's usually easy to book on arrival, but pre-booking is necessary for university graduation (July) and Cricket Week (Aug). Hotel chains include *BW, FP* and *Brook.* The nearest **HI** is Castle Hedingham and the closest **campsite** is **Colchester Camping and Caravan Park**, *Cymbeline Way, Lexden; (01206) 545551,* 1½ miles west.

SIGHTSEEING

There are **guided walks** departing from the VIC (book there) Mon–Sat at 1400, Sun at 1100 (June–Aug); daily at 1100 (Sept); £2. **Colchester Borough Transport**, *tel: (01206) 764029,* run **open-top bus tours** Mon–Sat at 1100, 1330 and 1500 (July–Aug), starting from Castle Park main gates; £4.50.

Colchester is Britain's oldest recorded town, mentioned by Pliny the Elder in AD 77. Invaded by the Romans in AD 43, burnt in revenge by the powerful Iceni tribe and their queen Boudicca (Boadicea) in AD 60, it subsequently became the first capital of Roman Britain. Now a busy university town, it has retained some of its old buildings and character.

The town's history is imaginatively interpreted, using hands-on displays, at the award-winning **Castle Museum**, *Castle Park, High St; tel: (01206) 282931,* open Mon–Sat 1000–1700 (all year); also Sun 1400–1700 (Mar–Nov); £3.50.

A collection of toys, costumes and decorative arts can be seen at **Hollytrees Museum**, *High St; tel: (01206) 282931,* open Tues–Sat 1000–1200 and 1300–1700; free, while **Tymperleys Clock Museum**, *Trinity St; tel: (01206) 282931,* open Tues–Sat 1000–1300 and 1400–1700 (Apr–Oct); free, displays Colchester-made clocks. Hands-on techniques are features of the **Natural History Museum**, *High St; tel: (01206) 282931,* open Tues–Sat 1000–1300 and 1400–1700; free. Also worth a look are the ruined **St Botolph's Priory**, *St Botolph's St,* and the **Roman wall** – this surrounds the town centre.

The award-winning **Colchester Zoo**, *Maldon Rd; tel: (01206) 330253;* open daily 0930–1800/1830 (closes one hour before dusk Oct–Apr); £7, is 2 miles south of centre.

OUT OF TOWN

Trips on a steam train can be enjoyed nearby: at the **Colne Valley Railway**, *Castle Hedingham; tel: (01787) 461174,* open daily 1000–1700 (Mar–Dec); £2 (£5 on steam days). 15 miles west. **Hedingham Castle**, *tel: (01787) 60261,* open daily 1000–1700 (Easter–Oct); £2.50, offers a great Norman keep, with peaceful woodland and lakeside walks.

Just north of Colchester lies the **Stour Valley**, which inspired John Constable, perhaps England's best loved landscape artist, to paint many of his most famous works; the village of **Dedham** and **Flatford Mill** (just over a mile from Dedham) are best visited during the week, when they are least busy. Also at Dedham is a **Rare Breeds Centre**, *Mill Rd; tel: (01206) 323111,* open daily 1000–1730 or one hour before dusk (Mar–Sept); £3.25. 10 miles north-east. For the unusual combination of a rare breeds farm and the

263

tallest Tudor gate tower in England, visit **Layer Marney Tower**, *Layer Marney; tel: (01206) 330784,* open Sun–Fri 1400– 1800 (Apr–Sept); Mon–Fri 1400–1800, Sun 1200–1800 July–Aug); public holidays 1100–1800; £3.50. 6 miles south.

Fingringhoe Wick Nature Reserve, *Fingringhoe; tel: (01206) 729678,* open Tues–Sun 0900–1700; free, but donations welcomed. 5 miles south. Set on the Colne estuary, this is a haven for sea birds.

IPSWICH

TIC: *St Stephen's Church, St Stephen's Lane, Ipswich, Suffolk IP1 1DP; tel: (01473) 258070,* open Mon–Sat 0900–1700. Services offered: local bed-booking and BABA (fee 10% of first night for all bookings). Tickets for local events, YHA/HI and NT membership sold. *Ipswich & District* is 50p (free by post) and includes accommodation listings.

264

GETTING AROUND

The majority of town attractions are an easy walk from the centre. General **transport enquiries**, freephone *tel: (0800) 919390.* **Ipswich Buses**, *tel: (01473) 232600,* operate most local services from **Tower Ramparts Bus Station**. The main **taxi** ranks are at the rail station, *Lloyds Ave* and *Old Cattle Market.*

ACCOMMODATION

There is a reasonable selection of hotel accommodation and a good range of b&bs and guesthouses. It is generally easy to book on arrival. Chains include *BW, CM* and *Nv.* **YMCA:** *2 Wellington St; tel: (01473) 252456.* The closest **campsites** are: **Orwell Meadows**, *Priory Lane, Nacton; tel: (01473) 726666;* and **Priory Park**, *Priory Lane, Nacton; tel: (01473) 727393,* both 4 miles south-east. Details of other sites from the TIC.

SIGHTSEEING

The TIC have a selection of walking trail leaflets (20p each) and **BBG guided walks** leave from the TIC Tues, Thur at 1415 (May–Sept); £1.25. Ipswich Buses operate a **circular city bus tour** on an open-top double-decker bus (late May– early Sept); £2 for a hop-on, hop-off dayticket.

Ipswich is one of England's oldest towns, continuously settled since Saxon times and now a busy port which has an interesting Victorian dockland: the *Ipswich Wet Dock Maritime Trail* gives a good insight into this historic area.

Although much of Ipswich was built or rebuilt in the 19th century, 12 medieval churches survive (ask the TIC about the *Historic Churches Trail*), as well as some fine timber-framed buildings. The **Unitarian Chapel** dates from 1699, while the elaborately plastered **Ancient House** (1670), *Buttermarket*, now contains a shop.

Another interesting old building (1548) is the **Christchurch Mansion and Wolsey Art Gallery**, *Christchurch Park; tel: (01473) 253246,* open Tues–Sat 1000– 1700, Sun, most public holidays 1430– 1630 (Apr–Oct); Tues–Sat 1000–1610 (Nov–Mar); free. It has period rooms and a fine selection of British art of all kinds, notably the Suffolk painters.

Ipswich Museum, *High St; tel: (01473) 213761,* open Tues–Sat 1000– 1700; free, houses many excellent displays, including *Anglo-Saxons come to Ipswich* and *Romans in Suffolk.*

Tolly Cobbold Brewery, *Cliff Rd; tel: (01473) 231723.* Tours daily at 1200 (May–Sept); the rest of the year there are tours only for groups, but you may be able to join one, so ask; £3.75. If you like beer, don't miss this tour of one of the finest Victorian breweries in the country (tasting included).

Ipswich Transport Museum, *Old Trolley Bus Depot, Cobham Rd; tel: (01473) 715666,* open Sun, public holidays 1100–1700 (Easter–Oct); Mon–Fri 1200–1600 (late-July–Aug); £2.25. 2 miles east. All the vehicles in the museum, were made in the Ipswich area.

ALDEBURGH

TIC: *The Cinema, High St, Aldeburgh, Suffolk IP15 5AU; tel: (01728) 453637,* open Mon–Fri 0900–1715, Sat–Sun, public holidays 1000–1715 (Mar–Oct). DP SHS services offered; local bed-booking and BABA (latest 1630). YHA/HI, Ramblers Association and NT memberships sold. *Suffolk Coast Holiday Guide,* including an accommodation listing, is 25p.

GETTING AROUND

The majority of attractions are not within walking distance and public transport is fairly patchy. The TIC can provide a town map and advise you on the best routes to take. There are several **taxi** companies: **Alde Taxis**, *tel: (01728) 452326;* **Coastal Cabs**, *tel: (01728) 832209;* **Millers**, *tel: (01728) 603279;* **Oscars**, *tel: (01728) 830614;* and **Pickering Pick-Ups**, *tel: (01728) 452095.*

ACCOMMODATION

Aldeburgh is very popular for weekend breaks, and it is advisable to book in advance for summer weekends, particularly during the Aldeburgh Festival (June). There are a handful of hotels, several b&bs and a few pubs offering rooms. Chains include *BW, Ct* and *Rg.*

HI: *Heath Walk, Blaxhall, Woodbridge; tel: (01728) 688206.* The nearest **campsites** are: **Church Farm Caravan and Camping Site**, *Thorpeness Rd; tel: (01728) 453433,* 1 mile north, **Cakes**

and **Ale Park**, *Abbey Lane, Theberton; tel: (01728) 831655,* 5 miles north-west.

EVENTS

This quietly fashionable seaside resort is famous for its annual music festival in June, founded by the composer Benjamin Britten, who made the town his home. The festival is now divided between Aldeburgh and Snape Maltings. Contact **The Aldeburgh Foundation**, *High St, Aldeburgh; tel: (01728) 452935.*

SIGHTSEEING

Bus tours of the area are organised by **Belle Coaches**, *tel: (01728) 830414,* and **Happy Wanderers**, *tel: (01728) 830358.*

Several companies offer **river trips** on the Alde Estuary and River Deben: **Lady Florence**, *tel: (0831) 698298;* **Jahan**, *tel: (01473) 736260;* **Snape**, *tel: (01728) 688303;* and **Regardless**, *tel: (01394) 450844.* Prices start from £3 an hour.

The seafront at Aldeburgh makes for a pleasant walk. Close to the beach is the quaint **Moot Hall Museum**, *Market Cross Pl.,* open variable times (Easter–Oct), so check; 50p.

There are good views from the **Town Steps** and up the hill is the fine **parish church** where Benjamin Britten is buried.

OUT OF TOWN

Snape Maltings consists of a collection of attractively-converted 19th-century granaries and malthouses, surrounded by Suffolk marshes. The complex offers a number of leisure facilities, including one of Europe's finest concert halls. **Snape Maltings Riverside Centre**, *Snape; tel: (01728) 688303,* open all year 1000–1700/1800; free. 6 miles west. Five miles south of Snape, is Henry II's magnificent keep of **Orford Castle** (EH), *Orford; tel: (01394) 450472,* open daily 1000–

265

1800 (Apr–Sept); daily 1000–1600 (Oct–Mar); £2.10. It occasionally closes 1300–1400.

The largest vegetated shingle spit in Europe, with a variety of habitats supporting a number of rare plants, as well as being a haven for breeding and migratory birds, is **Orford Ness** (NT), *Quay Office, Orford Quay, Woodbridge; tel: (01394) 450900*, open Thur–Sat (Easter–Oct). Outward ferries 1000–1240 (at 20-min intervals), maximum stay 3½ hrs; £3 (inc. ferry). Numbers are limited and pre-booking is recommended for the ferry; *tel: (01394) 450057*.

Sizewell Visitor Centre, *Sizewell, nr Leiston; tel: (01728) 642139*, open daily 1000–1600 – contact them directly for times of guided tours; free. Five miles north of Aldeburgh. The centre seeks to settle controversy about safety by explaining how nuclear power is generated.

266

LOWESTOFT

TIC: *East Point Pavilion, Royal Plain, Lowestoft, Suffolk NR33 0AP; tel: (01502) 523000; fax: (01502) 539023*, open daily 0900–1800 (May–Sept), Tues–Sun 1100–1700 (Oct–Apr).

Services offered: BABA and local accommodation bookings; reservations for harbour tours and trips at sea.

ACCOMMODATION

Hotels, guesthouses, self-catering establishments and holiday villages in Lowestoft are listed in *Suffolk Coast and Countryside Short Breaks*, available free from the TIC.

Hotel Hatfield, *The Esplanade, Lowestoft NR33 0QP; tel: (01502) 563337; fax: (01502) 511885*. Moderate.

Hotel Katherine, *49 Kirkley Cliff Rd, Lowestoft NR33 0DF; tel: (01502) 567858; fax: (01502) 581341*. Close to Lowestoft's south beach. Budget–moderate.

Abbé House Hotel, *322 London Rd South, Lowestoft NR33 0BG; tel/fax: (01502) 581083*. Budget.

SIGHTSEEING

Britain's most easterly town, Lowestoft is still a busy fishing port, but excellent beaches have helped it to develop as a popular holiday resort. Echoes of its traditional character, however, are to be found in The Scores, narrow cobbled alleyways with old buildings which were once fishermen's workshops and smokehouses.

Lydia Eva **Steam Drifter**, *Yacht Basin, Lowestoft Harbour*. The last of some 3000 drifters which once fished for herring off Lowestoft and Great Yarmouth now acts as a floating exhibition of the hardships of life ashore and afloat during the industry's heyday. Accessible Apr–Oct, but the vessel alternates between Lowestoft and Great Yarmouth, so check with the TIC.

Lowestoft and East Suffolk Maritime Museum, *Sparrows Nest Park, Whapload Rd; tel: (01502) 561963*, open daily 1000–1630 (end Mar–early Apr); 50p. Models of fishing vessels and commercial ships old and new are displayed.

Lowestoft Museum, *Broad House, Nicholas Everitt Park; tel: (01502) 511457*, open daily 1030–1300, 1400–1700 (mid May–early Oct); days and times vary in Mar–mid May and late Oct; free. The museum traces local history.

Royal Navy Patrol Service Museum, *Sparrows Nest Park, Whapload Rd; tel: (01502) 586250*, open Mon–Fri 1000–1200, 1400–1630, Sun 1400–1630 (mid May–mid Oct); free. The courage of officers and men who served on fisheries protection vessels during World War II is honoured through displays of photographs, memorabilia and ships' logbooks. Wartime posters and equipment are on show.

GREAT YARMOUTH

TIC: *Marine Parade, Great Yarmouth, Norfolk NR30 2EJ; tel: (01493) 842195; fax: (01493) 846332*, open Mon–Sat 0930–1730, Sun 1000–1700 (June–Sept); daily 1000–1300, 1400–1700 (Oct–Apr). The centre offers a complete range of services, including BABA and local accommodation reservations.

ACCOMMODATION

Great Yarmouth thrives on visitors, so there is no shortage of accommodation, especially at the budget end of the scale in the form of guesthouses and b&bs. Hotels maintain high standards.

Imperial Hotel, *North Drive, Great Yarmouth NR30 1EQ; tel: (01493) 851113; fax: (01493) 852229*. Well-appointed hotel with noted restaurant. Moderate–expensive.

Regency Hotel, *5 North Dr, Great Yarmouth NR30 1ED; tel: (01493) 843759; fax: (01493) 330411*. Small modern hotel. Budget–moderate.

Star Hotel, *24 Hall Quay, Great Yarmouth NR30 1HG; tel: (01493) 842294; fax: (01493) 330215*. Family-run hotel quietly located near the sea front. Moderate–expensive.

HI: *2 Sandown Rd, Great Yarmouth NR30 1EY; tel/fax: (01493) 843991*. The nearest camping/caravan grounds are **Clippesby Holidays**, *Clippesby, Great Yarmouth NR29 3BJ; tel: (01493) 369367; fax: (01493) 368181*; 6 miles north-west; and **Rose Farm Touring Park**, *Stepshort, Belton, Great Yarmouth NR31 9JS; tel/fax (01493) 780896*; 5 miles south-west.

SIGHTSEEING

Great Yarmouth wears at least three hats. It is still an active fishing port, although the industry is much smaller than it was in the past. It is an important base for the offshore oil and gas industries which have developed in recent years. Above all, it is a lively seaside resort with good beaches and enough attractions and distractions for rainy days. Details of **boat trips** and visits to the *Lydia Eva* steam drifter (see Lowestoft sightseeing, above) may be obtained from the TIC.

Elizabethan House Museum, *4 South Quay; tel: (01493) 855746*, open Sun–Fri 1000–1700 (end May–Sept); Mon–Fri 1000–1700, Sun 1400–1700 (two weeks from Mon before Easter); £1.10. Exhibits of 19th-century domestic life, Victorian toys and Lowestoft porcelain and glass.

Maritime Museum, *Marine Parade; tel: (01493) 842267*, open Sun–Fri 1000–1700 (end May–Sept), Mon–Fri 1000–1700, Sun 1400–1700 (two weeks from Mon before Easter); £1.10. The focus is on herring fisheries and Norfolk wherries, the wide-beamed sailing vessels that once plied the Norfolk Broads.

Old Merchant's House (EH), *South Quay; tel: (01493) 857900*, open Sun–Fri 1000–1300, 1400–1700 (first two weeks of Apr, end May–Sept); £1.50. A 17th-century town house standing among the ancient narrow alleyways known as the Rows. It has a splendid plaster ceiling and contains architectural and domestic fittings salvaged from other 'Row' houses destroyed during World War II air raids.

Tolhouse Museum, *Tolhouse St; tel: (01493) 858900*, open Sun–Fri 1000–1700 (end May–Sept), Mon–Fri 1000–1700, Sun 1400–1700 (two weeks from Mon before Easter); £1.10. One of the oldest municipal buildings in England, the museum was once the town's courthouse and jail – the old cells may be visited. Exhibits illustrate local history, and there is a brass-rubbing centre.

267

LONDON–NOTTINGHAM

Roman remains, a grand medieval castle overlooking the River Avon and two cathedrals – one ancient, one modern – lie along this route, which takes us into the heart of the English Midlands. We catch glimpses of history from pre-Christian times to the dark days of World War II, and see landscapes ranging from the sweeping grandeur of the shires to the smoking skylines of post-industrial revolution towns.

268

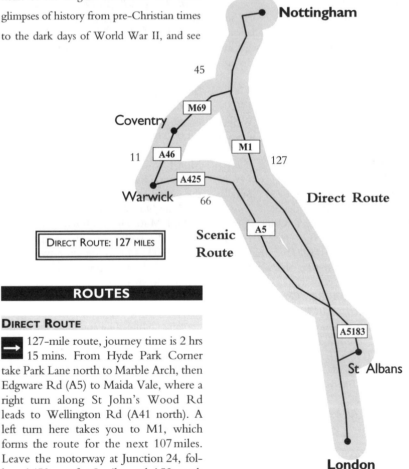

45

Coventry

M69

11   A46

M1

127

A425

Warwick   66

Nottingham

Direct Route

DIRECT ROUTE: 127 MILES

Scenic   A5
Route

ROUTES

DIRECT ROUTE

127-mile route, journey time is 2 hrs 15 mins. From Hyde Park Corner take Park Lane north to Marble Arch, then Edgware Rd (A5) to Maida Vale, where a right turn along St John's Wood Rd leads to Wellington Rd (A41 north). A left turn here takes you to M1, which forms the route for the next 107 miles. Leave the motorway at Junction 24, follow A453 east for 8 miles and A52 north for 1½ miles. A6005 leads to central Nottingham in a mile.

A5183

St Albans

London

SCENIC ROUTE

➡ This adds about 31 miles – allow 3½ hours travelling time. From Hyde Park Corner proceed to M1 as above and continue on the motorway for 11 miles, leaving at Junction 6. A405 and A5183 lead to the centre of St Albans. Leave St Albans on A5183 north and join A5 after 6 miles. Follow A5 for 42 miles, bearing left on to A45 (Daventry turn-off), and left again after 4 miles on to A425, which reaches **Warwick** after a further 20 miles. A46 leads from Warwick to Coventry in 11 miles. From **Coventry** follow signs north to M69, which intersects with M1 after 16 miles. Continue north on M1 for 19 miles to Junction 24, then follow A453 east for 8 miles to connect with A52, where you can follow signs for 2 miles to Nottingham city centre.

ST ALBANS

TIC: *Town Hall, Market Place, St Albans, Hertfordshire AL3 5DJ; tel: (01727) 864511*, open Mon–Sat 0930–1730 (Apr–Oct); Mon–Sat 1000–1600 (Nov–Mar); Sun 1030–1630 (mid June–mid Sept). DP services offered; local bed-booking and BABA (latest 30 mins before closing; small fee). *St Albans Official Guide* costs £1.

GETTING AROUND

The TIC has free transport maps. For **transport enquiries**, *tel: (0345) 244344*. The main **taxi** rank is on *St Peters St.*

ACCOMMODATION

For a relatively large city, St Albans is not too well endowed with accommodation. Hotel chains in the area include *FP, Ib, Ja, MH, Th*. There is a concentration of b&bs around City Station, about a mile east of the city centre. There is a plethora of pubs, many serving food.

The grandest establishment in the area

is **Sopwell House Hotel and Country Club**, *Cottonmill Lane, Sopwell, St Albans, AL1 2HQ; tel: (01727) 864477; fax: (01727) 844741*. Formerly the country home of Lord Mountbatten, the hotel is set in 11 acres of landscaped, wooded gardens. Expensive. **Noke Thistle Hotel**, *Watford Rd, St Albans AL2 3DS; tel: (01727) 854252; fax: (01727) 841906.*, is handy for the M1 and M25. Expensive.

SIGHTSEEING

There are (free) **guided walks** on Sun (Easter–Sept); from the Clock Tower at 1500. St Albans has some well-preserved streets, notably medieval *French Row* and Georgian *Fishpool St.*

The distinctive Norman cathedral has a glorious (and immensely long) nave and a tower of pillaged Roman brick. **Cathedral and Abbey Church**, *Sumpter Yard; tel: (01727) 860780*, open daily (services permitting) 0900–1745/1845; free.

Another landmark is the medieval **Clock Tower**, *Market Pl.; tel: (01727) 853301/860984*, open Sat–Sun, public holidays 1030–1700 (Easter–mid Sept); 25p, which offers fine views.

The history of the city is told at the **Museum of St Albans**, *Hatfield Rd; tel: (01727) 819340*, open Mon–Sat 1000–1700, Sun 1400–1700; free.

St Albans was an important Roman city: **Verulamium Park** contains part of the Roman wall, a good hypocaust (underfloor heating) and an excellent museum, where the collection includes well-preserved mosaics: **Verulamium Museum**, *St Michael's St; tel: (01727) 819339*, open Mon–Sat 1000–1730, Sun 1400–1730; £2.80. 1½ miles west of the centre. Nearby is the **Roman Theatre**, *Bluehouse Hill; tel: (01727) 835035/ 855000*, open daily 1000–1600/1700; £1.50.

269

OUT OF TOWN

Rose lovers are in paradise at the internationally renowned **Gardens of the Rose**, *Chiswell Green Lane, Chiswell Green; tel: (01727) 850461*, open Mon–Sat 0900–1700, Sun 1000–1800 (June–Oct); £4. 3 miles south-east. These consist of 20 acres, containing some 30,000 roses of different species.

Anyone interested in aviation should head for the selection of real aircraft and working displays at the base of one of the great designers: **de Havilland Mosquito Aircraft Museum**, *Salisbury Hall, London Colney; tel: (01727) 822051*, open Tues, Thur, Sat 1400–1730, Sun, public holidays 1030–1730 (Easter–Oct); £4.

Further afield is 17th-century **Hatfield House**, *Old Hatfield; tel: (01707) 262823/ 265159*, house open Tues–Sat 1200–1600, Sun 1300–1630, public holidays 1100–1630 (Easter–Sept); £5.20 (house and gardens). 7½ miles east. Notable features in the house itself are the long gallery (180 ft long, with gold-leaf ceiling) and a Flemish stained-glass window in the chapel. Items on display include tapestries, furniture, armour and model soldiers, while the gardens are in Elizabethan and Jacobean styles. There are three nature trails in the park. During the **Living Crafts Exhibition** (May), hundreds of craftspeople demonstrate their skills – and sell their wares. **Elizabethan banquets** are held throughout the year in the **Old Palace**; *tel (01707) 262055/ 272738 –* modern food, old-style entertainment.

Luton Hoo, *Luton; tel: (01582) 22955*, open Fri–Sun: 1330–dusk (Apr–mid Oct); public holidays (1030–dusk); £5. 9 miles north. The house imitates 18th-century French styles and contains very varied objects, from Fabergé photo frames to Gothic works of art, collected by a diamond millionaire and his descendants.

WARWICK

TIC: *The Court House, Jury St, Warwick CV34 4EW; tel: (01926) 492212*, open daily 0930–1630. DP SHS services offered; local bed-booking (latest 1615), BABA (latest 1600). Free accommodation list available. *Warwick Official Town Guide* is 50p.

The main **post office**, *Brook St*, is open Mon–Fri 0900–1730, Sat 0900–1230 (no poste restante).

GETTING AROUND

Most attractions are within walking distance of the centre. There is a good local bus service to Coventry, Leamington Spa, Kenilworth, Stratford and surrounding villages, operated by **Midland Red** and **Stratford Blue**, *tel: (01788) 535555*, and **Warwickshire Buses**, *tel: (01926) 414140*. There are evening services on some routes, but only sparse coverage on Sun. The main bus stop is in *Market Pl.* There is a **taxi** rank in *Market Pl.*

ACCOMMODATION AND FOOD

There is a small range available, with cheaper accommodation on the edge of the centre. It is usually easy to book a room on arrival, except during the Royal Show and Warwick Arts Festival (both July) and during the Folk Festival (Aug). The only chain is *Hn* – outside town, close to the M40.

Accommodation is often available at **Warwick University** during the holidays; *tel: (01203) 523523*. There are various **campsites** nearby – a list is available from the TIC for 26p.

There is a good selection of eateries, particularly of cheaper restaurants, pubs serving meals, cafés and tearooms. There are also regular medieval banquets throughout the year, in the Undercroft of the Castle, *tel: (01926) 495421.*

ENTERTAINMENT AND EVENTS

A free entertainments listing, *What's On in Warwick*, is available from the TIC and local newspapers give details. Nightlife in Warwick is largely peaceful with safe streets and good food. Live entertainment is offered by the **Warwick Folk Club** at the **Rose and Crown**, *Market Pl.*, Mon at 2030; and there's a folk session at **The Punch Bowl**, *The Butts*, Fri at 2000.

The main venue for more formal music, and for theatre, is **Warwick University Arts Centre**, *Gibbet Hill, Coventry; tel: (01203) 524524*, 7 miles away.

Warwick Festival (July) is an annual arts festival at various venues: information from **Warwick Arts Society**, *tel: (01926) 410747*. **Warwick Folk Festival** (Aug) is another big event taking place at different venues; *tel: (01203) 678738*. The TIC has a free events listing.

SHOPPING

The main shopping streets are *Market Pl, Swan St, Brook St, Smith St, Jury St* and *West St*. There is also an abundance of antique shops and centres. There is a **market** in *Market Place* every Sat.

Converted farm buildings house craft workshops at **Hatton Country World**, *George's Farm, Hatton; tel: (01926) 843411*, open daily 1000–1730, 4½ miles north.

SIGHTSEEING

Information about **guided walks** is available at the TIC.

Try to pick a quiet time to visit **Warwick Castle**, *tel: (01926) 495421/ 406600*, open daily 1000–1700 (Nov–Mar); daily 1000– 1800 (Apr–Oct); £9.95 (July–Aug); £8.95 (Sept–June). It's crowded when special events are staged at the castle, which is one of the most pop-ular visitor attractions in England. The curtain wall and tower defences are intact, while the state rooms (inhabited until the 1970s) are rich in treasures. There are also dungeons and a torture chamber for the ghoulish. The extensive grounds, land-scaped by Capability Brown, include a Victorian rose garden and woodland walks; the best view of the castle, towering above the Avon, is from Castle Bridge.

Warwick's compact centre is remark-ably harmonious: much of it was rebuilt in the 18th century, after a fire in 1694. *Northgate St* has some lovely façades. The fine **Court House** (1725), as well as hous-ing the TIC, has changing exhibitions of (mainly) military paraphernalia in the **Warwickshire Yeomanry Museum**, *Court House, Jury St; tel: (01926) 492212*, open Sat–Sun, most Fri, public holidays, 1000–1300 and 1400–1600 (Easter–Sept); free. At **Warwickshire Museum**, *Market Pl.; tel: (01926) 410410*, open Mon–Sat 1000–1730 (all year); Sun 1400–1700 (May–Sept); free, notable exhibits include the *Great Fire of Warwick* and Sheldon's tapestry map.

Housed in a Jacobean mansion, there are reconstructions of period rooms, exhibits including musical instruments and costumes at **St John's Museum**, *St John's; tel: (01926) 410410*, open Tues–Sat, public holidays 1000–1230 and 1330–1730 (all year); Sun 1430–1700 (May–Sept); free.

The limits reached by the fire are clearly defined by where the half-timbered houses begin. None of these is more charmingly irregular than the medieval **Lord Leycester Hospital and Master's Garden**, *High St; tel: (01926) 491422*. Hospital open Tues–Sun 1000–1700 (Easter–Sept); 1000–1600 (Oct–Easter); £2.50. The restored walled garden is open Tues–Sun 1400–1700 (Easter–Sept); £1.

271

Oken's House and Doll Museum, *Castle St; tel: (01926) 495546,* open Sat 1000–dusk (Oct–Easter); Mon–Sat 1000–1700, Sun 1300–1700 (Easter–Sept); £1. This Elizabethan timber-framed house, has a superb collection of early toys and dolls, including automata and dolls' houses.

Collegiate Church of St Mary, *Old Square; tel: (01926) 403940,* open daily 1000–1800 (Easter–Sept); 1000–1600 (Oct–Easter); free, but there's a small charge for the tower (accessible only when weather permits). The church is renowned for its outstanding 15th-century chapel, housing the lavish tomb of Richard Beauchamp.

OUT OF TOWN

Charlecote Park (NT), *Charlecote; tel: (01789) 470277,* open Fri–Tues 1100–1300 and 1400–1715 (Easter–Oct); £4.60. 5 miles south. Shakespeare allegedly poached deer from here (it dates from the 1550s) and there are still herds in the park.

Out of town is the dramatic ruin of once-mighty **Kenilworth Castle** (EH), *Kenilworth; tel: (01926) 852078,* open daily 1000–1800 (Apr–Sept); daily 1000–1600 (Oct–Mar); £2.50. 5 miles north. This forms a peaceful contrast to Warwick's fortress. Sir Walter Scott used it as a romantic backcloth for his novel *Kenilworth* (1821), a fictionalised account of Elizabeth I's visit here.

A historic waterwheel-worked mill is **Wellesbourne Watermill,** *Kineton Rd, Wellesbourne; tel: (01789) 470237,* open Thur–Sun, public holidays 1000–1630 (Easter–Sept); Tues–Sun 1000–1630 (mid-July–Aug); £3.50. 8 miles south. More recent history can be found in the nearby **Wellesbourne Wartime Museum,** *Wellesbourne Airfield, Wellesbourne; tel: (01789) 470237,* open Sun, some public holidays 1000–1600; £1. On the site of a wartime airfield, this offers miscellaneous war-related exhibits.

COVENTRY

TIC: *Bayley Lane, Coventry CV1 5RN; tel: (01203) 832303/4,* open Mon–Fri 0930–1630/1700, Sat–Sun 1000–1630. DP services offered; free local bed-booking (latest 30 mins before closing), BABA (latest 30 mins before closing). Tickets for events sold. There are several free guides, including one listing accommodation.

GETTING AROUND

Most attractions can be reached on foot from the centre; free town and transport maps available from the TIC. There is a good local bus service throughout the city and well into Warwickshire, operated by several different companies. **Shopmobility,** *tel: (01203) 832020.*

For enquiries about all public transport in the West Midlands: **Centro Hotline,** *tel: (01203) 559559.*

The main **taxi** ranks are at the rail and bus stations and on *Ironmonger Row.* Telephone: **Allens Taxis,** *tel: (01203) 555555;* or **Lewis's,** *tel: (01203) 666666.*

ACCOMMODATION

There is a good range of hotel and guest-house accommodation, but very little in the way of b&bs. **Freephone bed-booking service**: *tel: (0800) 243748.* Cheaper establishments can be found on the edge of town and it's usually easy to book on arrival, except during the Royal Agricultural Show (June–July). Hotel chains include *BW, Ca, DV, FP* and *Nv.* **University** accommodation is available July–Aug; *tel: (01203) 838318.* There is a **campsite** just 1½ miles south: **Canley Ford Milk Bar,** *off Kenilworth Rd; tel: (01203) 675286.* For other campsites ask at the TIC.

SIGHTSEEING

Walking city tours (£1.50) are organised daily, with qualified **Green Badge Guides**: book at the TIC.

Virtually obliterated by German bombs in 1940, Coventry is now a bright, modern industrial city. Though much of the post-war development is depressing, the city makes the most of the remnants of its past and it's worth seeking them out.

The statue of **Lady Godiva**, *Broadgate,* commemorates the lady who (in 1040) rode naked through the city streets in protest at the high taxes imposed by her husband.

Spon Street is a living reminder of the city's heritage, consisting largely of restored 15th- to 16th-century buildings, now being put to good use as shops, galleries and restaurants.

The two cathedrals stand as a powerful symbol of Coventry's regeneration. The haunting ruins of the **medieval cathedral** provide a startling contrast to Sir Basil Spence's neighbouring **St Michael's Cathedral** – a notable work of modern architecture, with Epstein's *St Michael and the Devil* adorning the exterior and Sutherland's tapestry, *Christ in Glory,* enhancing the inside, open daily (subject to services) 0930–1800 (Easter–Sept); 0830–1800 (July–Aug); 0930–1630 (Oct–Easter); free, but donations requested. **Visitor Centre**, *Priory Row; tel: (01203) 227597,* opens Mon–Sat 1000–1600 (Apr– Oct); Sat 1000–1600 (Nov–Mar); £1.25. In *St Michael's Hall* you can see treasures from both cathedrals.

In the cathedral quarter is the medieval **St Mary's Guildhall**, *Bayley Lane; tel: (01203) 833041,* open Sun–Thur 1000–1600 (Apr–Oct); free, but closes for civic functions. This contains excellent examples of good craftsmanship in stone, glass, timber and thread.

Modern art is well represented at the **Herbert Art Gallery and Museum**, *Jordan Well; tel: (01203) 832381,* open Mon–Sat 1000–1730, Sun 1400–1700; free. Paintings by Lowry and sculptures by Moore are among the exhibits.

Toy Museum, *Much Park St; tel: (01203) 227560,* open daily 1200–1800; £1.50. This offers toys and games from 1740 to 1951 – and a dolls' hospital.

Coventry was once the hub of Britain's motor industry, and the **Museum of British Road Transport**, *St Agnes Lane, Hales St; tel: (01203) 832425,* open daily 1000–1700; £3.30, has the largest collection of its kind, from an actual hobby horse to an audiovisual experience of *Thrust 2*: the vehicle in which Richard Noble reached the record-breaking speed of 633 mph.

Civil and military aircraft spanning 70 years are displayed at the **Midland Air Museum**, *Coventry Airport; tel: (01203) 301033,* open Mon–Sat 1030–1700, Sun, public holidays 1030–1800 (Apr–Oct); daily 1000–1630 (Nov–Mar); £3.

OUT OF TOWN

Ryton Organic Gardens, *Ryton-on-Dunsmore; tel: (01203) 303517,* open daily 1000–1700/dusk; £2.50 (halved Nov–Easter). 5 miles south-east. Ten acres of landscaped delight, in total harmony with nature, offer glorious displays.

National Motorcycle Museum, *Coventry Rd, Bickenhill, Solihull; tel: (01675) 443311,* open daily 1000–1800; £3.75. 10 miles west. Covers over 60 years of British motorcycle production, with over 700 machines in superb condition.

Royal Agricultural Society of England, *National Agricultural Centre, Stoneleigh Park; tel: (01203) 696969.* This is the venue for the **Royal Agricultural Show** (late June–early July).

LONDON–OXFORD

Oxford is an easy day trip from London. Taking the direct route described below, you can get there by car in less than 75 minutes, traffic permitting. Follow the scenic route, however, and you can also take in Royal Windsor and the picturesque Thames Valley.

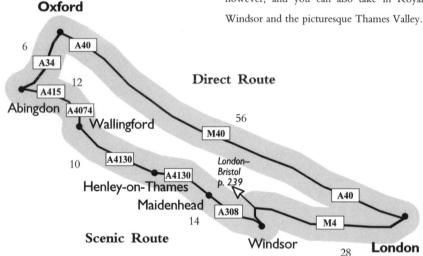

Oxford

6

A40

A34

12   **Direct Route**

A415

Abingdon   A4074

56

Wallingford   M40

10   A4130

A4130   London–Bristol *p. 239*

Henley-on-Thames

Maidenhead   A308   A40

14   M4

Scenic Route   **Windsor**   28   **London**

ROUTES

DIRECT ROUTE: 56 MILES

DIRECT ROUTE

This route of 56 miles takes 1 hr 15 mins. From Hyde Park Corner proceed north along Park Lane and at Marble Arch bear left into Bayswater Road. This is A40 west, which should be followed until it joins M40 Junction 1 after 18 miles. Continue on the motorway for 31 miles, leaving at Junction 8. Follow A40 for 4½ miles, and at Headington take A420 to the city centre.

SCENIC ROUTE

This route totals 70 miles allow 2 hours driving time. From Hyde Park Corner follow A4 west (Knightsbridge and Brompton Road) and after 8 miles, at Chiswick, join M4. Leave the motorway at Junction 6 and follow A332 into **Windsor**. From Windsor head west on A308 for 5 miles to **Maidenhead**, then follow A4 for 2 miles west, A423 for 1 mile and A4130 north-west to reach **Henley-on-Thames** after a further 6 miles. Continue west on A4130 for 10 miles to **Wallingford**. From Wallingford take A4074 north for 6 miles and at Berinsfield join A415 to reach Abingdon in 6 miles. Leave **Abingdon** on A4183 and after a mile join A34 for a further 2 miles. From South Hinksey follow signs for 3 miles to the centre of Oxford.

WINDSOR

Royal Windsor Information Centre: *24 High Street, Windsor, Berkshire SL4 1LH; tel: (01753) 852010,* open Mon–Sat 0930–1800, Sun 1000–1730 (Apr–Oct); daily 1000–1600 (Nov–Mar). DP SHS services offered; local bed-booking (latest 15 mins before closing; fee £2.50), BABA (fee £4). National Heritage passes sold. *Royal Windsor Visitor and Accommodation Guide* is £2.

GETTING AROUND

Most of the town's attractions are within walking distance of the centre. The major local operator is **Beeline**, based at **Brunel Bus Station**, *Slough, tel: (01753) 524144.* Bus services are reduced after 2000 and there are very few after 2200.

The main **taxi** rank is on *Thames St* (outside the castle). Registered taxi companies include: **Five Star**, *tel: (01753) 858888*; **Eton Taxis**, *tel: (01753) 866576*; and **Windsor Radio Cars**, *tel: (01753) 841414*.

ACCOMMODATION

Windsor is an easy day trip from London, but does offer a choice of accommodation. As well as a small range of hotels, there are plenty of b&b establishments and a few pubs offering accommodation in the centre. The majority of cheaper accommodation is located in the centre and the western suburbs. It is always advisable to book ahead in summer, essential during Royal Ascot (mid–late June) and the Royal Windsor Horse Show (mid May). **Accommodation hotline**: *tel: (01753) 841746* – free booking service available 7 days a week. Chain hotels in Windsor (and the immediate area) include: *CM, Cp, Ct, Gr* and *Hd*.

Oakley Court, *Windsor Rd, Water Oakley, SL4 5UR; tel: (01753) 609988;* *fax: (01753) 37011.* Victorian manor in 35 acres beside the River Thames. The public areas are spacious and relaxing. Pricey.

HI: *Edgworth House, Mill Lane, tel: (01753) 861710.* The TIC can provide full information on the two **campsites** not far from Windsor. The closest is **Amerden Camping and Caravan Site** (see Maidenhead, below).

SIGHTSEEING

Guide Friday, *tel: (01789) 294466*, operate **bus tours** in open-top double-deckers; £6 for a hop-on hop-off ticket that is valid all day. **Boat trips** (both cruises and hire your own boat) are offered by **French Brothers**, *tel: (01753) 851900*, and **Salters Bros**, *tel: (01753) 865832.* **Guided walks** are **Windsor Guide Services**, *tel: (01753) 852010.* The **White Bus Service** operates good routes for sightseeing.

The **Town & Crown Exhibition**, *above the TIC; tel: (01753) 852010*, open daily 1000–1600/1700; £1, presents an audiovisual history of Windsor and Eton. Picturesque Windsor grew in Victorian times and many of its buildings date from that period. It is completely dominated by **Windsor Castle**, *tel: (01753) 831118.* State functions mean that opening times can vary, so always check, but normally the castle is open daily 1000–1600/1700; £9.80 Mon–Sat, £7.70 Sun. England's largest palace has been a royal residence for more than 900 years. The Queen and her family make fairly frequent visits and it does have a lived-in atmosphere. The state rooms are magnificent (some recently refurbished after an extensive fire).

Opposite the castle, **The Dungeon**, *Thames St; tel: (01753) 868000*, open daily 1000–1730; £4.50, depicts the story of crime and punishment since the 13th century.

275

OUT OF TOWN

Savill Garden, *Wick Lane, Englefield Green, Egham, tel: (01753) 860222*, open daily 1000–1800 (Mar–Oct); 1000–1600 (Nov–Feb); £3.50. 6 miles, on the eastern boundary of Great Park. The beautiful garden consists of over 35 acres of woodland and borders, offering something spectacular and colourful whatever the season.

Dorney Court, *Dorney; tel: (01628) 604638*, open Mon–Thur 1300–1630 (July–Aug); May Day Bank Holiday Sun–Mon 1400–1730; £4. 5 miles northwest. This fine Tudor manor house, dating from 1440, includes family portraits spanning four centuries.

Ascot Racecourse, *Ascot; tel: (01344) 876456*; £5–£28; 7 miles south, is famous as the home of **Royal Ascot** – a race meeting that dates from 1711. It is one highlight of the London 'Season' and people travel for miles to see the hats worn on Gold Cup day, an occasion elegantly portrayed in *My Fair Lady*.

Eton is home to the famous public school founded in 1440 by Henry VI. **Eton College**, *High St, Eton; tel: (01753) 671177*, opening times vary according to term times. Admission £2.50; tours £3.50–£6.50. Across the Thames from central Windsor; 15 mins' walk – or Guide Friday tour bus.

Legoland Windsor, *Winkfield Rd; tel: (0990) 626375*, open daily 1000–1800/ dusk (Mar–mid July, Sept), daily 1000–2000 (mid July–Aug); £15. The park is closed when capacity is reached, so it's best to book in advance (by credit card) to ensure you get in. 2 miles south of the centre, to the west of the Great Park, it's a wonderful place for children.

Thorpe Park, *Staines Rd, Chertsey, tel: (01932) 569393*, open daily 1000–1800 (Easter–Oct); £11.25. Water-based theme park, with rides.

MAIDENHEAD

TIC: *Central Library, St Ives Rd, Maidenhead, Berks, SL6 1QU; tel: (01628) 781110*, open all year. Services offered: local accommodation bookings and BABA.

ACCOMMODATION

Boulters Lock Hotel, *Boulters Island, Maidenhead; SL6 8PE; tel: (01628) 21291, fax: (01628) 26048*. Moderate–expensive, maximum double room rate being £150.

Fredrick's Hotel and Restaurant, *Shoppenhangers Rd, Maidenhead SL6 2PZ; tel: (01628) 35934; fax: (01628) 771054*. Luxuriously furnished rooms in a quiet location near the M4's Junction 8/9 and is handy for Heathrow. Expensive.

Walton Cottage Hotel, *Marlow Rd, Maidenhead SL6 7LT; tel: (01628) 24394; fax (01628) 773851*. Also offers serviced luxury apartments and suites with kitchenettes. Moderate–expensive.

Clifton Guest House, *2 Craufurd Rise, Maidenhead SL6 1LR; tel/fax: (01628) 23572*. Budget. **Gables End**, *4 Gables Close, Maidenhead SL6 8QD; tel: (01628) 39630*. Non-smoking b&b. Budget. **Wylie Cottage**, *School Lane, Cookham, nr Maidenhead SL6 9QJ; tel: (01628) 520106*. Non-smoking household with garden. Budget.

Amerden Caravan Park, *Old Marsh Lane, Dorney Park, Maidenhead SL6 0EE; tel: (01628) 27461; fax: (01628) 27921*.

SIGHTSEEING

The main attraction for holidaymakers is the River Thames. On bright summer days **Boulters Lock** is crowded with onlookers as pleasure boats move up and down the river. Less than half a mile away the road bridge over the Thames is an elegant 18th-century stone structure, and less than a quarter of a mile is the red brick bridge which carries the railway over the Thames. Brunel built it with only two arches spanning the water, though narrower arches extend on the banks. Each span is 128 ft wide – the widest Europe had seen – and experts predicted it would collapse. That was in 1838, and the bridge is still in constant use.

Courage Shire Horse Centre, *Cherry Garden Lane, Maidenhead Thicket, Maidenhead SL6 3QD; tel: (01628) 824848*, open daily 1030–1700 (Mar–Oct), last admission 1600; £2.80. A dozen shire horses, retired from pulling brewery drays, give visitors rides around the site. A saddler can be seen at work most days. Bygones museum, aviary and audiovisual presentations.

Stanley Spencer Gallery, *Kings Hall, High St, Cookham, nr Maidenhead; tel: (01628) 520890*, open daily 1030–1730 (Easter–Oct), Sat and Sun 1100–1700 (Nov–Easter); 50p. Some of Spencer's paintings in his very individual style, including *Christ Preaching at Cookham Regatta* are exhibited, and there are also some of his personal possessions. Spencer, who was Cookham's most famous resident, died in 1959, aged 68.

HENLEY-ON-THAMES

TIC: *Town Hall, Market Place, Henley-on-Thames, Oxfordshire RG9 2AQ; tel: (01491) 578034*, open daily 1000–1900 (Apr–Sept); daily 1000–1600 (Oct–Mar). DP SHS services offered; local bed-booking (fee £3 or 10% of first night), BABA (latest 30 mins before closing; fee 10% of total stay). An accommodation guide, *Henley-on-Thames*, is free.

GETTING AROUND

Town maps (25p) and free transport maps are available from the TIC. Public transport is good in the centre, but patchy to outlying areas, and reduced in the evenings and on Sun. The main **taxi** rank is in *Falaise Sq.*, near the entrance to the *Greys Rd* car park.

ACCOMMODATION

There are only a few hotels in the town, but several pubs and inns offer accommodation in the centre and there are plenty of b&b establishments in the area. It is generally easy to book on arrival, except during Henley Royal Regatta. Two **campsites** only half a mile from town are: **Swiss Farm International Camping**, *Marlow Rd; tel: (01491) 573419*; and **Four Oaks Caravan Site**, *Marlow Rd; tel: (01491) 572312*.

EVENTS

Henley Royal Regatta, *tel: (01491) 572153* (last week June–first week July) is an international rowing event and part of the fashionable London 'Season'. **Henley Festival of Music and the Arts**, *tel: (01491) 411353* (early July), offers orchestral concerts, cabaret acts, jazz, dancing, marching bands and fireworks.

SIGHTSEEING

Boat trips are available with **Hobbs & Sons**, *Station Rd; tel: (01491) 572035*.

Henley-on-Thames is full of picturesque streets – like *New St* and *Hart St* – with delightful 18th- and 19th-century buildings. The **Town Hall, St Mary's Church** and 18th-century **Henley Bridge**, with its five arches, are of both architectural and historical interest. Nearby houses of note include 17th-century **Fawley Court**, *Marlow Road; tel: (01491) 574917*, open Wed–Thur, Sun 1400–1700 (Mar– Oct); £3. 1 mile north. This was designed by Sir Christopher Wren and stands in grounds landscaped by Capability Brown.

277

OUT OF TOWN

Greys Court (NT), *Rotherfield Greys; tel: (01491) 628529.* House open Mon, Wed, Fri 1400–1800 (Apr–Sept); £4.20 (house and garden). 3 miles west. The house was begun in Tudor times and is surrounded by beautiful gardens include a wisteria walk, a white garden and an ornamental vegetable garden.

Stonor House, *Stonor Park; tel: (01491) 638587,* open 1400–1730, but days vary: Sun, public holidays (Apr–Sept); Wed (May–Oct); Thur (July–Aug); Sat (Aug); £4 (house, chapel and gardens). 5 miles north-west. The ancestral home of the Stonors since it was built (*c.*1190), the house contains family collections that include rare furniture, tapestries and works of art. The medieval chapel is still in use.

WALLINGFORD

TIC: *Town Hall, St Martins St, Wallingford, OX10 AL; tel: (01491) 826972,* open all year. Services offered: BABA and local accommodation reservations.

ACCOMMODATION

Springs, *Wallingford Rd, North Stoke, OX10 6BE; tel: (01491) 836687; fax: (01491) 836877.* Nearly 40 comfortable rooms, many with balconies, in late 19th-century hotel. Expensive.

George Hotel, *High St, Wallingford OX10 0BS; tel: (01491) 836665; fax: (01491) 825359.* Formerly a coaching inn where according to legend Dick Turpin stayed. Moderate–expensive.

Ford's Farm, *Ewelme, Wallingford OX10 6HU; tel: (01491) 839272.* Accommodation on working farm, 4 miles from Wallingford. Budget.

SIGHTSEEING

Wallingford Museum, *Flint House, High St; tel: (01491) 835065.* £1.75, open

Tues–Fri 1400–1700, Sat 1030–1700 (Mar–Nov), also Sun and Bank Holiday Mon 1400–1700 (July and Aug). The museum, in part of a medieval hall house, contains a River Thames exhibit and presents the history of the 13th-century castle, now in ruins.

ABINGDON

TIC: *Abbey House, Abbey Close, Abingdon, OX14 3JD; tel: (01235) 522711,* open year-round. Services offered: local room reservations and BABA.

ACCOMMODATION

Abingdon Lodge, *Marcham Rd, Abingdon OX14 1TZ; tel: (01235) 553456; fax: (01235) 554117.* Modern hotel with good atmosphere. Moderate.

Upper Reaches, *Thames St, Abingdon OX14 3JA; tel: (01235) 522311; fax: (01235) 555182.* Forte Heritage hotel on a Thames island near Benedictine abbey ruins, using original abbey outbuildings to good effect. Moderate.

SIGHTSEEING

Abingdon is a pleasant town on the Thames with riverside walks and a mainly pedestrianised centre.

Abingdon Museum, *County Hall, Market Place, Abingdon OX14 3HA; tel: (01235) 523703),* open Tues–Sun 1100–1700 (summer), 1100–1600 (winter); free. Archways lead to the open ground floor market hall and the museum is above. The county hall was built in the late 17th century by master mason Christopher Kempster, who had worked for Sir Christopher Wren in London. As well as depicting local history, the museum stages regular events and exhibitions. The Southern Arts contemporary craft collection is housed here, and is available for study by appointment.

NEWCASTLE

A busy commercial city, Newcastle lies at the heart of a sprawling conurbation along the Tyne. It has more to offer than appears at first sight: its Norman castle, medieval quayside, fine 19th-century streets and squares and many museums, plus the north-east's best shops, repay at least a day's visit.

TOURIST INFORMATION

City and Tourist Information Service, *City Library, Princess Square, Newcastle upon Tyne NE99 1DX; tel: (0191) 261 0610/ 261 0691*, open Mon, Thur 0930–2000, Tues–Wed, Fri 0930–1700, Sat 0900–1700; closed public holidays Sat–Mon. DP services offered; local bed-booking (latest 15 mins before closing; refundable deposit of 10%), BABA (latest 30 mins before closing; refundable deposit of 10%). Theatres, tours, travel and events booked, YHA/HI membership and Great British Heritage Pass sold. Main city guide and mini guide free.

TIC: **Central Station**, *main concourse; tel: (0191) 230 0030*, open Mon–Fri 1000–2000, Sat 0900–1700, Sun 1000–1600 (June–Sept); Mon–Sat 1000–1700 (Oct– May). Same services offered as the main TIC.

ARRIVING AND DEPARTING

A1, the major north–south route, skirts to the west of the city centre, but there are well-marked link roads to the centre from all directions.

Rail Station: **Central**, *Neville St*, is just half a mile from the city centre, an easy walk, or take the metro. There is a taxi rank and the station has a branch of the TIC.

North Sea ferry services arrive at the **International Ferry Terminal**, *Royal Quays*, 7 miles east of the city centre, with bus connections to and from Central Station. For services to Bergen and Stavanger in Norway: **Colour Line**, *tel: (0191) 296 1313*. For Amsterdam, the Netherlands; Hamburg, Germany; and Gothenburg, Sweden: **Scandinavian Seaways**, *tel: (0191) 293 6262*.

GETTING AROUND

Most attractions are within walking distance of the city centre. Free city and transport maps are available from the TIC. Network tickets, which cover the metro and all buses in the area (not just the city services), include a **Day Rover** (£3.30) and a **weekly ticket** (£11.10).

There is an efficient metro system (underground in the centre) and several bus companies which, between them, cover all areas. Frequency is reduced in the evenings and on Sun, with last services 2300–2330. **General bus and metro enquiries**, *tel: (0191) 232 5325*. The main **taxi** rank is at Central Station.

STAYING IN NEWCASTLE

Accommodation
Accommodation hotline: *tel: (0191) 261 1405*.

There are a reasonable number of hotels in the middle range, but not much in the way of b&b or pub accommoda-

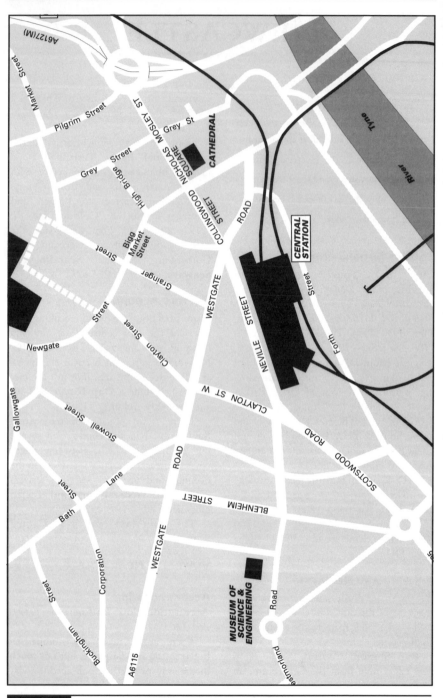

tion. Cheaper accommodation is situated a couple of miles out of the city centre, in the suburbs of Jesmond, Heaton, Fenham and Spital Tongues. Accommodation is generally easy to find on arrival, except during university graduation (July and Nov) and the Great North Run (Sept).

Hotel chains include *BW, CI, Cp, FP, MC, Mn, SW* and *Th*. University accommodation is available (July–Sept); *tel: (0191) 222 8150*.

The Copthorne-Newcastle, *The Close, Quayside, NE1 3RT; tel: (0191) 222 0333*. A large, modern hotel with excellent facilities, restaurant/coffee shops and an attractive riverside location; expensive.

Ferncourt Hotel, *34 Osborne Rd, Jesmond NE2 2AJ; tel: (0191) 281 5418; fax: 212 0783*. Handy for Hadrian's Wall and other attractions, the hotel has 23 rooms and a restaurant specialising in Texan and Mexican dishes; moderate.

Newcastle-Marriott Hotel, *Metro-Centre, Gateshead NE11 9XF; tel: (0191) 493 2233; fax: 493 2030*. Located opposite MetroCentre, the hotel has an indoor heated pool, lounge bar and restaurant; moderate.

Novotel-Newcastle, *Ponteland Rd, Kenton NE3 3HZ; tel: (0191) 214 0303*. An indoor swimming pool and restaurant/coffee shop are among the amenities; moderate.

HI: *107 Jesmond Rd, NE2 1NJ; tel: (0191) 222 8150*. The closest **campsites** are: **Lizard Lane Campsite**, *Marsden, South Shields; tel: (0191) 454 4982*, 10 miles south-east; **Sandhaven Campsite**, *Bents Park Rd, South Shields; tel: (0191) 454 5594*, 10 miles south-east; and **Derwent Park Campsite**, *Rowlands Gill; tel: (01207) 543383*, 6 miles south-west.

Eating and Drinking

The TIC has an excellent *Eating Out* guide for 50p, detailing Newcastle's wide range of eating places, including a good selection of international cuisine. Good areas are *Stowell St* (for Chinatown), *Bigg Market* and *Quayside*. Newcastle Brown Ale is a local speciality.

Sachins, *Forth Banks; tel: (0191) 261 9035*, open Mon–Sat 1200–1415, 1800–2315; moderate–pricey. Aficionados of Indian food will want to try this restaurant, which is renowned for its specialist Punjabi dishes.

Leela's, *20 Dean St; tel: (0191) 230 1261*; moderate. Vegetarians will find a good choice among a range of dishes from southern India.

Seafood is the speciality at **21 Queen Street**; *tel: (0191) 222 0755*; pricey. One of Newcastle's leading restaurants.

Communications

The main **post office**, *Sidgate, Eldon Square*, opens Mon–Fri 0900–1730, Sat 0900–1230. Poste restante facilities are available.

Money

There is a **Thomas Cook bureau de change** at *Midland Bank, 77 Grainger St*.

ENTERTAINMENT AND EVENTS

Entertainment leaflets, *Paint it Red* and *Northern Review* (both free), are available from the TIC and some other outlets.

Newcastle has five theatres, the most important being the **Theatre Royal**, *Grey St; tel: (0191) 232 2061*, which hosts the Royal Shakespeare Company in Sept–Oct. **City Hall**, *Northumberland Rd; tel: (0191) 261 2606*, is the main venue for classical music, while **Newcastle Arena**, *4 Arena Way; tel: (0191) 260 5000*, hosts a variety of musical events, as well as sporting concerts. There is an abundance of other live music, of all types, in the many

281

lively pubs and clubs (see the TIC's free *Nightlife* listing).

If you are visiting in June, don't miss **The Hoppings**, *Town Moor*, which is Europe's largest travelling fair – over a mile long (1 mile from the city centre). The annual **Great North Run** (mid-Sept) is a half-marathon from Newcastle to South Shields, one of the biggest fun-runs in Europe.

SHOPPING

Newcastle is a regional shopping centre for the north-east, with *Eldon Square, Eldon Garden* and *Monument Mall* forming a large shopping area in the city centre, featuring many department stores and chain stores, specialist shops and boutiques. Easily accessible by bus or metro. The most popular **street market** (of which there are a few) is **Quayside Market**, open every Sun 0930–1400. **Blackfriars Craft Centre**, *Monk St*, is a 13th-century Dominican friary with a variety of locally produced goods. Serious shoppers shouldn't miss the **MetroCentre** at Gateshead, said to be Europe's largest shopping mall; frequent trains from Newcastle (a 7 min journey) or 16 mins by bus100.

SIGHTSEEING

For an introduction to the city, there are **bus tours** and **guided walks** with **City Guides**, *tel: 261 0610*. **Boat trips** are offered by **River Tyne Cruises**, *tel: (0191) 251 5920*, and **Nexus**, *tel: (0191) 454 8183*, starting from *Quayside*.

Many of Newcastle's oldest buildings are found near the river. **Sandhill** is the historic heart of the city and **Bessie Surtees House** (EH), *41–44 Sandhill, Quayside; tel: (0191) 261 1585*, open

Mon–Fri 1000–1600; free, consists of two rare 16th- and 17th-century merchants' houses.

From the 19th-century battlements of the old Norman **Castle Keep**, *Castle Garth, St Nicholas St; tel: (0191) 232 7938*, open Tues–Sun 0930–1730 (1630 Oct–Mar); £1.80, there are good views of the six bridges across the Tyne: the two most famous are Robert Stephenson's double-decker **High Level Bridge** (1849), for both rail and road, and the 1920s single-span **Tyne Bridge**, almost half a mile long.

A delicate lantern tower from 1470 is the outstanding feature of **St Nicholas Cathedral**, *St Nicholas Square; tel: (0191) 232 1939*, open Mon–Fri 0700–1900, Sat 0800–1600, Sun outside services; free.

The north-east's prime art collection, including works by Joshua Reynolds, is housed in the **Laing Art Gallery**, *Higham Place; tel: (0191) 232 7734*, open Mon–Fri 1000–1730, Sat 1000–1630, Sun 1430–1730; free.

Many of the finds from Hadrian's Wall are displayed in the **Museum of Antiquities**, *Newcastle University; tel: (0191) 222 7844*, open Mon–Sat 1000–1700; free. **Newcastle Discovery**, *Blandford House, West Blandford Square; tel: (0191) 232 6789*, open Mon–Sat 1000–1700, Sun 1400–1700; free, has a plethora of galleries aimed at families, with subjects ranging from football to inventors.

Hancock Museum, *Claremont Rd; tel: (0191) 222 7418*, open Mon–Sat 1000–1700, Sun 1400–1700; £1.95. Don't miss the hands-on environmental gallery *Living Planet*; dinosaurs and ancient Egypt are among other subjects covered plus a collection of over 150,000 insects.

NEWCASTLE– LAKE DISTRICT

Hadrian's Wall, marking the northern limit of the Roman empire, is the major attraction over much of this route, but it is impossible to ignore the stunning beauty of the upper Tyne Valley and the fells of the North Pennines, often exceeding 2000 ft, to say nothing of the last leg of the trip which leads right into the heart of the Lake District. We offer two ways of making the journey, both scenic, though the second one provides more opportunity to examine Hadrian's Wall.

Scenic Route

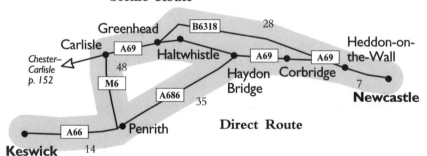

283

Direct Route

DIRECT ROUTE: 77 MILES

ROUTES

DIRECT ROUTE

■➡ This route covers 77 miles in 1 hr 45 mins. From central Newcastle follow A167 west for 2 miles, then A1 for a further 2 miles and bear right on to A69 west for 24 miles via **Corbridge** to Haydon Bridge. Follow A686 south-west for 35 miles to Penrith and continue on A66 for 14 miles to Keswick.

THE WALL ROUTE

■➡ Leave Newcastle as above and continue on A69 for 7 miles to Heddon-on-the-Wall, then follow B6318, rejoining A69 at Greenhead after 28 miles. Head east a couple of miles along the A69 to reach **Haltwhistle**. Continue on A69 to reach Carlisle (see p. 143) in 17 miles . From Carlisle you can travel south for 17 miles to Penrith on M6 or A6 – the two highways run more or less side by side (there is a service area on the motorway). Penrith is the north-east gateway to the Lake District and from here A66 travels west to reach Keswick in 17 miles.

CORBRIDGE

TIC: *Hill St, Corbridge NE45 5AA; tel: (01434) 632815.* Seasonal opening. BABA.

ACCOMMODATION

Dilson Mill, *Corbridge NE45 5QZ; tel: (01434) 633493.* Listed commended house, no smoking. Moderate.

Angel Inn, *Main St, Corbridge NE45 5LA; tel: (01434) 632119.* Commended inn. Children welcome. Moderate.

The Hayes Guest House, *Newcastle Rd, Corbridge NE45 5LP; tel: (01434) 632010.* Budget.

The Cottage, *Corbridge. Contact Mrs J. Coates, Southcroft, Ovington NE42 6EE; tel: (01661) 830651.* Self-catering.

SIGHTSEEING

Corbridge Roman Site and Museum (EH), *Hadrian's Wall, Corbridge; tel: (01434) 632349,* open daily 1000–1800 (Apr–Oct) Wed–Sun 1000–1600 (Nov–Mar); admission charge. Excavated remains provide evidence of a military depot and a town (Corstopitum), which in Roman times was on the main York–Scotland road.

Aydon Castle (EH), *Corbridge; tel: (01434) 632450,* open daily 1000–1300 and 1400–1800 (Easter–Oct); £1.80. 1 mile north-east. The 13th century fortified manor became a farmhouse in the 17th century and is well preserved – and in surroundings of great natural beauty.

OUT OF TOWN

Chesters Roman Fort (EH), *Chollerford; tel: (01434) 681379,* open daily 0930–1800/dusk (Apr–Sept); 1000–1600 (Oct–Mar); £2.50. 11 miles north-west. This is also beautifully sited and an exceptionally well-preserved example of a typical Roman fort; features include a Roman bath-

house and a museum displaying local archaeological finds.

HALTWHISTLE

TIC: In summer: *Church Hall, Main St, Haltwhistle NE49 0BE;* winter: *Swimming and Leisure Centre, Greencroft, Haltwhistle; tel: (year-round) (01434) 322002.*

ACCOMMODATION

Broomshaw Hill Farm, *Willia Rd, Haltwhistle NE49 9NP; tel/fax: (01434) 320866.* 18th century farmhouse; footpath to Hadrian's Wall. Budget.

Centre of Britain Hotel and Restaurant, *Haltwhistle NE49 0BH; tel: (01434) 322422.* Moderate.

Ashcroft, *Lantys Lonnen, Haltwhistle NE49 0DA; tel: (01434) 320213.* Vicarage building, elegantly furnished. Budget–moderate.

Camping and Caravanning Club Site, *Burnfoot Park Village, Haltwhistle NE49 0JP; tel: (01434) 320106.* Pitches for 60 touring caravans.

SIGHTSEEING

Housesteads Roman Fort and Museum (NT/EH), *Hadrian's Wall, Hexham NE47 6NN; tel: (01434) 344363,* open daily 1000–1800/dusk (Apr–Sept); 1000–1600 (Oct–Mar); £2.50. 6 miles north-east. Best preserved of the Roman forts, the site contains the only visible example of a Roman hospital in Britain and remarkably well-preserved Roman latrines with flush system. The most popular spot along Hadrian's Wall, for its dramatic ridge site, outstanding views and the walk along the wall to Steel Rigg.

Roman Army Museum, *Walltown, near Haltwhistle; tel: (01697) 747485,* open daily 100–1700/1830 dependin on season (Feb–Oct); £2.80. 3 miles north-west. Here the life of a soldier in the Roman

Hadrian's Wall

The most important monument built by the Romans in Britain is 73 miles long, nearly 2000 years old and a magnificent sight. Along its route, from Wallsend-on-Tyne in the east to Bowness-on-Solway in the west, are many features of interest – milecastles, turrets, forts, bathhouses, even Roman flushing latrines. Much of it is on the crags of the Whin Sill, a difficult and exposed part.

It is believed that the Emperor Hadrian ordered the building of the wall after he visited Britain in AD 122. A Roman biographer of Hadrian suggested it was 'to separate the Romans from the Barbarians'. But the most generally agreed theory is that Hadrian wanted to mark the northern boundary of his great empire.

Whatever the reason, legions of Roman soldiers were despatched to the unfamiliar and sometimes bitterly cold expanses of north-eastern England to carry out the sophisticated engineering project. Auxiliary forces from Germany, Belgium and the Balkans were brought in.

Sentries and guards kept watch from the milecastles and turrets, keeping a check on who and what was crossing the frontier. Forts built along the wall strengthened control and served as crossing points. Civilian settlements grew up around them.

Ditches were dug on either side of the wall. The entire project was completed in six years. Today, much of the wall is no longer visible and there are gaps where stone has been stolen for building use, but some sectors survive and the entire course is well documented. Along the route are museums, visitor centres, picnic sites and car parks – there is sometimes a small charge for parking.

One of the most memorable views is from the Sewingshields milecastle (between Chesters and Haltwhistle), where the wall stretches miles to the east of Housesteads. Near Cawfields, around Winshields Crag, is one of the most rugged sections. Heddon-on-the-Wall, just west of Newcastle upon Tyne, has another fine stretch.

At Carlisle, the award-winning Tullie House Museum has a wealth of knowledge to convey about the wall, and features the Roman town of Luguvalium.

The most spectacular part of the wall for hardy walkers is a 12 mile stretch in Northumberland National Park (Sewingshields to Greenhead) – pretty rough going in parts. Much of this is owned by the National Trust. Guided walks are held regularly.

The National Park centre at Once Brewed; *tel: (01434) 344396*, open daily (mid Mar–end Oct) interprets the wall's central sector.

Hadrian's Wall Tourism Partnership publishes an informative free leaflet, *A Visitor's Guide to Hadrian's Wall*. It has a map, details sites along the wall and gives information on the Hadrian's Wall Bus, which operates in summer, and on parts accessible by train. The leaflet is available from more than a dozen TICs along the wall's route and from the **Northumbria Tourist Board**, *Aykley Heads, Durham DH1 5UX; tel: (0191) 375300*. Please send stamped addressed envelope.

285

army in the garrisons of Hadrian's Wall is outlined through models, reconstructions, displays and artefacts.

Vindolanda Fort, *Chesterholm, Bardon Mill; tel: (01434) 344277*, open daily 1000–1700/1830 depending on season (Mar–Oct); site open (museum closed) 1000–1600 (Nov–Feb); £3.50. 5 miles north. As well as the remains of a chain of forts and civilian settlements, there is a museum containing some unusual artefacts from everyday Roman life.

NORWICH

Norwich is a beautiful and ancient city with a proud tradition of independence. From St James Hill, above the city on Mousehold Heath, the buildings of old Norwich can be seen clustered around the cathedral, within the circle of the old city walls and the river. The streets, alleys and many medieval churches illustrate the long-standing prosperity of Norwich. The city is also an ideal touring centre for the Norfolk countryside.

TOURIST INFORMATION

TIC: *The Guildhall, Gaol Hill, Norwich NR2 1NA; tel: (01603) 666071*, open Mon–Sat 1000–1700 (June–Sept); Mon–Fri 1000–1600, Sat 1000–1400 (Oct–May). Services offered: local bed-booking service (fee £2.50 and 10% of first night refundable deposit) and BABA (fee £2.50 and 10% of first night refundable deposit). National Express and Anglia Plus rail tickets and YHA/HI membership sold. Guided walking tours booked.

The guide *Norwich and the Norfolk Countryside* is available free and includes accommodation listings.

ARRIVING AND DEPARTING

With the A11 forming the major route from London, Norwich stands at the crossroads of the north–south A140 and the east–west A47. The A147 forms a ring road with excellent links to the city centre.

GETTING AROUND

The majority of the city's attractions are within walking distance of the town centre, except for the **Sainsbury Centre**.

The bulk of bus services are operated by **Eastern Counties** from the **central bus station**, *Surrey St; tel: (01603) 622800*. Information on all the county's bus servicesis available from **Norfolk Bus Information Centre (NORBIC)**, *Advice Arcade, 4 Guildhall Hill; (freephone) tel: (0500) 626116*, open Mon–Sat 0830–1700.

The main **taxi** ranks are at *Guildhall Hill* and Thorpe Station.

STAYING IN NORWICH

Accommodation and Food

Norwich has a good range of accommodation of all types, throughout the city and in the outlying areas. There are several budget hotels in the city centre and a wide choice of b & b establishments, mostly on the outskirts. Some farmhouses offer accommodation in the surrounding countryside.

Hotel chains in Norwich include *BW, Ct, FP, Ja, Mn* and *ST*.

HI: *112 Turner Rd; tel: (01603) 627647; fax: (01603) 629075*. There are also **YMCA**, *48 St Giles St; tel: (01603) 620269*, and **YWCA**, *61 Bethel St; tel: (01603) 622059*, both in the city centre.

The closest **campsite** is: **Lakenham Camping and Caravanning Club Site**, *Martineau Lane, Lakenham; tel: (01603) 620060*, 2 miles south.

The city centre has a wide selection of eating establishments in all price ranges.

Communications

The main **post office**, *Castle Mall*, opens

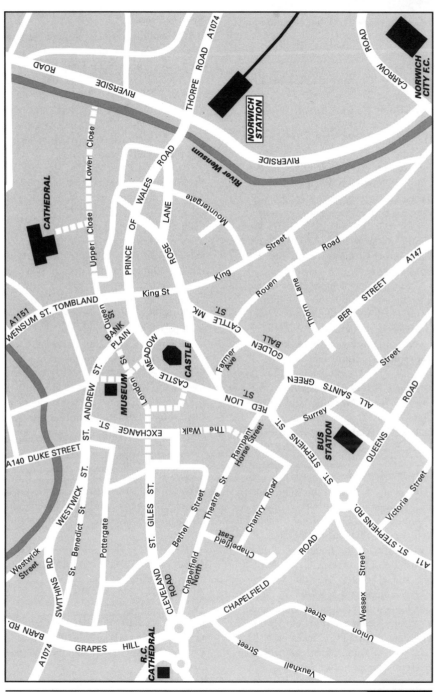

Mon–Sat 0900–1730, but closes on public holidays.

Money

There are **Thomas Cook bureaux de change** at *Midland Bank, 18 London St,* and also at *Norwich Airport.*

ENTERTAINMENT AND EVENTS

Theatres in Norwich include: **Maddermarket Theatre**, *St Johns Alley; tel: (01603) 620917;* **Norwich Puppet Theatre**, *St James, Whitefriars; tel: (01603) 629921;* **Sewell Barn Theatre**, *Constitution Hill; tel: (01603) 764764;* and **Theatre Royal**, *Theatre St; tel: (01603) 630000.* **Norwich City Football Club** is on *Carrow Rd; tel: (01603) 761661.*

Norwich has a number of nightclubs and discos, mostly located in the city centre; it also offers several arts centres and a wide range of leisure facilities.

Major annual events include the **Royal Norfolk Agricultural Show**, *Royal Norfolk Showground* (June); **The Lord Mayor's Street Procession**, in the city centre (July); **Norfolk and Norwich Arts Festival**, various venues (Oct); and **CAMRA (Campaign for Real Ale) Beer Festival**, *St Andrew's Hall* (Oct).

SHOPPING

The main shopping streets in Norwich are *St Benedict* for specialist clothes and furniture stores; *Elm Hill* and *Tombland* for craft shops, bookshops and jewellers; *St Giles St* for antiques and bookshops; *London St* for clothes and jewellers; **Castle Mall**, a 7-acre site adjacent to Norwich Castle, with over 75 shops; and *Magdalen St*, the oldest and longest shopping street in the city.

A large **open-air market**, *Market Place* (adjacent to the TIC), takes place Mon–Sat, with a wide variety of stalls selling everything from books to cheese.

SIGHTSEEING

BBG walking tours around historic Norwich can be booked at the TIC, and last about 1½ hrs; £2.25. Tours depart from the TIC at 1100 and/or 1430 Mon–Sat (mid May–Sept); 1100 Sat (Apr–mid May, Oct); 1100 Sun (June–July, Sept); and 1100 Easter Sun–Mon. There are also evening tours at 1700 on selected days (June–Aug). Ask the TIC for details.

Boat trips of 1–3 hrs are run by **Southern River Steamers**, *tel: (01603) 624051*, departing daily from Elm Hill Quay and Foundry Bridge Quay.

Norwich was already an important town at the time of the Norman conquest and, during most of the Middle Ages, rivalled London and York in size and wealth. This has left a heritage of medieval buildings (including the cathedral, the castle and over 30 fine churches) which is unsurpassed by any British city.

Norwich Cathedral, *Cathedral Close; tel: (01603) 764385*, open daily 0730–1800 (mid Sept–mid May); daily 0730–1900 (mid May–mid Sept); free. Founded in 1096, the cathedral has fine decorative work in the cloisters (1297–1430) and carved 15th-century choir stalls; the Visitor Centre offers audiovisual displays. The spire is the second highest in Britain.

The Riverside Walk, along the River Wensum to Carrow Bridge, passes **Cow Tower**, formerly a river tollhouse and prison, **Pull's Ferry**, the 15th-century

Colour section (i): Aldeburgh, Suffolk (p. 337); a view of Lindisfarne Castle (p. 340). (ii) Beamish Open Air Museum (p. 265); Windsor Castle (p. 275). (iii) The cloisters of Salisbury Cathedral (p. 311); Scarborough (p. 317–318). (iv) York Minister viewed from the city's side streets (p. 331).

water-gate to the cathedral close (Pull was the last ferryman), and the medieval **Bishop Bridge**. *Elm Hill* is a winding cobbled street with antique and craft shops, leading to the area next to the cathedral, **Tombland**, whose name has nothing to do with graves, but comes from an old word for market.

Norwich Castle provides an example of Norman military architecture second only to the Tower of London and houses the **Castle Museum**, *Castle Meadow; tel: (01603) 223624,* open Mon–Sat 1000–1700, Sun 1400–1700 (but Sun may be discontinued, so check); £2.30 (Oct–June), £3.10 (July–Sept), this includes admission to the Norfolk Regimental Museum (see below). Castle Museum has one of the country's finest regional collections of natural history, archaeology and art, the eclectic exhibits ranging from Celtic gold to a polar bear, from teapots to Egyptian mummies. A **battlement and dungeon tour** reflects the nine-century history of the castle; £1.50; to book, *tel: (01603) 223628.* The **Royal Norfolk Regimental Museum**, *Market Ave; tel: (01603) 223649,* open same hours as Castle Museum; £1.20, follows the regiment in peace and war – mostly on overseas tours of duty.

The church of **St Peter Mancroft**, near the market place, was founded in 1430 and is an exceptionally beautiful and imposing example of the Perpendicular Gothic style. Facing the church is the **Guildhall**, dating from the same period, which was the seat of the city's council until **City Hall**, now dominating the market place, was built in 1938.

After 500 years of obscurity, it is now possible to enter **Dragon Hall**, *115–23 King St; tel: (01603) 663922,* open Mon–Sat 1000–1600 (Apr–Oct); Mon–Fri 1000–1600 (Nov–Mar); £1, and to admire

the magnificent medieval timber-framed great hall and intricate carvings.

Norwich has a good selection of art galleries and museums. These include the **Assembly House**, *Theatre St; tel: (01603) 626402,* open Mon–Sat 1000–2000 (sometimes later); free. This is a fine Georgian house (1754). **Norwich Gallery**, *Norwich School of Art and Design, St George's St; tel: (01603) 610561,* opens for exhibitions only; free. **Bridewell Museum**, *Bridewell Alley; tel: (01603) 667228,* open public holidays, Tues–Sat 1000–1700 (Easter–Sept); £1.20. Once a prison, this is now a fun museum crammed with everyday items. A former (15th-century) church is **St Peter Hungate Church Museum and Brass Rubbing Centre**, *Princes St; tel: (01603) 667231,* open Mon–Sat 1000–1700; free. **Colman's Mustard Shop & Museum**, *Bridewell Alley; tel: (01603) 627889,* open Mon–Sat 0930–1700; free. The small exhibition is devoted to one of Norwich's best-known products.

The city also has plenty of parks and gardens. The major ones are **Castle Gardens**, *Castle Meadow* (ornamental gardens occupying what was once the castle's moat); **Chapel Field Gardens**, *Chapel Field Rd* (city centre gardens); **City Hall Gardens**, *St Peters St* (war memorial gardens); **Elm Hill Riverside Gardens**, *Elm Hill*; and **Ketts Heights**, entrances in *Ketts Hill* and *Gas Hill*; buses 19/20.

OUT OF TOWN

Sainsbury Centre for Visual Arts, *University of East Anglia, Watton Rd; tel: (01603) 456060,* open Tues–Sun 1100–1700 (all year, but closed for university's Christmas break); £2. 3 miles west. The superb building has won awards for its designer, Sir Norman Foster, and the Sainsbury Collection comprises over 1000 paintings, sculptures and ceramics.

289

NORWICH–LINCOLN

This route traverses north Norfolk and the Fens, following the coastline of the Wash from King's Lynn to Boston and on to the bracing old seaside resort of Skegness, before turning inland to cross the Lincolnshire Wolds and reach the stunning cathedral city of Lincoln.

Lincoln 22

A158

Horncastle

A158 21

Skegness

A52

Boston 23

A16

Sheringham 3 Cromer

44 34

A148

A17

A140

ROUTE: 171 MILES

King's Lynn

25

Norwich

ROUTE

Journey time is 4 hrs 10 mins for 171 miles. From central Norwich follow signs to **Cromer** (A140 north), which is reached after 25 miles. Continue on A149 west for 3 miles to **Sheringham**, then follow A148 west for 34 miles to the King's Lynn bypass and continue for 3 miles to the town centre. Leave **King's Lynn** on A149 south-west for 8 miles, pick up A17, go on for 25 miles to Algakirk, then turn right on to A16 to reach **Boston** in 8 miles. Less than a mile north of Boston follow A52 north-east for 22 miles to **Skegness**. A158 heads north-west from Skegness to reach **Horncastle** in 21 miles and Lincoln in a further 22 miles.

CROMER

TIC: *Bus Station, Prince of Wales Rd, Cromer, Norfolk NR27 9HS; tel: (01263) 512497*, open daily 1000–1700 (Apr–mid July and Sept–Oct), daily 0930–1900 (mid July–Aug); Mon–Sat 1000–1600 (Nov–Mar). Services offered: BABA and local accommodation bookings.

ACCOMMODATION

Cliftonville Hotel, *Seafront, Cromer NR27 9AS; tel: (01263) 512543;*

fax: (01263) 515700. Restored family-run Edwardian hotel 500 yds from Cromer Pier. Moderate.

Red Lion, *Brook St, Cromer NR27 9HD; tel: (01263) 514964; fax: (01263) 512834.* Moderate.

North Norfolk Holiday Homes, *Lee Warner Ave, Fakenham, Norfolk NR21 8ER; tel: (01328) 855322; fax: (01328) 851336,* offers self-catering properties in the Cromer and Sheringham areas, as well as throughout the county.

SIGHTSEEING

Sandy beach, fishing boats, crabs fresh from the sea and a theatre on the pier make the clifftop town of Cromer a popular holiday spot.

Cromer Museum, *East Cottages, Tucker St; tel: (01263) 512543,* open Mon–Sat 1000–1700, Sun 1400–1700; £1.20. Housed in a fisherman's cottage of the late Victorian era, the museum has displays on fishing, natural history, archaeology, local history and the town's heyday as a bathing resort.

Cromer Lifeboat Museum and Lifeboat, *The Pier and Gangway, Cromer; tel: (01263) 512503,* open daily 1000–1600 (Mar–Oct); donations welcome. In pride of place is the Oakley class lifeboat *H. F. Bailey*, in service at Cromer 1935–1947; the boat and crew saved 818 lives. The history of Cromer lifeboats unfolds through pictures, photographs and models. Visitors can also see the present lifeboat.

SHERINGHAM

TIC: *Station Approach, Sheringham NR26 8RA; tel: (01263) 824329.* Seasonal opening. Services offered: local accommodation bookings, BABA.

ACCOMMODATION

Beaumaris, *South St, Sheringham NR26*

8LL; tel (01263) 822370. Within walking distance of the town. Moderate.

Norfolk Country Cottages, *Carlton House, Market Place, Reepham, Norfolk NR10 4JJ; tel: (01603) 871872; fax: (01603) 870304,* is a local family-run agency.

Park Lodge *Sheringham Park, Upper Sheringham, NR26 8TB; tel: (01263) 822056,* is in the National Trust's list. There are lovely walks in the area. Budget.

Eastcourt, *2 Abbey Rd, Sheringham, c/o Mrs P. Cornish, The Old Chapel, Edgefield St, Melton Constable, Norfolk NR24 2AU; (freephone) tel: (0500) 400490.* Two flats sleeping two–four.

SIGHTSEEING

Sheringham is a relaxing country town by the sea, with a sandy beach and grassy dunes. There are cliff walks, narrow back streets, a theatre, and an indoor swimming complex.

North Norfolk Railway, *Sheringham Station, Station Approach; tel: (01263) 822045.* Station open daily 0930–1700 (year round); train services run daily 0930–1700 (Mar–Dec); £5.90. Steam trains (or vintage diesels) regularly run the 5 miles between Sheringham and the market town of Holt, through pine forest and heathland with sea views. A museum at Sheringham has railway memorabilia.

KING'S LYNN

TIC: *Custom House, Purfleet Quay, King's Lynn, Norfolk; tel: (01553) 763044/767711,* open daily 0915–1700. DP services offered; local bed-booking (latest 1650; 10% of first night deposit), BABA (latest 1630; variable fee). Tickets sold for local events. Ask about multi-attraction passes. *King's Lynn Mini Guide* and the *West Norfolk What to Do* and *Where to Stay* guides are free.

GETTING AROUND

Most of the attractions are within easy walking distance and free town maps are available from the TIC. General enquiries for all **west Norfolk buses**: *tel: (0345) 626116* – ask them for (free) timetables: in particular for the special **Coastliner**, which goes to most of the local attractions (June–Sept). There is a reasonable bus service in the centre, mostly operated by **Eastern Counties**, but it is patchy to outlying areas and there's a reduced service on most routes after 2000 and on Sun.

For taxis, contact: **Gaywood Taxis**, *tel: (01553) 764500*; **Lynn Cabs**, *tel: (01553) 760600*; **Star Cars**, *tel: (01553) 761152*; or **Taffy's Taxis**, *(01553) 760900*.

ACCOMMODATION

There is a fair range of hotel and guesthouse accommodation, with cheaper rooms on the edge of town and a few pubs with rooms in outlying villages. Accommodation is generally easy to book on arrival, except during the King's Lynn Festival (July). Hotel chains include *BW*.

HI: *Thoresby College, College Lane; tel: (01553) 772461*.

SIGHTSEEING

BBG town walks are operated regularly (May–Oct): details and bookings at the TIC. In medieval times, King's Lynn was a major port that had strong trading links with Germany and there is still a Germanic feel to some of the many elegant buildings which remain in the old town, bordering the Great Ouse river and along *King St*.

Diverse exhibits and some hands-on displays recreate Lynn life since Tudor times at the **Town House Museum**, *46 Queen St; tel: (01553) 773450*, open Mon–Sat 1000–1700, Sun 1400–1700 (May–Sept); Mon–Sat 1000–1600 (Oct–Apr); £1. The rooms vary from a

Victorian kitchen to a 1950s living room, while exhibits include costumes and toys. There's also a Victorian herb garden. **Lynn Museum**, *Market St; tel: (01553) 775001*, open Tues–Sat 1000–1700; 60p, in a former Victorian chapel, is devoted to west Norfolk people since prehistoric times and contains everything from a Saxon skeleton to carousel horses.

The chequered-fronted **Trinity Guildhall** (1421), *Saturday Market Pl*, is home to a new attraction, *Tales of King's Lynn*.

An engraver can personalise anything you buy at **Caithness Crystal**, *10–12 Paxman Rd, Hardwick Industrial Estate; tel: (01553) 765111*. Glass-making demonstrations Mon–Fri 1100–1500 (Jan–Mar); 0915–1600 (Apr–Dec); Sat–Sun 1100–1600 (mid June–mid Sept); free. 1½ miles south-east.

True's Yard, *North St; tel: (01553) 770479*, open daily 0930–1630; £1.90, is a fishing museum in the form of a fully restored fishermen's yard. **St Nicholas Chapel**, *St Ann's St*, is usually open Tues, Thur, Sat 1000–1400 (June–Aug); free. If it's closed, at any reasonable time, you can borrow a key from True's Yard. The beautiful **St Margaret's Church**, *Saturday Market Pl.*, open daily 1000–1800; free, has some impressive 12th-century windows and brasses.

OUT OF TOWN

The most famous estate in the area is the royal country retreat of **Sandringham House**, *Sandringham; tel: (01553) 772675*, open mid Apr–mid Oct, but only between royal visits, so check with the TIC; £4.50 (inclusive); £3.50 (museum and grounds). 8 miles north. As well as the grounds and museum, you can see many rooms used by the Royal Family and admire a variety of priceless collections. There's a land train (free) for those who want to enjoy the

60 acres of glorious grounds without a long walk.

Castle Rising Castle (EH), *Castle Rising; tel: (01553) 631330*, open daily 1000–1800/dusk (Easter–Oct), Wed–Sun 1000–1600 (Nov–Easter); £2. 4 miles north-east. The great 12th-century keep stands at the centre of impressive earthworks and many of the fortifications are still intact.

There's a superb art collection at **Holkham Hall**, *Wells-next-the-Sea; tel: (01328) 710227*, open Sun–Thur 1330–1700 (late May–Sept), public holidays Sun–Mon 1130–1700 (Easter, early May, Aug); £6 inclusive, £4 (hall alone), £4 (bygones). 30 miles north-east. The Palladian mansion houses paintings by Rubens, Van Dyck and Gainsborough and has a good Bygones collection, as well as offering a 3000-acre deer park by the sea.

The largest lavender grower and distiller in the country is **Norfolk Lavender**, *Caley Mill, Heacham; tel: (01485) 570384*, open daily 1000–1700 (mid Jan–mid Dec); free. You can learn all about the fragrant shrub and its uses: there are tours daily (May–Sept) and a minibus to the lavender fields (mid June–end of harvest). 13 miles north.

Park Farm, *Snettisham; tel: (01485) 542425*, open daily 1000–1700 (Feb–Dec); £3.50 (£6 including safari). 11 miles north. The main attractions are scenic walking trails and a deer safari, but children can enjoy a pony ride or the large adventure playground, while adults browse round the craft centre.

Houghton Hall, *Harpley; tel: (01485) 528569*, open Thur, Sun, public holidays 1400–1730 (Easter–Sept); £5.50. 13 miles east. Houghton is a Palladian mansion, magnificently decorated and furnished in style, and boasting one of the world's best collections of model soldiers – over 20,000 – some set up to recreate battles.

Oxburgh Hall (NT), *Oxborough; tel: (01366) 328258*. House open public holidays 1100–1700, Sat–Wed 1300–1700 (Easter–Oct); £4.60 (house, garden and estate). 15 miles south-east. This is a 15th-century moated building with an impressive 25 m high gatehouse, parterre garden and woodland walks. Inside, you can trace progress from medieval times to the Elizabethan period.

BOSTON

TIC: *Market Place, Boston, Lincolnshire PE21 6NN; tel: (01205) 356656*, open Mon–Sat 0900–1700. Services offered: local bed-booking and BABA (latest 1630). *Boston: The Original*, and an accommodation listing, are free.

GETTING AROUND

Most attractions are within walking distance of the centre and a town map is available from the TIC. **Transport Hotline**, *tel: (01522) 553135*, covers general transport enquiries. The main **taxi** rank is on *Market Pl*. Details of companies can be obtained from the TIC.

ACCOMMODATION

There is a small range of accommodation (hotel, b&b and guesthouse) in town and a number of b&bs and pubs with rooms in the surrounding area. It's sensible to book in advance. The nearest **campsite** is **Orchard Park Caravan Park**, *Hubbert's Bridge; tel: (01205) 290328*, 3½ miles north-west. The TIC has details of other sites.

SIGHTSEEING

For details of **river cruises** into **the Wash**, contact the TIC. A weekly **market** has been a tradition since 1308 and still takes place every Wed and Sat in the town centre (on Wed there is also an open-air auction).

The Pilgrim Fathers, who sailed from Boston in 1630, named their Massachusetts settlement after this still-busy inland port. An earlier attempt at escape led to the Puritans' imprisonment (in 1607) in the 15th-century **Guildhall**, now a museum of Boston's history and maritime heritage. An audio guide is available for the **Guildhall Museum**, *South St; tel: (01205) 365954*, open Mon–Sat 1000–1700 (all year); Sun 1330–1700 (Apr–Sept); £1.20.

Boston has some pleasant buildings, the most famous of which is the 14th-century **St Botolph's Church**, *Market Pl.; tel: (01205) 362864*, open Mon–Sat 0830–1630 and for Sun services; church free (donations appreciated), but charges for photography and £2 to climb the tower. The church (dating from 1309) is magnificent in both size and detail, with a 272ft tower – the **Boston Stump** – which is the region's best-known landmark: 365 steps to the top, for a magnificent view over the Wash.

On the edge of town is the tallest working mill in England, **Maud Foster Windmill**, *Willoughby Rd; tel: (01205) 352188*, open Wed–Sun 1100–1700 (July–Aug); Wed, public holidays 1000–1700, Sat 1100–1700, Sun 1300–1700 (Sept–June); £1.50. The five-sailed mill dates from 1819 and was restored in 1988 – you can climb to the top while observing it in action.

Blackfriars Arts Centre, *Spain Lane; tel: (01205) 363108*, open Mon–Sat 1000–1800; free. What was left of the old Dominican friary has been converted into a fully equipped arts centre.

OUT OF TOWN

Pilgrim Fathers Memorial (monument), *Fishtoft*. Freely accessible, the monument is 4½ miles south-east.

SKEGNESS

TIC: *Embassy Centre, Grand Parade, Skegness, Lincolnshire PE25 2UP; tel: (01754)*, open year round. Services offered: BABA and local bed-booking.

ACCOMMODATION

Savoy Hotel, *North Parade, Skegness PE25 2UB; tel: (01754) 763371; fax: (01754) 761256*. Friendly seafront property. Good short break deals. Budget–moderate.

North Shore Hotel and Golf Course, *North Shore Rd, Skegness PE25 1DN; tel: (01754) 763298*. Close to beach. Moderate.

Saxby Hotel, *12 Saxby Ave, Skegness PE25 3LG; tel/fax: (01754) 763905*. Family-run property in quiet area. Budget.

White Lodge Guest House, *129 Drummond Rd, Skegness PE25 3DW; tel: (01754) 764120*. Close to bowling green, golf course and nature reserve. Budget.

Chequers Holiday Flats, *64 Sandbeck Ave, Skegness PE25 3PZ; tel: (01754) 765317*. Self-catering flats for two to four people.

Skegness has nearly a dozen camping and caravan parks. The closest to the town centre is **Richmond Holiday Centre**, *Richmond Drive, Skegness; tel: (01754) 762097*, open Mar–Nov.

Sycamore Lakes Touring Site, *Skegness Rd, Burgh-le-Marsh, Skegness; tel: (01754) 810749*, open Feb–Dec. Quiet rural site near village 4 miles from Skegness seafront. The site is adjacent to 4 acres of fishing lakes. Prices from £5.50.

SIGHTSEEING

Skegness was a busy port until the North Sea suddenly enveloped it in 1571. Three hundred years later, the arrival of the railway put the little town firmly on the seaside holiday map. The first Butlin's Holiday Camp was established here in 1936. Today, the accent is on family amusements and children's adventure and recreational pursuits. Donkey rides on the sand are as popular as ever.

Skegness Model Village, *South Parade; tel: (01754) 762262*, open daily (weather permitting) 1000–dusk (Good Fri–late Oct); admission charge. In peak season the village is illuminated from dusk.

Skegness Nature and Seal Sanctuary, *North Parade; tel: (01754) 764345*, open daily 1000–1700 (Apr–Sept, but opens until 1730 July–Aug), 1000–1600 (Nov– Mar); £3.40. It combines education, conservation and entertainment. As well as seals there are penguins, crocodiles, snakes, tropical birds and a pets' corner.

Church Farm Museum, *Church Rd South; tel: (01754) 766658*, open daily 1030–1730 (Apr–Oct); £1. Life on a dairy farm a century ago is demonstrated by costumed guides. There's a 'mud and stud' thatched cottage and a traditionally furnished farmhouse. The farm has some Lincoln Longwool sheep. Sunday afternoon craft demonstrations are held and various events take place during the season.

Hardy's Animal Farm, *Anchor Lane, Ingoldmells, Skegness; tel: (01754) 872267*, open daily 1000–1800 (Easter–early Oct) last admission 1700; admission charge. A present day farm is seen at work here. Occupants of the pig unit can be observed through a glazed viewing area, and there are sheep, cattle, goats and poultry.

HORNCASTLE

TIC: *The Trinity Centre, Spilsby Rd, Horncastle, Lincolnshire LN9 9AW; tel: (01507) 525536*. Seasonal opening. Services offered: local accommodation reservations; BABA.

ACCOMMODATION

Admiral Rodney Hotel, *North St, Horncastle LN9 5DX; tel: (01507) 523131*. Comfortable well-equipped rooms. Moderate.

The Bull Hotel, *The Bull Ring, Horncastle LN9 5HU; tel: (01507) 524011*. 16th-century former coaching inn with traditional English tea shop. Budget–moderate.

The Old Rectory, *Fulletby, nr Horncastle; tel: (01507) 533533*. B&b in tranquil Wolds countryside. Lovely home in 5 acres of grounds, off A153. Budget–moderate.

Poplar Tree Farm, *Low Toynton, Horncastle LN9 6JU; tel: (01507) 523547*. Tennis and fishing on site. Budget.

Greenfield Farm, *Minting, Nr Horncastle LN9 5RX; tel: (01507) 578457*. Modern en suite facilities in farmhouse. Budget.

Stamford Farm House, *Miningsby, Nr Horncastle PE22 7NW; tel: (01507) 588682*. Self-catering in comfortable two-bedroom converted barn. Scenic walks in Tennyson country.

Ashby Park, *Horncastle LN9 5PP; tel: (01507) 527966*, open all year. Pitches for 55 caravans on site with six fishing lakes in 52 acres.

SIGHTSEEING

Set at the confluence of two small rivers, the Bain and the Waring, Horncastle is a pretty market town of 5000 people, close to the Wolds. A number of the quaint old buildings are antique shops, which attract many browsers and buyers to the area.

Snipe Dales Country Park, *tel: (01522) 552821*, open year round; free (charge for car park). North of the B1195, between Spilsby and Horncastle, the 210-acre park has trails by ponds and streams.

NOTTINGHAM

Best known as the (real or mythical) home of Robin Hood, Friar Tuck and Maid Marian, Nottingham was also once the centre of a thriving lace industry. It has a lively and cosmopolitan atmosphere, many good museums and plenty to see in the surrounding area.

TOURIST INFORMATION

TIC: *1–4 Smithy Row, Nottingham NG1 2BY; tel: (0115) 915 5330*, open Mon–Fri 0830–1700, Sat 0900–1700 (all year); Sun 1000–1600 (Apr–Sept). DP SHS services offered; local bed-booking (latest 30 mins before closing; 10% of first night taken as deposit), BABA (latest 1 hr before closing; 10% of first night taken as deposit). Guided tours booked, tickets sold for local theatre and concerts. The *Robin Hood Country Holiday Guide* and an accommodation guide are available free.

ARRIVING AND DEPARTING

M1, 5 miles west of Nottingham, is the most direct north-south route to the city, which is accessed from Junction 26 and A610. A52 provides links to the east and west. Parking is sparse in the immediate city centre, but there is plenty within a quarter of a mile or so.

GETTING AROUND

Most attractions are within easy walking distance of the centre. Free town and transport maps are available from the TIC. There is good public transport within the city and to most nearby towns. The main **taxi** ranks are on *Market Sq.*, at the Victoria Centre and Midland Station.

Streamline, *tel: (0115) 947 5964*, have distinctive black and white taxis.

STAYING IN NOTTINGHAM

There is a good range of hotels and guesthouses, with most of the cheaper accommodation located in the suburbs of West Bridgford (1 mile south) and Beeston (4–5 miles west). It is generally easy to book on arrival, except during the Nottingham Goose Fair (Oct). Hotel chains include *BW, CI, FP, Hd, MH, Mn, Nv, ST* and *Th*. For budget accommodation, there are the **YMCA**, *4 Shakespeare St; tel: (0115) 956 7600*, and **Nottingham Igloo**, *110 Mansfield Rd; tel: (0115) 947 5250*, open 0800–1000 and 1600–midnight. The closest **campsite** is **Holmepierrepont Caravan and Camping Park**, *Adbolton Lane, Holmepierrepont; tel: (0115) 982 1212*, 3 miles south.

Money

There are **Thomas Cook bureaux de change** at *Midland Bank, 16 Long Row* and *6 Victoria St*.

SIGHTSEEING

For information about all the **in-town attractions**, *tel: (0115) 915 5555*. **Robin Hood bus tours**, *tel: (0115) 978 6111*, leave from Nottingham Castle – on request only. There are **guided walking tours** on Sat at 1400 (June–Sept), or contact **BBG**, *tel: (01909) 482503*.

Nottingham Castle and Gardens, *Castle Rd*. Castle open daily 1000–1700 (all year); usually free, but £1.50 Sat–Sun, public holidays. The castle (not Prince John's home, but a mainly 17th-century rebuild) was where Charles I raised his standard at the start of the Civil War; the **Castle Museum** within tells the town's story. At the foot of the sandstone rock upon which the castle stands is one of the most plausible contenders for the title of oldest pub in England, **Ye Olde Trip to Jerusalem**, which was used by crusaders (1189).

Several museums focus on the lace and textile industries, notably **Lace Hall**, *High Pavement*, open daily 1000–1700 (all year); £2.85, which has working machinery and audiovisual demonstrations to explain the making of Nottingham lace; and the **Museum of Costume and Textiles**, *51 Castle Gate*, open 1000–1700 (all year); free, which displays costumes from the 1730s to the 1960s, in period rooms.

To find out what it was like to be on the receiving end of 19th-century justice, visit the award-winning **Galleries of Justice – Condemned!**, *Shire Hall, Lace Market*, open Tues–Sun, public holidays 1000–1800 (Apr–Aug); 1000–1700 (Sept–Mar); £4.25.

Brewhouse Yard Museum, *Castle Boulevard*, open daily 1000–1700 (all year); £1.50 Sat, Sun, public holidays – otherwise free, depicts Nottingham life in post-medieval times; while the **Canal Museum**, *Canal St*, open Wed–Sun 1000–1700 (all year); free, relates the history of the River Trent.

The Tales of Robin Hood, *30–38 Maid Marian Way*, open daily 1000–1800 (Easter–Sept); 1000–1700 (Oct–Easter); £4.25. This themed museum takes visitors in adventure cars on a search for the legendary hero (allow at least 1½ hrs).

To see a working tower mill, visit **Green's Mill and Science Centre**, *Windmill Lane*, open Wed–Sun, public holidays 1000–1700 (all year, but may close 1200–1300); free.

A unique set of man-made caves, used for different purposes over the centuries, can now be explored at **The Caves of Nottingham**, *Drury Walk, Broad Marsh Centre*, open Mon–Sat 1000–1700, Sun 1100–1700; £2.95.

OUT OF TOWN

Wollaton Hall, Park and Natural History Museum, *Wollaton; tel: (0115) 915 5555*, hall and Museum open Mon–Sat 1000–1700, Sun 1300–1700 (Apr–Sept); Mon–Sat 1000–1630, Sun 1330–1630 (Oct–Mar); usually free, but £1.50 Sat–Sun, public holidays. 3 miles west. After enjoying the sometimes unusual aspects of nature in the museum, you can see the real thing in the surrounding 500-acre park.

Holme Pierrepont Hall, *Holme Pierrepont; tel: (0115) 933 2371*. Hall open 1400–1800: Easter, public holidays Sun–Tues (all year); Sun (June); Thur, Sun (July); Tues, Thur–Fri, Sun (Aug); £3 (hall and garden). 5 miles south-east.

For the literary-minded, poetic memorabilia are preserved at the romantic ancestral home of Lord Byron: **Newstead Abbey**, *Linby; tel: (0115) 915 5555*. House open daily 1200–1800 (Apr–Sept); £3.50 (house and grounds). 8 miles north.

D.H. Lawrence Birthplace Museum, *8a Victoria St, Eastwood; tel: (01773) 763312*, open daily 1000–1700 (Apr–Oct); 1000–1600 (Nov–Mar); £1.75. 8 miles north-west. Humble Victorian terrace in the Nottinghamshire coalfield, giving an insight into the novelist's childhood.

North of the city lie the small remnants of what was once a great forest, including the ancient and massive **Major Oak**. **Sherwood Forest Country Park and Visitor Centre**, *Edwinstowe, nr Mansfield; tel: (01623) 823202*. Visitor Centre open daily 1030–1630 (Nov–Mar); 1030–1700 (Apr–Oct); free. 20 miles north.

297

OXFORD

The world-famous university of Oxford offers plenty of attractions for the visitor, from punting on the River Cherwell to the 'dreaming spires' of 35 university colleges, whose hidden courtyards and neat lawns are a timeless haven of tranquillity. Oxford University was established by 1214 and the city now offers a mix of attractive old streets, riverside walks and historic colleges – with bicycles everywhere!

TOURIST INFORMATION

TIC: *The Old School, Gloucester Green, Oxford OX1 2DA; tel: (01865) 726871,* open Mon–Sat 0930–1700; Sun, summer public holidays 1000–1300 and 1330–1530. DP services offered; local bed-booking and BABA (latest 30 mins before closing; fee for both £2.50 plus 10% refundable deposit). Bus tours, guided walks and individual guides booked. *This Month in Oxford* is a free entertainment/events listing and the TIC supply free town maps, but the accommodation listing is 50p.

Guide Friday Tourism Centre, *Railway Station, Park End St; tel: (01865) 790522,* handles accommodation bookings (for £2) and runs a regular shuttle bus into the city centre half a mile away. There's also a taxi rank outside.

ARRIVING AND DEPARTING

The A40 crosses north of Oxford; 5 miles east of the city it connects with M40 which links London and the Midlands. A34 runs north–south to the west of Oxford: 20 miles south it joins M4 to south-west England and South Wales.

Oxford city centre has acute traffic and parking problems, so day visitors and shoppers are encouraged to use the Park and Ride scheme. Park and Ride car parks are clearly signposted on the city's ring road.

GETTING AROUND

Most attractions are within walking distance of the centre. Bus services within the city and in outlying areas are excellent. The city's transport hub, **Gloucester Green Bus Station**, is just by the TIC. **Shopmobility**, *tel: (01865) 248737.*

Oxford is served by two **bus** companies. **Thames Transit**, *tel: (01865) 772250,* have minibuses operating every 4–5 mins throughout the central area and to the surrounding countryside. **Oxford Bus Company**, *tel: (01865) 785400,* have a comprehensive network of buses. The main **taxi** rank is at Gloucester Green, near the TIC. The others are at the rail station and St Giles.

STAYING IN OXFORD

Accommodation and Food

There is a large selection of accommodation of most types in the city centre. Hotel chains include *FP, Hn* and *Ja.* **University** accommodation is not available to visitors.

HI: *32 Jack Straw's Lane; tel: (01865) 762997.* **Backpackers Hostel**, *9 Hythe Bridge St; tel: (01865) 721761,* close to the station. There are several **campsites**, the nearest being **Oxford Camping International**, *426 Abingdon Rd; tel: (01865) 246551,* 1½ miles south.

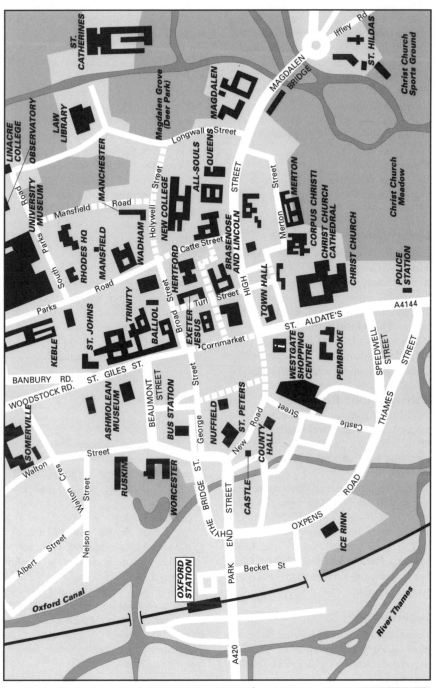

Oxford has a large and varied selection of restaurants. Being a city with many students, it is possible to eat well without spending much, but there are also many gourmet restaurants.

Communications

The main **post office**, *St Aldates*, is open Mon–Fri 0900–1730, Sat 0900–1800.

Money

There is a **Thomas Cook bureau de change** at *Midland Bank, 65 Cornmarket St.*

ENTERTAINMENT AND EVENTS

Oxford has two principal theatres. **Apollo Theatre**, *George St; tel: (01865) 244544*, is traditionally Oxford's premier venue. Audiences enjoy the best from many international professional touring companies. **The Oxford Playhouse**, *11–12 Beaumont St; tel: (01865) 798600*, is an intimate, historic theatre, presenting drama, dance, opera, musicals and concerts in comfortable period surroundings. **Holywell Music Room**, *Holywell St,* is the setting for many concerts; tickets for most of them from **Blackwell's**, *Holywell St; tel: (01865) 261384*. Established in 1965, the **City of Oxford Orchestra** is now the leading regional orchestra and presents regular series of concerts in such settings as the Holywell Music Room, Merton College Chapel, Sheldonian Theatre and Christ Church Meadows.

The main annual event is the **Lord Mayor's Parade and Gala**, held in May. For a comprehensive listing of events, contact the TIC.

SHOPPING

Oxford has a wonderful selection of bookshops, notably **Blackwell's**, *48–51 Broad St.*, one of the finest and largest booksellers in the world. At the **Oxford University Press Bookshop,** *116–17 High St*, you can get all their titles. **The Oxford Antique Trading Company**, *40–41 Park End St*, has enormous showrooms full of antiques and can deliver worldwide.

The main shopping area is compact and easy to explore on foot. To the north of Oxford's central crossroads – known as Carfax – runs *Cornmarket St*, where there are branches of chains, plus many smaller shops and the **Clarendon Shopping Centre**. West from Carfax runs *Queen St*, at the west end of which is the **Westgate Shopping Centre**. Tucked behind the modern façades of *Cornmarket St* is the **Covered Market**, built in 1774. Traditionally, this is where the colleges do their shopping and it's a gourmet's paradise. There's also an **open market**, every Wed at Gloucester Green. In beautifully designed buildings set around the market square, the **Gallery** houses a mixture of specialist shops and restaurants.

SIGHTSEEING

Tours

The best way to explore Oxford is on foot, with a guide. The TIC and Guide Friday offer a variety of **themed walks** (mostly £4), starting at 1100 and 1400 daily all year.

Guide Friday also run open-top double-decker **city bus tours** (Mar–Sept); £7.50 for a hop-on, hop-off day ticket.

Walking tours beginning at **Carfax Tower**, *tel: (01865) 792653 (or 726871 when tower closed)* on Sat–Sun at 1345 (£4) include free admission to Christ Church (see below). The Tower itself is open daily 1000–1730 (Apr–Oct); daily 1000–1530 (Nov–Mar); £1.20, and provides stupendous views (72 ft – 99 steps).

Colleges

Most travellers come to visit the lovely **university colleges** in the heart of Oxford. Most are usually open in the afternoons and during holidays (though liable to close at short notice). You should respect the fact that these are places of study, keep the noise down and heed privacy notices. A few colleges charge entry fees.

Most of the historic colleges lie east of *St Giles/Cornmarket/St Aldates*. The most famous, to the south, is **Christ Church** (or 'The House'), founded in 1525 by Cardinal Wolsey; £3. It has the largest quadrangle in Oxford, known as 'Tom Quad' after the bell, Great Tom, in Wren's Tom Tower: Great Tom still rings 101 times at 2105 each night, marking a long-defunct undergraduate curfew. The college chapel doubles as **Christ Church Cathedral**: the smallest cathedral in England, it predates the college, being part of what was an 8th-century convent – its spire was the first in England. Now mainly Norman, it has a magnificent Early English chapter house. In Canterbury Quad is **Christ Church Picture Gallery**, open Mon–Sat 1030–1300 and 1400–1630/1730, Sun 1400–1630/1730; £1, which includes Italian, Flemish and Dutch works.

To the south and east of Christ Church sprawls the pastoral **Christ Church Meadow**, Oxford's answer to Cambridge's 'Backs'.

East of here, along *Merton St*, is 13th-century **Merton College**, one of the oldest in Oxford; its peaceful gardens are partly enclosed by the old city wall.

Beside Magdalen Bridge lies **Magdalen College**, perhaps the most attractive in the city; its buildings have changed little since the 15th century, apart from the addition of the harmonious New Buildings in 1733. At sunrise on May Day, the college choir sings from the top of the tower, witnessed by crowds of inebriated students emerging from May Ball revels. Magdalen has its own deer park and there are peaceful walks along the River Cherwell.

Back along *High St* are **Queen's College**, with buildings by Wren and Hawksmoor, and **St Edmund Hall**, with a dining hall from 1659; the best view in town is from the 13th-century tower of **St Mary the Virgin**, the university church. *Queen's Lane* leads to another gem, **New College**, famed for its gardens, hall and cloisters. The **Bridge of Sighs**, spanning *New College Lane*, forms part of **Hertford College**. Next to the Bodleian Library (see below) is the imposing **Sheldonian Theatre**, designed by Sir Christopher Wren in 1664 to resemble a Roman theatre, and used for university functions and concerts. Westwards, along *Broad St*, are famous rivals neo-Gothic **Balliol College** and **Trinity College**, which has renowned gardens. **Wadham College**, along *Parks Rd*, has beautiful 17th-century buildings. Worth a slightly longer walk, for a contrast to all the sandstone, is red-brick **Keble College**, a Victorian *tour de force*.

Other Attractions

Bate Collection of Musical Instruments, *Faculty of Music, St Aldates; tel: (01865) 276139*, open Mon–Fri 1400–1700 (all year); Sat 1000–1200 during full terms; free. England's most comprehensive collection of European woodwind, brass and percussion instruments.

A 17th-century gateway leads into Oxford's **Botanic Garden**, *Rose Lane; tel: (01865) 276920*, open daily 0900–1630/1700 (greenhouses 1400–1600); usually free, but £2 June–Aug. This was founded in 1621 and is the oldest in Britain.

Ashmolean Museum, *Beaumont St; tel: (01865) 278000*, open Tues–Sat

301

1000–1600, Sun 1400–1600, public holidays 1400–1700; free. The oldest museum in Britain; it houses treasures from the time of early man to 20th-century art.
Bodleian Library, *Broad St; tel: (01865) 277000*. Tours (compulsory) Mon–Fri 1030, 1130, 1400 and 1500, Sat 1030 and 1130 (Easter–Oct); Wed 1430, Sat 1100 (Nov–Easter); £3.50. The oldest library in the world is one of the five copyright libraries of the UK, receiving a copy of every book published in Britain. The original Duke Humphrey's Library (1480) is among the parts open to the public. The great, domed **Radcliffe Camera** nearby, built in 1737, acts as one of the reading rooms.

University Museum, *Parks Rd; tel: (01865) 270949*, open Mon–Sat 1200–1700; free, is the city's natural history museum and has collections dedicated to zoology, entomology and geology, all housed in an imposing Victorian Gothic building. Under the same roof is the eclectic **Pitt Rivers Museum**, open Mon–Sat 1300–1630; free – less well known, but definitely worth a visit.

One of Oxford's newer attractions is the imaginative presentation of the city's story from a moving medieval scholar's desk. **The Oxford Story**, *6 Broad St; tel: (01865) 790055*, open daily 0930–1700 (Apr–June, Sept–Oct), 0900–1800 (July–Aug); 1000–1630 (Nov–Mar); £4.75.

OUT OF TOWN

There are many attractions around Oxford, including the **Didcot Railway Centre**, *Station Yard, Didcot; tel: (01235) 817200*, open daily 1100–1700 (Easter–Sept); Sat–Sun 1100–1700 (all year); £3.50–£5.50, depending on whether it is a steam day. 10 miles south. Here you can relive the golden age of steam and the

Great Western Railway. There are over 20 locomotives on display, including steam and diesel engines, and dozens of carriages dating from the 1880s to the 1950s.

The ancient village of Cogges is home to **Cogges Manor Farm Museum**, *Church Lane, Cogges, Witney; tel: (01993) 772602*, open Tues–Fri, public holidays 1030–1730, Sat–Sun 1200–1730 (Easter–Sept); Tues–Fri 1030–1630, Sat–Sun 1200–1630 (Oct); £3. 10 miles west. This is a fascinating display of farming and the countryside, complete with stone outbuildings and manor house, furnished as it would have been at the turn of the century.

A few miles north of Oxford is the attractive town of **Woodstock**, home of fabulous **Blenheim Palace**, *tel: (01993) 811325/811091*. Palace open daily 1030–1730 (Easter–Oct); £7.80 covers all attractions except the maze and rowing boats. 8 miles north-west. Blenheim was built for warrior hero John Churchill, the first Duke of Marlborough, and is the early 18th-century work of Sir John Vanbrugh. It is the only English palace which was not built for royalty and was Sir Winston Churchill's birthplace. There are tours of the interior, with its fine pictures and furnishings. The parkland and gardens were landscaped by Capability Brown.

In Woodstock itself is a 16th-century fletcher's home, which now houses the **Oxfordshire County Museum**, *Fletcher's House, Park St, Woodstock; tel: (01993) 811456*, open Tues–Sat 1000–1700, Sun 1400–1700 (May–Sept); Tues–Fri 1000–1600, Sat 1000–1700, Sun 1400–1700 (Oct–Apr); £1.50. This tells the story of Oxfordshire through the ages, using a variety of archaeological, craft and industrial exhibits.

PLYMOUTH

Plymouth sits at the mouth of the River Tamar and has been a seaport of note since the 13th century. The city has a rich maritime heritage and, in the past, many famous explorers have set sail from its natural harbour: Sir Walter Raleigh and Sir Francis Drake sailed from here in Elizabethan times; the Pilgrim Fathers left for the New World in the *Mayflower* in 1620; and Captain James Cook set sail in the 18th century.

TOURIST INFORMATION

TIC: *Island House, 9 The Barbican, Plymouth PL1 2LS; tel: (01752) 264849 or 227865,* open Mon–Sat 0900–1700 (all year); also Sun 1000–1600 (Easter–Oct). DP services offered; local bed-booking (£2 booking fee), BABA (£3 booking fee). Heritage passes, local theatre and attractions tickets sold. The *Plymouth Guide* is available free from the TIC and contains accommodation listings.

TIC: *Discovery Centre, Marsh Mills, Crabtree, Plymouth PL3 6RN; tel: (01752) 266030,* opening hours and services as for Barbican TIC.

ARRIVING AND DEPARTING

A38, stretching from Exeter to Bodmin, is Plymouth's major east-west route. A386 heads north, skirting Dartmoor National Park and passing through Tavistock and Okehampton to reach Bideford in North Devon. Plymouth is generously endowed with car parks and has more than a dozen in the city centre alone.

GETTING AROUND

The majority of attractions in Plymouth are within walking distance of the centre. Free town and public transport maps are available from the TIC.

Taxi ranks are situated in *Old Town St, Royal Parade* and *Raleigh St.*

STAYING IN PLYMOUTH

Accommodation and Food

Plymouth has a wide range of accommodation. The majority of cheaper places are found near the seafront and rail station. It is generally easy to find accommodation on arrival, but book in advance during the 'Navy Days' event (August bank holiday). Chains include *BW, Ca, Cp, FP, MC, MH, Mn* and *Nv.*

HI: *Belmont House, Belmont Place, Stoke; tel: (01752) 562189.* There's also the **Backpackers Hostel**, *172 Citadel Rd, The Hoe; tel: (01752) 225158.* The TIC can provide information on local **campsites,** including **Riverside**, *Longbridge Rd, Marsh Mills; tel: (01752) 344122,* 4 miles from town; and **Smithaleigh Camping Park**, *Smithaleigh; tel: (01752) 893194,* 7 miles east.

The TIC provides a free list of local restaurants, most of which are concentrated in the Barbican area, near Sutton Harbour, and in *Mayflower St/Cornwall St* in the shopping area. There is a wide choice of styles and many tea shops and pubs offer cheap eating.

Traditional Plymouth Gin is produced in **The Distillery**, *Southside St, The Barbican,* and Devonshire teas with clotted cream are offered in most cafés and restaurants.

303

Communications

The main **post office**, *St Andrews Cross*, is open Mon–Fri 0900–1700, Sat 0900–1230. Poste restante facilities.

Money

There are **Thomas Cook bureaux de change** at *Midland Bank, 4 Old Town St* and *Millbay Docks, Millbay Rd.*

ENTERTAINMENT AND EVENTS

The free publication *What's On and Where to Go* is produced monthly. The local *Evening Herald* also has listings. The main theatre venue is the **Theatre Royal**, *Royal Parade; tel: (01752) 267222*

The **Navy Days** event, when Devonport Dockyard is open to the public, takes place every 2 years (uneven years) on August holiday weekend and Plymouth becomes very busy.

SHOPPING

Big stores are located in *Royal Parade, New George St, Old Town St, Cornwall St* and *Armada Way*, while antique and craft shops can be found in the Barbican. There is also a large daily covered **market** at *Pannier St.*

SIGHTSEEING

Book at the TIC for **guided walks** round the Royal Citadel and the Barbican (daily May–Sept; £2.50). **Bus tours** are operated by **Guide Friday**, *tel: (01752) 222221*; £4.00. **Plymouth Boat Cruises**, *tel: (01752) 822797*, and **Tamar Cruising**, *tel: (01752) 822105*, offer **boat trips** from the Barbican.

Plymouth Hoe, the grassy area overlooking Plymouth Sound, was where Sir Francis Drake casually finished playing his game of bowls before setting out to fight the approaching Spanish Armada in 1588. Plymouth's seafaring history is vividly brought to life, at the **Plymouth Dome**,

The Hoe; *tel: (01752) 603300*, open daily 0900–1930 (June–mid Sept); 0900–1730 (Easter–May, mid Sept–Oct); 0900–1800 (Nov–Easter); £3.95.

City Museum and Art Gallery, *Drake Circus; tel: (01752) 264878*; open Tues–Fri 1000–1730; Sat, public holidays 1000–1700; free, has displays of local archaeological finds, porcelain and paintings, including some by Sir Joshua Reynolds, who was a local man.

Most of old Plymouth was destroyed during World War II, although there are some old-town remains around the harbour area of the **Barbican**.

OUT OF TOWN

Saltram House (NT), *Merafield Rd, Plympton; tel: (01752) 336546*, house open Sun–Thur, Good Fri 1230–1730 (Easter–Oct); £5.30 (house and garden). The magnificent Georgian mansion comes complete with its original contents and extremely ornate decor, overlooks landscaped grounds to Plymouth Sound.

Mount Edgcumbe House and Earl's Garden, *Cremyll, Torpoint; tel: (01752) 822236*, open Wed–Sun, public holidays 1100–1700 (Apr–Oct); £3.50. 10 miles south-west. The house is beautifully furnished and adorned with family treasures, from Irish Bronze Age horns to Chinese porcelain. The Earl's Garden, beside the house, was created in the 18th century and contains such rare trees as a 400-year-old lime and a Mexican pine. The grounds (free access all year) cover over 800 acres.

Dartmoor Wildlife and Conservation Park, *Sparkwell; tel: (01752) 837209*, open all year 1000–dusk; £5.45. 3 miles east. On the south-western edge of Dartmoor, the park occupies 30 acres of beautiful countryside and contains around 1000 animals, including big cats and falcons.

PLYMOUTH–PENZANCE

This route takes us along the southernmost edge of the south-west Peninsula after crossing the River Tamar from Devon into Cornwall. Because of space restrictions, we have chosen only the major holiday towns, but there are dozens of picture-postcard fishing villages, coves and hidden beaches along the route for those with the time to explore. Be warned, however, that some Cornish lanes are very narrow and difficult for cars to negotiate and that swimming may be dangerous in some places. Always seek local advice.

DIRECT ROUTE: 78 MILES

Direct Route

71

A38 Saltash
A30
A390
A38
A39 Truro 39
Looe 19
A394 14
Penzance Falmouth Plymouth
28 **Scenic Route**

305

ROUTES

DIRECT ROUTE

This route takes 1 hr 45 mins. From central Plymouth follow signs to A38 and continue west for 7 miles to Saltash (toll bridge over River Tamar) and head west for 24 miles to Bodmin. Take A30 west to reach Penzance in a further 47 miles.

SCENIC ROUTE

This route is about 22 miles longer – allow another hour's driving time. Proceed from central Plymouth as above. From Saltash continue on A38 for 9 miles, then take B3251 and B3252, followed by A387 to arrive in **Looe** after 3 miles. Leave Looe on A387 west and after 2 miles head north on B3359, which connects with A390 after 6 miles. Turn left and follow A390 for 24 miles, then join A39 to reach **Truro** in a further 7 miles. Continue west on A39, arriving at **Falmouth** in 14 miles. Return along A39 for 4 miles, then bear left on to A394 and continue for 21 miles. A30 west covers the last 3 miles into Penzance (see p. 108).

(see p. 108)

LOOE

TIC: *The Guildhall, Fore St, East Looe, Cornwall PL13 1AA; tel: (01503) 26072*, open Mon–Sat 1000–1700 (Apr–Oct). DP services offered; local bed-booking and BABA. *South East Cornwall Guide* is free; *tel: (01579) 341035.*

GETTING AROUND

Free town maps are available from the TIC. The main local bus operators are **Hambly's**, *tel: (01503) 220660/220385* and **Western National**, *tel: (01752) 222666*. For details of registered **taxi** companies, contact the TIC.

ACCOMMODATION

There is a good spread of accommodation, from mid-range hotels to b&bs. It is generally easy to book on arrival, except during Aug. The only hotel chain is *Mo*.

Commonwood Manor Hotel, *St Martins Rd, East Looe PL13 1LP; tel: (01503) 262929; fax: (01503) 262632.* Victorian villa in 6 acres of garden and woodland with spectacular views. Moderate.

Coombe Farm, *Widegates, Near Looe PL13 1QN; tel: (01503) 240223; fax: (01503) 240895.* Small hotel, surrounded by meadows, woods and streams, with superb sea views, and heated outdoor pool. Moderate.

Fieldhead Hotel, *Portuan Rd, Looe PL13 2DR; tel: (01503) 262689; fax: (01503) 264114.* Edwardian house overlooking the sea. Moderate.

Bucklawren Farm, *St Martin-by-Looe PL13 1NZ; tel: (01503) 240738; fax: (01503) 240481.* Set in glorious countryside with sea views. Budget.

Kantara Licensed Guesthouse, *7 Trelawney Terrace, West Looe PL13 2AG; tel: (01503) 262093.* Close to beach and shops. Budget.

The TIC has details of **campsites**. The nearest are: **Tencreek Caravan Park**, *Looe; tel: (01503) 262447*; a little over a mile west; **Polborder House Caravan and Camping Park**, *Bucklawren Rd, St Martin-By-Looe; tel: (01503) 240265*; 2½ miles east.

SIGHTSEEING

Looe is a fishing port which has long been a centre for touring Cornwall – it is an attractive town, with many old buildings, and wears its tourist commercialisation well.

The only 'attraction' is **The Monkey Sanctuary**, *tel: (01503) 262532*, open Sun–Thur 1030/1130–1630/1700 (Easter, May–Sept); £4. 5 miles east of town. Woolly monkeys have lived happily here for four generations and behave quite naturally – except that they trust humans, so physical contact is common.

TRURO

TIC: *Municipal Buildings, Boscawen St, Truro, Cornwall TR1 2NE; tel: (01872) 74555*, open Mon–Thur 0900–1700, Fri 0900–1645 (Nov–Mar); Mon–Fri 0900–1715, Sat 1000–1300 (Apr–May, Oct); Mon–Fri 0900–1800, Sat 1000–1700 (June–Sept). DP services offered; local bed-booking and BABA (latest 30 mins before closing). *Truro City Guide* costs 50p, but *Truro Accommodation Register* is free.

GETTING AROUND

A free town map is available from the TIC. **Western National**, *tel: (01209) 719988*, operate throughout the town and most of the county. The main **taxi** rank is by the War Memorial on *Boscawen St*.

ACCOMMODATION

There are a few medium-sized hotels, but the best choice lies in smaller hotels, guesthouses and b&bs. Book ahead during the summer. The city's best-known and most central hotel is **The Royal**, *Lemon St, Truro TR1 2QB; tel: (01872) 70345; fax: (01872) 42453*. Moderate–expensive.

Alverton Manor, *Tregolls Rd, Truro TR1 1XQ; tel: (01872) 76633; fax: (01872) 222989*. A former convent, the hotel has 34 rooms stylishly furnished with reproduction antique furniture.

Bissick Old Mill, *Ladock, Near Truro TR2 4PG; tel: (01726) 862557; fax: (01726) 884057*; 5 miles east, off B3275. Elegant country hotel. Moderate.

Marcorrie Hotel, *20 Falmouth Rd, Truro TR1 2HX; tel: (01872) 277374; fax: (01872) 241666*. 5 min walk to city centre. Budget–moderate.

Arrallas, *Ladock, Near Truro TR2 4NP; tel: (01872) 510379; fax: (01872) 510200*. Stylish guesthouse with six well-furnished en suite rooms. Budget.

Trevispian-Vean Farm Guesthouse, *Tresillian, Truro TR2 4BL; tel: (01872) 279514; fax: (01872) 263730*; 2 miles east. Noted for its comfort and meals. Budget.

Polsue Manor Farm, *Tresillian, Truro TR2 4BP; tel: (01872) 520234; fax: (01872) 520616*. Six rooms in a manor overlooking the Tresillian river. Budget.

HI: Perranporth; *tel: (01872) 573812* (8 miles west); and **Falmouth** (see below). The nearest **campsites** are **Carnon Downs Camping and Caravan Park**, *Carnon Downs; tel: (01872) 862283*, 3 miles south; **Leverton Place Caravan and Camping Park**, *Greenbottom; tel: (01872) 560462*, 3 miles west; **Summer Valley Touring Park**, *Shortlanesend; tel: (01872) 277878*, 3 miles north; and **Chacewater Park**, *Cox Hill, Chacewater; tel: (01209) 820762*, 6 miles west.

SIGHTSEEING

Bus tours around the area are available from **F.T. Williams Travel**, *tel: (01209) 717152*, while **boat trips** are operated by **Enterprise Boats**, *tel: (01326) 374241*.

Once a river port and tin-mining centre, Truro had its heyday in the 18th century, as its elegant and well-preserved Georgian streets (especially *Boscawen St, Lemon St* and *Walsingham Place*) bear witness. A good introduction to Cornish history and industry (it also boasts a number of Old Masters) is the **Royal Cornwall Museum and Art Gallery**, *River St; tel: (01872) 272205*, open Mon–Fri 0900–1700, Sat 1000–1700; £2.

Truro Cathedral, *High Cross; tel: (01872) 276782*, open daily; free, but donation requested, had its foundation stone laid only in 1880, when Cornwall was finally granted its own bishop. It is an impressive example of the Gothic Revival style.

OUT OF TOWN

The gardens in this part of southern Cornwall's so-called 'Riviera' testify to its subtropical climate. **Trelissick Gardens** (NT), *Feock; tel (01872) 862090*, open Mon–Sat 1030–1730 (Apr–Sept); Mon–Sat 1030–1700 (Mar, Oct); £4. 4 miles south. From the gardens there are unrivalled views of the Fal estuary, as well as beautiful woodland and sheltered flower gardens; Trelissick is noted for its variegated shrubs.

Trewithen House and Gardens, *Grampound Rd, Probus; tel: (01726) 883647*, house open (with compulsory tour) Mon–Tues 1400–1600 (Apr–July and Aug public holidays); £3.20 (house and garden). Gardens open Mon–Sat 1000–1630 (Mar–Sept); Sun 1000–1630 (Apr–May); £2.80. 5 miles east. The 18th-century house has a particularly magnificent dining room, as well as a 30-acre landscaped garden of international fame, containing many rare species. If you need help in choosing plants to suit specific conditions, don't miss nearby **Probus Gardens**, *Probus; tel: (01726) 882597*, open daily 1000–1700 (Apr–Sept); Mon–Fri 1000–1600 (Oct–Mar); £2.70.

St Austell Brewery Visitor Centre, *Trevarthian Rd; tel: (01726) 66022*. Tours by appointment Mon–Fri 0930–1630 (Apr–Oct). The working brewery was established in 1851 and tours include a beer sampling. Just north of St Austell is **Wheal Martyn China Clay Heritage Centre**, *Carthew; tel: (01726) 850362*, open daily 1000–1800 (Apr–Oct); £4.25. Varied points of interest include a nature trail, a large waterwheel, a view of a modern working clay pit, a play area, exhibitions and audiovisual shows – mostly related to the production of china clay.

FALMOUTH

TIC: *28 Killigrew St, Falmouth, Cornwall TR11 3PN; tel: (01326) 312300*, open Mon–Thur 0845–1715, Fri 0900–1645, Sat 0900–1700 (Easter–Sept); Sun 1000–1600 (July–Aug); Mon–Thur 0845– 1300 and 1400–1715, Fri 0900–1300 and 1400–1645 (Sept–Easter). DP Services offered: local bed-booking and BABA (latest booking 1630). The *Falmouth Guide* is available free and includes an accommodation listing.

GETTING AROUND

Falmouth's attractions are within walking distance of the centre. Free town and transport maps are available from the TIC. Most buses are operated by **Western National**, *tel: (01209) 719988*. Services are good in town, but patchy elsewhere. Very limited services operate after 1800 and on Sun. The main **taxi** rank is on the Moor (in the centre).

ACCOMMODATION

There is a good range of accommodation, most cheaper establishments being in the centre (the seafront is expensive). It is generally easy to find accommodation on arrival, except during Falmouth Sailing Week (Aug). Hotel chains in Falmouth include *BW* and *Ct*.

Falmouth Hotel, *Castle Beach, Falmouth TR11 4NZ; tel: (01326) 312671; fax: (01326) 319533*. The 73 rooms in this charming establishment overlook either the river or the sea. Moderate–expensive.

Green Lawns Hotel, *Western Terrace, Falmouth TR11 4QJ; tel: (01326) 312734; fax: (01326) 211427*. This château-style hotel stands in beautifully landscaped grounds just a stroll from the town and main beaches. Moderate.

Home Country House Hotel, *Penjerrick, Budock Water, Falmouth TR11 5EE; tel: (01326) 250427; fax: (01326) 250143*. Located between the town and the Helford River, the Home has fine views over the countryside and the sea, open Mar–Oct. Budget.

Hotel Anacapri, *Gyllngvase Beach, Falmouth TR11 4DJ; tel/fax: (01326) 311454*. Enjoying a delightful position overlooking Falmouth Bay. Budget.

Penmere Manor, *Mongleath Rd, Falmouth TR11 4PN; tel: (01326) 211411; fax: (01326) 317588*. Tranquil hotel noted for its cuisine. Moderate.

Tresillian House Hotel, *3 Stracey Rd, Falmouth; tel: (01326) 312425*. Family-run hotel in a quiet location close to beach and coastal walks. Budget.

Ivanhoe, *7 Melvill Rd, Falmouth TR11 4AS; tel: (01326) 319083*. Charming Edwardian b&b close to town centre and beaches. Budget.

Grove Hotel, *Grove Place, Falmouth TR11 4AU; tel/fax: (01326) 319577*.

Overlooking Falmouth harbour. Budget. **The Trevelyan**, *6 Avenue Rd, Falmouth TR11 4AZ; tel: (01326) 311545.* Guesthouse with a licensed bar. Budget. **HI: Pendennis**, *The Headland; tel: (01326) 311435.* The closest **campsites** are: **Pennance Mill Farm**, *Maenporth, tel: (01326) 312616*; **Tregedna Farm**, *Maenporth, tel: (01326) 250529*; **Main Valley Caravan and Camping Park**, *Maenporth; tel: (01326) 312190,* all 2 miles south-west; and **Tremorrah Tent Site**, *Swanpool Rd; tel: (01326) 312103,* 1½ miles south-west.

The **Falmouth–Penzance** bus offers particularly good views of the surrounding countryside. Alternatively, there are **bus tours** around the area, bookable at the TIC. A variety of boats operates from Prince of Wales Pier: **St Mawes Ferry**, *tel: (01326) 313813/313201*; **Enterprise Boats**, *tel: (01326) 313234* (cruises and Truro ferry); **Falmouth Passenger Boat Co**, *tel: (01326) 313813*; and **K & S Cruises**, *tel: (01326) 376347/211056* (both offering cruises and deep-sea fishing). **Falmouth Sailing Week** (early Aug) is a major sailing regatta.

The largest town in Cornwall, Falmouth has a vast natural harbour, rimmed by grand hotels and mansions, and is renowned for its exceptionally mild climate and splendid beaches.

Two wonderfully preserved castles built by Henry VIII guard the harbour entrance: take the ferry across from one to the other and (from Black Rock) enjoy the stunning view up the wooded Fal estuary. **Pendennis Castle** (EH), *Pendennis Headland; tel: (01326) 316594,* open daily 1000–1800 (Apr–Oct); 1000–1600 (Nov–Mar); £2.70. **St Mawes Castle**, *St Mawes; tel: (01326) 270526,*

open daily 1000–1800 (Apr–Oct); 1000–1600 (Nov–Mar); £1.70. **Cornwall Maritime Museum**, *2 Bells Court, Market St; tel: (01326) 316745,* open Mon–Sat 1000–1600 (Easter–Oct); 1000–1500 (Nov–Easter); £1. Run entirely by enthusiastic volunteers, the museum's fascinating displays cover the entire history of Cornish shipping.

OUT OF TOWN

The **National Seal Sanctuary**, *Marine Animal Rescue Centre, Gweek, nr Helston; tel: (01326) 221361,* open daily 0900–1730 (Mar–Oct); 1000–1700 (Nov–Feb); approx. £5.50 (seasonal), 5 miles south-west, is the largest in Europe, rescuing many sick and injured seals and returning them to the wild.

A number of gardens in the area boast subtropical species, including two at Mawnan Smith, 4 miles south-west: **Glendurgan Gardens** (NT), *tel: (01326) 250906*; open Tues–Sat, public holidays 1030–1730 (Mar–Oct); £3; a delightful, informal valley garden, with walled and water gardens and a laurel maze; and **Trebah Gardens**, *tel: (01326) 250448,* open daily 1030–1700; £3. The 25-acre garden descends steeply through a ravine, dropping 200 ft between the 18th-century house and a private beach (visitors are allowed to swim), with natural waterfalls and many subtropical plants, which form a spectacular kaleidoscope of colour and scent.

Flambards Village Theme Park, *Culdrose Manor, Helston; tel: (01326) 564093,* open most days 1000/1030–1700 /1800 (Easter–Oct), but check early and late in the season; £5.99 (£4.60 after 1400). 13 miles south-west. A Victorian village, *Britain in the Blitz* and a log flume ride are among the varied attractions of this rather unthemed theme park.

309

SALISBURY

Built around one of England's great cathedrals – with the country's tallest spire – Salisbury is claimed by some as Britain's loveliest cathedral city. It is certainly a joy to explore. The extensive cathedral close has a range of buildings covering architectural styles from the 13th to the 18th centuries.

TOURIST INFORMATION

TIC: *Fish Row, Salisbury, Wiltshire SP1 1EJ; tel: (01722) 334956*, open Mon–Sat 0930–1700 (Oct–Apr); Mon–Sat 0930–1700, Sun 1030–1630 (May); Mon–Sat 0930–1800, Sun 1030–1630 (June, Sept); Mon–Sat 0930–1900, Sun 1030–1700 (July–Aug). DP SHS services offered; local bed-booking and BABA (latest bookings for both 1700; fee 10% of first night). Explorer and local theatre tickets sold. Free town and accommodation guides available.

The TIC also operates a kiosk at the railway station, *South Western Rd*, a quarter mile west of the centre, open Mon–Sat (not public holidays) 0930–1630 (late Mar–Sept), offering general information and local bed-booking (fee 10% of first night).

ARRIVING AND DEPARTING

Salisbury stands at the intersection of a number of important routes. The major east–west route is the A30, which stretches from London to Land's End. The A36 connects Southampton, to the south-east, and Bath, to the north-west. The A338 is the north–south link between Bournemouth and Oxford. The A354 strikes south-west

to Dorchester and Weymouth. There are plenty of car parks around the city centre, but parking may be difficult on market days – Tues and Sat.

GETTING AROUND

The majority of attractions in Salisbury are within walking distance of the centre. Free town and bus maps are available from the TIC. Buses are operated by **Wilts & Dorset**, *Endless St; tel: (01722) 336855*. There are **taxi** ranks at New Canal and the railway station.

STAYING IN SALISBURY

Accommodation and Food

Salisbury has a good range of central accommodation, including several cheaper hotels, a wide choice of guesthouses and b&bs and several pubs offering accommodation. Pre-booking is recommended June–Sept. Hotel chains include *BW, FH, MH.*

Rose and Crown, *Harnham Rd, Harnham, Salisbury SP2 8QJ; tel: (01722) 399955; fax: (01722) 3 39816*. With gardens bordering the River Avon, the main part of this 29-room hotel dates from 13th century. Expensive.

White Hart, *1 St John's St, Salisbury SP1 2SD; tel: (01722) 327476; fax: (01722) 412761*. City centre hotel, handy for the cathedral and shops. Expensive.

King's Arms Hotel, *St John's St, Salisbury SP1 2SB; tel: (01722) 327629; fax: (01722) 414246*. The oldest part of this atmospheric old inn dates from early 12th century. Moderate.

Alderbury Caravan Park, *Southampton Rd, Whaddon, Salisbury SP5 3HP; tel:*

(01722) 710125. Off the A36, 4 miles south-east of the city centre, the park is open all year and has 39 touring pitches, 20 with hook-up electricity.

HI: *Milford Hill House, Milford Hill; tel: (01722) 327572.* The TIC can provide information on **campsites**. The closest accessible by public transport is **Hudsons Field Campsite**, *Castle Rd; tel: (01722) 320713,* 1½ miles north.

The majority of restaurants are situated in the *Market Square* vicinity. There are some luxury restaurants and several pubs offer very good food.

Money

There is a **Thomas Cook bureau de change** at *Midland Bank, 19 Minster St.*

ENTERTAINMENT AND EVENTS

The TIC produces a free monthly entertainment listing, *What's On.* **The City Hall**, *Malthouse Lane; tel: (01722) 327676,* is an entertainment centre attracting a variety of quality events. **Salisbury Playhouse**, *Malthouse Lane; tel: (01722) 320333,* has a good theatre programme and **The Salisbury Arts Centre**, *Bedwin St; tel: (01722) 321744,* presents a range of performing and visual arts.

Major annual events in Salisbury include the **Salisbury Festival** (May–June) and **St George's Spring Festival** (Apr).

SIGHTSEEING

A variety of **guided walks** is available from the TIC; the basic town walks are £2.

Salisbury Cathedral, *The Close; tel: (01722) 328726,* open daily 0800–1830 (mid Sept–mid May); daily 0800–2015 (mid May–mid Sept); free, but £2.50 donations requested. This is the purest example of the Early English style: it was built entirely between 1220 and 1258 – apart from the spire (the highest in the country), which was added 1334–80. The intrepid can climb 360 steps up the tower to the base of the (leaning) spire. Take time to explore the cloister, the octagonal chapter house with its medieval frieze carved with scenes from *Genesis* and *Exodus* and the peaceful, walled **Cathedral Close**. The latter preserves a happy mix of 13th–18th-century houses. These include the 1710 **Mompesson House** (NT), *Choristers' Green; tel: (01722) 335659,* open Sat–Wed 1200–1730 (mid Mar–Oct); £3.20, which has fine plasterwork, Queen Anne furniture and a collection of rare 18th-century drinking glasses; and **Malmesbury House**, *15 The Close; tel: (01722) 327027,* open Tues–Sat 1030–1730 (Apr–Sept); £3.50, where the composer Handel once lived. Also within the Close, in the 13th-century King's House, is the **Salisbury and South Wiltshire Museum**, *65 The Close; tel: (01722) 332151,* open Mon–Sat 1000–1700 (all year); Sun 1400–1700 (July–Aug); £3. This contains many archaeological treasures from Old Sarum and Stonehenge, as well as a reconstructed pre-NHS doctor's surgery. North of the cathedral, towards *Market Square*, is a network of medieval streets and alleys, with many overhanging half-timbered houses.

OUT OF TOWN

To the north of the present city are the massive ramparts of **Old Sarum** (EH), open daily 1000–1800/dusk (Apr–Oct); 1000–1600 (Nov–Mar); £1.90. 2 miles north. Originally an Iron Age hill fort, the site was successively used by Romans, Saxons and Normans. The inconvenience of its windswept site led to the foundation of New Sarum, beside the River Avon, and thus was born modern Salisbury.

SALISBURY–EXETER

This route starts in one cathedral city and finishes in another, with some wonderful countryside and delightful small towns and villages in between. It touches four of England's prettiest counties – Wiltshire, Dorset, Somerset and Devon – and offers plenty of scope for dawdling.

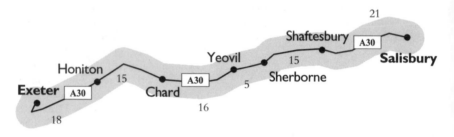

ROUTE: 90 MILES

ROUTE

This 90-mile route takes 2hrs 30mins. Leave Salisbury on A36 west for 4 miles, then bear left on A30 which continues west for 17 miles to **Shaftesbury**, 15 miles to **Sherborne**, and a further 5 miles to **Yeovil**. Continue on A30 west to reach **Chard** in 16 miles, **Honiton** in 15 miles and Exeter after a final 18 miles.

SHAFTESBURY

TIC: *8 Bell St, Shaftesbury, Dorset SP7 8AE; tel: (01747) 853514,* open daily 1000–1700 (Apr–Oct); Mon–Thur 1000–1300, Fri–Sat 1000–1700 (Nov–Mar). DP services offered; local bed-booking and BABA (latest bookings 1630; fee 10% of first night). *Shaftesbury Visitors Guide* is 20p, *Where to Stay in Shaftesbury & District* and *Where to Stay in Rural Dorset* are free.

GETTING AROUND

Town and transport maps are available from the TIC. Local **buses** cover nearby towns, but sporadically – with no service after 1900 or on Sun. The main **taxi** rank is on High St, near the Town Hall.

ACCOMMODATION

It is advisable to book accommodation in advance, particularly during the Great Dorset Steam Fair (Aug–Sept). There are a few smallish hotels and around 50 guesthouses and b&bs within a 10 mile radius of Shaftesbury, as well as several pubs offering accommodation. Hotel chains include *BW*. The nearest **campsites** are: **Shaftesbury Football Club**, *Coppice St; tel: (01747) 854132 (daytime), (01747) 853990 (after 1830)*, **Blackmore Vale Caravan Park**, *Sherborne Causeway; tel: (01747) 852573,* 2 miles west along A30; and **Thorngrove Centre**, *Common Mead Lane, Gillingham; tel: (01747) 822242 (daytime), (01747) 825384 (evenings/weekends)*, 6 miles.

SIGHTSEEING

Shaftesbury, one of England's oldest towns, appears in Thomas Hardy's novels under the name of 'Shaston' and offers wonderful views over Blackmore Vale. The town's attractions are close to each other: much-photographed **Gold Hill** is a picturesque, steep, cobbled street. At the top is **Shaftesbury Town Museum**, *Gold Hill; tel: (01747) 852157*, open daily 1100–1700 (Easter–Sept); Sun 1100–1600 (Oct–Easter); 75p. The displays are mainly of such everyday items as lace, dolls, old maps and photos, Dorset buttons, toys and coins.

The now-ruined medieval Benedictine abbey was founded by King Alfred the Great in AD 888. It's in a walled garden with a reconstructed Anglo-Saxon herb bed: the **Shaftesbury Abbey Museum**, *Abbey Walk; tel: (01747) 852910*, open daily 1000–1730 (Easter–Oct); £1, displays carved stonework, medieval floor tiles, pottery and the like.

OUT OF TOWN

Old Wardour Castle (EH), *nr Tisbury; tel: (01747) 870487*, open daily 1000–1800/dusk (Apr–Oct); Wed–Sun 1000–1600 (Nov–Mar); £1.50. 8 miles east. Built in 1393, for social rather than defensive reasons (although it was damaged in the Civil War), the castle is peacefully sited by a lake and the view from the top is worth the climb.

Stourhead House and Garden (NT), *Stourton, Warminster; tel: (01747) 841152*. House open Sat–Wed 1200–1730/dusk (Apr–Oct); £7.70 (house and garden). 12 miles north-west. Dating from the 18th century, the house contains fine works of art, but the main attraction is the landscaped garden, with a series of lakes, temples, rare trees and marvellous vistas.

SHERBORNE

TIC: *3 Tilton Court, Digby Road, Sherborne, Dorset DT9 3NL; tel: (01935) 815341*, open Mon–Sat 0930–1730 (mid Mar–mid Oct); Mon–Sat 1000–1500 (mid Oct–mid Mar). DP SHS services offered; local bed-booking and BABA, local theatres and ferries booked. *West Dorset Accommodation Guide* is free, *Sherborne Visitor Guide* is 40p.

GETTING AROUND

The town's attractions are mostly within walking distance of the centre. Free transport maps are available from the TIC. The main bus operator is **Southern National**, *tel: (01935) 76233*. There are regular services during the day, but little after 2200 or on Sun. The main **taxi** rank is outside the station.

ACCOMMODATION

Most of the accommodation in Sherborne consists of pubs and b&bs; there are a couple of mid-range hotels. The cheaper accommodation is on the edge of the centre. It is generally easy to book on arrival, except July–Aug and public holidays. The TIC has details of **campsites** in the area – the nearest is **Giants Head Caravan and Camping Park**, *Old Sherborne Rd, Cerne Abbas; tel: (01300) 341242*, 12 miles south.

SIGHTSEEING

The TIC can book **bus tours, boat trips** and **guided walks**.

The lovely medieval buildings of Sherborne are dominated by **Sherborne Abbey**, *tel: (01935) 812452*, open daily 0900–1800 (May–Sept); 0900–1600 (Oct–Apr); free. Tours Tues 1030, Fri 1430 (June–Sept). Founded in 705 and rebuilt several times over the centuries, there are traces of many styles and it's even more interesting inside than out.

313

This small country town boasts two castles. **Sherborne Castle**, *tel: (01935) 813182*, open Thur, Sat–Sun public holidays 1330–1700 (Easter–Sept); *£4.80*. A furnished house built by Sir Walter Raleigh in 1594, the castle is enhanced by a variety of priceless family heirlooms. Across a tranquil stretch of water is the ruined 12th-century **Sherborne Old Castle** (EH), *tel: (01935) 812730*, open daily 1000–1800/dusk (Easter–Oct); Wed–Sun 1000–1600 (Nov–Mar); *£1.50*.

Over 15,000 items trace local history since Roman times in the **Sherborne Museum**, *Abbey Gate House; tel: (01935) 812252*, open Tues–Sat 1030–1630, Sun, public holidays 1430–1630 (Easter–Oct); *£1*.

The Almshouse of St John the Baptist and John the Evangelist, *Half Moon St; tel: (01935) 813245*, open Tues, Thur–Sat 1400–1600 (May–Sept); *50p*. This dates from the 15th century, when it was intended to house 'pore, feeble and ympotent' men (12) and women (5).

OUT OF TOWN

Worldlife, *Compton House; tel: (01935) 474608*, open daily 1000–1700 (Apr–Sept); *£3.95*. 3 miles west. Established to promote awareness of conservation, the original butterfly jungle is still a major feature, but now many other creatures (some wild) can be found on the premises.

YEOVIL

TIC: *Petters House, Petters Way, Yeovil, Somerset BA20 1SH; tel: (01935) 471279*, open Mon–Sat 0915–1800 (Apr–Oct), Mon–Fri 0930–1700 (Nov–Mar). Services offered: local accommodation bookings, BABA, coach tour reservations and tickets for regional events and attractions; YHA enrolments.

ACCOMMODATION

Workaday Yeovil is stronger on hotel accommodation than guesthouses and b&bs – check with the TIC.

Little Barwick House, *Barwick Village, Near Yeovil BA22 9TD; tel: (01935) 423902; fax: (01935) 420908*. Six excellent en suite rooms in a listed Georgian house miles south of Yeovil. Rooms moderate; restaurant pricey.

Manor House, *Hendford, Yeovil BA20 1TG; tel: (01935) 231161; fax: (01935) 706607*. Close to town centre. Moderate.

Preston Hotel and Motel, *64 Preston Rd, Yeovil BA20 2RG; tel: (01935) 474400; fax: (01935) 410142*. Family-run hotel. Moderate.

Yeovil Court, *West Coker Rd, Yeovil BA20 2NE; tel: (01935) 863746; fax: (01935) 863990*. Modern hotel on the western edge of town. Moderate.

EATING AND DRINKING

The Pall Tavern, *Silver St; tel: (01935) 76521*. Steaks and grills are the specialities – but look out for the daily blackboard specials – in this evocatively restored medieval tavern, open daily 1200–1415, 1830–2200. Moderate.

Rose and Crown, *Trent, Dorset; tel: (01935) 850776*; 4 miles north-east. Award-winning cuisine includes Cajun and Creole dishes as well as traditional fish and game. Restaurant and bar meals served daily 1200–1400, 1900–2130. Moderate.

The Black Piper, *1 High St, Stoke-sub-Hamdon; tel: (01935) 822826*. 5 miles north-west. Popular seafood restaurant. Dinner from 1900. Lunch by arrangement. Expensive.

SIGHTSEEING

Yeovil itself is a busy market town rather than a tourism centre, but its major attractions are within 5 miles by car.

Fleet Air Arm Museum, *RNAS Yeovilton, Ilchester, Somerset; tel: (01935) 840565,* open daily 1000–1630 (Nov–Mar); 1000–1730 (Apr–Oct); £6.50. 5 miles north. Stand on the deck of a carrier, take a navy flight, stroll through Concorde: it's all possible.

Ilchester Museum, *Town Hall, High St, Ilchester; tel: (01935) 841247,* open Thur, Sat 1000–1600; free. 5 miles north. The town's story from prehistoric times to the present day is told in text, pictures, photographs and local archaeological finds.

Montacute House (NT), *Montacute, Somerset; tel: (01935) 823289.* House open Wed–Mon 1200–1730 (Easter–Oct); £5 (house and grounds). 4 miles north-west. This late 16th-century house has a notable long gallery and great hall and some fine furniture.

Museum of South Somerset, *Hendford, Yeovil; tel: (01935) 424774,* open Tues–Sat 1000–1600 (Apr–Oct), Tues–Fri 1000–1600 (Nov–Mar); free. Reconstructed Roman and Georgian rooms are featured in the museum, which also houses collections of costumes and glassware.

CHARD

TIC: *The Guildhall, Fore St, Chard, Somerset TA20 1PP; tel: (01460) 67463,* open Mon–Sat 1000–1630 (Easter–Nov), Mon–Fri 1100–1600, Sat 1000–1300 (Dec–Easter). Services offered: local bed-booking, BABA. The centre also sells theatre and coach trip tickets, maps and souvenirs.

ACCOMMODATION

The Lordleaze Hotel and Restaurant, *Chard TA20 2HW; tel: (01460) 61066; fax: (01460) 66468.* Country hotel on the edge of Chard with 16 en suite rooms. Noted for good food. Moderate.

George Hotel and Courtyard Restaurant, *Market Sq., Crewkerne TA18 7LP; tel: (01460) 73650; fax: (01460) 72974.* 6 miles east. Historic coaching inn with 13 rooms (most en suite) and an indoor swimming pool. Caters for vegetarians and special diets. Budget–moderate.

Keymer Cottage, *Buckland St Mary, Chard TA20 3JF; tel: (01460) 234460; fax: (01460) 234226.* Non-smoking b&b with three en suite rooms. Evening meals, including vegetarian dishes. Budget.

Watermead Guesthouse, *83 High St, Chard TA20 1QT; tel: (01460) 62834.* The guesthouse has nine rooms (six en suite). Evening meals, including vegetarian and special diets. Budget.

Hawthorne House, *Bishopswood Chard TA20 3RS; tel: (01460) 234482.* 4 miles north-west. Cosy stone-built 19th-century house with six comfortable rooms. Good food (take your own wine); vegetarians welcomed. Budget.

315

SIGHTSEEING

Chard and District Museum, *Godworthy House, High St; tel: (01460) 65091,* open daily 1030–1630 (July–Aug), Mon–Sat 1030–1630 (Sept–Oct and May–June); £1.70. Farm implements and machinery and domestic appliances from the past are on display and there are exhibits featuring cider-making and local history.

Ferne Animal Sanctuary, *Wambrook, Chard; tel: (01460) 65214,* open Wed, Sat, Sun, public holidays 1400–1700 (end Mar–mid Oct); free. Some 300 animals, ranging from terrapins to shire horses on a 50-acre site. Nature trail.

Hornsbury Mill, *Eleighwater, Chard; tel: (01460) 63317,* open daily 1000–1630 (mid Feb–Dec); £2. A 200 year old working water mill and museum standing in landscaped water gardens.

OUT OF TOWN

Perry's Cider Mills, *Dowlish Wake, Ilminster; tel: (01460) 52681.* 4 miles north, open Mon–Fri 0900–1730, Sat 0930–1630, Sun 1000–1300; free. A working cider farm, where you can visit a museum containing cider presses, wagons and farm tools. A video shows how cider is brewed, and there's a shop where you can taste and buy the finished product.

Cricket St Thomas Wildlife Park, *Chard; tel: (01460) 30755.* 2 miles east, open daily 1000–1800 (dusk if earlier); £4. Elephants, sealions, heavy horses and other animals, plus Mr Blobby, a woodland railway, fun village, safari rides and lots more – all on the estate used as the location for the BBC TV series *To The Manor Born*.

HONITON

TIC: *Lace Walk Car Park, Honiton, Devon EX14 8LT; tel: (01404) 43716,* open Mon–Sat 0930–1630 (Apr–Oct), Tues, Thur–Sat 1000–1500 (Nov–Mar).

ACCOMMODATION

Colestocks House Hotel, *Payhembury Rd, Feniton, nr Honiton EX14 0JR; tel: (01404) 850633; fax: (01404) 850901.* 3 miles west. A 16th-century thatched farmhouse has been tastefully converted into an hotel with ten en suite bedrooms, open Apr–Oct. Moderate.

Greyhound Inn, *Fenny Bridges, nr Honiton EX14 0BJ; tel: (01404) 850380; fax: (01404) 850812.* 4 miles west. Thatched roof inn with oak beams and huge open fireplace; ten en suite rooms. Moderate.

Barn Park Farm, *Stockland Hill, Cotleigh, nr Honiton EX14 9JA; tel/fax: (01404) 861297.* 5 miles east. Three guest-rooms in an old farmhouse with flintstone walls on a working dairy farm. Budget.

Stonehenge

To include Stonehenge on this route, take A345 north for 8 miles from Salisbury to Amesbury, then head west on A303. The monument will be reached after 2 miles at the junction of A303 and A344; *tel: (01980) 624715*, open daily 0930–1800 (mid Mar–May and Sept–mid Oct); daily 0900–1900 (June–Aug); daily 0930–1600 (mid Oct–mid Mar); £3.90.

One of the world's most famous heritage sites, mysterious Stonehenge draws thousands of visitors, who have to be kept at some distance from the monument in the interests of preservation. There are snacks and a shop, but at the time of writing there was still no decision on plans to build a visitor centre and improved access to the site.

On leaving Stonehenge continue west on A303 for 18 miles, then head south on A350 to reach Shaftesbury in 8 miles. Follow A30 west to continue the route to Exeter.

Lane End Farm, *Broadhembury, Honiton EX14 0LU; tel: (01404) 841563.* 4 miles north-west. Five rooms in a farmhouse in a picturesque village with many thatched cottages. Lovely gardens, superb views, good food. Budget.

SIGHTSEEING

Famous for lace-making – its lace is said to have been worn by every royal bride and Speaker of the House of Commons – Honiton is a former coaching town with a wide main street of elegant Georgian buildings.

Examples of Honiton lace can be seen at the **Allhallows Museum**, *High St.* The town is noted for its antiques and antiquarian bookshops and its twice-weekly market.

SCARBOROUGH

Lively Scarborough is said to be Britain's oldest seaside resort. It has been a spa since 1662 and was regarded as the country's premier holiday destination during Victorian times. It has two sweeping crescents of golden sand separated by a small harbour and a narrow headland with a Norman castle built in 1130. The Yorkshire author Anne Brontë, who died in the town in 1849, is buried in the graveyard of nearby St Mary's Church.

TOURIST INFORMATION

TIC: *Unit 3, Pavilion House, Valley Bridge Rd, Scarborough, North Yorkshire YO11 1UZ; tel: (01723) 373333*, open daily 0930–1800 (May–Sept); 1000–1630 (Oct–Apr). DP SHS services offered; local bed-booking and BABA. *Scarborough, Whitby and Filey Holiday* brochure and an accommodation listing are free. Accommodation guide for disabled travellers is available from Disablement Action Group, *5 West Parade Rd; tel: (01723) 379397.*

ARRIVING AND DEPARTING

Located at north-east edge of the North Yorks Moors National Park, Scarborough is approached from York by A64 and from Bridlington and Humberside to the south by A165. A170 links with A1 by way of Pickering and Thirsk. A171 follows the coast north through the national park to Whitby and Teesside.

GETTING AROUND

The attractions in town are all within walking distance of the centre. Town maps are available from the TIC (£1), who also have limited information about buses. **Bus** services are good in the centre and frequent to surrounding towns, but most services are reduced after 2000 (Mon–Sat) and all day Sun. The main local bus company is **Scarborough and District**, *tel: (01723) 375463*, who operate Skipper buses from various points in the town. Other bus companies include: **Tees and District**, *tel: (01642) 210131*; **United Buses** *tel: (01325) 468771*; and **Yorkshire Coastliner**, *tel: (01653) 692556*.

Registered taxi companies include: **Nippy Taxis**, *tel: (01723) 370888*; **Castle Taxis**, *tel: (01723) 378161*; and **Boro Taxis**, *tel: (01723) 366144.*

STAYING IN SCARBOROUGH

Accommodation

A good range of accommodation is available, particularly cheaper to mid-range hotels, but there are also many large independent hotels. Cheaper accommodation and rooms in pubs and inns can be found in all areas. It is usually easy to find accommodation on arrival, except July–Aug and public holiday weekends. Hotel chains represented include *Pn*.

Ambassador Hotel, *South Cliff, Scarborough YO11 2AY; tel/fax: (01723) 362841*. Clifftop hotel with tropical lounge, sauna and heated pool. Moderate.

Avoncroft Hotel, *Crown Terrace, Scarborough YO11 2BL; tel/fax: (01723) 372737*. Standing in a Georgian terrace a few minutes' walk from the beach and

317

town centre. Budget–moderate.

Blacksmith's Arms, *High Street, Cloughton, Scarborough YO13 0AE; tel: (01723) 870244*. Located on the edge of the national park, 4 miles north of Scarborough. Quaint country pub. Budget–moderate.

East Ayton Lodge Country House Hotel and Restaurant, *Moor Lane, East Ayton, Scarborough YO13 9EW; tel: (01723) 864227; fax: (01273) 862680*. Attractive hotel in a lovely 3-acre setting in the North Yorkshire Moors National Park. Budget–moderate.

HI: White House, *Burniston Rd; tel: (01723) 361176*. The TIC has information on local **campsites**. The nearest is: **Scalby Manor Caravan Park**, *Burniston Rd; tel: (01723) 366212*, 2 miles north.

Eating and Drinking

As might be expected of a popular seaside resort, Scarborough offers a wide choice of eating places and pubs.

Copper Horse, *15 Main St, Seamer, Scarborough YO12 4RF; tel: (01723) 862029*. Good English fare served in a friendly pub atmosphere; moderate.

Golden Grid Fish Restaurant, *4 Sandside, Scarborough YO11 1PE; tel: (01723) 360922*. Seafood fresh daily from the North Sea, open daily 1030–2200; moderate.

Lanterna, *33 Queen St, Scarborough YO11 1HQ; tel: (01723) 363616*. One of Scarborough's best-known restaurants serves authentic Italian dishes, open Mon–Sat 1900–2200; pricey.

Money

There is a **Thomas Cook bureau de change** at *47 Westborough*.

SIGHTSEEING

Applebys, *tel: (01723) 366659*, operate a **bus tour** around Scarborough, bookable

at the TIC, where you can also get information on **boat trips** and **guided walks**.

Scarborough Castle (EH), *Castle Rd; tel: (01723) 372451*, open daily 1000–1800/dusk (Easter–Oct); Wed–Sun 1000–1600 (Nov–Easter); £1.80, over-looks two sandy beaches. The town has a wide variety of seaside attractions, such as an exciting water theme park: **Atlantis**, *North Bay; tel: (01723) 372744*, open daily 1000–1800 (June–Aug); £4.80 July–Aug, £4 June – both reduced slightly after 1400.

Scarborough Millennium *Harbourside; tel: (01723) 501000*, open daily 1000–2200 (May–Sept); 1000–1700, but with variations (Oct–Apr); £4.50. This is a journey back through time and the history of the town, covering the period AD 966–1966.

OUT OF TOWN

To the south-west is **Eden Camp**, *nr Malton; tel: (01653) 697777*, open Mon–Fri 1000–1700 (mid Jan–mid Feb); daily 1000–1700 (mid Feb–mid Dec); £3. 22 miles south-west. The name derives from the fact that this museum is housed in genuine prisoner-of-war huts. In each, modern technology is used to recreate some aspect of life during World War II, in a way designed to make you part of the experience: from being in a torpedoed submarine to coping with rationing.

Sea Life Centre, *Scalby Mills; tel: (01723) 376125*, open daily 1000–2000 (school summer holidays); daily 1000–1800 (rest of the year); £4.75. 2 miles north. Three pyramids display over 30 separate marine habitats – and there's a seal rescue unit.

West of Scarborough, take a steam train ride on the **North Yorkshire Moors Railway** or visit **Flamingo Land Family Fun Park** (see Whitby, p.320).

SCARBOROUGH– NEWCASTLE

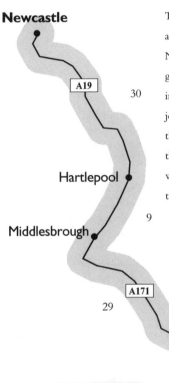

The first 35 miles or so of this route take us along the magnificent coastal edge of the North Yorkshire Moors National Park – a good start to a trip that travels across alternating rural, urban and industrial landscapes. The journey also provides an opportunity to see the estuary areas of those two great rivers of the North-East – the Tees and the Tyne – as well as visiting Count Dracula's old haunt, the very sanguine seaside town of Whitby.

ROUTE: 89 MILES

319

ROUTE

Allow 2 hrs for this route if driving non-stop. From Scarborough head north on A165 for 4 miles and continue north on A171 for 17 miles to **Whitby**. Continue on A171, crossing the north-east tip of the North Yorkshire Moors National Park, travelling through Guisborough, and turning right on to A174 after 27 miles. After 2 miles turn right on to A1032 to reach central **Middlesbrough** in less than a mile. Leave Middlesbrough on A178, passing Hartlepool Power Station on the

right and reaching **Hartlepool** town centre in 9 miles. Continue north on A1086 to Peterlee, reached in 8 miles, then turn right on to A19. Follow A19 for 15 miles, turn left on to A184 for 5 miles to

Gateshead. From here A167 crosses the River Tyne and the centre of Newcastle (p. 279) is reached in less than 2 miles.

WHITBY

TIC: *Langborne Rd, Whitby, North Yorkshire YO21 1YN; tel: (01947) 602674,* open daily 0930–1800 (May–Sept); daily 1000–1230 and 1300–1630 (Oct–Apr). DP services offered; local bed-booking and BABA (latest 30 mins before closing). Free accommodation guide available.

GETTING AROUND

Most attractions are within walking distance of the centre. The TIC issues free transport maps. **Tees Buses** is the main operator for local buses. For information contact the **Travel Office**, *Station Sq.; tel: (01947) 602146.* There is a good town service, but it is patchy to outlying areas. The main **taxi** rank is on *Langborne Rd,* outside the TIC.

ACCOMMODATION

Whitby has a good range of accommodation, particularly guesthouses and b&bs. The majority of cheaper hotels are in the West Cliff area. There are about a dozen pubs in the centre that offer accommodation. It's usually relatively easy to book on arrival, but sensible to pre-book for July–Aug, especially public holiday weekends.

HI: *East Cliff, Whitby; tel: (01947) 602878.* The TIC can provide listings of **campsites**; the nearest is **Sandfield House Farm Caravan Park**, *Sandsend Rd; tel: (01947) 602660,* 1 mile north.

SIGHTSEEING

A number of tours operated by **Coastal & Country**, *tel: (01947) 602922,* can be booked through the TIC. **Fishing trips** and **guided walks** can also be arranged.

Whitby manages to be both a popular resort and an active fishing port. Although crammed with souvenir shops, the steep narrow streets of the old town above the river have much charm. Looming above the harbour on the East Cliff – reached via 199 steps – is the dramatic ruin of **Whitby Abbey** (EH), *East Cliff; tel: (01947) 603568,* open daily 1000–1800/dusk (Easter–Oct); 1000–1600 (Nov–Easter); £1.60.

Captain Cook's former home, which contains miscellaneous memorabilia of the great 18th-century Pacific explorer, is now the **Captain Cook Memorial Museum**, *Grape Lane; tel: (01947) 601900,* open daily 0945–1700 (Easter–Oct); Sat–Sun 1100–1500 (Nov–Easter); £2.20.

Whitby is notorious as the setting for Bram Stoker's novel *Dracula*; the ghoulish can follow a *Dracula Trail* (30p from TIC) or shudder at the mixture of live actors, electronics and waxworks in the **Dracula Experience**, *9 Marine Parade; tel: (01947) 601923,* open daily 1000–1800 (Easter–Oct); Sat–Sun 1000–1800 (Nov–Easter); £1.75.

For those interested in maritime tradition, one of the best of its kind is the **Whitby Lifeboat Museum**, *Pier Rd; tel: (01947) 602001,* open daily in high season, but irregular hours – so check with the TIC; free.

Whitby Museum and Art Gallery, *Pannett Pk; tel: (01947) 602908,* open Mon–Sat 0930–1730, Sun 1400–1700 (May–Sept); Wed–Sat, public holidays 1030–1600, Mon–Tues 1030–1300, Sun 1400–1600 (Oct–Apr); museum £1.50; gallery free. This is a charming small museum with eclectic exhibits about the town.

St Mary's Parish Church, *East Cliff; tel: (01947) 603421,* open daily 1000–1500/1700 (Easter–Oct); 1000–1200 (Nov–Easter); free, has an audiovisual presentation about Whitby; £1.

320

OUT OF TOWN

Flamingo Land Theme Park and Zoo, *Kirby Misperton; tel: (01653) 668287*, open daily 1000–variable closing (Easter–Sept); also Sat–Sun, half-term holidays (Oct); £9.50. 25 miles south-west. The mixture of white-knuckle rides, children's amusements and animals makes this an excellent dayout for families.

MIDDLESBROUGH

TIC: *51 Corporation Rd, Middlesbrough, TS1 1LT; tel: (01642) 243425*, open Mon–Fri 0900–1700, Sat 0900–1300 year round. Closed public holidays. Services offered: BABA, local accommodation reservations, tourist guide services.

ACCOMMODATION

Marton Way Toby Hotel, *Marton Rd, Middlesbrough TS1 3BA; tel: (01642) 817651; fax: (01642) 829409*. 2 miles south of town centre. Moderate.

Baltimore Hotel, *250 Marton Rd, Middlesbrough TS4 2EZ; tel: (01642) 224111; fax: (01642) 226156*. Within a mile of the town centre and railway station. Moderate–expensive.

Chadwick Hotel, *27 Clairville Rd, Middlesbrough TS4 2HN; tel: (01642) 245340*. Friendly family-run hotel. Budget–moderate.

Grey House Hotel, *79 Cambridge Rd, Linthorpe, Middlesbrough TS5 5NL; tel/fax: (01642) 817485*. Edwardian property in garden setting. Moderate.

Hospitality Inn, *Fry St, Middlesbrough, TS1 1JH; tel: (01642) 232000; fax: (01642) 232655*. High-rise hotel in town centre. Expensive.

Southern Cross Hotel, *Dixons Bank, Middlesbrough, TS7 8NX; tel: (01642) 317539*. Small licensed hotel. Budget.

University of Teesside, *Middlesbrough; TS1 3BA; tel: (01642) 218121;*

fax: (01642) 342067. Good quality accommodation in Easter and summer vacations. Budget.

Prissick Caravan Park, *Marton Rd, Middlesbrough*. Contact *Lesrirue, PO Box 69, Vancouver House, Middlesbrough TS1 1QP; tel: (01642) 300202; fax: (01642) 300276*, open Easter–end Sept, then flexible arrangements with limited facilities.

SIGHTSEEING

Captain James Cook was born at Middlesbrough, and although there are several Cook-related attractions, which include a one-fifth scale replica of the *Endeavour* on the self-guided **Captain Cook Town Tour**, Middlesbrough has a variety of interesting places to see. Teesside is part of the fastest-growing tourism area in Britain. The countryside spills into the town at some points – the 'beck valleys' – little waterways with wooded banks which are pleasant to walk by.

Middlesbrough Art Gallery, *320 Linthorpe Rd, Middlesbrough; tel: (01642) 247445*, open Tues–Sat and public holidays 1000–1730. Free. One of the finest collections of 20th-century British art in the north of England is housed here.

Cleveland Crafts Centre, *57 Gilkes St, Middlesbrough; tel: (01642) 262376*, open Tues–Sat 1000–1700. Free. Popular museum and gallery exhibiting a wide range of crafts.

Nature's World at the Botanic Centre, *Ladgate Lane, Acklam, Middlesbrough; tel: (01642) 594895*, open daily Mon–Sat 1000–1700, Sun 1000–1800 (April–Sept), 1030–1600 (Oct–Mar); £3. A working model of the River Tees can be seen at this environmental centre, with gardens, ponds and livestock corner.

Captain Cook Birthplace Museum, *Stewart Park, Marton, Middlesbrough; tel: (01642) 311211*, open Tues–Sun

321

1000–1730 (summer), 0900–1600 (winter). Last entry 45 minutes before closing; £2. Interactive displays and a time travel machine which enables visitors to join Cook on his voyages.

Transporter Bridge, *Ferry Rd, Middlesbrough; tel: (01642) 247563*, open Mon–Sat 0500–2305, Sun 1400–2305. Pedestrians 26p, cars 72p. The only working transporter bridge in the country, it moves across the River Tees carrying traffic.

Stewart Park, *Ladgate Lane* and **Albert Park**; for both *tel: (01642) 300202*, both open 0730–dusk (summer), 1000–1600 (winter) are particularly worth visiting. As well as the Captain Cook Museum (see above), Stewart Park's attractions include a children's zoo, lakes, parkland and a conservatory containing plants that Captain Cook and his botanist, Joseph Banks, would have seen on their travels.

HARTLEPOOL

TIC: *Hartlepool Art Gallery and Information Centre, Church Sq., Hartlepool, TS14 6HI; tel: (01429) 869706*, open year round. Services offered: local accommodation reservations, BABA.

ACCOMMODATION

Grand Hotel, *Swainson St, Hartlepool, TS24 8AA; tel: (01429) 266345; fax: (01429) 265217.* Victorian hotel in the heart of the town and business district. Moderate–expensive.

Ash Vale Homes and Holiday Park, *Easington Rd, Hartlepool TS24 9RF; tel: (01429) 862111.* Pitches for 24 touring caravans from £3 per night.

SIGHTSEEING

Hartlepool Historic Quay, *Marine Ave, Hartlepool; tel: (01429) 860006*, open daily 1000–1700 all year and to 1900 (mid July and Aug). £4.95. This is Teesside Development Corporation's authentic reconstruction of a north-east seaport in Nelson's time. The project cost £200 million and there is much to see – life-size ship interiors, quayside shops and market, Teesside-made crafts, children's playground, gardens, marina walkways, seafront promenade, pubs and restaurants.

Museum of Hartlepool, *Jackson's Dock, Marina, Hartlepool; tel: (01429) 222255*, open daily 1100–1800 all year. The original light from the town's lighthouse is among local historical and archaeological exhibits in the new museum building.

Hartlepool Art Gallery, *Church Sq., Hartlepool; tel: (01429) 869706.* A varied programme of art and craft exhibitions in a church building which also contains the TIC. A bell-tower platform provides a view of Hartlepool.

Hartlepool Power Station Visitor Centre, *Tees Rd, Hartlepool; tel: (01429) 853888* for opening times; free. Guided tour includes the control room and giant turbo generator. Interactive galleries and audiovisual presentations.

HMS Trincomalee, *Jackson Dock, Hartlepool; tel: (01429) 223193*, open Mon–Fri 1300–1630, Sat, Sun and public holidays 1000–1630. £2.50. One of the oldest British warships afloat, the vessel was built in Bombay in 1817 and is undergoing restoration. Guided tours, visitor centre and shop.

PSS *Wingfield Castle*, *Jackson Dock, Hartlepool; tel: (01429) 022255*, open daily 1000–1800 all year; free. The paddle steamer, built in 1934 for the LNER as a passenger and vehicle ferry operating between Kingston-upon-Hull and New Holland, is now on show at Hartlepool.

STRATFORD-UPON-AVON

The claim to fame of this small market town in central England rests on one accident of birth: England's greatest playwright was born here in 1564, in the upstairs room of a timber-framed house. Stratford has attracted literary pilgrims ever since the Bard's death, and the Shakespeare connection is inescapable, from pub and café names to the main tourist attractions which have a link, however tenuous, with the man himself.

TOURIST INFORMATION

TIC: *Bridgefoot, Stratford-upon-Avon, Warwickshire CV37 6GW; tel: (01789) 293127*, open Mon–Sat 0900–1800, Sun 1100–1700 (Mar–Oct); Mon–Sat 0900–1700 (Nov–Mar). DP SHS services offered; local bed-booking (latest 15 mins before closing), BABA (latest 1 hr before closing), guided tours booked, bureau de change. Tickets booked for Guide Friday tours and Shakespeare Properties (reductions if you combine them). Great British Heritage Pass and Town Heritage Pass sold. Ask for free town guide *Stratford-upon-Avon, Shakespeare's Country* and accommodation guide.

Guide Friday Tourism Centre, *Civic Hall, 14 Rother St; tel: (01789) 294466*, open 0900–1730 (May–Sept); 0930–1600 (Mar–Apr, Oct); 1000–1400 (Nov–Feb). DP services offered; local bed-booking and BABA (fee £3), guided tours booked (with discounts on Shakespeare Properties). Local events booked.

ARRIVING AND DEPARTING

At the heart of the English Midlands, Stratford-upon-Avon is easily reached from all directions. Birmingham is barely 20 miles to the north, while Junction 15 of M40 – the major route between London and Birmingham – is 7 miles north-east. The M5, the main link between Exeter and Birmingham, passes near Worcester, 25 miles to the west.

GETTING AROUND

Free town and transport maps are available from the Bridgefoot TIC. Local bus services are good in the town centre but less frequent to outlying areas.

Busline (general bus information); *tel: (01788) 535555*. **Stratford Blue** run local buses, from *Bridge St* and *Wood St*. Buses X16 (to Coventry), 18 (to Leamington) and X20 (to Birmingham) operate a reduced service on Sun, other buses Mon–Sat only. Weekly **Blue Rider** tickets (£4.95, from the bus driver) are for use only on Stratford Blue buses within Stratford.

Taxi ranks can be found at *Bridgefoot, Bridge St, Union St* and *Rother Market* (near White Swan Hotel). The TIC has a list of registered taxi companies. **Stratford Taxis**, *tel: (01789) 415888*, offer wheelchair transport.

STAYING IN STRATFORD

Accommodation

Stratford itself offers predominantly guesthouse accommodation, but there is a wide range of accommodation around the

323

town. It is necessary to book ahead for July–Aug and over public holiday weekends. Cheaper accommodation can be found on the outskirts – try *Alcester Rd*, *Shipston Rd*, *Evesham Rd* and *Evesham Place*. For **accommodation advice** (not bookings), *tel: (01789) 293127* (busiest Fri and Sat mornings).

Hotel chains in Stratford include *BW*, *FH*, *FP*, *MH*, *Mo*, *QI* and *Th*.

Arden Park Hotel, *6 Arden St, Stratford-upon-Avon CV37 6PA; tel/fax: (01789) 296072*. B&b accommodation in seven en suite rooms. Close to town centre. Budget.

Arden Thistle, *44 Waterside, Stratford-upon Avon CV37 6BA; tel: (01789) 294949; fax: (01789) 415874*. Directly opposite the Royal Shakespeare and Swan theatres. Outdoor terrace dining is available in summer. Moderate–expensive.

Craig Cleeve House, *67–69 Shipston Rd, Stratford-upon-Avon CV37 7LW; tel: (01789) 296573; fax: (01789) 299452*. Within strolling distance of the town centre, this private hotel has 15 rooms. Budget–moderate.

Sequoia House Hotel, *51 Shipston Rd, Stratford-upon-Avon CV37 7LN; tel: (01789) 268852; fax: (01789) 414559*. In a charming riverside setting opposite the Royal Shakespeare Theatre, this private hotel has 24 rooms. Moderate.

Swan House Hotel, *The Green, Wilmcote CV37 9XJ, off the A3400 three miles north of Stratford; tel: (01789) 267030; fax: (01789) 204875*. Overlooking Mary Arden's House and itself a listed building, the hotel has eight rooms with four-poster beds. Budget–moderate.

White Swan, *Rother St, Stratford-upon-Avon CV37 6NH; tel: (01789) 297022; fax: (01789) 268773*. Ancient beams and solid oak furniture help to preserve the Elizabethan ambience of this inn which

Shakespeare himself would easily recognise; moderate.

HI: *Hemmingford House, Alveston; tel: (01789) 297093*. There are various **campsites** within easy reach of town: **Avon Caravan Park**, *Warwick Rd; tel: (01789) 293438*, 1 mile east; **Dodwell Park**, *Evesham Rd; tel: (01789) 204957*, 2 miles south-west; **Stratford Racecourse**, *Luddington Rd; tel: (01789) 267949*, 1½ miles south-west.

Eating and Drinking

The TIC has a free list of places to eat and drink. The range is good, with half a dozen gourmet restaurants and plenty of cheaper options, including a wide choice of pubs. Places in the centre are more expensive. The largest concentration of restaurants is in *High St* and *Sheep St*.

Bell Bistro, *Alderminster CV37 8NY, off A3400, 4½ miles south of Stratford; tel: (01789) 450414*, open daily 1200–1400, 1900–2130. Blackboard menus, beams, flagstone floors and open fires contribute to an atmosphere that matches the food in this old coaching inn; moderate.

Marlowes Restaurant, *18 High St, Stratford-upon-Avon CV37 6AU; tel: (01789) 204999*, open daily 1200–1430, 1745–2230. Famous actors and actresses are among the regular clientele of this first-class restaurant set in a former Elizabethan town house. The menu is as celebrated as the famous guests; moderate–pricey.

The Vintner, *5 Sheep St, Stratford-upon-Avon CV37 6ES; tel: (01789) 297259*, open daily 1030–2330. Café-wine bar with authentic Elizabethan surroundings offers value-for-money steaks, salads and vegetarian dishes; moderate.

The Dirty Duck, *Waterside, Stratford-upon-Avon CV37 6BA; tel: (01789) 297312*. Autographed photographs of famous actors

324

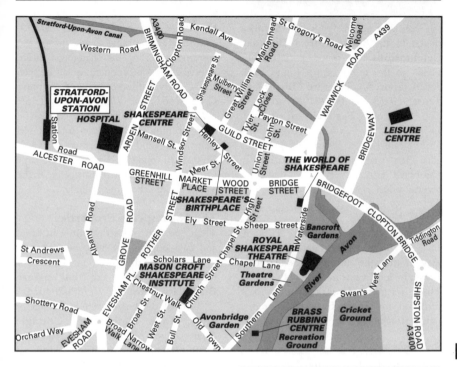

325

adorn the walls in this old riverside inn overlooking the Royal Shakespeare Theatre gardens. Snacks are served in the bar and there is a separate restaurant. Budget–moderate.

Slug and Lettuce, *38 Guild St, Stratford-upon-Avon CV37 6QY; tel: (01789) 299700*. The pub's unappealing name fails to repel Stratford's young set, who turn up in droves, especially at weekends. Real ales and an imaginative range of snacks, light meals and more substantial dishes add to the attraction. Budget–moderate.

Communications and Money

The main **post office**, *Henley St*, is open Mon–Fri 0900–1730, Sat 0900–1230. Poste restante facilities are available.

There is a **Thomas Cook bureau de change** at *Midland Bank, 13 Chapel St*.

ENTERTAINMENT AND EVENTS

The TIC has its own free entertainments listing, as well as the *Visitor Magazine* (free) and *Herald Press* (28p). In addition to the excellent theatres for which Stratford is famous, there are four nightclubs, and a great number of pubs.

The best way to appreciate Shakespeare is to see one of his plays performed, especially by the **Royal Shakespeare Company (RSC)** at the **Royal Shakespeare Theatre** (it's best to book 2–3 months in advance, but always worth checking for returns at the box office on the day). Alternatively, try the **Swan Theatre**, *Waterside,* and the **Other Place**, *Southern Lane; tel: (01789) 414999,* which have performances Mar–Jan.

For horse-racing enthusiasts, there is **Stratford Racecourse**, *Luddington Rd; tel: (01789) 267949.* 1½ miles south-west.

Every year on 23 Apr (or the Saturday closest to it), **Shakespeare's Birthday Celebrations** take place, with various events in the town centre (some free): details from **Shakespeare Birthplace Trust**, *Henley St; tel: (01789) 204016.* The **Stratford Festival**, *tel: (01789) 267969,* is a wide-ranging, non-Shakespeare-related festival of performance arts that attracts internationally renowned artists every July, staged at several venues.

Shopping

The main shopping streets are *High St, Bridge St, Bell Court* and *Bard's Walk*. You may notice the unusual resin figures crafted by local artists in some of the shops. There is a **general market** on *Rother St* (Fri) and, for those who are interested, a **cattle market** on *Alcester Rd* (Thur).

Sightseeing

Bus tours (with open-top buses and a guide) are operated by **Guide Friday**, *tel: (01789) 299866;* daily 0930/1000–1530/ 1830 (seasonal) every 15–20 mins (May–Sept), every 20–30 mins (Oct–Apr). The full circuit takes an hour, but the tickets (£7.50) are valid all day, allowing you to jump on and off at places of interest, including all five Shakespeare Properties.

If you want to get further afield and see some of the lovely countryside and picturesque villages, a **Guide Friday Cotswold Tour** is available daily at 1615 (Easter–Oct); £15.

The TIC can also book **river cruises**, **guided walks** and **individual guides**.

Stratford is now a Mecca for coach parties and, if your enjoyment is likely to be marred by having to share the experience with hordes of others, visit the major sites early – before 1100.

The **RSC** offer **backstage tours**: £4.

For times and bookings, *tel: (01789) 412602.* On the same theme, props and costumes revealing the changing fashions in Shakespearean productions can be seen at the **Royal Shakespeare Company Collection**, *Swan Theatre, Waterside; tel: (01789) 412602,* open Mon–Sat 0915– after evening performance interval (all year); Sun 1200–1630 (Easter–mid Oct); 1100–1530 (mid Oct–Easter); £1.50 (free for those attending a performance at the Swan Theatre the same evening).

The Shakespeare Properties

There are five properties, three in town and two outside; £8.50 covers all five; £5.50 covers the three in town. For information, contact the **Shakespeare Birthplace Trust**, *tel: (01789) 204016.*

Two of the biggest draws are out of town. **Anne Hathaway's Cottage**, *Shottery*, open Mon–Sat 0900–1700, Sun 0930–1700 (Easter–mid Oct); Mon–Sat 0930–1600, Sun 1000–1600 (mid Oct–Easter); £2.50. Tour bus – or frequent Stratford Blue Avon Shuttle bus from *Bridge St* – or signed 1-mile walk from *Evesham Place*. The 'cottage' is, in fact, a substantial thatched farmhouse, where Anne Hathaway lived with her wealthy family before her marriage to Shakespeare. It's arranged to reveal Tudor domestic life and has a pretty garden.

The childhood home of William's mother is **Mary Arden's House and Shakespeare's Countryside Museum**, *Wilmcote*, open Mon–Sat 0930–1700, Sun 1000–1700 (Easter–mid Oct); Mon–Sat 1000–1600, Sun 1030–1600 (mid Oct–Easter); £3.50. Train to Wilmcote Station (3½ miles), then a 5 min walk. The house was restored in the 19th century. Its extensive outbuildings house displays of farming and rural life, including a working blacksmith's forge and falconry demonstrations.

In Stratford itself, Bard memorabilia and Elizabethan exhibits are on display at **Shakespeare's Birthplace**, *Henley St* (times as Anne Hathaway's Cottage); £3.60. **Hall's Croft**, *Old Town* (times as Mary Arden's House); £2.20, is an impressive gabled house with a beautiful walled garden. It was the home of Dr John Hall, who married Shakespeare's daughter Susanna, and has an exhibition on medicine in Dr Hall's time. Only the foundations remain of **New Place**, where Shakespeare spent his final years and died in 1616; an Elizabethan garden marks the site, and entry is through a museum of local history and furniture; **Nash's House**, *Chapel St* (times as Mary Arden's House); £2.20.

Other Attractions

Shakespeare was baptised, and is buried, in the beautiful **Holy Trinity Church**, *Old Town; tel: (01789) 266316*, open Mon–Sat 0830–1800, Sun 1400–1700 (Apr–Oct); Mon–Sat 0830–1600, Sun 1400–1700 (Nov–Mar); church free; Shakespeare's grave 60p.

World of Shakespeare, *13 Waterside; tel: (01789) 269190*, open daily 0930–2130 (May–Sept); 0930–1700 (Oct–Apr); £4. With the auditorium in the centre, a 360° audiovisual diorama takes you back to Elizabethan England. Shows are every half hour.

Shakespeare is not the town's only noteworthy inhabitant. The mother of John Harvard, founder of Harvard University, lived at modest **Harvard House** (1596), *High St; tel: (01789) 204016*, open daily 1000–1600 (Easter–mid Oct); £2.

Stratford Brass Rubbing Centre, *Avonbank Garden, nr Holy Trinity Church;*

tel: (01789) 297671, open daily 1000–1800 (Easter–mid Oct); 1100–1600 (mid Oct–Easter); centre free; brass rubbing from £1.50.

The **Teddy Bear Museum**, *19 Greenhill St, nr Market Pl.; tel: (01789) 293160*, open daily 0930–1800 (Mar–Dec); 0930–1700 (Jan–Feb); £2.25, contains every conceivable kind of stuffed ursine creature, including the original Sooty and reproductions of other famous bears.

Stratford-upon-Avon Butterfly Farm, *Tramway Walk, Swan's Nest Lane; tel: (01789) 299288*, open daily 1000–1800/ dusk; £3.25. This is the place to enjoy the natural beauty of some thousand exotic (live) butterflies.

OUT OF TOWN

Coughton Court (NT), *Alcester; tel: (01789) 762435*, open Sat–Wed 1200–1700 (May–Sept); Sat–Sun 1200–1700 (Apr–Oct); Easter Mon–Wed 1200–1700; £4.95 (house and grounds). 9 miles north-west. This is a splendid, winged Tudor gatehouse, with two churches and a lake in its grounds.

Heritage Motor Centre, *Gaydon; tel: (01926) 641188*, open daily 1000–1800 (Apr–Oct); 1000–1630 (Nov–Mar); £5.50. 13 miles from town. The centre tells the story of the UK motor industry from the 1890s to the present. Huge collection of historic cars and many themed displays.

Ragley Hall, *Alcester; tel: (01789) 762090*, house open Thur–Sun, public holidays 1100–1700 (Easter–Sept); £4.50 (house and gardens). 8 miles north-west. This is a fine Palladian mansion in a 400-acre park designed by Capability Brown – a refreshing contrast to half-timbered Stratford.

327

YORK

The River Ouse flows through the beautiful and historic city of York. Originally settled by the Romans, followed by the Vikings and the Normans, the town became prosperous with the medieval wool trade. Much of York's history can be seen within its city walls, built on Roman foundations and entered by one of four medieval gates. The centre is a maze of ancient streets with narrow alleys, known as *snickelways*. Today, the city is a fascinating mixture of architecture and treasures from Roman, Viking, Norman, medieval and Georgian times, much of it made more accessible by modern technology.

TOURIST INFORMATION

TIC: *York Tourism Bureau, 6 Rougier St, York YO1 1JA; tel: (01904) 611690,* open Mon–Sat 0900–1800, Sun 1000–1600 (Apr–Oct); Mon–Sat 0900–1700 (Nov–Mar). DP SHS services offered; local bed-booking and BABA (latest 30 mins before closing; fee £3.50 for all bookings). Guided tours booked. The *York Guide* (including accommodation listing) is available free of charge. Bureau de change. Theatre tickets, National Express and Scottish Citylink tickets booked.

ARRIVING AND DEPARTING

All roads lead to York, it seems. The A64 Leeds–Scarborough route intersects with A1237 to form an outer ring road. Other major routes converging on the city are A59 from Preston and A1079 from Kingston-upon-Hull. The A1, the artery to the north from London, steers to the west of York, but intersects with A64 four miles west of Tadcaster. The M62, which crosses the country from Manchester and intersects with M1 just south of Leeds, runs some 20 miles to the south, but a number of intersecting roads form connections with York.

GETTING AROUND

Most attractions are within walking distance of the centre. In deciphering street maps, remember that 'gate' means 'street' in York, as in many other English towns which were Viking settlements. A town map is available from the TIC. Local transport is very good within the city, but frequency to outlying areas varies. A **Minster Card**, covering the whole city's transport system, is available weekly (£9) or monthly (£31).

Rider York, *tel: (01904) 435637,* is the main operator of local **buses** and can supply a route map. The main **taxi** rank is outside York Station; *tel: (01904) 623332.* Registered taxi companies include: **Station Taxis**, *tel: (01904) 623332;* **Streamline**, *tel: (01904) 638833;* and **Fleetways**, *tel: (01904) 645333.* Details of further companies are available from the TIC.

STAYING IN YORK

Accommodation

There is a good range of accommodation. Most of the cheaper places are to be found on the edge of town and in the suburbs. It is generally easy to book on arrival, except July–Sept, public holidays and during the

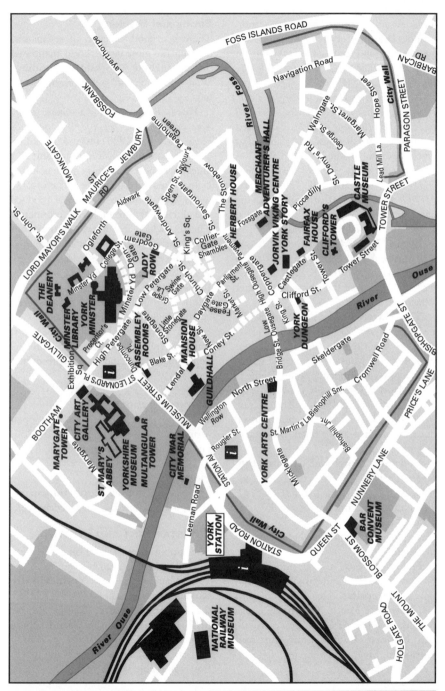

Jorvik Festival (February). Accommodation includes large, mid-range and small hotels, guesthouses and pubs. Hotel chains in York include: *BW, Ct, FP, Ja, MH, Nv, Pn, QI, ST* and *SW*.

Abbots Mews Hotel, *6 Marygate Lane, Bootham, York YO3 7DE; tel: (01904) 622395; fax: (01904) 612848*. Converted from an old coach-house and stables. Bar lunches available Mon–Fri. Moderate.

Ascot House, *80 East Parade, York YO3 7YH; tel: (01904) 426826; fax: (01904) 431077*. Less than a mile from the city centre, this Victorian guesthouse has 15 air-conditioned rooms. Budget.

Byron House Hotel, *7 Driffield Terrace, The Mount, York YO2 2DD; tel: (01904) 632525; fax: (01904) 638904*. Within walking distance of the Minster and other attractions. Budget.

The Hazelwood, *24–25 Portland St, Gillygate, York YO3 7EH; tel: (01904) 626548; fax: (01904) 628032*. A 5 min walk from the Minster, this elegant guest-house enjoys a secluded location. Budget.

Hudson's Hotel, *60 Bootham, York YO3 7BZ; tel: (01904) 621267; fax: (01904) 654719*. Two city centre town houses converted into a hotel. Moderate–expensive.

Red Lion Motel and Country Inn, *Upper Poppleton, York YO2 6PR; tel: (01904) 781141; fax: (01904) 785143*. Three miles west of the city, on A59, this cheerful country inn is handy for trips to Harrogate and the Yorkshire Dales. Budget–moderate.

HI: *Water End, Clifton; tel: (01904) 653147*. The TIC can provide information on **campsites**. The closest to town are: **Rawcliffe Manor Campsite**, *Manor Rd; tel: (01904) 624422*, 2 miles north, and **Naburn Locks Camping and Caravan Site**, *Naburn; tel: (01904) 728697*, 4 miles south.

Eating and Drinking

There is a good selection of restaurants, catering for most tastes. Local traditional dishes include Yorkshire pudding, Wensleydale cheese and Yorkshire curd tart.

Kites Restaurant, *13 Grape Lane, York YO1 2HU; tel: (01904) 641750*, open Mon–Sat 1200–1400, 1830–2230. This intimate second-floor restaurant, in a quiet street near the Minster, offers imaginative international cuisine and affordable wines. The emphasis is on local produce and all herbs are grown by the proprietor. Cheeses include an unusual selection from the Yorkshire Dales; Moderate–pricey.

Plunkets, *9 High Petergate, York YO1 2EN; tel: (01904) 637722*, open daily 1200–2300. The atmosphere is relaxed and the surroundings bright. Set in a 17th-century building, the restaurant offers an eclectic menu which includes Mexican and Thai cuisine as well as more conventional meat, fish and vegetarian dishes; moderate.

Communications

The main **post office**, *Lendal*, is open Mon–Fri 0900–1700, Sat 0900–1230. Poste restante facilities are available.

Money

There is a **Thomas Cook bureau de change** at *Midland Bank, 13 Parliment St*.

ENTERTAINMENT AND EVENTS

The publication *York Diary*, detailing entertainments, is available free from the TIC. Main venues are: **York Theatre Royal**, *St Leonard's Pl.; tel: (01904) 623568*; the **Barbican Centre**, *Barbican Rd; tel: (01904) 656688*; and the **Grand Opera House**, *Clifford St; tel: (01904) 671818*.

York's main annual event is the **Jorvik Festival** (Feb), which recalls the Viking origins of the city. Many different events take place all over the city throughout the two weeks of the festival; some are free. For further information contact **Fibbers**, *tel: (01904) 651250*. The **Early Music Festival** takes place in July; details from **York Festival Office**, *PO Box 226, York YO3 6ZU, tel: (01904) 658338*.

SHOPPING

York is a treasure trove for shoppers – the winding medieval streets house famous names in some of the city's most beautiful buildings. Visit **The Shambles, Stonegate Walk, Petergate** and **Coppergate Centre** for specialist shopping. There is a daily **market** in *Market Sq*.

SIGHTSEEING

Guide Friday, *tel: (01904) 640896*, operate a daily York tour on their open-topped double-decker buses; *£6.50*. **Eddie Brown Tours**, *8 Tower St; tel: (01904) 641737*, run excellent guided tours of Yorkshire by luxury coach. the **Original Ghost Walk of York**, *tel: (01904) 764222/(01759) 373090*, conducts nightly walks (*£2.50*), starting from the Kings Arms (*Ouse Bridge, King's Staith*); the **Victorian Ghost Walk**, *tel: (01904) 640031/640036 (£3.50)*, starts from James Tea Rooms (*75 Low Petergate*).

York has many attractions and most of them are within walking distance of each other. The historic city centre is a maze of narrow, twisting streets, such as **The Shambles**, with its overhanging medieval houses and shops.

In the castle area is the extensive **York Castle Museum**, *The Eye of York; tel: (01904) 653611*, open Mon–Sat 0930–1730, Sun 1000–1730 (Apr–Oct); Mon–Sat 0930–1600, Sun 1000–1600 (Nov–Mar); *£4.50*. This presents a fascinating reminder of bygone days, complete with reconstructed

shop fronts, furnished rooms and hundreds of everyday objects. You should allow an hour and a half, so don't go late. In the heart of the area is a 13th-century tower that was formerly the keep of York Castle – it provides fine views across the city: **Clifford's Tower** (EH), *York Castle; tel: (01904) 646940*, open daily 1000–1800/ dusk (Easter–Oct); daily 1000–1600 (Nov–Easter); *£1.60*.

A few streets away is the **York Dungeon**, *12 Clifford St; tel: (01904) 632599*, open daily 1000–1830 (Apr–Sept); 1000–1730 (Oct–Mar); *£4.25*. This is a museum depicting scenes of execution, torture and other past horrors and featuring such personalities as Guy Fawkes and Dick Turpin.

England's largest medieval cathedral towers above the surrounding streets. It took 250 years to complete, 1220–1470, and is famous for its spectacular windows of medieval stained glass. **York Minster**, *Deangate*, open dawn–dusk; free, but there's a donation box. Information from The **Visitors Officer**, *Church House, Ogleforth; tel: (01904) 624426*. Voluntary guide service available. Nearby is an elegant house that was originally the home of the treasurers of York Minster: **Treasurer's House** (NT), *Chapter House St; tel: (01904) 624247*, open Sat–Thur 1030–1700 (Easter–Oct); *£3.30*. The elegant building in *Minster Close* contains a series of period rooms which provide a perfect setting for the superb collections of furniture and other items.

One of England's finest 18th-century town houses, and with a superb furniture collection, is **Fairfax House**, *Castlegate; tel: (01904) 655543*, open Mon–Thur, Sat 1100–1700, Sun 1330–1700 (mid Feb– mid Jan); also Fri 1100–1700 (Aug–Sept); *£3.50*. Another fine historic building is the mid 14th-century guild hall: **Merchant**

Adventurers' Hall, *Fossgate; tel: (01904) 654818*, open daily 0830–1700 (Easter–Oct); Mon–Sat 0830–1500 (Nov–Easter, but with a long break over Christmas); £1.90.

On the site of the excavation of the Viking street of Coppergate is the remarkable **Jorvik Viking Centre**, *Coppergate; tel: (01904) 643211*, open 0900–1930 (Apr–Oct); 0900–1730 (Nov–Mar); £4.95. Here, 'time cars' transport visitors through the centuries to the authentic sights, sounds and smells of 10th-century Viking York, complete with houses, a market and a quayside. There is also an exhibition of artefacts discovered during the dig.

The ARC (Archaeological Resource Centre), *St Saviourgate; tel: (01904) 643211*, open Mon–Fri 1000–1600, Sat 1300–1600 (Jan–mid Dec); £3.50, is in a restored medieval church. It offers hands-on archaeology and the opportunity to try out ancient crafts, such as spinning and weaving.

Yorkshire Museum, *Museum Gdns; tel: (01904) 629745*, open daily 1000–1700 (Apr–Oct); Mon–Sat 1000–1700, Sun 1300–1700 (Nov–Mar); £3.50, has ancient treasures of Roman, Viking and medieval Yorkshire origin. **York City Art Gallery**, *Exhibition Sq.; tel: (01904) 551861*, open Mon–Sat 1000–1630, Sun 1430–1630; free, houses a splendid collection of British and European paintings.

Cross over the river Ouse to reach the **National Railway Museum**, *Leeman Rd; tel: (01904) 621261*, open daily 1000–1800; £4.80. The largest railway museum in the world, this tells the story of British railways from the 1820s onwards. It includes luxurious carriages used by Queen Victoria and Edward VII; and *Mallard*, the world's fastest steam locomotive.

Another esoteric museum is the **Regimental Museum**, *3 Tower St; tel: (01904) 662790*, open Mon–Sat 0900–1630; £1. This traces three centuries of the Royal Dragoon Guards and the Prince of Wales's Own Regiment of Yorkshire: a great display of regimental pageantry.

OUT OF TOWN

Beningbrough Hall and Gardens (NT), *Shipton-by-Beningbrough; tel: (01904) 470666*. Hall open Good Fri, Sat–Wed 1100–1700 (Easter–Oct); also Fri 1100–1700 (July–Aug); £4.50 (house, garden and exhibition); £3 (garden and exhibition only). Guided garden walks on most weekends at 1330 and 1500; free. 8 miles north-west. This is a beautifully restored Georgian (1716) country house with 18th and 19th-century exhibits, but little electricity – so avoid dull days if you want to study details. Features include a Victorian laundry, a cantilevered staircase, a potting shed, a walled garden and a gallery exhibition about the hall.

Better known is 18th-century **Castle Howard**, *tel: (0653) 648333*. House open 1100–1630 (Easter–Oct); £6.50 (castle and grounds). 15 miles north-east; *tel: (01904) 645151*, call most days. This is the ancestral home of the Howard family – the largest and most spectacular stately home in Yorkshire. It is filled with family treasures and surrounded by over 1000 acres of parkland, with lakes and fountains. Castle Howard was thesetting for the acclaimed TV drama *Brideshead Revisited*.

YORK–BERWICK

This route takes us north from the serene landscapes of North Yorkshire to the rugged beauty of the countryside on the border of Scotland. It is a journey with a wide variety of scenery and sights, from drowsy dales hamlets to the grandeur of Durham Cathedral. The scenic route, especially, is quite long but there are plenty of interesting overnight stops along the way.

ROUTES

DIRECT ROUTE

➡️ The 146-mile route takes 3 hrs. Leave York on A19 north and continue for 90 miles to connect with A1 north of Newcastle upon Tyne, then follow A1 north for a further 56 miles to Berwick-upon-Tweed.

SCENIC ROUTE

➡️ Meandering from the main route clocks up around 190 miles and about 5 hrs driving time. Leave York as above and follow A19 for 22 miles to **Thirsk**. Follow A168 north to reach **Northallerton** in 10 miles. Continue north on A167 for a mile, then head north-west on B6271, reaching **Richmond** in 12 miles. From there take A6108 north-east to connect with A1(M) after 7 miles. After a further 3 miles, follow A66M east, and town centre signs to reach **Darlington** in 5 miles. Leave Darlington on A167 north and after 4 miles join A1(M) and continue for 15 miles to A690 east which reaches **Durham** in under

Berwick-upon-Tweed

23 — A1

Alnwick — A1 — 50

Newcastle–Lake District p. 283 — **Newcastle**

Hexham — 28 — A68 — A19 — **Direct Route**

Durham

Scenic Route — 17 — A690 — 101

Darlington — 15

Richmond — 13 — A167

Northallerton — A168 — 10 — **Thirsk**

22

A19

DIRECT ROUTE: 146 MILES

York

333

2 miles. To get to **Hexham** from Durham follow A691 for 12 miles to Consett, A692 west for 2 miles, then A68 north for 8 miles to connect with A69, which reaches Hexham in a further 6 miles. Head north from Hexham on A6079 and after 9 miles turn left on to A68. After 12 miles turn right on to B6320 to reach

Otterburn in 2 miles. From Otterburn follow B6341 east for 27 miles to **Alnwick**, then take A1 for the final 23 miles to **Berwick-upon-Tweed**.

THIRSK

TIC: *14 Kirkgate, Thirsk, North Yorkshire YO7 1PQ; tel: (01845) 522755.* Seasonal opening. BABA; local accommodation bookings.

ACCOMMODATION

Doxford House, *73 Front St, Sowerby, Thirsk YO7 1JP; tel: (01845) 523238.* Georgian house overlooking the village green. Budget. **Golden Fleece Hotel**, *42 Market Pl., Thirsk YO7 1LL; tel: (01523) 523108; fax: (01523) 523996.* Olde worlde inn. Moderate. **Three Tuns Hotel**, *Market Pl., Thirsk, YO7 1AJ; tel: (01845) 523124; fax: (01845) 526126.* Comfortable former Georgian dower house. Budget–moderate.

Hambleton House, *78 St James Green, Thirsk YO7 1AJ; tel: (01845) 525532; fax: (01845) 523369.* Overlooking quiet green, close to the town centre. Budget. **Sheppard's**, *Church Farm, Front St, Sowerby, Thirsk YO7 1JF; tel: (01845) 523655; fax: (01845) 524720.* This popular small hotel has an agricultural theme. Moderate–expensive. **Old Red House**, *Station Rd, Thirsk YO7 4LT; tel: (01845) 524383; fax: (01845) 525902.* Welcoming good-value pub. Moderate.

SIGHTSEEING

Trees to Treske Visitor Centre, *Station Maltings, Thirsk; tel: (01845) 522770,* open daily 1000–1700 (Easter-Sept), 1100–dusk (Oct–Easter); £2.50. This unusual and interesting place demonstrates how a living tree 'works' and a tree is transformed into furniture. Factory tour, displays, games and inter-active exhibits.

Sion Hill Hall and Bird of Prey and Conservation Centre, *Kirby Wiske, Thirsk; tel: (01845) 587206.* Hall open Wed–Sun and public holidays 1230–1620 (late Mar–Oct); £4; birds daily 1030–1730 (Mar–Oct); £4. The Mawer Collection of antique furniture, paintings, porcelain and clocks can be seen in 20 room settings. More than 90 birds of prey can be visited in the Victorian walled garden.

Thirsk Museum, *16 Kirkgate; tel: (01845) 522755,* open Mon–Sat 0930–1700, Sun 1400–1600 (Easter–Oct). Veterinary equipment from James Herriot's surgery, agricultural bygones, mementoes of Thirsk life, cricketing memorabilia and the odd legend detailed.

NORTHALLERTON

TIC: *Applegarth Car Park, Northallerton DL7 7LZ; tel: (01609) 776864.* BABA and local accommodation bookings.

Solberge Hall Hotel, *Newby Wiske, Northallerton DL7 9ER; tel: (01609) 77919,* a secluded Georgian country house. Expensive.

Mount Grace Priory (EH), *Saddlebridge, Northallerton; tel: (01609) 883494,* open daily 1000–1800 (Apr–Sept, to dusk Oct), Wed–Sun 1000–1600 (Nov–Mar); £2.70. Considered the best-preserved Carthusian priory in the country, in a woodland setting, with a restored two-storey monastic cell and a herb garden.

RICHMOND

TIC: *Friary Gdns, Victoria Rd, Richmond, North Yorkshire DL10 4AJ; tel: (01748) 850252/825994,* open daily 0930–1730 (Apr–Oct); Mon–Sat 0930–1630 (Nov–Mar). DP services offered; local bed-booking and BABA (latest booking 30 mins before closing). Swaledale Festival tickets sold. The *Yorkshire Dales Holiday Guide* is available free and contains accommodation listings. Separate mini-guide to the Northern Dales also available.

ACCOMMODATION

There is a wide range in the local area, particularly b&bs, and it is generally easy to find accommodation. Hotel chains include *Ct.* **HI**: *Grinton; tel: (01748) 884206.* TIC will provide details of local **campsites**. The closest are: **Swale View Caravan Park**, *Reeth Rd, Richmond; tel: (01748) 823106*, 3 miles west of the centre; and **Brompton on Swale Caravan and Camping Park**, *Brompton on Swale, Richmond; tel: (01748) 824629*, 3 miles east.

SIGHTSEEING

Guided walks are arranged by the TIC and can be booked by phone.

Richmond is an attractive market town, dominated by the ruined 11th-century **Richmond Castle** (EH), *tel: (01748) 822493*, open daily 1000–1800 (Easter–Oct); daily 1000–1600 (Nov–Easter); £1.80. Wonderful views across the **Vale of York**.

Regimental uniforms and campaign relics from 1688 onwards can be seen at the **Green Howards Museum**, *Trinity Church Sq.; tel: (01748) 822133*, open Mon–Sat 0930–1630, Sun 1400–1630 (Apr–Oct); Mon–Sat 1000–1630 (Mar, Nov); Mon–Fri 1000–1630 (Feb); £2.

Georgian Theatre Royal and Museum, *Victoria Rd; tel: (01748) 823021*. Theatre and museum open Mon–Sat 1030–1630, Sun 1100–1400 (Easter–Oct); £1.50. The theatre is one of England's oldest – originally built in 1788, it has been restored and reopened. The museum contains interesting memorabilia.

Richmondshire Museum, *Ryder's Wynd; tel: (01748) 825611*, open daily 1100–1700 (Apr–Oct); £1. This concentrates on the history of the area.

OUT OF TOWN

Lively displays depict the past lifestyles of the Dales people at the **Swaledale Folk Museum**, *Reeth Green, Reeth; tel: (01748) 884373*, open daily 1030–1730 (Easter–Oct); £1. 8 miles west. The emphasis is on hill farming and lead-mining.

Yorkshire Museum of Carriages and Horsedrawn Vehicles, *Yore Mill, Aysgarth Falls, Leyburn; tel: (01969) 663399*, open daily 0930–dusk; £2. 8 miles south-west. Museum consists of 57 Victorian coaches, housed in a 200-year-old mill overlooking **Aysgarth Falls**.

DARLINGTON

Information Darlington: *13 Horsemarket, Darlington, Co. Durham DL1 5PW; tel: (01325) 388666*, open Mon–Tues 0900–1700, Wed 0930–1700, Thur–Fri 0900–1700, Sat, public holidays 1000–1600. Services offered: local bed-booking and BABA (latest 15 mins before closing). Theatre and coach daytrip tickets booked. Free *Darlington Leisure Breaks Guide* and map. The main **taxi** rank is on *Market Sq.* Information Darlington can provide information about registered taxi companies.

ACCOMMODATION

There is a good choice of hotel accommodation, as well as plenty of b&b establishments. It is generally possible to book accommodation on arrival, except during the Beer Festival (Mar) and Darlington Dog Show (Sept). Hotel chains include *MC* and *SW*. **Blanche Pease House**, *The Arts Centre, Vane Terrace; tel: (01325) 483271*, offers hostel-style b&b accommodation, open Mon–Sat 0900–2200.

SIGHTSEEING

A selection of **countryside walks** around Darlington is available (15p per walk); contact Information Darlington for details.

The industrial town of Darlington boomed in the 19th century, as a rail and engineering centre: the world's first fare-paying steam train ran from here to Stockton-on-Tees. You can see George Stephenson's pioneering engine, *Locomotion*, at the **Darlington Railway Centre and Museum**, *North Rd Station; tel: (01325) 460532*, open daily 1000–1700; £1.90.

The **Darlington Museum**, *Tubwell Row; tel: (01325) 463795*, open Mon–Tues, Thur–Sat 1000–1300 and 1400–1630; free, is devoted to local history: social, industrial and natural.

19th-century Darlington Waterworks is being developed into a museum: **Tees Cottage Pumping Station**, *Coniscliffe Rd; tel: (01325) 388666*. Steaming and open days on a few weekends each year, 1100–1700; £1.50. 2 miles west of centre.

OUT OF TOWN

Barnard Castle (EH), *Barnard Castle; tel: (01833) 638212*, open daily 1000–1800 (Easter–Oct); Wed–Sun 1000–1600 (Nov–Easter); £2 (more if there's a special event). 15 miles west. The extensive ruins of the castle, with its imposing Round Tower, perch high above the Tees, in the town which shares its name.

A little west of the castle is the isolated **Bowes Museum**, *Barnard Castle; tel: (01833) 690606*, open Mon–Sat 1000–1730, Sun 1400–1700 (May–Sept); Mon–Sat 1000–1700 (Mar–Apr, Oct); Mon–Sat 1000–1600 (Nov–Feb); £3.50. This houses a superb collection of ceramics, furniture, textiles and paintings.

There are reminders of a medieval way of life at the tranquil, picturesquely sited ruins of 12th-century **Egglestone Abbey** (EH), *nr Barnard Castle; tel: (0191) 261 1585*, open daily dawn–dusk; free.

Preston Hall Museum and Park, *Yarm Rd, Stockton-on-Tees; tel: (01642) 781184*, museum open daily 1000–1730 (Easter–Sept); 1000–1630 (Oct–Easter); free. 12 miles east. Attractions include a Victorian period street, a tropical aviary, craftsmen at work and 112 acres of parkland, with riverside walks.

Raby Castle, *Staindrop; tel: (01833) 660202*, castle open Wed, Sun 1300–1700 (May–June); Sun–Fri 1300–1700 (July–Sept); public holiday weekend Sat–Wed 1300–1700 (all year); £4 (castle, park and gardens). 17 miles west. The 14th-century castle contains fine furniture and Meissen porcelain and is surrounded by 200 acres of deer park.

DURHAM

TIC: *Market Pl., Durham DH1 3NJ; tel: (0191) 384 3720*, open Mon–Sat 1000–1700 (Sept–June); Mon–Sat 1000–1800, Sun 1400–1700 (July–Aug). DP services offered; local bed-booking and BABA (latest 30 mins before closing). Local theatre tickets sold. Free *County Durham Holiday Guide* includes accommodation listing. Pick up the very detailed *Places to Visit* leaflet.

GETTING AROUND

The majority of attractions are within a walkable area of the centre. Free town and transport maps are available from the TIC. For information on bus and train services, contact **Durham Bus Station**, *North Rd, tel: (0191) 384 3323*. There are **taxi** ranks on *North Rd* and at the station.

ACCOMMODATION

There is a small choice of hotels and a good range of b&b and guesthouse accommodation. It is usually easy to book on arrival, except during university graduation (June) and the beginning of university term (Oct). Chains include *SW*.

Accommodation is available in the university colleges during the holidays (details in the TIC's accommodation guide). The closest **campsite** is **Grange Camping and Caravan Site**, *Meadow Lane, Carville; tel: (0191) 384 4778*, 2 miles north-east.

ENTERTAINMENT AND EVENTS

Event details are available in the *Durham Advertiser*. The **Miner's Gala** (dating back to 1891) takes place in July, with marching bands parading through the city streets. In June there is the **Durham Regatta**.

SIGHTSEEING

BBG, *tel: (0191) 384 3720*, offer free **city walking tours**, from the TIC Wed and Sat at 1415 (June–Sept).

Durham's setting, in a wooded loop of the River Wear, and its magnificent cathedral, make it one of England's most visually memorable cities. Being so small, and with restricted access to motor traffic, it is an excellent place to explore on foot, by its medieval streets and alleys, riverside paths and the footbridges that are among seven bridges spanning the Wear. There are especially good views from *South St.*

Durham Cathedral, *North Bailey; tel: (0191) 386 4266*, open daily 0715–2000 (May–Aug); 0715–1800 (Sept–Apr); free, but donation requested and optional extras. Guided tours; £2. Audiovisual; 50p. Tower, open Mon–Sat 0930/1000–1500/ 1600; £2. Monks' dormitory, open Mon–Sat 1000–1530, Sun 1230–1530 (Apr–Oct); 80p. The building is the greatest piece of Norman church architecture in Britain – no other cathedral has preserved so much period character, and the rich ornamentation on the pillars and arcades is unforgettable. The cathedral's **Treasury Museum** (open Mon–Sat 1000–1630, Sun 1400–1630; £1) houses the coffin and cross of St Cuthbert, the

most revered of northern saints, and many valuable and beautiful ecclesiastical objects.

Across Palace Green, the 11th-century (*c.*1070) castle guards the approach to the historic city. Now part of England's third oldest university, it was, until 1836, the seat of the powerful prince-bishops of Durham, and has a fine Norman chapel. **Durham Castle**, *Palace Green; tel: (0191) 374 3800*, open for guided tours Mon–Sat 1000–1230 and 1400–1600, Sun 1400–1600 (Easter–Sept); Mon, Wed, Sat–Sun 1400–1600 (Oct–Easter); £2.75

Durham University Oriental Museum, *Elvet Hill Rd; tel: (0191) 374 2911*, open Mon–Fri 0930–1300 and 1400–1700, Sat–Sun 1400–1700; £1.50. 2 miles south. This is the only museum in Britain that is devoted entirely to the Orient, with art and archaeology from all the Oriental cultures.

Durham Heritage Centre, *St Mary le Bow Church, North Bailey; tel: (0191) 386 8719*, open daily 1400–1630 (Easter week); Sat–Sun 1400–1630 (Easter–May); daily 1400–1630 (June, Sept); daily 1130–1630 (July–Aug); 80p. A medieval church, partly rebuilt in the 17th century, housing items connected with the town's heritage.

Durham University Museum of Archaeology, *Old Fulling Mill* (between Framwelgate and Prebends Bridges); *tel:(0191) 374 3623*, open daily 1100–1600 (Easter–Oct); Wed–Sun 1230–1500 (Nov–Easter); 80p. Displays include a collection of local finds.

OUT OF TOWN

In the 13th century, the Benedictine monks from Durham went for their retreats to **Finchale Priory** (EH), *Brasside; tel: (0191) 386 3828*, open daily 1200–1700 (Easter–Sept), £1; otherwise open but unattended, free. 4 miles north.

337

Beamish North of England Open Air Museum, *Beamish, Co. Durham; tel: (01207) 231811*, open daily 1000–1800 (July–Aug); £7.99, open daily 1000–1700 (Easter–June, Sept–Oct); £6.99, open Tues–Thur, Sat–Sun 1000–1600 (Nov–Easter); £1.99–£2.99. 6 miles north-west. Beamish is a reminder of the more recent industrial past; a recreation of a northern town at the turn of the century, complete with trams and people in costume.

Auckland Castle, *Bishop Auckland; tel: (01388) 601627*. Castle open Fri, Sun 1400–1700 (May–June, Sept); Thur, Fri, Sun 1400–1700 (July); Thur–Sun 1400–1700 (Aug); £3. 10 miles south-west. This was the principal country residence of the bishops of Durham in Norman times, and is now their official residence, but much is open to the public.

Rokeby Park, *nr Barnard Castle; tel: (01833) 37334*, open Mon–Tues 1400–1700 (May–early Sept); £3.50. 22 miles south-west. This Palladian house has a unique collection of needle-paintings.

HEXHAM

TIC: *Hallgate, Hexham, Northumberland NE46 1XD; tel: (01434) 605225/652348*, open Mon–Sat 0900–1800/1830, Sun 1000–1700 (mid May–Sept); Mon–Sat 0900–1700 (Oct–mid May). SHS services offered; local bed-booking and BABA (latest 15 mins before closing), guided tours booked. Tickets sold for local bus excursions. *Hadrian's Wall Country Holiday Guide* is 50p (free to postal enquiries) and includes an accommodation listing. The TIC has free town and transport maps.

ACCOMMODATION

There is a small selection of hotels including one chain (*BW*), a good number of b&b establishments on the edge of town, and pubs with rooms in outlying villages.

It is generally easy to find accommodation on arrival. **HI**: **Acomb**, *Main St, Acomb; tel: (01434) 602864.*

SIGHTSEEING

Hexham Guild of Guides, *tel: (01434) 605225*, conduct **guided walks** starting from the TIC, in return for a donation to the Guild. **Bus tours and walks** can be booked at the TIC.

Hexham is a small, attractive market town, preserving many fine medieval buildings. It makes a good base from which to explore the best bits of **Hadrian's Wall**, the 74-mile barrier which served as ancient Rome's northern frontier. For details of sites along the wall see p.285.

Border History Museum, *The Old Gaol, nr Market Pl.; tel: (01434) 652351*, open daily 1000–1630 (Easter–Sept); Sat–Tues 1000–1600 (Feb–Easter, Oct–Nov); £1.50. The museum is devoted to the reivers (border families) of the 15th and 16th centuries.

Hexham Abbey, *Market Pl.; tel: (01434) 602031*, open daily 0900–1900 (May–Sept); 0900–1700 (Oct–Apr); free. The 12th-century abbey is very well preserved, retaining the original Saxon crypt, with some superb medieval wood carving; it is still the parish church.

OUT OF TOWN

Cherryburn (NT), *Mickley, Stocksfield; tel: (01661) 843276*, open Thur–Mon 1300–1730 (Easter–Oct); £2.70. 11 miles east. The 19th-century farmhouse was the birthplace of Thomas Bewick, Northumbrian artist, engraver and naturalist.

Prudhoe Castle (EH), *Prudhoe; tel: (01661) 833459*, open daily 1200–1700 (Easter–Sept); £1.60. 12 miles east. There are extensive 12th-century remains and a small exhibition.

OTTERBURN

Accommodation: **YMCA**, *Otterburn Hall, Otterburn, Northumberland NE19 1HE; tel: (0191) 385 2822.* Single, double, twin, triple and multiple rooms, mostly with en suite facilities.

Otterburn Mill; *tel: (01830) 520225*, open Mon–Sat 0900-1730, Sun 1100-1700 (year round); free. The woollen mill's artefacts and records from the 1870s to the 1970s, when production ceased, can be seen at this museum which tells the story of the border woollen trade and the mill's history. Much of the Victorian machinery, including textile machine and water turbines, is still in its original working position. Craft shop.

The Border Reiver, *Otterburn; tel: (01830) 520682.* An award-winning village shop with gift gallery and visitor information point.

ALNWICK

TIC: *The Shambles, Alnwick, Northumberland NE66 1TN; tel: (01665) 510665,* open all year. Services offered: BABA and local accommodation bookings.

ACCOMMODATION

Several agencies for self-catering properties serve the area, including: **Causeway Cottages**, *Causeway House, 15 Grousemoor Drive, Ashington NE63 8LU; tel: (01670) 522580*; **Dales Holiday Cottages**, *Carleton Business Park, Carleton New Rd, Skipton BD23 2DG; tel: (01756) 790919*; **Northumbrian Byways**, *Crosby House, Crosby-on-Eden, Carlisle CA6 4QZ; tel: (01228) 573337*; **Northumbrian Coast and Country Cottages**, *Carpenter's Court, Riverbank Rd, Alnmouth NE66 2RH; tel: (01665) 830783.*

Bondgate House Hotel, *20 Bondgate Without, Alnwick NE66 1PN; tel: (01665) 602025.* Budget. **Oronsay Guest**

House, *18 Bondgate Without, Alnwick NE66 1PP; tel: (01665) 603559.* Budget.
White Swan Hotel, *Bondgate Within, Alnwick NE66 1TD; tel: (01665) 602109.* Town centre hotel. Moderate. **Rock Farmhouse**, *Rock Village, Embleton, Alnwick NE66 3SB; tel: (01665) 579235.* 14th-century creeper-covered house with walled garden. Budget–moderate.

SIGHTSEEING

Alnwick Castle; *tel: (01665) 510777*, open Sat–Thur 1100–1700 (mid Apr–Sept), last admission 1615; £4.70, grounds only £2.50. Set in Capability Brown landscaping, the castle is the home of the Duke of Northumberland whose kin, the Percy family, have lived here since 1309 and is said to be the second largest inhabited castle in the country. The interior is in the Renaissance style; art treasures include paintings by Van Dyck, Titian and Canaletto. Visitors can see the Regimental Museum of the Royal Northumberland Fusiliers, a museum of early British and Roman relics, the coach house, dungeons, gun terrace and grounds.

House of Hardy Museum and Country Store, *Willowburn, Alnwick; tel: (01665) 510027*, open Mon–Fri 0900–1700, Sat 1000–1700 (year round), also Sun 1330–1700 (Mar–Oct); free. Tells the history of the House of Hardy, makers of world-famous fishing tackle.

BERWICK-UPON-TWEED

TIC: *Castlegate Car Park, Berwick-upon-Tweed, Northumberland TD15 1JS; tel: (01289) 330733*, open Mon–Sat 0930–1900, Sun 1000–1700 (Easter–Oct); Mon–Sat 1000–1600 (Nov–Easter). DP services offered; local bed-booking and BABA (latest 1 hr before closing). *Berwick Holiday Guide* is 50p; an accommodation listing is free.

339

Northumbria National Park

Wild and remote, with Kielder Water one of Europe's largest man-made lakes at its edge, Northumbria National Park provides mile after mile of glorious unspoilt country, some of it forested. If seclusion is what you seek, you will find it here in the least known of all the national parks.

The park stretches from Hadrian's Wall, designated a World Heritage Site in 1987, to the market town of Wooler, in the foothills of the Cheviots, where the most northerly of England's youth hostels is conveniently placed. For information contact Northumbria National Park headquarters; *tel: (01434) 605555.*

A free town map is available from the TIC. All the in-town attractions are within easy walking distance of the centre. **Public Transport Helpline**, *tel: (01670) 533128.* The TIC have details of taxis.

ACCOMMODATION

Accommodation in all price categories is readily available. Accommodation booking, *tel: (01289) 330733.* **HI**: *30 Cheviot St, Wooler; tel: (01668) 281365.* Nearest campsite is **Marshall Meadow House Campsite**, *Marshall Meadows; tel: (01289) 307375,* 2 miles north.

SIGHTSEEING

This border town, on the unspoilt Northumbrian coast, changed hands between England and Scotland 13 times before 1482. The Elizabethan ramparts encircling the old town – the first in Europe designed to incorporate cannon – are exceptionally well preserved. The 2-mile walk round them is highly recom-mended; guided tours are available in summer. From Meg's Mount there is a splendid view of Berwick and the River Tweed, which is spanned by the Three Bridges. What life was like in one of the first purpose-built army barracks is recreated at **Berwick-upon-Tweed Barracks and Art Gallery** (EH), *The Parade; tel: (01289) 304493/307427,* open daily 1000–1800/dusk (Easter–Oct); Wed–Sun 1000–1300 and 1400–1600 (Nov–Easter); £2.30. It also houses three museums.

Berwick Town Hall and Cell Block Museum, *Town Hall; tel: (01289) 330900.* Tours Mon–Fri 1030 and 1400 (Easter–Oct); £1. There are mementoes of historic Berwick and a chance to ring the town bells.

OUT OF TOWN

Give priority to **Holy Island**, accessible by a causeway, but only at low tide – so check both tide tables and opening times before you go. The island is home to 'the cradle of Christianity' in northern England, the beautiful **Lindisfarne Priory** (EH), *tel: (01289) 89200,* open daily 1000–1800/dusk (Easter–Oct), daily 1000–1600 (Nov–Easter); £2.50. The atmospheric museum traces the priory's history. About 10 mins' walk away is **Lindisfarne Castle** (NT), *tel: (01289) 389244,* open Sat–Thur, Good Fri 1300–1730 (Easter–Oct); sometimes from 1100 (July–Aug); £3.80. Built in 1550, the castle was converted into a private house in 1903 by Sir Edwin Lutyens.

Bamburgh Castle, *Bamburgh; tel: (01668) 214515,* open daily at 1100 (Easter–Oct) – closing times variable; £3.50. 20 miles south-east. The present building has evolved over several centuries, so it's interesting architecturally and contains wide-ranging collections.

YORK–
THE LAKE DISTRICT

One of the most attractive routes in England. An introduction to the stunning beauty of the Yorkshire Dales, it takes in the spa resort of Harrogate and the wonderful old market towns of Knaresborough, Skipton and Settle, and ends at Kendal, gateway to the English Lake District.

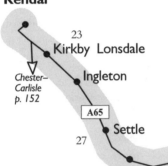

Kendal

23
Kirkby Lonsdale

Chester–
Carlisle
p. 152

Ingleton

A65

Settle
27

A59

Skipton
26

Knaresborough
A59

Harrogate 19

York

341

ROUTE: 96 MILES

ROUTE

The 96 miles take around 2 hrs 30 mins. Leave York on A59 and travel west to reach **Knaresborough** in 19 miles and **Harrogate** in a total of 23 miles. Continue west on A59 for a further 22 miles to **Skipton**, then head north-west on A65 to Settle (16 miles), **Ingleton** (11 miles), **Kirkby Lonsdale** (7 miles) and Crooklands (7 miles). Continue on A65 for a mile, follow A590 for 4 miles and take A591/A6 for the final 5 miles to Kendal.

KNARESBOROUGH

TIC: *9 Castle Courtyard, Knaresborough, North Yorkshire HG5 8AE; tel: (01423) 866886,* open Apr–Oct. Services offered: BABA, local accommodation booked.

ACCOMMODATION

Ebor Mount Guest House, *18 York Place, Knaresborough HG5 0AA; tel: (01423) 863315.* 18th-century town house. Budget.

General Tarleton Inn, *Ferrensby, Knaresborough HG5 0QB; tel: (01423) 340284 fax: (01423) 340288.* Mid 18th-century inn with log fires. Moderate.

Newton House Hotel, *5–7 York Place, Knaresborough HG5 0AD; tel: (01423) 863539, fax: (01423) 869748.* Moderate.

The Yorkshire Lass, *High Bridge, Harrowgate Rd, Knaresborough HG5 8DA; tel: (01423) 862962, fax: (01423) 869091.* Riverside pub. Budget–moderate.

SIGHTSEEING

Knaresborough Castle and Old Courthouse Museum, *Castle Grounds; tel: (01423) 503340*, open daily 1030–1700 (Easter, May–Sept); £1.75. The castle encompasses the museum which features the legends and characters of medieval Knaresborough.

Mother Shipton's Cave and Petrifying Well, *Prophecy House, Knaresborough: tel: (01423) 864600*, open daily 0930–1745 (Easter–Halloween); daily 1000–1645 (Halloween–Easter); £3.95. Mother Shipton was an Elizabethan prophetess who forecast the Spanish Armada and the Great Fire of London. She was born in a cave beside the geological phenomenon known as the Petrifying Well – it turns ordinary objects into stone.

HARROGATE

342

TIC: *Royal Baths Assembly Rooms, Crescent Rd, Harrogate HG1 2RR; tel: (01423) 537300*, open Mon–Fri 0900–1715, Sat 0900–1230 (Oct–May); Mon–Sat 0900–1800, Sun 1300–1600 (June–Sept). DP services offered; local bed-booking and BABA. Tickets for local events sold. *Harrogate District* guide 50p, accommodation listing free.

GETTING AROUND

Most attractions are within walking distance of the centre, but the town is very busy during conference times and the Spring Flower Show (Apr). A free town map is available from the TIC and a transport map from **Harrogate and District Travel**, *20a Lower Station Parade; tel: (01423) 566061*. There are several bus operators in the area: **United Automobile Services**, *tel: (01765) 602093*; **Harrogate and District**, *tel: (01423) 566061*; **Stephenson Nationwide**

Travel, *tel: (01347) 838990*. For **general bus enquiries**, *tel: (01423) 566061*. The main **taxi** rank is in *Station Parade*.

ACCOMMODATION

There are a number of central hotels, but the majority of guesthouses and b&b establishments are on the edge of the centre. It is generally easy to find accommodation on arrival, but not when there is a conference at the Harrogate International Centre, so check before planning a stay. Hotel chains include *Ct, MC, MH, Pn, QI, Rg* and *SW*. There are four **campsites** in the immediate area (details from the TIC): **Ripley Caravan Park**, *Ripley; tel: (01423) 770050*, is 3 miles north.

SIGHTSEEING

Coach tours can be booked through **Wrays**, *tel: (01423) 522466*, starting from *St Mary's Walk*. Free **guided walks** can be arranged through **Harrogate Council**, *tel: (01423) 500600, ext. 3212*.

Harrogate has a rich spa heritage and a modern role as a cosmopolitan visitor venue. The town has a reputation as one of the most florally attractive towns in Britain.

Following the discovery of the first mineral spring in 1571, the town evolved as a fashionable spa. The Pump Room, built in 1842 to enclose the old sulphur well, has now been restored as a museum. **Royal Pump Room Museum**, *Crown Pl.; tel: (01423) 503340*, open Mon–Sat 1000–1600/1700, Sun 1400–1600/1700; £1.75.

Harlow Carr Botanical Gardens, *Crag Lane; tel: (01423) 565418*, open daily 0930–1800/dusk; £3.40. The most prestigious gardens in the north of England. A special feature is the **Museum of Gardening History**, which closes two hours before the gardens.

OUT OF TOWN

Fountains Abbey and Studley Royal Water Garden (NT/EH), *Fountains, nr Ripon; tel: (01765) 608888*, opening times vary with special events, but usually: daily 1000–1900 (Apr–Sept); daily 1000–1700/dusk (Oct, Feb–Mar); Sat–Thur 1000–1700/dusk (Nov–Jan); £4.20. 10 miles north. The romantic ruins of a 12th-century abbey, an Elizabethan mansion and a Georgian water garden combine delightfully at this World Heritage site.

Lightwater Valley, *North Stainley, Ripon; tel: (01765) 635368* (24 hr information), open daily (June–Aug); sporadically (Mar–May, Sept–Oct); £9.95–£11.95 (seasonal). 6 miles north, opening times vary, so ask the TIC. Lightwater is the north's leading theme park and home to the world's longest roller-coaster.

Ripley Castle, *Ripley; tel: (01423) 770152*, castle open Sat–Sun, public holidays 1000–1500 (Easter, Apr–May, Oct); Thur–Fri 1130–1630, Sat–Sun 1000–1500 (June, Sept); Mon–Fri 1130–1630, Sat–Sun 1000–1500 (July–Aug); £4 (castle and gardens). 3 miles north. The castle is crammed with fine furnishings and personal touches. The charmingly varied grounds are home to the national hyacinth collection (best Apr–May).

SKIPTON

TIC: *9 Sheep St, Skipton BD23 1JH; tel: (01756) 792809/700679*, open Mon–Sat 1000–1700, Sun 1400–1700 (Easter–Oct); Mon–Sat 1000–1600, Sun 1300–1600 (Nov–Easter). There is a staff member with BSL qualifications. Services offered: local bed-booking and BABA. Free accommodation listings.

GETTING AROUND

The majority of attractions in Skipton are within walking distance of the centre and the TIC provide free town and transport maps.

Most **buses** operate from **Skipton Bus Station**, *Keighley Rd*. The two main bus companies are: **Keighley and District**, *tel: (01756) 795331*, and **Pennine Buses**, *tel: (01756) 749215*.

The main **taxi** rank is at the bus station.

ACCOMMODATION

There are few hotels – the majority of accommodation is in guesthouses and b&bs. It is usually easy to find something on arrival, but pre-booking is advisable for public holidays.

The nearest **campsite** is **Eshton**, *Eshton Rd, Gargrave; tel: (01756) 749229*, 5 miles north-east.

SIGHTSEEING

Boat trips along the **Leeds and Liverpool Canal** are possible, with **Pennine Boat Trips**, *Waterside Court, Coach St; tel: (01756) 790829*, daily (Apr–Oct); £3 for a 90-min trip.

With its cobbled streets and alleyways, Skipton is an attractive market town and an ideal touring base for the Yorkshire Dales. One of the best preserved medieval fortresses in England is **Skipton Castle**, *High St; tel: (01756) 792442*, open Mon–Sat 1000–1800, Sun 1400–1800 (Mar–Sept); Mon–Sat 1000–1600, Sun 1400–1600 (Oct–Feb); £3.60.

Holy Trinity Parish Church, *High St; tel: (01756) 798804*, open daily 0900–dusk; free, has close historical links with the castle.

OUT OF TOWN

The majestic ruins of **Bolton Priory** are the centrepiece of the **Bolton Abbey Estate**, a recreational park with 75 miles of moorland, woodland and riverside

343

footpaths. **Bolton Abbey**, *Skipton; tel: (01756) 710533*, open daily dawn–dusk; £3 per car, pedestrians free. 6 miles north-east. You can get there on the **Embsay and Bolton Abbey Steam Railway**, *tel: (01756) 794727*, which runs every Sun (all year) and extra days in summer; £4 round trip between the abbey and Embsay (2 miles from Skipton).

SETTLE

TIC: *Town Hall, Cheapside, Settle, North Yorkshire, BD24 9EJ; tel: (01729) 825192*, open Mon–Sat 0930–1730. Services offered: local accommodation reservations. BABA.

ACCOMMODATION

Falcon Manor Hotel, *Skipton Rd, Settle, BD24 9BD; tel: (01729) 823814; fax: (01729) 822087*. Good base for exploring Wharfedale. Moderate.

Golden Lion Hotel, *Duke St, Settle BD24 9DU; tel: (01729) 822203; fax: (01729) 824103*. Former coaching inn. Budget–moderate.

Ottawa, *Station Rd, Giggleswick, nr Settle D24 0AE; tel: (01729) 822757*. A welcoming household in one of the prettiest Dales villages. Budget–moderate.

SIGHTSEEING

Settle–Carlisle Railway, *Watershed Mill, Langcliffe Rd, Settle; tel: (0345) 484950*, open year round, daily in summer, less in winter. Minimum return fare £14.20. This is generally acknowledged to be England's most scenic rail journey.

INGLETON

TIC: *Community Centre Car Park, Ingleton LA6 3HJ; tel: (015242) 41049*, open daily 1000–1630 (May–Oct). BABA, local accommodation bookings. Material of interest to cavers, climbers and hikers.

ACCOMMODATION

Wheatsheaf Inn and Hotel, *22 High St, Ingleton, via Carnforth LA6 3AD; tel: (015242) 41275*. 17th-century former coaching inn. Budget–moderate. **Dales Guest House**, *1 Ingleborough View, Main St, Ingleton LA6 3HH; tel: (015242) 41401*. Budget. **Thorngarth House**, *Ingleton LA6 3HN; tel: (015242) 41295*. Family-run hotel offering gourmet dining. Moderate. **Langber Country Guest House**, *Tatterthorn Rd, Ingleton LA6 3DT; tel: (015242) 41587*. Uninterrupted mountain and farmland views. Budget.

Riverside Lodge, *24 Main St, Ingleton LA6 3HJ; tel: (015242) 41359*. Private access to river. Great views from guest-rooms. Sauna and games room. Budget–moderate.

HI: *Greta Tower, Sammy Lane, Ingleton tel: (015242) 41444; fax: (015242) 41854*.

KIRKBY LONSDALE

TIC: *24 Main St, Kirkby Lonsdale, Cumbria, LA6 2AE; tel: (015242) 71437*, open daily 0900–1700 (Easter–Oct) Mon and Thur–Sat 0900–1700 (Nov–Easter). Services offered: BABA, local accommodation reservations, tour guide bookable.

Pheasant Inn, *Castleton, Kirkby Lonsdale, LA6 2RX; tel/fax: (015242) 71230*. Friendly traditional old inn in unspoilt countryside. Moderate. **Plough Hotel**, *Cow Brow, Lupton, nr Kirkby Lonsdale LA6 1PJ; tel: (015395) 67227*. A range of real ales and good menus at country inn with 14 guest rooms. Moderate.

The little market town close to the Yorkshire border is on the River Lune. A circular, mainly elevated, walk beside the river takes you via 87 steps up to **Ruskin's View**, immortalised in a painting by Turner. Ruskin called it 'a priceless place'.

344

DRIVING DISTANCES AND TIMES

A selection of longer distances between major cities and tourist centres, other than those covered by recommended routes in this book, is given below; journeys follow the fastest roads, i.e. motorways and trunk roads wherever possible. Driving times are meant as an average indication only, allowing for the nature of the roads but not for traffic conditions, which can be very variable. They do not include allowance for stops or breaks en route.

	Miles	Hours		Miles	Hours
LONDON to . . .			**Cardiff to . . .**		
Aberystwyth	238	5	Birmingham	108	1¾
Birmingham	120	2	Bristol	47	¾
Cardiff	155	3	London	155	3
Carlisle	313	5½	Manchester	192	3¼
Exeter	200	4¾	**Carlisle to . . .**		
Manchester	203	3½	Aberystwyth	236	4¾
York	212	3½	Birmingham	198	3½
Aberystwyth to . . .			London	313	5½
Birmingham	123	2½	Manchester	120	2
Bristol	132	2¾	York	115	2¼
Carlisle	236	4¾	**Exeter to . . .**		
London	238	5	Birmingham	162	3¼
Manchester	131	2¾	London	200	4¾
Birmingham to . . .			**Manchester to . . .**		
Aberystwyth	123	2½	Aberystwyth	131	2¾
Bristol	88	1½	Birmingham	88	1½
Cambridge	113	2¼	Bristol	172	3
Cardiff	108	1¾	Cardiff	192	3¼
Carlisle	198	3½	Carlisle	120	2
Exeter	162	3¼	London	203	3½
London	120	2	Oxford	161	2¾
Manchester	88	1½	York	71	1¼
Oxford	68	1¼	**Oxford to . . .**		
Bristol to . . .			Birmingham	68	1¼
Aberystwyth	132	2¾	Bristol	74	1½
Birmingham	88	1½	Manchester	161	2¾
Cardiff	47	¾	**York to . . .**		
Manchester	172	3	London	212	3½
Oxford	74	1½	Carlisle	115	2¼
Cambridge to . . .			Manchester	71	1¼
Birmingham	113	2¼			

345

HOTEL CODES
AND CENTRAL BOOKING NUMBERS

The following abbreviations have been used throughout the book to show which chains are represented in a particular town or city. Central booking service phone numbers are shown – use these numbers while in England and Wales to make reservations at any hotel in the chain. Some telephone numbers are free, usually incorporating *800*.

BW	**Best Western** (0345) 737373	HI	**Hostelling International** (0171) 248 6547	Pn	**Principal** (0171) 413 8877
Ca	**Campanile** (0181) 569 6969	Hn	**Hilton** (0800) 856 8000	QI	**Quality Inn** (0800) 444444
CI	**Comfort Inn** (0800) 444444	Ib	**Ibis** (0181) 746 3233	Rg	**Regal** (0345) 334400
CM	**Courtyard by Marriott** (0800) 221222	Ic	**Intercontinental** (0345) 581237	RH	**Ryan Hotel Group** (00 343) 1 878 7933
Cp	**Copthorne** (0800) 414741/ (01342) 717888	Ja	**Jarvis** (0345) 581237	Rm	**Ramada** (0800) 181737
Ct	**Consort** (0800) 272829	Ju	**Jurys** (00 353) 1 607 0000	Sc	**Scandic** see Holiday Inn for number
DV	**De Vere** (01925) 403202	Ma	**Marriott** (0800) 221222	Sh	**Sheraton** (0800) 353535
FC	**Forte Crest** (0345) 404040	MC	**Mount Charlotte** (0800) 181716	ST	**Stakis** (0990) 909090
FH	**Forte Heritage** (0345) 404040	MH	**Moat House** (0645) 102030	SW	**Swallow** (0500) 303030
FP	**Forte Posthouse** (0345) 404040	Mo	**Minotel** (01253) 292000	Th	**Thistle** (0800) 181716
Gr	**Granada** (0800) 555300	Nv	**Novotel** (0181) 748 3433	Tl	**Travel Inns** (01582) 414341
Hd	**Holiday Inn** (0800) 897121	PL	**Premier Lodge** (0800) 118833		

346

CONVERSION TABLES

DISTANCES (approx. conversions)
1 kilometre (km) = 1000 metres (m)   1 metre = 100 centimetres (cm)

Metric	Imperial/US	Metric	Imperial/US	Metric	Imperial/US
1 cm	3/8 in	9 m	(10 yd) 29 ft	0.75	½ mile
1 m 0 cm	3 ft 3 in	10 m	(11 yd) 33 ft	1 km	5/8 mile
2 m 0 cm	6 ft 6 in	20 m	(22 yd) 66 ft	5 km	3 miles
3 m 0 cm		50 m	(54 yd) 164 ft	10 km	6 miles
4 m 0 cm	13 ft 0 in	100 m	(110 yd) 330 ft	20 km	12½ miles
5 m 0 cm	16 ft 6 in	200 m	(220 yd) 660 ft	30 km	18½ miles
6 m 0 cm	19 ft 6 in	250 m	(275 yd) 820 ft	50 km	31 miles
7 m 0 cm	23 ft 0 in	300 m	(330 yd) 984 ft	75 km	46 miles
8 m 0 cm	26 ft 0 in	500 m	(550 yd) 1640 ft	100 km	62 miles

24-HOUR CLOCK
(examples)

0000 = Midnight	1200 = Noon	1800 = 6.00 p.m.
0600 = 6.00 a.m.	1300 = 1.00 p.m.	2000 = 8.00 p.m.
0715 = 7.15 a.m.	1415 = 2.15 p.m.	2110 = 9.10 p.m.
0930 = 9.30 a.m.	1645 = 4.45 p.m.	2345 = 11.45 p.m.

TEMPERATURE
Conversion Formula: $°C × 9 ÷ 5 + 32 = °F$

°C	°F	°C	°F	°C	°F	°C	°F
-20	-4	-5	23	10	50	25	77
-15	5	0	32	15	59	30	86
-10	14	5	41	20	68	35	95

347

WEIGHT
1 kg = 1000 g   100 g = 3½ oz

Kg	Pounds	Kg	Pounds	Kg	Pounds
1	2¼	5	11	25	55
2	4½	10	22	50	110
3	6½	15	33	75	165
4	9	20	45	100	220

FLUID MEASURES
1 litre(l) = 0.88 Imperial quarts = 1.06 US quarts

Litres	Imp.gal.	US gal.	Litres	Imp.gal.	US gal.
5	1.1	1.3	30	6.6	7.8
10	2.2	2.6	35	7.7	9.1
15	3.3	3.9	40	8.8	10.4
20	4.4	5.2	45	9.9	11.7

MEN'S CLOTHES

UK	Europe	US
36	46	36
38	48	38
40	50	40
42	52	42
44	54	44
46	56	46

MENS' SHOES

UK	Europe	US
6	40	7
7	41	8
8	42	9
9	43	10
10	44	11
11	45	12

LADIES' CLOTHES

UK	France	Italy	Rest of Europe	US
10	36	38	34	8
12	38	40	36	10
14	40	42	38	12
16	42	44	40	14
18	44	46	42	16
20	46	48	44	18

MEN'S SHIRTS

UK	Europe	US
14	36	14
15	38	15
15½	39	15½
16	41	16
16½	42	16½
17	43	17

LADIES' SHOES

UK	Europe	US
3	36	4½
4	37	5½
5	38	6½
6	39	7½
7	40	8½
8	41	9½

AREAS
1 hectare = 2.471 acres

1 hectare = 10,000 sq meters

1 acre = 0.4 hectares

INDEX

References are to page numbers. **Bold** numbers refer to map pages.

349

READER SURVEY

If you enjoyed using this book, or even if you didn't, please help us improve future editions by taking part in our reader survey. Every returned form will be acknowledged, and to show our appreciation we will give you £1 off your next purchase of a Thomas Cook guidebook. Just take a few minutes to complete and return this form to us.

When did you buy this book?

Where did you buy it? (Please give town/city and if possible name of retailer)

When did you/do you intend to travel around England and Wales?

    For how long (approx.)?
    How many people in your party?

Which towns, cities, parks and other locations did you/do you intend mainly to visit?

351

Did you/will you:
    ☐ Make all your travel arrangements independently?
    ☐ Travel on a fly-drive package?
Please give brief details:

Did you/do you intend to use this book:
    ☐ For planning your trip?
    ☐ During the trip itself?
    ☐ Both?

Did you/do you intend also to purchase any of the following travel publications for your trip?
    Thomas Cook Travellers: *London*
    A road map/Atlas (please specify)
    Other guidebooks (please specify)

Have you used any other Thomas Cook guidebooks in the past? If so, which?

Please rate the following features of On the Road around England and Wales for their value to you (Circle VU for 'very useful', U for 'useful', NU for 'little or no use'):

The 'Travel Essentials' section on pages 15–25	VU	U	NU
The 'Driving in England and Wales' section on pages 26–31	VU	U	NU
The 'Themed Itineraries' on pages 41–45	VU	U	NU
The recommended driving routes throughout the book	VU	U	NU
Information on towns and cities, etc	VU	U	NU
The maps of towns, cities, etc	VU	U	NU
The colour planning map	VU	U	NU

Please use this space to tell us about any features that in your opinion could be changed, improved, or added in future editions of the book, or any other comments you would like to make concerning the book:

352

Your age category: ☐ 21-30 ☐ 31-40 ☐ 41–50 ☐ over 50

Your name: Mr/Mrs/Miss/Ms
(First name or initials)
(Last name)

Your full address: (Please include postal or zip code)

Your daytime telephone number:

Please detach this page and send it to: The Project Editor, On the Road around England and Wales, Thomas Cook Publishing, PO Box 227, Peterborough PE3 6PU, United Kingdom.

We will be pleased to send you details of how to claim your discount upon receipt of this questionnaire.

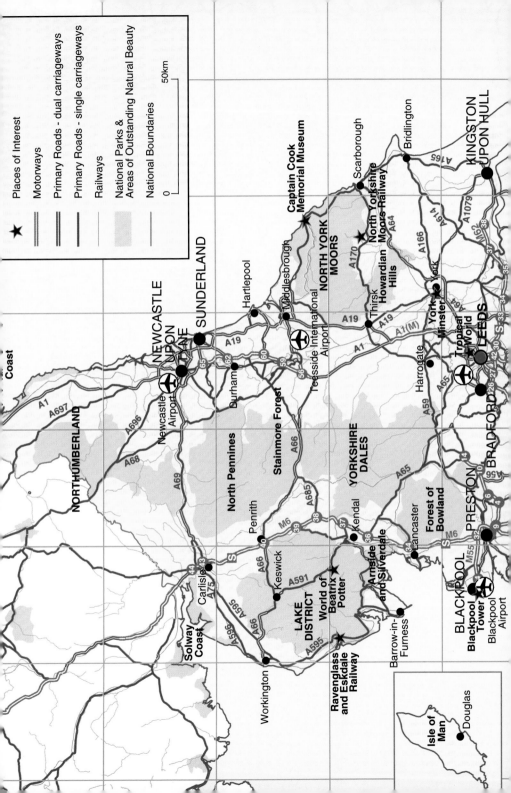

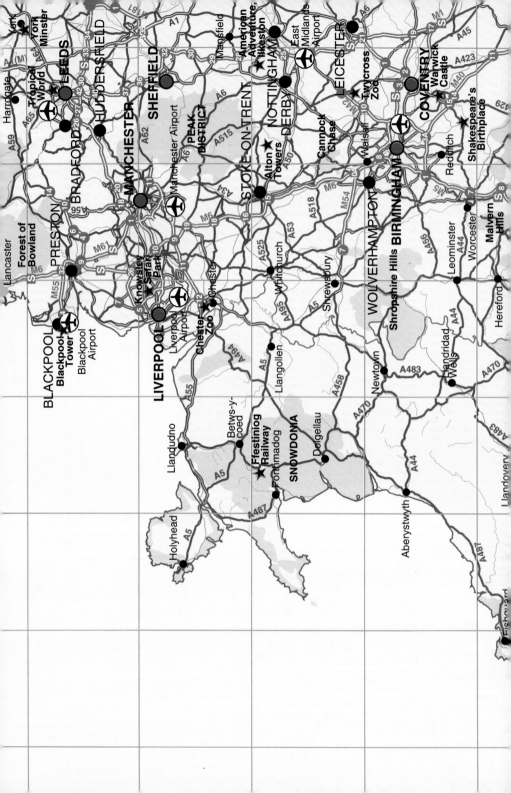

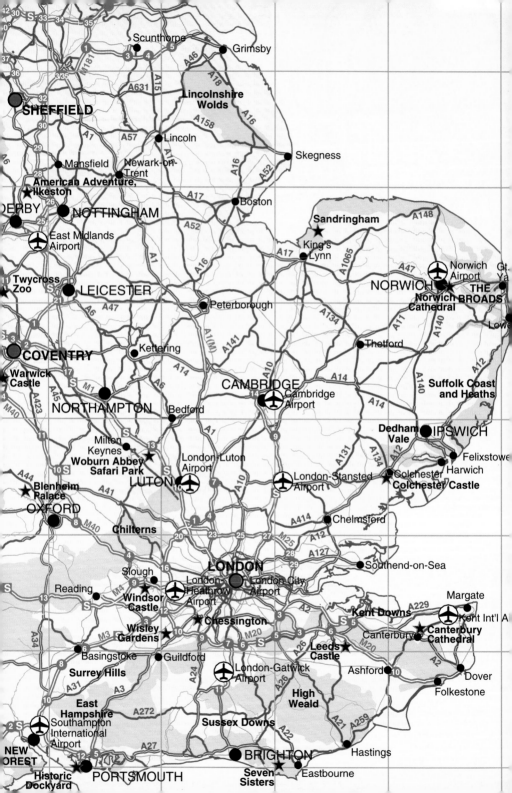